Lecture Notes in Computer Science 3989

Commenced Publication in 1973
Founding and Former Series Editors:
Gerhard Goos, Juris Hartmanis, and Jan van Leeuwen

T0189823

Jianying Zhou   Moti Yung   Feng Bao (Eds.)

Applied Cryptography and Network Security

4th International Conference, ACNS 2006
Singapore, June 6-9, 2006
Proceedings

 Springer

Volume Editors

Jianying Zhou
Feng Bao
Institute for Infocomm Research
21 Heng Mui Keng Terrace, 119613, Singapore
E-mail: {jyzhou, baofeng}@i2r.a-star.edu.sg

Moti Yung
Columbia University, RSA Laboratories
1214 Amsterdam Avenue, New York, NY 10027, USA
E-mail: moti@cs.columbia.edu

Library of Congress Control Number: 2006926666

CR Subject Classification (1998): E.3, C.2, D.4.6, H.3-4, K.4.4, K.6.5

LNCS Sublibrary: SL 4 – Security and Cryptology

ISSN   0302-9743
ISBN-10   3-540-34703-8 Springer Berlin Heidelberg New York
ISBN-13   978-3-540-34703-3 Springer Berlin Heidelberg New York

Springer is a part of Springer Science+Business Media

springer.com

© Springer-Verlag Berlin Heidelberg 2006
Printed in Germany

Typesetting: Camera-ready by author, data conversion by Scientific Publishing Services, Chennai, India
Printed on acid-free paper   SPIN: 11767480   06/3142   5 4 3 2 1 0

Preface

The 4th International Conference on Applied Cryptography and Network Security (ACNS 2006) was held in Singapore, during June 6-9, 2006. ACNS 2006 brought together individuals from academia and industry involved in multiple research disciplines of cryptography and security to foster exchange of ideas. This volume (LNCS 3989) contains papers presented in the academic track.

ACNS was set a high standard when it was initiated in 2003. There has been a steady improvement in the quality of its program in the past 4 years: ACNS 2003 (Kunming, China), ACNS 2004 (Yellow Mountain, China), ACNS 2005 (New York, USA), ACNS 2006 (Singapore). The average acceptance rate is kept at around 16%. We wish to receive the continued support from the community of cryptography and security worldwide to further improve its quality and make ACNS one of the leading conferences.

The Program Committee of ACNS 2006 received a total of 218 submissions from all over the world, of which 33 were selected for presentation at the academic track. In addition to this track, the conference also hosted an industrial track of presentations that were carefully selected as well. All submissions were reviewed by experts in the relevant areas. We are indebted to our Program Committee members and the external reviewers for the great job they have performed. The proceedings contain revised versions of the accepted papers. However, revisions were not checked and the authors bear full responsibility for the content of their papers.

More people deserve thanks for their contribution to the success of the conference. We sincerely thank General Chair Feng Bao for his support and encouragement. Our special thanks are due to Ying Qiu for managing the website for paper submission, review and notification. Shen-Tat Goh and Patricia Loh were kind enough to arrange for the conference venue and took care of the administration in running the conference. Without the hard work of the local organizing team, this conference would not have been possible. We would also like to thank all the authors who submitted papers and the participants from all over the world who chose to honor us with their attendance.

Last but not the least, we are grateful to the Institute for Infocomm Research for organizing and sponsoring the conference.

April 2006   Jianying Zhou
                                                                    Moti Yung

ACNS 2006

4th International Conference on
Applied Cryptography and Network Security

Singapore
June 6-9, 2006

Organized and Sponsored by

Institute for Infocomm Research, Singapore

General Chair

Feng Bao .... Institute for Infocomm Research, Singapore

Program Chairs

Jianying Zhou .... Institute for Infocomm Research, Singapore
Moti Yung .... Columbia University, USA

Program Committee

Carlisle Adams .... Univ. of Ottawa, Canada
Tuomas Aura .... Microsoft Research, UK
Roberto Avanzi .... Ruhr Univ., Germany
Giampaolo Bella .... Univ. of Catania, Italy
Kefei Chen ....Shanghai Jiaotong Univ., China
Ed Dawson ....QUT, Australia
Robert Deng ....SMU, Singapore
Xiaotie Deng .... City Univ., Hong Kong
Yvo Desmedt ....UCL, UK
Marc Girault .... France Telecom, France
Dieter Gollmann .... TU Harburg, Germany
Stefanos Gritzalis .... Univ. of the Aegean, Greece
Jens Groth .... UCLA, USA
Peter Gutmann ....Univ. of Auckland, New Zealand
Yongfei Han ....ONETS, China
Amir Herzberg .... Bar-Ilan Univ., Israel
John Ioannidis .... Columbia Univ., USA
Jonathan Katz .... Univ. of Maryland, USA
Angelos D. Keromytis .... Columbia Univ., USA
Taekyoung Kwon .... Sejong Univ., Korea
Wenke Lee .... Georgia Institute of Tech., USA
Ninghui Li ....Purdue Univ., USA

Javier Lopez .... Univ. of Malaga, Spain
Stefan Lucks .... Univ. of Mannheim, Germany
Subhamoy Maitra .... ISI, India
Patrick McDaniel .... PSU, USA
Chris Mitchell .... RHUL, UK
Refik Molva .... Eurecom, France
Sang-Jae Moon .... KNU, Korea
David Naccache .... ENS, France
Rolf Oppliger .... eSECURITY Technologies, Switzerland
Elisabeth Oswald .... Graz Univ. of Tech., Austria
Guenther Pernul .... Univ. of Regensburg, Germany
Raphael Phan .... Swinburne UT, Malaysia
Michael Roe .... Microsoft Research, UK
Rei Safavi-Naini .... Univ. of Wollongong, Australia
Kouichi Sakurai ....Kyushu Univ., Japan
Pierangela Samarati .... Univ. of Milan, Italy
Vitaly Shmatikov .... UT Austin, USA
Masakazu Soshi .... JAIST, Japan
Francois-Xavier Standaert .... UCL, Belgium
Ravi Sundaram .... Northeastern Univ., USA
Tsuyoshi Takagi .... Future Univ., Japan
Pim Tuyls .... Philips Research, The Netherlands
Wen-Guey Tzeng .... NCTU, Taiwan
Guilin Wang .... I2R, Singapore
Xiaofeng Wang .... Indiana Univ., USA
Brent Waters .... Stanford Univ., USA
Yuliang Zheng .... UNCC, USA

Publicity Chair

Yongfei Han .... ONETS, China

Organizing Committee

Shen-Tat Goh .... Institute for Infocomm Research, Singapore
Patricia Loh .... Institute for Infocomm Research, Singapore
Ying Qiu .... Institute for Infocomm Research, Singapore

Steering Committee

Yongfei Han .... ONETS, China
Moti Yung .... Columbia University, USA
Jianying Zhou .... Institute for Infocomm Research, Singapore

External Reviewers

Abhinav Kamra
Ajay Mahimkar
Angelos Stavrou
Avishek Adhikari
Benoit Libert
Bessie Hu
Boniface Hicks
Chae Hoon Lim
Chen-Kang Chu
Christian Schlager
Christoph Herbst
Christopher Wolf
Colin Boyd
Costas Karafasoulis
DaeHun Nyang
Dibyendu Chakrabarti
Dieter Schmidt
Duncan S. Wong
Duong Hieu Phan
Eike Kiltz
Elisavet Constantinou
Eric Dahmen
Eric Peeters
Ewan Fleischmann
Fabien Pouget
Frederik Armknecht
Gaurav Kc
Gene Beck Hahn
George Kambourakis
Greg Rose
Gregory Neven
Guerric Meurice
Guomin Yang
Herve Denar
Herve Sibert
Hidenori Kuwakado
Hovav Shacham
Hui Li
Jacques Traore
Jan Kolter
Jason Gower
Jeong Ok Kwon
Jian Wen
Jiangtao Li

Jie Guo
Ji-Won Byun
Joerg Gilberg
Johann Groszschaedl
John Canny
Juan Gonzalez Nieto
Julien Cathalo
Katja Schmidt-Samoa
Ke Wang
Keisuke Hakuta
Kenji Imamoto
Kenny Paterson
Kevin Butler
Khoongming Khoo
Kris Gaj
Kun Peng
Kurt Dietrich
Lan Nguyen
Larry Washington
Laurent Butti
Lifeng Guo
Lihua Wang
Ling Dong
Liqun Chen
Ahmad-Reza Sadeghi
Lisa Johanson
Liu Yang
Lizhen Yang
Ludwig Fuchs
Manfred Aigner
Marc Fischlin
Maria Karyda
Martin Feldhofer
Masahiro Mambo
Masayuki Terada
Mathieu Ciet
Benoit Feix
Matthew Burnside
Melek Onen
Mi Wen
Michael Jacobson
Michael Locasto
Nasir Memon
Olivier Lepetit

Olivier Pereira
Palash Sarkar
Patrick Traynor
Petros Belsis
Pierre Creut
Qi Qi
Qiang Tang
Qianhong Wu
Qihua Wang
Raylin Tso
Rodrigo Roman
Rolf Schillinger
Routo Terada
Rui Xue
Sabrina De Capitani di Vimercati
Sandra Dominikus
Shengli Liu
Shiao-Ying Lin
Shinsaku Kiyomoto
Shiqun Li
Shlomo Hershkop
Shuhong Wang
Siamak Fayyaz
Soonhak Kwon

Stanislas Francfort
Stelios Sidiroglou
Stehane Socie
Seastien Canard
Tae Hyun Kim
Tanja Lange
Tanmoy Kanti Das
Theodoros Balopoulos
Toru Nakanishi
Vanessa Gratzer
Wei Gao
Wei-Jen Li
Wolfgang Dobmeier
Xavier Boyen
Xinming Ou
Xinyi Huang
Yong-Sork Her
Yoshifumi Ueshige
Young Ho Park
Yu Long
Yunlei Zhao
Yvonne Hitchcock
Zhuowei Li

Table of Contents

Key Management

Cryptanalysis

Security of Limited Devices

Cryptography

Security and Privacy

Adaptive Detection of Local Scanners

Ahren Studer and Chenxi Wang

Carnegie Mellon University
{astuder, chenxi}@ece.cmu.edu

Abstract. Network attacks often employ scanning to locate vulnerable hosts and services. Fast and accurate detection of local scanners is key to containing an epidemic in its early stage. Existing scan detection schemes use statically determined detection criteria, and as a result do not respond well to traffic perturbations. We present two adaptive scan detection schemes, *Success Based* (SB) and *Failure Based* (FB), which change detection criteria based on traffic statistics. We evaluate the proposed schemes analytically and empirically using network traces. Against fast scanners, the adaptive schemes render detection precision similar to the traditional static schemes. For slow scanners, the adaptive schemes are much more effective, both in terms of detection precision and speed. SB and FB have non-linear properties not present in other schemes. These properties permit a lower *Sustained Scanning Threshold* and a robustness against perturbations in the background traffic.

Keywords: Scan Detection, Internet Worms, Security.

1 Introduction

Network based attacks commonly employ port scans to locate vulnerable machines. A large amount of scan activity is therefore a strong indicator of malicious reconnaissance activities, often to be followed by exploits or infections. To thwart attackers and contain epidemics an important piece in a network defense is fast and accurate detection of local scanners. With few exceptions, existing scan detectors are exclusively what we call *static rate schemes*. Such schemes rely on a statically determined arrival rate of suspicious events to delineate the behaviors of legitimate hosts from those of scanners. For instance, NSM [1] permits a host to contact a maximum number of distinct addresses in a given time window. Any host that exceeds this rate is flagged as a potential scanner. These schemes work well for fast scanners whose behaviors are distinctively different from legitimate hosts. Detecting slow scanners, however, is more difficult because slow scans tend to blend in with the background traffic. If you set the rate too low, false positives can occur whilst a large rate will permit a liberal amount of scans.

In this paper, we investigate *adaptive rate* schemes concerning the detection of slow scanners in the presence of background traffic. We show that adaptively changing the permitted rate of suspicious events achieves "non-linear" properties not present in other schemes. These properties are more robust and effective against various forms of scanning behavior. We introduce two adaptive schemes, one changes the permitted rate (of suspicious events) based on the host's connection success statistics (we call it *Success*

J. Zhou, M. Yung, and F. Bao (Eds.): ACNS 2006, LNCS 3989, pp. 1–17, 2006.

Based(SB)) and the other one based on the failure statistics (we call this one *Failure Based(FB)*). Both SB and FB are able to catch slow scanners while remaining effective against fast scanners.

Throughout this paper, we use a *token-based framework* to describe and analyze each scan detection scheme. More specifically, in this framework a scan detector begins by allocating a number of tokens to each host. Each ensued suspicious event constitutes the removal of some number of tokens, and tokens are rewarded back in an algorithm-specific fashion. The net rate at which tokens are rewarded determines the permitted arrival rate of suspicious events—a host that exceeds this rate is labeled as a scanner. In a static-rate scheme, the permitted arrival rate of suspicious events is constant. In an adaptive scheme, this rate is dynamically determined, based on traffic characteristics.

It is easily seen how some of the existing scan detectors fit into this framework. For instance, we can use the token balance to represent the state of the random walk in TRW [2]; a step in the walk toward the scanner hypothesis represents the consumption of tokens, and a step in the opposite direction constitutes the accumulation of tokens. The use of this framework simplifies the representation of specific schemes; sometimes a family of algorithms can be described with a single token-based representation (e.g., TRW and RHT). It abstracts away superfluous details and permits the direct comparison of core design choices.

To contrast and compare the adaptive schemes with others, we focus on these aspects of detection performance; *error rates*, *detection speed*, and *Sustained Scanning Threshold*(SST). Error rates are specifically false positive and false negative rates. We use the metric Escaped_Count to measure detection speed. Escaped_Count is defined as the number of scans permitted from a scanning host before detection occurs. The Sustained Scanning Threshold (SST)[2] is the maximum failure rate a host can maintain without being labeled as a scanner. SST is an especially important metric concerning slow scanners.

To investigate these aspects, we tested each scheme against both real and synthetic network and scan traces. Our analysis shows that both SB and FB produce a lower SST while maintaining comparable false positive levels to the other detectors. More specifically, SB and FB are as effective against fast scanners as the static-rate schemes, but are faster and more precise against stealth scanners. A sensitivity analysis shows that, while the adaptive detectors do not strictly render better detection precision, they are robust, in the sense that their performances are only slightly affected by traffic perturbations.

2   Related Work

Many scan detection schemes have been proposed in the literature. The earlier ones, such as NSM [1], Snort [3], and Bro [4], are static rate schemes that simply count the number of distinct destinations or failures of each host within a given window of time, and label the host as a scanner if a pre-determined rate is exceeded. These schemes tend to adopt generous permitted rates for fear of false positives. As a result, they are not as effective against slow scanners.

Jung et al. [5] developed a scheme that uses a threshold random walk (TRW) to detect scanners. In this scheme, a connection success results in a step in one direction, while a failure is a step in the opposite direction. A pre-determined distance traveled in a direction labels the host either as a scanner or a safe host. Reverse Hypothesis Testing (RHT) [6] and the Approximate TRW [2] are variations of TRW. Ganesh et al. [7] developed another scheme where optimal detection is possible if traffic characteristics are known. In this scheme, the time between failures dictates the number of tokens removed or rewarded. These algorithms are closest to our schemes and also belong in the class of adaptive algorithms. We present an analytic comparison between our proposals and these other schemes and show that our adaptive algorithms are less susceptible to intelligent gaming, more robust to background perturbations, and more effective against slow scanning worms.

Other defenses against worms include automatic containment and signature generation. Rate limiting such as Williamson's [8], Chen et al's [9], and Wong et al.'s DNS-based scheme [10] are examples of containment schemes. This class of mechanisms focuses on containing potentially anomalous traffic and has different goals and constraints than detection schemes. Signature generation techniques such as Earlybird [11], Autograph [12], and Polygraph [13] have great potential but thus far proved to be difficult against zero-day worms, in particular against slow spreading worms.

3   A Token Based Framework

To facilitate analysis, throughout this paper we use a token-based framework to represent the different detection schemes. In this framework, each host has a bank of tokens. Tokens are removed when suspicious events occur (e.g., connection failures), and accrued at a pre-specified rate or in the absence of suspicious events. The consumption of tokens models the occurrence of suspicious events, and an increase in the token balance indicates benign/good behavior. The scan detector regulates the subtraction and addition of tokens and reports that the host is a scanner if the token balance reaches a pre-determined level.

We map the logic of each detection scheme into this framework. To normalize the discussion, token consumption occurs only when outbound connections fail.[1] How many tokens are removed and the conditions under which tokens are rewarded are algorithm-specific.

In this study, we represent the connection rate of legitimate traffic with a random variable, η, that follows a probability density function $f_\eta(\cdot)$ with an expected value of μ. We assume that both legitimate and scan traffic exhibit a consistent success probability over time, p_n and p_s, respectively. We further assume that scans are emitted at a constant rate, r_s. Table 1 summarizes the different parameters used in the paper.

The maximum scan rate that a scanner can sustain without being detected is the *Sustained Scanning Threshold*, or *SST* [2]. The SST of a detector denotes the optimal worm scan rate against the detector. The expected value for SST is shown in Equation 1.

$$E[SST] = \frac{a/\gamma - \mu(1 - p_n)}{1 - p_s} \tag{1}$$

Another metric we use is Escaped_Count, which measures the timeliness of the detector. Escaped_Count is defined as the number of scans permitted before detection. A

---

[1] The outgoing SYN elicits a TCP_RST or timeout before receiving a SYN_ACK.

Table 1. Token Equation Parameters

Symbol	Meaning	Symbol	Meaning
a	token reward rate	γ	token penalty
n	initial token balance (also maximum)	μ	expected background traffic rate
r_s	rate of scan connections	p_n	background traffic success probability
p_s	scan traffic success probability		

scanner that evades detection (a false negative) would have an infinite Escaped_Count. Equation 2 gives the expected Escaped_Count.

$$E[\text{Escaped\_Count}] \approx \frac{E[Tokens]}{\gamma(r_s(1 - p_s) + \mu(1 - p_n)) - a} \cdot r_s \tag{2}$$

4   Static Rate Schemes

In this section we explore a generic token-based representation for static rate schemes. A static rate detector stipulates that the permitted rate of suspicious events remains constant throughout time. In a token-based form, this translates to as follows—failures result in the removal of a constant number of tokens, and tokens are accrued at a constant rate, independent of the state of the system.

To give the best performance, our token-based formulation stipulates that tokens are consumed only when first-contact connections fail. (A first-contact connection is the very first connection to a particular destination [5].) A connection is considered *failed* when the outgoing SYN elicits a TCP_RST or a timeout without a SYN_ACK. To determine whether a connection is a first-contact connection, the host must maintain statistics of previously contacted addresses. While we do not specify how these statistics should be maintained at the host level, we stipulate that there exist many efficient mechanisms (e.g, hash tables, bloom filters) to store and look up a list of previously seen destination addresses without incurring a high performance overhead. Prior results [6, 10] suggest that a list of 64 or more addresses render sufficiently accurate results.

The static rate algorithm works as follows: When the host sends an outgoing SYN packet, the destination IP is checked against the list of maintained addresses. If the destination is not in the list, it is added to the list and the connection is monitored. If the connection fails, a token is removed from the host's token pool. Detection occurs when the host exhausts its token pool.

If we model the timing of packets transmitted by the background traffic as a Poisson process with rate parameter μ, the arrival of non-scan failures is then a Poisson process with rate parameter $\mu(1 - p_n)$. The probability for false positive for a period of time τ is therefore

$$P_{FP} = \Sigma_k \frac{e^{-\mu(1-p_n)\tau}(\mu(1 - p_n)\tau)^k}{k!} \qquad \text{s.t.} \qquad k > n_0 + a\tau \tag{3}$$

where n_0 is the token balance at the beginning of the interval τ. The false negative probability is,

$$P_{FN} = e^{-\mu(1-p_n)R}(1 + \mu(1 - p_n)R) \qquad \text{s.t.} \qquad R = \frac{1}{a - r_s(1 - p_s)} \tag{4}$$

If $R < 0$, the scan will consume all the tokens independent of the background traffic and $P_{FN} = 0$.

In the remainder of the paper we will use this static rate scheme as a baseline for comparison and contrast it with the adaptive schemes.

5   Adaptive Rate Scan Detection

The main problem with the static rate scheme is that the permitted rate of suspicious events is statically determined, which leaves little freedom for legitimate traffic pertur- bation. If one sets the token reward rate too low, it will result in false positives while a high rate permits a liberal amount of scans to escape the network. In this section, we investigate adaptive rate schemes, which give rise to a dynamically changing rate of permitted suspicious events. As we shall see later in this section, making this rate dynamic in the manners detailed below has significant impact on scan detection.

We propose two adaptive detectors, *Success Based (SB)* and *Failure Based (FB)*. SB changes the token reward rate, a, based on the connection success characteristics of the host. FB changes the token penalty, γ, based on the failure statistics. We analyze and contrast them with the static rate scheme described in Section 4 and other dynamic schemes such as RHT [6] and the CUSUM detector by Ganesh et al.[7] in Section 6.

5.1   Success Based (SB)

The fundamental observation behind SB is that a legitimate host will exhibit a greater percentage of connection successes than a scanning host. As such, SB adjusts the to- ken reward rate based on the connection success statistics of the host. The high-level strategy of SB is simple: more successful hosts are rewarded with a larger token reward rate. This approach is different from RHT [6] and the CUSUM detector by Ganesh et al. [7]; RHT uses only the ratio of success to failure while the CUSUM detector uses only the rate of failures. SB uses both and as a result gives rise to a better overall performance.

To keep track of success statistics, we use the concept of *success index*. The success index of a host after the ith first-contact connection, ρ_i, is calculated as

$$\rho_i = \text{connectionResult}_i \cdot \alpha + \rho_{i-1}(1 - \alpha) \qquad (5)$$

α is a smoothing factor we set to 0.1. connectionResult$_i$ is a binary value indicating the success (1) or failure (0) of the ith connection. ρ_0 is initialized as the percentage of successful connections within the initialization period. Equation 5 renders a weighted index that slightly favors recent connection results, which is more sensitive to short- term traffic pattern changes than a straightforward success ratio. However, the success index calculation is also robust against short traffic bursts, assuming reasonable values for α (typically 0.05 to 0.2).

To put things in perspective, a typical desktop client (with web surfing and email ac- tivities) has a success index greater than 0.6. However, we observed that hosts involved in P2P applications tend to exhibit a wide range of success indices sometimes as low as 0.2. The scan traffic recorded in our traces has a success index less than 0.1.

Table 2. Success Index to Token Reward Rate Mapping (ϵ: desired false positive rate)

Host Success Index (ρ)	Token Reward Rate (a)
$0 \le \rho < 0.1$	$a = $ Desired SST (σ)
$0.1 \le \rho < 0.9$	$a \approx \dfrac{\sigma(1-\rho)e^{(10\ln(\omega/\sigma)\rho)/9}}{\epsilon^{1/n} - 0.146}$
$0.9 \le \rho \le 1$	$a = $ Maximum-to-be-tolerated failure rate (ω)

Once we have the success index, the token reward rate, a, is determined in the fashion detailed in Table 2. Hosts with success indices below 0.1 receive the lowest a set to be the desired SST. For instance, $a = 0.01$ (1 token every 100 seconds) matches an SST of 1 scan per 100 seconds. Similarly, we set the largest token reward rate to the maximum to-be-tolerated legitimate failure rate and allocate this rate to hosts whose success indices are above 0.9. For the mid-range success indices, a is determined by the formula shown in Table 2 where ϵ is the desired false positive rate, and n is the maximum token balance. These values reflect SB's design philosophy that benign hosts are rewarded for good behavior while potentially malicious hosts are progressively restricted. For hosts whose success indices are low (likely scanners), token reward rates should approximate the desired SST. When a host's success index is above 0.9 (likely legitimate), its token reward rate reflects the largest to-be-tolerated failure rate for the host; anything lower could result in false positives. The mid-range mapping in Table 2 was selected with the goal of maintaining a low SST and low false positives. To see the derivation of this formula, please refer to our tech report [14].

Table 2 provides a general guideline for setting token reward rates based on the success index. To avoid adjusting the token reward rate for small changes in ρ one can set incremental values for a based on the relationship guideline laid out in Table 2. An example is shown in Table 3 (σ is 0.01, ω is 4.0, and ϵ is 2%).

Excluding the calculation of the success index and the dynamic token reward rate, SB operates exactly the same as the static rate scheme–one token is removed for each first-contact failure and only first-contact connections are considered in the calculation of the success index.

The probability for false positive with SB is as follows,

$$P_{FP} = \Sigma_k \frac{e^{-\mu(1-p_n)\tau}(\mu(1-p_n)\tau)^k}{k!} \qquad \text{s.t.} \qquad k > n_0 + f(\rho)\tau \qquad (6)$$

where μ is the background traffic rate, and $f(\rho)$ represents the mapping between ρ and the token reward rate as defined by Table 2. The false negative probability for SB is,

$$P_{FN} = e^{-\mu(1-p_n)T}(1 + \mu(1-p_n)T) \qquad \text{s.t.} \qquad T = \frac{1}{f(\rho) - r_s(1-p_s)} \qquad (7)$$

Note that a scanner can inflate ρ by generating successful first-contact connections. This way the host will receive a greater token reward rate and thereby increasing the SST. Unlike RHT, the SST of SB increases at a substantially lower rate. A detailed comparison and analysis of SB vs. other schemes appears in Section 6.

Table 3. Example Reward Rates for SB

Host Success Index	Token Reward Rate	Host Success Index	Token Reward Rate
$0 \leq \rho < 0.1$	0.01	$0.5 \leq \rho < 0.6$	0.75
$0.1 \leq \rho < 0.2$	0.10	$0.6 \leq \rho < 0.7$	1.0
$0.2 \leq \rho < 0.3$	0.25	$0.7 \leq \rho < 0.8$	2.0
$0.3 \leq \rho < 0.4$	0.40	$0.8 \leq \rho < 0.9$	3.0
$0.4 \leq \rho < 0.5$	0.50	$0.9 \leq \rho \leq 1.0$	4.0

5.2 Failure Based (FB)

Instead of changing the token reward rate, FB adjusts the token penalty, γ, based on the host's failure behavior. FB achieves dynamic rates with a decidedly different focus than SB; FB is more restrictive and achieves faster detection by manipulating γ. This, however, necessitates an increase in false positives, but the success test here is a lower false positive rate than that of a static-rate scheme with the same SST.

At a high level: FB increases γ as the host's failure rate increases and reduces it as the failure rate decreases. The token reward rate, a, remains constant in FB. We will detail how a is determined below. To determine the token penalty, FB periodically estimates the host's failure rate as follows: after each interval i, the failure rate, ϕ_i, is calculated as

$$\phi_i = \text{current\_failure\_rate} \cdot \alpha + \phi_{i-1} \cdot (1 - \alpha) \tag{8}$$

where current_failure_rate is the average failure rate for the current period (i) and α is the smoothing factor. We use an α of 0.25 here. ϕ_0 is the average failure rate for the first interval.

In addition to ϕ, FB uses two other quantities; 1) a, the constant token reward rate, is set to the maximum, to-be-tolerated, failure rate (a may reflect a legitimate bursty failure rate) and 2) β, the maximum length of legitimate failure bursts, also the length of estimation interval for failure rates. Both a and β are configurable parameters. For our network, failure bursts for legitimate hosts typically last fewer than 5 seconds, and therefore a five-second interval window seems appropriate.

FB adjusts the token penalty per failure, γ, based on the failure rate, ϕ, in a fashion detailed in Table 4. For each range of failure rate, the interval-until-depletion number specifies the desired number of intervals until the depletion of tokens, assuming the failure rate remains stable. These numbers are system-specific parameters, set based on traffic characteristics and the target false negative and false positive probability. More specifically,

- If ϕ, is less than $0.2a$, the host is considered normal and γ is set to 1 to allow the maximum permitted failure rate a (note that the permitted failure rate for the host is a/γ). For these values, the interval-until-depletion is infinite.
- Hosts whose failure rates are within $[0.2a, 0.4a]$ should primarily be legitimate hosts. However, we increase the penalty to 2 to allow only 50% of the maximum permitted failure rate. This would shorten the detection time should the failure rate continue to increase (e.g. due to a scan).

- If ϕ is close to a ($\phi \geq 0.8a$), the host has been generating failures close to the maximum rate for more than one interval (see Equation 8). Continued failures at this rate are well outside what is considered acceptable. The token penalty is therefore set to $a\beta$ to ensure that all tokens will be depleted before the end of the next interval.
- For hosts whose failure rate is within $[0.4a, 0.8a]$, one selects the desired number of intervals until depletion; they are system-specific parameters. x_1 and x_2 should be progressively smaller. γ can be calculated subsequently using the formula in Table 4. Such a penalty will give rise to the desired number of interval-until-depletion, if the failure rate remains within the same range . In our network, we set x_1 and x_2 to 4 and 2, respectively. The corresponding token penalties are therefore 3 and 4.

Assuming the background traffic as Poisson with a rate μ, the false positive probability for FB as,

$$P_{FP} = \Sigma_j \left(\frac{e^{-\mu(1-p_n)\tau}(\mu(1-p_n)\tau)^j}{j!} \right) \quad \text{s.t.} \quad j \geq \frac{n_0 + a\tau}{g(\phi)} \quad (9)$$

where a is the constant token reward rate and $g(\cdot)$ is the function defined by Table 4 such that $\gamma \leftarrow g(\phi)$.

The probability of false negative is,

$$P_{FN} = e^{-\mu(1-p_n)T}(1 + \mu(1-p_n)T) \quad \text{s.t.} \quad T = \frac{1}{a/g(\phi) - r_s(1-p_s)} \quad (10)$$

where r_s is the scan rate and p_s is the scan success probability.

Table 4. Penalties for FB Detection

Estimated Failure Rate (ϕ)	Desired intervals until token depletion	Penalty γ(# tokens)
$0 \leq \phi < 0.2a$	∞	1
$0.2a \leq \phi < 0.4a$	∞	2
$0.4a \leq \phi < 0.6a$	x_1	$\left(\frac{n}{x_1\beta} + a\right) 1/\phi$
$0.6a \leq \phi < 0.8a$	x_2	$\left(\frac{n}{x_2\beta} + a\right) 1/\phi$
$\phi \geq 0.8a$	1	$a\beta$

FB cannot by gamed; the only way to evade detection with FB is to reduce the failure rate of the host. For scanning worms, doing so necessitates a reduction in the scan rate, which leads to a slower propagation.

5.3   Probability of Error

Figures 1(a) and (b) show the false positives and negatives probabilities for SB, FB and the baseline static rate scheme. Figure 1(a) shows the false positive probability against 5-second traffic bursts. The parameters of the schemes plotted here are selected such that static and FB would have the same SSTs.

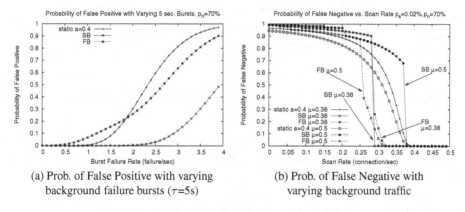

(a) Prob. of False Positive with varying
background failure bursts (τ=5s)

(b) Prob. of False Negative with
varying background traffic

Fig. 1. Error Probabilities for SB, FB and Static Schemes

A number of observations are significant here. First, when the SSTs are similar, in Figure 1(a) the false positive probability for the static rate scheme increases at a greater rate than the others as the burst failure rate increases–the static rate scheme is less robust against background failure bursts. Second, SB exhibits the least chance of false positive. This is not surprising since one of the design goals for SB was the accommodation of such bursts for hosts with a large success index. In our experience, legitimate hosts can generate short bursts with up to 3 or 4 failures/second. The parameter setting plotted in Figure 1(a) stipulates that the static-rate scheme will likely generate false positives with at least 40% probability during such bursts. To remedy this, we can increase the token reward rate, but doing so would increase the SST. Within the three schemes, SB has a visibly lower false positive rate and is in general less sensitive to changes in the background traffic rate.

The false negative plot in Figure 1(b) shows the detection capabilities of the schemes with respect to scan rates and two different background traffic rates $\mu = 0.38$ and 0.5. We opt for low background traffic rates to better represent average long term traffic characteristics. When $\mu = 0.38$, the three detectors have approximately the same SST (0.3scans/second). Both SB and FB have a sharper decreasing false negative probability than the static scheme. This is intentional, since both aim for fast detection of scanners beyond their SSTs. When the background traffic rate, μ, increases, SB's SST pulls away from the others since its success index will likely be higher due to more background successes. We will address the SST inflation issue of SB in Section 6.2.

Overall, FB provides fast detection but is susceptible to false positives when bursty failures occur, and hence is more appropriate for a controlled environment with well-understood traffic characteristics. SB, on the other hand, is more robust against traffic perturbation and is also able to quickly detect scanners. SB would work well in an open network with diverse traffic characteristics. Table 5 provides the expected SST and Escaped_Count for each scheme mentioned so far in the paper.

To put things in perspective, assume normal traffic success probability $p_n = 0.7$, scan success probability $p_s = 0.02\%$, and the expected rate of non-scan traffic $\mu = 0.4$ (4 connections in 10 seconds), a token reward rate of $a = 1$ for static and FB, a penalty

Table 5. Expected Sustained Scanning Threshold and Escaped_Count Equations

Scheme	$E[SST]$	$E[\text{Escaped\_Count}]$
Static Rate	$\frac{a/\gamma - \mu(1-p_n)}{1-p_s}$	$\frac{E[Tokens]}{\gamma(r_s(1-p_s)+\mu(1-p_n))-a} \cdot r_s$
SB	$\frac{f(\rho)-\mu(1-p_n)}{1-p_s}$	$\frac{E[Tokens]}{r_s(1-p_s)+\mu(1-p_n)-f(\rho)} \cdot r_s$
FB	$\left(\frac{a}{g(\mu(1-P_n)+r_s(1-p_s))} - \mu(1-p_n)\right)/(1-p_s)$	$\frac{E[Tokens]}{g(\phi)(r_s(1-p_s)+\mu(1-p_n))-a} \cdot r_s$

of $\gamma = 1$ for static, and the remaining parameters configured as described in the paper. The expected SST for the static rate scheme, SB, and FB would be 0.8802, 0.3, and 0.28, respectively.

6   Analysis

In this section we present a detailed analysis of SB and FB, comparing against the static scheme and other adaptive detectors. We show that, both analytically and empirically, SB and FB are capable of rendering lower SSTs than the others while maintaining comparable or better detection precisions.

6.1   Other Adaptive Detectors

Two scan detectors, *Reverse Hypothesis Test* (RHT) [6] and the CUSUM detector [7], are of particular interest to this work because both fall in the category of adaptive scan detection. Due to space constraints, we give only a brief description of RHT and CUSUM. Readers should refer to the original papers for more details.

RHT is a random walk based detector that operates in the range of real numbers. The position of the walk is increased by a pre-determined range for each first-contact failure and decreased by a pre-determined range for a first-contact success. If the random walk exceeds a certain threshold, the algorithm terminates and reports that the host is a scanner. Translating RHT into a token-based form entails taking log of the step function values as the subtraction and addition operation of tokens. If we use the original parameter setting as defined in [6], the token representation of RHT calls for the removal of one token for every first-contact failure and the addition of 1.77 tokens for each first-contact success. The expected value of token reward rate for RHT is therefore, $E[a] = 1.77(r_s p_s + \mu p_n)$, and the expected SST and Escaped_Count for RHT are as follows, using the expected token reward rate.

$$E[SST_{RHT}] = \frac{\mu(2.77p_n - 1)}{1 - 2.77p_s} \tag{11}$$

$$E[\text{Escaped\_Count}_{RHT}] = \frac{E[Tokens]}{r_s(1 - 2.77p_s) + \mu(1 - 2.77p_n)} \cdot r_s \tag{12}$$

RHT is susceptible to gaming in that a scanner can generate successful cover traffic to accrue more tokens. If the cover traffic is able to generate more tokens than the scan traffic consumes, detection will not occur.

The CUSUM detector by Ganesh et al. [7] is analogous to FB in that both are only concerned with failure characteristics. CUSUM assumes that the detector knows the failure rate of both non-scan and scan traffic, which they call λ_0 and λ_1, respectively. CUSUM also provides a *suboptimal* way to estimate λ_1 based on λ_0, the maximum token balance and the scan success probability. Central to CUSUM is the concept of inter-failure time; the detector rewards more tokens for a larger inter-failure time, and removes more tokens for a smaller inter-failure time.

Equations 13 and 14 provide the expected SST and Escaped_Count, respectively.

$$E[SST_{CUSUM}] = \left(\frac{\lambda_1 - \lambda_0}{\log(\lambda_1/\lambda_0)} - \mu(1 - p_n) \right) / (1 - p_s) \tag{13}$$

$$E[\text{Escaped\_Count}_{CUSUM}] = \frac{E[Tokens]}{\log(\lambda_1/\lambda_0)(r_s(1 - p_s) + \mu(1 - p_n)) - (\lambda_1 - \lambda_0)} \tag{14}$$

If we assume the non-scan failure rate λ_0 is 1 failure/second and we calculate λ_1 using the suboptimal method, $\lambda_1 = 1.003$, for CUSUM and use the original parameter settings for RHT. The same example where $\mu = 0.4$, $p_n = 70\%$, and $p_s = 0.02\%$ renders SSTs of 0.882 and 0.375 scans per second for CUSUM and RHT, respectively. It is important to mention that for CUSUM, the larger the difference between λ_1 and λ_0, the larger the number of tokens removed for quick inter-failure times, which results in faster detection. However, increasing λ_1 will lead to a higher SST. As such, there is a trade-off between SST and detection speed for CUSUM as λ_1 varies and λ_0 stays constant.

6.2 Sustained Scanning Threshold Analysis

Figure 2(a) shows the expected SST for all the schemes discussed thus far with varying background traffic rate, μ. In this plot, we use a non-scan success probability $p_n = 70\%$ and a token reward rate of $a = 1$ for both static-rate and FB. For CUSUM, we plotted two configuration settings; the suboptimal λ_1 and $\lambda_1 = 3$. For both configurations the expected background failure rate, λ_0, is set to match the background failure rate.

As shown in Figure 2, compared to the other schemes, both SB and FB render a substantially lower SST's for a wide range of background traffic rates. The CUSUM suboptimal configuration yielded a near zero SST. However, the suboptimal configuration's Escaped_Count in Figure 2(b) is magnitudes larger and off the chart. It is important to note that with the scan probability of success, p_s, used in calculation the basic reproduction number for the infected hosts would be slightly less than one. On average another host would not be infected. However, this long delay still permits a large number of scans to escape the network before the host is detected. As such, the CUSUM suboptimal detector is not a good choice in practice. The other CUSUM detector, when λ_1 is a larger fixed value of 3, fared better in that its Escaped_Count is comparable to the other schemes once the scan rate surpasses the SST. For a fixed λ_0, as λ_1 increases the SST increases and the Escaped_Count decreases.

RHT's SST increases with background traffic. In our experience, normal desktop machines tend to initiate connections in the neighborhood of 0.5 connections/second.

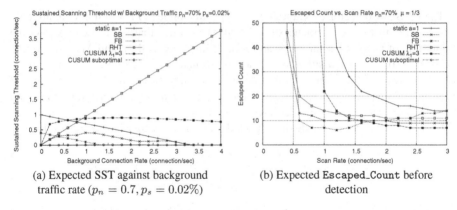

(a) Expected SST against background
traffic rate ($p_n = 0.7, p_s = 0.02\%$)

(b) Expected `Escaped_Count` before
detection

Fig. 2. Sustained Scanning Thresholds and Escaped Counts

These hosts are well suited for SB, FB, or RHT. For more active hosts with traffic rates over 0.5 connections/second, SB and FB are a better choice if slow scanners are concerned. Note that SB has consistently low SSTs across the different values of μ; as such, SB is better suited for hosts with diverse traffic patterns.

Assuming a constant p_n and p_s, the static rate and FB schemes give rise to an expected SST value that is inversely proportional to the background traffic rate. As the background traffic rate grows, so does the background failure rate, which leaves less tokens for scan traffic, thereby reducing the SST. For RHT the expected value of SST grows linearly with the rate of the background traffic (as indicated by Equation 11). For SB, this increase is slower and tapers off as the background traffic rate hits 1 connection/second. This disparity of behavior between RHT and SB is important. For RHT, it would require a significant amount of time to detect a scanner on a host with a near 100% success rate (numerous failures are needed to counteract the addition of tokens). With SB, however, the limited token reward rate allows consecutive failures to quickly exhaust the token balance.

Figure 2(b) shows the expected `Escaped_Count` for each scheme with varying scan rates. For this plot, we assume a constant background traffic rate of 1/3 connection/second and success probability of 70%. For each scheme, when the scan rate surpasses its SST (where the `Escaped_Count` approaches infinity), the number of permitted scans decreases exponentially. Note that SB and FB exhibit a faster decrease in `Escaped_Count` than the other schemes. One of the fundamental differences between our schemes and the others is that both SB and FB have a non-linear relationship between the traffic failure rate and the token balance. In SB and FB, the token balance decreases superlinear to the increase of the connection failure rate when the failure rate is near the SSTs. As such, these schemes provide faster detection than others.

A graphical depiction of the epidemic growth of worms at the cusp of SST is shown in Figure 3(a). This plot includes the estimated, "untampered" growth of Blaster as a baseline comparison to the epidemic growth when scan detectors are in place. The graph uses a constant μ of 0.4 connection/second, p_n of 70%, and the scheme configurations mentioned in the individual sections. Compared with other detectors, SB and FB can

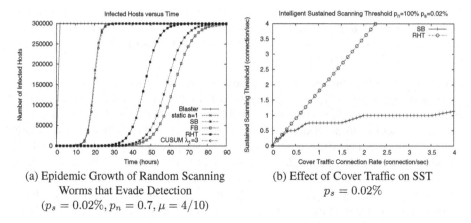

(a) Epidemic Growth of Random Scanning
Worms that Evade Detection
$(p_s = 0.02\%, p_n = 0.7, \mu = 4/10)$

(b) Effect of Cover Traffic on SST
$p_s = 0.02\%$

Fig. 3. Permitted Worm Spread and Effect of Cover Traffic on the Schemes

deter worm growth significantly—reaching 15% of the susceptible population with SB or FB requires more than twice the amount of time as with CUSUM or the static rate detector.

Gaming of SST. A scanner can game RHT and SB by adding successful cover traffic. To be effective, the cover traffic needs to have a high success probability. Figure 3(b) plots the SSTs for SB and RHT versus the rate of cover traffic. For simplicity, we assume that all non-scan traffic is cover traffic that succeeds with 100% probability (i.e., p_n=1). As shown, SB's SST increases at a much slower rate that that of RHT's.

According to Equation 11, RHT's SST increases linearly to the cover traffic rate, μ, assuming p_n and p_s are constants. In contrast, SB's SST is upperbounded by $\frac{\omega}{1-p_s}$ where ω is the max to-be-tolerated failure rate (see Table 5 when p_n is 1).

6.3   Error Rates

In this section, we present an empirical analysis of the various detectors using both real and simulated network traffic.

Trace Data. We use four traffic traces in this study. Traces I and II were collected at the boundary of a 1200-host network. The network serves approximately 1500 users and has a variety of operating systems and applications. The traces include TCP headers of traffic entering and exiting the network. Trace I is a 25-day outbound trace that contains the outbreak of *Blaster* [15] and *Welchia* [16], scanning worms that infected 103 local hosts in our network. Trace II is a 10-day outbound trace with no internal scan activity; it is used to investigate false positives.

Traces III and IV are synthetic traffic that include simulated slow scans and traffic bursts. In both traces there are 1100 hosts of which 100 perform 1 scan every two seconds. 75% of the hosts generate background traffic that succeeds 70% of the time and is a Poisson process with a rate of 0.1. The other 25% generate traffic that succeeds with a 30% probability and is a Poisson process with a mean of 0.05. This mix of traffic is a simplification of the real traffic seen in our network. In both traces, the more active hosts (75%) have five-second bursts. These bursts occur uniformly with 1% probability for each five second interval. Trace III has relatively slow bursts at the rate of 0.5 connections/second. Trace IV has faster bursts at the rate of 2 connections/second to simulate traffic during business hours.

Simulation Results. The token-based implementation of our algorithms is straightforward; each host is originally allocated n tokens and first-contact connections are differentiated using a set of Previously-Contacted-Hosts, as in RHT [6]. For the static-rate detector, we set the token reward rate, a, to 1 per second, and each first-contact failure consumes a token. For SB, a is set based on the success index (see Table 2) and 10 connections are used for the initialization period. For FB, we estimate the host's failure rate and use Table 4 to determine the penalty for each subsequent first-contact failure. RHT and CUSUM were implemented as described in [6] and [7] and several configurations were simulated. In particular, ident resulted in many false positives for RHT. Since ident can be easily whitelisted, we present results for RHT with and without ident.

The CUSUM detector requires estimates for the non-scan failure rate, λ_0, and the scan failure rate, λ_1. We set λ_0 to match the permitted failure rate/token reward rate of the static-rate scheme. We used two values for λ_1. The first one was 10 failures/second to approximate the optimal situation when the worm scanning rate is known.[2] The second one uses the "suboptimal" estimate with a scan success of probability, p_s, of 0.02.

Table 6. Experimental Results

Scheme	Settings	FN Rate(%)	Mean Esc. Count			FP Rate (%)			
Trace		I	I	III	IV	I	II	III	IV
Static Rate	$a = 1$	0	13.1	–	–	0.35	0.71	–	–
	$a = 0.4$	–	–	34.0	32.3	–	–	0	48.5
RHT	normal	0	10.2	–	–	27.216	4.876	–	–
	no Ident	0	10.2	8.98	8.93	2.216	4.876	21.2	23.1
CUSUM	$\lambda_1 = 10$	0	13.4	–	–	0.62	0.17	–	–
$\lambda_0 = 1$	suboptimal	26.2	8367	–	–	0	0	–	–
$\lambda_0 = 0.4$	$\lambda_1 = 0.5$	–	–	423	376	–	–	0	0
	optimal	–	–	8.21	8.07	–	–	1.5	71.7
SB	$\sigma = 0.01, \omega = 4$	0	10.4	13.53	13.39	0.798	0.355	1.4	8.8
FB	$a=1, \beta=5$ $x_1=4, x_2=2$	0	10.1	15.1	14.7	0.62	1.24	0.2	29.6

Table 6 shows the results of our experiments. False negative (FN) rate is defined as the portion of scanners that elude detection. False positive (FP) rate is the portion of legitimate hosts incorrectly labeled as scanners. The mean Escaped_Count is the average number of scans from infected hosts before the scanner is detected.

All but the "suboptimal" CUSUM were able to detect all the scanners. Most schemes rendered a similar detection efficiency, as indicated by the mean Escaped_Count. This is primarily due to the fact that Blaster is a fast scanning worm whose behavior is

---

[2] Infected hosts in Trace I generated roughly 10 scans/second with a success of 0.02%.

clearly different from normal traffic. In our experiments Blaster managed to deplete all tokens before a single new token was awarded. For this reason, Trace I is not ideal for studying detection efficiency. The experiments with Traces III and IV have more descriptive results.

Note that CUSUM performs well only if the estimates of λ_0 and λ_1 are close to the real failure rates. The "suboptimal" estimation method renders a λ_1 significantly smaller than the real scan rates. This configuration missed over 25% of the scanners and resulted in a large Escaped_Count. The CUSUM work is of theoretical interest because it shows that there exists an optimal detector if scan and traffic rates are known. In practice these assumptions often do not hold.

Overall SB and FB performed well with Traces I and II and yielded a lower false positive rate than RHT. This is because RHT considers the cumulative number of failures rather than the failure rate. Consequently, RHT can not handle legitimate hosts that experience persistent but slow failures. In contrast, SB and FB consider both failure numbers and rates. To present meaningful results with Trace III and IV, we changed a few parameters to ensure that the slow scans in these traces are detectable. The permitted failure rate for static and "suboptimal" CUSUM is altered to render an SST similar to the other schemes. The optimal configuration of CUSUM has a background failure rate of $\mu(1 - p_n)$ and a scan failure rate of $r_s(1 - p_s)$. FN Rate columns are not included for Traces III and IV because all scans are detected. Traces III and IV include traffic bursts to show the impact of background traffic perturbation. Recall that Trace III has near constant traffic with slower bursts, while Trace IV includes larger bursts representative of work day network traffic.

As shown, the static-rate scheme had a false positive rate of 48.5% with bursty background traffic. This is consistent with our sensitivity analysis in Section 5.3 that showed the static-rate scheme is more sensitive to traffic perturbation. The optimal CUSUM detector had a large error rate for Trace IV because it assumes that failure rates remain constant and therefore cannot accommodate traffic perturbations.

SB and FB performed well in the presence of bursty traffic. SB in particular maintained a low false positive rate and Escaped_Count throughout. FB showed a larger increase in the false positive rate when traffic became burstier, but was still on par with RHT. When traffic is predictable (Trace III), SB's and FB's detection speeds are only slightly worse than optimal (as compared to the optimal CUSUM detector), and their false positive rates are extremely low.

7   Summary

In this paper, we present two adaptive local scan detectors, Success Based (SB) and Failure Based (FB). In the token-based framework, SB regulates the token reward rate based on the host's connection successes. FB, on the other hand, adjusts the token penalty based on the failure behavior of the host.

Both SB and FB can quickly detect slow scanners while maintaining similar detection precisions to other detectors. More importantly, we show that SB and FB are less susceptible to intelligent gaming and more robust against traffic variations. We show that previously proposed detectors fail to achieve similar goals. The desirable properties of the adaptive detectors arise from their non-linear nature, which allows the detector to change its detection threshold dynamically, based on both long and short term statistics. This ultimately gives rise to faster detection and decreased sensitivity to short-term traffic perturbation.

The desirable properties of the adaptive detectors arise from their non-linear nature. This is in contrast to the previously proposed, largely linear detectors. Traditionally, detectors label a host a scanner if the rate or the number of suspicious events exceeds a pre-determined threshold. The adaptive algorithms allow the detector to change its threshold based on both long and short term statistics. This gives rise to faster detection and decreased sensitivity to short-term traffic perturbation.

Acknowledgments

This material is based upon work supported by the National Science Foundation under Grant No. 0326472 and an SRS grant by DARPA.

References

1. Heberlein, L.T., Dias, G.V., Levitt, K.N., Mukherjee, B., Wood, J., Wolber, D.: A network security monitor. In: Proc. IEEE Symposium on Research in Security and Privacy. (1990) 296–304
2. Weaver, N., Staniford, S., Paxson, V.: Very fast containment of scanning worms. In: Proceedings of the 13th USENIX Security Symposium. (2004)
3. Roesch, M.: Snort: Lightweight intrusion detection for networks. In: Proceedings of the 13th Conference on Computer and Communication Security (LISA-99). (1999) 229–238
4. Paxson, V.: Bro: a system for detecting network intruders in real-time. Computer Networks **31(23-24)** (1999) 2435–2463
5. Jung, J., Paxon, V., Berger, A.W., Balakrishman, H.: Fast portscan detection using sequential hypothesis testing. In: Proceedings of 2004 IEEE Symposium on Security and Privacy. (2004)
6. Schechter, S., Jung, J., Berger, A.W.: Fast detection of scanning worm infections. In: Recent Advances In Intrusion Detection (RAID) 2004, France (2004)
7. Ganesh, A., Gunawardena, D., Key, P., Massoulie, L., Scott, J.: Efficient quarantining of scanning worms: Optimal detection and coordination. In: Proceedings of IEEE INFOCOM 2006. (2006)
8. Williamson, M.: Throttling viruses: Restricting propagation to defeat malicious mobile code. In: Proceedings of the 18th Annual Computer Security Applications Conference, Las Vegas, Nevada (2002)
9. Chen, S., Tang, Y.: Slowing down internet worms. In: Proceedings of 24th International Conference on Distributed Computing Systems, Tokyo, Japan (2004)
10. Wong, C., Bielski, S., Studer, A., Wang, C.: Empirical analysis of rate limiting mechanisms. In: Recent Advances In Intrusion Detection (RAID) 2005, Seattle (2005)
11. Singh, S., Estan, C., Varghese, G., Savage, S.: Automated worm fingerprinting. Proceedings of the 6th ACM/USENIX Symposium on Operating System Design and Implementation (2004)
12. Kim, H., Karp, B.: Autograph: Toward automated, distributed worm signature detection. In: Proceedings of the 13th USENIX Security Symposium, San Diego, California, USA (2004)
13. Newsome, J., Karp, B., Song, D.: Polygraph: Automatic signature generation for polymorphic worms. In: Proc. IEEE Symposium on Research in Security and Privacy. (2005)

14. Studer, A., Wang, C.: Fast detection of local scanners using adaptive thresholds. Technical Report CMU-Cylab-06-004, Carnegie Mellon University (2006)
15. Symantec: W32.Blaster.Worm. http://securityresponse.symantec.com /avcenter/venc/data/ w32.blaster.worm.html (2003)
16. Symantec: W32.Welchia.Worm. http://securityresponse.symantec.com /avcenter/venc/data/ w32.welchia.worm.html (2003)

Probabilistic Proof of an Algorithm to Compute TCP Packet Round-Trip Time for Intrusion Detection

Jianhua Yang[1] and Yongzhong Zhang[2]

[1] Department of Computer Science, University of Houston
4800 Calhoun Rd. Houston, TX, 77204 USA
jhyang@cs.uh.edu
[2] Department of Computer Science, Shanghai TV University
288 Guoshun Rd, Shanghai, 200433 China
yzhang@shtvu.edu.cn

Abstract. Most network intruders tend to use stepping-stones to attack or invade other hosts to reduce the risks of being discovered. One typical approach for detecting stepping-stone intrusion is to estimate the number of connections of an interactive session by using the round-trip times (RTTs) of all Send packets. The key of this approach is to match TCP packets, or compute the RTT of each Send packet. Previous methods, which focus on matching each Send packet with its corresponding Echo packet to compute RTTs, have tradeoff between packet matching-rate and matching-accuracy. In this paper, we first propose and prove a clustering algorithm to compute the RTTs of the Send packets of a TCP interactive session, and show that this approach can compute RTTs with both high matching-rate and high matching-accuracy.

Keywords: Network security, intrusion detection, stepping-stone, round-trip time, TCP packet-matching.

1 Introduction

Computer and network security has been becoming more and more important as people depend on the Internet to conduct business, and the number of the Internet attacks has increased greatly [1], [2], [3]. To detect and traceback intruders on the Internet have become more and more difficult than before because most intruders are using some sophisticated technologies and usually launching their attacks indirectly to reduce the risks of being discovered. One prevalent way used by intruders is to take advantage of stepping-stones [4], which are computer hosts compromised by intruders to hide themselves deeply, to launch their attacks. Bunch of techniques have been proposed and developed to detect such kind of attacks, called stepping-stone intrusion.

One representative of the techniques is to estimate the downstream length (in number of connections) of a connection chain from the monitor host where a monitor program resides to the destination host to detect the existence of a stepping-stone intrusion. Yung [5] firstly published the idea to do it in 2002. In that paper, Yung proposed to use the RTT between one Send packet and its corresponding Echo packet to measure the length of a connection chain. The problem is that Yung did not

J. Zhou, M. Yung, and F. Bao (Eds.): ACNS 2006, LNCS 3989, pp. 18–32, 2006.

propose a way to match each Send and Echo packet exactly. Instead he used statistical method to estimate the RTT of a Send packet, which is not accurate, especially when send-echo pairs are overlapped deeply, which happens often on the Internet. Yang and Huang [6] published an idea to estimate the RTT of a Send packet by matching a TCP Send packet with its corresponding Echo packet; it results in the Conservative and the Greedy algorithms. Yang [6] makes use of TCP Send and Echo packet sequence number and takes advantage of the gap between two consecutive Send packets to match TCP packets. However, even though Yang claimed that the Conservative algorithm can estimate the RTT accurately, but only few packets are matched especially under the scenario that send-echo pairs are overlapped deeply. The Greedy algorithm can cover most of the Send packets, but with some incorrectly matches. Neither of them can obtain both high packet matching-rate and high packet matching-accuracy. The problem is that they always search for a 'candidate' Echo packet locally, rather than globally, when they try to match a Send packet.

In this paper, we propose a clustering algorithm that matches most of Send packets, and computes the RTTs of Send packets more accurate. This algorithm is based on a result that is a cluster with smallest standard deviation has the highest probability to represent the true RTTs, which can be proved by using Chebyshev inequality. The clustering algorithm can get both high packet matching-rate and high packet matching-accuracy in computing packet RTTs because it looks for a 'candidate' Echo packet globally when it tries to match a Send packet. The way used in the Conservative and the Greedy algorithms is that once an Echo packet is captured, we must determine its matched Send packet immediately even though sometimes we could not. Unlike this way, the clustering algorithm takes the approach that once we catch an Echo packet, we do not determine its matched Send packet immediately even though occasionally we are pretty sure the matched Send packet.

The contributions of this paper are the two points. 1) We prove a result that is the cluster, which is generated from the Send and Echo packets of a TCP interactive session, with smallest standard deviation has the highest probability to represent the true RTTs of the Send packets. 2) We propose a clustering algorithm based on the proved result to compute the RTTs by matching each TCP Send and Echo packets globally.

The rest of this paper is arranged as following. In Section 2, we talk about the motivations of proposing the clustering algorithm to compute RTTs. Section 3 presents the clustering algorithm and its probabilistic proof. In section 4, some experimental results and comparisons are presented. Section 5 presents some related work. Finally, in Section 6, the whole work is summarized, and the future work is presented.

2   The Motivation

Detecting a long interactive connection chain is a very important method to detect stepping-stone intrusion because it has no false alarms. The key issue of estimating the length of a connection chain is to match the TCP packets flowing through a connection chain, or to compute the RTTs of TCP Send packets. If each Send packet is followed immediately by one or more Echo packets, such as the sequence $\{s_1, e_1, s_2,$

e_2, e_3, s_3, e_4} in which each element represents the timestamp of the corresponding Send or Echo packet, the gaps e_1-s_1, e_2-s_2, and e_4-s_3 would be the true RTT of each Send packet s_1, s_2, and s_3 respectively. The complexity of matching TCP packets is in the situation that more Send packets are followed by more Echo packets, which is overlap of send-echo pair. For example, if the above case became the sequence {s_1, s_2, e_1, e_2, e_3, s_3, e_4}, there would be several possible packet-matching schemes. 1) Send packet s_1 together with s_2 are matched by e_1, e_2, and e_3; 2) s_1 is matched with e_1, as well as s_2 is matched with e_2, and e_3; 3) s_1 is matched with e_1 and e_2, thus s_2 matches e_3; 4) s_1 matches e_1, e_2, and e_3, therefore, s_2 and s_3 match e_4. If you look at the four schemes, s_1 must match e_1 whatever the matching scheme is. This is just the idea of the Conservative algorithm [4], which has low matching-rate because it ignores to match s_2 in the above case. The Greedy algorithm [4] takes a very rapacious way to match the rest Send packets, which is FIFO. As a result, for the above case, the Greedy algorithm would match s_1 with e_1, in addition, match s_2 with e_2. This is why it is possible that the Greedy algorithm has low matching-accuracy because the matches determined by FIFO policy might not be correct.

However, we are aware of one fact that each Echo packet must correspond to one or more Send packets which timestamps are smaller than that of the Echo packet. When we capture an Echo packet, even though we are not sure its matched Send packet, but we do know there is at least one Send packet matched with it. We simply assume that every Send packet is supposed to match the Echo packet, and compute each gap between each Send packet and the Echo packet. For each Echo packet, we have one gap set in which one of the gaps must be the true RTT of the Echo packet. The problem is that we are not sure which gap is the right one. The interesting thing is if we observe more such gap sets, we found that for most of the gap sets, each gap set has one element that is very close to the ones in other gap sets. The only sound explanation is those tight elements are the true RTTs of the Send packets unless this is a coincidence. The more gap sets we observe, the lower probability that it is a coincidence. After we explore the distribution of true RTTs, we believe the probability of coincidence is extremely small. The feature of the distribution of the true RTTs motivates us a way to extract the RTTs from the gap sets observed. This way is the algorithm to be discussed in Section 3.

The RTT of a Send packet is the sum of processing delay, queuing delay, transmission delay and propagation delay [10] for the packet in a connection chain on the Internet. Further research pointed out that a RTT is mainly determined by the propagation delay and the queuing delay [10]. The propagation delay determines mainly its constant part, and the queue delay determines mainly its varying part, which can be simulated by an exponential distribution. In other words, the variation of the RTTs can be modeled as an exponential distribution, which indicates that most of the true RTTs are scattered in a very small range. The true RTTs can be different because the Internet traffic always fluctuates but they vary slightly. If we use standard deviation to measure the variation degree of RTTs, it should be small. If we combine the elements in the gap sets to form clusters, the cluster with smallest standard deviation should have the highest probability to represent the true RTTs. If we could prove this point, the way to pull out the true RTTs from the gap sets would become to find the cluster with smallest standard deviation.

Table 1 shows the comparison of standard deviation over different clusters in a real world example that can give us some practical sense on the above analysis. In this example, a connection chain, which contains six connections, is established by using OpenSSH. We monitor the connection chain at the start of the session for a period of time, and capture all the Send and Echo packets. First, for each Echo packet, we form one gap set; second, we form all the clusters by combining the elements in all the gap sets (for details to form the clusters, see Section 3). We compute the standard deviation (with unit microsecond) of each cluster and show only part of the results in Table 1. It is apparently that the standard deviation of the RTTs (one of the clusters) is much smaller than that of any other cluster.

Table 1. Comparison of standard deviations of time gap clusters

RTTs	cluster1	cluster2	cluster3	cluster4	cluster5
2.8E3	4.4E7	3.3E6	2.7E5	1.7E7	8.5E6

There are two problems needed to mention. One is to process resend packet. Another is to process the Send packets without reply. Resend packets are easy to handle because they have the same sequence (Seq) and acknowledgement (Ack) number. We do not record the Send packet if it has the same Seq and Ack number as its previous packet. We know that is not every Send packet is replied by the victim site (or the host at the end of a session). There are still few Send packets only acknowledged by the downstream neighbor host or not replied at all, such as ignore packet, keep-alive packet, and key re-exchange packet [7], [8], [9]. These packets are not intended for the target machine, so we cannot capture their Echo packets. The question is if they affect the result of packet-matching or computing RTTs. First, it does not affect our clustering algorithm much because the amount of these packets is very small comparing to the whole Send packets. Second, if a Send packet is not echoed by the final destination host, it does not matter due to the two reasons. 1) Its gap is not involved into the cluster that represents the RTTs because this gap is probably either smaller or larger than a regular RTT. 2) Even though we assume that the gap between this Send packet and the other Echo packet is close to the true RTTs and involved into the RTT cluster accidentally, but the only effect is we have one more packet-matching. It does not affect the estimation of RTTs. To simplify our analysis, we assume every Send packet is replied by the final destination host.

3   Clustering Algorithm and Its Proof

Given two sequences $S=\{s_1, s_2, ..., s_n\}$ and $E=\{e_1, e_2, ..., e_m\}$, where s_i is a Send packet, as well as its timestamp, and so is e_j. We assume that the packets in these two sequences are captured from the monitor host in a connection chain at the same period of time. We can use S and E to generate different data sets, which are actually aggregations of gaps between each Send packet in S and each Echo packet in E. There are two ways to create the data sets: one is to compute the gaps based on each Echo packet in E, while another is based on each Send packet in S. Obviously the data sets created by the two ways are fundamentally equivalent.

If we create each data set based on each Send packet in S, we have the following n data sets in which the negative elements are not taken into consideration:

$$S_1=\{s_1e_1, s_1e_2,\ldots, s_1e_m\},$$
$$S_2=\{s_2e_1, s_2e_2,\ldots, s_2e_m\},$$
$$\ldots$$
$$S_n=\{s_ne_1, s_ne_2,\ldots, s_ne_m\}.$$

Here, S_i represents i^{th} data set based on the Send packet s_i; $s_ie_j=e_j-s_i$ represents the time gap between the timestamp of ith Send packet and the jth Echo packet. There is one and only one gap which represents the true RTT in each data set because we have assumed that each Send must be replied by the victim site (final destination host).

If we create the data sets based on each Echo packet in E, we have the following m data sets in which the negative elements are also not taken into consideration:

$$E_1=\{s_1e_1, s_2e_1,\ldots, s_ne_1\},$$
$$E_2=\{s_1e_2, s_2e_2,\ldots, s_ne_2\},$$
$$\ldots$$
$$E_m=\{s_1e_m, s_2e_m,\ldots, s_ne_m\}.$$

Similarly, E_j represents the jth data set based on the Echo packet e_j in E. We are not sure if we have and only have one gap to represent the RTT in each data set E_i. The reason is that one Send is possibly replied by one or more Echo packets. We need to define which one represents the true RTT of the Send exactly. Under this situation, we define the gap between the Send and the first Echo to represent the true RTT. A similar situation is that more Send packets are perhaps responded by only one Echo, under which we define the gap between the last Send and the Echo to represent the true RTT. Anyway, we prefer to define the smallest gap to represent the true RTT.

For convenience, we first consider the data sets based on each Send in S. We already knew that each data set must contain one and only one true RTT, but we are not sure which one in a data set is the right one. We simply assume that each gap in each data set S_i has the same probability to represent the RTT. We make a combination by picking up one element from each data set and call each combination a cluster, so we have m^n clusters altogether. The true RTTs must be one of the m^n clusters because all the possibilities of combination are enumerated. We can prove that the cluster with the smallest standard deviation has the highest probability to represent the true RTTs. The following clustering algorithm to compute the true RTTs of TCP Send packets is rooted in this statement.

3.1 A Clustering Algorithm

We monitor an interactive TCP session established by using OpenSSH for a period of time, capture all the Send and Echo packets, and put them in two sequences S with n packets and E with m packets, respectively. The following clustering algorithm with inputs S and E can compute the true RTTs for all the Send packets in S.

A Clustering Algorithm (S, E):
Begin
1. Create data sets S_i, $1 \leq i \leq n$, and $S_i=\{t(i,j) \mid t(i,j)=t(e_j)-t(s_i), 1 \leq j \leq m\}$;
2. Generate clusters C_k $(1 \leq k \leq m^n)$ from data sets S_i $(1 \leq i \leq n)$, and $C_k=\{t(i, j_i) \in S_i \mid \forall 1 \leq i \leq n \ \& \ j_i \in [1, m] \ \& \ j_1 \leq j_2 \leq \cdots \leq j_n\}$;

3. Filter out each cluster C. For any cluster C_k: (a) if $t(i, u)$, $t(i, v) \in C_k$ & $u<v$, then delete $t(i, u)$, and (b) if $t(u, j)$, $t(v, j) \in C_k$ & $u<v$, then delete $t(v, j)$
4. Compute the standard deviation σ of each cluster C;
5. Output the cluster C_u to represent the true RTTs of the Send packets in S, and $C_u=C_q \mid \sigma_q \leq \sigma_v$ for all $1 \leq v \leq m^n$.

End

Here we use $t(i,j)$ to represent the time gap between i^{th} Send packet and j^{th} Echo packet, $t(e_j)$, and $t(s_i)$ to represent the timestamp of jth Echo and i^{th} Send packet, respectively.

In Step 1, we create n data sets, one of which has at most m elements because the negative elements are not considered. In Step 2, we take one element from each data set and combine them into one cluster, thus at most form m^n clusters because each data set has at most m elements. For any two clusters C_u and C_v, they must have at least one element different. The condition $j_1 \leq j_2 \leq \cdots \leq j_n$ can compress largely the space of the clusters. This condition is reasonable because once a Send packet, such as s_i, is assumed to match an Echo packet, such as e_j, it is impossible that any Send packet after s_i will match an Echo packet before e_j. In Step 3, we focus on handling the case that is either more Send packets are responded by one Echo packet or one Send packet is responded by more Echo packets. In Step 5, we select the cluster with the smallest standard deviation to represent the true RTTs of the Send packets in S. Step 5 is guaranteed by the following *Theorem 1*.

Theorem 1. *If given two sequences S (n Sends) and E (m Echoes) from the same session at same period of time, and generate clusters C_1, C_2, ..., C_k from S and E according to the clustering algorithm, then the cluster with the smallest standard deviation has the highest probability to represent the true RTTs of the packets in S.*

Proof

Given any cluster C of clusters C_1, C_2,..., C_k with distribution Z which has standard deviation σ_1 and mean μ_1. We assume that the Echo packets inter-arrival distribution is Y with mean μ_2, standard deviation σ_2, and the smallest inter-arrival is L. We first compute the probability of selecting an incorrect gap to represent the true RTT.

Suppose c_i, which is any element in cluster C, is selected from $S_i=\{s_ie_1, s_ie_2,..., s_ie_{k-1}, s_ie_k, s_ie_{k+1}, ..., s_ie_m\}$, we assume the correct selection should be s_ie_k, but other element in S_i is selected. To satisfy the condition that C has the smallest standard deviation, the element in S_i selected incorrectly must be closer to μ_1 than s_ie_k. The reason is that for any distribution, if we add one more element, the closer to the mean the one is, the smaller the standard deviation. Only one of the two elements s_ie_{k-1}, s_ie_{k+1} has the highest probability to be selected incorrectly because the elements in S_i are in ascending order. Here, we assume s_ie_{k+1} is closer to μ_1 than s_ie_{k-1}, so we have the inequality (1) which indicates that s_ie_{k+1} is selected incorrectly to represent the true RTT,

$$\left| s_i e_{k+1} - \mu_1 \right| < \left| s_i e_k - \mu_1 \right| \tag{1}$$

We have assumed that L is the smallest interval in distribution Y, so we have

$$t(e_{k+1}) - t(e_k) \geq L = 2q\sigma_1 \tag{2}$$

Here q is a real number. From inequality (2), for any Send packet s_i, we have

$$t(e_{k+1}) - t(s_i) - (t(e_k) - t(s_i)) \geq 2q\sigma_1$$
$$s_i e_{k+1} - s_i e_k \geq 2q\sigma_1$$
$$s_i e_{k+1} - \mu_1 + \mu_1 - s_i e_k \geq 2q\sigma_1$$
$$|s_i e_{k+1} - \mu_1| + |s_i e_k - \mu_1| \geq 2q\sigma_1 \tag{3}$$

From inequality (1) and (3), we derive

$$|s_i e_k - \mu_1| \geq q\sigma_1$$

The probability that c_i is selected incorrectly can be estimated by using Chebyshev inequality [11], [12],

$p(c_i$ is selected incorrectly$)=p(s_i e_{k+1}$ is selected$)$

$$= p(|s_i e_{k+1} - \mu_1| < |s_i e_k - \mu_1|)$$
$$= p(|s_i e_k - \mu_1| > q\sigma_1) < \frac{1}{q^2}$$

In other words, the probability to make a correct selection of a Send packet's RTT can be estimated by the following inequality,

$p(c_i) = p(c_i$ is selected correctly$)$
$= 1 - p(c_i$ is selected incorrectly$)$

$$\geq 1 - \frac{1}{q^2} \tag{4}$$

Given any two clusters C_i and C_j with standard deviation σ_i and σ_j respectively, we know that:

$$\sigma_i < \sigma_j \tag{5}$$

and

$$q_i \sigma_i = q_j \sigma_j = L \tag{6}$$

Here, q_i and q_j are two real numbers. From Step 2 of the clustering algorithm, we know that C_i, and C_j have n elements respectively,

$C_i = \{c_{i1}, c_{i2}, \ldots, c_{in}\}$
$C_j = \{c_{j1}, c_{j2}, \ldots, c_{jn}\}$

Each Send packet is independent from the others, and from inequality (4) we have

$p(C_i$ is the RTTs$)=p(c_{i1}$ is the RTT of s_1, c_{i2} is the RTT of s_2, $\ldots c_{in}$ is the RTT of $s_n)$
$=p(c_{i1})*p(c_{i2})\ldots*p(c_{in})$

$$\geq \left(1 - \frac{1}{q_i^2}\right)^n$$

$p(C_j$ is the RTTs$)=p(c_{j1}$ is the RTT of s_1, c_{j2} is the RTT of s_2, $\ldots c_{jn}$ is the RTT of $s_n)$
$=p(c_{j1})*p(c_{j2})\ldots*p(c_{jn})$

$$\geq \left(1 - \frac{1}{q_j^2}\right)^n$$

From (5), (6) we know that

$$\left(1-\frac{1}{q_i^2}\right)^n \geq \left(1-\frac{1}{q_j^2}\right)^n$$

This indicates that each cluster C has a probability to represent the true RTTs, but the one with the smallest standard deviation has the highest probability to represent the true RTTs. Therefore, we select the cluster with smallest standard deviation among all the clusters created to represent the true RTTs of the Send packets in S. **End Proof.**

We prove that the cluster with smallest standard deviation has the highest probability to represent the true RTTs. Even though the algorithm can give us the best answer when we find the RTTs of Send packets in S, but it is not efficient because of the time complexity which is $O(m^n)$ in worst case. This algorithm cannot be used in real time. In the following section, we propose an efficient clustering algorithm that can be used in real time. Unfortunately, we cannot prove if we can get the best answer with the efficient algorithm, but we can justify it by comparing its result with that of the clustering algorithm in the same context in Section 4.

3.2   The Efficient Clustering Algorithm

The inefficiency of the above clustering algorithm is that the cluster space complexity is $O(m^n)$. Our goal is to shrink the space without losing useful information to make the clustering algorithm efficient. Here we still suppose that we monitor an interactive TCP session for a period of time, and capture n Send packets and m Echo packets, as well as assuming that all the n Send packets are echoed and only echoed by the m Echo packets. We form data sets S_1, S_2, ..., S_n upon the n Send packets and m Echo packets. The reason that we have huge combination space in the clustering algorithm is that we combine the elements in data sets S_1, S_2, ..., S_n freely, without any restrictions, and enumerate all the possibilities. Some combinations that are apparently impossible to represent the true RTTs are still involved into the final cluster space.

We take some measures in the efficient clustering algorithm to reduce the size of the final cluster space. We have n data sets, and know that each element of the true RTTs is hidden in different one of the data sets as well. For all the m elements in S_1, we simply assume that each one is possible to represent the true RTT of the Send packet s_1, even though we know that actually only one element in S_1 is qualified to represent the true RTT of s_1. We take any element in S_1, such as the ith element s_1e_i, to be the first element of cluster C_i, and look at all the elements in S_2 to find the one that makes C_i more possible to represent the true RTTs and add it to C_i. Similarly, we check all the elements in S_3, S_4, ..., S_n respectively, and find one suitable element in each data set and add them to C_i respectively, which finally has n elements. We eventually have m clusters because S_1 has m elements each of which can be used to form one cluster. From *Theorem 1*, it is obvious to take the cluster that has the smallest standard deviation among the m clusters to represent the true RTTs.

However, we still have two problems here. First, when we check a data set to find one element to make the current cluster to be more possible to represent the true RTTs, we have the question that is how to make the current cluster to be more possible to represent the true RTTs. Second, from the whole process to generate the m clusters, we cannot guarantee that the cluster that represents the true RTTs is involved in the final m clusters. For the first problem, the way we take is to select an element that makes the current cluster have the smallest standard deviation. Upon each element in data set S_1, we could have m^{n-1} combinations in the worst case. The cluster generated by ensuring the smallest standard deviation every time to select one element from a data set could not guarantee the smallest standard deviation among its whole m^{n-1} combinations. This is why the second problem is. To be more understandable, we explain the second problem in details through an example.

Suppose we have four data sets $S_1= \{20, X\}$, $S_2= \{15, 18\}$, $S_3= \{18, 19\}$, $S_4= \{7, 8\}$, it does not matter whatever the second element in S_1 is because we only check the clusters formed upon the first element of S_1. If we traverse all the possibilities upon the first element in S_1, we have eight clusters, which are $C_1=\{20,15,18,7\}$, $C_2=\{20,15,18,8\}$, $C_3=\{20,15,19,7\}$, $C_4=\{20,15,19,8\}$, $C_5=\{20,18,18,7\}$, $C_6=\{20,18,18,8\}$, $C_7=\{20,18,19,7\}$, $C_8=\{20,18,19,8\}$ with standard deviation 5.71, 5.25, 5.91, 5.45, 5.91, 5.42, 6.06, 5.56, respectively. From the *Theorem 1*, the good answer should be $C_2=\{20,15,18,8\}$. However, from the efficient algorithm, cluster C only has one element at first, that is C= $\{20\}$. Then we check the elements in S_2, we find that the second element is our best choice because it makes C have the smallest standard deviation, so C= $\{20, 18\}$. For similar reason, we check the elements in S_3, and S_4 respectively, finally find the cluster C should be $\{20, 18, 19, 8\}$ which is different from the one obtained from the first algorithm. This is the second problem that cannot be solved in theory so far.

Fortunately, even though there is possibility theoretically that the efficient clustering algorithm could get an incorrect answer, but that possibility is very low when we apply this algorithm to a real world example. We have justified hundreds of real world examples, the above case happened in a very small chance. In Section 4, we give some real world experimental examples to justify the efficient clustering algorithm. Here we give the detailed efficient clustering algorithm.

The Efficient Clustering Algorithm (S, E)
Begin
1.   Do i=1, n
              $S_i=\phi$;
              Do j=1, m
                     $t(i, j) = t(e_j)-t(s_i)$;
                     $S_i=S_i \cup t(i, j)$;
              End Do
        End Do
2.   For each $t(1, i)\in S_1$, form cluster C_i:
      Do k=2, n
              $\sigma = stdev(C_i \cup t(k,1))$;
              $t_s = t(k,1)$;
              Do u=1, m

$$\text{If stdev}(C_i \cup t(k,u)) \leqslant \sigma$$
$$\sigma = \text{stdev}(C_i \cup t(k,1));$$
$$t_s = t(k,u);$$

      EndIf

   End Do

   $C_i = C_i \cup t(k,1)$

End Do

3. Filter out each cluster C. For any cluster C_k $(1 \leqslant k \leqslant n)$: (a) if $t(i, u)$, $t(i, v) \in C_k$, $u<v$, then delete $t(i, u)$, and (b) if $t(u, j)$, $t(v, j) \in C_k$, $u<v$, then delete $t(v, j)$

4. $\sigma = \text{stdev}(C_1);$

   $C_s = C_1;$

  Do k=1, n

      If $\text{stdev}(C_k) \leqslant \sigma$

        $\sigma = \text{stdev}(C_k);$

        $C_s = C_k;$

     End If

  End Do

5. Output cluster C_s as the RTTs of the Send packets in S.

End

In Step 1, at first, we suppose that each data set is empty which is denoted ϕ. We use sign '$\cup$' to express adding one more element to a data set. In Step 2, we use σ to denote the standard deviation of the cluster, and t_s to denote the element in each data set that makes the current cluster get the smallest standard deviation. We use 'stdev' as a function to compute the standard deviation of a given cluster. In Step 3, C_s stands for a cluster which has the smallest standard deviation among all the clusters considered.

Let us analyze the complexity of this algorithm. Suppose we have n Send packets, and m Echo packets, from the efficient clustering algorithm, we need to select one cluster from the m clusters. The complexity of this algorithm is dominated by Step 2. Considering there are n elements in each cluster, and there are m elements in each data set, the complexity of this algorithm is $O(m*n*(m-1))=O(n*m^2)$ under the worst case. Comparing with the complexity of the previous algorithm, $O(m^n)$, obviously, this algorithm is largely improved in time and space complexity.

4 Empirical Study

We have proposed and proved a clustering algorithm to compute the true RTTs of the Send packets of a TCP session, as well as an efficient one. *Theorem 1* only means among all the clusters created, the cluster with smallest standard deviation has the highest probability to represent the true RTTs of the Send packets. Therefore, from *Theorem 1*, we get the possibility in what extent that the result of the clustering algorithm could stand for the true RTTs. We are not able to prove the result of the clustering algorithm can be the true RTTs definitely. Hence, we design three experiments to evaluate the performance of the above two algorithms and give readers more practical sense. The first experiment is used to justify the correctness of the results of the clustering by comparing them with the known correct RTTs. The second experiment is designed to evaluate the performance of the clustering algorithm by comparing it with the best packet-matching algorithm. The third experiment is used to evaluate the performance of the efficient algorithm by comparing it with the clustering algorithm.

We made a program by using Libpcap [13], [14] to capture the Send and Echo packets of an interactive TCP session on the Internet. We set up a connection chain that spanned U.S. and Mexico and was long enough so as to generate the overlap of send-echo pair which makes matching packets harder. The connection chain used in our experiment is: Host 1→ Acl08 → Mex→ Themis → Mex → Bayou, in which Host 1, Acl08, Themis and Bayou are hosts located in Houston, and Mex is a host located in Mexico which we have a legal user to access. Acl08 is our monitor host on which one program was running to capture the Send and Echo packets of a TCP session. The sign '→' represents a connection established by using OpenSSH. We did each experiment hundreds of times but here with only one of the results presented.

4.1 Justifying the Correctness of the Clustering Algorithm

In this experiment, we examine the correctness of the clustering algorithm by comparing its results with the known correct RTTs. The problem is how to obtain the correct RTTs of the Send packets of a TCP session for a real world case. The reason to bother packet-matching is the overlap of send-echo pair as we have discussed.

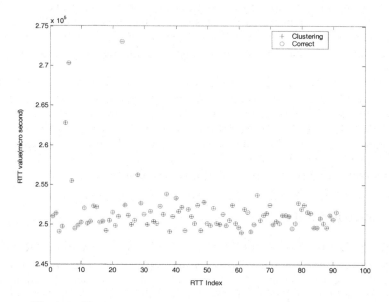

Fig. 1. Justify the correctness of the result of the clustering algorithm

We would avoid such overlap by controlling the keystroke speed to make matching TCP packets easier, and thus obtain the correct RTTs. We did not type each character until we are sure that the previous one (a Send packet) had been replied. It is trivial to compute the correct RTT for each Send packet by simply matching it with the closest Echo packet following it. Meanwhile, we collect all the Send and Echo packets, and apply the clustering algorithm to them to output the results for the Send packets. Then we can compare these results with the correct RTTs and be sure if they are consistent. The comparison result is showed in Fig. 1, in which X axis represents the Send packet index number, and Y axis represents the RTT value with unit microsecond. For clarity, Fig. 1 only shows us part of the results. It shows obviously that the result of the clustering algorithm is the same as the correct RTTs.

4.2 Comparison Between the Clustering and the Best Packet-Matching Algorithm

In the experiment of Section 4.1, we have justified the correctness of the clustering algorithm, but need to control the keystroke speed to get the correct RTTs. In the real world, it is impossible to do so because intruders control the keystroke speed of an interactive session. Here, we use different way to evaluate the performance of the clustering algorithm under the context very close to the real world. The way is to evaluate the performance of the clustering algorithm by comparing it with the best packet-matching algorithm, the Conservative algorithm [6], which claims to match TCP packet correctly, or computing RTTs correctly, but with few packets matched.

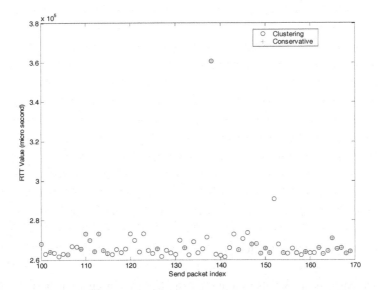

Fig. 2. Comparison between the Conservative and the clustering algorithm

We monitor the TCP connection chain at Acl08 by running the Conservative algorithm to compute the RTTs, while we capture all the Send and Echo packets, and apply the clustering algorithm to them to compute the RTTs. In this experiment, we captured 232 Send packets, but the Conservative algorithm only gave 107 send-echo matches, while the clustering algorithm can obtain 232 RTTs that are equal to 232 send-echo matches. For clarity, we only show part of the RTTs (Send packet index number 100-170) in Fig. 2. From this comparison, we draw the following two points. 1) All the RTTs obtained by the Conservative algorithm are the same as the part of the RTTs found by the clustering algorithm. 2) Even though we cannot judge the correctness of the rest of the RTTs, but from their distribution, we see they are very close to the results of the Conservative algorithm.

4.3   Justifying the Efficient Clustering Algorithm

The efficient clustering algorithm cannot guarantee to compute the best RTTs theoretically just as we have analyzed in Section 3.2. However, this algorithm is still useful to compute the RTTs in practice because the empirical study showed that the efficient clustering algorithm could obtain the RTTs, which are the same as the results of the clustering algorithm for most real world examples. Even though in a very few cases, they are different, but the RTTs from the efficient clustering algorithm are still useful in detecting stepping–stone intrusion because it does not affect to identify one level of a connection chain.

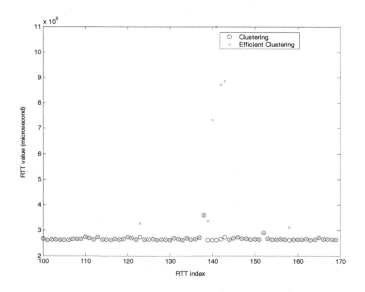

Fig. 3. Verifying the efficient clustering algorithm

In this experiment, we also monitored the connection chain at host Acl08, and collected all the Send and Echo packets in a period of time. We applied the two algorithms to these packets respectively, and compared their results. We did this experiment hundreds of times, and found their results are the same in more than 99% cases. Fig. 3 shows one exception in which their results are different slightly.

In Fig. 3, the circles represent the part of the RTTs found by the clustering algorithm, while the crosses stand for the part of the results obtained from the efficient clustering algorithm. It is obvious that the most of the RTTs computed by the two algorithms respectively are identical. Only a few RTTs computed by the efficient clustering algorithm are different from the ones obtained from the clustering algorithm. Compare to number of the whole RTTs computed, the number of these RTTs is relatively small (in this experiment, it is 8 out of 232), so we can still figure out one level of a connection chain upon the RTTs found by the efficient algorithm, and thus make this algorithm useful in detecting stepping-stone intrusion.

5 Related Work

The related work can be classified into two categories: a) detecting stepping-stone; b) detecting stepping-stone intrusion. Category a) includes the approaches proposed in papers [4], [15], [16], [17], [18], [19]; Category b) includes the algorithms proposed in papers [5], [6]. The difference between the two categories is that the approaches in category a) can only predict if a host is used as a stepping-stone, the approaches in category b) can predict not only a host is used as a stepping-stone, but also if the host is used by an intruder. Being used as a stepping-stone does not mean being used by an intruder because some legal users also need a host to be used as a stepping-stone. In this paper, we propose an algorithm to compute the RTTs, which eventually can be used to detect stepping-stone intrusion. It is not necessary to compare this algorithm with the approaches in category a).

To determine if a host is used as a stepping-stone is easier than to determine if a host is used by an intruder. Most approaches in category a) are to compare an incoming connection with an outgoing connection to determine if a host is used as a stepping-stone, such as content-based method [19], time-based method [4], [18], packet-number-based method [16]. They all suffer from not only a problem of being vulnerable to intruders' evasion except the method in paper [6], but also high false alarm rate in detecting stepping-stone intrusion. The detecting method based on the RTTs from the clustering algorithm can detect intruders' evasion. We discuss this point in another paper. It is obvious that the approaches in category b) have no false alarm problem in detecting stepping-stone intrusion.

6 Conclusions and Future Work

In this paper, we have proved a theory and proposed a clustering algorithm the theory to compute the RTTs of the Send packets of a TCP interactive session, which are useful in detecting stepping-stone intrusion. We also proposed an efficient clustering algorithm to compute the RTTs with less computation cost, which is possible to be used in real-time detection. The empirical study showed: 1) the RTTs found by the clustering algorithm are the same as the correct ones; 2) the clustering algorithm can match packets with both high matching-rate and high matching-accuracy; 3) the efficient clustering algorithm can compute the RTTs almost the same as the results from the clustering algorithm in most cases.

The clustering algorithm can only figure out estimation of single level RTTs. Even though it is useful in detecting stepping-stone intrusion, but computing multi-level RTTs is more useful and challenging to detect intrusion. One future work is to improve the current clustering algorithm to compute multi-level RTTs.

References

1. R. Base: A New Look at Perpetrators of Computer Crime. Proceeding of 16th Department of Energy Computer Security Group Conference, Denver, CO, May (1994).
2. Richard Power: Current and Future Danger. Computer Security Institute, San Francisco, CA, (1995).
3. CERT: CERT/CC Statistics 1988-2005.,http://www.cert.org, Accessed July (2005)
4. Yin Zhang, Vern Paxson: Detecting Stepping-Stones. Proceedings of the 9th USENIX Security Symposium, Denver, CO, August (2000) 67-81.
5. Kwong H. Yung: Detecting Long Connecting Chains of Interactive Terminal Sessions. RAID 2002, Springer Press, Zurich, Switzerland, October (2002) 1-16.
6. Jianhua Yang, Shou-Hsuan Stephen Huang: Matching TCP Packets and Its Application to the Detection of Long Connection Chains, Proceedings (IEEE) of 19th International Conference on Advanced Information Networking and Applications (AINA'05), Taipei, Taiwan, China, March (2005) 1005-1010.
7. University of Southern California: Transmission Control Protocol. RFC 793, September (1981).
8. Ylonen, T.: SSH Protocol Architecture. draft IETF document, http://www.ietf.org/internet-drafts/draft-ietf-secsh-architecture-16.txt, June (2004).
9. Ylonen, T. : SSH Transport Layer Protocol. draft IETF document, http://www.ietf.org/ internet-drafts/ draft-ietf-secsh-transport-18.txt, June (2004).
10. Qiong Li, David L. Mills: On the Long-range Dependence of Packet Round-trip Delays in Internet. Proceedings of International Conference on Communications (ICC'98), Atlanta, USA, June (1998) 1185-1192.
11. E. Kao: An Introduction to Stochastic Processes. Duxbury Press, New York (1996) 47-87.
12. W. Feller: An Introduction to Probability Theory and Its Applications. Volume I, John Wiley & Sons, Inc., New York (1968) 212-237.
13. Lawrence Berkeley National Laboratory (LBNL): The Packet Capture library. ftp://ftp.ee.lbl.gov/libpcap.tar.z, accessed March (2004).
14. Data Nerds Web Site: Winpcap and Windump. http://www.datanerds.net, accessed July (2004).
15. D. L. Donoho (ed.): Detecting Pairs of Jittered Interactive Streams by Exploiting Maximum Tolerable Delay. Proceedings of International Symposium on Recent Advances in Intrusion Detection, Zurich, Switzerland, September (2002) 45-59.
16. A. Blum, D. Song, And S. Venkataraman: Detection of Interactive Stepping-Stones: Algorithms and Confidence Bounds. Proceedings of International Symposium on Recent Advance in Intrusion Detection (RAID), Sophia Antipolis, France, September (2004) 20-35.
17. X. Wang, D.S. Reeves: Robust Correlation of Encrypted Attack Traffic Through Stepping-Stones by Manipulation of Interpacket Delays. Proceedings of the 10th ACM Conference on Computer and Communications Security (CCS 2003), Washington DC, Oct (2003).
18. K. Yoda, H. Etoh: Finding Connection Chain for Tracing Intruders. Proc. 6th European Symposium on Research in Computer Security (LNCS 1985), Toulouse, France, September (2000) 31-42.
19. S. Staniford-Chen, L. Todd Heberlein: Holding Intruders Accountable on the Internet. Proc. IEEE Symposium on Security and Privacy, Oakland, CA, August (1995) 39-49.

DSO: Dependable Signing Overlay

Guofei Gu, Prahlad Fogla, Wenke Lee, and Douglas Blough

Georgia Institute of Technology
{guofei, prahlad, wenke}@cc.gatech.edu
doug.blough@ece.gatech.edu

Abstract. Dependable digital signing service requires both high fault-tolerance and high intrusion-tolerance. While providing high fault-tolerance, existing approaches do not satisfy the high intrusion-tolerance requirement in the face of availability, confidentiality and integrity attacks. In this paper, we propose Dependable Signing Overlay (DSO), a novel server architecture that can provide high intrusion-tolerance as well as high fault-tolerance. The key idea is: replicate the key shares and make the signing servers anonymous to clients (and thus also to the would-be attackers), in addition to using threshold signing. DSO utilizes structured P2P overlay routing techniques to provide timely services to legitimate clients. DSO is intended to be a scalable infrastructure for dependable digital signing service. This paper presents the architecture and protocols of DSO, and the analytical models for reliability and security analysis. We show that, compared with existing techniques, DSO has much better intrusion-tolerance under availability, confidentiality and integrity attacks.

Keywords: intrusion-tolerance, fault-tolerance, P2P overlay, dependable, digital signing service.

1 Introduction

Digital signing is an integral part of a modern computer security architecture. It is one of the basic services provided by any CA (Certificate Authority) or PKI (Public Key Infrastructure) system. Dependable digital signing service should continue to provide service despite system failures and malicious attacks. In other words, it needs to be both high fault-tolerant and high intrusion-tolerant (also called attack-tolerant).

Researchers have been studying techniques to provide both fault-tolerant and intrusion-tolerant service (not limited to signing service) using multiple servers. Traditional fault-tolerant approaches (e.g., replication and Byzantine quorum systems [9, 18]) mainly provide redundancy. Secret sharing [24, 6, 10] and threshold cryptography [5, 21, 25] can be used to provide certain level of fault-tolerance and intrusion-tolerance. For instance, a (k, m) threshold scheme divides a secret into m pieces such that any k or more pieces can be used to reconstruct the secret. Knowledge of any $k - 1$ or fewer pieces does not provide any information of the secret. These threshold schemes can provide intrusion-tolerance up to a given threshold, above which there is no security at all. For example, using a (k, m) scheme can tolerate confidentiality and integrity attacks

J. Zhou, M. Yung, and F. Bao (Eds.): ACNS 2006, LNCS 3989, pp. 33–49, 2006.

up to $k - 1$ shares. If k or more shares are compromised, the attacker can reconstruct or modify the secret data successfully. Similarly, if $m - k + 1$ or more nodes are under an availability attack (e.g., Denial of Service, or DoS), then the signing service becomes unavailable.

We propose a novel architecture, Dependable Signing Overlay (DSO), to enhance intrusion-tolerance and fault-tolerance for digital signing service. The key idea is: replicate the key shares and make the signing servers anonymous to the other hosts including the clients, in addition to using threshold signing. The threshold signing scheme and replication technique provide fault-tolerance. The threshold signing scheme and anonymous signing servers provide intrusion-tolerance because the attackers cannot know which signing servers to attack in order to deny signing service, steal, or corrupt the secret signing key. By systematically combining these three techniques, DSO can provide not only very high fault-tolerance but also very high intrusion-tolerance. Although DSO technique can be extended as a general architecture to provide other dependable services, we focus our effort on providing a scalable infrastructure or platform for dependable signing service in this paper. The design and evaluation of DSO are presented. Specifically, we make the following contributions:

– **Architecture and Protocol Design.** A key goal in DSO is to make the signing servers anonymous, or "hidden" among a large number of DSO nodes, so that all an adversary can do is just to randomly attack some nodes on DSO. Thus, the chance of a successful attack on confidentiality, availability, and integrity is low. On the other hand, an important goal is that legitimate client requests are served correctly and in a timely manner. We accomplish these goals by designing DSO as a P2P (peer-to-peer) overlay server network and adopting the techniques of structured P2P overlay routing based on DHT (Distributed Hash Table). Section 3 presents the architecture and main protocols of DSO.

– **Reliability and Security Analysis.** We derive analytical models so that we can concretely analyze and evaluate the reliability (fault-tolerance) and security (intrusion-tolerance) of DSO. The security analysis considers confidentiality, availability, and integrity attacks under both static and dynamic (with recovery) situations. Our results show that DSO provides very high fault-tolerance. For example, if the reliability of a single node is just 0.6 and we use a (6,10) threshold scheme in a 100 node DSO, the reliability of the service is more than 0.999. DSO also provides very high intrusion tolerance. For example, using a (6,10) threshold scheme in a 100 node DSO, when 30 nodes are attacked, the probability of successfully compromising availability is only 0.0000034754. The details of the analysis are in Section 4.

– **Comparison with Existing Schemes.** We show that, compared with existing representative techniques, DSO provides high fault-tolerance and much higher intrusion-tolerance. For example, a (6,10) threshold signing scheme can tolerate only up to 5 compromised nodes. If we use a (6,10) threshold signing scheme in a DSO with 100 nodes and an attacker compromises 30 nodes, the probability that the attacker obtains the signing key is just 0.0473. Section 5 discusses the comparison of DSO with existing schemes.

2   Related Work

Fault-tolerance and intrusion-tolerance have been studied intensively by the research community. Traditionally, fault tolerance is addressed by replicating the service and building quorum systems [9, 18].

Different threshold schemes were designed to build intrusion-tolerant services which can tolerate successful intrusions on less than k servers. Shamir's secret sharing [24] is a simple threshold scheme based on polynomial interpolation. Later, verifiable secret sharing schemes were proposed in [6, 4] for the verification of secret shares by share holders and share combiner. Proactive secret sharing schemes [10, 15] were proposed for the renewal of the shares without reconstructing the secret. Unlike secret sharing schemes that require secret data to be reconstructed at a trusted host, Threshold cryptography [5, 21, 25, 11] can use or generate secret key in a distributed fashion without the need of any trusted host. They used to provide decryption service, signing service and other CA services. The Intrusion Tolerance via Threshold Cryptography (ITTC) project at Stanford [28] used threshold cryptography to provide basic public key services without ever reconstructing the key. Zhou *et al.* and Luo *et al.* have applied threshold cryptography into Ad-hoc networks [29, 14, 17] to provide CA service to solve key management and membership problems. Narasimha *et al.* [19, 20] used threshold cryptography in P2P and MANET to provide efficient member control and node admission.

Recently, [30, 16, 2] tried to use traditional fault-tolerance techniques (e.g. replications, Quorums) along with secret sharing or threshold cryptography to provide both high fault-tolerance and intrusion-tolerance. Cornell Online CA (COCA [30]), combined quorum and threshold cryptography techniques to provide a secure distributed certificate authority. Lakshmanan [16] proposed a scheme to combine replication with secret sharing to provide secure and reliable data storage. MAFTIA [2] is a comprehensive approach for tolerating both accidental faults and malicious attacks in large-scale distributed systems.

One main problem with the above described systems is that it is easy for an attacker to find the address of the servers used in the system and directly attack them. A possible solution is to use anonymity and randomness techniques, as seen in some censorship-resistant publishing systems like Eternity Service [1], Publius [27], free haven [7]. These systems focus on providing distributed document storage and censorship-resistant publishing, which is different from the target of DSO. Secure Overlay Service (SOS [13]) also used the anonymity and randomness of the overlay network to make it difficult for the attacker to target any particular node for DoS attacks. We also try to exploit the anonymity provided by structured peer-to-peer networks to hide the actual service providers from the attacker. To take over any service, an attacker needs to randomly attack the nodes in the overlay network and hope for the best. In DSO, we couple service provider anonymity with threshold schemes and replication to provide a highly secure digital signing service which has both high reliability and security.

3   Architecture and Protocol Design

3.1   Design Goals

DSO aims to provide dependable digital signing service that can tolerate a large number of faulty nodes or malicious attacks. This security goal is achieved by making the signing servers anonymous, so that an attacker does not know which signing servers to attack. This reduces the chance of successful attacks on the system. Even though the servers are anonymous, legitimate client requests should be served efficiently. We choose structured P2P network for the architecture because it provides anonymity of the servers with minimal network overhead. An initial signing server generates the pair of public and secret keys, then distributes the secret key (signing key) to a number of nodes in the overlay using secret sharing. Later, a client requesting the signing service may obtain the partial signature from required nodes and reconstruct the signature using threshold signing scheme.

3.2   Structured P2P

Recently, many services are deployed on peer-to-peer networks. P2P is a fault-tolerant network because it provides redundancy (through replication) and it can automatically adapt itself to the failure or arrival/departure of nodes. Current structured P2P systems (e.g. Chord [26], Pastry [22]) are based on distributed hash table (DHT) technique to efficiently route the packets from source to destination. A typical structured P2P system based on DHT provides the following guarantees:

- Communication to any peer (or query to any data) identified by some key ID (a hash value) is guaranteed to succeed if and only if the peer (or data) corresponding to the key ID is present in the system;
- Communication to any peer (given ID) is guaranteed to terminate within a small and finite number of hops;
- The key ID space is uniformly divided among all currently active peers;
- The system is capable of handling dynamic peer joins and leaves.

In DSO, we can use a routing technique similar to Chord [26], which guarantees that a packet will get to its destination in no more than $log(N)$ hops (N is the size of the overlay) by looking up the ID (a hash value) of the destination. We can create multiple destination nodes for a given identifier by using multiple hash functions. By carefully choosing the proper class of hash functions, the sequences of nodes used to route a packet from a node to the destination can be independent from one another. Chord is robust to changes in overlay membership: each node's list is adjusted to account for nodes leaving and joining the overlay. This is called the self-healing feature of structured P2P networks. Note the original Chord directly maps a node's IP address to the ID using a hash function. Given the size of network (typically smaller than a million), an attacker can calculate the ID of each host in the network and store it. Now given the ID, he can easily determine the address of the host. This is not safe in DSO because our security guarantees rely on the anonymity of the servers in the network: no one should be able to convert node's ID to its IP address. Thus we do not use the original Chord's node identifier mapping mechanism. We can use a Pastry-like mechanism [22] (node IDs are assigned randomly with uniform distribution from a circular ID space) for DSO that makes it very hard to determine the IP address of the host given its ID. At the same time we should take care of the security of node ID assignment as in [3].

3.3   System Architecture and Process

The basic system architecture is shown in Figure 1. The three main components are share holders (SH), beacons and access points (AP). Brief functionalities of these three components are described below. Details are in Section 3.4.

DSO can provide multiple signing services at the same time. Any signing service is recognized using a service key tag. Each service has its own secret signing key, also called service key. This private key is divided into m parts using a secret sharing scheme (k, m). Each of these m shares are replicated to n_h distinct hosts selected by the initial signing server. Thus, there are n_h copies of each share of the service key in the system. All these shares are sent to selected SHs by the initial signing server.

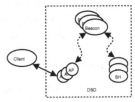

On receiving the share, a share holder calculates the index keys using a number of (n_b) well-known consistent hash functions as in SOS[13] operated on the service key tag. These index keys will identify the IDs of a set of overlay

Fig. 1. Dependable Signing Overlay (DSO)

nodes that will act as beacons. Beacons will be contacted and store IDs of these SHs at the end of service initialization process (see Section 3.4).

Certain nodes in DSO act as Access Points (AP) which have the capability to authenticate clients. Before acquiring signing service, a client should first contact an overlay AP to request a certain signing service (indicated by the service key tag). After authenticating and authorizing the request, the AP securely routes the request from the client to the correct beacons (whose IDs are identified with hash values of the service key tag) using the underlying routing mechanisms. (Each node in the path determines the next hop by applying appropriate hash function to the service key tag.)

After a beacon receives the signing request, it will route the packet to the proper share holders which will perform threshold signing and produce partial signatures according to the request. These partial signatures are then combined by a beacon to produce the final signature. The combiner (beacon) then sends the result to AP. The result is finally forwarded to the client. During the whole process, the original secret (private key) is never disclosed to anyone. The message sent from the client can be blinded (see Section 3.4) to achieve confidentiality.

This scheme is robust because:

- Each secret in the system is shared by different nodes and all of the shares are replicated to multiple servers. This provides good redundancy while maintaining the secrecy of the data.
- There are multiple access points, beacons, and share holders on DSO for every service. Any node in this overlay can be AP, beacon or share holder. In fact, in our discussion we assume all nodes are access points.
- As there are lots of APs available, failure of one AP does not have much effect on the system. Client can simply choose another AP to enter the overlay.
- The communication to some target node given its ID (not IP address) is most likely not direct, but indirect through a set of intermediate peer forwarding. This provides anonymity.

- If some beacon fails, DSO service can self-heal by choosing a new node as the beacon with using some new hash function.
- If some share holders are compromised or targeted by attackers, the service provider can choose an alternate set of share holders and such operations are transparent to clients.
- All the beacons and SHs are anonymous to the clients (clients do not know the IP address of any SH or beacon for a service). Even if some beacon is compromised, the attacker can only get the IDs of SHs. As we mentioned above, with only IDs an attacker cannot know the real addresses. Thus, the SHs are still anonymous to attackers even though they know the IDs. Similarly, if any access point is compromised, the attacker can only get the IDs of beacons, but not the real address.

3.4 Protocol Design

In this paper, we choose threshold RSA signing [25, 19, 20, 11] as our basic signing scheme because it is one of the most popular schemes (one can also use threshold DSA or other threshold signing techniques [19, 20]). In a threshold RSA scheme, q is the RSA modulus, K_e is the public key, and the private key K_d is shared by the servers and is used for signing. Secret shares corresponding to K_d are generated by the initial service provider and distributed to the SHs. There are three main protocols in DSO:

1. Service initialization: initializes the share holders, beacons for certain service key;
2. Service provision: provides the desired signing service;
3. Share update: periodically update the secret shares.

Service Initialization. This protocol creates multiple shares of the service key K_d and distributes them to randomly selected DSO nodes. The protocol is described in following steps.

- Using Shamir's classical secret sharing scheme [24], the service provider generates a $k - 1$ degree sharing polynomial $f(x) = a_0 + a_1 x + ... + a_{k-1} x^{k-1} \pmod{q}$ where $a_0 = K_d$. It also computes the partial share as $S_i = f(i) \pmod{q}$ for each share holder i, $i = 1, ..., m$. For the purpose of verification of share, we use Feldman's verifiable secret sharing scheme [6], which involves a large prime p such that q divides $p - 1$ and a generator g which is an element of Z_p^* of order q. Also, k public witness of the sharing polynomial's coefficients denoted as $g^{a_0}, ..., g^{a_{k-1}}$ are generated.
- The service provider randomly selects m nodes in the DSO as share holders and then gives every share holder its share S_i together with the k witnesses.
- When the share holders receive their shares they can verify the integrity by checking $g^{S_i} \equiv \prod_{j=0}^{k-1} (g^{a_j})^{i^j} \pmod{p}$. If it is valid, each SH_i calculates its own partial secret key $d_i = S_i l_i(0) \pmod{q}$, where $l_i(0)$ is lagrange coefficients and $l_i(0) = \prod_{j=1, j \neq i}^{k} \frac{0-j}{i-j} \pmod{q}$.
- Each SH replicates its share and partial secret key d_i to other $n_h - 1$ randomly selected server nodes. All these SHs will notify all beacons (whose IDs are identified with hash values of the service key tag) their roles and ask them to store IDs of the SHs for this certain signing service.

Service Provision. Once a signing service is initialized, DSO can provide signing service that requires the signing key.

- The client sends service request to DSO, asks for signing message m with the service private key corresponding to a service key tag K_t. The request is forwarded by AP to beacons, then to the proper SHs.
- When the share holders receive the signing request, each SH_i generates its partial signed result (partial signature) $P_i = m^{d_i} \bmod q$ using its partial secret key d_i. These partial results are sent to a beacon (combiner). In order for the beacon to verify the validity of the partial results, we use the following scheme [23]. When SH_i sends P_i, it also sends g^{S_i}, r, c, A_1, A_2. Here $A_1 = g^u, A_2 = m^u$ where u is a random number. $r = u - cS_i, c = hash(g^{S_i}, P_i, A_1, A_2)$. All calculations are on mod p.
- When the beacon receives k or more distinct partial results, it first verifies the following three equations (on mod p):

$$g^{S_i} \equiv \prod_{j=0}^{k-1} (g^{a_j})^{i^j}; \ g^r(g^{S_i})^c \equiv A_1; \ m^r(P_i)^c \equiv A_2$$

If these equations hold, then it means that the partial result is valid. After verifying k number of shares, the beacon can generate the final result F.

$$F = \prod_i P_i = \prod_i m^{d_i} = m^{\sum_i d_i} = m^{\sum_i (S_i l_i(0))} \ (mod \ q).$$

Note $m^{\sum_i (S_i l_i(0))} \ (mod \ q) \neq m^{k_d} \ (mod \ q)$. We must apply K-bounded coalition offsetting algorithm [14] to obtain the final signature $m^{k_d} \ (mod \ q)$. Note the original K-bounded coalition offsetting algorithm in [14] has a robustness problem, which was pointed in [19, 12] and corrected in [12, 11].

- The final signature is then sent to the AP who forwards it to the client.

Blinding the message: For privacy and confidential reason, the client can use blinding technique to hide the original message from the beacon and other nodes in DSO. Instead of sending the original message m, it chooses a blinding factor b at random and computes $s = b^{K_e}$ (again, all these and following calculations are on mod q) using public key K_e. The client then sends $m \cdot s = mb^{K_e}$ to the overlay, which returns $F' = (m \cdot s)^{K_d} = m^{K_d}b$. Finally the client can remove the blinding factor b by $F = F'/b$. Thus, the client obtains the final signature and does not leak any original information to DSO.

Share Update. To enhance security, we use proactive secret sharing scheme [10] to update each share holder's share periodically without reconstructing the service key K_d. In the update procedure, all share holders with the same share copies elect one representative SH to take part in the update protocol. After the update procedure, representatives will replicate the updated share to the other SHs.

- Representative share holder SH_i generates a random update polynomial $f_i(x) = b_{i,0}x + \dots + b_{i,k-1}x^{k-1} \ (mod \ q)$ with secret part as 0. SH_i computes m subshares $S_{i,j} = f_i(j) \ (mod \ q)$ and securely sends it to $SH_j, j = 1, \dots, m$.

– After collecting m subshares $S_{i,j}, j = 1, ..., m$, representative SH_i can calculate the new updated share as $S_i' = S_i + \sum_{j=1}^m S_{j,i} \pmod q$.

4 Reliability and Security Analysis

In this section, we analyze the fault-tolerance and security of DSO. Table1 list the notations we will use in the following analysis.

Table 1. Some Notations

N_n	total number of nodes in overlay	n_a	number of APs
n_t	number of attacked nodes	k	threshold value of secret sharing
n_b	number of beacons per service	m	number of distinct shares per service
n_h	number of each share's copies	x	total number of services provided by DSO

4.1 Fault-Tolerance Analysis

Fault tolerance of the system is measured as the probability that the service will be available to the clients in spite of the failures of individual nodes. For a given service, $R_{sys}(t)$ represents the probability that the service is available during time interval $(0, t)$. Since there are three components of the service, namely APs, beacons and SHs, all of them need to be operating correctly for the service to be available. Reliability of the system can be written as $R_{sys}(t) = \Pr$(At least one AP operates correctly during $(0, t)$) $\times \Pr$(At least one beacon operates correctly during $(0, t)$) $\times \Pr$(At least k distinct share holders operate correctly during $(0, t)$).

Every node in the DSO can act as an AP. We are assuming the beacons and share holders for the service are chosen independently. Thus, a given node in the system may have more than one role. To further simplify the computation, we assume that the reliability of every node in the network is equal to $R(t)$. If there are n parallel modules in the system each with reliability $R(t)$ which provide identical service, then the probability that at least one of them will be operating correctly is $R_n(t) = 1 - (1 - R(t))^n$. Reliability of the three components in the service can be represented using the following equations: $R_{AP}(t) = 1 - (1 - R(t))^{n_a}$, $R_{Be}(t) = 1 - (1 - R(t))^{n_b}$, $R_{SH}(t) = 1 - (1 - R(t))^{n_h}$.

Then, we compute the reliability of the system using Eq.(1).

$$R_{sys}(t) = R_{AP}(t) \cdot R_{Be}(t) \cdot \left(\sum_{i=k}^m \binom{m}{i} R_{SH}(t)^i (1 - R_{SH}(t))^{n_h(m-i)} \right) \tag{1}$$

$$= (1 - (1 - R(t))^{n_a}) (1 - (1 - R(t))^{n_b}) \left(\sum_{i=k}^m \binom{m}{i} (1 - (1 - R(t))^{n_h})^i (1 - R(t))^{n_h(m-i)} \right)$$

Using the reliability equation of the system, it is easy to calculate the mean time to failure as $MTTF = \int_0^\infty R_{sys}(t)$.

Consider an overlay network containing 100 nodes. Suppose we have 10 different services each using $(6, 10)$ to share the secret. Suppose the reliability of a single node is 0.9 during a certain time interval. If these services are deployed in a separate set of nodes with no replication, then the reliability of each service during the time interval is equal to 0.9984 which is two 9s after the decimal point. (For the remainder of this paper, we will write reliability in terms of number of 9s after the decimal point.)

Now, we group $10 \times 10 = 100 = N_n$ nodes together as DSO. We still use the $(6, 10)$ scheme for every service as before. Assume there are ten beacons and each share has four copies, i.e. $n_a = 100, n_b = 10, n_h = 4$. Then according to Eq.(1), the reliability for every service becomes nine 9s, which is much higher than the 2 9s for the services deployed separately.

Note that when using DSO we have much more nodes than required by the service. Many of these overlay nodes are used only for light-weight routing purposes and are not involved in threshold signing or replication. This is not a limitation but a design choice. DSO is designed as a scalable infrastructure to provide a platform for a large number of services. DSO may have a very large overlay and not limited to be within a single organization.

Table 2 shows the reliability of a pure threshold scheme and DSO, given different single node reliability. We can see that for the same threshold parameter $(6, 10)$ DSO has a much higher reliability than the pure threshold scheme. Even when the pure threshold scheme uses $(60, 100)$, which requires 100 servers for a single service, our DSO with following parameters $N_n = 100, n_a = 100, n_h = 4, n_b = 15, k = 8, m = 15$ can still beat the pure threshold scheme when the single node's reliability is not very high. When the single node reliability is very high (greater than 0.9), then both the (60,100) threshold scheme and DSO scheme can achieve high enough reliability (larger than 14 9's). We can see that the pure threshold scheme is very sensitive to the single reliability and the total number of servers. It can only achieve good reliability when using many servers with high single reliability. Whereas DSO can use a small number of servers (here servers mean the nodes really involved in threshold signing or replication) to achieve better performance even when the single reliability is not high.

Table 2. Reliability Comparison ($N_n = 100, n_a = 100, n_h = 4$ in DSO)

Single reliability	0.7	0.8	0.9	0.99		0.7	0.8	0.9	0.99
(6,10) scheme	0.8497	0.9672	0.9984	7 9's	(60,100) scheme	0.9875	5 9's	15 9's	53 9's
DSO ($n_b = 10$)	4 9's	6 9's	9 9's	15 9's	DSO ($n_b = 15$)	7 9's	10 9's	14 9's	15 9's

4.2 Intrusion-Tolerance Analysis

The Threat Model. Before security analysis, we first make clear the threat model of DSO. The goal of DSO is to enhance the tolerance to faults and attacks from architecture level. DSO itself is not able to solve all the security problems in the distributed environments. We assume the basic techniques in use, i.e., threshold cryptography, secret sharing and structured P2P routing, are secure. Furthermore we assume that proper authentication, secure communication based on cryptography, traffic analysis prevention and intrusion detection techniques can be used. All these can provide us the following guarantees.

- The overlay network is secure and it prevents the routing attacks.
- The communication between overlay nodes is secure in that authentication and encryption are used between overlay nodes. Also traffic pattern analysis is prevented.
- Every node in the overlay can verify and identify the illegitimate traffic sent to them. Attacker cannot control the node for a long time. Once a node is found under attack/control, it will go off-line and be repaired.
- Attackers do not know the addresses of the beacons and the share holders. Like clients and other routing nodes of overlay, attackers only know the service key tag and its neighbor overlay nodes.

With the above security guarantees, nodes in DSO can still be denied of service or temporarily broken/controlled by the attackers. An attacker can launch three kind of attacks.

1. Availability attack: Attacker can launch DoS attacks on n_t nodes in the network. This may deny the signing service provided by the system to clients.
2. Confidentiality attack: Attacker can attack the nodes to obtain the shares and try to acquire the original service private key (signing key).
3. Integrity attack: Attacker can modify the shares on nodes in the overlay.

In the following sections, we will analyze the intrusion-tolerance of DSO under these three attacks in detail.[1]

Static Intrusion-Tolerance. In static attack mode, we assume that there are n_t nodes under attack and there is no recovery.

(1) Availability Attack
Suppose we have a set of a nodes and we randomly select b nodes from it. Let $P_h(a, b, c)$ denotes the probability that selected nodes contains a given set of c nodes. Using elementary combinatorics, one can see that $P_h(a, b, c) = \binom{a-c}{b-c} / \binom{a}{b} = \binom{b}{c} / \binom{a}{c}$ when $b \geq c$, and $P_h(a, b, c) = 0$ when $b < c$.

When n_t nodes are attacked, the probability that at least one AP still works is $1 - P_h(N_n, n_t, n_a)$ and the probability that at least one beacon still works is $1 - P_h(N_n, n_t, n_b)$. For each distinct share having n_h copies, the chance of at least one copy available is $1 - P_h(N_n, n_t, n_h)$. A given service will still be available if at least one AP is available, at least one beacon is available and k out of m distinct shares are available. Thus, the probability of successfully denying a given service is

$$Pr_{d1} = 1 - (1 - P_h(N_n, n_t, n_a))(1 - P_h(N_n, n_t, n_b)) \times$$
$$\left(\sum_{i=k}^{m} \binom{m}{i} (1 - P_h(N_n, n_t, n_h))^i P_h(N_n, n_t, n_h)^{m-i} \right) \tag{2}$$

Figures 2(a) shows a small DSO example. The size of DSO is only 100 ($N_n = 100$). We select all 100 nodes as APs and 10 nodes as beacons. The threshold scheme we use is 6 out of 10. Every share has four replicated copies ($n_h = 4$). When there are $n_t = 10$ nodes attacked, the probability of a successful service availability attack is

---

[1] Due to space limit, the dynamic analysis is put into an extended version [8] of this paper.

almost negligible (1.1546×10^{-13}). When attacked nodes increase to 30, the probability comes to be 3.4754×10^{-6}. Even when half of the nodes are attacked, the successful attack probability is still low (0.0013). From the figure we can see that only when the number of attacked nodes is more than 70, the probability increases rapidly. Only after more than 90 nodes are attacked, does the probability become near to 1. Also, given a fixed m, using a larger k will slightly increase the chance of a successful attack. This is because, with a larger k, an attacker needs to attack fewer servers to deny the service.

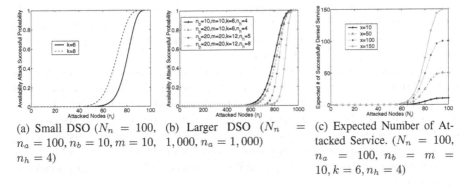

(a) Small DSO ($N_n = 100$, $n_a = 100$, $n_b = 10$, $m = 10$, $n_h = 4$)

(b) Larger DSO ($N_n = 1,000$, $n_a = 1,000$)

(c) Expected Number of Attacked Service. ($N_n = 100$, $n_a = 100$, $n_b = m = 10$, $k = 6$, $n_h = 4$)

Fig. 2. Availability Attack

In Figure 2(b) we see a larger DSO with $N_n = 1,000$. It is clear that a larger DSO can tolerate more attacks even with other parameters same as Figure 2(a). It is also clear that increasing the number of beacons, SHs and the number of copies of each share (n_h) will somewhat reduce the success probability of an availability attack. However, when less than 600 nodes are attacked, successful attack probabilities are close to zero. This indicates that the size of DSO is a very important factor to enhance the intrusion-tolerance.

We have so far calculated the successful attack probability to a specific service. Consider that the overlay provides x number of services. In this situation when an attacker compromises certain number of nodes, it may deny more than one service. Suppose we are interested in knowing the probability of denying at least one service. Prob(At least one service compromised) $= 1 -$ Prob(no service is compromised) $= 1 - \prod_{i=1}^{x}(1 - Pr_{d1})$. The upper bound on this probability is xPr_{d1}. Suppose there are total of 1,000 nodes DSO and a total of 1,000 different services on DSO. For $n_a = 1,000$, $n_b = 10$, $m = 10$, $k = 6$, $n_h = 4$, if attacker attacks 200 nodes, the probability of denying one or more service is less than $1,000 \times 1.7047 \times 10^{-7} = 1.7047 \times 10^{-4}$. This value is still negligible.

Now we want to compute the probability of denial of exactly y services in DSO. This probability will be a binomial distribution $Pr_d(y) = \binom{x}{y}(Pr_{d1})^y(1 - Pr_{d1})^{x-y}$. We can calculate the expected number of services brought down by the attacker as $\sum_{i=1}^{x} i \cdot Pr_d(i) = xPr_{d1}$.

Figure 2(c) plots the expected number of services that are denied given a certain number of attacks. Here we only use a small DSO with small parameters: $N_n =$

$100, n_a = 100, n_b = m = 10, k = 6, n_h = 4$ (using a larger DSO will obviously improve the performance). The result shows that when the number of attacked nodes is less than 60, almost no services are denied on DSO when the total number of services varies from 10 to 150. For example, when $x = 100$, attacking 30 random nodes can expect to denial 0.00034754 service on DSO. This shows that DSO can provide high availability.

(2) Confidentiality Attack

To analyze the probability of a successful confidentiality attack, Pr_{s1}, we first introduce another new function $P_g(a, b, c)$. Suppose we have a set of a nodes and we randomly select b nodes from it. $P_g(a, b, c)$ denotes the probability that selected nodes do not contain any of the nodes from a given set of c nodes. Evidently, $P_g(a, b, c) = \binom{a-c}{b}/\binom{a}{b}$ when $b \leq a - c$, $P_g(a, b, c) = 0$ when $b > a - c$.

A confidentiality attack may succeed only when an attacker can successfully get at least k distinct shares for a certain service. Since the attacker has no knowledge of where the share holders are located in the network, he needs to randomly attack a large set (n_t) of nodes on DSO. The probability of successfully stealing given service secret key Pr_{s1} is that of at least k out of m distinct shares be stolen. For each distinct share, $P_g(N_n, n_t, n_h)$ means no copy of this share is stolen while $1 - P_g(N_n, n_t, n_h)$ indicates that at least one copy is stolen. The probability of a successful confidentiality attack can be computed as

$$Pr_{s1} = \sum_{i=k}^{m} \binom{m}{i} (1 - P_g(N_n, n_t, n_h))^i P_g(N_n, n_t, n_h)^{m-i} \tag{3}$$

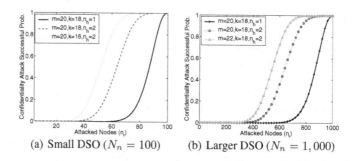

(a) Small DSO ($N_n = 100$)   (b) Larger DSO ($N_n = 1,000$)

Fig. 3. Confidentiality Attack

Figure 3(a) shows a small DSO example. Here $N_n = 100, n_a = 100, n_b = 10, m = 20, n_h = 2$. Assume $k = 18$, when attacker attacks $n_t = 20$ nodes, the chance of success is negligible (9.1880×10^{-7}). Even when half of nodes are attacked, the chance of a successful confidentiality attack is still low (0.0954). We can see from the figure that the confidentiality attack is very sensitive to the number of shares in DSO. Smaller n_h will achieve better attack tolerance than larger n_h. This makes sense because more copies of shares mean higher chance to leaking the shares. Given a fixed m, using a larger k will also enhance intrusion-tolerance. This is obvious because attackers need to attack more nodes in order to acquire at least k distinct shares.

In Figures 3(b), we see a larger DSO with 1,000 server nodes. For a fixed k, increasing m or increasing n_h will both enhance the attack probability because increasing m or n_h increases the number of shares in the system. Thus the attacker has more chance of getting k shares. For $m = 20, k = 18, n_h = 1$, when less than about 600 node are attacked, the probability of the success of attack is nearly zero.

The analysis of the probability of acquiring at least one service key, acquiring y service secret key and the expected number of service secret keys attacker can steal is similar to the analysis of that of availability attack.

We use different parameters in availability and confidential attack tolerance analysis. This is because availability and confidentiality has contradicting requirements. For example, larger n_h will achieve high availability attack tolerance but low confidentiality attack tolerance. As we can see there is some trade-off between availability and confidentiality. We will present some trade-off techniques in Section 5.1.

(3) Integrity Attack

One aspect of the integrity attack aims to corrupt enough shares so that attacker can forge the secret signing key. In this case the intrusion-tolerance against integrity attacks is the same as that against confidentiality attacks because when a node is attacked its share can either be disclosed or corrupted. Once an attacker has modified k copies of distinct shares, a client might receive the corrupted signature when beacon contacts those k nodes with corrupted shares.

Another aspect of the integrity attack is that the attacker modifies all copies of $n - k + 1$ distinct shares. Now no client will ever be able to use the signing service. This integrity attack is similar to Denial of Service. The successful attack probability is the same as that of availability attacks analyzed before.

As both aspects of the integrity attack are covered by the availability and confidentiality analysis, we will not further discuss this attack separately in this paper.

5   Discussion

Availability and confidentiality have conflicting requirements. If we try to improve one by changing parameters like k, m, n_h then the other will suffer and vice versa. We would like to find a trade-off between these two depending on the relative importance of availability and confidentiality ($A = lC$). Availability and confidentiality of the system can be measured as $(1 - Pr_{d1})$ and $(1 - Pr_{s1})$ respectively in DSO. If the desired ratio of availability to confidentiality is l, then $(1 - Pr_{d1}) = l(1 - Pr_{s1})$. Given l and some of the parameters, one can set the proper values of the rest of the parameters.

5.1   Intrusion-Tolerance Comparison

Other popular schemes which provide similar functionalities as DSO are pure replication, pure threshold scheme, threshold scheme plus replication, threshold scheme plus quorum. In pure replication, the key is replicated to all m_r servers. Pure threshold scheme uses (k_s, m_s) scheme where key is divided into m_s shares and at least k_s shares are required to reconstruct the secret. As the name suggests, threshold scheme plus share replication creates n_h replications of each m_{sr} shares.

In all these schemes, an attacker may know the servers providing the service and attack them. The attacker can easily determine the set of minimum servers it needs to attack to bring the system down. If the number of attacked nodes is below this threshold then the chance of successful attack is zero. If an attacker compromises more servers than the threshold, it will succeed with probability one. Table 3 lists the comparison of all existing schemes in terms of availability and confidentiality.

Table 3. Intrusion-tolerance Comparison (Attack Successful Probability)

	Availability Attack	Confidentiality Attack
Pure Replication	$\begin{cases} 0 & n_t < m_r \\ 1 & n_t \geq m_r \end{cases}$	$\begin{cases} 0 & n_t < 1 \\ 1 & n_t \geq 1 \end{cases}$
Pure threshold scheme	$\begin{cases} 0 & n_t < m_s - k_s + 1 \\ 1 & n_t \geq m_s - k_s + 1 \end{cases}$	$\begin{cases} 0 & n_t < k_s \\ 1 & n_t \geq k_s \end{cases}$
Threshold scheme+Replication	$\begin{cases} 0 & n_t < (m_{sr} - k_{sr} + 1)n_h \\ 1 & n_t \geq (m_{sr} - k_{sr} + 1)n_h \end{cases}$	$\begin{cases} 0 & n_t < k_{sr} \\ 1 & n_t \geq k_{sr} \end{cases}$
DSO	Eq. (2)	Eq. (3)

Let's compare the different schemes using a specific example. In order to have a fair comparison between other replication or threshold schemes and DSO, we need to use the same number of original servers. It will not be fair to compare a (50,100) pure threshold scheme and a 100 node DSO with a (6,10) scheme with no replication. Even though DSO has a network size of 100, only 10 servers are being used for this particular service. All other nodes are just part of the network. This case is similar to any distributed service provided on top of WAN or the Internet. We do not count routers or hosts in the path of routing as a part of servers. Thus, for all the schemes we compare, we assume that the total number of servers is 10. For DSO, we assume the overlay has 100 nodes.

Let's examine the intrusion-tolerance of each scheme. All schemes except DSO cannot get high intrusion-tolerance under both attacks. We use the importance comparison equation $A = lC$ to optimize the parameters for each scheme. To simplify matters, we will choose $l = 1$ which means attack-tolerance for availability and confidentiality is equally important. For other schemes, importance can be measured using the threshold.

For the pure replication scheme, threshold for availability attack-tolerance is m_r. But confidentiality is compromised even if a single server is successfully attacked.

For pure threshold scheme, we have the equation $m_s - k_s + 1 = k_s$. From this equation we get $k_s = (m_s + 1)/2 = 11/2 \approx 5$ which is the optimized value in order to achieve both attack-tolerance. So we take (5, 10) for pure threshold scheme.

Threshold plus replication scheme uses (k_{sr}, m_{sr}) secret sharing scheme and each share has n_h copies. Thus, the total number of servers in the system is $n_{sr} = m_{sr} \times k_{sr}$. By plugging in the values of availability and confidentiality in the importance equation we have $(m_{sr} - k_{sr} + 1)n_h = k_{sr}$. Thus $k_{sr} = (n_{sr} + n_h)/(n_h + 1) = 1 + (n_{sr} - 1)/(n_h + 1)$. This indicates that k_{sr} increases as n_h decreases. For $n_h = 2$, $k_{sr} = 12/3 = 4$. For $n_h = 1$ this becomes pure threshold scheme. For this scheme we take the optimized parameters as $k_{sr} = 4, m_{sr} = 5, n_h = 2$.

We place 10 servers into an overlay with 100 nodes. Note that we still use only 10 nodes as SHs for threshold signing or replication. Other nodes are just overlay nodes in charge of P2P routing. For these 10 servers, we use two strategies: one is a (5,10) threshold scheme ($k = 5, m = 10, n_h = 1$), the other is a (4,5) threshold scheme plus each share has 2 replications ($k = 4, m = 5, n_h = 2$).

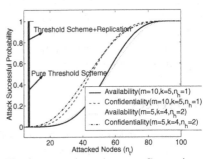

Figure 4 plots the intrusion-tolerance of three schemes (pure threshold scheme, threshold scheme plus replication, DSO) given the same number of total servers $n = 10$. It is obvious that DSO has the best intrusion-tolerance. The probability of intrusion-tolerance is still high even when there are many overlay nodes attacked.

Fig. 4.   Intrusion-tolerance Comparison of Three Schemes

5.2 Performance Evaluation

There are two types of overhead in the system, computation and communication. Distributed signing requires partial signing at SHs and combining at the combiner. The cost of one partial signing operation is the same as the signing using a complete RSA private key. Combining of data takes more time than partial signing. Time taken to partially sign the certificate and combine the partial signature by the combiner is proportional to the number of different shares. In DSO architecture, we do not need to use very high values of k and m to provide high security. As we have a smaller number of shares, time to sign or combine the shares is not very large. But in other system like pure threshold scheme one needs to have a large k and m to provide high security. Thus, these schemes require more time to combine the shares.

"MessageHop" is used as a metric to evaluate the communication cost. MessageHop is defined as the number of overlay nodes covered by the packet to reach the destination. The communication cost in DSO is the routing cost from AP to a beacon and then to m_{DSO} distinct SHs. The average number of hops for DHT-based routing to any destination is $log(N_n)/2$. So the total cost for sending request to share holders is $log(N_n)/2 \times (1 + m_{DSO})$. $log(N_n)$ can range from 5 to 30 depending on the size of the overlay. Although this involves some communication cost, it is still reasonable considering the fault- and intrusion-tolerance benefits provided by the overlay.

6 Conclusion

In this paper, we have discussed the importance of as well as the challenges in building dependable systems with both high fault-tolerance and intrusion-tolerance. Using digital signing service as a motivated example, we proposed a novel architecture, Dependable Signing Overlay (DSO). The fault-tolerance feature is achieved via using the threshold scheme plus replication. The intrusion-tolerance feature is obtained via using the threshold scheme plus anonymous servers, so the attackers cannot know which servers to attack in order to deny signing service or steal/corrupt signing key. We designed DSO as a P2P overlay server network and adopted the techniques of structured P2P overlay routing based on DHT. We derived analytical models and presented reliability (fault-tolerance) and security (intrusion-tolerance) analysis. Our results show that DSO provides very high fault-tolerance and intrusion-tolerance. We also compared DSO with other existing techniques. Our results showed that DSO provides high fault-tolerance and much higher intrusion-tolerance.

In conclusion, we believe that DSO is a promising and scalable platform to build dependable signing services.

References

1. Ross J. Anderson. The eternity service. http://www.cl.cam.ac.uk/users/rja14/eternity/eternity.html.
2. C. Cachin and J. Poritz. Secure intrusion tolerant replication on the internet. In *DSN 2002*, 2002.
3. Miguel Castro, Peter Druschel, Ayalvadi Ganesh, Antony Rowstron, and Dan S. Wallach. Security for peer-to-peer routing overlays. In *OSDI '02*, December 2002.
4. B. Chor, S. Goldwasser, S. Micali, and B. Awerbuch. Verifiable secret sharing and achieving simultaneity in the presence of faults. In *Proceedings of the 26th IEEE Symposium on the Foundations of Computer Science*, 1985.
5. Y. Desmedt and Y. Frankel. Threshold cryptosystems. In *Crypto'89*, 1989.
6. P. Feldman. A practical scheme for non-interactive verifiable secret sharing. In *Proceedings of IEEE 28th Annual Symposium on the Foundations of Computer Science*, October 1987.
7. The free haven project. http://www.freehaven.net/.
8. Guofei Gu, Prahlad Fogla, Wenke Lee, and Douglas Blough. DSO: Dependable Signing Overlay (full version). http://www.cc.gatech.edu/~guofei/paper/Gu_ACNS06_DSO_full.pdf, 2006.
9. Maurice Herlihy. A quorum-consensus replication method for abstract data types. *ACM Trans. Comput. Syst.*, 4(1):32–53, 1986.
10. A. Herzberg, S. Jarecki, H. Krawczyk, and M. Yung. Proactive secret sharing, or: How to cope with perpetual leakage. In *Proceedings of CRYPTO'95*, 1995.
11. Stanislaw Jarecki and Nitesh Saxena. Futher simplifications in proactive rsa signature schemes. In *TCC'05*, 2005.
12. Stanislaw Jarecki, Nitesh Saxena, and Jeong Hyun Yi. An attack on the proactive rsa signature scheme in the ursa ad hoc network access control protocol. In *SASN '04*, pages 1–9, New York, NY, USA, 2004. ACM Press.
13. Angelos Keromytis, Vishal Misra, and Dan Rubenstein. SOS: Secure Overlay Services. In *ACM SIGCOMM'02*, August 2002.
14. J. Kong, P. Zerfos, H. Luo, S. Lu, and L. Zhang. Providing robust and ubiquitous security support for mobile ad-hoc networks. In *ICNP'01*, November 2001.
15. Cachin K. Kursawe, A. Lysyanskaya, and R. Strobl. Asynchronous verifiable secret sharing and proactive cryptosystems. In *ACM CCS'02*, 2002.
16. Subramanian Lakshmanan, Mustaque Ahamad, and H. Venkateswaran. Responsive security for stored data. In *ICDCS'03*, 2003.
17. H. Luo, P. Zerfos, J. Kong, S. Lu, and L. Zhang. Self-securing ad hoc wireless networks. In *ISCC'02*, July 2002.
18. D. Malkhi and M. Reiter. Byzantine quorum systems. *Distributed Computing*, 11(4), 1998.
19. Maithili Narasimha, Gene Tsudik, and Jeong Hyun Yi. On the utility of distributed cryptography in p2p and manets: The case of membership control. In *ICNP '03*, 2003.

20. Maithili Narasimha, Gene Tsudik, and Jeong Hyun Yi. Efficient node admission for short-lived mobile ad hoc networks. In *ICNP '05*, 2005.
21. T. Rabin. A simplified approach to threshold and proactive rsa. In *Crypto'98*, 1998.
22. A. Rowstron and P. Druschel. Pastry: Scalable, decentralized object location and routing for large-scale peer-to-peer systems. In *Middleware'01*, 2001.
23. B. Schoenmakers. A simple publicly verifiable secret sharing scheme and its application to electronic voting. In *Crypto'99*, 1999.
24. A. Shamir. How to share a secret. *Communications of ACM*, 24(11), 1979.
25. V. Shoup. Practical threshold signatures. In *Proceedings of EUROCRPT'00*, 2000.
26. I. Stoica, R. Morris, D. Karger, M. F. Kaashoek, and H. Balakrishnan. Chord: A scalable peer-to-peer lookup service for internet applications. In *ACM SIGCOMM'01*, 2001.
27. Marc Waldman, Aviel D. Rubin, and Lorrie Faith Cranor. Publius: A robust, tamper-evident, censorship-resistant, web publishing system. In *Proc. 9th USENIX Security Symposium*, pages 59–72, August 2000.
28. T. Wu, M. Malkin, and D. Boneh. Building intrusion tolerant applications. In *Proceedings of 8th USENIX Security Symp (Security'99)*, 1999.
29. L. Zhou and Z. J. Haas. Securing ad hoc networks. *IEEE Networks*, 13(6), 1999.
30. L. Zhou, F.B. Schneider, and R. Van Renesse. A secure distributed online certification authority. *ACM Transactions on Computer Systems*, 20(4), 2002.

Do Broken Hash Functions Affect the Security of Time-Stamping Schemes?

Ahto Buldas[1,2,3,*] and Sven Laur[4,**]

[1] Cybernetica, Akadeemia tee 21, 12618 Tallinn, Estonia
[2] Tallinn University of Technology, Raja 15, 12618 Tallinn, Estonia
[3] University of Tartu, Liivi 2, 50409 Tartu, Estonia
Ahto.Buldas@ut.ee
[4] Helsinki University of Technology, Laboratory for Theoretical Computer Science,
P.O. Box 5400, FI-02015 TKK, Finland
slaur@tcs.hut.fi

Abstract. We study the influence of collision-finding attacks on the security of time-stamping schemes. We distinguish between *client-side hash functions* used to shorten the documents before sending them to time-stamping servers and *server-side hash functions* used for establishing one way causal relations between time stamps. We derive necessary and sufficient conditions for client side hash functions and show by using explicit separation techniques that neither collision-resistance nor 2nd preimage resistance is necessary for secure time-stamping. Moreover, we show that server side hash functions can even be not one-way. Hence, it is impossible by using black-box techniques to transform collision-finders into wrappers that break the corresponding time-stamping schemes. Each such wrapper should analyze the structure of the hash function. However, these separations do not necessarily hold for more specific classes of hash functions. Considering this, we take a more detailed look at the structure of practical hash functions by studying the Merkle-Damgård (MD) hash functions. We show that attacks, which are able to find collisions for MD hash functions with respect to *randomly chosen initial states*, also violate the necessary security conditions for client-side hash functions. This does not contradict the black-box separations results because the MD structure is already a deviation from the black-box setting. As a practical consequence, MD5, SHA-0, and RIPEMD are no more recommended to use as *client-side hash functions* in time-stamping. However, there is still no evidence against using MD5 (or even MD4) as *server-side* hash functions.

1 Introduction

Cryptographic hash functions are intended for transforming a message X of an arbitrary length into a digest $h(X)$ of a fixed length, which, in a way, represents the original message. Hash functions have several applications, such as electronic signatures,

---

* Partially supported by Estonian SF grant no. 5870, and by EU FP6-15964: "AEOLUS".
** Partially supported by Finnish Academy of Sciences, and by Estonian Graduate School in Information and Communication Technologies.

J. Zhou, M. Yung, and F. Bao (Eds.): ACNS 2006, LNCS 3989, pp. 50–65, 2006.

fast Message Authentic Codes (MACs), secure registries, time-stamping schemes, etc. Without any doubt, modern information technology needs hash functions as much as it needs stream and block ciphers. Therefore, the importance of research on hash function security can hardly be overestimated.

Unfortunately, the speed of developing suitable theoretical basis for hash function security cannot be compared to the expansion rate of hash function applications. Not much is known about suitable design criteria, nor about how to formalize the security requirements that originate from practical applications. A remarkable fact which characterizes the shortage of information in this field is that in many cases when theoreticians are looking for ways of modeling hash functions they just replace them with "random oracles".

Theoretical models of hash functions often deal with a limited number of "universal" security properties – collision-freedom, one-wayness, etc. –, which are possibly neither sufficient nor necessary in the context of particular practical applications. Recent success in finding collisions for practical hash functions (MD4,MD5, RIPEMD, SHA-0) by Wang et al [16, 17, 19] and later improvements [12, 18, 9, 10] raise an important question: For which practical implementations are the collisions a real threat? Modifications in software are always expensive and it would clearly not be economical to replace hash functions in all applications "just in case".

The problem addressed in this paper is to clarify and formalize the security properties of hash functions which are necessary and sufficient in the context of time-stamping schemes, and more general in secure registries. Considering the increasing use of electronic registries and databases, it is important to know to what extent and how their security depends on the security of hash functions:

- Which properties of hash functions would guarantee the security of time-stamping schemes?
- What kind of practical attacks (collisions, second preimages, etc.) are a suitable basis for replacing the hash functions in time-stamping schemes?

Just a few years after the birth of the first practical hash functions, it was pointed out that the specific security properties as well as their mutual relationships should deserve more attention. For example, Ross Anderson [1] listed several "freedom properties" (different from collision-freedom) arising from cryptographic constructions and applications. Rogaway and Shrimpton [13] presented an exhaustive study about "classical" security properties of hash functions and their mutual relationships. Hsiao and Reyzin [7] pointed out a fundamental difference between so-called *public-coin* hash functions and *secret-coin* hash functions by showing that the former cannot be constructed from the latter in a black-box way.

In the context of time-stamping, it has been shown [4] that the *chain-resistance* property, which is necessary in time-stamping schemes, is not implied by classical properties like collision-resistance or one-wayness. As a positive result, it was shown recently [5] that if time-stamping schemes have an additional audit functionality, then even the strongest reasonable (*universally composable*) security level is achievable if the hash functions used are universally one-way, which is a weaker property than collision resistance.

Time-stamping schemes use hash functions for two different goals: (1) to shorten the messages on the client side and (2) create one-way temporal (casual) relationships on the server side. Hence, it is natural to think that the client-side hash function and the server-side hash function have different security requirements. Thus far, the security proofs of time-stamping schemes [4, 5] assume the collision-resistance of client-side hash functions. Hence, it is important to study if we can replace collision-resistance on the client side with weaker requirements like *2nd preimage resistance* or *one-wayness*.

In this paper, we derive necessary and sufficient conditions for client side hash functions and show by using explicit separation techniques that neither collision-resistance nor 2nd preimage resistance is necessary for secure time-stamping. Moreover, we also show that server side hash functions can even be not one-way. More precisely, we prove that if secure hash-based time-stamping (as used in practical schemes like [15]) is possible at all, then we can replace client side hash functions with hash functions that are not 2nd preimage resistant and use server side hash functions, which are not one-way. In spite of using two "insecure" hash functions, we are able to achieve a new and rather strong security requirement for time-stamping schemes. Hence, it is impossible by using black-box techniques to transform collision-finders into wrappers that break the corresponding time-stamping schemes. Each such wrapper should analyze the structure of the hash function. Still, the results mentioned above do not necessarily apply to more specific classes of hash functions.

Considering the above, we will take a more detailed look at the structure of practical hash functions by studying the Merkle-Damgård (MD) style hash functions. We will show that the attacks which are able to find collisions to MD hash functions with respect to *randomly chosen initial state* also violate the necessary security conditions for client-side hash functions. This still does not mean that the recent attacks to MD hash functions render the practical hash functions insecure, because the attacks mostly consider the fixed (standard) initial state (IV) of the hash function. However, it is claimed by Klima [9, 10] that MD5 collisions can be find for random initial states, which (when true) would mean that MD5 cannot be used as a *client-side hash function* in time-stamping schemes. However, there are still no convincing arguments against using MD5 (or even MD4) as a *server-side hash function*.

This paper mainly focuses on the so called *hash-based time-stamping*, in which cryptographic (signature) keys are not used. However, the results about *client-side hash functions* also apply to the so-called *signature-based time stamps* [11] that consist of client-computed hash values, time values, and digital signatures of trusted servers.

The paper is organized as follows. Section 2 provides the reader with necessary notation and definitions. Section 3 outlines the basics of secure hash-based time-stamping schemes. Section 4 introduces a new security requirement and derives sufficient conditions for the client side and the server side hash functions that together imply the new condition. In Section 5, we show that 2nd preimage resistance is not necessary for client side hash functions. Section 6 shows that server side hash functions are not necessarily one-way. In Section 7, we show that certain multi-collision attacks to MD hash functions violate the necessary condition for client side hash functions. Section 8 presents some open problems related to this work.

2 Notation and Definitions

By $x \leftarrow \mathcal{D}$ we mean that x is chosen randomly according to a distribution $\mathcal{D}$. If A is a probabilistic function or a Turing machine, then $x \leftarrow A(y)$ means that x is chosen according to the output distribution of A on an input y. By $\mathcal{U}_n$ we denote the uniform distribution on $\{0,1\}^n$. If $\mathcal{D}_1, \ldots, \mathcal{D}_m$ are distributions and $F(x_1, \ldots, x_m)$ is a predicate, then $\Pr[x_1 \leftarrow \mathcal{D}_1, \ldots, x_m \leftarrow \mathcal{D}_m \colon F(x_1, \ldots, x_m)]$ denotes the probability that $F(x_1, \ldots, x_m)$ is true after the ordered assignment of $x_1, \ldots, x_m$. For functions $f, g \colon \mathbb{N} \to \mathbb{R}$, we write $f(k) = O(g(k))$ if there are $c, k_0 \in \mathbb{R}$, so that $f(k) \leq cg(k)$ $(\forall k > k_0)$. We write $f(k) = \omega(g(k))$ if $\lim_{k \to \infty} \frac{g(k)}{f(k)} = 0$. If $f(k) = k^{-\omega(1)}$, then f is *negligible*. A Turing machine M is *polynomial-time (poly-time)* if it runs in time $k^{O(1)}$, where k denotes the input size. Let FP be the class of all probabilistic functions $f \colon \{0,1\}^* \to \{0,1\}^*$ computable by a poly-time M.

A distribution family $\{\mathcal{D}_k\}_{k \in \mathbb{N}}$ is *poly-sampleable* if there is $D \in$ FP with output distribution $D(1^k)$ equal to $\mathcal{D}_k$. A poly-sampleable distribution family $\{\mathcal{D}_k\}$ is *unpredictable* if $\Pr[x' \leftarrow \Pi(1^k), x \leftarrow \mathcal{D}_k \colon x = x'] = k^{-\omega(1)}$ for every predictor $\Pi \in$ FP. Two distribution families $\mathcal{D}^{(1)}$ and $\mathcal{D}^{(2)}$ are *indistinguishable* if for every distinguisher $\Delta \in$ FP$\colon |\Pr[x \leftarrow \mathcal{D}_k^{(1)} \colon \Delta(1^k, x) = 1] - \Pr[x \leftarrow \mathcal{D}_k^{(2)} \colon \Delta(1^k, x) = 1]| = k^{-\omega(1)}$.

Let $\{\mathfrak{F}_k\}_{k \in \mathbb{N}}$ be a distribution family such that every $h \leftarrow \mathfrak{F}_k$ is a (deterministic) function $h \colon \{0,1\}^{\ell} \to \{0,1\}^k$, where ℓ is polynomial in k. We say that $\{\mathfrak{F}_k\}$ is a *function distribution family*. For every $x, x' \in \{0,1\}^k$ let $C(x, x')$ denote the condition that (x, x') is a collision for h, i.e. $x \neq x'$ and $h(x) = h(x')$. By following the security notions in [13] we say that a randomly chosen $h \leftarrow \mathfrak{F}_k$ is:

- *Collision-Resistant* if $\forall A \in$ FP$\colon \Pr[(x, x') \leftarrow A(1^k, h) \colon C(x, x')] = k^{-\omega(1)}$.
- *Everywhere 2nd Preimage Resistant* (eSec) if $\forall A \in$ FP:

$$\max_{x \in \{0,1\}^{\ell}} \Pr[x' \leftarrow A(1^k, h) \colon C(x, x')] = k^{-\omega(1)} \ .$$

- *2nd Preimage Resistant* if $\forall A \in$ FP$\colon \Pr[x \leftarrow \mathcal{U}_{\ell}, x' \leftarrow A(x) \colon C(x, x')] = k^{-\omega(1)}$.
- *One-Way* if $\forall A \in$ FP$\colon \Pr[x \leftarrow \mathcal{U}_{\ell}, x' \leftarrow A(h(x)) \colon h(x') = h(x)] = k^{-\omega(1)}$.

If for every k there exists h_k so that $\Pr[h \leftarrow \mathfrak{F}_k \colon h = h_k] = 1$ then we have a fixed family of functions, i.e. for each k we have a single unkeyed hash function, e.g. SHA-1.

3 Security of Time-Stamping Schemes

In this paper, we focus on the security of *hash functions* used in time-stamping schemes. The other primitives supporting the time stamping schemes (like signature schemes or encryption schemes) are not studied in this paper. A time-stamping procedure consists of the following general steps:

- Client computes a hash $x = H(X)$ of a document X (where H is called a *client-side hash function*) and sends x to the Server.
- Server binds x with a time value t (a positive integer), either by using a digital signature or a hash-chain created by using another (server-side) hash function h.

For the self-consistency of this paper, we outline the basic facts about hash-chains and how they are used in time-stamping. In the definition of a hash-chain we use the following notation. We will follow the notation and definitions introduced in [4] except some technicalities which we change in order to make the definitions more usable for this work. By $\lfloor\rfloor$ we mean the empty string. If $x = (x_1, x_2) \in \{0,1\}^{2k}$ and $x_1, x_2 \in \{0,1\}^k$ then by $y \in x$ we mean $y \in \{x_1, x_2\}$.

Definition 1 (Hash-Chain). *Let* $h\colon \{0,1\}^{2k} \to \{0,1\}^k$ *be a hash function.*[1] *By an* h*-chain from* $x \in \{0,1\}^k$ *to* $r \in \{0,1\}^k$ *we mean a (possibly empty) sequence* $c = (c_1, \ldots, c_\ell)$ *of pairs* $c_i \in \{0,1\}^{2k}$*, such that the following two conditions hold:*

(1) if $c = \lfloor\rfloor$ *then* $x = r$*; and*
(2) if $c \neq \lfloor\rfloor$ *then* $x \in c_1$*,* $r = h(c_\ell)$*, and* $h(c_i) \in c_{i+1}$ *for every* $i \in \{1, \ldots, \ell - 1\}$*.*

We denote by $F_h(x; c) = r$ *the proposition that* c *is an* h*-chain from* x *to* r*. Note that* $F_h(x; \lfloor\rfloor) = x$ *for every* $x \in \{0,1\}^k$*.*

Time-stamping involves Server, Publisher, and two procedures for *time-stamping* a bit-string and for *verifying* a time stamp. It is assumed that Publisher is write-once and receives items from Server in an authenticated manner. Time-stamping procedure is divided into rounds of equal duration. During each round, Server receives requests $x_1, \ldots, x_N \in \{0,1\}^k$ from the users. If the t-th round is over, Server computes a digest $r_t = T^h(x_1, \ldots, x_N) \in \{0,1\}^k$ by using a hash function $h\colon \{0,1\}^{2k} \to \{0,1\}^k$ and a tree-shaped hashing scheme T^h. After that, Server issues a hash chain c (*certificate*) for each request x, such that $F_h(x; c) = r_t$. In the scheme of Fig. 1, the time-certificate for x_2 is $((x_1, x_2), (y_1, z_1))$, where $y_1 = h(x_1, x_2)$. Certificate c of a request x is verified by obtaining a suitable r_t form Publisher and checking whether $F_h(x; c) = r_t$. Intuitively, this proves that x existed at time t when r_t was published.

Security condition for time-stamping [4] is inspired by the following simplistic attack-scenario with a malicious Server:

- Server computes $r \in \{0,1\}^k$ (not necessarily by using T^h) and publishes it.
- Alice, an inventor, creates a description $X_A \in \{0,1\}^*$ of her invention and (possibly) obtains a certificate for the hash $x_A = H(X_A)$ of the description.
- Some time later, the invention is disclosed to the public and Server tries to steal it by showing that the invention was known to Server long before Alice time-stamped it. He creates a slightly modified version X of X_A, i.e. changes invertor's name, modifies the creation time, and possibly rewords the document in a suitable way (to have a "desired" hash value).
- Finally, Server computes a hash $x = H(X)$, and back-dates x, by finding a certificate c, so that $F_h(x; c) = r$.

---

[1] Twice-compressing hash functions are sufficient in the server side, and strictly for this purpose it is not necessary to apply hash functions with long input length. When h is implemented by using a practical hash function like MD5, it is sufficient to use only one input block. This detail is very important for the conclusions of this work.

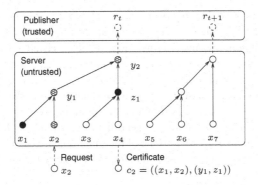

Fig. 1. Time-stamping by using a hash-function h

To formalize such a scenario, a two-staged adversary $A = (A_1, A_2)$ is used. The first stage A_1 *computes* r (and an advice string a) after which the second stage A_2 on input a *new bit-string* $x \in \{0,1\}^k$ (modeled as an output of an unpredictable distribution $\mathcal{D}_k$) tries to find c, so that $F_h(x; c) = r$. The second stage can also use the advice string a if necessary. As h is the only cryptographic primitive used in the formal scenario, the security condition can be represented as a general requirement for a hash functions:

Definition 2 (Chain resistance – Chain). *A function distribution family $\{\mathfrak{F}_k\}$ of two-to-one hash functions $h: \{0,1\}^{2k} \to \{0,1\}^k$ is chain resistant if for every unpredictable poly-sampleable distribution family $\{\mathcal{D}_k\}_{k \in \mathbb{N}}$ on $\{0,1\}^k$:*

$$\Pr[h \leftarrow \mathfrak{F}_k, (r, a) \leftarrow A_1(1^k, h), x \leftarrow \mathcal{D}_k, c \leftarrow A_2(x, a): F_h(x, c) = r] = k^{-\omega(1)} \ . \quad (1)$$

Remark. In the definition above, a denotes *state information* stored by A_1 when computing the digest r. The reason why a is introduced is completely technical – we prefer *ordinary* Turing machines, which (unlike *interacting* machines) cannot save the state information between two calls. Informally, A_1 and A_2 are parts of a single adversary, and hence *all inputs and random coins of A_1 are available to A_2.*

To be more practical, we should take into account that lengthy documents are shortened by using another hash function $H: \{0,1\}^{\ell(k)} \to \{0,1\}^k$, which is not necessarily the same hash function as h, which is used by Server. Let $\{\mathfrak{F}_k^c\}$ and $\{\mathfrak{F}_k^s\}$ be the corresponding function distribution families producing functions of types $\{0,1\}^{\ell(k)} \to \{0,1\}^k$ and $\{0,1\}^{2k} \to \{0,1\}^k$ respectively.

Definition 3 (Secure (H, h)-time-stamping). *For every $A = (A_1, A_2) \in FP$ and for every unpredictable $\mathcal{D}_k$ on $\{0,1\}^{\ell(k)}$ the following probability is negligible:*

$$\Pr[H \leftarrow \mathfrak{F}_k^c, h \leftarrow \mathfrak{F}_k^s, (r, a) \leftarrow A_1(1^k, H, h), X \leftarrow \mathcal{D}_k, c \leftarrow A_2(X, a): F_h(H(X), c) = r] \ . \quad (2)$$

This security definition may seem confusing for those who have got used to a "folklore" belief that collision-resistance is essential for time-stamping. What if the inventor creates two colliding files, time-stamps one, and later tries to claim credits for the other? It is important here to notice that *this is not an attack in terms of time-stamping*! Indeed, both colliding files were created by the inventor approximately at the same time, and so there is nothing wrong in proving that the other file also existed at that time.

So far, security proofs exist only for time-stamping schemes which are "bounded" somehow. For example, if H and h are collision-resistant, then a (H, h)-time-stamping can be proven secure if the number of the allowed hash chain "shapes" is restricted to polynomial [4], or if there is an additional audit functionality included into the scheme [5]. It is also known [4] that the claim "h is collision-resistant $\Rightarrow$ h is chain-resistant" cannot be proven in a black-box way. One of the main objectives of this paper is to clarify whether collision-resistance of h (and of H) is necessary for secure time-stamping.

4   New Security Condition

There are several concerns related to the security condition (2). First, chain-resistance is a *necessary* property for h but it is not yet known whether it is *sufficient*, i.e. if H is collision resistant and h is chain-resistant, there are no known results for concluding that the time-stamping scheme (that uses H and h) is secure.

Another concern about (2) is that the adversary does not participate in the generation of X, i.e. X is picked independent of the adversary. This does not match with the informal description of the back-dating attack, where X was created by the adversary based on another document X_A and hence it is quite natural to assume that the adversary is able to "tune" the distribution $\mathcal{D}_k$ according to which the new document X is chosen. Based on these ideas, we give a new stronger security condition for (H, h)-time-stamping in which X is chosen by A_2. We still have to assume that X is unpredictable and hence we have to allow only those adversaries that produce unpredictable X. It is also important to require that A_2 adds "his own randomness" into X, i.e. X should be unpredictable even if the output and the random coins of A_1 are known.

We derive a necessary and sufficient security condition for the client side hash function H. Roughly saying, H must not destroy the computational entropy in a catastrophic way – unpredictable input distributions transform to unpredictable output distributions.

We prove that the new condition is not weaker than (2). We also propose a new stronger condition for h – *Strong Chain-Resistance* (sChain), which is sufficient for secure time-stamping. We prove that if H is unpredictability-preserving and h is strongly chain-resistant, then we have a secure (H, h)-time-stamping scheme in terms of (2).

4.1   New Security Definition

Let FPU be the class of all two-staged probabilistic poly-time adversaries (A_1, A_2), such that the first output component is unpredictable, even if the output of A_1 is known to the predictor, i.e. for every poly-time predictor Π:

$$\Pr[(r, a) \leftarrow A_1(1^k), x' \leftarrow \Pi(r, a), (x, c) \leftarrow A_2(a): x' = x] = k^{-\omega(1)} \ .$$

Note that as the additional inputs (r, a) of Π are generated by a uniform machine $A_1(1^k)$ this definition does not imply unpredictability in the *non-uniform* model. Note also that is is reasonable to assume that the advice string a contains all internal random coins of

A_1 because concealing these coins by A_1 certainly would not make any attacks easier. Moreover, as the main role of Π is to measure the capability of A_1 to predict the future, then for this measure to be adequate Π has to know the random coins of A_1.

Definition 4 (Secure (H, h)-time-stamping). *A (H, h)-time-stamping scheme is secure if for every $(A_1, A_2) \in$ FPU the next probability is negligible:*

$$\Pr[H \leftarrow \mathfrak{F}_k^c, h \leftarrow \mathfrak{F}_k^s, (r, a) \leftarrow A_1(1^k, H, h), (X, c) \leftarrow A_2(a) \colon F_h(H(X); c) = r] \ . \quad (3)$$

It is easy to see that (3) implies the old condition (2). Indeed, if $(A_1, A_2) \in$ FP breaks (H, h)-time-stamping in terms of (2) with success $\delta(k)$, then define $A_2'(a)$ that picks $x \leftarrow \mathcal{D}_k$, computes $c \leftarrow A_2(x, a)$, and outputs (x, c). By definition, $(A_1, A_2') \in$ FPU breaks (H, h)-time-stamping in terms of (3) with success $\delta(k)$.

Remark. It is insufficient to assume that X is unpredictable without advice, because then the condition (3) would be not achievable. Indeed, let A_1 be an adversary who generates X at random and outputs $(H(X), X)$ (where H is the client-side hash function) and let $A_2(1^k, a)$ be an adversary who always outputs $(a, \lfloor\rfloor)$. For such an adversary

$$\Pr[H \leftarrow \mathfrak{F}_k^c, h \leftarrow \mathfrak{F}_k^s, (r, a) \leftarrow A_1(1^k, H, h), (x, c) \leftarrow A_2(a) \colon F_h(H(x), c) = r] = 1.$$

4.2 Necessary and Sufficient Requirements for H

Finding collisions for H does not mean that the time-stamping scheme is insecure according to our definitions. A single collision is not sufficient to produce probability distribution with high uncertainty. In a way, one single collision allows one to backdate a single document that is known before the digest is produced, leaving the majority of temporal dependencies intact. It turns out that the following entropy-preservation property is necessary and sufficient for the client-side hash function H.

Definition 5 (Unpredictability preservation – uPre). *A function distribution family $\{\mathfrak{F}_k\}$ is unpredictability preserving, if for every unpredictable poly-sampleable distribution family $\{\mathcal{D}_k\}$ and for every predictor $\Pi \in$ FP:*

$$\Pr[H \leftarrow \mathfrak{F}_k, y \leftarrow \Pi(1^k, H), x \leftarrow \mathcal{D}_k \colon y = H(x)] = k^{-\omega(1)} \ .$$

A fixed $H \colon \{0, 1\}^{\ell(k)} \to \{0, 1\}^k$ is uPre iff it converts unpredictable poly-sampleable distributions $\mathcal{D}_k$ to unpredictable output distributions $H(\mathcal{D}_k)$.

Remark. Poly-sampleability of $\mathcal{D}_k$ is crucial, because if $H_k \colon \{0, 1\}^{\ell(k)} \to \{0, 1\}^k$ and $\ell(k) = k + \omega(\log k)$, then there exists a family $\mathcal{D}_k$ with Rényi entropy $H_2[\mathcal{D}_k] = \omega(\log k)$, such that $H_2[H(\mathcal{D}_k)] = 0$. Indeed, $\exists y \in \{0, 1\}^k$ for which $|H^{-1}(y)| = (2^{k+\omega(\log k)})/2^k = k^{\omega(1)}$. Define $\mathcal{D}_k$ as the uniform distribution on $H^{-1}(y)$.

Theorem 1. *Unpredictability preservation is a necessary requirement for H: in every secure (H, h)-time-stamping scheme, the client-side hash function H is uPre.*

Proof. Let $\mathcal{D}_k$ be unpredictable and Π be a predictor for $H(\mathcal{D}_k)$ with success probability $\pi(k) = \Pr[H \leftarrow \mathfrak{F}_k^c, y \leftarrow \Pi(1^k, H), x \leftarrow \mathcal{D}_k \colon H(x) = y]$. Define $A_1(1^k, H, h) \equiv \Pi(1^k, H)$ and A_2 which on input x outputs $(x, \sqcup)$. As $F_h(H(x); \sqcup) = H(x) = y$ whenever Π is successful, the success of (A_1, A_2) in terms of (2) is $\pi(k)$. Hence, $\pi(k)$ must be negligible and H is uPre. $\qquad\square$

Definition 6 (Strong chain-resistance – sChain). *A function distribution family* $\{\mathfrak{F}_k\}$ *is strongly chain-resistant, if for every* $(A_1, A_2) \in$ FPU:

$$\varepsilon(k) = \Pr[h \leftarrow \mathfrak{F}_k, (r, a) \leftarrow A_1(1^k, h), (x, c) \leftarrow A_2(a) \colon F_h(x; c) = r] = k^{-\omega(1)} \ .$$

Theorem 2. *For secure* (H, h)*-time-stamping in terms of (3) it is sufficient that* h*-is* sChain, H *is* uPre *and the distribution* $H \leftarrow \mathfrak{F}_k^c$ *is poly-sampleable.*

Proof. Let $(A_1, A_2) \in$ FPU an adversary with success

$$\varepsilon(k) = \Pr[H \leftarrow \mathfrak{F}_k^c, h \leftarrow \mathfrak{F}_k^s, (r, a) \leftarrow A_1(1^k, H, h), (X, c) \leftarrow A_2(a) \colon F_h(H(X); c) = r] \ .$$

Define $A_1'(1^k, h)$ that picks $H \leftarrow \mathfrak{F}_k^c$, computes $(r, a) \leftarrow A_1(1^k, H, h)$ and outputs (r, a'), where $a' = (a, H)$. Define $A_2'(a')$ that parses a' to obtain a and H, calls $(X, c) \leftarrow A_2(a)$ and outputs $(H(X), c)$. We have $(A_1', A_2') \in$ FPU, because H is uPre. Obviously, (A_1', A_2') breaks h in terms of sChain with success $\varepsilon(k)$. $\qquad\square$

5   Unpredictability Preservation vs 2nd Preimage Resistance

It is known that every collision-resistant function is uPre [5]. However, it turns out that 2nd preimage resistance does not imply uPre and *vice versa*, which means that client-side hash functions need not be 2nd preimage resistant.

Theorem 3. *If* uPre *hash functions exist (i.e. if secure time-stamping with client side hashing is possible at all), then there are hash functions which are* uPre *but not 2nd preimage resistant.*

Proof. Let $H \colon \{0, 1\}^{\ell(k)} \to \{0, 1\}^k$ (chosen randomly from $\mathfrak{F}_k$) be uPre. Define $H'(X') = H(X' \text{ or } 1)$ for every $X' \in \{0, 1\}^{\ell(k)}$, where or denotes the logical bitwise OR-operation. Let $\mathfrak{F}_k'$ denote the distribution of H'. Obviously, H' is not 2nd preimage resistant. To show that H' is uPre, let us assume that $\mathcal{D}_k$ is an unpredictable distribution and Π is a poly-time predictor for $H'(\mathcal{D}_k)$. As the distribution $\mathcal{D}_k' = (\mathcal{D}_k \text{ or } 1)$ is also unpredictable, the success probability of Π is

$$\begin{aligned} \pi(k) &= \Pr[H' \leftarrow \mathfrak{F}_k', y \leftarrow \Pi(1^k, H'), X' \leftarrow \mathcal{D}_k \colon H'(X') = y] \\ &= \Pr[H \leftarrow \mathfrak{F}_k, y \leftarrow \Pi'(1^k, H), X \leftarrow \mathcal{D}_k' \colon H(X) = y] = k^{-\omega(1)} \ , \end{aligned}$$

because H is uPre. Here $\Pi'(1^k, H)$ just transforms H to H' and returns $\Pi(1^k, H')$. $\quad\square$

On the other hand, it turns out that 2nd preimage resistance does not imply uPre and is thereby also insufficient for client side hash functions. Recall that collision-resistance was sufficient on the client side (but still not on the server side [4]).

Theorem 4. *If there are hash functions which are 2nd preimage resistant, then there are hash functions that are 2nd preimage resistant but not* uPre.

Proof. Let $H\colon \{0,1\}^{\ell(k)} \to \{0,1\}^k$ be 2nd preimage resistant and $\ell(k) = k+\omega(\log k)$. We construct a function $H'\colon \{0,1\}^{\ell'(k)} \to \{0,1\}^k$ which is 2nd preimage resistant but not uPre. Let $\ell'(k) = \ell(k-1)$ for all $k > 1$, and for every $X \in \{0,1\}^{\ell'(k)}$:

$$H'_k(X) = \begin{cases} 0^k & \text{if } X = 0^{k-1}\|X_1 \text{ for an } X_1 \in \{0,1\}^{\ell(k-1)-k+1} \\ 1\|H_{k-1}(X) & \text{otherwise.} \end{cases}$$

Define $\mathcal{D}$ on $\{0,1\}^{\ell'(k)}$, so that $\mathcal{D}_k = 0^{k-1}\|\mathcal{U}_{\ell(k-1)-k+1}$. $\mathcal{D}$ is unpredictable because it has Rényi entropy $H_2(\mathcal{D}_k) = \ell(k-1) - k + 1 = \omega(\log k)$. As the output distribution $H'(\mathcal{D})$ has no entropy at all, we conclude that H' is not uPre. At the same time, H' is 2nd preimage resistant because the probability that the first $k-1$ bits of a uniformly chosen $X \leftarrow \mathcal{U}_{\ell(k)}$ are all zeroes is $2^{-(k-1)}$, which is negligibly small. □

It is interesting to note that if in the everywhere second preimage-resistance (eSec) condition the adversary is prevented from abusing a small set of pre-computed existential collisions (which do not affect the security of time-stamping schemes) then we obtain a weaker condition weSec which turns out to be equivalent to uPre. This shows that eSec is a sufficient (but not necessary) condition for client-side hash functions. In this weaker requirement, the class of adversaries is restricted by requiring that the second pre-image X' produced by an adversary is distributed according to a high-entropy distribution. Though the following theorem holds for a fixed family H, it is possible to generalize the definition and the proof to arbitrary function distribution families.

Theorem 5. *For fixed families $H = \{H_k\}$,* uPre *is equivalent to the following* weak *everywhere 2nd preimage resistance (weSec) condition: For every poly-sampleable unpredictable distribution family $\mathcal{A}_k$ on $\{0,1\}^{\ell(k)}$:*

$$\max_{X\in\{0,1\}^{\ell(k)}} \Pr[X' \leftarrow \mathcal{A}_k \colon X' {\neq} X, H(X'){=}H(X)] = k^{-\omega(1)} .$$

Proof. weSec $\Longrightarrow$ uPre: Let $\mathcal{D}_k$ be unpredictable and Π be a predictor for $H(\mathcal{D}_k)$ with success $\pi(k) = \Pr[y \leftarrow \Pi(1^k), X' \leftarrow \mathcal{D}_k \colon y = H(X')] \neq k^{-\omega(1)}$. Hence, there is $y \in \{0,1\}^k$ such that $\Pr[X' \leftarrow \mathcal{D}_k \colon y = H(X')] \geq \pi(k)$ and we have

$$\max_{X\in\{0,1\}^{\ell(k)}} \Pr[X' \leftarrow \mathcal{D}_k \colon H(X'){=}H(X)] \geq \pi(k) \neq k^{-\omega(1)} .$$

As $\Pr_{X'\leftarrow\mathcal{D}_k}[H(X'){=}H(X)] = \Pr_{X'\leftarrow\mathcal{D}_k}[X'{=}X] + \Pr_{X'\leftarrow\mathcal{D}_k}[X'{\neq}X, H(X'){=}H(X)]$ and the first probability in the sum is negligible (because $\mathcal{D}_k$ is unpredictable), the second one must be non-negligible and hence $\mathcal{D}_k$ breaks H in the sense of weSec.

uPre $\Longrightarrow$ weSec: Let $\mathcal{A}_k$ be a unpredictable distribution on $\{0,1\}^{\ell(k)}$ and let $X \in \{0,1\}^{\ell(k)}$ be a bit-string such that $\delta(k) = \Pr_{X'\leftarrow\mathcal{A}_k}[X'{\neq}X, H(X'){=}H(X)] \neq k^{-\omega(1)}$. Therefore, $\Pr_{X'\leftarrow\mathcal{A}_k}[H(X'){=}H(X)] \geq \delta(k) \neq k^{-\omega(1)}$ and $H(\mathcal{A}_k)$ predicts itself with success $\pi(k) = \Pr[X' \leftarrow \mathcal{A}_k, X'' \leftarrow \mathcal{A}_k \colon H(X''){=}H(X')] \geq \delta^2(k) \neq k^{-\omega(1)}$. □

6   Strong Chain-Resistance vs One-Wayness

In this section, we show that the server side hash function h is not necessarily one-way.

Theorem 6. *For every secure (H, h)-time-stamping scheme, there is a secure (H, h')-time-stamping scheme, where h' is not one-way (and hence not collision-resistant and not 2nd preimage resistant).*

Proof. Define h' that behaves like h, except that $h'(x, x) = x$ for every $x \in \{0, 1\}^k$. The new function h' is clearly not one-way. To show that h' is strongly chain-resistant, let $A_1 \in FP$ and $A_2 \in FPU$ be an adversaries for h' with success

$$\varepsilon(k) = \Pr[(r, a) \leftarrow A_1(1^k), (X, c) \leftarrow A_2(a) : F_{h'}(H(X); c) = r] \neq k^{-\omega(1)} .$$

Define a new A_2' that calls $(x, c) \leftarrow A_2$ and outputs (x, c'), where c' is produced from c by deleting all elements c_i of the form (y, y). It is easy to verify that $F_h(H(X); c') = F_{h'}(H(X); c) = r$ (which is true even if c' is empty) and hence (A_1, A_2') breaks the (H, h)-time-stamping scheme. A contradiction.   □

Note that the proof also shows that strong chain resistant functions are not necessarily one-way functions, i.e. the chain resistance property is quite separated from other standard requirements for hash functions. Recall that there are no black-box proofs [4] for showing that collision-resistance implies chain resistance.

7   Implications to Practical Iterated Hash Functions

In this section, we will study what kind of collision-finding attacks to practical (client side) hash functions would make them insecure for time-stamping. We use the fact that most of the practical hash functions use the Merkle-Damgård construction, which (in order to compute hash for long messages) iterates a fixed compression function f.

Definition 7 (Merkle-Damgård Hash). *Let $f_k : \mathcal{S}_k \times \mathcal{M}_k \to \mathcal{S}_k$ be a family of poly-time compression functions and $g_k : \mathcal{S}_k \to \mathcal{T}_k$ be a family of poly-time output functions. Let the state update function $F_k : \mathcal{S}_k \times \mathcal{M}_k^* \to \mathcal{S}_k$ be defined by $F_k(s, x_1, \ldots, x_r) = f_k(\cdots f_k(s, x_1), \ldots, x_r)$. Then $h_k : \mathcal{S}_k \times \mathcal{M}_k^* \to \mathcal{T}_k$, defined by $h_k(s, x) = g(F_k(s, x))$, is a family of iterative (Merkle-Damgård) hash functions.*

Definition 8 (Collision-resistance w.r.t random initial state). *A family $\{h_k\}$ of MD hash functions is* collision resistant *(w.r.t. to random initial state) if for every $A \in FP$:*

$$\Pr\left[s \leftarrow \mathcal{S}_k, (x_0, x_1) \leftarrow A(1^k, s, h_k) : x_0 \neq x_1, h_k(s, x_0) = h_k(s, x_1)\right] = k^{-\omega(1)} .$$

The internal state of $\{h_k\}$ is said to be collision resistant w.r.t. random initial state *if the state update function family $\{F_k\}$ is collision-resistant w.r.t. random initial state.*

Definition 9 (Collision-resistance w.r.t fixed initial state s_0). *A family of MD hash functions $\{h_k\}$ is* collision resistant *(w.r.t. to a fixed initial state s_0) if for every $A \in FP$:*

$$\Pr\left[(x_0, x_1) \leftarrow A(1^k, f) : x_0 \neq x_1, h_k(s_0, x_0) = h_k(s_0, x_1)\right] = k^{-\omega(1)} .$$

The internal state of $\{h_k\}$ is said to be collision resistant w.r.t. fixed initial state s_0 *if the state update function family $\{F_k\}$ is collision-resistant w.r.t. fixed initial state.*

7.1 Discussion on Practical Hash Functions

In practical MD-hash functions the initial state s_0 (so called *Initial Value – IV*) is fixed by standards and is not chosen randomly. In order to formally define the collision-resistance of such functions, we have to assume that the compression function f is chosen randomly in accordance to a distribution $\mathfrak{F}$. Otherwise, an adversary can abuse a single existential collision which always exists because hash functions compress data.

It is important to distinguish between two kinds of collision-finding attacks: (1) attacks that find collisions for a fixed (standard) initial state, or more general, for a limited number of "weak" initial states, and (2) attacks that find collisions for random initial states (i.e. for a non-negligible fraction of initial states). In some sense these two types of attacks are incomparable in strength. For example, if the standard initial value s_0 is weak but still almost all other values are strong, then there are attacks of the first type but no attacks of the second type. If in turn the standard s_0 is strong and a non-negligible fraction of other states are weak, then there exist attacks of the second type but no attacks of the first type. However, these cases are ruled out by the following heuristic assumptions about the design of practical hash functions:

- *Reasonable choice of the standard IV:* Widely used hash functions are designed by specialists with good experience. Hence, it is reasonable to believe that *the choice of standard IV is at least as good as a random choice.* Hence, the situation where the standard IV is weak but almost all other IV-s are strong is extremely unlikely.
- *Reasonably efficient encoding of the internal state:* It is reasonable to believe that hash functions are designed quite efficiently, i.e. there is no considerable amount of redundancy in the initial state. Hence, it is also unlikely that the standard IV is strong but still a non-negligible fraction of other IV-s are weak. This is because the output of the compression function (in case of random inputs) is intuitively viewed as a random value, which would mean that weak initial states will eventually occur. (See the Computational Uniformity assumption below)

Therefore, it is reasonable to believe that efficient collision finders w.r.t. fixed IV imply the existence of efficient collision-finders w.r.t. random IV. Still, this does not mean that we *know* how to find collisions for random IV, though the heuristic assumptions above suggest that such attacks exist. The latest attacks against MD5 by Wang [16, 17] and by Klima [10] are claimed to be able to find collisions for arbitrary IV.

We show that *collision-finding attacks w.r.t. random IV are sufficient to render the client-side hash function H insecure for time-stamping*, i.e. H is no more uPre. This means that MD5 and MD4 are probably insecure as *client-side hash functions* in time-stamping. However, as we show later, this still does not mean that MD5 (or even MD4) are insecure as *server-side hash functions*.

The next property of MD hash functions (*Computational Uniformity*) is not an explicit design goal, but is often implicitly assumed in heuristic discussions about hash functions. Indeed, it has been shown [3] that hash functions must be almost regular to withstand birthday attacks. This suggests that some kind of statistical uniformity must hold for secure hash functions and hence the computational indistinguishability from uniform distribution is not a so far-fetched assumption.

Definition 10 (Computational uniformity). *Let ℓ be a polynomial and $U_{\ell(k)}$ denote uniform distribution on $\mathcal{M}_k^{\ell(k)}$. We say that iterative hash function family $\{h_k\}$ is computationally uniform w.r.t. length restriction ℓ, if $h_k(s, U_{\ell(k)})$ is computationally indistinguishable from uniform distribution on $\mathcal{T}_k$ for any $s \in \mathcal{S}_k$.*

7.2   Collisions of MD-Hash Functions Affect uPre

In the following, we will prove two results. First, if a collision finder has non-negligible success probability for every initial state, then the iterative hash function violates the uPre property. The second result states that the average-case and worst-case complexities for collision finding are roughly the same, if we assume *computational uniformity* from the compression function. Thus, it is quite likely that uPre implies collision resistance w.r.t. random initial value for all practical iterative hash functions.

Theorem 7. *Let $\{h_k\}$ be a fixed family of iterative hash functions. Then unpredictability preservation implies negligible worst-case success probability for all collision finders of $\{F_k\}$, i.e. for every $A \in FP$:*

$$\min_{s_0 \in \mathcal{S}_k} \Pr\left[(x_0, x_1) \leftarrow A(s_0) : x_0 \neq x_1, F_k(s_0, x_0) = F_k(s_0, x_1)\right] = k^{-\omega(1)} \ .$$

Proof. For the sake of contradiction, assume that there exists an algorithm A that the worst-case success probability is larger than k^{-c} for infinitely many indices. Then running A sufficiently many times (polynomial in k) assures that we fail with negligible probability. Denote this algorithm by A'. Then we start A' on s_0 and get a collision pair (x_1^0, x_1^1) such that $s_1 = F_k(s_0, x_1^0) = F_k(s_0, x_1^1)$. Similarly, we can find the following collisions $s_i = F_k(s_{i-1}, x_i^0) = F_k(s_{i-1}, x_i^1)$, $i = 1, \ldots, k$. The total failure probability is still negligible. Now, for any $b \in \{0,1\}^k$, the corresponding hash value $h_k(x_1^{b_1} \ldots x_k^{b_k})$ is the same. The distribution $\mathcal{D} = \{x_1^{b_1} \ldots x_k^{b_k} : b \in \{0,1\}^k\}$ is polysampleable and has min-entropy k, but $H(\mathcal{D})$ has no min-entropy. A contradiction.   □

Theorem 8. *Let $\{F_k\}$ be a fixed family of computationally uniform compression functions. Then the negligible worst-case success probability for all collision finders of $\{F_k\}$ implies collision resistance w.r.t. random initial state.*

Proof. Since $\{F_k\}$ is computationally uniform for a polynomial $\ell(k)$, we know that $F_k(s, U_{\ell(k)})$ must be computationally indistinguishable from the uniform distribution on $\mathcal{S}_k$. The latter implies that the success probability of any collision finder A that works on the initial state $s = F_k(s_0, x), x \leftarrow U_{\ell(k)}$ can differ from the average case probability

$$\Pr\left[s \leftarrow \mathcal{S}_k, (x_0, x_1) \leftarrow A(s) : x_0 \neq x_1, F_k(s, x_0) = F_k(s, x_1)\right]$$

by a negligible amount. Otherwise, we convert A to an efficient distinguisher that outputs 1 if a collision was found, and 0 otherwise. Hence, if $\{F_k\}$ is not collision resistant (w.r.t. random IV), the worst-case success is not negligible for all collision finders.   □

Having an adversary that finds collisions for random IV, it is possible to construct a poly-sampleable high-entropy distribution $\mathcal{D}$ and launch the next back-dating attack:

1. Given 1^k as input, A_1 computes a list $a = [(x_1^0, x_1^1), (x_2^0, x_2^1), \ldots, (x_k^0, x_k^1)]$ of colliding pairs like in Theorem 7, computes $d = H(x_1^0 x_2^0 \ldots x_k^0)$ and outputs (d, a).
2. Given (d, a) as input, A_2 picks $b_1, \ldots, b_k \leftarrow \{0, 1\}$ and outputs $(x_1^{b_1} x_2^{b_2} \ldots x_k^{b_k}, \sqcup)$.

The adversary (A_1, A_2) has success probability 1 in terms of Definition 4, which means that the time-stamping scheme is insecure. Note however that this still does not mean one is able to back-date *meaningful documents* in practice.

7.3   MD-Hash Functions at the Server Side

If the server side hash function $h: \{0, 1\}^{2k} \rightarrow \{0, 1\}^k$ is implemented by using a practical MD hash function, then it is sufficient to apply the compression function f only once: $h(x_1, x_2) = f(IV, x_1 \| x_2 \| \mathsf{Padding})$, where IV denotes the standard initial value. In the proof of Theorem 7 we needed multiple applications of f to construct the high-entropy distribution $\mathcal{D}$ that was mapped to a single output value. Hence, Theorem 7 does not have practical implications for server-side hash functions.

To break h as a server-side hash function (i.e. to back-date "new" hash values), we should be able to find collisions for f, if one of the arguments x_1 or x_2 is randomly fixed, i.e. an attacker A is successful if for randomly chosen $x_1 \leftarrow \{0, 1\}^k$ it is able to find a pair $x_2 \neq x_2'$ such that $f(IV, x_1 \| x_2 \| \mathsf{Padding}) = f(IV, x_1 \| x_2' \| \mathsf{Padding})$.

To our knowledge, no such attacks have been presented to MD5 or even to MD4, which means that there are no rational reasons not to use MD5 as the server-side hash function in a time-stamping scheme.

7.4   Separation of Collision Resistance and Computational Uniformity

The proof above may raise the following concern. We assumed that the hash function is broken in terms of collisions but still the compression function is computationally uniform. Hence, if collision-resistance is implied by computational uniformity, then the proof above does not make any sense. We will show that this is not the case.

Theorem 9. *There exist Merkle-Damgård hash functions that are not collision-resistant w.r.t. random initial state but have computationally uniform compression functions.*

Proof. Let $\mathcal{M}_k = \{0, 1\}^{p(k)}$ and $\mathcal{S}_k = \{0, 1\}^k$, where $p(k) > k$. Define the compression function $f_k: \mathcal{S}_k \times \mathcal{M}_k \rightarrow \mathcal{S}_k$, so that $f_k(s, x) = x_{\{1, \ldots, k\}}$, i.e. $f_k(s, x)$, independent of s, returns the first k bits of x. Obviously, the corresponding MD-hash function h_k and its internal state F_k are not collision-resistant w.r.t. random initial state, but the compression function is regular, which implies computational uniformity.   □

Just for interest, we will also prove a dual separation result, which shows that computational uniformity does not follow from collision-resistance (w.r.t. random initial state) and hence it is not an ultimate design criterion for collision-free hash functions.

Theorem 10. *If there exist collision-resistant Merkle-Damgård (MD) hash functions, then there exist collision-resistant MD-hash functions in which the compression function is not computationally uniform.*

Proof. Let $f_k \colon \{0,1\}^k \times \{0,1\}^{p(k)} \to \{0,1\}^k$ be a compression function, so that the corresponding MD hash function h_k is collision-resistant w.r.t. random initial state. Define a new compression function $f'_k \colon \{0,1\}^{k+1} \times \{0,1\}^{p(k)} \to \{0,1\}^{k+1}$, so that $f'_k(b\|s, x) = 1\|f_k(s, x)$. The new compression function is collision-resistant, because every collision for h' w.r.t. initial state $b\|s$ implies a collision for h w.r.t. initial state s. However, h' is not computationally uniform, because the first output bit of F'_k is 1 with probability 1, whereas in the case of uniform distributions this probability is $\frac{1}{2}$.   □

8   Conclusions and Open Questions

Collision-resistance is unnecessary if the hash-functions in time-stamping schemes are viewed as black-box functions, i.e. without considering particular design elements it is impossible to prove that collision-resistance is necessary for secure time-stamping. This also means that not every collision-finding attack is dangerous for time-stamping.

Still, we proved that for an important and wide class of practical hash functions (MD hash functions) certain multi-collision attacks also violate uPre, which we proved is a necessary and sufficient condition for client-side hash functions in time-stamping schemes (both the hash-based and for the signature based ones). We proved that uPre implies *collision resistance w.r.t. random initial state* whenever the state function is *computationally uniform*, which is a natural (though, not ultimate) design criterion for practical MD hash-functions. Heuristic arguments show that if the standard IV of a practical hash function turns out to be weak, then probably also a randomly chosen IV is weak. Still, in order to draw conclusions on the (in)security of time-stamping it is important to check whether the collision-finding attacks work in the case of random IV.

We also proved that in hash-based time-stamping, the server side hash functions may even be not one-way. Twice-compressing hash functions $h \colon \{0,1\}^{2k} \to \{0,1\}^k$ in the server side can be implemented with practical MD hash functions (like MD4, MD5, SHA-1, etc.) by calling the compression function f only once. Although we proved that the chain-resistance condition implies uPre, we cannot apply Theorem 7 because to construct a high-entropy input distribution $\mathcal{D}$ (with no output entropy) in the proof, we used multiple calls to f. So, it needs further research, whether there are efficient attacks that are able to find preimages for the *compression functions* of practical hash functions (MD4, MD5, SHA-1, etc.) in case a considerable number of input bits are (randomly) fixed. Only such attacks would be dangerous for *server-side* hash functions.

Considering very black scenarios it would be interesting to study whether secure time-stamping is possible in case *no hash function is collision-free*, i.e. if all the known practical hash functions have collisions or if one proves that the collision-resistance is not achievable. Recent results suggest that the former situation could be very likely. We conjecture that even in such a situation, secure time-stamping is still possible. Analogous to the result by Simon [14], this can probably be proven via oracle separation by constructing an oracle that provides access to a universal collision-finder but relative to which secure time-stamping schemes still exist.

References

1. Ross Anderson. The classification of hash functions. In *Proc. of the Fourth IMA Conference on Cryptography and Coding*, pp. 83–93, 1993.
2. Dave Bayer, Stuart Haber, and W.-Scott Stornetta. Improving the efficiency and reliability of digital time-stamping. In *Sequences II: Methods in Communication, Security, and Computer Science*, pp.329-334, Springer-Verlag, New York 1993.
3. Mihir Bellare and Tadayoshi Kohno. Hash Function Balance and Its Impact on Birthday Attacks. In *Advances in Cryptology – EUROCRYPT 2004, LNCS 3027*, pp. 401–418. 2004.
4. Ahto Buldas and Märt Saarepera. On Provably Secure Time-Stamping Schemes. In *Advances in Cryptology – Asiacrypt 2004, LNCS 3329*, pp. 500–514. 2004.
5. Ahto Buldas, Peeter Laud, Märt Saarepera, and Jan Willemson. Universally Composable Time-Stamping Schemes with Audit. In *Information Security Conference – ISC 2005*, LNCS 3650, pp.359–373. 2005. (IACR ePrint Archive 2005/198, 2005).
6. Stuart Haber and W.-Scott Stornetta. Secure Names for Bit-Strings. In *ACM Conference on Computer and Communications Security*, pp. 28–35, 1997.
7. Chun-Yuan Hsiao and Leonid Reyzin. Finding Collisions on a Public Road, or Do Secure Hash Functions Need Secret Coins? In *Advances in Cryptology – Crypto 2004, LNCS 3152*, pp. 92–105. 2004.
8. Antoine Joux. Multicollisions in Iterated Hash Functions. Application to Cascaded Constructions. In *Advances in Cryptology – CRYPTO 2004, LNCS 3152*, pp. 306–316, 2004.
9. Vlastimil Klima. Finding MD5 Collisions – a Toy For a Notebook. *Cryptology ePrint Archive*, Report 2005/075.
10. Vlastimil Klima. Finding MD5 Collisions on a Notebook PC Using Multi-message Modifications. *Cryptology ePrint Archive*, Report 2005/102.
11. RFC 3161: Internet X.509 Public Key Infrastructure Time-Stamp Protocol (TSP).
12. Vincent Rijmen and Elisabeth Oswald. Update on SHA-1. In *Topics in Cryptology - CT-RSA 2005, LNCS 3376*, pp. 58–71. 2005.
13. Phillip Rogaway and Thomas Shrimpton. Cryptographic Hash-Function Basics: Definitions, Implications, and Separations for Preimage Resistance, Second-Preimage Resistance, and Collision Resistance. In *Fast Software Encryption – FSE 2004*. 2004.
14. Daniel Simon. Finding Collisions on a One-Way Street: Can Secure Hash Functions Be Based on General Assumptions? In *Advances in Cryptology – Eurocrypt 1998, LNCS 1403*, pp. 334–345. 1998.
15. Homepage of Surety: www.surety.com
16. Xiaoyun Wang, Xuejia Lai, Dengguo Feng, Hui Chen, and Xiuyuan Yu. Cryptanalysis of the Hash Functions MD4 and RIPEMD. In *Advances in Cryptology – Eurocrypt 2005, LNCS 3494*, pp. 1–18, 2005.
17. Xiaoyun Wang and Hongbo Yu. How to Break MD5 and Other Hash Functions. In *Advances in Cryptology – Eurocrypt 2005, LNCS 3494*, pp. 19–35, 2005.
18. Xiaoyun Wang, Yiqun Lisa Yin, Hongbo Yu. Finding Collisions in the Full SHA-1. *Advances in Cryptology – CRYPTO 2005, LNCS 3621*, pp. 17-36, 2005.
19. Xiaoyun Wang, Hongbo Yu, Yiqun Lisa Yin. Efficient Collision Search Attacks on SHA-0. In *Advances in Cryptology – CRYPTO 2005, LNCS 3621*, pp.1-16, 2005.

A Handy Multi-coupon System

Sébastien Canard, Aline Gouget, and Emeline Hufschmitt

France Telecom Research and Development,
42 rue des Coutures, BP 6243, F-14066 Caen cedex
{sebastien.canard, aline.gouget, emeline.hufschmitt}@francetelecom.com

Abstract. A coupon is an electronic data that represents the right to access a service provided by a service provider (e.g. gift certificates or movie tickets). At *Financial Crypto'05*, a privacy-protecting multi-coupon system that allows a user to withdraw a predefined number of single coupons from the service provider has been proposed by Chen *et al*. In this system, every coupon has the same value which is predetermined by the system. The main drawbacks of Chen *et al*. proposal are that the redemption protocol of their system is inefficient, and that no formal security model is proposed. In this paper, we consequently propose a formal security model for coupon systems and design a practical multi-coupon system with new features: the quantity of single coupons in a multi-coupon is not defined by the system and the value of each coupon is chosen in a predefined set of values.

Keywords: Electronic coupons, security model, proof of knowledge.

1 Introduction

The issues of *electronic money* [8, 11, 6, 15, 13] and *electronic coupons* [16] are closely related since both are electronic data for payment. The former involves a *Bank* $\mathcal{B}$, a *User* $\mathcal{U}$ and a *Merchant* $\mathcal{M}$; $\mathcal{B}$ delivers electronic coins to $\mathcal{U}$, $\mathcal{U}$ spends them to get goods or services delivered by $\mathcal{M}$, $\mathcal{M}$ deposits the coins at the bank $\mathcal{B}$ and in exchange $\mathcal{B}$ credits the banking account of $\mathcal{M}$. The latter involves a *Service Provider* $\mathcal{SP}$ playing both the roles of $\mathcal{B}$ and $\mathcal{M}$, and a *User* $\mathcal{U}$ that withdraws electronic coupons from the $\mathcal{SP}$ and later redeems these coupons to get an access to specific services offered by the $\mathcal{SP}$.

Similarly, the usually required security properties of electronic coin systems and those of electronic coupons systems are closely related. For instance, the privacy of the users must be protected, i.e. , it must be impossible to link a withdrawal protocol with a user identity as well as to link two spending/redemption protocols, and it must be impossible to link a spending/redemption protocol to a withdrawal protocol (except for the owner of the coin/coupon).

As it is easy to duplicate electronic data, an electronic payment system requires a mechanism that prevents a user from spending the same coin/coupon twice. The problem of detecting the double-redemption of a coupon is at most as difficult as the problem of detecting the double-spending of a coin. Indeed,

J. Zhou, M. Yung, and F. Bao (Eds.): ACNS 2006, LNCS 3989, pp. 66–81, 2006.

in a coupon system, every coupon is redeemed to the service provider that has previously delivered it; the service provider can then easily check the redeemed coupons database in order to detect a double-redemption. In an electronic coin system, the merchant cannot detect a double-spending during a payment protocol since the coins delivered by the bank can be spent at several merchants. Then, the detection of a double-spending is done by the bank.

For a practical use, it is important to consider the efficiency of each protocol of the electronic coin/coupon scheme. For instance, the withdrawal of m coins/coupons should be more efficient than m executions of the withdrawal protocol of one coin/coupon; an efficient solution has been recently proposed [8]. In the same way, the spending/redemption of m coins/coupons should be more efficient than m executions of the spending/redemption protocol; this is still an open problem. Another practical property that should be considered is the size of the electronic wallet/multi-coupon.

In real life, coupons are widely used by vendors. For instance gift certificates are useful means to draw the attention of potential customers. Due to the diversification of the activities of more and more shops, it becomes common that a vendor gives to customers a money-off coupon book with coupons of different values or dedicated to different parts of the goods shop. Then, an electronic coupon system must not only be secure and efficient, but it should also offer such features of real life multi-coupon systems.

1.1 Related Works

The coupon system proposed by Chen *et al.* [16] allows to create multi-coupons where a multi-coupon is a set of m coupons (m is a predetermined value of the system) and every coupon has the same value V. This system does not require the existence of a trusted third party. The usual security properties required in the context of electronic payment are fulfilled by this coupon scheme, i.e. the unforgeability (of a multi-coupon or of a coupon), the unlinkability (of a withdrawal protocol with a redemption protocol, or between several redemption protocols), and the detection of the double-redemption of a coupon. In [16], a multi-coupon is composed of *non-detachable* coupons (i.e. if a user wants to transfer coupons to another user, she must give all her coupons or nothing). This property can be suitable when coupons are used as drug prescriptions from a doctor. However, this property seems to be inconvenient in many other applications such as movie tickets or reduction tickets, for which a user must be allowed to detach a single coupon from her multi-coupon. The redemption protocol proposed in [16] is not efficient. Indeed, it is based on a proof of OR statement that is proportional to the number of withdrawn coupons and consequently unpractical.

Camenisch *et al.* [8] have recently proposed an efficient *compact e-cash* system[1] that allows a user to withdraw a wallet with 2^ℓ coins such that the space required to store these coins, and the complexity of the withdrawal protocol

---

[1] In [8], an extension of this system provides traceable coins without any trusted third party but this property is not relevant in our context.

are proportional to ℓ rather than to 2^ℓ. This scheme fulfills the anonymity and unlinkability properties usually required for electronic cash schemes. The compact e-cash scheme combines Camenisch-Lysyanskaya's signature [7], Dodis-Yampolskiy's verifiable random function (VRF) [18] and an innovative system of serial numbers and security tags. As for the coupon system of Chen *et al.*, the number of coins withdrawn during a withdrawal protocol and the coin values are predetermined by the system. The main drawback of the compact e-cash system is that it does not address the problem of *divisibility*: the property that payments of any amount up to the monetary amount of a withdrawn coin can be made. This functionality is considered by the *divisible* e-cash systems.

In [22, 21], the authors proposed *unlikable divisible* e-cash systems, i.e. schemes allowing a user to withdraw a single coin and next to spend this coin in several times by dividing the value of the coin. The usual properties of anonymity and unlinkability are fulfilled by these unlinkable divisible e-cash schemes. Contrary to the schemes mentioned above, the unlinkable divisible e-cash scheme requires a trusted third party. The scheme of Nakanishi and Sugiyama is less efficient than the compact e-cash scheme since it uses double decker proofs of knowledge that are expensive.

Note that all schemes mentioned above suffer from the fact that it is not possible to choose the number of coins/coupons and to choose the value of each coin/coupon.

1.2 Our Contribution

We first propose a security model suitable for electronic multi-coupon systems that includes the usual security properties, i.e. the unforgeability and the un-linkability but also the propery for a user to split her multi-coupon. In the coupon system of Chen *et al.*, a user can give either her whole multi-coupon or nothing. The protection against splitting of a multi-coupon can be suitable when coupons are used such as drug prescriptions from a doctor. However, this protection seems to be unsuitable in many other real life applications such as movie tickets or reduction tickets, for which a user must be allowed to detach a coupon from her multi-coupon and transfer it to another user. Then, we propose a model suitable for electronic multi-coupon systems that allows the transfer of coupons.

We then propose a new multi-coupon scheme that is more efficient than the proposal of Chen *et al.* [16] and in addition offers new features. For instance, the quantity of coupons of a multi-coupon can be chosen during a withdrawal protocol. In our scheme, the data of a set of coupons are treated as a clear text in the withdrawal protocol, but kept secret in the redemption protocol whereas in [16] scheme, they were kept secret in the withdrawal protocol, but opened in the redemption protocol. This change offers the interesting property that a set of coupons can easily include a number of different values where the set of possible values is predetermined by the system. The owner of a multi-coupon can redeem each coupon of her multi-coupon to the appropriate service provider. Furthermore, the owner of a multi-coupon can give a part of her multi-coupon to another user, which means that a first user can transfer a set of coupons to a second user and then the first user looses the possibility to redeem the coupons she gave and the second user can redeem only the coupons she received. Our redemption protocol is based on a proof of the OR statement that is only proportional to the logarithm of the maximum number of withdrawn coupons, which is far more efficient than the one of Chen et al. [16].

Very recently, some of the ideas present in this paper have been independently proposed by Nguyen [23].

1.3   Organization of the Paper

This paper is organized as follows. Section 2 describes the security model and requirements for a multi-coupon system. In Section 3, we list and describe the cryptographic tools we need. Section 4 is the main one: it contains the new multi-coupon system. Section 5 gives the security theorem of our scheme (the proof is included in the full paper) and Section 6 compares it to Nguyen's coupon system. Section 7 concludes this paper.

2   Security Model

An electronic coupon system involves a service provider and several users. The Service Provider is denoted by $\mathcal{SP}$ and a user by $\mathcal{U}$. The set of authorized values for coupons is $\mathcal{V} = \{V_1, \ldots, V_n\}$. A coupon C is formed by an identifier I_C and a value $V_i \in \mathcal{V}$. A multi-coupon is formed by a multi-coupon identifier I and the set $\mathcal{S} = \{(J_i, V_i); i \in [1, n]\}$ where J_i is the number of coupons of value V_i. We set $\mathcal{J}_i = \{0, \ldots, J_i - 1\}$.

2.1   Algorithms

- **ParamKeyGen**: a probabilistic algorithm taking as input the security parameter k. This algorithm outputs some secret parameters $sParams$ and some public parameters $pParams$ including the authorized values of the coupons $\mathcal{V} = \{V_1, \ldots, V_n\}$.
- **SPKeyGen**: a probabilistic algorithm executed by $\mathcal{SP}$ taking as inputs the security parameter k and the parameters of the system $sParams$ and $pParams$. This algorithm outputs the key pair $(sk_{\mathcal{SP}}, pk_{\mathcal{SP}})$ of $\mathcal{SP}$.
- **Withdraw**: an interactive protocol between the service provider $\mathcal{SP}$ taking as inputs $(sk_{\mathcal{SP}}, pk_{\mathcal{SP}})$ and $pParams$, and a user $\mathcal{U}$ taking as inputs $pk_{\mathcal{SP}}$ and $pParams$. For every $i \in [1, n]$, the user chooses the number J_i of coupons of value V_i she wants to withdraw. At the end of the protocol, the user's output is the multi-coupon, i.e. an identifier I and the set $\mathcal{S} = \{(J_i, V_i); i \in [1, n]\}$, or an error message. The Service Provider's output is its view $V_{\mathcal{SP}}^{\mathtt{Withdraw}}$ of the protocol.
- **Redeem**: an interactive protocol between a user $\mathcal{U}$, taking as inputs a multi-coupon, i.e. an identifier I and the set $\mathcal{S} = \{(J_i, V_i); i \in [1, n]\}$, the public

key pk_{SP} and $pParams$, and the service provider SP, taking as inputs the public key pk_{SP} and $pParams$. The user U chooses the value V_j of the coupon she wants to redeem. At the end of the protocol, the Service Provider SP obtains from the User U a coupon C of value V_j with a proof of validity and outputs its view V_{SP}^{Redeem} of the protocol. U outputs an updated multi-coupon, i.e. the identifier I and the set $\{(J_i', V_i); i \in [1, n]\}$ where $J_j' = J_j - 1$ and $J_i' = J_i$, $i \in [1, n]$ and $i \neq j$, or an error message.

– **Transfer**: an interactive protocol between a user U_1, taking as inputs a multi-coupon, i.e. an identifier I and the set $S = \{(J_i, V_i); i \in [1, n]\}$, the public key pk_{SP} and $pParams$, and a second user U_2 taking as inputs pk_{SP} and $pParams$. For every $i \in [1; n]$, the user U_1 chooses the number J_i', $J_i' \leq J_i$, of coupons of value V_i she wants to transfer to U_2. At the end of the protocol, the user U_2 outputs a new multi-coupon, i.e. an identifier I' and the set $\{(J_i', V_i); i \in [1, n]\}$, and the user U_1 outputs an updated multi-coupon, i.e. the identifier I and the set $\{(J_i - J_i', V_i); i \in [1, n]\}$, or an error message.

2.2   A Formal Model

In this section, we propose a formal model for secure multi-coupon systems. A valid coupon is a coupon obtained from a valid `Withdraw` or `Transfer` protocol and notpreviously redeemed.

– **Correctness:** if an honest user U runs `Withdraw` with an honest Service Provider SP, then neither will output an error message; if an honest user U runs `Redeem` with an honest service provider SP, then SP accepts the coupon if it is valid; if an honest user U_1 runs `Transfer` with an honest user U_2, then U_2 gets a valid coupon (possibly by assuming that SP is honest).

– **Unforgeability:** from the Service Provider's point of view, what matters is that no coalition of users can ever spend more coupons than they withdrew. Let an adversary A be a p.p.t. Turing Machine. At the begining of the game, A is given the public key pk_{SP} and the public parameters $pParams$ of the system. Furthermore, at any time during the game:

  1. A can execute in a concurrent manner `Withdraw` protocols with honest service providers,
  2. A can execute `Redeem` protocols with honest service providers,
  3. A can execute `Transfer` protocols with honest users playing the role of U_1 or U_2.

At some point of the game, the adversary A can legitimately extract, from these protocols, a list L of valid coupons C with identifiers I's. At the end of the game, A outputs a coupon $C \notin L$ and a `Redeem` protocol (or a `Transfer` protocol) is played by A with an honest service provider SP (resp. an honest user U).

We require that for every adversary playing the previous game, the probability that the honest Service Provider SP (resp. the honest user U) accepts the `Redeem` protocol (resp. the `Transfer` protocol) is negligible.

- **Unlinkability:** from the privacy point of view, what matters to users is that the service provider, even cooperating with any collection of malicious users, cannot learn anything about the user's spendings other than what is available from side information from the environment. Let an adversary $\mathcal{A}$ be a p.p.t. Turing Machine. At the begining of the game, $\mathcal{A}$ is given the key pair $(pk_{\mathcal{SP}}, sk_{\mathcal{SP}})$ of the Service Provider $\mathcal{SP}$ and the public parameters *pParams* of the system. Furthermore, at any time during the game:

  1. $\mathcal{A}$ can execute in a concurrent manner `Withdraw` protocols with honest users,
  2. $\mathcal{A}$ can execute `Redeem` protocols with honest users,
  3. $\mathcal{A}$ can execute `Transfer` protocols with honest users playing the role of $\mathcal{U}_1$ or $\mathcal{U}_2$.

  At some point of the game, the adversary $\mathcal{A}$ outputs two views $\mathcal{V}_{\mathcal{A}}^{\text{Withdraw}_1}$ and $\mathcal{V}_{\mathcal{A}}^{\text{Withdraw}_2}$ of previously executed `Withdraw` protocols. Then, for the two challenged withdrawn multi-coupon, the adversary outputs a value V_i and the rank $j \in \mathcal{J}_i$ of a coupon that has not been already redeemed. We require that these two coupons must not be redeemed by the adversary. A further step of the game consists in choosing secretly and randomly a bit b. Then, a `Redeem` protocol (or a `Transfer` protocol) is played by $\mathcal{A}$ with the owner of the multi-coupon outputted from Withdraw_b. Finally, $\mathcal{A}$ outputs a bit b'.

  We require that for every adversary playing the previous game, the success probability that $b = b'$ differs from $1/2$ by a fraction that is at most negligible.

2.3   Comparison Between our Security Model and Chen *et al.*'s

Let us now show that our formulation is strong enough to capture all informal security requirements introduced in [16].

Unforgeability. Chen *et al.* defined the unforgeability as the infeasibility to create new multi-coupons, to increase the number of unspent coupons, or to reset the number of spent coupons. In addition, Chen *et al.* defined a property called *redemption limitation* that consists in limiting the number of times by at most m that a service provider accepts an m-redeemable coupon M. The property of *redemption limitation* means that the user is not able to increase the quantity of coupons contained in her multi-coupon, that is, the user is not able to create a new coupon in her multi-coupon. In our security model, the property of *unforgeability* includes the property of *redemption limitation*.

Double-redemption detection. The property of *double-redemption detection* is defined in the security model of Chen *et al.* However, in the context of coupon systems, this property is useless. Indeed, before accepting a coupon, a service provider checks that the coupon is fresh, i.e. the coupon has not been redeemed before. Then, a double-redemption is impossible. We consequently include the impossibility to use twice the same coupon in the correctness of the system.

Unlinkability and minimum disclosure. The property of unlinkability is similar of those given in [16]. Here, the unlinkability must be ensured between a withdrawal protocol and a redemption protocol, between a withdrawal protocol and a transfer protocol, between a redemption protocol and a transfer protocol, between two redemption protocols and between two transfer protocols.

The property of minimum disclosure defined by Chen *et al.* is that the number of unspent coupons cannot be inferred from any redemption protocol run. Chen *et al.* separate the property of minimum disclosure from the property of unlinkability. However, since the minimum disclosure property is included in the unlinkability property, we do not keep the separation of the two properties.

Coupon transfer property / protection against splitting. The main difference between the issues of our coupon system and Chen *et al.*'s is the property of transferability or untransferability.

It is trivially not possible to prevent a user to give all her multi-coupon to another user. Beyond that, a first possibility, which was chosen by Chen *et al.*, consists in preventing a user to give a part of her multi-coupon to another user without giving her whole multi-coupon, i.e. protect a multi-coupon system against splitting. The protection against splitting is defined in [16] as follows: a coalition of customers $\mathcal{U}_i$ should not be able to split an m-redeemable multi-coupon M into (disjoint) s_i-redeemable shares M_i with $\sum_i s_i \leq m$ such that M_i can only be redeemed by customer $\mathcal{U}_i$ and none of the other customers $\mathcal{U}_j$, $j \neq i$, or a subset of them is able to redeem M_i or a part of it.

Chen *et al.* defined a *weak protection against splitting* property, assuming that users trust each other not to spend (part of) the multi-coupon they have not. With this assumption, user $\mathcal{U}_1$ (resp. is $\mathcal{U}_2$) is sure that user $\mathcal{U}_2$ (resp. $\mathcal{U}_1$) will not use one of the coupon of the multi-coupon $\mathcal{C}'$ (resp. $\hat{\mathcal{C}}$).

A second possibility, that we adopt in this paper, is to permit the splitting of a multi-coupon by adding a new algorithm called `Transfer` as defined above. A user $\mathcal{U}_1$ with the coupons $\mathcal{C} = \{C_0, \ldots, C_{m-1}\}$ can transfer to a user $\mathcal{U}_2$ part of $\mathcal{C}$. At the end of the protocol, $\mathcal{U}_1$ obtains the coupons $\mathcal{C}'$ and $\mathcal{U}_2$ obtains the coupons $\hat{\mathcal{C}}$ such that $\hat{\mathcal{C}} \cup \mathcal{C}' = \mathcal{C}$ and $\hat{\mathcal{C}} \cap \mathcal{C}' = \emptyset$.

In this paper, we consequently add an optional secure `Transfer` algorithm that implies an honest service provider during the `Transfer` algorithm which is responsible for the creation of two new multi-coupons $\mathcal{C}'$ and $\hat{\mathcal{C}}$ from $\mathcal{C}$.

3   Useful Tools

In this section, we first introduce the notation and the complexity assumptions that we will use all along the paper. We next present some cryptographic tools: proofs of knowledge, a type of signature schemes introduced by Camenisch and Lysyanskaya and the Dodis-Yampolskiy pseudorandom function.

3.1   Notation

Throughout the paper, the symbol $\|$ will denote the concatenation of two strings. The notation "$x \in_R E$" means that x is chosen uniformly at random from the set E. For an integer p, $\mathbb{Z}_p$ denotes the residue class ring modulo p and $\mathbb{Z}_p^*$ the multiplicative group of invertible elements in $\mathbb{Z}_p$. $\mathcal{G}$ denotes a cyclic group. $PK(\alpha/f(\alpha,\dots))$ will denote a proof of knowledge of a value α that verifies the predicate f. $PedCom(x_1,\dots,x_l)$ is the Pedersen commitment [24] on values $x_1,\dots,x_l$. Other notations and definitions will be set as needed.

3.2   Complexity Assumptions

Flexible RSA assumption [19]: given an RSA modulus n of special form pq, where $p = 2p' + 1$ and $q = 2q' + 1$ are safe primes, and a random element $g \in \mathbb{Z}_n^*$, it is hard to output $h \in \mathbb{Z}_n^*$ and an integer $e > 1$ such that $h^e = g \mod n$.

y-Strong Diffie-Hellman assumption [4]: given a random generator $g \in \mathcal{G}$ where $\mathcal{G}$ has prime order p, and the values $(g, g^x, \dots, g^{x^y})$, it is hard to compute a pair (c, s) such that $s^{x+c} = g$.

y-Decisional Diffie-Hellman Inversion assumption [3]: given a random generator $g \in \mathcal{G}$ where $\mathcal{G}$ has prime order p and the values $(g, g^x, \dots, g^{x^y})$ for a random $x \in \mathbb{Z}_p$, and a value $R \in \mathcal{G}$, it is hard to decide if $R = g^{1/x}$ or not.

3.3   Proofs of Knowledge

The zero-knowledge proofs of knowledge that we use are constructed over a cyclic group $\mathcal{G} = <g>$ either of prime order q or of unknown order[2] (but where the bit-length of the order is $l_\mathcal{G}$). The base of each building block is either the Schnorr authentication scheme [27] or the GPS authentication scheme [20, 25]. These are interactive proofs of knowledge where the prover sends a commitment and then responds to a challenge from the verifier. In our scheme, we need the proof of knowledge of a representation, the proof of equality of two known representations [14, 10], the proof of the OR statement [17, 26], the proof that a committed value lies in an interval [5, 10, 12, 2] and the proof that a committed value is less than another committed value. We only detailled the proof that a committed value is less than another committed value since it is, to the best of our knowledge, a new building block.

Proof that a committed value is less than another committed value. A proof that a committed value is less than another committed value consists in proving that $0 \leq x < y$ where x and y are committed with $C = g^x h^r$ and $D = g^y h^w$, where g and h are generators of the group $\mathcal{G}$. This interactive proof is denoted by

$$PK(\alpha, \beta, \gamma, \delta / C = g^\alpha h^\beta \wedge D = g^\gamma h^\delta \wedge 0 \leq \alpha < \gamma).$$

In our case, x and y are l-bit integers with l relatively small (see below), that is $x = x_0 + x_1 2 + \dots + x_{l-1} 2^{l-1}$ and $y = y_0 + y_1 2 + \dots + y_{l-1} 2^{l-1}$. The proof can consequently be done using the fact that $y - x - 1 \geq 0$.

---

[2] Under the Flexible RSA Assumption, standard proofs of knowledge protocols working for a group of known order are also proofs of knowledge in this setting [19].

1. The prover randomly chooses $r, r_0, \ldots, r_{l-1}, w, w_0, \ldots, w_{l-1} \in_R \mathbb{Z}_p$. We note $u = y - x - 1 = u_0 + u_1 2 + \ldots + u_{l-1} 2^{l-1}$. The prover then computes

$$
\begin{aligned}
C &= g^x h^r, & C_0 &= g^{x_0} h^{r_0}, \ldots, C_{l-1} = g^{x_{l-1}} h^{r_{l-1}} \\
D &= g^y h^w, & D_0 &= g^{u_0} h^{w_0}, \ldots, D_{l-1} = g^{u_{l-1}} h^{w_{l-1}} \\
\widetilde{C} &= \textstyle\prod_{i=0}^{l-1} C_i^{2^i}, & \widetilde{D} &= \textstyle\prod_{i=0}^{l-1} D_i^{2^i}, \overline{D} = D/(gC)
\end{aligned}
$$

Note that the elements $\widetilde{C}$, $\widetilde{D}$ and $\overline{D}$ can be computed by the prover and the verifier. Moreover, note that $\overline{D} = g^{y-x-1} h^{w-r} = g^u h^{w-r}$. By noting $\widetilde{C} = g^{\tilde{x}} h^{\tilde{r}}$ and $\widetilde{D} = g^{\tilde{u}} h^{\tilde{w}}$, we consequently obtain that $C\widetilde{C}^{-1} = g^{x-\tilde{x}} h^{r-\tilde{r}}$ and that $\overline{D}\widetilde{D}^{-1} = g^{u-\tilde{u}} h^{w-r-\tilde{w}}$.

2. Then, the prover and the verifier make the following interactive proof of knowledge

$$
\begin{aligned}
PK\Big(&\alpha, \beta, \gamma_0, \ldots, \gamma_{l-1}, \delta, \epsilon, \zeta, \eta_0, \ldots, \eta_{l-1}, \theta, \rho, \iota / \\
&(C_0 = h^{\gamma_0} \vee C_0/g = h^{\gamma_0}) \wedge \ldots \wedge (C_{l-1} = h^{\gamma_{l-1}} \vee C_{l-1}/g = h^{\gamma_{l-1}}) \wedge \\
&(D_0 = h^{\eta_0} \vee D_0/g = h^{\eta_0}) \wedge \ldots \wedge (D_{l-1} = h^{\eta_{l-1}} \vee D_{l-1}/g = h^{\eta_{l-1}}) \wedge \\
&C = g^{\alpha} h^{\beta} \wedge C\widetilde{C}^{-1} = h^{\delta} \wedge D = g^{\epsilon} h^{\zeta} \wedge \overline{D} = g^{\rho} h^{\iota} \wedge \overline{D}\widetilde{D}^{-1} = h^{\theta}\Big).
\end{aligned}
$$

This proof contains $\mathcal{O}(l)$ proof of OR statement. If the order of the group is public, this proof needs $2^l < p/2$ (which is not very restrictive in many cases[3]).

One may use Boudot's proof [5] but this implies necessarily the use of a group of unknown order, and consequently larger parameters (e.g. exponent of size 1024 bits instead of 160 bits in our case). Thus, even if Boudot's proof is proportional to $\mathcal{O}(1)$ w.r.t. the size of x and y, instead of $\mathcal{O}(l)$ for us, the value of l will be smaller enough in practice to make Boudot's proof less efficient.

3.4 CL Type Signature Schemes with Pedersen Commitment

The Pedersen commitment scheme [24] permits a user to commit to some values $x_1, \ldots x_l \in \mathbb{Z}_p$ without revealing them, using some public elements of a cyclic group $\mathcal{G}$ of prime order p with generators $(g_1, \ldots, g_l)$. To do that, the user computes the commitment $C = \prod_{i=1}^{l} g_i^{x_i}$. Such commitment is secure under the Discrete Logarithm assumption.

Camenisch et Lysyanskaya [9] have proposed various signature schemes based on Pedersen's scheme to which they add some specific protocols:

- an efficient protocol between a user and a signer that permits the user to obtain from the signer a signature σ of some commitment C on values $(x_1, \ldots, x_l)$ unknown from the signer. The latter computes $\texttt{CLSign}(C)$ and the user obtains $\sigma = \texttt{Sign}(x_1, \ldots, x_l)$.

---

[3] This restriction does not permit an attacker to use its knowledge of the order p of g to use the representation between 0 and p of a negative integer.

– an efficient proof of knowledge of a signature of some committed values. The proof is divided into two parts: the computation of a witness, denoted $witness(\sigma)$, and the following proof of knowledge

$$PK(\alpha_1, \ldots, \alpha_l, \beta/\beta = \texttt{Sign}(\alpha_1, \ldots, \alpha_l)).$$

These constructions are quite close to group signature schemes. This is the case of the two following examples, one based on the ACJT signature scheme [1], secure under the Flexible RSA assumption, and the other based on the BBS one [4], secure under the y-SDH assumption.

3.5   Dodis-Yampolskiy Pseudorandom Function

A cryptographically secure pseudorandom function (PRF) is an efficient algorithm that when given a seed and an argument returns a new string that is undistinguishable from a truly random function. Such function takes as input some public parameters, a seed s and a value x and outputs a pseudorandom value (plus a proof of validity). In our paper, we will use the Dodis-Yampolskiy pseudorandom function [18] which is secure under the y-DDHI assumption.

The construction of Dodis and Yampolskiy works as follows. Let $\mathcal{G}$ be a group of order p, g a generator of $\mathcal{G}$ and s a seed in $\mathbb{Z}_p$. The Dodis-Yampolskiy pseudorandom function f takes as input $x \in \mathbb{Z}_p$ and outputs $f_{g,s}(x) = g^{\frac{1}{s+x+1}}$.

4   Description of the *handy* Multi-coupon System

In this section, we present our new construction of a multi-coupon system based on the compact e-cash scheme of Camenisch *et al.* [8]. We first give the general principle of our improvement and then describe all algorithms.

4.1   General Principle

A user $\mathcal{U}$ can withdraw a number of coupons of her choice. Futhermore, a user can also choose the value of each coupon from a set of values $\mathcal{V} = \{V_1, \ldots, V_n\}$ predetermined by the service provider. For each possible value V_i, the user decides, with the service provider, the number J_i of coupons of value V_i that she withdraws. In our construction, due to the used proof of knowledge, the possible number of coupons she can withdrawn must be less than a fixed value 2^l. This is not really restrictive in practice. The numbers $J_1, \ldots, J_n$ are chosen by the user[4], known and signed by the service provider during the withdrawal protocol, but unrevealed during the redemption protocol. Each value V_i is linked to a random value $\tilde{g}_i$ in $\mathcal{G}$ that is used to trace a designated coupon. During a redemption protocol of a coupon of value V_i, a user chooses a *fresh* integer in the set $\mathcal{J}_i = \{0, \ldots, J_i - 1\}$ in such a way that for each redemption protocol of a coupon of value V_i, the user must choose an integer distinct from the

---

[4] The values $J_1, \ldots, J_n$ can also be chosen by the service provider if required by the application.

ones revealed during previous redemption protocols of coupons of the same value V_i. Consequently, we can associate the monetary value of the coupon, the set $\mathcal{J}_i = \{0, \ldots, J_i - 1\}$ and the generator $\tilde{g}_i$ in $\mathcal{G}$.

Remark 1. Another solution (not addressed in this paper) is to choose the value j in the set $\mathcal{J} = \{0, \ldots, J_m - 1\}$ in such a way that $\mathcal{J}_1 = \{0, \ldots, J_1 - 1\}$ corresponds to the value V_1, $\mathcal{J}_2 = \{J_1, \ldots, J_2 - 1\}$ corresponds to the value V_2, etc. and $\mathcal{J}_n = \{J_{n-1}, \ldots, J_n - 1\}$ corresponds to the value V_n. All values $J_1, \ldots, J_n$ are chosen by the user, known and signed by the bank but unrevealed during the redemption protocol. This solution is nevertheless less efficient.

4.2   Setup

Let k be a security parameter. We consider a group $\mathcal{G}$ of order p. $\tilde{g}_1, \ldots, \tilde{g}_n, g,$ $h, h_0, \ldots, h_{n+1}$ are randomly chosen in $\mathcal{G}$. All these data compose the public parameters $pParams$ of the system. The service provider $\mathcal{SP}$ computes the key pair $(sk_{\mathcal{SP}}, pk_{\mathcal{SP}})$ of a Camenisch-Lysyanskaya signature scheme that will permit it to sign multi-coupons, using the CLSign algorithm (see Section 3.4 for details). The number 2^l of coupons a user can withdraw for each value V_i must be less than $p/2$, due to the use of the proof that a committed value is less than another committed value described in Section 3.3.

4.3   Withdrawal Protocol

During a withdrawal protocol (Figure 1), a user $\mathcal{U}$ takes as inputs $pParams$ and $pk_{\mathcal{SP}}$ and interacts with a service provider $\mathcal{SP}$, that takes as inputs $pParams$ and $(sk_{\mathcal{SP}}, pk_{\mathcal{SP}})$, as follows.

1. $\mathcal{U}$ and $\mathcal{SP}$ both participate to the randomness of the secret s. First, $\mathcal{U}$ selects a random value $s' \in \mathbb{Z}_p$, sends to $\mathcal{SP}$ a commitment $C' = PedCom(s', r)$ and the numbers $J_1, \ldots, J_n$ corresponding to the number of coupons of values $V_1, \ldots, V_n$ she wants to withdraw. $\mathcal{SP}$ sends a random $r' \in \mathbb{Z}_p$ and $\mathcal{U}$ can compute the secret s as $s = s' + r'$.
2. $\mathcal{U}$ and $\mathcal{SP}$ run the CL protocol's for obtaining $\mathcal{SP}$'s signature on committed values contained in the commitment $C = PedCom(s, J_1, \ldots, J_n, r)$. As a result, $\mathcal{U}$ obtains $\sigma = \text{Sign}(s, J_1, \ldots, J_n, r)$.
3. $\mathcal{U}$ saves the multi-coupon, i.e. the identifier $I = (s, r, \sigma)$ and the set $\mathcal{S} = \{(J_i, V_i); i \in [1, n]\}$.

4.4   Redemption Protocol

When a user wants to redeem a coupon from her multi-coupon $(I, \mathcal{S})$, she first has to choose the value V_i of the coupon she wants to redeem. Then, the user chooses the rank j of the coupon she wants to redeem in the set of all possible coupons of value V_i, that is between 0 and $J_i - 1$.

As explained in Figure 2, a redemption protocol consists in the following.

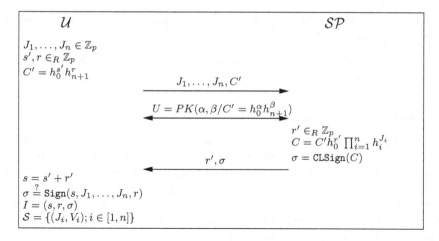

Fig. 1. Withdrawal protocol

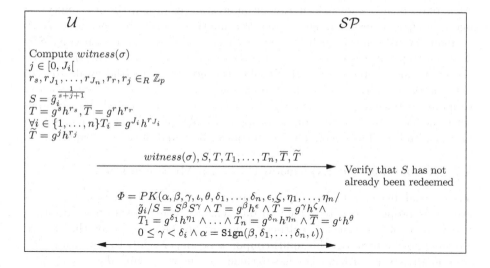

Fig. 2. Redemption protocol

1. Computing the coupon's identifier as the Dodis-Yampolskiy pseudorandom function with seed s and generator $\tilde{g}_i$ associated to the monetary value V_i, on the input j: $S = \tilde{g}_i^{\frac{1}{s+j+1}}$.
2. A proof of validity of this coupon, that is an interactive proof of knowledge[5] of a $\mathcal{SP}$ signature on the secrets $(s, J_1, \ldots, J_n, r)$, plus a proof that the selected coupon belongs to the set $\mathcal{J}_i = \{0, \ldots, J_i - 1\}$.

---

[5] This proof consequently does not necessitate the Fiat Shamir heuristic and a hash function. Thus, our construction is on the standard model.

Note that the proof of knowledge Φ (see Figure 2) includes a challenge c sent by the service provider $\mathcal{SP}$.

Remark 2. $S = \tilde{g}_i^{\frac{1}{s+j+1}}$ can also be written $\tilde{g}_i/S = S^s S^j$, which explains the proof of knowledge.

4.5   Multi-redemption Protocol

The multi-redemption protocol consists in redeeming several coupons of a multi-coupon in a single interactive protocol with $\mathcal{SP}$. The global protocol is more efficient than simply executing the redemption protocol in Figure 2 for each redeemed coupon. In fact, the proof of knowledge of the $\mathcal{SP}$ signature $\sigma = \mathtt{Sign}(s, J_1, \ldots, J_n, r)$ only needs to be done once whereas the computation involving the rank of each redeemed coupon needs to be done for each coupon. This protocol can be found in the full paper.

4.6   Transfer Protocol

As explained in Section 2.3, it can be interesting to design the possibility for one user $\mathcal{U}_1$ to transfer some coupons of a multi-coupon to another user $\mathcal{U}_2$. A straightforward solution includes the participation of the Service Provider $\mathcal{SP}$. The first step consists for $\mathcal{U}_1$ in choosing the coupons she wants to transfer and to redeem them by interacting with $\mathcal{SP}$. The second step is a withdrawal protocol between the user $\mathcal{U}_2$ and $\mathcal{SP}$ with the number and the right values of transfered coupons. At the end of this global protocol, $\mathcal{U}_1$ obtains an updated multi-coupon since she has withdraw some of her coupons. $\mathcal{U}_2$ obtains a new multi-coupon, as after a withdrawal protocol. This protocol can be found in the full paper.

4.7   Revocation and Expiration Date of a Multi-coupon

The revocability of a multi-coupon is not a property considered in [16]. However, this property can be added to our scheme. The revocation means that the coupons of a designated multi-coupon must not be accepted by the Service Provider if it decides that this multi-coupon is no longer valid. To revoke a multi-coupon, the service provider $\mathcal{SP}$ has to calculate a new key pair $(sk_{\mathcal{SP}}, pk_{\mathcal{SP}})$ and the users have to update $pk_{\mathcal{SP}}$ and their multi-coupon. It consists in revoking the signature made during the corresponding withdrawal protocol. The revocation scheme of our multi-coupon system thus relies on the revocation mechanism of the group signature underlying the CL signature scheme. When using a BBS signature scheme we can use the revocation scheme described in [4]. For an ACJT signature scheme, the revocation can be done as in [7].

We can also add an expiration date to the multi-coupon in case the Service Provider wants to limitate its use. To do so, we simply modify the withdrawal and redemption protocols. During the Withdraw protocol the Service Provider adds to the signature a value which represents the expiration date. Then, during the Redeem protocol, the user proves to the Service Provider that the date contained in her signature is more than the current date.

5   Security Arguments

Let us now give the security theorem that our proposal is secure under the definition given above.

Theorem 1. *In the standard model, under the y-DDHI assumption and the security assumptions of the used CL signature scheme (Flexible RSA if ACJT and y-SDH if BBS), the multi-coupon system described in Section 4 is secure w.r.t. the security model described in Section 2.*

The proof can be found in the full paper.

6   Recent Work on Coupon Systems

Recently, Nguyen [23] has independently proposed a multi-coupon system and a formal security model. Our model is quite close to Nguyen's, except that we include a transfer protocol, which is not compatible with his property of unsplittability.

As we do in this paper, Nguyen adapted the compact e-cash system [8] to the electronic coupon context. In his adaptation, Nguyen focused on the efficiency of the redemption protocol and consequently had a protocol with constant cost for communication and computation. However the size of the multi-coupon increases proportionally to the number of coupons, whereas in our scheme, the multi-coupon has a small constant size.

Apart from the adaptation of the compact e-cash system, Nguyen also permitted the revocation of a multi-coupon, as we do. He also suggested a solution, different from ours, to permit the user to choose the number of coupons she wants to withdraw. It will be interesting in the future to study the efficiency of these two solutions w.r.t. the size of the multi-coupon, the number of withdrawn coupons and the application (efficiency of withdrawal protocol vs. efficiency of redemption protocol).

Finally, we also add the possibility to have coupons of different values, which is not studied by Nguyen.

7   Conclusion

In this paper, we first introduced a strong and formal model suitable for electronic multi-coupon systems. We then proved the existence of a system, meeting our requirements, based on standard complexity assumptions, in the standard model. We introduced in the context of electronic coupon schemes the transfer of coupons which seems to be suitable for most of the applications of the real life. Furthermore, our scheme allows a user to choose the number of coupons she wants to withdraw, and the value of each coupon of a multi-coupon is chosen by the user among a set of pre-defined values; as far as we know, our electronic coupon scheme is the first scheme that propose these features. Moreover, the latter improvements can also be used in an electronic cash system such as the compact e-cash of Camenisch *et al.*

It will be useful in the future to design a transfer protocol which does not involve the service provider, as is it closer to reality and consequently more practical. Moreover, the multi-redeem protocol may be run more efficiently, possibly by permitting the computation of coupon identifiers iteratively for each redeemed coupon.

Acknowledgment. We would like to thank Jacques Traoré and Marc Girault for their help and anonymous referees for their useful comments. This work is partially supported by the French Ministry of Research RNRT Project "CRYPTO++".

References

1. G. Ateniese, J. Camenisch, M. Joye, and G. Tsudik. A practical and provably secure coalition-resistant group signature scheme. Advances in Cryptology - Crypto'00, volume 1880 of LNCS, pages 255-270, 2000.
2. M. Bellare and S. Goldwasser. Verifiable partial key escrow. In ACM Conference on Computer and Communications Security, pages 78-91, 1997.
3. D. Boneh and X. Boyen. Short signatures without random oracles. Advances in Cryptology - Eurocrypt'04, volume 3027 of LNCS, 2004.
4. D. Boneh, X. Boyen, and H. Shacham. Short group signatures. Advances in Cryptology - Crypto 04, volume 3152 of LNCS, pages 41-55, 2004.
5. F. Boudot. Efficient proofs that a committed number lies in an interval. Advances in Cryptology - Eurocrypt'00, volume 1807 of LNCS, pages 431-444, 2000.
6. S. Brands. Untraceable off-line electronic cash in wallets with observers. Advances in Cryptology - Crypto'93, volume 773 of LNCS, pages 302-318, 1993.
7. J. Camenisch and A. Lysyanskaya. A signature scheme with efficient protocols. SCN'02, 2576:268-289, 2002.
8. J. Camenisch, S. Hohenberger, and A. Lysyanskaya. Compact e-cash. Advances in Cryptology - Eurocrypt'05, volume 3494 of LNCS, pages 302-321, 2005.
9. J. Camenisch and A. Lysyanskaya. Signature schemes and anonymous credentials from bilinear maps. Advances in Cryptology - Crypto 04, volume 3152 of LNCS, pages 56-72, 2004.
10. J. Camenisch and M. Michels. Proving in zero-knowledge that a number is the product of two safe primes. Advances in Cryptology - Eurocrypt'99, volume 1592 of LNCS, pages 107-122, 1999.
11. S. Canard and J. Traoré. On fair e-cash systems based on group signature schemes. ACISP'03, volume 2727 of LNCS, pages 237-248, 2003.
12. A.H. Chan, Y. Frankel, and Y. Tsiounis. Easy come - easy go divisible cash. Advances in Cryptology - Eurocrypt'98, volume 1403 of LNCS, pages 561-575, 1998.
13. D. Chaum, A. Fiat, and M. Naor. Untraceable electronic cash. Advances in Cryptology - Crypto'88, volume 403 of LNCS, pages 319-327, 1988.
14. D. Chaum and T. Pedersen. Transferred cash grows in size. Advances in Cryptology - Eurocrypt'92, volume 658 of LNCS, pages 390-407, 1993.
15. D. Chaum and T. Pedersen. Wallet Databases with Observers. Advances in Cryptology - Crypto'92, volume 740 of LNCS, pages 89-105, 1993.
16. L. Chen, M. Enzmann, A.-R. Sadeghi, M. Schneider II, and M. Steiner. A privacy-protecting coupon system. In Financial Cryptography'05, LNCS, pages 93-108, 2005.

17. R. Cramer, I. Damgard, and B. Schoenmakers. Proofs of partial knowledge and simplified design of witness hiding protocols. Advances in Cryptology - Crypto'94, volume 839 of LNCS, pages 174-187, 1994.
18. Y. Dodis and A. Yampolskiy. A verifiable random function with short proofs and keys. PKC'05, volume 3386 of LNCS, pages 416-431, 2005.
19. E. Fujisaki and T. Okamoto. Statistical zero-knowledge protocols to prove modular polynomial relations. Advances in Cryptology - Crypto'97, volume 1294 of LNCS, pages 16-30, 1997.
20. M. Girault. An identity-based identification scheme based on discrete logarithms modulo a composite number. Advances in Cryptology - Eurocrypt'90, volume 473 of LNCS, pages 481-486, 1991.
21. T. Nakanishi, M. Shiota, and Y. Sugiyama. An efficient online electronic cash with unlinkable exact payments. ISC'04, pages 367-378, 2004.
22. T. Nakanishi and Y. Sugiyama. Unlinkable divisible electronic cash. ISW'00, pages 121-134, 2000.
23. L. Nguyen. Privacy-protecting coupon system revisited. In Financial Cryptography'06 LNCS (to appear), 2006.
24. T. Pedersen. Non-interactive and information-theoretic secure verifiable secret sharing. Advances in Cryptology - Crypto'91, volume 576 of LNCS, pages 129-140, 1992.
25. G. Poupard and J. Stern. Security analysis of a practical "on the fly" authentication and Signature Generation. Advances in Cryptology - Eurocrypt'98, volume 1403 of LNCS, pages 422-436, 1998.
26. A. De Santis, G. Di Crescenzo, G. Persiano, and M. Yung. On Monotone Formula Closure of SZK. FOCS 1994, pages 454-465, 1994.
27. C. P. Schnorr. Efficient identification and signatures for smart cards. Advances in Cryptology - Crypto'89, volume 435 of LNCS, pages 239-252, 1990.

An Efficient Single-Key Pirates Tracing Scheme Using Cover-Free Families

Dongvu Tonien and Reihaneh Safavi-Naini

School of Information Technology and Computer Science,
University of Wollongong, Australia
{dong, rei}@uow.edu.au

Abstract. A cover-free family is a well-studied combinatorial structure that has many applications in computer science and cryptography. In this paper, we propose a new public key traitor tracing scheme based on cover-free families. The new traitor tracing scheme is similar to the Boneh-Franklin scheme except that in the Boneh-Franklin scheme, decryption keys are derived from Reed-Solomon codes while in our case they are derived from a cover-free family. This results in much simpler and faster tracing algorithms for *single-key pirate* decoders, compared to the tracing algorithms of Boneh-Franklin scheme that use Berlekamp-Welch algorithm. Our tracing algorithms *never* accuse innocent users and identify *all* traitors with overwhelming probability.

1 Introduction

In a public key traitor tracing scheme, the encryption key is made public and everyone can use this public key to encrypt messages and broadcast the resulting ciphertexts to all users. Each user is given a unique secret key which can be used to decrypt the broadcasted ciphertexts. Malicious users may combine their decoder keys to construct a pirate decoder that can decrypt the broadcast. A pirate decoder contains a secret key different from all of the colluders' secret keys, or a different decryption algorithm. Pirate decoders can be sold to unauthorised users allowing them to illegally access the content. A tracing algorithm takes a pirate decoder and outputs one of the colluders. Typical applications of such systems are distribution of content in pay-per-view television and web-based content distribution.

Traitor tracing was first introduced by Chor, Fiat and Naor [3]. The first public key traitor tracing scheme was proposed by Boneh and Franklin [2]. In their scheme, two models of pirate decoders are considered. The first model is the *single-key pirate* model and assumes that there are two separate parties called the *key-builder* and the *box-builder*. The key-builder is a group of malicious users who combine their secret keys to create a new pirate decryption key. The pirate key is then handed over to the box-builder who implements the decryption box freely based on this single pirate key. The single-key pirate model is thus a simple but a realistic model of the pirate market. The second pirate model is more sophisticated and allows a pirate decoder with more than one pirate key.

J. Zhou, M. Yung, and F. Bao (Eds.): ACNS 2006, LNCS 3989, pp. 82–97, 2006.

In Kiayias and Yung's model [10, 11], a pirate decoder may also have several built-in self protection functionalities, for example, remembering previous tracer queries, erasing internal keys and shutting down when it "detects" that it is being queried by a tracer. "Crafty pirates" require more advanced tracing algorithms.

A common technique in tracing general pirate decoders is the black box confirmation technique which has been used in many schemes including [2, 20, 29, 17, 5, 14, 15]. Even though, this technique achieves the goal of tracing sophisticated pirate decoders, however, it is obviously not an efficient technique. If c denotes the maximum number of malicious users who have created a pirate decoder, a traitor tracing algorithm using the back box confirmation technique should implement a sub-procedure that takes a subset of c users and determines whether the subset contains the whole set of traitors or not. Thus, for a scheme of n users, up to $\binom{n}{c}$ executions of the sub-procedure may be required. While there has not been any known efficient tracing algorithm for the crafty pirate model, it may be argued that this pirate model is not very realistic as a self protection mechanism in a crafty pirate decoder usually requires the embedding of several keys [30, 31]. It remains as an open problem to design a public key traitor tracing with efficient tracing algorithm against crafty pirates.

In this paper, we only deal with single-key pirates. We propose a new public key traitor tracing scheme with an efficient *combinatorial* traitor tracing algorithm against single-key pirate decoders based on cover-free families. At present, Boneh-Franklin's tracing algorithm [2] is the most efficient algorithm for tracing single-key pirates. This is an *algebraic* algorithm which uses Berlekamp-Welch [1] decoding algorithm for generalized Reed-Solomon codes. Two other traitor tracing schemes [20, 13] also use Berlekamp-Welch algorithm. Our traitor tracing scheme is similar to the Boneh-Franklin scheme except that in the Boneh-Franklin scheme, decryption keys are derived from Reed-Solomon codes, but in our scheme, decryption keys are derived from a cover-free family, resulting in simpler and faster tracing algorithms compared to the tracing algorithms of Boneh-Franklin scheme.

Cover-free families (CFF) are well-studied combinatorial structures with many applications in computer science and cryptography such as information retrieval, data communication, magnetic memories, group testing, key distribution and authentication [9, 25, 24]. It is interesting to discover yet another application of cover-free families for traitor tracing. A c-CFF(m,n) is a pair $(\mathcal{S}, \mathcal{B})$ where $\mathcal{S}$ is a set of m *points* and $\mathcal{B}$ is a collection of n subsets (or *blocks*) of $\mathcal{S}$ with the property that the union of any c blocks cannot cover another block. A cover-free family can be constructed with large n and relatively small m. In our scheme, there are n users that are used to label the n blocks, and m modular linear equations that are used to label the m points. Secret keys of the n users are generated as vector solutions of a certain number of modular equations based on the incidence matrix of the cover-free family. Our tracing algorithms identify traitors by taking intersection of certain subsets derived from the cover-free family and so are simpler and faster than Boneh-Franklin tracing algorithms. The drawback is that our tracing algorithms may not identify all traitors, although we show that they will identify *all* traitors with an *overwhelming probability*. In addition, our algorithms are *error-free*, meaning that an innocent user is never wrongly accused by the algorithms.

Our method of generating secret keys using a number of modular linear equations is inspired by the work of Narayanan et al. [21], although in [21] the set of equations satisfied by a certain secret key is chosen randomly, whereas in our scheme the equations are deterministically determined using the incidence matrix of the cover-free family. In [21], an innocent user may be mistakenly identified as a traitor. In our scheme however, due to the cover-free property, the traitor tracing algorithms will *never* accuse innocent users. We also note that Narayanan et al's scheme is not a public key scheme. Finally, flaws in the key generation algorithm of Narayanan et al's scheme are reported in [27].

Organization of the paper. Section 2 introduces cover-free families. Section 3 briefly presents our intuition behind the scheme. Section 4 describes our new traitor tracing scheme; and the tracing algorithms are presented separately in Section 5. We conclude our paper in Section 6. Many proofs have been omitted due to lack of space, we refer readers to [28].

2   Cover-Free Families

Cover-free families were first introduced in 1964 by Kautz and Singleton [9] to investigate superimposed binary codes. Since then, these combinatorial structures have been studied extensively and appeared to have many applications in information theory, combinatorics and cryptography including information retrieval, data communication, magnetic memories, group testing, key distribution and authentication [9, 25, 24].

Definition 1. *A c-cover-free family is a pair $(\mathcal{S}, \mathcal{B})$, where $\mathcal{S}$ is a set of m elements and $\mathcal{B}$ is a collection of n subsets (called* blocks*) of $\mathcal{B}$ with the following property: for any $1 \leq c' \leq c$, the union of any c' blocks cannot contain any other block. We use the notation c-CFF(m, n) to denote a c-cover-free family $(\mathcal{S}, \mathcal{B})$ with $|\mathcal{S}| = m$ and $|\mathcal{B}| = n$.*

For the ease of presentation, through out this paper, we assume $\mathcal{S} = \{1, 2, \ldots, m\}$. The following theorem gives a lower bound for the parameter m in term of parameters c and n. See [7, 8, 23] for different proofs of this theorem.

Theorem 1. *For a c-CFF(m, n), it holds that*

$$m \geq \theta \frac{c^2}{\log c} \log n$$

for some constant θ.

The constant θ in Theorem 1 is shown to be approximately $1/2$ in [7], approximately $1/4$ in [8] and approximately $1/8$ in [23]. Slightly stronger bounds are given in [26]. A simple construction of cover-free families is based on concatenated codes [6].

For our traitor tracing scheme construction, we want to choose a c-cover-free family with large n and small m since as we will see later, the parameter c becomes the collusion threshold, the parameter n becomes the number of users, and traitor tracing complexity depends on the parameter m.

Suppose we have a c-CFF(m, n) $(\mathcal{S}, \mathcal{B})$ with $\mathcal{S} = \{1, 2, \ldots, m\}$ and $\mathcal{B} = \{B_1, B_2, \ldots, B_n\}$. We construct its *incidence matrix* $\mathcal{M}$ as follows. The matrix has n rows and m columns. Label n rows by n blocks of $\mathcal{B}$ and label m columns by m elements of the set $\mathcal{S}$. The entry $\mathcal{M}[i, j]$ at row labeled by B_i and column j is 1 if $j \in B_i$ and is 0 if $j \notin B_i$. The c-cover-free property is interpreted in the incidence matrix as follows. For any c' blocks $B_{i_1}, B_{i_2}, \ldots, B_{i_{c'}}$, where $1 \le c' \le c$, and any other block B_k, since $B_{i_1} \cup B_{i_2} \cup \ldots \cup B_{i_{c'}}$ does not contain B_k, there must exist $j \in B_k$ such that $j \notin B_{i_1}$, $j \notin B_{i_2}$, $\ldots$, and $j \notin B_{i_{c'}}$. It means that if we take arbitrary c' rows $i_1, i_2, \ldots, i_{c'}$ and any other row k, then there exists at least a column j such that $\mathcal{M}[i_1, j] = \mathcal{M}[i_2, j] = \ldots = \mathcal{M}[i_{c'}, j] = 0$ and $\mathcal{M}[k, j] = 1$. The *complementary incidence matrix* $\mathcal{M}'$ is obtained from the incidence matrix $\mathcal{M}$ by replacing the entries 1 by 0 and replacing 0 by 1. The following property of the complementary incidence matrix $\mathcal{M}'$ plays the crucial role in constructing our new traitor tracing scheme. That is, for any $1 \le c' \le c$, if we take arbitrary c' rows and another row of $\mathcal{M}'$, then there exists at least a column whose entries on these c' rows are all 1 and the entry on the other row is 0.

3   Idea

Suppose we want to construct a public key traitor tracing scheme with n users and c is the collusion threshold. Then we need to use a c-CFF(m, n) $(\mathcal{S}, \mathcal{B})$ with an $n \times m$ *complementary incidence matrix* $\mathcal{M}'$. We will generate m random *modular linear equations*:

$$
\begin{aligned}
\text{equation 1 } (E_1): & \quad \mu_{1,1}X_1 + \mu_{1,2}X_2 + \ldots + \mu_{1,t}X_t = 0 \quad (\text{mod } N_1) \\
\text{equation 2 } (E_2): & \quad \mu_{2,1}X_1 + \mu_{2,2}X_2 + \ldots + \mu_{2,t}X_t = 0 \quad (\text{mod } N_2)
\end{aligned}
$$

$$\vdots \qquad\qquad\qquad\qquad \vdots$$

$$\text{equation } m \ (E_m): \mu_{m,1}X_1 + \mu_{m,2}X_2 + \ldots + \mu_{m,t}X_t = 0 \quad (\text{mod } N_m)$$

where parameters t and N_1, N_2, ..., N_m will be described in details later. We now label m columns of $\mathcal{M}'$ by these m equations E_1, E_2, ..., E_m, and label n rows of $\mathcal{M}'$ by n user keys v_1, v_2, ..., v_n.

$$\mathcal{M}' \quad \begin{array}{c|cccc} & E_1 & E_2 & \dots & E_m \\ \hline v_1 & 0 & 1 & \dots & 0 \\ v_2 & 1 & 1 & \dots & 0 \\ \vdots & \vdots & \vdots & & \vdots \\ v_i & 1 & 0 & \dots & 1 \\ \vdots & \vdots & \vdots & & \vdots \\ v_n & 0 & 1 & \dots & 1 \end{array}$$

User i decryption key has the form $v_i = (v_{i,1}, v_{i,2}, \dots, v_{i,t}) \in \mathbf{N}^t$ and is generated in such a way that, for each $1 \le j \le m$, if $\mathcal{M}'[i,j] = 1$ then v_i satisfies the equation E_j, and if $\mathcal{M}'[i,j] = 0$ then v_i does not satisfy the equation E_j. For example, if the row i of $\mathcal{M}'$ is $(1, 0, \dots, 1)$ then $v_i = (v_{i,1}, v_{i,2}, \dots, v_{i,t})$ is generated such that v_i satisfies equation E_1, *not* satisfy equation E_2, ..., and satisfies equation E_m.

We will show that in our new traitor tracing scheme, if c' traitors i_1, i_2, ..., $i_{c'}$ collude then from their keys v_{i_1}, v_{i_2}, ..., $v_{i_{c'}}$ they can only create pirate key v_{pirate} that has the form

$$v_{pirate} = \alpha_1 v_{i_1} + \alpha_2 v_{i_2} + \dots + \alpha_{c'} v_{i_{c'}},$$

where α_1, α_2, ..., $\alpha_{c'}$ are integer numbers such that $\alpha_1 + \alpha_2 + \dots + \alpha_{c'} = 1$.

Consider the set $\mathcal{E}$ of equations that are satisfied by all of the vectors v_{i_1}, v_{i_2}, ..., $v_{i_{c'}}$. The linearity implies that the pirate vector v_{pirate} also satisfies all equations in the set $\mathcal{E}$. However, from the property of the matrix $\mathcal{M}'$, any innocent user k, there exists at least one equation in the set $\mathcal{E}$ that is *not* satisfied by v_k.

$$\mathcal{M}' \quad \begin{array}{c|c} & \dots \; set\; \mathcal{E} \; \dots \\ \hline \vdots & \vdots \; \vdots \; \vdots \; \vdots \\ v_{i_1} & \dots 1\;1\;1\;1 \dots \\ v_{i_2} & \dots 1\;1\;1\;1 \dots \\ \vdots & \vdots \; \vdots \; \vdots \; \vdots \\ v_{i_{c'}} & \dots 1\;1\;1\;1 \dots \\ \vdots & \vdots \; \vdots \; \vdots \; \vdots \\ v_k & \dots \quad 0 \quad \dots \\ \vdots & \vdots \; \vdots \; \vdots \; \vdots \\ v_{pirate} & \dots 1\;1\;1\;1 \dots \end{array}$$

Therefore, from a pirate key v_{pirate}, we trace the traitors as follows. First, we identify the set $\mathcal{E}$ of equations that are satisfied by v_{pirate}. Next, for each equation in $\mathcal{E}$, take the corresponding set of vectors that satisfy this equation. Finally, find the intersection of these sets. The set of indices of the vectors in this intersection identifies the traitors. From the above analysis, we can see that no vectors corresponding to innocent users can remain in the intersection because, a vector corresponding to an innocent user must fails at least one equation in the set $\mathcal{E}$.

4   The Proposed Traitor Tracing Scheme

In this section, we present a new public-key traitor tracing scheme based on the idea outlined in the previous section. We show that our proposed scheme is semantically secure against passive adversary assuming the difficulty of the standard DDH problem. The scheme has two tracing algorithms: open-box tracing and black-box tracing which will be presented in the next section.

4.1   Key Generation

Let n be the number of users, c be the collusion threshold, and λ, Δ be security parameters.

1. Select a c-CFF(m, n) $(\mathcal{S}, \mathcal{B})$ with an $n \times m$ *complementary incidence matrix* $\mathcal{M}'$ where $m = \theta \frac{c^2}{\log c} \log n$ and θ is a small constant.
2. Choose a group G of Δ-bit order such that it is infeasible to find a multiple of order of G (we can choose G as the group $\mathbf{Z}_M^*$ where $M = pq$ is a RSA modulo). Choose a group element g of high order. Choose $2c + 1$ random numbers d, d_1, ..., d_{2c} such that $\gcd(d_{2c}, |G|) = 1$. Let $y = g^d$, $g_1 = g^{d_1}$, ..., $g_{2c} = g^{d_{2c}}$.
3. Set the *public encryption key* to be $PK = (y, g_1, \ldots, g_{2c})$.
4. Let $z = \lceil m/(2c-2) \rceil$. Generate z random λ-bit primes $p_1, p_2, \ldots, p_z$. Pick m numbers $N_1, N_2, \ldots, N_m$ from $\{p_1, p_2, \ldots, p_z\}$ such that each prime is picked at most $2c - 2$ times.
5. Generate a random $m \times (2c - 1)$ matrix $(\mu_{i,j})$ such that any $2c - 2$ rows of the matrix are linear independent. Consider the following m random *modular linear equations*

$$
\begin{aligned}
\textit{equation 1 } (E_1): & \quad \mu_{1,1}X_1 + \mu_{1,2}X_2 + \ldots + \mu_{1,2c-1}X_{2c-1} = 0 \quad (\bmod\ N_1) \\
\textit{equation 2 } (E_2): & \quad \mu_{2,1}X_1 + \mu_{2,2}X_2 + \ldots + \mu_{2,2c-1}X_{2c-1} = 0 \quad (\bmod\ N_2)
\end{aligned}
$$

$$
\vdots \qquad\qquad\qquad\qquad \vdots
$$

$$
\textit{equation m } (E_m): \mu_{m,1}X_1 + \mu_{m,2}X_2 + \ldots + \mu_{m,2c-1}X_{2c-1} = 0 \quad (\bmod\ N_m)
$$

Label m columns of $\mathcal{M}'$ by m equations and label n rows of $\mathcal{M}'$ by n vectors $v_1, v_2, \ldots, v_n$. Each vector is of the form $v_i = (v_{i,1}, v_{i,2}, \ldots, v_{i,2c-1})$ and is generated in such a way that, for each $1 \le j \le m$, if $\mathcal{M}'[i, j] = 1$ then v_i satisfies E_j, and if $\mathcal{M}'[i, j] = 0$ then v_i does *not* satisfy E_j. By Chinese Remainder Theorem, we can choose each vector component $v_{i,k}$ as a natural number less than the product $(p_1 p_2 \ldots p_z)$.

6. For each user i, calculate

$$v_{i,2c} = d_{2c}^{-1}(d - d_1v_{i,1} - d_2v_{i,2} - \ldots - d_{2c-1}v_{i,2c-1}) \pmod{|G|}$$

and set the *secret decryption key* of user i to be

$$dk_i = (\boldsymbol{v_i}, v_{i,2c}) = (v_{i,1}, v_{i,2}, \ldots, v_{i,2c-1}, v_{i,2c}).$$

Example. Let look at steps 4 and 5 in the following toy example with $m = 5$ and $c = 2$.

Step 4: $z = \lceil 5/2 \rceil = 3$. Generate 3 random primes p_1, p_2, p_3. Pick 5 numbers N_1, N_2, N_3, N_4, N_5 from $\{p_1, p_2, p_3\}$ such that each prime is picked at most 2 times. Let's pick $N_1 = N_2 = p_1$, $N_3 = N_4 = p_2$, $N_5 = p_3$.

Step 5: Generate 5 random *modular linear equations*

$$
\begin{array}{llll}
equation\ 1 & (E_1): & \mu_{1,1}X_1 + \mu_{1,2}X_2 + \mu_{1,3}X_3 = 0 & (\bmod\ p_1) \\
equation\ 2 & (E_2): & \mu_{2,1}X_1 + \mu_{2,2}X_2 + \mu_{2,3}X_3 = 0 & (\bmod\ p_1) \\
equation\ 3 & (E_3): & \mu_{3,1}X_1 + \mu_{3,2}X_2 + \mu_{3,3}X_3 = 0 & (\bmod\ p_2) \\
equation\ 4 & (E_4): & \mu_{4,1}X_1 + \mu_{4,2}X_2 + \mu_{4,3}X_3 = 0 & (\bmod\ p_2) \\
equation\ 5 & (E_5): & \mu_{5,1}X_1 + \mu_{5,2}X_2 + \mu_{5,3}X_3 = 0 & (\bmod\ p_3)
\end{array}
$$

Suppose the first row of $\mathcal{M}'$ is $(1, 1, 0, 1, 0)$ then the $\boldsymbol{v_1} = (v_{1,1}, v_{1,2}, v_{1,3})$ is generated so that

$$
\begin{array}{llll}
equation\ 1 & (E_1): & \mu_{1,1}v_{1,1} + \mu_{1,2}v_{1,2} + \mu_{1,3}v_{1,3} = 0 & (\bmod\ p_1) \\
equation\ 2 & (E_2): & \mu_{2,1}v_{1,1} + \mu_{2,2}v_{1,2} + \mu_{2,3}v_{1,3} = 0 & (\bmod\ p_1) \\
equation\ 3 & (E_3): & \mu_{3,1}v_{1,1} + \mu_{3,2}v_{1,2} + \mu_{3,3}v_{1,3} \neq 0 & (\bmod\ p_2) \\
equation\ 4 & (E_4): & \mu_{4,1}v_{1,1} + \mu_{4,2}v_{1,2} + \mu_{4,3}v_{1,3} = 0 & (\bmod\ p_2) \\
equation\ 5 & (E_5): & \mu_{5,1}v_{1,1} + \mu_{5,2}v_{1,2} + \mu_{5,3}v_{1,3} \neq 0 & (\bmod\ p_3)
\end{array}
$$

We first solve for $(v_{1,1}, v_{1,2}, v_{1,3})$ in (E_1) and (E_2) in modulo p_1, then solve for $(v_{1,1}, v_{1,2}, v_{1,3})$ in (E_3) and (E_4) in modulo p_2, and solve for $(v_{1,1}, v_{1,2}, v_{1,3})$ in (E_5) in modulo p_3, and finally, using Chinese Remainder Theorem to derive the final solution in modulo $p_1p_2p_3$.

Remark

1. The public encryption key $PK = (y, g_1, \ldots, g_{2c})$ contains $2c + 1$ group elements, so PK is approximately $(2c + 1)\Delta$-bit long.
2. User decryption key $dk_i = (\boldsymbol{v_i}, v_{i,2c})$. Since each component of $\boldsymbol{v_i}$ is a natural number less than $p_1p_2 \ldots p_z$, it is $z\lambda$-bit long. Thus, $\boldsymbol{v_i}$ is $(2c-1)z\lambda$-bit long. So dk_i is $\Delta + (2c - 1)z\lambda \approx \Delta + \lambda\theta\frac{c^2}{\log c}\log n$-bit long.

4.2   Encryption and Decryption

Encryption. A message $M \in G$ is encrypted as

$$(M\,y^r, g_1^r, g_2^r, \ldots, g_{2c}^r),$$

where r is a random number.

Decryption. User i using the secret decryption key dk_i to decrypt

$$\frac{M\,y^r}{(g_1^r)^{v_{i,1}}\,(g_2^r)^{v_{i,2}}\,\cdots\,(g_{2c}^r)^{v_{i,2c}}} = M.$$

The correctness of the decryption algorithm can easily be verified as follows. In the step 6 of the key generation, we have

$$v_{i,2c} = d_{2c}^{-1}(d - d_1 v_{i,1} - d_2 v_{i,2} - \ldots - d_{2c-1}v_{i,2c-1}) \quad (\bmod\ |G|),$$

so $d_1 v_{i,1} + d_2 v_{i,2} + \ldots + d_{2c-1}v_{i,2c-1} + d_{2c}v_{i,2c} = d \quad (\bmod\ |G|)$. Thus

$$g^{d_1 v_{i,1}} g^{d_2 v_{i,2}} \cdots g^{d_{2c}v_{i,2c}} = g^d,$$

and

$$g_1^{v_{i,1}} g_2^{v_{i,2}} \cdots g_{2c}^{v_{i,2c}} = y.$$

Therefore,

$$\frac{M\,y^r}{(g_1^r)^{v_{i,1}}\,(g_2^r)^{v_{i,2}}\,\cdots\,(g_{2c}^r)^{v_{i,2c}}} = \frac{M\,y^r}{y^r} = M.$$

4.3   Security of the Encryption Scheme

We show that our encryption scheme is semantically secure against a passive adversary assuming the difficulty of the decision Diffie–Hellman problem in G.

The decision Diffie–Hellman problem in G is to distinguish between tuples of the form $(\nu, \nu^a, \nu^b, \nu^{ab})$ and the form $(\nu, \nu^a, \nu^b, \nu^c)$ where ν is chosen random from G and a, b, c are random number.

With the assumption that the decision Diffie–Hellman problem in G is hard we show that the probability for an adversary to win in the following game is negligible over one half. In this game, the challenger executes the key generation procedure and gives the public encryption key to the adversary. The adversary then produces two messages M_0 and M_1 and gives them to the challenger. The challenger randomly chooses $\delta \in \{0,1\}$ and gives the adversary a ciphertext of M_δ. The adversary then answers $\delta' \in \{0,1\}$ and she wins if $\delta' = \delta$.

Theorem 2. *The encryption scheme is semantically secure against a passive adversary assuming the difficulty of the DDH problem.*

Similar to the Boneh–Franklin [2] scheme, our scheme can be modified to achieve security against chosen ciphertext attacks using Cramer–Shoup [4] approach.

5   Traitor Tracing Algorithms

This section is divided into three parts. In the first part, we will show that if the traitors do not know a non-zero multiple of the order of the group G and the discrete log problem in G is hard then the only pirate key that the traitors can construct is a *convex* pirate key. Convex pirate key is a key of the type

$$dk_{pirate} = \alpha_1 dk_{i_1} + \alpha_2 dk_{i_2} + \ldots + \alpha_{c'} dk_{i_{c'}},$$

where $\alpha_1, \alpha_2, \ldots, \alpha_{c'}$ are integer numbers such that $\alpha_1 + \alpha_2 + \ldots + \alpha_{c'} = 1$. Here $dk_{i_1}, dk_{i_2}, \ldots, dk_{i_{c'}}$ are decryption keys of c' traitors with $1 \leq c' \leq c$.

In the second part, we present open-box traitor tracing algorithm. That is how to trace traitors given a convex pirate key dk_{pirate}. Finally, black-box traitor tracing algorithm is presented in the third part.

5.1   Pirate Keys

In the key generation procedure, the public key is set to $PK = (y, g_1, g_2, \ldots, g_{2c})$ where $y = g^d$, $g_1 = g^{d_1}, g_2 = g^{d_2}, \ldots, g_{2c} = g^{d_{2c}}$. A tuple $(e_1, e_2, \ldots, e_{2c}) \in \mathbf{Z}^{2c}$ is said to be a (discrete log) representation of y with respect to the base $g_1, g_2, \ldots, g_{2c}$ if $y = g_1^{e_1} g_2^{e_2} \ldots g_{2c}^{e_{2c}}$, or equivalently,

$$e_1 d_1 + e_2 d_2 + \ldots + e_{2c} d_{2c} = d \pmod{|G|}.$$

It is clear that each user decryption key $dk_i = (\boldsymbol{v_i}, v_{i,2c}) = (v_{i,1}, \ldots, v_{i,2c-1}, v_{i,2c})$ is a representation of y with respect to $g_1, \ldots, g_{2c}$. Any representation $(e_1, e_2, \ldots, e_{2c})$ can be used for decrypting a ciphertext $(M y^r, g_1^r, g_2^r, \ldots, g_{2c}^r)$ as

$$\frac{M y^r}{(g_1^r)^{e_1} (g_2^r)^{e_2} \ldots (g_{2c}^r)^{e_{2c}}} = M.$$

A group of malicious users $\{i_1, i_2, \ldots, i_{c'}\}$, where $1 \leq c' \leq c$, can use their keys $dk_{i_1}, dk_{i_2}, \ldots, dk_{i_{c'}}$ to construct a pirate key as follows. They select random integer numbers $\alpha_1, \alpha_2, \ldots, \alpha_{c'}$ such that $\alpha_1 + \alpha_2 + \ldots + \alpha_{c'} = 1$ and calculate

$$dk_{pirate} = \alpha_1 dk_{i_1} + \alpha_2 dk_{i_2} + \ldots + \alpha_{c'} dk_{i_{c'}}.$$

It is easy to see that dk_{pirate} is a representation of y with respect to $g_1, g_2, \ldots, g_{2c}$ so it can be use as a pirate key for decryption.

In this construction of pirate key, we call $\{i_1, i_2, \ldots, i_{c'}\}$ as *active traitors* if all the linear coefficients $\alpha_1, \alpha_2, \ldots, \alpha_{c'}$ are *non-zero*. The purpose of traitor tracing is to identify these active traitors.

There may be some *inactive traitors* who support the collusion but they did not contribute their keys into the formation of pirate key. It is impossible to trace these inactive traitors. So we only focus on tracing active traitors. For this purpose, we define the following set

$\mathsf{Convex}(i_1, i_2, \ldots, i_{c'})$
$$= \{\alpha_1 dk_{i_1} + \ldots + \alpha_{c'} dk_{i_{c'}} : \alpha_1, \ldots, \alpha_{c'} \in \mathbf{Z} \setminus \{0\}, \alpha_1 + \ldots + \alpha_{c'} = 1\}.$$

In the following lemma, we show that if the active traitors $\{i_1, i_2, \ldots, i_{c'}\}$ do not know a non-zero multiple of the order of the group G and the discrete log problem in G is hard then the only pirate keys that they can construct are convex pirate keys in the above set $\mathsf{Convex}(i_1, i_2, \ldots, i_{c'})$.

Lemma 1. *Let $(y, g_1, g_2, \ldots, g_{2c})$ be a public key. Suppose an adversary is given the public key and c private keys $dk_{i_1}, \ldots, dk_{i_c}$. If the adversary can generate a new representation of y with respect to g_1, g_2, $\ldots$, g_{2c} that is not in the set*

$$\bigcup_{U \subset \{i_1, i_2, \ldots, i_c\}} \mathsf{Convex}(U)$$

then either the adversary knows a non-zero multiple of $|G|$ or the adversary can effectively compute discrete logs in G.

5.2   Open-Box Tracing Algorithm

In open-box tracing, we assume that the tracer can open the pirate decoder and obtain the pirate key dk_{pirate}. Let $\boldsymbol{v}_{pirate}$ be the vector formed by the first $2c-1$ components of dk_{pirate}. Then

$$\boldsymbol{v}_{pirate} = \alpha_1\,\boldsymbol{v}_{i_1} + \alpha_2\,\boldsymbol{v}_{i_2} + \ldots + \alpha_{c'}\,\boldsymbol{v}_{i_{c'}}$$

where $\alpha_1, \alpha_2, \ldots, \alpha_{c'}$ are *non-zero* integers whose sum is equal to 1.

Recall that in the key generation algorithm, we generate n vectors $\boldsymbol{v}_1, \boldsymbol{v}_2, \ldots, \boldsymbol{v}_n$ and m equations $E_1, E_2, \ldots, E_m$ so that each of the vectors satisfies a number of equations based on the $n \times m$ matrix $\mathcal{M}'$.

For an equation E, let $\mathsf{Vector}(E)$ denote the set of all vectors that satisfy E.

Let denote by $\mathsf{Equation}(\boldsymbol{v}_{i_1}, \boldsymbol{v}_{i_2}, \ldots, \boldsymbol{v}_{i_{c'}})$ the set of all equations that are satisfied by all of the vectors $\boldsymbol{v}_{i_1}, \boldsymbol{v}_{i_2}, \ldots, \boldsymbol{v}_{i_{c'}}$, and similarly, let denote by $\mathsf{Equation}(\boldsymbol{v}_{pirate})$ the set of all equations that are satisfied by $\boldsymbol{v}_{pirate}$.

By linearity, any equation that is satisfied by all of the vectors $\boldsymbol{v}_{i_1}, \boldsymbol{v}_{i_2}, \ldots, \boldsymbol{v}_{i_{c'}}$ must be satisfied by $\boldsymbol{v}_{pirate}$. Thus, $\mathsf{Equation}(\boldsymbol{v}_{i_1}, \boldsymbol{v}_{i_2}, \ldots, \boldsymbol{v}_{i_{c'}})$ must be a subset of $\mathsf{Equation}(\boldsymbol{v}_{pirate})$.

The following theorem states that it is likely that these two sets are equal and the probability that $\mathsf{Equation}(\boldsymbol{v}_{i_1}, \boldsymbol{v}_{i_2}, \ldots, \boldsymbol{v}_{i_{c'}})$ is a proper subset of $\mathsf{Equation}(\boldsymbol{v}_{pirate})$ is negligible.

Theorem 3. *It must hold that*

1. $\mathsf{Equation}(\boldsymbol{v}_{i_1}, \boldsymbol{v}_{i_2}, \ldots, \boldsymbol{v}_{i_{c'}}) \subset \mathsf{Equation}(\boldsymbol{v}_{pirate})$;
2. $Pr_{\alpha_1, \ldots, \alpha_{c'}}[\mathsf{Equation}(\boldsymbol{v}_{i_1}, \boldsymbol{v}_{i_2}, \ldots, \boldsymbol{v}_{i_{c'}}) \neq \mathsf{Equation}(\boldsymbol{v}_{pirate})] < \frac{2m}{2^\lambda}$.

Let k be an innocent user (i.e. outside of the set of active traitors $i_1, i_2, \ldots, i_{c'}$). The special property of the matrix $\mathcal{M}'$ states that there must exist an equation E_j such that E_j is satisfied by all of the vectors $\boldsymbol{v}_{i_1}, \boldsymbol{v}_{i_2}, \ldots, \boldsymbol{v}_{i_{c'}}$ but E_j is *not* satisfied by $\boldsymbol{v}_k$. It means that there exists $E_j \in \mathsf{Equation}(\boldsymbol{v}_{pirate})$ such that E_j is *not* satisfied by $\boldsymbol{v}_k$.

This leads to the following tracing algorithm: first identify the set of all equations, $\mathsf{Equation}(\boldsymbol{v}_{pirate})$, that are satisfied by $\boldsymbol{v}_{pirate}$, then find the set V of all vectors among $\boldsymbol{v}_1, \boldsymbol{v}_2, \ldots, \boldsymbol{v}_n$ that satisfy all equations in $\mathsf{Equation}(\boldsymbol{v}_{pirate})$. The index set of the vector set V is then the set of traitors. This set V can be formulated as

$$V = \bigcap_{E \in \mathsf{Equation}(\boldsymbol{v}_{pirate})} \mathsf{Vector}(E).$$

The algorithm. *Input:* A convex pirate key dk_{pirate}

1. Form $\boldsymbol{v}_{pirate}$ from the first $2c - 1$ components of dk_{pirate};
2. Go through m equations and identify the set $\mathsf{Equation}(\boldsymbol{v}_{pirate})$ of all equations that are satisfied by $\boldsymbol{v}_{pirate}$.
3. Each equation $E \in \mathsf{Equation}(\boldsymbol{v}_{pirate})$ has the associated set $\mathsf{Vector}(E)$. Find the intersection V of all these vector sets.
4. Output the index set X of V.

The following theorem guarantees the correctness of the open-box tracing algorithm.

Theorem 4. *Let* $dk_{pirate} \in \mathsf{Convex}(i_1, i_2, \ldots, i_{c'})$ *where* $1 \leq c' \leq c$, *and* X *be the output of the open-box tracing algorithm executed on the input* dk_{pirate}. *Then*

1. *X does not contains any innocent users, i.e. for all* $1 \leq k \leq n$ *if* $k \notin \{i_1, \ldots, i_{c'}\}$ *then* $k \notin X$;
2. *X is a subset of active traitors, i.e.* $X \subset \{i_1, i_2, \ldots, i_{c'}\}$;
3. *the probability that X contains all active traitors is close to 1, more specifically,*

$$Pr[X = \{i_1, \ldots, i_{c'}\}] > 1 - \frac{2m}{2^\lambda}.$$

Example. Let look at the following toy example with $c = 2$, $n = 5$, $m = 6$. We use a 2-CFF(6,5) $(\mathcal{S}, \mathcal{B})$ with $\mathcal{S} = \{1, 2, 3, 4, 5, 6\}$ and $\mathcal{B}$ has 5 blocks $B_1 = \{1\}$, $B_2 = \{2, 4\}$, $B_3 = \{3\}$, $B_4 = \{4, 5\}$ and $B_5 = \{6\}$ *(Note to readers: generally n is much larger than m, please do not get the wrong impression by this toy example!).*

$$\mathcal{M} \quad \begin{array}{l|l} & 1\,2\,3\,4\,5\,6 \\ \hline B_1 = \{1\} & 1\,0\,0\,0\,0\,0 \\ B_2 = \{2,4\} & 0\,1\,0\,1\,0\,0 \\ B_3 = \{3\} & 0\,0\,1\,0\,0\,0 \\ B_4 = \{4,5\} & 0\,0\,0\,1\,1\,0 \\ B_5 = \{6\} & 0\,0\,0\,0\,0\,1 \end{array} \qquad \mathcal{M}' \quad \begin{array}{l|llllll} & E_1 & E_2 & E_3 & E_4 & E_5 & E_6 \\ \hline v_1 & 0 & 1 & 1 & 1 & 1 & 1 \\ v_2 & 1 & 0 & 1 & 0 & 1 & 1 \\ v_3 & 1 & 1 & 0 & 1 & 1 & 1 \\ v_4 & 1 & 1 & 1 & 0 & 0 & 1 \\ v_5 & 1 & 1 & 1 & 1 & 1 & 0 \end{array}$$

Based on the matrix $\mathcal{M}'$, we have six equations and five vectors are generated for five users. For example, v_1 satisfies E_2, E_3, E_4, E_5, E_6 but does *not* satisfy E_1.

The associated Vector sets for these equations are:

$$\mathsf{Vector}(E_1) = \{v_2, v_3, v_4, v_5\}, \quad \mathsf{Vector}(E_2) = \{v_1, v_3, v_4, v_5\},$$
$$\mathsf{Vector}(E_3) = \{v_1, v_2, v_4, v_5\}, \quad \mathsf{Vector}(E_4) = \{v_1, v_3, v_5\},$$
$$\mathsf{Vector}(E_5) = \{v_1, v_2, v_3, v_5\}, \quad \mathsf{Vector}(E_6) = \{v_1, v_2, v_3, v_4\}.$$

Remark that these Vector sets are independent to the generation of equations and vectors. We can find these sets by either looking at matrix $\mathcal{M}'$ or $\mathcal{M}$. For example, based on matrix $\mathcal{M}'$ then $\mathsf{Vector}(E_1)$ is identified by the entries 1 on the first column, and based on matrix $\mathcal{M}$ then $\mathsf{Vector}(E_1)$ is identified by the entries 0 on the first column. These Vector sets can be easily precomputed based on the c-CFF $(\mathcal{S}, \mathcal{B})$.

Now suppose that user 2 and user 3 are active traitors, they construct dk_{pirate}. We will go through the open-box tracing algorithm step by step:

1. Form $\boldsymbol{v}_{pirate}$ from the first three components of dk_{pirate}; $\boldsymbol{v}_{pirate}$ must be an active convex combination of $\boldsymbol{v_2}$ and $\boldsymbol{v_3}$;
2. Go through six equations and identify the set of all equations that are satisfied by $\boldsymbol{v}_{pirate}$. Since $\boldsymbol{v_2}$ and $\boldsymbol{v_3}$ both satisfy E_1, E_5, E_6, $\boldsymbol{v}_{pirate}$ satisfies E_1, E_5, E_6. As stated in Theorem 3,

$$\mathsf{Equation}(\boldsymbol{v}_{pirate}) \supset \mathsf{Equation}(\boldsymbol{v_2}, \boldsymbol{v_3}) = \{E_1, E_5, E_6\}.$$

and it is likely that $\mathsf{Equation}(\boldsymbol{v}_{pirate}) = \{E_1, E_5, E_6\}$.
We assume $\mathsf{Equation}(\boldsymbol{v}_{pirate}) = \{E_1, E_5, E_6\}$;
3. Identify the intersection of Vector sets associated with the equations E_1, E_5, E_6:

$$\begin{aligned}
V &= \mathsf{Vector}(E_1) \cap \mathsf{Vector}(E_5) \cap \mathsf{Vector}(E_6) \\
&= \{\boldsymbol{v_2}, \boldsymbol{v_3}, \boldsymbol{v_4}, \boldsymbol{v_5}\} \cap \{\boldsymbol{v_1}, \boldsymbol{v_2}, \boldsymbol{v_3}, \boldsymbol{v_5}\} \cap \{\boldsymbol{v_1}, \boldsymbol{v_2}, \boldsymbol{v_3}, \boldsymbol{v_4}\} \\
&= \{\boldsymbol{v_2}, \boldsymbol{v_3}, \boldsymbol{v_5}\} \cap \{\boldsymbol{v_1}, \boldsymbol{v_2}, \boldsymbol{v_3}, \boldsymbol{v_4}\} \\
&= \{\boldsymbol{v_2}, \boldsymbol{v_3}\};
\end{aligned}$$

4. Output the index set of V: $X = \{2, 3\}$ – these are active traitors.

Rationale. *Firstly*, in the step 2 of the above example, one can wonder what would happen if $\mathsf{Equation}(\boldsymbol{v}_{pirate})$ contains more than $\{E_1, E_5, E_6\}$, eventhough Theorem 3 asserts that this scenario only happens with a very small probability. The answer is, if this happens then we only catch a subset of active traitors. Indeed, suppose $\mathsf{Equation}(\boldsymbol{v}_{pirate}) = \{E_1, E_3, E_5, E_6\}$ then in step 3,

$$\begin{aligned}
V &= \mathsf{Vector}(E_1) \cap \mathsf{Vector}(E_3) \cap \mathsf{Vector}(E_5) \cap \mathsf{Vector}(E_6) \\
&= \{\boldsymbol{v_2}, \boldsymbol{v_3}, \boldsymbol{v_4}, \boldsymbol{v_5}\} \cap \{\boldsymbol{v_1}, \boldsymbol{v_2}, \boldsymbol{v_4}, \boldsymbol{v_5}\} \cap \{\boldsymbol{v_1}, \boldsymbol{v_2}, \boldsymbol{v_3}, \boldsymbol{v_5}\} \cap \{\boldsymbol{v_1}, \boldsymbol{v_2}, \boldsymbol{v_3}, \boldsymbol{v_4}\} \\
&= \{\boldsymbol{v_2}\};
\end{aligned}$$

Thus, the algorithm outputs one active traitor $X = \{2\}$, and does not detect the other active traitor. We would like to emphasize here that, in all cases, there will be *no* innocent users are mistakenly output as traitors.

Secondly, one can question the significance of the usage of the cover-free family. The answer is, if we do not use cover-free families then the algorithm will output innocent users as traitors.

Consider the following example where $\mathcal{B}$ has one more blocks $B_6 = \{2,3\}$. Now $(\mathcal{S}, \mathcal{B})$ is no longer 2-cover-free because $B_6 = \{2,3\}$ is covered by $B_2 = \{2,4\}$ and $B_3 = \{3\}$. We have one more user, user 6, and the new matrices are

	1 2 3 4 5 6
$B_1 = \{1\}$	1 0 0 0 0 0
$B_2 = \{2,4\}$	0 1 0 1 0 0
$\mathcal{M}$ $B_3 = \{3\}$	0 0 1 0 0 0
$B_4 = \{4,5\}$	0 0 0 1 1 0
$B_5 = \{6\}$	0 0 0 0 0 1
$B_6 = \{2,3\}$	0 1 1 0 0 0

	E_1 E_2 E_3 E_4 E_5 E_6
v_1	0 1 1 1 1 1
v_2	1 0 1 0 1 1
$\mathcal{M}'$ v_3	1 1 0 1 1 1
v_4	1 1 1 0 0 1
v_5	1 1 1 1 1 0
v_6	1 0 0 1 1 1

The new associated Vector sets are:

$$\mathsf{Vector}(E_1) = \{v_2, v_3, v_4, v_5, v_6\}, \quad \mathsf{Vector}(E_2) = \{v_1, v_3, v_4, v_5\},$$
$$\mathsf{Vector}(E_3) = \{v_1, v_2, v_4, v_5\} \quad , \quad \mathsf{Vector}(E_4) = \{v_1, v_3, v_5, v_6\},$$
$$\mathsf{Vector}(E_5) = \{v_1, v_2, v_3, v_5, v_6\}, \quad \mathsf{Vector}(E_6) = \{v_1, v_2, v_3, v_4, v_6\}.$$

If user 2 and user 3 are active traitors and in step 2 of the tracing algorithm we have $\mathsf{Equation}(v_{pirate}) = \{E_1, E_5, E_6\}$ then in step 3,

$$V = \mathsf{Vector}(E_1) \cap \mathsf{Vector}(E_5) \cap \mathsf{Vector}(E_6)$$
$$= \{v_2, v_3, v_4, v_5, v_6\} \cap \{v_1, v_2, v_3, v_5, v_6\} \cap \{v_1, v_2, v_3, v_4, v_6\}$$
$$= \{v_2, v_3, v_6\}.$$

The algorithm has mistaken output user 6 as an active traitor.

Comparison with Boneh–Franklin's Scheme. While our encryption scheme is the same as the encryption scheme of Boneh–Franklin [2], our tracing algorithm is much simpler. Tracing algorithm in Boneh–Franklin's scheme involves solving a linear system of dimension n (the total number of users) and decoding BCH error-correcting codes using Berlekamp's [1] algorithm. Whereas, in our tracing algorithm, it only has two simple steps:

Step 1: Finding the set $\mathsf{Equation}(v_{pirate})$ of equations that are satisfied by v_{pirate}. There are totally $m = \theta \frac{c^2}{\log c} \log n$ equations. This step involves m number of testings whether the vector v_{pirate} satisfies each equation or not.

Step 2: Finding the intersection V of Vector sets associated with equations in $\mathsf{Equation}(v_{pirate})$. This is a very simple step because m Vector sets associated with m equations are precomputed.

Let r be a small positive integer (for example $r = 2$). The intersection step is performed even faster if we precompute and store $\binom{m}{r}$ intersection sets

$$V_{\{i_1, i_2, \dots, i_r\}} = \mathsf{Vector}(E_{i_1}) \cap \mathsf{Vector}(E_{i_2}) \cap \dots \cap \mathsf{Vector}(E_{i_r}),$$

where $1 \le i_1 < i_2 < \dots < i_r \le m$. These intersection sets have small cardinalities compared to n. If $|\mathsf{Equation}(v_{pirate})| < r$ then V is an intersection of small number $(<r)$ of sets Vector. If $|\mathsf{Equation}(v_{pirate})| \ge r$ then V is the intersection of $|\mathsf{Equation}(v_{pirate})|/r < m/r$ number of intersection sets $V_{\{i_1, i_2, \dots, i_r\}}$.

With a much simpler tracing algorithm, our scheme achieves almost the same goals as the Boneh–Franklin scheme:

Error Free Tracing: There are no innocent users mistakenly output by the tracing algorithm as traitors. Output of the tracing algorithm are active traitors.

Full Tracing: While the tracing algorithm in the Boneh–Franklin scheme always outputs *all* active traitors, our tracing algorithm outputs all active traitors with probability almost near 1. Our algorithm outputs a proper subset of active traitors with only a negligible probability.

5.3   Black-Box Tracing Algorithm

A black-box tracing algorithm for single-key pirate can be developed using Boneh–Franklin's [2] approach. In this approach, we need to choose a underlying group G so that the tracer can efficiently solve the discrete log problem in the group such as those used in [22]. If this is the case, then suppose $dk_{pirate} = (v_1, v_2, \ldots, v_{2c})$ is a pirate key, we can find the values $v_1, v_2, \ldots, v_{2c}$ as follows. Query the pirate device by invalid ciphertexts of the form $C' = (Y, g^{r_1}, \ldots, g^{r_{2c}})$. The pirate device will respond with the value $Y/g^{r_1 v_1 + \cdots + r_{2c} v_{2c}}$. Hence, we can calculate $g^{r_1 v_1 + \cdots + r_{2c} v_{2c}}$. After $2c$ queries, the tracer can calculate $g^{v_1}, \ldots, g^{v_{2c}}$, and with the above assumption, all the components of the pirate key $v_1, \ldots, v_{2c}$ can be derived by the tracer. From here, the tracer can identify the set of active traitors as it does in the open-box tracing algorithm.

6   Conclusion

In this paper, we show yet another application of cover-free families in cryptography. We show how to use a cover-free family to construct a public-key traitor tracing scheme. The encryption system of our proposed traitor tracing scheme is similar to that of Boneh–Franklin [2] scheme, thus it is semantically secure against passive adversary assuming the intractability of the standard DDH problem. Our scheme can easily modified as the Boneh–Franklin's scheme to obtain chosen ciphertext security against active adversary. The main advantage of our scheme over the Boneh–Franklin is in traitor tracing algorithms. While tracing algorithm in Boneh–Franklin's scheme involves solving a linear system of dimension n (the total number of users) and decoding BCH error-correcting codes using Berlekamp's [1] algorithm, our tracing algorithm only has two simple steps related to $O(\frac{c^2}{\log c} \log n)$ number of modular linear equations (c is the collusion threshold).

References

1. E.R. Berlekamp and L. Welch, *Error Correction of Algebraic Block Codes*, U.S. Patent No. 4633470, 1986.
2. D. Boneh and M. Franklin, An Efficient Public Key Traitor Tracing Scheme, *Proceedings of CRYPTO 1999, Lecture Notes in Computer Science* 1666, 338–353.

3. B. Chor, A. Fiat and M. Naor, Tracing traitors, *Proceedings of CRYPTO 1994*, *Lecture Notes in Computer Science* 839, 257–270, 1994.

4. R. Cramer and V. Shoup, A Practical Public Key Cryptosystem Provably Secure Against Adaptive Chosen Ciphertext Attack, *Proceedings of CRYPTO 1998*, *Lecture Notes in Computer Science* 1462, 13–25.

5. Y. Dodis and N. Fazio, Public Key Trace and Revoke Scheme Secure against Adaptive Chosen Ciphertext Attack, *Proceedings of PKC 2003*, *Lecture Notes in Computer Science* 2567, 100–115, 2003.

6. A.G. D'yachkov, A.J. Macula and V.V. Rykov, New Constructions of Superimposed Codes, *IEEE Transactions on Information Theory* **46** (2000), 284–290.

7. A.G. D'yachkov and V.V. Rykov, Bounds on the Length of Disjunctive Codes, *Problemy Peredachi Informatsii* **18** (1982), 7–13. [Russian]

8. Z. Füredi, On r-Cover-Free Families, *Journal of Combinatorial Theory A* **73** (1996), 172–173.

9. W.H. Kautz and R.C. Singleton, Nonrandom Binary Superimposed Codes, *IEEE Transactions on Information Theory* **10** (1964), 363–377.

10. A. Kiayias and M. Yung, Self Protecting Pirates and Black-Box Traitor Tracing, *Proceedings of CRYPTO 2001*, *Lecture Notes in Computer Science* 2139, 63–79, 2001.

11. A. Kiayias and M. Yung, On Crafty Pirates and Foxy Tracers, *Proceedings of DRM 2001*, *Lecture Notes in Computer Science* 2320, 22–39, 2002.

12. A. Kiayias and M. Yung, Traitor Tracing with Constant Transmission Rate, *Proceedings of EUROCRYPT 2002*, *Lecture Notes in Computer Science* 2332, 450–465, 2002.

13. A. Kiayias and M. Yung, Breaking and Repairing Asymmetric Public-Key Traitor Tracing, *Proceedings of DRM 2002*, *Lecture Notes in Computer Science* 2696, 32–50, 2003.

14. C.H. Kim, Y.H. Hwang and P.J. Lee, An Efficient Public Key Trace and Revoke Scheme Secure against Adaptive Chosen Ciphertext Attack, *Proceedings of ASIACRYPT 2003*, *Lecture Notes in Computer Science* 2894, 359–373, 2003.

15. C. H. Kim, Y. H. Hwang and P. J. Lee, TTS without Revocation Capability Secure Against CCA2, *Proceedings of ACISP 2004*, *Lecture Notes in Computer Science* 3108, 36–49, 2004.

16. K. Kurosawa and Y. Desmedt, Optimum Traitor Tracing and Asymmetric Schemes with Arbiter, *Proceedings of EUROCRYPT 1998*, *Lecture Notes in Computer Science* 1403, 145–157, 1998.

17. K. Kurosawa and T. Yoshida, Linear Code Implies Public-Key Traitor Tracing, *Proceedings of PKC 2002*, *Lecture Notes in Computer Science* 2274, 172–187, 2002.

18. T. Matsushita and H. Imai, A Public-Key Black-Box Traitor Tracing Scheme with Sublinear Ciphertext Size against Self-Defensive Pirates, *Proceedings of ASIACRYPT 2004*, *Lecture Notes in Computer Science* 3329, 260–275.

19. M. Naor and B. Pinkas, Threshold Traitor Tracing, *Proceedings of CRYPTO 1998*, *Lecture Notes in Computer Science* 1462, 502–517, 1998.

20. M. Naor and B. Pinkas, Efficient Trace and Revoke Schemes, *Proceedings of Financial Cryptography 2000*, *Lecture Notes in Computer Science* 1962, 1–20, 2001.

21. A. Narayanan, C.P. Rangan and K. Kim, Practical Pay TV Schemes, *Proceedings of ACISP 2003*, *Lecture Notes in Computer Science* 2727, 192–203, 2003.

22. P. Paillier, Public-Key Cryptosystems Based on Discrete Logarithms Residues, *Proceedings of EUROCRYPT 1999*, *Lecture Notes in Computer Science* 1592, 223–238, 1999.

23. M. Ruszinkó, On the Upper Bound of the Size of the r-Cover-Free Families, *Journal of Combinatorial Theory A* **66** (1994), 302–310.
24. R. Safavi-Naini and H. Wang, Multireceiver Authentication Codes: Models, Bounds, Constructions, and Extensions, *Information and Computation* **151** (1999), 148–172.
25. D.R. Stinson, Tran van Trung and R. Wei, Secure Frameproof Codes, Key Distribution Patterns, Group Testing Algorithms and Related Structures, *Journal of Statistical Planning and Inference*.
26. D.R. Stinson, R. Wei and L. Zhu, Some New Bounds for Cover-Free Families, *Journal of Combinatorial Theory A* **90** (2000), 224–234.
27. D. Tonien, *On a Traitor Tracing Scheme from ACISP 2003*, Cryptology ePrint Archive 2005/371.
28. D. Tonien and R. Safavi-Naini, *An Efficient Single-Key Pirates Tracing Scheme USing Cover-Free Families*, Cryptology ePrint Archive 2006/099.
29. W. Tzeng and Z. Tzeng, A Public-Key Traitor Tracing Scheme with Revocation Using Dynamic Shares, *Proceedings of PKC 2001, Lecture Notes in Computer Science* 1992, 207–224, 2001.
30. J. Yan and Y. Wu, *An Attack on Black-box Traitor Tracing Schemes*, Rump session, IEEE Symposium on Security and Privacy, Oakland, USA, May 2001.
31. J. Yan and Y. Wu, *An Attack on A Traitor Tracing Scheme*, Cryptology ePrint Archive Report 2001/067.

Efficient Memory Bound Puzzles
Using Pattern Databases

Sujata Doshi, Fabian Monrose, and Aviel D. Rubin

Johns Hopkins University, Computer Science Department, MD, USA
{sdoshi, fabian, rubin}@cs.jhu.edu

Abstract. CPU bound client puzzles have been suggested as a defense mechanism against connection depletion attacks. However, the wide disparity in CPU speeds prevents such puzzles from being globally deployed. Recently, Abadi *et. al.* [1] and Dwork *et. al.* [2] addressed this limitation by showing that memory access times vary much less than CPU speeds, and hence offer a viable alternative. In this paper, we further investigate the applicability of memory bound puzzles from a new perspective and propose constructions based on heuristic search methods. Our constructions are derived from a more algorithmic foundation, and as a result, allow us to easily tune parameters that impact puzzle creation and verification costs. Moreover, unlike prior approaches, we address client-side cost and present an extension that allows memory constrained clients (e.g., PDAs) to implement our construction in a secure fashion.

1 Introduction

The Internet provides users a plethora of services, but at the same time, it is vulnerable to several attacks. Denial of Service (DoS) attacks, for example, represent a potentially crippling attack vector by which a user or organization is deprived of legitimate services, and may be forced to temporarily cease operation. While many approaches have been suggested as countermeasures to DoS attacks, one of the more promising avenues for defending against such attacks is based on the notion of client puzzles [3, 4, 5, 6].

Juels *et. al.* present one of the first practical solutions that employs CPU puzzles to defend against connection depletion attacks. [3]. That approach attempts to overcome the limitations of SYN-cookies [7] and random dropping of connections [8] by instead issuing puzzles constructed from time-sensitive parameters, secret information held by the server, and additional client request information.

To date, the design of client puzzles are bound by either CPU or Memory constraints of the client. Memory bound puzzles, however, overcome a notable obstacle in the widespread adoption of client puzzles, namely the large disparity in client CPU speeds. Recently, Abadi *et. al.* [1] proposed the first memory-bound puzzle construction aimed at addressing this disparity, and provide a solution based on performing a depth first search through a large array.

Unfortunately, while that approach and subsequent work [2] has indeed validated the conjecture regarding the low disparity in memory access times, we find

J. Zhou, M. Yung, and F. Bao (Eds.): ACNS 2006, LNCS 3989, pp. 98–113, 2006.

that prior work in this area lacks a thorough algorithmic foundation. Specifically, the constructions presented to date involve accessing random locations in a large array, but unlike some CPU-bound instances, these accesses are not semantically associated to solving any known hard problem. Furthermore, the memory-bound puzzle constructions presented thus far incur high creation and verification costs which themselves can lead to a form of DoS attack. While it may be argued that by appropriately adjusting the parameters of these constructions the task remains memory rather than CPU bound, a rigorous empirical evaluation has yet to be presented.

In this paper we propose a new memory bound puzzle construction based on heuristic search using pattern databases. One of the primary advantages of such an approach is that there already exists an equivalence class of problems (such as the Sliding Tile [9] and the Rubik cube problems [10]) that have been solved efficiently using memory based heuristics [11, 12], and that can be used as building blocks in our constructions. Furthermore, this class of problems enhances the flexibility in controlling the hardness of the client puzzle.[1]

In what follows, we present constructions based on the Sliding Tile problem, but note that it can be easily replaced with an equivalent problem. Additionally, the algorithmic nature of our constructions allows for simple and efficient extensions. Specifically, we consider the case of constrained clients (e.g, PDAs) that may not have sufficient memory to implement our constructions, and propose an enhancement which reduces the memory overhead at the client while still maintaining the security of the scheme.

2   Preliminaries

Our primary goal is to explore memory bound puzzles and appropriate constructions that meet the definition below. For the most part, the properties enlisted have been introduced elsewhere [3, 1, 2, 13], but we restate them here for completeness. We also introduce a new *Relaxed State* property for client puzzles.

Definition 1. *Memory Bound Client Puzzles are computable cryptographic problems which provide the following properties:*

- *Stateless: The server can verify the puzzle solution without maintaining state.*
- *Time-Dependent: The client is allowed limited time range in which the puzzle must be solved.*
- *Inexpensive Server-Side Cost: Creation and verification of the puzzle is inexpensive for the server.*
- *Controlled Hardness: The server can control the hardness of the puzzle it sends to the client.*

---

[1] For instance, the branching factor of the problem controls the number of paths that need to be explored in order to reach a solution. Hence, as technology evolves the building blocks of our constructions can be replaced with ones having a higher branching factor.

- **Hardware Independent:** *The puzzle should not be hardware dependent — ensuring that the puzzle can be widely deployed.*
- **Hardness of Pre-computation:** *It is computationally hard for the client to pre-compute the puzzle solution. This ensures that while the puzzle can be reused, its solution is not reusable.*
- **Random Memory Access:** *A memory bound function should access random memory locations in such a way that the cache memory becomes ineffective.*
- **Slower CPU bound solution variants:** *A client puzzle, can be solved by a memory bound or a CPU bound method. However the Memory Bound algorithm should converge faster than the corresponding CPU bound variant.*
- **Relaxed State:** *The server is allowed to maintain a limited amount of state for puzzle creation and verification. This property is applicable where additional storage is not a primary concern.*

3   Related Work

CPU Bound: Cryptographic puzzles were first introduced by Merkle [14] in the context of key agreement protocols where the derived session key is the solution to the puzzle. Juels *et. al.* [3] further extended the idea of puzzles in an attempt to provide a countermeasure to connection depletion attacks. Essentially, the client is forced to perform multiple hash reversals to correctly solve the puzzle. While [3] addresses server-side issues, little attention is given to client-side overhead.

Another approach to building CPU bound puzzles is the use of Hashcash [15]. HashCash was originally proposed as a countermeasure to email spam, and hence requires non-interactive cost-functions. The drawback, however, of a non-interactive approach is that an attacker can pre-compute all the tokens (solutions) for a given day and temporarily overload the system on that day.

Dean *et. al.* [4] show the applicability of CPU bound puzzles in protecting SSL against denial of service attacks and Wang *et. al.* [16] introduce the notion of congestion puzzles to defend against DDoS attacks on the IP layer. Wang and Reiter [5] address the issue of setting puzzle difficulty in the presence of an adversary with unknown computing power. They present a mechanism of puzzle auctions where each client bids for resources by tuning the difficulty of the puzzles it solves. More recently, Waters *et. al.* [6] point out that the puzzle distribution itself can be subject to attack, and present a defense mechanism which outsources the puzzle via a robust external service called a bastion. Both puzzle auctions and puzzle outsourcing can be adapted to use both CPU and Memory Bound Puzzles.

Memory Bound: Dwork *et. al.* consider memory bound constructions for fighting against spam mail [2]. The basic idea is to accompany email with proof of effort, in order to reduce the motivation for sending unsolicited email. Here, puzzle construction involves traversing a static table T of 2^{22} random 32-bit integers, and the sender is forced to perform a random walk of l steps through this table.

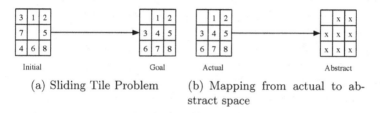

(a) Sliding Tile Problem   (b) Mapping from actual to abstract space

Fig. 1. The Sliding Tile Problem and its Abstract Mapping

The walk computes a one-way value R and success is defined when R contains a number of 0's in the least significant bit positions. The recipient accepts the proof (a hash on R and a path identification number i) if i lies under a specific threshold and the hash is correct. While Dwork *et. al.* show that the memory bound running times vary much less compared to the CPU bound variants, a drawback is the high verification cost on the server side. Rosenthal [17] further points out that with Dwork's solution, the sender of an email could have performed less work than that stated in the accompanying proof. To mitigate this scenario a modification was proposed that instead requires the sender to explore an entire range of paths rather than stopping at the first index.

Abadi *et. al.* [1] also propose memory bound constructions which involve accessing random locations in a very large array. There, the server applies a function $F(\cdot)$ k times to a random number, x_0, to obtain x_k. The server then sends x_k and the checksum over the path, $x_0 \cdots x_k$, and a keyed hash $H(K, x_0)$ (where K is a secret key of the server) to the client. Note that the hash is used for verification of the solution sent by the client. The client builds a table of the inverse function $F^{-1}(\cdot)$ and performs random accesses through this table to arrive at x_0. Unfortunately, the construction imposes constant work on the server for puzzle creation which is undesirable.

4   Memory Based Heuristic Search

In this paper we consider heuristic search for the Sliding Tile problem proposed by Sam Lyod [9]. Figure 1(a) illustrates the basic 3x3 Sliding Tile Problem. Here, eight numbers are arranged in a 3 x 3 grid of tiles where one tile is kept blank. The idea is to find a set of moves from the set $\{Left, Right, Up, Down\}$ which transforms the initial configuration to the goal configuration. A widely known, and very efficient, CPU bound method of solving such a problem is to use the A^* algorithm [18, 19, 20] along with the Manhattan Distance heuristic. In this case, a heuristic function $h(s)$ computes an *estimate* of the distance from state s to a goal state. A more efficient way of solving such a problem is to use a memory based heuristic, instead of the Manhattan Distance heuristic, whereby one precomputes the *exact* distance from a state s to the abstract goal state and stores that in a lookup table indexed by s. This lookup table is called a *pattern database* or a *heuristic table*.

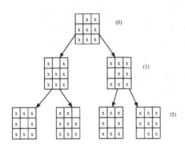
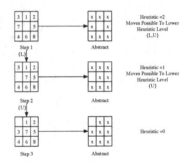

Fig. 2. Pattern Database Creation. The numbers near the configurations depict the heuristic values.

Fig. 3. Solving a Sliding Tile problem with a coarse abstraction

Pattern databases were introduced by Culberson and Schaeffer [21] to find optimal solutions to the 4 x 4 Sliding Tile problem, and have been instrumental in solving large problems efficiently [11]. The primary motivation behind using pattern databases is that they enable search time to be reduced by using more memory [12, 22]. When creating a pattern database, the goal configuration is first mapped to an abstract goal state (as in Figure 1(b)) and then the heuristic values are computed by performing a breadth first search backwards from the abstract goal (as in Figure 2).

5   Memory Bound Constructions

In what follows we describe two constructions—a naïve algorithm that does not meet all the properties of Definition 1, and then extend that to achieve a better construction. Section 5.1 presents the initialization steps and some notation common to both constructions.[2]

5.1   Initialization

The client and server have an agreed upon goal state(s). The client initially precomputes the pattern database corresponding to the goal. For example, Figure 1(b) shows the coarse mapping from the actual state space to the abstract space for the 3 x 3 Sliding tile problem; such a mapping yields a database consisting of 9 heuristic values corresponding to the 9 unique locations of the blank tile.

With this abstraction the database can be used to solve sub-versions of the original problem. However, notice that while the goal state might be reached in the abstract space, the goal might not be reached in the actual state space. Consequently, one will also have to explore search paths in the actual state space

---

[2] Note that in our protocols we do not focus on adapting the puzzle hardness in accordance with the changing memory size of the client. However, such a mechanism can be incorporated along the lines of the auction protocol provided by Wang and Reiter [5].

without using the database, hence, the client needs to also use an exhaustive CPU bound search to completely solve the problem. Figure 3 illustrates the process of solving the puzzle in Figure 1(a) given a database with this abstraction. Notice that Steps 1 and 2 are memory bound and lead to the goal in the abstract space. However, the client still has to perform additional moves from Step 3 to the actual Goal state. This implies that the given abstraction leads to a partially memory-bound search. Note, however, that a one-to-one mapping between the actual and abstract goal yields a larger pattern database which stores the exact heuristic values and that the corresponding search is completely memory bound. We use such a mapping in the various constructions introduced. Also note that precomputing this database is computationally expensive and hence it must be created offline.

Additionally we assume there exists a publicly accessible random oracle which can be queried to obtain a checksum value C. (In our case the oracle is implemented using a cryptographic hash function). Furthermore the server has access to a pseudorandom function $\mathcal{F}_K(\cdot)$ (such as HMAC-SHA1 [23]) where K is a secret key known only by the server.

5.2   Naïve Construction

The client and server have an agreed upon goal state G. The client precomputes the pattern database corresponding to the goal G. The protocol steps are:

- PUZZLE CREATION: The server applies d moves at random to G, from the set { *Left, Right, Up, Down* }, to arrive at the configuration P. Let M_i denote the opposite of the ith move on the puzzle where i takes values in $[1, d]$. Note that the parameter d controls the puzzle difficulty. The server computes a checksum C over $(M_d \ldots M_1)$.[3] The server also computes a verification value $V = \mathcal{F}_K(T, M_1, \ldots M_d)$ where T is the time stamp associated with the client visit. The server sends P, C, V, and T to the client.
- PUZZLE SOLVING: The client uses the pattern database and performs a guided search from P until he reaches the goal G and the checksum over the moves performed from P to G matches C. A guided search essentially involves following paths which lead closer to the goal. The client returns T, V and the d moves $\{M_1' \ldots M_d'\}$ to the server.
- PUZZLE VERIFICATION: The server verifies that the d moves sent by the client are correct using the verification value $V \stackrel{?}{=} \mathcal{F}_K(T, M_1' \ldots M_d')$.

Experimental Analysis. We implemented the above construction using the 2 x 4 Sliding Tile problem and evaluated it on machine M6 in Table 1. We chose a 2 x 4 configuration instead of a larger configuration (e.g. 3 x 3), to prevent a pattern database for one goal state from occupying too much main memory. This consideration becomes important in Section 5.3 where the client needs to store a pattern database for a large pool of goal states.

---

[3] The checksum is computed in the opposite direction over the moves as the client solves the puzzle from P towards G.

Table 1. Machine Specifications

Label	Processor	CPU (GHz)	Cache (KB)	Memory (MB)
M1	Pentium 2	0.4	512	128
M2	PowerMac G4	1.33	256 L2 2048 L3	1024
M3	Pentium 4	1.6	512	256
M4	PowerPC G4	1.67	512	1024
M5	PowerMac G5	2	512	3072
M6	Pentium 4	3.2	1024	1024

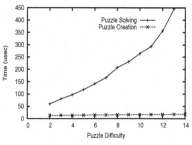

Fig. 4. Client and Server Costs

Figure 4 compares the client versus server cost for varying puzzle difficulty d. It can be seen that the work ratio between the client and server is substantial—for instance, at $d = 12$ moves, the server takes merely $17.3\mu sec$ to create the puzzle while solving the puzzle takes approximately $356.8\mu sec$. Additionally, the server does not maintain any database to verify the puzzle solution and so this construction meets the *Statelessness* property of Definition 1.

To determine if the memory bound approach is more effective than CPU bound methods for *solving* the puzzle, we compare our naïve construction against the best known (to our knowledge) CPU-bound method for solving the Sliding Tile problem — namely, the A^* algorithm[18, 19] with the Manhattan Distance Heuristic. Let $P(x)$ denote the fraction of nodes with heuristic value $\leq x$. If b denotes the branching factor of the problem and d denotes the solution depth (i.e puzzle difficulty) then the average case time complexity of A^* is $\frac{1+\sum_{i=0}^{d} b^i P(d-i)}{2}$ [24, 25]. Note, however, that the regular A^* algorithm does not incorporate the checksum into the search algorithm and so once an optimal path is found the result is returned. On the other hand, our setting requires that the client returns the path for which the checksum matches. In this way, the naive construction forces the client to search through non-optimal paths as well.

Figure 5 compares the time complexity for various search methods in terms of node expansion at a given solution depth. Note that node expansion is a valid metric for complexity because it inherently affects the search time. The results in Figure 5 show that the time complexity of the Naive Construction is higher than that of A^* algorithm with Pattern Database heuristic, indicating that the checksum forces the client to search non-optimal paths, thus confirming our previous argument. Note also that the performance of the Naïve Construction tends to follow the plot of A^* with Manhattan Distance. These results indicate that given an algorithm that incorporates the checksum into A^* with Manhattan Distance we can safely claim that the time complexity for such an algorithm would be more inline with that of the Brute Force approach. As such, we argue that brute force search is indeed a reasonable baseline for comparing our memory-bound approach.

Figure 6 compares the search component of the naïve construction to the brute force depth-first search approach which explores all paths until it reaches the goal, and the checksum matches. The results clearly indicates that the naïve

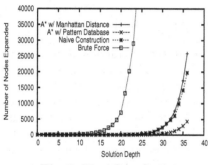

Fig. 5. Time Complexity   **Fig. 6.** Naïve vs Brute Force on M6

approach achieves better performance than the brute force algorithm and shows that the construction achieves the *Slower CPU bound solution variants* property of Definition 1. Unfortunately, this naïve construction suffers from a number of significant limitations, most notably that it fails to meet the following criteria:

- **Hardness of Pre-computation:** If the client is presented with an initial configuration P' whose moves to the goal state is a superset of the moves of a previously solved configuration P, then the client can re-use his old solution. While this issue cannot be completely resolved, the probability of re-using old solutions can be reduced by increasing the pool of initial configurations available to the server.
- **Random Memory Access:** The accesses in the pattern database are not random. More specifically, if we consider the number of unique puzzle configurations at a given heuristic level for the 2 x 4 Sliding Tile problem, then the maximum number of configurations between two consecutive heuristic levels is only 2000. This corresponds to at most 100 KB of memory and so the consecutive moves made by the client will not be cache misses. Moreover, the total number of configurations for the 2 x 4 Sliding Tile problem is just over 20,000 which results in a table of roughly 1 MB—which can easily be cached. Hence, this naïve solution is not memory bound.

In what follows we present a variant that overcomes the limitations of the naïve construction.

5.3   A Construction Using Multiple Goals

Again, assume that the client and server have an agreed upon pool of goal states $\{G_0, \ldots G_n\}$. The client precomputes the pattern database corresponding to all of these goal states and stores it in one table. The database is indexed by the tuple $(G_i, P), i \in \{0 \ldots n\}$ where P denotes the current configuration. The indexed location contains the heuristic value — the distance from the current configuration P to the goal configuration G_i. We define puzzle difficulty based on two parameters, namely the *horizontal puzzle difficulty* which denotes the number of Sliding Tile problems that have to be solved simultaneously, and the *vertical puzzle difficulty* which denotes the number of moves required to reach the goal state for a given initial configuration. The protocol steps are:

- PUZZLE CREATION: The server chooses f goal states at random from $\{G_0, \ldots G_n\}$. Let the set $\mathcal{G}$ contain these f goal states. The server then applies d moves at random to each goal $G_k \in \mathcal{G}$, from the set $\{$ *Left, Right, Up, Down* $\}$, to arrive at the f initial configurations P_k. Note that the parameter d controls the vertical puzzle difficulty and the parameter f controls the horizontal puzzle difficulty. The server also computes checksums over the moves as follows. Let $M_j^k, 1 \leq j < d$ denote the opposite of the jth move on the goal G_k. For difficulty level $j, 1 \leq j < d$, the checksum C_j is taken over $M_j^k, \forall G_k \in \mathcal{G}$.

  The server also computes a verification value $V = \mathcal{F}_K(T, d$ moves over f configurations $)$ where T is the time stamp associated with the client visit. The server sends the goal configurations chosen $G_k \in \mathcal{G}, |\mathcal{G}| = f$, corresponding initial configurations P_k, checksums $C_j, 1 \leq j \leq d$, V, and T to the client.

- PUZZLE SOLVING: The client uses the pattern database and performs a guided search from each P_k. The client solves all the initial configurations simultaneously. This implies that the client first infers the right set of moves $M_j^k, \forall G_k \in \mathcal{G}$ for a given difficulty level $j, d \geq j \geq 1$ such that the checksum over those moves matches C_j. Then he proceeds to do the same for the next level $j - 1$. This procedure is followed until the client reaches the goal configurations $G_k \in \mathcal{G}$. The client returns T, V and the d moves over these f initial configurations to the server.

- PUZZLE VERIFICATION: The server verifies that the d moves for all the f Sliding Tile problems sent by the client are correct using the verification value $V \stackrel{?}{=} \mathcal{F}_K(T, d$ moves over f configurations $)$.

If b is the brute force branching factor of the problem, then in the worst case, the time complexity of our multiple goals construction is $O((b - c)^f d)$ where c is a constant that depends on the number of paths pruned by the pattern database heuristic at a given horizontal level.

Experimental Analysis. We now evaluate this construction using a pool of 100 configurations for the 2 x 4 Sliding Tile problem on the machines given in Table 1. The pattern database for 100 configurations took approximately 30 minutes to build on M6 indicating that the database must be created offline. Note, however, that this is a one time cost. The database occupies around 169MB of the main memory and cannot be cached given that typical cache sizes are less than 8MB. Figures 7(a) and 7(b) compares the cost for solving a puzzle with a brute force search and a memory bound search against varying horizontal difficulty f. There, the vertical difficulty was set at $d = 20$ which yields a larger pool of 1194 sliding tile puzzles (per goal configuration) to choose from.

Observe that even though the worst case time complexity of brute force is $O(b^f d)$, up to a horizontal difficulty of $f \leq 15$ brute force search is more effective

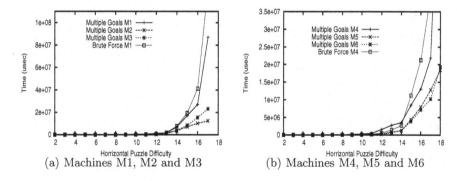

Fig. 7. Multiple Goals vs Brute Force

on all the machines.[4] However, beyond $f = 15$ our memory bound approach is considerably faster suggesting that for $d = 20$ the horizontal difficulty should be set above 15. Moreover, our results show that the time for solving a puzzle is on the order of seconds for $f \in [15, 18]$, indicating that our construction performs as well as or better than prior work. For example, in the solution presented by Waters et. al. [6] a client may need to wait for roughly 20 minutes before she can gain access to server resources. In addition, our solution is considerably better than that of [1] in terms of puzzle solving times, indicating that our approach reduces end user wait time compared to Abadi's approach.

Comparison with HashCash: For completeness, we also compared our results with the CPU bound algorithm, HashCash. Table 2 indicates the time to solve a puzzle with parameters, $f = 16$, $d = 20$ and a pattern database for 100 2 x 4 goal configurations. We compare our results with the time to mint 100, 20 bit hash cash tokens—more than 20 bit tokens take considerably longer to mint. Our results show that with the memory bound approach, the disparity in puzzle solving times across machines is much less when compared to HashCash. Specifically, the maximum ratio of the time to solve a CPU bound puzzle (HashCash) across machines is 9.17, but only 5.64 in the memory bound case. Furthermore, the puzzle solving times are much lower in the memory bound case—our slowest machine (M1) takes 291.88 seconds to mint a HashCash token versus only 33.91 seconds to solve the memory bound puzzle—indicating that our approach may be even better suited for global deployment than HashCash.

Comparison to the Naïve Approach: Unlike the naïve approach, this alternative does meet the *Random Memory Access* property of Definition 1. This is achieved by choosing f goals at *random* from the available pool of goals. This ensures that the pattern databases corresponding to each of these f goals would not be located at contiguous regions in memory. The client is thus forced to access these random locations when solving the Sliding Tile problems simultaneously.

---

[4] On M2, M3 and M5 the bound is at $f = 15$. On machines M4 and M6 brute force is more effective up to $f = 14$ and on M1 the bound is at $f = 13$.

Table 2. Memory Bound vs Hash Cash

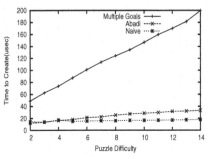

Fig. 8. Puzzle Creation Costs

Machine	Memory Bound (seconds)	Ratio	Hash Cash (seconds)	Ratio
M1	33.91	**5.64**	291.88	**9.17**
M2	14.75	2.45	71.01	2.23
M3	14.2	2.36	152.65	4.8
M4	17.44	2.9	37.9	1.19
M5	8.93	1.48	78.38	2.46
M6	6.01	1	31.8	1

As it stands, the approach does not meet the property of *In-expensive Server Side Cost* of Definition 1. Specifically, the puzzle creation cost in this approach remains high. Figure 8 compares the cost of creating a puzzle to that of Abadi *et. al.* [1]. While the naïve algorithm outperforms Abadi's approach, puzzle creation in the multiple goals approach is 5 times as slow. This high work factor can in itself lead to a DoS attack. In what follows, we show how server side puzzle creation cost can be reduced considerably. We note that in doing so we forgo the *Stateless* property in Definition 1 but achieve the *Relaxed state* property suggesting that our construction is still of practical value.

5.4 Reducing Server Side Cost

In puzzle creation and verification the server side work involves performing d moves on f goal configurations, computing d checksums (hashes), a MAC to compute the verification value V, and a final MAC for puzzle verification. This overhead is unfortunately much higher than [1] which involves only d moves, 1 checksum, a hash for the verification value, and a final hash for puzzle verification. We can address this limitation by having the server create p puzzles offline, and storing these puzzles in a table. Each location of the table simply contains:

1. **Puzzle to be sent to the client.** The goal configurations chosen $G_k \in \mathcal{G}, |\mathcal{G}| = f$, corresponding initial configurations P_k, checksums $C_j, 1 \leq j \leq d$
2. **Solution to Puzzle.** The d moves for the f goal configurations $G_k \in \mathcal{G}, |\mathcal{G}| = f$

On a client visit, the server computes the time stamp T associated with the visit and generates a random number R. The server computes an index into the table I choosing $\log(p)$ bits of $\mathcal{F}_K(T, R)$ deterministically. Recall that $\mathcal{F}_K(\cdot)$ is a pseudo random function and K is the server's secret key. The server sends to the client, T, R and the puzzle at index I. The client returns the solution to the puzzle with T and R and the server simply recomputes the index I and verifies that the solution sent by the client matches the solution at index I. In doing so, we reduce the online server work for puzzle creation and verification to computing two MAC's per client connection. This server work is a slight improvement over Abadi *et. al* which adds additional online work on the server

Table 3. Server storage per puzzle

State Table Items	Storage (bytes)
16 Goal Configurations	32
16 Initial Configurations	32
20 Checksums	400
Puzzle Solution	320
(20 moves for	
16 configurations)	
Total Storage per Puzzle	784

Table 4. Memory Read Time

Machine	Read Time (μsec)
M1	0.27
M2	0.18
M3	0.20
M4	0.27
M5	0.26
M6	0.15

for computing the d moves and the checksum over the path. Furthermore, this approach outperforms that of Dwork *et. al.* [2] which adds additional overhead on the server side during puzzle verification.

In the following discussion we show how an upper bound on the parameter p is obtained, depending on the expected server load.

Setting the state parameters: Similarly to [3], we assume that the server issues puzzles to defend against TCP SYN-flooding attacks. Let τ denote the total time for the client server protocol, including the time for which the TCP buffer slot is reserved. Let the server buffer contain p additional slots for legitimate TCP connections when under attack. Note that the client induces at least fd memory accesses when solving a puzzle. Hence, to solve p puzzles an adversary will take at least pfd time steps. To mount a successful attack the adversary must solve p puzzles in τ seconds. If m denotes the number of memory accesses that an adversary can perform per second, then to prevent a flooding attack p should be set to $\frac{\tau m}{fd}$. This is an upper bound on p, because fd is the minimum number of memory accesses required to solve a given puzzle.

Assuming that a client server connection takes around $\tau = 150$ seconds [3] and that the average read time is $0.2\mu sec$ (see Table 4), then this allows for $m = 5000000$ accesses per second. Hence, for $d = 20$ and $f = 16$ a maximum of $p = 2,500,000$ puzzles need to be created offline. Additionally, each puzzle requires the server to store 784 bytes of information (see Table 3). Under these parameters the resulting state table is at most 1.96 GB, which can be easily stored in the main memory of a storage server. This confirms that our construction is practical.

5.5   Improving Client Side Cost

Earlier we noted that the pattern database for heuristic values corresponding to 100 goal configurations is approximately 169 MB in size. For some devices, however, 169 MB is prohibitively large. As such, it is desirable to have a method by which the pool of configurations available stays the same, but the size of the pattern database is reduced. Specifically, it would be ideal if a given pattern database could be used for multiple goal configurations. Intuitively, we can do so as follows: assume that a client has a pattern database for goal configuration G. Our task is to adapt this pattern database for goal configuration G'. One way of achieving this is by providing the client a hint in the form of the relative distance r (either positive or negative) between G and G'. The client augments the heuristic values stored in the table with r when performing the guided search to the goal G'. In this case, the protocol steps are now as follows:

- PUZZLE CREATION: The client and server have an agreed upon pool of goal states $\{G_0 \ldots G_n\}$. The client maintains pattern database corresponding to these goal states. The server picks f goal states at random from the pool (say $\mathcal{G}$ contains these f goals) and performs a set of d moves from the f goals in $\mathcal{G}$ to arrive at the corresponding initial configurations. This operation is the same as presented in Section 5.3. The server also performs a set of r moves from the randomly chosen goals to the actual goal states $\mathcal{G}'$. The checksum is computed over all levels starting from the actual goal states up to the initial configurations. Along with this puzzle the server sends a hint, r, which is the distance between the actual goal states in $\mathcal{G}'$ and the database goal states in $\mathcal{G}$ and the verification value V as before.
- PUZZLE SOLVING: The client performs a guided search as before, but also augments the heuristic values with this relative distance, r, when deciding which path should be followed.
- PUZZLE VERIFICATION: The server uses the verification value V to verify that the $d + r$ moves for all the f Sliding Tile problems are correct.

Adding relative distance thus allows the client to use the same pattern database for multiple goal configurations, and still meets all the properties of Definition 1. Additionally, this enhancement provides more flexibility in controlling vertical difficulty of a puzzle. Furthermore, the simplicity of this extension is an added benefit of our algorithmic approach.

We argue that considering both the client and the server side improvements the multiple goals construction offers a viable memory bound puzzle construction.

6   Security Analysis

In this section we informally justify the claims that our constructions meet the (security) properties outlined in Section 2. Note that the justifications assume a computationally bounded adversary $\mathcal{A}$.

Claim 1. *The Sliding Tile problem is more efficiently solved with a memory bound approach (i.e., A^* with pattern database heuristic) compared to the best known CPU bound approaches (to date).*

Korf *et.al* [11] showed that memory based heuristics for this class of problem provide a significant reduction in search time at the cost of increasing the available memory. Specifically, if n denotes the number of states in the problem space and m the amount of memory used for storing the heuristic values, then the running time t of A^* is governed by the expression $t \approx n/m$. This analysis was later revisited by Holte *et. al.* [22] who subsequently showed a linear relation between

$log(t)$ and $log(m)$. Specifically, as m increases, the number of states explored in the heuristic search diminishes, which inherently reduces the running time. These results [11, 22] show that memory bound heuristics are indeed the most efficient method to date to reduce search time, and so we argue that Claim 1 is satisfied. To address the security of the underlying approach we first restate the properties of a pseudo random function [26].

Definition 2. *A cryptographically secure pseudorandom function $\mathcal{F}_K(\cdot)$ is an efficient algorithm that when given an l-bit key, K, maps n-bit argument x to an m-bit string such that it is infeasible to distinguish $\mathcal{F}_K(x)$ for random K from a truly random function.*

Claim 2. *The multiple goals scheme is secure against an adversary, $\mathcal{A}$, in the random oracle model as long as Claim 1 holds and the verification value, V, is the output of a pseudorandom function.*

Following from Claim 1, and assuming that the pattern database heuristic is computed using a one-to-one mapping between the abstract and actual state space (see Section 5.1), then $\mathcal{A}$ can not solve the puzzle faster using a CPU bound approach. Furthermore, even though $\mathcal{A}$ can perform multiple queries to the random oracle, it is computationally hard to determine information about the underlying moves from C_i. In addition since V is computed using a pseudo random function $\mathcal{F}_K(\cdot)$, it is difficult for $\mathcal{A}$ to determine the moves, considering that K is a secret random key of the server.

Claim 3. *A parallelizable solver can not solve the puzzle more efficiently than a brute force approach when puzzle difficulty is set appropriately.*

To see why that is the case, assume that $\mathcal{A}$ uses multiple processes to simultaneously solve the multiple goal configurations. Note that in order to arrive at a correct solution, the moves obtained by each process must collectively match the checksum. In other words, given the set of moves obtained by each process, $\mathcal{A}$ needs to determine the correct permutation of these moves that will match the given checksum. However, the process of determining the correct set is essentially a brute force search, which we showed to be ineffective for $d = 20$ and $f > 15$.

7   Conclusion

In this paper we introduce the first heuristic search based memory bound puzzle, and present several constructions accompanied by rigorous experimental analysis. Our constructions address the issues of non-reusable solutions, random memory access, and easily parametrized client and server-side tuning. Additionally, we present several improvements to our multiple goals construction that limit server and client side overhead. From the client's perspective, we also address a major concern regarding limited memory on constrained clients such as PDAs, and present an enhancement that allows the client to use the same pattern database for multiple goals—without violating the general properties of client puzzles. Our client puzzle protocol is interactive and hence is applicable to defend against DoS attacks such as TCP SYN flooding. Exploring methods to extend our construction to defend against spam and DDoS attacks remains a possible area of future work.

Acknowledgements

We thank Patrick McDaniel and Seny Kamara for their invaluable feedback on this research. We also thank the anonymous reviewers for their insightful comments on this paper. This work is funded by the NSF grant CNS-0524252.

References

1. Abadi, M., Burrows, M., Manasse, M., Wobber, T.: Moderately hard, memory-bound functions. In: Proceedings of Network and Distributed Systems Security Symposium, San Diego, California, USA. (February 2003) 107–121
2. Dwork, C., Goldberg, A., Naor, M.: On memory-bound functions for fighting spam. In: Proceedings of the 23rd Annual International Cryptology Conference. (2003) 426–444
3. Juels, A., Brainard, J.: Client puzzles: A cryptographic countermeasure against connection depletion attacks. In: Proceedings of Networks and Distributed Security Systems. (February 1999) 151–165
4. Dean, D., Stubblefield, A.: Using client puzzles to protect TLS. In: Proceedings of the 10th USENIX Security Symposium. (August 2001) 1–8
5. Wang, X., Reiter, M.K.: Defending against Denial-of-Service attacks with puzzle auctions. In: Proceedings of the IEEE Symposium on Security and Privacy, IEEE Computer Society (2003) 78–92
6. Waters, B., Juels, A., Halderman, J.A., Felten, E.W.: New client puzzle outsourcing techniques for DoS resistance. In: Proceedings of the 11th ACM conference on Computer and Communications Security. (2004) 246–256
7. Bernstein, D.J.: SYN cookies (1996) http://cr.yp.to/syncookies.html.
8. Floyd, S., Jacobson, V.: Random early detection gateways for congestion avoidance. IEEE/ACM Transactions on Networking **1(4)** (1993) 397–413
9. Loyd, S.: Mathematical Puzzles of Sam Loyd. Dover (1959) Selected and Edited by Martin Gardner.
10. Singmaster, D.: Notes on Rubik's Magic Cube. Enslow Pub Inc. (1981)
11. Korf, R.: Finding Optimal Solutions to Rubik's Cube Using Pattern Databases. In: Proceedings of the 14th National Conference on Artificial Intelligence and 9th Innovative Applications of Artificial Intelligence Conference, Rhode Island, AAAI Press/MIT Press (July 1997) 700–705
12. Hern'advolgyi, I.T., Holte, R.C.: Experiments with automatically created memory-based heuristics. In: Proceedings of the 4th International Symposium on Abstraction, Reformulation, and Approximation, London, UK, Springer-Verlag (2000) 281–290
13. Bocan, V.: Threshold puzzles: The evolution of DoS-resistant authentication. Periodica Politechnica, Transactions on Automatic Control and Computer Science **49(63)** (2004)

14. Merkle, R.C.: Secure communications over insecure channels. Communications of ACM **21(4)** (April 1978) 294–299
15. Back, A.: Hash cash - A Denial of Service Counter-Measure. Technical report (2002) http://www.hashcash.org/.
16. Wang, X., Reiter, M.K.: Mitigating bandwidth-exhaustion attacks using congestion puzzles. In: Proceedings of the 11th ACM conference on Computer and Communications Security, New York, NY, USA, ACM Press (2004) 257–267
17. Rosenthal, D.S.H.: On the cost distribution of a memory bound function. Computing Research Repository **cs.CR/0311005** (2003)
18. Hart, P.E., Nilsson, N.J., Raphael, B.: A formal basis for the heuristic determination of minimum cost paths. IEEE Transactions on Systems Science and Cybernetics **4(2)** (1968) 100–107
19. Hart, P.E., Nilsson, N.J., Raphael, B.: Correction to a formal basis for the heuristic determination of minimum cost paths. ACM SIGART Bulletin (37) (1972) 28–29
20. Parberry, I.: A real-time algorithm for the $(n^2 - 1)$-puzzle. Information Processing Letters **56**(1) (1995) 23–28
21. Culberson, J.C., Schaeffer, J.: Searching with pattern databases. In: Advances in Artificial Intelligence, 11th Biennial Conference of the Canadian Society for Computational Studies of Intelligence, Springer (1996) 402–416
22. Holte, R.C., Hern'advolgyi, I.T.: A space-time tradeoff for memory-based heuristics. In: Proceedings of the 16th national conference on Artificial Intelligence and the 11th Innovative Applications of Artificial Intelligence conference, Menlo Park, CA, USA, American Association for Artificial Intelligence (1999) 704–709
23. FIPS: The Keyed-Hash Message Authentication Code (HMAC). (2002) http://csrc.nist.gov/publications/fips/fips198/fips-198a.pdf.
24. Korf, R.E.: Recent progress in the design and analysis of admissible heuristic functions. In: Proceedings of the 17th National Conference on Artificial Intelligence and 12th Conference on Innovative Applications of Artificial Intelligence, AAAI Press / The MIT Press (2000) 1165–1170
25. Korf, R.E., Reid, M.: Complexity analysis admissible heuristic search. In: Proceedings of the 15th national/10th conference on Artificial Intelligence/Innovative Applications of Artificial intelligence, Menlo Park, CA, USA, American Association for Artificial Intelligence (1998) 305–310
26. Goldreich, O., Goldwasser, S., Micali, S.: How to construct random functions. J. ACM **33**(4) (1986) 792–807

Effect of Malicious Synchronization

Mun Choon Chan, Ee-Chien Chang, Liming Lu, and Peng Song Ngiam

Department of Computer Science,
National University of Singapore
{chanmc, changec, luliming, ngiampen}@comp.nus.edu.sg

Abstract. We study the impact of malicious synchronization on computer systems that serve customers periodically. Systems supporting automatic periodic updates are common in web servers providing regular news update, sports scores or stock quotes. Our study focuses on the possibility of launching an effective low rate attack on the server to degrade performance measured in terms of longer processing time and request drops due to timeouts. The attackers are assumed to behave like normal users and send one request per update cycle. The only parameter utilized in the attack is the timing of the requests sent. By exploiting the periodic nature of the updates, a small number of attackers can *herd* users' update requests to a cluster and arrive in a short period of time. Herding can be used to discourage new users from joining the system and to modify the user arrival distribution, so that the subsequent *burst attack* will be effective. While the herding based attacks can be launched with a small amount of resource, they can be easily prevented by adding a small random component to the length of the update interval.

Keywords: Network security, Distributed Denial of Service (DDoS) attacks, low rate DDoS attack, synchronization, periodicity, herding.

1 Introduction

There are many applications in the Internet that utilize periodic updates. Some common examples are stock quote update, news update and sport score update. Less common examples, but gaining popularity, are web cameras that provide images of highways, scenic views, or various sites under surveillance. Popular news web sites like CNN (www.cnn.com), Wall Street Journal (www.wsj.com) and The New York Times (www.nytimes.com) perform automatic refresh every 1800s, 900s and 900s respectively. For sport events, many sport related web sites provide periodic score updates, commonly in the intervals of 30s, 60s or 90s. In global events like the Olympics, tremendous amount of traffic reaches a relatively small number of servers for periodic updates. In this paper, we study the potential of malicious synchronization on such systems.

The main role of periodic updates is to "spread" the users over the update interval, so as to obtain a trade-off between the server's resources and timeliness of the service. An implicit assumption is that since users arrive randomly, it is likely the arrivals are also randomly distributed over the update interval.

J. Zhou, M. Yung, and F. Bao (Eds.): ACNS 2006, LNCS 3989, pp. 114–129, 2006.

In general, periodic updates can be performed in an *absolute* or *relative* manner. In absolute periodic update, once a user begins an update at T_0, subsequent updates are performed at time T_i^a, $i = 1, 2, 3...$, where $T_i^a = T_0 + i * P$ and P is the update period. On the other hand, in relative update, the next update is scheduled P seconds after the completion of the current update. Hence, $T_i^r = T_{i-1}^r + N_i + P$, where N_i is a positive component that reflects the network and processing delays. Relative update is easy to implement and is the common approach used. Many web-pages evoke automatic updates using the Refresh META tag. For instance, including the following line in a web-page automatically refreshes the page every 30 seconds in a relative manner.

```
<meta http-equiv="Refresh" content="30">
```

Relative update is not only easy to implement; in the absence of maliciously synchronized requests, it has an implicit adaptive behavior in response to various load levels and the distribution of initial user arrivals. Through the self-correction mechanism, it is more stable and outperforms the absolute update, as will be shown in Section 4.

However, the adaptivity of relative update can be exploited by attackers. Through a process of *herding*, a small number of attackers can gather a significant portion of the normal users to arrive in a relatively small interval, causing temporary overload, even though the average load over the entire update period is low. As a result, some new users may receive highly degraded service and decide to leave the system. Furthermore, herding can condition the user arrival distribution so that subsequent Denial-of-Service attacks can be effective, even with a small number of attackers. The combined herd-burst attack can be executed even when each attacker adheres to the normal application semantics, without excessively consuming resources. Such behavior makes detection very difficult. The only "tool" needed by the attackers is the timing of the request arrivals. Experiments show that herding attacks can be successful even when the total users and attackers load is only a fraction of the server capacity.

The rest of the paper is organized as the following. In Section 2, the related work on DDoS and synchronization problems in the network is presented. In Section 3, the model of periodic update is presented. In Section 4, the behavior of relative update and its advantage over absolute update in high load condition is examined. The herding behavior and related attacks are discussed in Sections 5 and 6. Implementation results on test-bed are presented in Section 7. Finally, a prevention measure to stop such attacks is described in Section 8 and the conclusion is drawn in Section 9.

2   Related Work

One of the most prevalent forms of network attacks is Distributed Denial of Service (DDoS) attack. In DDoS, many compromised hosts send a large amount of network traffic to the victim network elements such that the resources of the elements are exhausted and the performance seen by legitimate users is severely degraded. A comprehensive overview of common DDoS attacks can be found in [1].

Normal DDoS attacks are very different from the attacks described in this paper. Usually in a DDoS attack, the amount of attack traffic is extremely high which easily overwhelms the victims. Hence, DDoS defense mechanisms always assume that they are operating in an overloaded system. However, the attacks to be presented are effective even when the total traffic from attackers and users is a fraction of the system capacity. In this sense, they are similar to the low rate attacks described in [2] and [3]. In [2], a low rate attack designed to disrupt TCP connections is proposed. By sending a burst of well-timed packets, this attack is able to create packet loss and retransmission timeout for certain TCP flows (in particular, those with small RTTs). The signature for such an attack is the existence of a "square wave". Defense mechanisms like [4] have been proposed to detect such attacks. In [3], the attack proposed degrades the performance by disrupting the feedback mechanism of a control system, with a small amount of attack traffic. Interestingly, the authors also made the observation that the vulnerabilities resulting from adaptation of dynamics are potentially serious. The example used for illustration is a bottleneck queue with Active Queue Management(AQM) employing Random Early Detection (RED). The attack effectiveness is measured in terms of the reduction of quality (RoQ) compared to the original system. The impact of our attacks is similar to [2] and [3] in that using only low rate attack traffic, the victim's service is disrupted; and that the affected users experiencing prolonged delay are driven to leave the system.

The proposed attacks rely on the periodicity and synchronization of update requests. Risks caused by periodicity and synchronization have been explored in domains such as routing updates, NTP and Wireless Sensor Network (WSN) MAC protocols. [5] highlights the problem that periodic routing messages can be synchronized unintentionally, causing significant delay in the routing update. [6] discusses similar problems in ACK compression. It is reported in [7] and [8] that defective NTP configuration can direct a massive amount of synchronized requests at a particular NTP server. As a response, the server can explicitly send a "kiss-of-death" packet, requesting the clients to back off. In [9] and [10], several jamming attacks against representative WSN MAC protocols are presented. In these attacks, the sensor's sleep-listen schedule and the temporal pattern in packet inter-arrivals are exploited to create collisions energy efficiently. In [10], the proposed solutions include the use of link layer encryption to hide the schedule, spread spectrum hardware and TDMA.

3   Periodic Updates

Figure 1 illustrates a periodic update system. At any time, a new user may join the system; and users existing in the system may periodically send requests for updates, or leave the service. The delay of a request is measured as the duration between the initiation of the request and the reception of the reply by the user. In the case of *relative update*, after the request is served, the user waits for T seconds before sending the update request. Due to network delay and the service time, the actual interval between two update requests is more than T. In the

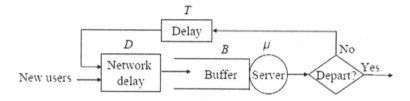

Fig. 1. Periodic updates

case of *absolute update*, the time between consecutive update request initiations is always T. An attacker behaves exactly like a user, except for the timing of the requests.

In this paper, two settings are considered:

1. The server's buffer is unlimited and the user requests do not timeout.
2. The server has a finite buffer of size B and a request is dropped when the buffer is full. Timeout occurs when a request is not served within the initial timeout period T_A. Timeout can occur either due to a dropped request or the request waiting for more than T_A seconds in the buffer. After a timeout occurs, the user retransmits his request. In addition, each subsequent timeout period is twice of the previous one. If the user's request is not served after N_T number of timeouts, the user will depart and is considered *lost*.

Below is a summary of the relevant parameters for the model:

- N_A: Number of attackers
- N_U: Number of users
- μ: Mean service time of a request
- T: Update period
- δ: One-way network delay
- B: Buffer size at the server
- N_T: Number of timeouts allowed
- T_A: Initial timeout period
- α: Probability of a user to depart

4   Absolute and Relative Update

Before presenting the low rate attack strategies, we first explore the advantage of relative update over absolute update.

Figure 2 shows the average processing delay vs. the normalized server load, where the normalized server load is computed as $\rho = \mu N_U / T$ and the mean service time $\mu = 50$ ms. For ρ below 0.90, the performances of the absolute and relative updates are very similar and have average processing delays below 0.3s. However, when ρ approaches 1, the average processing delay for absolute update increases rapidly. Yet for relative update, the average delay increases slightly to 0.90s when $\rho = 1$. Even at an extremely high load of $\rho = 1.1$, the average delay is only 2.95 seconds. Such robustness is due to the indirect "increase" of the update period by increasing waiting time in the queue.

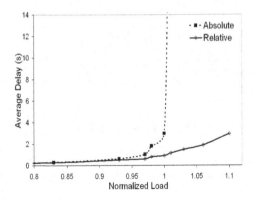

Fig. 2. Comparison of absolute and relative updates

While the self correcting behavior of relative update makes the approach more robust, this dynamic behavior, which is absent in the absolute update, can be exploited by attackers.

5   Herding

5.1   Concept of Herding

Herding allows attackers to influence the timing of the users such that the users become part of the attack. The herding action is executed by having a small amount of attackers performing *approximately synchronized* updates. Note that it is not necessary to have perfect synchronization. The idea of herding is illustrated in Figure 3. User arrivals are (initially) distributed over the update period. In each herding round, the attackers delay their update time by a duration of T_{off} in addition to the usual update period T.

To simplify the explanation, μ is assumed to be constant, $\delta = 0$, and the attackers are perfectly synchronized. Let N_A attackers commence herding at

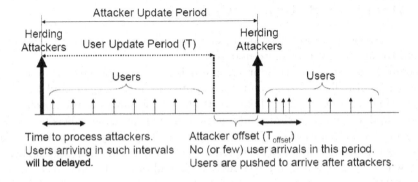

Fig. 3. The herding behavior

time T_h and send N_A simultaneous requests to the server. The buffer size B is assumed to be large enough that there is no request drop. Under such a deterministic scenario, all attacker requests arrive at the server at the same time and for a period of μN_A, only attackers are served. Users arriving during this period are queued behind the attackers. Their request completion times become more clustered. Since the updates are performed in a *relative* manner, the compact completion times entail compact update requests in subsequent rounds. In fact, a period of μN_A is removed from serving users in each herding round.

By setting $T_{off} \leq \mu N_A$, the attackers commence the next herding action at time $T_h + T + T_{off}$. With a constant μ and $\delta = 0$, there will be no user update requests between $T_h + T$ and $T_h + T + \mu N_A$. A herding offset of $T_{off} = \mu N_A$ per round for the herding scheme in this static scenario is the most efficient. A smaller offset reduces the speed of the herding process whereas a larger offset lets some users be served before the attackers and escape from the cluster of compact request arrivals.

Formally, we say that a user request q is *herded* if there is no delay between the completion time of the previously served request $\widetilde{q}$ and the time the server starts to serve q. Furthermore, the previously served request $\widetilde{q}$ is either (1) from an attacker, or (2) from another herded user.

In a probabilistic environment, the network delay and the service time are not deterministic. In addition, the number of users joining or departing the service varies. Hence, more analysis is required to determine the optimal offset.

5.2   Modelling of Herding Behavior

In this section, we present a model for the herding behavior. Such model is useful in estimating the optimal attack offset T_{off} and monitoring the effectiveness of herding. We first consider the effect of variable network and processing delay, and next handle the case with new and departed users. We make the simplification that the attackers are synchronized. This is a reasonable approximation as the attackers can estimate the network delay they experience. In the simulation, we evaluate the impact of synchronization error on the performance.

The two main components in the model are the *escape probability*, the probability that herded users become no longer herded, and the average number of freshly herded users in a period.

Variable Network and Processing Delay. For each herded user, we want to estimate its escape probability which depends on the duration between the arrival of the request and that of the attacker requests. Suppose the attackers arrive at T_0, they will return at $T_1 = T_0 + T + T_{off} + \delta$.

Consider the requests in the current period. Let the i-th herded user served after the attackers be u_i and its service time after T_0 be t_i. Hence, for u_i, it will have its service completed at $T_0 + t_i$ and will return at $T_0 + t_i + T + 2\delta$. The user u_i will not be herded in the next update period if it arrives (early) before the attackers, therefore if $T_0 + t_i + T + 2\delta < T_1$. The converse may not be true but the chances that u_i escapes by arriving late is low. Therefore, we can approximate,

$$Pr(u_i \text{ escapes}) = Pr(t_i + \delta < T_{\text{off}}). \tag{1}$$

Let us assume that the processing time is exponentially distributed with mean μ. The distribution of t_i is the Gamma distribution where

$$f_n(t) = \lambda e^{-\lambda t} \frac{(\lambda t)^{(n-1)}}{(n-1)!} \quad \text{with } n = N_A + i, \lambda = \frac{1}{\mu}. \tag{2}$$

Suppose there are k_1 herded users in the current update period, for a specific N_A, T_{off} and a constant δ, using equation 1, the expected number of users escaping in the next period can be written as

$$esp(k_1) = \sum_{j=1}^{k_1} Pr(u_j \text{ escapes}). \tag{3}$$

Note that the escape probability is heavily dependent on T_{off}. It increases with increasing T_{off} since users are more likely to arrive before the attackers but decreases with increasing δ since the reverse is true.

New and Departed Users. After his request is served, a user may depart with probability $\alpha > 0$. For simplicity, we consider a model where the number of users in an update period is kept constant. In other words, for every user departure during the current period, a new user will join in the next period, and its arrival time is uniformly distributed over $[T_0 + T, T_0 + 2T]$.

Let $r = T_{\text{off}}/T$. Suppose the number of herded users in the current update period is k_1, the expected number of users captured in the next period can be approximated by

$$cap(k_1) = r\alpha k_1 + r(N_U - k_1), \tag{4}$$

where the first term gives the average number of new users who join and are captured immediately; the second term gives the average number of un-herded users that are captured in each round. Assuming a small α, the first term increases with i but the second term decreases with i. Overall, as i increases, $cap(k_1)$ decreases.

H_i, the expected number of herded users in the i-th update period can be computed using equations 3 and 4. We calculate H_i iteratively as

$$H_i = H_{i-1} - esp(H_{i-1}) + cap(H_{i-1}). \tag{5}$$

5.3   Simulation Results on Herding

In this section, we use simulations to demonstrate the effect of herding. For the experiments reported here and in Section 7, the parameters are set as (unless otherwise specified): the update period $T = 30s$, the number of attackers

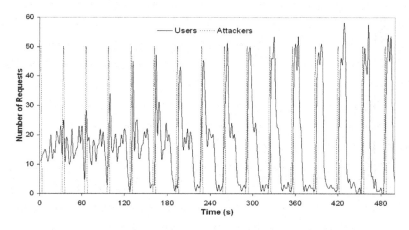

Fig. 4. Request arrivals with herding

$N_A = 50$ and the number of users $N_U = 250$. The service time of a request is
exponentially distributed with mean $\mu = 50$ms. So the normalized server load is
$\rho = (250 + 50)0.050/30 \approx 50\%$. The herding offset is chosen as 2.25s, which is
slightly less than $\mu N_A = 50 \times 50$ms. In addition, in every update period, 5% of
new users join the system and 5% of existing users leave.

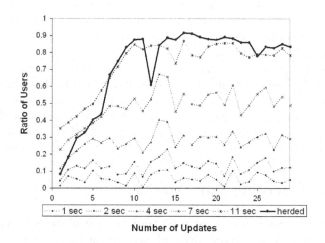

Fig. 5. The effect of herding as ratio of users herded

Figure 4 illustrates the user behavior during herding. As herding progresses,
user requests become increasingly clustered after the attacker requests.

Figure 5 presents the progress of herding in each period as the ratio of users
clustered. The graph shows 6 lines, each line corresponds to the percentage of
users herded or arriving within 1, 2, 4, 7 and 11 seconds after the attackers.
Initially, user arrivals are uniformly distributed. The ratio of herded users gradually increases to 90% after 10 rounds and stabilizes. The partial escape of

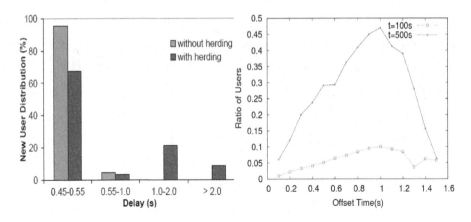

Fig. 6. The effect of herding on new user delay

Fig. 7. Impact of T_{off}

users from herding is caused by variation in the network delay and the server's processing time. Figure 6 compares the delay experienced by new users when herding is present and absent. For the case with herding, the delay experienced by new users is measured after 10 rounds of herding, when the herding effect has stabilized. When herding is absent, the new user delays average at 0.50s. With herding, close to 40% of the new users experience prolonged delay. Among which, 22.1% has delay greater than 1.5s and 8.8% has delay greater than 2s.

The choice of herding offset T_{off} greatly impacts the effectiveness of herding, because a small T_{off} takes much longer to herd the users; while a large T_{off} allows many users to escape herding. Figure 7 shows how the ratio of herded users varies with different T_{off} after 100 and 500 seconds of herding. In this simulation, the number of attackers $N_A = 100$, and the expected service time $\mu = 10$ms ($\mu N_A = 1$s). The result shows that when $T_{\text{off}} = 0.1$s, herding is too slow while the effect of herding decreases dramatically for T_{off} larger than 1.2s. Herding is most effective when T_{off} approximates μN_A, which is between 0.9 to 1.1s in this scenario.

6   Effect of Herding and Attacks

Herding achieved two results. Firstly, by herding most of the users into a much smaller time interval, the average delay of many normal users increases substantially. In particular, the delay experienced by new users who arrive during the herding interval will be excessive. In the context of web server, the new users requesting for web pages are more sensitive to delays. A noticeable delay is sufficient to discourage a new user from browsing further. Recent studies show that a user usually decides whether he satisfies with the web page quality within 50ms [11]. Hence, herding alone is sufficient to turn away a significant number of new users.

Secondly, by making many users arrive in a small time interval, the impact of a burst attack can be magnified. In other words, herding can be used as a means to "condition" the user distribution so that subsequent attacks can be effectively carried out.

In the previous discussion, we assume the buffer size is unlimited. As mentioned in Section 3, limited buffer can lead to request drop, entailing timeouts and retransmissions, which in turn leads to user lost. In the next few subsections, we will consider limited buffer when comparing three attacks: *flood*, *burst* and *herd-burst* attacks.

6.1 Attacks Without Herding

DDoS attacks are typified by *flood* attacks. In such attacks, a large amount of attack traffic is generated to overwhelm the server. Success of such attacks is achieved when the combined load from the users and attackers exceeds the server capacity.

In a *burst* attack, attackers are synchronized and the attack packets are sent at the same time to the server. Such attack achieves short term congestion, yet it still requires a large amount of attack traffic for an ongoing congestion.

6.2 Combining Herding and Burst Attack

Intuitively, burst attacks are effective when the aggregated user and attacker request rate is close to or exceeds the system capacity. On the other hand, with herding, short term congestion can be created. This motivates the following herd-burst attack.

The strategy is to alternate herding and burst attack. When herding creates sufficient short term congestion, burst attack can then be used for maximum impact. The attack strategy is presented below:

- Perform herding using N_H ($< N_A$) attackers for R_1 rounds
- Repeat
    - Perform burst attack using N_A attackers
    - Perform herding for R_2 rounds

At the start of the attack, R_1 rounds of herding are performed to increase user density over a short period of time which will help in the later attack stages.

The above attack can be stealth, since during herding, *there is no request drop or excessive processing delay*. Hence, unless details on arrival time are captured and analyzed, it is difficult for the system administrator to notice that the herding process is going on. When the initial "preparation" herding is done, burst attack commences.

Figure 8 shows the result of a herd-burst attack with $R_1 = 20$ and $R_2 = 2$. The simulated duration is 1500 seconds, and the parameters are $N_H = 100$, $N_A = 300$, $B = 100$ and $T = 30$s. The μ and δ are exponentially distributed with mean 10ms and 50ms respectively. The initial timeout T_A is uniformly distributed between 1s and 2s. Each subsequent timeout value is twice of its previous one. The user always retransmits in case of timeout. Three lines are shown in Figure 8, indicating the percentage of users experiencing processing delay of more than

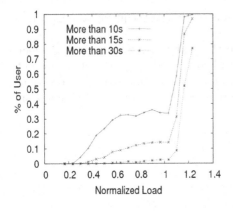
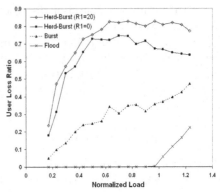

Fig. 8. Delay of user access   **Fig. 9.** Comparing user request lost

10, 15 and 30 seconds at least once. For example, at a normalized load of 60%, 40% of the users experience a processing delay of more than 10s, 8% experience delay of more than 15s and 0.5% experience delay of more than 30s. Depending on the application level timeout specified or user impatience, the number of users who feel unsatisfied with the service and leave the system can range from 0.5% to 40% if the application level timeout is between 10s to 30s.

6.3   Comparison of Herd-Burst, Flood and Burst Attacks

In this section, we compare the performance of the proposed attack to the flooding and the burst attacks. For the herd-burst attack, there are two experiments. The first experiment sets R_1 to 0, meaning there is no pre-herding and the alternating herd-attack starts immediately. In the second experiment, herding is first performed for 20 rounds. The number of users, N_U, is varied from 200 to 3400. Therefore, the normalized load, $\rho = (N_A + N_U)\mu/T$, varies from 0.17 to 1.23. The rest of the parameter values follow those from the previous subsection for all attacks, except $N_T = 1$, that is, one retransmission is allowed, a user will be lost if the retransmission also timeouts. This definition is used in the rest of the simulation in this section.

Figure 9 illustrates that the proposed herd-burst strategy is much more effective. With $R_1 = 0$, $R_2 = 2$, the user lost rate is 72.2% at 60% load. When 20 rounds of pre-herding are performed to cluster users ($R_1 = 20$), the attack efficiency is improved to 82.7% user loss at 60% load.

6.4   Effect of Network Delay and Attacker Synchronization Error

In this section, we study the effect of network delay and synchronization error on the effectiveness of herding.

Figure 10 shows the impact of increasing the network delay variation. The network delay is exponentially distributed with mean varying from 0ms to 200ms. As expected, as network delay variation increases, the attack efficiency decreases.

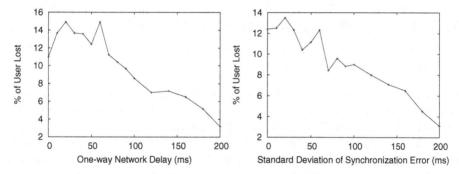

Fig. 10. Impact of network delay

Fig. 11. Impact of attacker synchronization error

In Figure 11, the attacker synchronization error is assumed to have a normal
distribution with 0 mean. The standard deviation of the distribution is varied
from 0ms to 200ms. The result is similar to the variation in the network delay.
The attack efficiency remains high for standard deviation less than 50ms.

6.5   Effect of Buffer Size

In previous experiments, we assume that the buffer size is known and herding
can be performed by sending the exact number of attacker requests. However,
such values may not be available and needs to be estimated by probing. Figure 12
shows the impact of estimation errors in the server buffer size, with the attacker
assuming that $B = 100$. For herding to work correctly, it is important for the
attackers to not over-estimate the buffer size as it will result in missing too many
users in the herding process. The figure shows that if the buffer is less than 60,
the attackers are progressing too quickly and too many users are left behind.
The resulting lost rate is 0. The herding process is sufficiently robust such that
when the actual buffer size is between 80 to 120, the lost rate remains high,

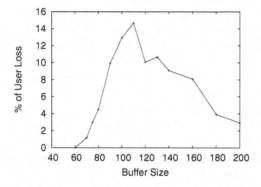

Fig. 12. Impact of buffer size

between 10% to 14%. However, if the buffer size is beyond 120, attack efficiency drops. When the buffer size reaches 200, the loss rate drops to 3%.

7   Results on Test-Bed

In order to validate that herding can indeed be carried out in practice, we repeat the experiments done in Section 5.3 using PlanetLab (http://www.planet-lab.org). 10 nodes from U.S.A, Canada, Spain, Italy and Singapore were used to make the experiments as realistic as possible. Attackers and users are emulated on PlanetLab nodes and each node emulates a total of about 30 to 50 users and attackers. Our server is represented by a Java program that places arrived requests in a First-In-First-Out queue. For each request, the server provides some dummy calculations as service.

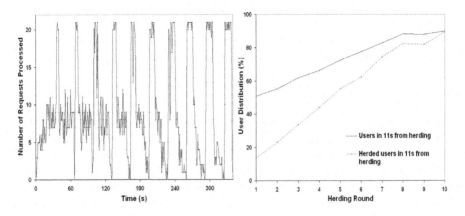

Fig. 13. Number of requests served per second

Fig. 14. The effect of herding

In the first set of experiments, we observe the temporal pattern of user requests during herding. Figure 13 illustrates the serving rate at the server as herding progresses. Observe that after each herding round, herded users are pushed forward. Also notice that the service rate in between peaks is non-zero. This is due to new users entering the system periodically. Figure 14 shows the effect of herding by measuring the percentage of users herded and that arrives within 11s from a herding round. Note that after 10 rounds of herding, almost all users within 11s are herded.

Next, we repeat the experiment with different herding offsets and compare the values after 10 herding rounds. Figure 15 shows the effectiveness of the different offsets for herded users and users arriving within 11s. Note that the optimal herding offset is approximately $\mu N_A = 2.5$s which corresponds to the optimal offset analyzed from the model.

Finally, we conduct another set of experiments to illustrate the effect of herding on new users. As before, in every period, 5% of new users join the system and

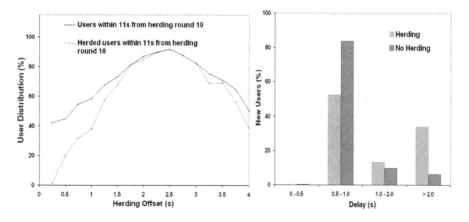

Fig. 15. The effect of herding offset

Fig. 16. Delay experienced by new users

5% of existing users leave the update cycle. Compared to the existing users, a new user is more sensitive to the delay because he initiates the first request. We first conduct herding with 50 attackers for 10 rounds by which the system behavior has stabilized. Next we measure the delay experienced by new users over 30 update periods. We also consider the case in which no herding is performed. Figure 16 shows that with herding, 40% of new users are likely to experience a delay of more than 2s. Compared to Figure 6, measurements from the test-bed display larger delays. This is because the network nodes employed for test-bed experiments have longer links and larger network delay variation to reach the server.

8   A Prevention Approach

In this section, we present an approach to negate the effect of the proposed herd-burst attack. Though the herd-burst attack is shown effective and robust,

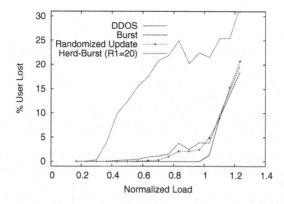

Fig. 17. Effect of adding a randomization component of 3s

it depends on the constant period of updates. In particular, herding relies on the periodicity to work correctly. Therefore, one simple way to prevent herding is to add a small random component with mean 0 to the length of the update interval.

In Figure 17, the same parameter setting used to generate Figure 9 is used. The experiment on herd-burst attack without pre-herding is modified. It is executed over an update period uniformly distributed between 27 and 33 seconds. With such randomization added to the update period, the herding process fails and the user lost rate drops slightly lower than the burst attack. This is because with $R_2 = 2$, the herd-burst attack only burst once every three rounds.

9   Conclusion

Periodic updates can be viewed as a feedback queue whereby the served requests are further delayed before rejoining the queue. Due to the growing popularity of the use of automatic refreshment of web services, it is interesting to investigate such model. In this paper, we first study the advantages of relative update verse absolute update. We show that relative update gives better performance in term of average service delay. More interestingly, we found that relative updates indirectly provides a self-correcting mechanism, and can be stable even when the system is overloaded. Although relative updates provides good performance, potentially it can be manipulated by a small number of attackers. We give a herding strategy whereby a small number of attackers can herd a significant portion of the users to arrive in a small time interval. Such herding can be used as a way to "condition" the request arrival distribution so that subsequent burst attacks can be effectively carried out. It can also be employed to discourage new users from joining the system. The herding can be performed by adhering to the normal application semantics, and thus it is difficult to identify individual attackers. Fortunately, herding can be easily prevented by introducing randomness to the length of the update interval.

References

1. Mirkovic, J.: D-WARD: Source-End Defense Against Distributed Denial-of-Service Attacks. PhD thesis, UCLA (2003)
2. Kuzmanovic, A., Knightly, E.: Low-Rate TCP-Targeted Denial of Service Attacks. Proc. ACM SIGCOMM (2003) 75–86
3. Guirguis, M., Bestavros, A., Matta, I.: Explaining the Transients of Adaptation for RoQ Attacks on Internet Resources. Proc. Int. Conf. Network Protocols (2004) 184–195
4. Sun, H., Lui, John C.S, Yau, David K.Y.: Defending against Low-Rate TCP Attacks: Dynamic Detection and Protection. Proc. Int. Conf. Network Protocols (2004) 196–205
5. Floyd, S., Jacobson, V.: The Synchronization of Periodic Routing Messages. IEEE/ACM Trans. Networking, Vol. 2. (1994) 122–136

6. Mogul, J.: Observing TCP Dynamics in Real Networks. Proc. ACM SIGCOMM (1992) 305–317
7. Plonka, D.: Flawed Routers Flood University of Wisconsin Internet Time Server Netgear Cooperating with University on a Resolution. http://www.cs.wisc.edu/~plonka/netgear-sntp (2003)
8. Mills, David L.: Survivable, Real Time Network Services. DARPA Report (2001)
9. Law, Y., Hartel, P., Hartog, J. den, Havinga, P.: Link-Layer Jamming Attacks on S-MAC. Proc. IEEE 2nd European Workshop on Wireless Sensor Networks (EWSN) (2005) 217–225
10. Law, Y., van Hoesel, L., Doumen, J., Hartel, P., Havinga, P.: Energy-Efficient Link-Layer Jamming Attacks against Wireless Sensor Network MAC Protocols. Proc. 3rd ACM Workshop on Security of Ad Hoc and Sensor Networks (SANS) (2005) 76–88
11. Lindgaard, G., Dudek, C., Fernandes, G., Brown J.: Attention web designers: you have 50 milliseconds to make a good first impression. J. Behaviour & Information Technology, Vol. 25 (2005) 115–126

Misusing Unstructured P2P Systems to Perform DoS Attacks: The Network That Never Forgets

Elias Athanasopoulos[1], Kostas G. Anagnostakis[2], and Evangelos P. Markatos[1]

[1] Institute of Computer Science (ICS)
Foundation for Research & Technology Hellas (FORTH)
{elathan, markatos}@ics.forth.gr
[2] Institute for Infocomm Research, Singapore
kostas@i2r.a-star.edu.sg

Abstract. Unstructured P2P systems have gained great popularity in recent years and are currently used by millions of users. One fundamental property of these systems is the lack of structure, which allows decentralized operation and makes it easy for new users to join and participate in the system. However, the lack of structure can also be abused by malicious users. We explore one such attack, that enables malicious users to use unstructured P2P systems to perform Denial of Service (DoS) attacks to third parties. Specifically, we show that a malicious node can coerce a large number of peers to perform requests to a target host that may not even be part of the P2P network, including downloading unwanted files from a target Web Server. This is a classic form of denial-of-service which also has two interesting characteristics: (a) it is hard to identify the originator of the attack, (b) it is even harder to stop the attack. The second property comes from the fact that certain unstructured P2P systems seem to have a kind of "memory", retaining knowledge about (potentially false) queries for many days. In this paper we present real-world experiments of Gnutella-based DoS attacks to Web Servers. We explore the magnitude of the problem and present a solution to protect innocent victims against this attack.

1 Introduction

With the explosion of file sharing applications and their adoption by large numbers of users, P2P systems exposed a wealth of interesting design problems regarding scalability and security.

In this paper we examine one such problem that may arise from the implicit trust that is inherent in current unstructured P2P systems. We show how a malicious user could launch massive DoS attacks by instructing peers to respond positively to all queries received, pretend to provide all possible files, and pretend to share everything. Such peers usually respond to all queries in order to trick ordinary users to download files which contain garbage, advertisements, or even malware. In this paper we show that the responses provided by such bogus peers may result in DoS attacks to unsuspected victims, which may not even

J. Zhou, M. Yung, and F. Bao (Eds.): ACNS 2006, LNCS 3989, pp. 130–145, 2006.

be part of the P2P network. Indeed, with modest effort we have managed to develop techniques, which, if adopted by bogus peers, can result in DoS attacks to third parties by redirecting a large number of peers to a single target host. In a nutshell, whenever they receive a query, these bogus peers respond by saying that the victim computer has a file that matches the query. As a result, a large number of peers may try to download files from the unsuspected victim, increasing its load significantly. Furthermore, we have developed mechanisms which *trick* this large number of peers to actually download files from the unsuspected victim. To make matters worse, in our methods, the victim does not even need to be part of the P2P network but could also be an ordinary Web Server. Therefore, it is possible for a significant number of peers attempt downloading files from a Web Server, increasing its load and performing the equivalent of a DoS attack.

The rest of this paper is organized as follows. Section 2 presents the architecture of the Gnutella P2P system focusing on the lookup and data transfer process. Section 3 illustrates the techniques we developed to perform DoS attacks by misusing the Gnutella system, and Section 4 presents experiments for the measurement of the effectiveness of the DoS attacks. Section 5 presents an algorithm to protect third parties from Gnutella based DoS attacks. Section 6 provides an overview of related work and Section 7 summarizes our findings and presents directions for further work.

2   Gnutella Architecture

The Gnutella system is an open, decentralized and unstructured P2P system. This Section describes the architecture of the Gnutella system and highlights the basic components that are used as part of the attack.

2.1   Query-QueryHit Exchange Mechanism

Information lookup in the Gnutella system is performed using Query flooding or controlled Query flooding, known as Dynamic Querying. In both cases, nodes broadcast a Query packet, which embeds the search criteria, to some or all of their first-hop neighbors. The Query packet is forwarded to the system until its TTL becomes zero. In each forwarding step the TTL of the Query packet TTL is decremented by one and a "HOPs" counter is incremented. Along the paths on which the Query propagates, every node of the system is free to answer by issuing a QueryHit packet. A QueryHit packet travels back to the originator of the Query following the same path of the Query packet. It is important to note that there is no central mechanism to confirm whether peers generating QueryHit packets actually hold a file that matches the search criteria of the original Query.

A QueryHit packet consists of a standard Gnutella header describing the TTL and HOPs of the packet and the actual QueryHit payload. Among other fields, the QueryHit payload specifies the IP address and the port number of the node holding the requested data file and a list of entries matching the search criteria of the Query. Each entry is formed by the file name of the object, its local

index and sometimes a SHA1 hash, to assist in the parallel download of a file
from multiple locations (e.g., *swarming*). Upon receiving a QueryHit the node
that issued the query can directly connect to the host listed in the QueryHit
packet and try to perform the download. It is important to note that there is
no central authority to verify that the IP address and the port number listed
in the QueryHit packet match the IP address and the port number of the node
issued the QueryHit packet. In addition, a peer may generate QueryHit messages
with a spoofed "HOPs" field, to imitate QueryHits that have been generated by
another peer.

2.2   Data Transfer Protocol

The actual data transfer among two Gnutella peers is performed using an HTTP
based request/response mechanism. Specifically, when a servent receives a Query-
Hit and is willing to download the data file, it connects to the IP address and
port number listed in the QueryHit packet and issues a request that has the
following form:

```
GET /get/<File Index>/<File Name> HTTP/1.1\r\n
User-Agent: Gnutella\r\n
Host: 123.123.123.123:6346\r\n
Connection: Keep-Alive\r\n
Range: bytes=0-\r\n
\r\n
```

On the receiving end, the servent generates a response in the following form:

```
HTTP/1.1 200 OK\r\n
Server: Gnutella\r\n
Content-type: application/binary\r\n
Content-length: 4356789\r\n
\r\n
```

It is obvious that the data transfer process is an HTTP transaction, identical to
those exchanged between Web browsers and Web Servers. One small difference
is the "/get/<File Index>" part of the initial GET request, which is entered
only by Gnutella servents and not by Web browsers.

3   Exploiting Gnutella

The content lookup process and the data transfer mechanism can lead to serious
attacks against the system itself but also against third parties. Malicious users
can exploit the absence of a mechanism for verifying the integrity of the information exchanged among peers and pollute the system with fake information.
In this Section we explore techniques that can lead to DoS attacks against any
machine connected to the Internet and to degradation of the Gnutella system
itself.

3.1 Exploiting the Query-QueryHit Mechanism

As already noted, there is no central mechanism to verify that a node which replies with a QueryHit to a Query is trustworthy. That is, malicious nodes can reply to any Query they receive with a QueryHit which embeds the IP address and the Port number of any remote Server. For example, a malicious node can reply to every Query it receives and redirect peers to another Gnutella peer. In the general case, a QueryHit can embed the IP address and the Port number of any computer machine connected to the Internet, including Web Servers. This may lead a large number of Gnutella peers to connect and try downloading a non-existent data file from the Web Server. The Web Server may respond with an HTTP 404, meaning that it was unable to locate the requested data file. As we will show later in our experiments, Gnutella peers will persistently try to to download the data file from the Web Server, even though they have received an HTTP-level failure message.

3.2 Exploiting the HTTP protocol

A large number of HTTP requests that result in an HTTP 404 response code may not be difficult to handle for a Web Server. The attack can be more efficient if we can force the Gnutella peers to perform an actual download from the Web Server. The download may not even be relevant to their search criteria Server. This can be achieved by embedding a specifically constructed file name in the QueryHit packet. For example, consider that a Query with search criteria "foo bar" is received. The file name:

```
../../live HTTP/1.0\r\n\r\nfoo bar.mp3
```

will be displayed to the user's client as:

```
../../live HTTP/1.0____foo bar.mp3
```

If the user decides to download the above data file, the targeted Web Server will receive a request[1]:

```
GET /get/1/../../live HTTP/1.0\r\n\r\nfoo bar.mp3 HTTP/1.1\r\n
User-Agent: Gnutella\r\n
Host: 123.123.123.123:6346\r\n
Connection: Keep-Alive\r\n
Range: bytes=0-\r\n
\r\n
```

Since any Web Server will try to process the request as soon as it parses the \r\n\r\n sequence, the above request is equivalent to:

```
GET /get/1/../../live HTTP/1.0\r\n\r\n
```

---

[1] Note that we have constructed an HTTP 1.0 request, which is accepted by the majority of current Web Server software.

which, in turn, is equal to:

```
GET /live HTTP/1.0\r\n\r\n
```

Assuming there is a data file with the filename "live" in the Document Root of the targeted Web Server, the tricked Gnutella peers will be forced to download it. Depending on the file size, the Web Server may be unable to cope with the incoming malicious requests.

3.3   Attacking Gnutella

Malicious peers that use this attack are hard to detect by the Gnutella system. A malicious peer can spoof the HOPs field of a Gnutella message and thus hide its origin. Consider that peer A constructs a QueryHit message and sends it to its neighbors, but instead of inserting a HOPs=0 field, it inserts a HOPS=s field. The neighbors of A, upon receiving the QueryHit (which in reality is constructed by A), will think that another peer, s HOPs away from A, has constructed the QueryHit and forwarded it to A.

A peer which receives fake QueryHits may consider the node which constructed these QueryHits as a spammer. Unfortunately, the identity which is embedded in the QueryHit message is not the identity of the peer which constructed the QueryHit message. That is, Gnutella peers believe that it is the victim peer that produces spam messages.

The problem of isolating spam nodes is actively investigated by the developers of most Gnutella clients. To the best of our knowledge, the identification of spammers is currently still a manual process. If some IP addresses of a subnet qualify as belonging to nodes generating spam, the whole subnet is isolated from the system by entering its range to a "black list" used by the Gnutella client. Although this is a slow process requiring human intervention, a few misbehaving nodes can lead to isolation of large subnets, something that an attacker might exploit. This means that an attack to the Gnutella itself can be constructed by producing fake QueryHits, which embed IP addresses of active Gnutella peers that belong to known large subnets. These IP addresses are easy to be collected by crawling the Gnutella system[8].

4   Experimental Results

We performed experiments in order to measure the effect of a DoS attack produced by the Gnutella system to Web Servers of our lab. The Web Server software which we used was the standard pre-configured Apache[2] of the Debian GNU/Linux Operating System[3]. We modified a well-known Gnutella servent[4] to respond to every Query it receives with one and only QueryHit. This policy was one of the fundamental choices that we made, since we wanted to perform an attack with minimal effort. The Web Server was installed on the same host with the Gnutella servent. The Gnutella servent was trying to maintain from 80 up to 100 simultaneous connections to the Gnutella system and besides issuing QueryHits it operated at the ultrapeer level implementing the whole Gnutella protocol as is. In the rest of this Section we present the results of our experiments.

4.1 Simple Query-QueryHit Exploitation

In the first experiment, our malicious servent was replying to every Query it received with one and only QueryHit which embedded a file with advertised size of 3,240,000 bytes. The filename provided in the QueryHit was the product of the concatenation of the search criteria with the ".mp3" extension. That is, a Query for "foo" had as a result a QueryHit for "foo.mp3". Again, following the "least effort" principle, we chose not to create a sophisticated engine that will eventually understand the semantics of the Query, such as the format and size of the file the remote user issuing the Query wants to download. Instead, we chose to have the malicious servent generate QueryHits in the most obvious and naive way.

We connected our malicious servent to Gnutella and let it to answer every incoming Query for a period of two days. Figure 1 presents the requests which were logged in the Apache log file by our Web Server. After careful examination of the Apache log file, we found out that our Web Server had also recorded some Gnutella Handshake requests in addition to HTTP GET requests. That is, our

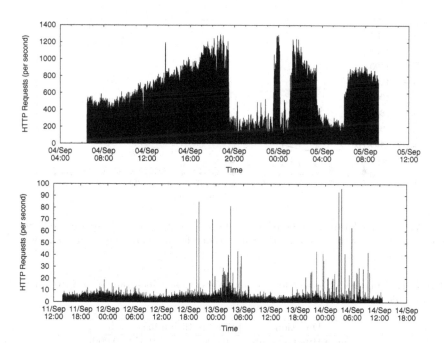

Fig. 1. The rate of HTTP Requests per second that our Web Server recorded. The first graph presents the period that our malicious client was connected to Gnutella. The second one presents the period after over 10 days of the experiment.

Web Server was considered as a good peer to connect to by other peers of the system, since it was advertising that it had a lot of content to provide.

It is important to note that the second graph in Figure 1 depicts the HTTP requests which were logged by our Web Server 10 days after the end of the experiment. We observe that peers that could not receive the content they were looking for, kept on trying for many days. It seems that Gnutella has a kind of "memory", with the information contained in QueryHits having a long lifetime inside the system. It appears that a DoS attack based on generating malicious QueryHit packets is hard to stop, since the Gnutella system will continuously try to access the victim machine. This means that even if the original attacker is discovered and shut down, the attack may still go on.

4.2   Adding HTTP Exploitation

In the next experiment we want to experiment with a DoS attack to a Web Server using a single servent connected to the Gnutella system. We modified our client to create QueryHits that carried filenames constructed in the fashion we explained in Section 3.2. For each incoming Query we constructed a QueryHit with the filename:

```
../../high_quality HTTP/1.0\r\n\r\n search_criteria.mp3
```

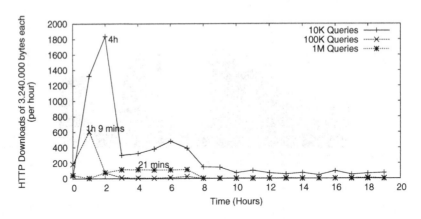

Fig. 2. Download rate (per hour) of a file of 3,240,000 bytes from the Web Server. Each curve has a caption noting the time needed for the malicious client to answer the amount of Queries.

Table 1. Statistics collected for the experiment, in which our Web Server actually serves a file with 3,240,000 bytes

Duration	21 mins	1h 9 mins	4 h
QueryHits Generated	10,000	100,000	1,000.000
Downloads Recorded	696	1,017	6,061
Unique IP Addresses	30	332	1,988

Table 2. Statistics collected for the experiment, in which our Web Server actually serves a file with 0 bytes. Denote that Duration is related to the time period needed by the malicious client to serve the amount of Queries specified in the 2nd row. The last two rows represent information collected for the whole experiment.

Duration	10 mins	1h 10 mins	4 h 30 mins
QueryHits Generated	10,000	100,000	1,000,000
Downloads Recorded	133	10,639	258,769
Unique IP Addresses	10	192	2,698

Our Web Server had a file with filename "high_quality" with an actual size of 3,240,000 bytes in its Document Root directory. That is, every request performed by a Gnutella peer had as a result an actual file download of 3,240,000 bytes.

We performed the experiments for 10K Queries, 100K Queries and 1M Queries respectively. That is, our malicious servent was generating a fixed amount of QueryHit packets in each experiment. The attacked Web Server was instantiated on a new port before the beginning of each experiment. Note that our Web Server was isolated from all other traffic, since it was always listening to non-standard port numbers. The download requests per hour recorded by our Web Server are presented in Figure 2.

We observe that in contrast with the previous experiment, the request rate per hour is quite low. This is obvious, since the Web Server is quickly saturated and thus unable to serve all incoming requests. That is, many requests are not recorded because they never manage to complete the TCP/IP handshake with the Web Server.

One could argue that the decrease of the request rate is due to our HTTP exploitation trick. However, we have found that is not the case. We repeated the experiment but instead of using a file of 3,240,000 bytes we used a file with the

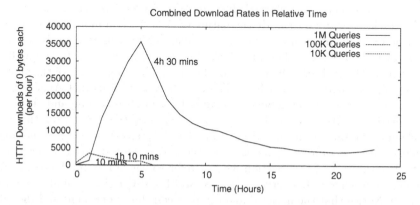

Fig. 3. Download rate (per hour) of a file of 0 bytes from the Web Server. Each curve has a caption noting the time needed for the malicious client to answer the amount of Queries.

filename identical but empty (e.g., zero-size). The file size was again advertised as 3,240,000 bytes in our QueryHits. The results of this experiment are presented in Figure 3.

As we can see the request rate is quite high. This confirms the observation that our Web Server was under a DoS attack during the first experiment, since a lot of its incoming requests were never recorded in the log file.

In Tables 1 and 2 we present the results for both experiments. (These Tables actually contain the aggregate numbers used in Figures 2 and 3.) At first, we observe that in the case where the Web Server actually serves a file with a size of 3,240,000 bytes, more than 5,000 complete downloads have taken place in a few hours. This corresponds to more than 15 GB of data and represents the amount of data transmitted from our attacked Web Server during the experiment. Furthermore, we observe that in the second experiment where our Web Server responds with an empty file, we recorded downloads for more than one quarter of the amount of QueryHits produced by our malicious servent. This number does not represent unique requests, since the unique IPs which were logged were less than 3,000. On the other hand, because of the existence of NAT and Proxy gateway configurations, it is quite likely that less than 3,000 unique IPs map to a larger number of unique users.

It is interesting to observe that users seem to download files with obscured filenames. We believe that besides naive users that download everything, some automated clients must exist that are pre-configured to download everything in batch mode. This suspicion is supported by our logfiles, which contained records of download entries with names like "foo.mpg.mp3". That is, due to the naive way that our malicious servent respond to incoming Queries, it generated completely bogus QueryHits, and, surprisingly, some of them were actually selected for downloading.

4.3   Measurements of a Simultaneous DoS Attack

Since previous experiments showed that our Web Server was persistently under a DoS attack, we wanted to study the nature of the attack in more detail. We set up a new experiment with five malicious clients acting simultaneously against five distinct Web Servers. The malicious clients were configured to serve 10K, 100K, 1M, 10M and 100M Queries using HTTP-exploitation. Each of the clients was running in a dedicated machine. The targets were five distinct Apache processes running on a dedicated Server, isolated from other incoming and outgoing traffic, except for Web and SSH. We decided to discard the traces from the first two clients (the ones that served 10K and 100K Queries) since the generated download rate was quite low compared to the rate produced by the other three clients. For the rest of this Section we will refer to the traffic produced by the three malicious clients that served 1M, 10M and 100M Queries as small, medium and large. Notice that the major difference between this experiment and the one in Section 4.2 is that the malicious clients run simultaneously and all the DoS attacks are taking place at the same time.

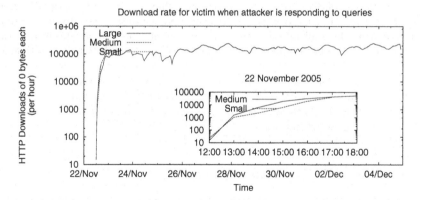

Fig. 4. Download rate per hour of a file of 0 bytes from the Web Servers during a simultaneous DoS attack, while each of the malicious client is connected to the Gnutella system. Y axis is on logarithmic scale.

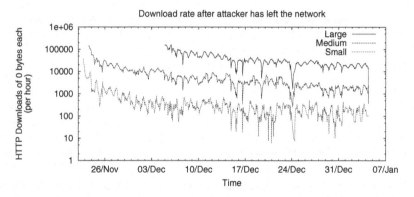

Fig. 5. Download rate per hour of a file of 0 bytes from the Web Servers during a simultaneous DoS attack, after the time each of the malicious client got disconnected from the Gnutella system. Y axis is on logarithmic scale.

Table 3 presents the results of our last experiment. In addition, in Figures 4 and 5 we present the request rate recorded by our Web Servers while the malicious clients were serving Queries and after the time they stopped. Observe that the attack does not stop at the time the malicious clients end their action, but continues for many days.

It is very interesting to observe the fluctuations of the curves for specific daily time periods. We believe that this effect relates to non-business hours and holiday periods in different locations, e.g., when users are more likely to be using their Gnutella clients or more likely to be engaged in other activities. For example, notice in Figure 5 that on December 24 and at the end of December (e.g., on Christmas eve and around New Year's day) the request rate is quite low.

Table 3. Statistics collected for the final experiment, in which we issued a simultaneous DoS attack in three distinct Web Servers. Denote that Duration is related to the time period needed by the malicious client to serve the amount of Queries specified in the 2nd row. The last two rows represent information collected for the whole experiment.

Duration	303 mins	1,529 mins	18,273 mins
QueryHits Generated	1,000,000	10,000.000	100,000,000
Downloads Recorded	731,625	10,161,472	70,952,339
Unique IP Addresses	5,272	52,473	421,217

4.4   Analysis of the Attacking Population

We take a closer look at characteristics of the population of peers participating in the attack. As we have already explained the attack is the result of one and only malicious Gnutella client, which is able to act maliciously by serving a fixed amount of incoming Queries with fake QueryHits.

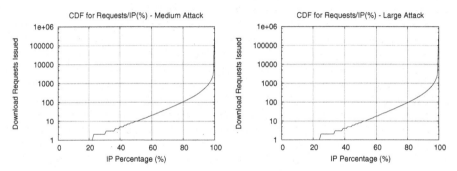

Fig. 6. The CDF of the percentage of the download requests issued per IP address for the medium and the large attack respectively

In Figure 6 we show the distribution of the number of download requests per IP address, for the medium and large attack respectively. Recall, from Table 3, that in the medium attack trace more than 10 million downloads were recorded from 52,473 unique IP addresses[2]. On the other hand, the large attack trace embeds near 71 millions of downloads issued by 421,217 IP addresses.

The CDFs of both the medium and large attack are quite similar. We observe that roughly 80% of IP addresses issue less than 100 requests, and a small percentage, about 0.5%, issue thousands of requests. This result is expected, since normal users will not try to download a file more than a few times. The small fraction of the IP addresses that generate massive download requests are very likely to be automated downloaders that try to download everything, or Gateways/Proxies that shield large subnetworks. It is interesting to note, that

---

[2] This is likely to be more, since some of the IP addresses are mapped to Internet Gateways/Proxies.

although the two CDFs of Figure 6 are very similar, the IP addresses of the two traces are different.

Figure 6 leads to two important observations. First, it shows that the attack has a very distributed nature resembling flash crowds. Second, a small fraction of the tricked nodes, those that perform massive downloading, are the ones that maintain the request rate. Even if someone manages to filter out the few IPs that generate thousands of requests, it would still be difficult to stop the attack, since the attack is the cumulative effect of normal clients that perform some tens of download requests.

Finally, beyond the saturation of the communication channel, which is used by the attacked Web Server, we must note that there are also other implications. For example, the download requests are logged in the same fashion as ordinary requests. That is, the attack garbles the traffic of the Web Server. Statistics based on log files will produce misleading results. Akamized Web sites will also face problems, since the Akamai Service is based on the magnitude of a Web Site's traffic.

5   Countermeasures

As demonstrated in the previous Section, a DoS attack can be launched by malicious peers that answer all Queries received and hereby direct unsuspected Gnutella peers to request a non-existing file from a third party such as a Web Server. Furthermore, by embedding specific file names in the QueryHit packet, malicious peers can force ordinary peers to download an existing file from a Web Server. If a great amount of ordinary peers is tricked to download a large file from a Web Server, the Server will soon be unable to serve its ordinary requests, since its available capacity will be exhausted by the requests performed by the tricked Gnutella peers.

One could argue that the existing Gnutella software can be changed to detect HTTP-exploitable filenames in QueryHit packets, but this would not cover attacks against Gnutella peers. Another practical solution would be to prevent URL escaping in HTTP GET requests, in a fashion similar to Web Browsers. Network-level intrusion detection and prevention systems could also be used to filter Gnutella traffic from the traffic a Web Server receives.

However, we believe that it is worth examining whether it is possible to tackle the problem "head-on" rather than relying on partial fixes or workarounds such as the ones presented above. We next describe an algorithm that aims to detect and mitigate the impact of DoS attacks to non-Gnutella participants and present a preliminary evaluation.

5.1   Short Term Safe Listing: The SEALING Algorithm

Our algorithm mainly focuses on protecting innocent victims such as non-Gnutella participants from DoS attacks originated from Gnutella. We consider a non-Gnutella participant as any host advertised to Gnutella (i.e. with an IP address and port number delivered in a Gnutella QueryHit) that does not support the Gnutella protocol. That is, the following Validation Criterion is used to distinguish between third parties that are potential victims of a DoS attack from normal Gnutella peers:

SEALING Validation Criterion: *Any host advertised in a Gnutella QueryHit packet which can not respond correctly to a Gnutella Handshake process is considered as a non-Gnutella participant and a potential victim for a Gnutella-based DoS attack.*

The SEALING algorithm is shown in Figure 7. The goal of the algorithm is to place potential DoS victims in a Safe List based on the SEALING Validation Criterion. This Safe List keeps track of machines that should not be contacted for downloads. Each Gnutella node keeps a Safe List and periodically updates its records. Each record has a lifetime of a fixed time interval. For the purposes of our evaluation, we used a fixed time interval of 30 minutes.

```
0    SafeListLifeTime := 30 mins;
1    if (GnutellaPacket(pkt) == QueryHitPacket) {
2        GnutellaExtractNode(pkt, &GnutellaNode);
3        if (SafeListContains(GnutellaNode)) {
4            if (CurrentTime() -
5                SafeListGetTimeOfNode(GnutellaNode) <
6                SafeListLifeTime)
7                GnutellaDropPacket(pkt);
8        }
9        else
10           GnutellaParseHits(pkt);
11   }
12   ...
13   onDownloadAttempt(node, file) {
14       if (GnutellaHandShake(node))
15           GnutellaDownload(node, file);
16       else
17           SafeListAdd(node);
18   }
19   ...
```

Fig. 7. SEALING Algorithm

5.2   SEALING Evaluation

We attempt to evaluate the SEALING algorithm using the trace collected from the Middle DoS attack. We group the download requests by the IP address recorded by the Web Server during the attack. We consider the first download request as a download attempt that, according to SEALING, will fail since the Web Server will not respond correctly to the Gnutella Handshake. Based on SEALING, all the download requests following the first download and for the next 30 minutes will be filtered out by the Gnutella peer and eventually will not make it to the Web Server. That is, we assume that the Gnutella peer that received the QueryHit, will add the Web Server to its Safe List after failing to Handshake with it.

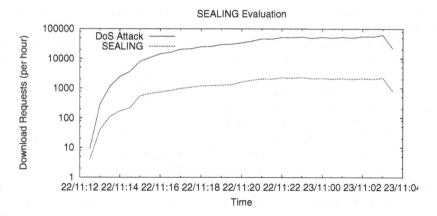

Fig. 8. The evaluation graph of the SEALING algorithm. The solid curve represents the amount of download requests during a DoS attack using Gnutella. The dashed curve represents the amount of download requests that will be eventually exposed to a Web Server, if Gnutella nodes utilize the SEALING algorithm.

For every download request we find in the trace we compare its timestamp with the first one encountered in the trace, which serves as the time offset of the SEALING algorithm. If the timestamp of a download request is found to be over 30 minutes after the time offset, then we consider that the download request serves as a new Handshake, which will also eventually fail. Again, we filter out the next download requests we encounter in the trace that have relative time difference less than 30 minutes with the new time offset. The results of the evaluation, as shown in Figure 8, indicate that SEALING reduces the effectiveness of the DoS by roughly two orders of magnitude in terms of the number of download requests to the victim site. We believe that this is sufficient to downgrade the threat of Gnutella-based DoS attacks to the level of mere nuisance for the majority of potential victims.

6   Related Work

There are many studies on security issues of unstructured P2P systems such as Gnutella. Daswani end Garcia-Molina[5] propose a number of strategies for limiting Query flooding attacks through Query traffic balancing an the Ultrapeer level. Mishra[6] describes extensively a number of existing attacks in P2P systems and proposes a new protocol called Cascade. One of the main features of Cascade is iterative search. In iterative search, a peer controls the Query flow. In contrast with pure flooding, iterative search forwards the Query to a peer's neighbors and requests the neighbors of each neighbor. Then, it proceeds on connecting to them and performing the Query recursively.

Zeinalipour-Yazti[10] considers the spam generation problem in Gnutella and proposes for each peer to perform a direct connection to the peer it wants to download from, using the system protocol and the download protocol, re-querying the peer and then performing the download.

AusCERT[1] has published an anonymous article which presents a traffic analysis from Gnutella traces. The analysis discusses IP addresses and Port numbers in PONG and QueryHit messages that are not Gnutella peers, implying that DoS attacks via Gnutella may have already been performed.

Paxson[7] has studied the problem of reflectors in DoS attacks, where Gnutella is also listed as a major threat. According to Paxson, a Gnutella network can be used as a reflector in a DoS attack by generating fake PUSH messages. A PUSH message is sent to a firewalled peer which can not accept incoming connections, so as to initiate the connection for a data transfer.

Finally, some proposed enhancements to Gnutella may further amplify the attack presented in this paper. For instance, in an attempt to address to the freeriders problem Sun and Garcia-Molina have proposed SLIC[9], a technique that rewards data share holders and isolates freeriders. Because it does so based on the number of Queries and QueryHits forwarded, SLIC is likely to be a prosperous environment for the attack presented in this paper, since it promotes peers that have seemingly great answering power.

7   Concluding Remarks

We have demonstrated how unstructured P2P systems can be misused for launching DoS attacks against third parties. We have developed an attack that exploits a number of weaknesses of unstructured P2P systems and manages to instruct innocent Gnutella peers to generate a significant amount of traffic to a victim host. The victim can be another Gnutella peer, but also a host outside the Gnutella system, such as a Web Server.

Although the basic attack relies primarily on the ability to spoof QueryHit responses, we also took advantage of the HTTP protocol used by Gnutella peers for data transfers. This allowed us to construct malicious QueryHits that result in downloads of arbitrary files from a target Web Server. An interesting observation is that the use of HTTP in this case allowed the attack to "leak" to other systems as well.

Finally, we have developed SEALING, an algorithm which aims at keeping a local "Safe List" on each peer, containing IP addresses and port numbers of hosts that have been characterized as non-Gnutella participants. Our algorithm assumes that any connection from Gnutella participants to non-Gnutella participants is a possible DoS attack.

7.1   Future Work

To ensure prompt mitigation of Gnutella-based DoS attacks we believe that it is necessary to further strengthen our defenses. The SEALING algorithm presented in this paper is sufficient, but only if it is adopted by a large fraction of Gnutella users, as its effect is proportional to the fraction of nodes that support it. Until most nodes implement SEALING, it may be worth considering countermeasures that can be effective even if only deployed on a smaller fraction of nodes, such as superpeers. One solution that we are currently exploring is probabilistic validation of QueryHits on superpeers.

Another direction worth exploring is how the basic attack can be used against third parties other than Web Servers and Gnutella peers, and for launching attacks other than DoS. For example, it may be possible to embed buffer-overflow URLs in QueryHit responses, so that Gnutella peers unintentionally assist in the dissemination of malware-carrying exploit code to victim Servers. Determining the feasibility and effectiveness of such an attack requires further investigation and experimental analysis.

Acknowledgments

We thank, in alphabetical order, the following members of the Distributed Computing Systems Laboratory (ICS, FORTH) for their valuable remarks during a series of meetings regarding the material presented in this paper: Periklis Akritidis, Spiros Antonatos, Demetres Antoniades, Manos Athanatos, Demetres Koukis, Charalambos Papadakis, Michalis Polychronakis, and Vivi Fragopoulou. This work was supported in part by project SecSPeer (GGET USA-031), funded in part by the Greek Secretariat for Research and Technology and by the Core-Grid Network of Excellence.

References

1. Anonymously Launching a DDoS Attack via the Gnutella Network. http://www.auscert.org.au/render.html?it=2404.
2. Apache web server. http://www.apache.org/.
3. Debian gnu/linux os. http://www.debian.org/.
4. Gtk-gnutella servent. http://gtk-gnutella.sourceforge.net.
5. N. Daswani and H. Garcia-Molina. Query-flood dos attacks in gnutella networks. In *ACM Conference on Computer and Communications Security*, 2002.
6. M. Mishra. Cascade: an attack resistant peer-to-peer system. In *the 3rd New York Metro Area Networking Workshop*, 2003.
7. Vern Paxson. An analysis of using reflectors for distributed denial-of-service attacks. *SIGCOMM Comput. Commun. Rev.*, 31(3):38–47, 2001.
8. Daniel Stutzbach and Reza Rejaie. Characterizing the two-tier gnutella topology. *SIGMETRICS Perform. Eval. Rev.*, 33(1):402–403, 2005.
9. Qixiang Sun and Hector Garcia-Molina. Slic: A selfish link-based incentive mechanism for unstructured peer-to-peer networks. In *ICDCS '04: Proceedings of the 24th International Conference on Distributed Computing Systems (ICDCS'04)*, pages 506–515, Washington, DC, USA, 2004. IEEE Computer Society.
10. D. Zeinalipour-Yazti. Exploiting the security weaknesses of the gnutella protocol. Technical Report CS260-2, Department of Computer Science, University of California, 2001.

Password Based Server Aided Key Exchange[*][**]

Yvonne Cliff, Yiu Shing Terry Tin, and Colin Boyd

Information Security Institute, Queensland University of Technology,
GPO Box 2434, Brisbane Q 4001, Australia
y.cliff@isi.qut.edu.au, {t.tin, c.boyd}@qut.edu.au

Abstract. We propose a new password-based 3-party protocol with a formal security proof in the standard model. Under reasonable assumptions we show that our new protocol is more efficient than the recent protocol of Abdalla and Pointcheval (FC 2005), proven in the random oracle model. We also observe some limitations in the model due to Abdalla, Fouque and Pointcheval (PKC 2005) for proving security of such protocols.

Keywords: Key agreement, password authentication, three-party.

1 Introduction

A major goal of modern cryptography is to enable two or more users on an insecure (adversary controlled) network to communicate in a confidential manner and/or ensure that such communications are authentic. Symmetric key cryptographic tools are often used for such communications, due to their efficiency. However, due to the impracticality of every pair of users sharing a large secret key, public key and/or password based techniques are used to generate such a key when it is required. We focus on password-based key exchange, which is useful in situations where the secure storage of full length cryptographic keys is infeasible, such as in mobile environments. However, because of the short length of the password, special care must be taken when designing protocols to ensure that both the password and the key finally agreed remain secret.

One area of recent attention is password-based 3-party protocols with a formal security proof. These protocols enable two clients to exchange a secret key where each client shares a (different) password with a common server. Such protocols overcome the problem associated with 2-party password-based protocols (such as all of the password-based protocols being standardized in IEEE P1363.2 and ISO/IEC FDIS 11770-4) whereby a single user must hold as many passwords as there are parties with whom it wishes to communicate.

Although such protocols have received some attention in the literature, formal proofs have only recently been provided. Abdalla, Fouque and Pointcheval

[*] Research funded by Australian Research Council through Discovery Project DP0345775.
[**] Extended abstract; for the full version see: http://sky.fit.qut.edu.au/~boydc/papers

[AFP05] proved the security of a generic construction (called GPAKE) that uses any two-party authenticated key exchange protocol as well as a three party key distribution protocol, and combines them with a Diffie-Hellman key exchange authenticated using a message authentication code (MAC). They proved this construction secure in a new model (which we call the AFP model) based on the models of Bellare et al. [BR93, BR95, BPR00]. However, protocols constructed according to this method can be quite inefficient.

The AFP model contains two variants. The first, called the find-then-guess (FTG) model, is similar to existing models, since it allows Reveal queries (to disclose the session key of a requested instance to the adversary) and only one Test query (where the adversary must guess whether it was told the actual session key of a session it selected). The other variant is called the real-or-random (ROR) model, and disallows Reveal queries, but allows multiple Test queries, where the keys returned by the test queries are either all real or all random. It is shown that the ROR model is stronger than the FTG model when password-based protocols are being studied. However, when high-entropy keys are used rather than passwords, protocols secure in one variant are secure in the other also.

The AFP model also defines a new notion, *key privacy*, which means that the server cannot deduce the value of the secret key shared between the clients. Key privacy may be proven separately to the protocol's semantic security. However, the AFP model does have the shortcoming of not allowing adaptive corrupt queries; corrupted parties are chosen statically at the beginning of a proof in the AFP model.

The GPAKE protocol was proven secure in the ROR variant of the AFP model, assuming that the two-party authenticated key exchange protocol used with it is also secure in the ROR model. Although most suitable password based protocols have been proven secure in the FTG model, it is claimed that most proofs, including the KOY one [KOY01], can be modified easily to meet the ROR model requirements.

Abdalla and Pointcheval [AP05] later proposed another 3-party password-based protocol, to which we refer as the AP protocol. It was proven secure using the FTG variant of the AFP model, using the random oracle (RO) model (note that earlier versions, including the conference version, have an error in the protocol description that leads to an attack [CBH05b]). The proof requires new and stronger variants of the Decisional Diffie-Hellman (DDH) assumption. The authors claim that their protocol is quite efficient, requiring 2 exponentiations and a few multiplications per party, or less than half the cost for the server compared with using GPAKE.

In this paper we propose another 3-party password-based protocol, proven secure using the Canetti-Krawczyk (CK) proof model [CK01]. This model allows the adversary to make adaptive corrupt queries. In contrast, the AFP model only allows static corrupt queries. We therefore select the CK model as it can model a wider variety of attack scenarios and allows the modular design of protocols by enabling key exchange and authentication mechanisms to be proven secure separately.

We regard it as a significant advantage that our proof is in the standard model, in contrast to the AP protocol which requires the RO model. We also examine the AP protocol efficiency claims more closely and claim that our new protocol can be more efficient with reasonable assumptions.

The rest of this paper proceeds as follows. Section 2 reviews the CK model, and is followed by a description of the protocol and its security proof in Section 3. Section 4 then discusses the efficiency, advantages and disadvantages of the proposed scheme in comparison to the AP and GPAKE protocols.

2   The Canetti–Krawczyk Model

In this section the CK approach is reviewed. Further details of the model can be found in the original papers [BCK98, CK01], a paper extending the model to justify optimization techniques [HBGN05], or the full version.

In the CK model a protocol π is modelled as a collection of n programs running at different parties, $P_1, \ldots, P_n$. Each program is an interactive probabilistic polynomial-time (PPT) machine. Each invocation of π within a party is defined as a *session*, and each party may have multiple sessions running concurrently. The communications network is controlled by an adversary $\mathcal{A}$, also a PPT machine, which schedules and mediates all sessions between the parties. Three different models exist:

- The *authenticated-links model (AM)* defines an idealized adversary, $\mathcal{A}$, that is restricted to delivering messages faithfully (but possibly out of order) between uncorrupted parties, if at all. $\mathcal{A}$ is not allowed to fabricate, modify, or replay messages of its choice except if the message is purported to come from a corrupted party.
- The *unauthenticated-links model (UM)* allows the adversary, $\mathcal{U}$, to fabricate messages and deliver any messages of its choice.
- The *hybrid model (HM)*, with adversary $\mathcal{H}$, combines the above models, and messages are marked by the sender as authentic (so that AM rules apply to the message) or unauthentic (so that UM rules apply). $\mathcal{H}$ may fabricate unauthentic messages.

Upon activation, the parties perform some computations, update their internal state, generate local output and may output messages. Local output records the occurrence of important, security-related events, such as key establishment (recorded by P_i as "Established (P_i, P_j, s, κ)" to denote that a key κ has been established with party P_j). The adversary's view consists of all parties' public authentication information, output messages and local outputs, except for the established keys (κ-values) of completed sessions. Two sessions $(P_i, P_j, s, role)$ and $(P_i', P_j', s', role')$ are said to be *matching sessions* if $P_i = P_i'$, $P_j = P_j'$, and $s = s'$, i.e. if their session-ids are identical and they recognized each other as their respective communicating partner for the session.

In addition to activating parties, $\mathcal{A}$ can corrupt a party to obtain its long term keys, request a session's session-key or session-state, request session-expiration to erase the session key or select a test-session to receive either the real key or a random one with equal probability. A protocol is session key (SK) secure if uncorrupted parties who complete matching sessions output the same key and the probability of $\mathcal{A}$ guessing correctly whether it received the real key from its test query is no more than $\frac{1}{2}$ plus a negligible function in the security parameter.

Protocols that are SK-secure in the AM can be converted into SK-secure protocols in the UM by applying an *authenticator* to them. Authenticators can be constructed from *message transmission (MT) authenticators*, which authenticate each message almost independently of all other messages. To translate an SK-secure protocol in the AM to an SK-secure protocol in the UM an MT-authenticator can be applied to each message and the resultant sub-protocols combined to form one overall SK-secure protocol in the UM. An MT-authenticator emulates the MT protocol, in which the sender A outputs 'A sent m to B.' and sends (A, B, m) to party B, and upon receipt of the authentic message, B outputs 'B received m from A.'

Constructing an authenticator by using an MT-authenticator for each message can lead to very inefficient protocols due to the large number of messages generated and the requirement that the session identifier be known before the protocol begins. Until recently, heuristic arguments were made as to why optimized versions of protocols where messages were shifted and nonces reused were secure. However, recent work [HBGN05] has provided a formal basis for such optimizations by showing and/or proving how to define a session identifier part way through the protocol, that more than one MT-authenticator may be used to construct an authenticator for an entire protocol, that certain *preamble* authenticator messages can be shifted to earlier points in the protocol if some conditions are met, that the message m being authenticated need not form part of every authenticator message, and that nonces used in some authenticators only need to be previously unused by that party in that authenticator and may be replaced with other values from the protocol. The techniques presented in that work will be used throughout this paper.

3   Conversion from Two-Party to Three-Party Protocol

In this section, we propose a new protocol, labelled 3DH, that uses a server's assistance to perform the Diffie-Hellman key agreement between two parties. The protocol's purpose is to enable the use of a password-based authenticator between each of the parties and the server, S. The server is a gateway responsible for connecting parties A and B faithfully and providing assurance of the identify of each party to the other.

Figure 1 shows an HM template describing the possible actions for party A, the initiator or responder of the protocol, and specifies which actions are prerequisites for others, and which may be performed in parallel. It also specifies which actions must be performed in a single activation. The use of such a template has been recommended [HBGN05] to clearly show the security requirements of a

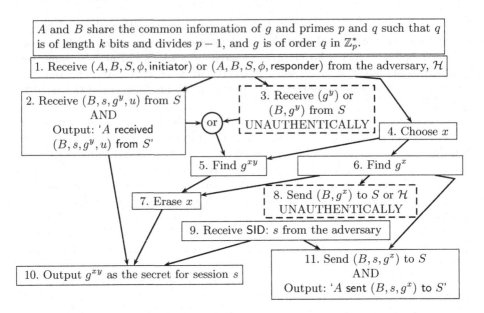

Fig. 1. Possible step order for receiver and responder in the 3DH protocol in the HM

protocol and yet allow it to be easily adapted to suit different authenticators or objectives, without breaking the security proof.

In the diagram, all messages are assumed to be authentic, unless otherwise specified, and actions that must be performed in the same activation are shown in the one box and joined with "AND." An arrow from one step to another indicates that the first step must be completed before the second is begun. Optional steps are shown using dashed boxes. The session identifier s received from the adversary must be the same as that received in the authentic message from B, otherwise the protocol halts without outputting a secret key. The template for party B is identical, except for the renaming of A to B, B to A, x to y and y to x. The value u received from S is not used in the template. Its purpose is described below.

In Figure 2, the possible interaction between the server and any party B is shown (i.e. B in Figure 2 may correspond to either A or B in Figure 1). In a single protocol run, such interaction may occur between the server and more than one party. The value u is included to ensure the requirement that all authentic messages are unique [BCK98, full version p.8, footnote 2] is met. Some authenticator proofs require this property.

An examination of Figures 1 and 2 shows that a number of steps can be performed if one party has possession of the other's unauthentic Diffie-Hellman value. Therefore, it seems logical to specify an HM protocol such as the one shown by Protocol 1 that allows a party to receive an unauthentic Diffie-Hellman value and then carry out as many actions as possible. Messages not labelled "unauth'c" are authentic. In this version, the adversary chooses the Diffie-

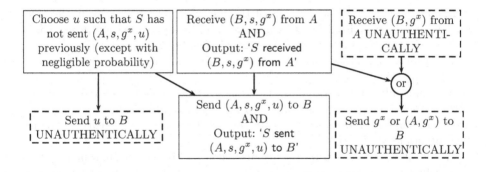

Fig. 2. Possible step order for the server of the 3DH protocol in the HM, with optional steps in dashed boxes

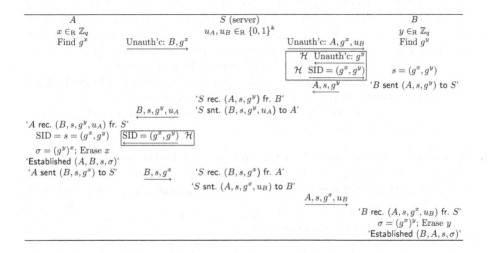

Protocol 1. A possible server aided 3DH HM protocol

Hellman values, (g^x, g^y), to be the session identifier, and the unauthentic message g^y from B to the HM adversary, $\mathcal{H}$, facilitates this. Later changes will allow the clients to choose the session identifier, so the messages in boxes will then be removed.

Our new protocol differs from the ordinary Diffie-Hellman key exchange in that protocol participants do not directly make contact with each other. Although password-based protocols where the participants communicate directly with one another do exist and have been proven secure in other proof models [KOY01, Mac02], they do not use a public key for the server and are not amenable to the CK-model, since their key exchange and authentication mechanisms cannot be separated [HK99]. Furthermore, such protocols require a party to maintain a list of passwords for each of the targets with whom it wishes to communicate. Thus the advantages of the modular approach used by the CK-model cannot be realized by such protocols, and they are inappropriate when storage constraints exist, such as those in wireless networks.

The proposed protocol uses a common trusted server for authentication, a common practice in networking. The server is unable to calculate the session key; it can only be generated by two authenticated clients. Moreover, client authentication uses passwords which can be memorized by users, eliminating the need for shared secrets to be stored in the users' devices, and greatly reducing the potential security risk.

We disallow server corruption because there is no way of guaranteeing the establishment of secure session keys using a corrupted server controlled by the adversary. A corrupted server would effectively allow an adversary to inject authentic messages from the server into the network. In addition, session-state reveals on S have been disallowed to keep the partner and session identity definitions simple. However, if server session-state reveal queries were allowed, it would not affect the security of the protocol when used in conjunction with existing authenticators. This is because the server only forwards messages between the two clients. Since such messages are not secret, session-state reveals do not reveal any information that can be used effectively in an attack.

Proving the security of 3DH requires the use of the decisional Diffie-Hellman (DDH) assumption [Bon98]. The definition and proof are based in $\mathbb{Z}_p^*$ but the protocol may also be run in an elliptic curve group where the elliptic curve version of the DDH assumption holds.

Assumption 1 (Decisional Diffie-Hellman (DDH)). *Let k be a security parameter. Let primes p and q be such that q is of length k bits and divides $p - 1$, and let g be of order q in $\mathbb{Z}_p^*$. Then the probability distributions $Q_0 = \{\langle p, g, g^x, g^y, g^{xy}\rangle\} : x, y, \xleftarrow{R} \mathbb{Z}_q\}$ and $Q_1 = \{\langle p, g, g^x, g^y, g^z\rangle\} : x, y, z \xleftarrow{R} \mathbb{Z}_q\}$ of quintuples are computationally indistinguishable.*

Theorem 1. *Any Diffie-Hellman based HM protocol where the actions of each party satisfy the requirements specified in Figures 1 and 2 is SK-secure[1], provided the DDH assumption holds.*

The proof is similar to Canetti and Krawczyk's Theorem 8 [CK01] and Hitchcock et al.'s Theorem 4 [HBGN05] and is provided in the full version.

Protocol 2 shows another version of the Diffie-Hellman protocol where the adversary no longer inputs the session identifier to the parties. In addition, messages containing the same term twice have had the second term removed, and the unauthentic message to the adversary has been removed. The proof of the following theorem is very similar to that of Theorem 5 of Hitchcock et al. [HBGN05] and may be found in the full version.

Theorem 2. *If Protocol 1 is secure then so is Protocol 2.*

---

[1] We use the 2-party SK-security definition, since S provides authentication only, cannot be corrupted or have its sessions revealed, and does not share the secret key.

A	S (server)	B
$x \in_R \mathbb{Z}_q$	$u_A, u_B \in_R \{0,1\}^k$	$y \in_R \mathbb{Z}_q$
Find g^x $\xrightarrow{\text{Unauth'c: } B, g^x}$		
	$\xrightarrow{\text{Unauth'c: } A, g^x, u_B}$	Find g^y
		Set SID $= s = (g^x, g^y)$
	'S rec. (A, g^x, g^y) fr. B' $\xleftarrow{A, g^x, g^y}$	'B snt. (A, g^x, g^y) to S'
	$\xleftarrow{B, g^x, g^y, u_A}$ 'S snt. (B, g^x, g^y, u_A) to A'	
'A rec. (B, g^x, g^y, u_A) fr. S'		
Set SID $= s = (g^x, g^y)$		
$\sigma = (g^y)^x$; Erase x		
'Established (A, B, s, σ)'		
'A snt. (B, g^y, g^x) to S' $\xrightarrow{B, g^y, g^x}$ 'S rec. (B, g^y, g^x) fr. A'		
	'S snt. (A, g^y, g^x, u_B) to B'	
	$\xrightarrow{A, g^y, g^x, u_B}$	
		'B rec. (A, g^y, g^x, u_B) fr. S'
		$\sigma = (g^x)^y$; Erase y
		'Established (B, A, s, σ)'

Protocol 2. Secure 3DH protocol suitable for optimization

We now focus on the authenticators to be used in conjunction with Protocol 2. The password-based authenticator, $\lambda_{\text{P-ENC}}$, shown in Protocol 3, has been chosen, so that clients do not need keep secret a large key. It has a proof [HTB+03] of password-based session key (PBSK-) security, when the encryption scheme is indistinguishable under chosen ciphertext attack (IND-CCA secure), $H(m) \stackrel{\text{def}}{=} m$, $\mathcal{E}_e$ denotes encryption with key e and $\mathcal{D}_d$ denotes decryption with key d. This means that if the server refuses to complete sessions with a client after γ unsuccessful login attempts for that client, then the adversary has an advantage negligibly greater than the advantage due to simply guessing a password and attempting to impersonate the user online. The nonce N_B may be any value of B's choice, including one chosen by the adversary, if it has not been used as a nonce in this authenticator before, except with negligible probability. Since N_B is a preamble message it may be sent before the first authenticator message.

In order to increase the efficiency of the authenticator (and hence the resulting protocols) we now alter the authenticator slightly, replacing the message m by $H(m)$. The authenticator is still PBSK-secure if H is chosen to be a collision resistant one-way hash function. This new authenticator is labelled $\lambda_{\text{P-ENC-H}}$. The proof is deferred to the full version, but proceeds by observing that $\lambda_{\text{P-ENC-H}}$ sends the same messages as would be required to authenticate $H(m)$ (rather than m) using $\lambda_{\text{P-ENC}}$. Therefore, breaking $\lambda_{\text{P-ENC-H}}$ involves breaking the hash function or else breaking $\lambda_{\text{P-ENC}}$.

Another authenticator is required for messages from the server to the clients. The only suitable existing authenticators are the signature based and the encryption based authenticators [BCK98] (denoted λ_{SIG} and λ_{ENC}), as other available authenticators would require the clients to hold secret keys. If signature and encryption schemes are chosen that have proofs of security in the standard model,

A (Client)	$\lambda_{\text{P-ENC}}$	B (Server)
Known: Password, π		Known: Password of A, π
Public key of B, e_B		Public/private keys, (e_B, d_B)
	$\xrightarrow{m}$	$N_B \in_R \{0,1\}^k$
	$\xleftarrow{m, N_B}$	
$c = \mathcal{E}_{e_B}(H(m), N_B, A, \pi)$	$\xrightarrow{m, c}$	$v = \mathcal{D}_{d_B}(c)$
		Check $v \overset{?}{=} (H(m), N_B, A, \pi)$

A (Server)	λ_{ENC}	B (Client)
Known: Public/private keys, (e_A, d_A)		Known: Public key of A, e_A
'A sent m to B'	$\xrightarrow{m}$	$r_B \in_R \{0,1\}^k$
$r_B = \mathcal{D}_{d_A}(c)$	$\xleftarrow{m, c}$	$c = \mathcal{E}_{e_A}(r_B)$
$z = \mathcal{M}_{r_B}(m, B)$; Erase r_B	$\xrightarrow{m, z}$	Check $z \overset{?}{=} \mathcal{M}_{r_B}(m, B)$
		'B received m from A'

Protocols 3 and 4. Password and encryption based authenticators

the encryption and signature schemes have about the same efficiency. Therefore, we use λ_{ENC}, shown in Protocol 4, to minimize the number of separate crypto-graphic primitives that must be implemented. We observe that c is a preamble message, but r_B must be erased in the same activation as c is decrypted for the authenticator to be secure [CBH05a]. Further details of the efficiency of these au-thenticators and the associated signature and encryption schemes having proofs in the standard model are in the full version.

Protocol 5 shows the result of applying $\lambda_{\text{P-ENC-H}}$ and λ_{ENC} to Protocol 2. S has two encryption keys to keep the state of each authenticator independent, as required by the proof that two or more authenticators may be applied to the one protocol [HBGN05].

We can begin to improve Protocol 5 by removing the authentic message (i.e. "m" in the authenticator description) from the first and second messages of each authenticator. Since the authentic message is still being delivered in the last message of each authenticator, this is not a problem [HBGN05]. The parts to be deleted have been boxed in Protocol 5.

The optimization process can now be completed by replacing a and b with u_A and u_B respectively to reduce the number of values generated and transmitted, and by moving messages and piggybacking them together. Values a and b may be replaced since they are only required to be not previously used as a nonce with $\lambda_{\text{P-ENC-H}}$. Since u_A and u_B have negligible probability of being generated previously, they may be used in place of a and b [HBGN05]. The four messages shifted to earlier points in the protocol (those containing only b, c_{A2}, a and c_{B2}) are all preamble messages. The values u_A and u_B are already known to the adversary at the time they are used in place of a and b, so this requirement for shifting and replacing the nonces is also met. The final result is shown in Protocol 6.

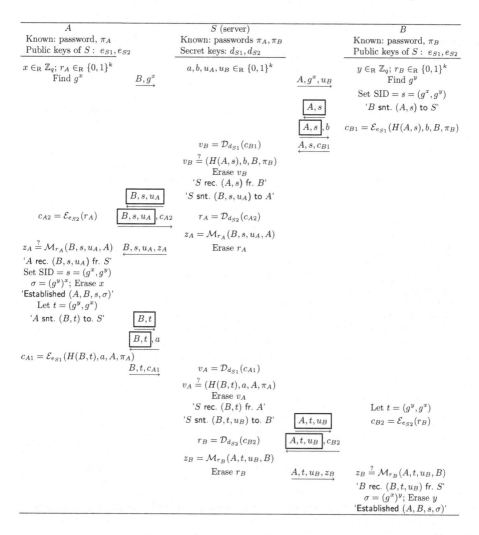

Protocol 5.   Unoptimized authenticated server aided 3DH

4   Comparison of Protocols

This section provides a comparison of the proposed, AP and GPAKE protocols. It assumes there is only one server (so the server's identity or public key may be used in offline computations), the password may not be used in offline computations, and the time for hashes and MACs is generally ignored. Exponentiations use a 1024 bit modulus with a 160 bit exponent unless otherwise specified. If the shared secret DH value generated by using the key agreement protocol can be used directly as a key, then k in Assumption 1 would typically be 160 bits for 80-bit security. However, if a uniformly distributed key (e.g. a 128-bit key)

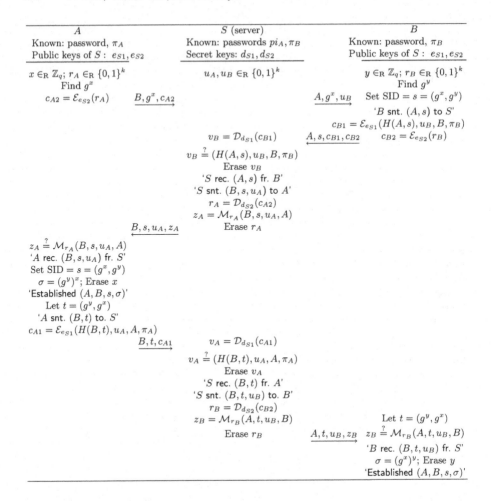

Protocol 6. Optimized authenticated serve   r aided Diffie–Hellman protocol

is to be derived from the DH value, k would need to be larger unless a random oracle model is used to extract randomness from the DH value (e.g. using the left over hash lemma, $k = 160 + 128 = 288$ bits for 79-bit security when the key is derived using a universal hash function). However, the exponents may remain at 160 bits if the 160-Discrete Log Short Exponent (DLSE) assumption is made. Further details are available in works by Dodis et al. [DGH+04] and Gennaro et al. [GHR04].

Abdalla and Pointcheval claim that the AP protocol only requires 2 exponentiations and a few multiplications per party. However, this figure does not take into account the G_1 and G_2 hash functions used by the protocol, which are modelled as random oracles in the proof, and map into the group, G, in which the protocol operates. The algebraic setting for the AP protocols is not specified, but a typical choice for G would be a subgroup of order q (where q is 160 to 288 bits) in $\mathbb{Z}_p^*$ where p is a 1024 bit prime. How should G_1 and G_2 be implemented in such a setting? The most natural choice seems to be that used by MacKenzie [Mac02] for his suite of PAK protocols, and by IEEE P1363.2 [IEE06] in the DLREDP-1 (Discrete Log Random Element Derivation Primitive), in which the functions are implemented as a hash of the inputs raised to a power to map the hash output into the subgroup. This power will be quite large ($1024 - 288 = 736$ bits long), and the computation would take the time of about 4.6 exponentiations with 160 bit exponents. Table 1 shows the equivalent number of exponentiations for this option. We should note, however, that a more efficient implementation may be possible when using DLREDP-2 from IEEE P1363.2 [IEE06] (but this requires adding two extra values to the domain parameters) or when $\frac{p-1}{q}$ is small or G is an elliptic curve group (since the co-factor in these cases is much smaller).

The efficiency of GPAKE mainly depends on which 2-party password based key exchange protocol is used by it. Use of the KOY protocol [KOY01] is assumed here, since it is in the standard model and was suggested as a suitable protocol in the GPAKE proposal. (Other protocols recommended, although faster, were in the RO model.) The equivalent number of exponentiations for the KOY protocol, excluding those for the one-time signature, is shown in Table 1. (Some exponentiations may be performed more efficiently together, and we have accounted for this.) The Bellare and Rogaway [BR95] key distribution scheme was suggested for use with GPAKE, and requires 1 symmetric decryption for each client, and 2 symmetric encryptions for the server. The GPAKE protocol itself requires 2 exponentiations for each client.

The proposed protocol requires 1 offline and 1 online public key encryption, and 1 offline and 1 online exponentiation for each client, as well as 4 public key decryptions for the server.

From the summary in Table 1, we see that the GPAKE protocol is the least efficient of all the schemes, especially if offline computations are considered. Including G_1 and G_2 evaluations in the efficiency analysis of AP makes its online efficiency similar to that of GPAKE, although it requires fewer offline computations. In comparison with these two schemes, our scheme performs quite favourably. However, some symmetric operations required for the public key encryption and decryption operations in the proposed scheme have been omitted from the analysis; symmetric operations have not been included in the GPAKE totals, either. In addition, it may be possible to optimize these schemes with precomputations to make the exponentiations run faster.

Another consideration in the choice of a protocol is the number of rounds it requires. The protocol proposed here seems, at first, inefficient in the number of rounds, as it requires six. In comparison, the GPAKE protocol requires 3 rounds for the KOY protocol, 3 rounds for the key distribution (although a small change to the key distribution protocol would result in 2 rounds), and 1 round for the exchange of the DH and MAC values, making a total of 6 or 7 rounds. The AP protocol requires only two rounds. However, by reordering the messages of the proposed protocol, the number of rounds can be substantially reduced to

Table 1. Protocol Efficiency Comparison

Protocol	Client Efficiency			Server Efficiency		
	Operation	Equivalent Exp. Offline	Online	Operation	Equivalent Exp. Offline	Online
Proposed	1 offline exp.	1				
	1 online exp.		1			
	1 online PK enc.	3	1	4 online PK dec.		12
	1 offline PK enc.	4				
	Proposed Total:	8	2	Proposed Total:		12
GPAKE ...KOY	One-time signature key gen.			Per KOY key exchange:		
	One-time signature			One-time verification		
	Validity check		5	Validity check		5
	2 offline exp.	2		3 offline exp.	3	
	2 double exp.		2.6	1 double exp.		1.3
	2 multi-exp.	2	3.3	2 multi-exp.	2	3.3
	KOY Total:	4	11	KOY Total per key:	5	9.6
...key dist.	1 symm. dec.			2 symm. enc.		
...other	2 exp.	1	1			
	GPAKE Total	5	12	GPAKE Total:	10	19.3
AP	2 exp.	1	1	2 exp.		2
	1 G_1 evaluation		4.6	2 G_1 evaluations		9.2
	1 G_2 evaluation		4.6	2 G_2 evaluations		9.2
	AP Total:	1	10.2	AP Total:		20.4

only three rounds, making its round complexity slightly worse than that of the AP protocol, but better than that of the GPAKE protocol. The details of this optimization are in the full version.

In addition to the above efficiency considerations, there are a number of other points to consider when selecting a protocol:

Random oracle v. standard model. Our proof is in the standard model, whereas that of the AP protocol is in the RO model. The proof of GPAKE may be in either model, depending upon the components used with it.

Corrupt queries. The CK model, which is used for our proof, allows the use of adaptive Corrupt queries to model a malicious insiders. This is contrary to the AFP model. In fact, an attack on the AP protocol has been described [CBH05b] that uses a corrupt query. The original proof did not rule out this attack because corrupt queries were not allowed in the proof model. Therefore, we can rule out a wider range of attacks on our protocol because of the more general model.

Session-state reveal queries. The CK model also allows session-state reveal queries. These queries model the exposure of data that must be kept between activations, and the requirement that exposure of such data in one session should not compromise other sessions. However, the AFP model does not allow such queries, and the AP protocol would be insecure in the presence of such queries. This is because an adversary could find a party's secret

Diffie-Hellman exponent using a session-state reveal query, and then use the exponent to find the secret password from the party's first protocol message.

Key privacy. The AFP model includes the key privacy requirement, but the CK model does not. However, the proposed protocol fulfills the requirement, since the server only forwards authentic messages in Protocol 1, and does not create any messages with new content. These messages are also known to the adversary, who cannot find any information about the key. Since the server knows no more than the adversary, it is also unable to deduce any information about the secret key. However, the CK model may need some modification to include the requirement if needed for other protocols.

Concurrency. The proof of the AP protocol does not allow concurrency, so that only one instance of a player can exist at a time. On the other hand, the proposed protocol allows full concurrency. Although instructions are given on how to modify the AP protocol to achieve partial and full concurrency, the correctness of these instructions is not proven. In addition, provision of full concurrency requires two extra message flows from the server at the beginning of the protocol.

Assumptions. The AP protocol proof requires the use of some non-standard assumptions based on the Diffie-Hellman problem. Our proposed protocol only requires the DDH assumption, a collision-resistant one-way hash function, and an IND-CCA secure encryption scheme. The use of standard assumptions may be less risky than the use of new assumptions that have not been extensively studied.

Online attack detection. It is always possible for the adversary to make an online attack by guessing a party's password and running the protocol using the guessed password. If the final key is correct, then the password must have been correct. Otherwise another password may be guessed and the protocol run again until the correct password is found. To prevent such attacks, the definition of PBSK-security for the CK model requires the server to refuse to run the protocol with any party who has made more than a certain number of incorrect guesses of the password. However, the server in the AP and KOY protocols cannot detect whether a client has made an incorrect password guess, and although the proofs differentiate active and passive attacks, this cannot be done in practice. In addition, such attacks are tolerated by the AFP security definition where the problem is that the adversary's advantage must only be less than $O(n/|\mathfrak{D}|)$ plus a negligible function, where n is the number of active sessions and $|\mathfrak{D}|$ is the size of the password dictionary. No small bound is placed on the number of (unsuccessful) online attacks; it may be the same as the maximum number of online sessions.

In conclusion, we have proposed a new password-based three-party protocol, one of the few such protocols with a security proof. Our proof is in the standard model, in contrast to a recently proposed protocol with a proof in the RO model, and has a number of other advantages that have been discussed above.

References

AFP05.   M. Abdalla, P.-A. Fouque, and D. Pointcheval. Password-based authenticated key exchange in the three-party setting. In *Public Key Cryptography— PKC 2005*, volume 3386 of *LNCS*, pages 65–84. Springer, 2005.

AP05.   M. Abdalla and D. Pointcheval.   Interactive Diffie-Hellman assumptions with applications to password-based authentication. In *Financial Cryptography and Data Security—FC 2005*, volume 3570 of *LNCS*, pages 341–356. Springer, 2005.   Full version: http://www.di.ens.fr/$\sim$pointche/pub.php?reference=AbPo05.

BCK98.   M. Bellare, R. Canetti, and H. Krawczyk.   A modular approach to the design and analysis of authentication and key exchange protocols. In *Proceedings of the thirtieth annual ACM symposium on Theory of computing*, pages 419–428. ACM Press, 1998.   Full version: http:// www-cse.ucsd.edu/users/mihir/papers/key-distribution.html.

Bon98.   D. Boneh. The decision Diffie-Hellman problem. In *Proceedings of the Third Algorithmic Number Theory Symposium*, volume 1423 of *LNCS*, pages 48– 63. Springer, 1998.

BPR00.   M. Bellare, D. Pointcheval, and P. Rogaway. Authenticated key exchange secure against dictionary attacks. In *Advances in Cryptology – Eurocrypt 2000*, volume 1807 of *LNCS*, pages 139–155. Springer, 2000.

BR93.   M. Bellare and P. Rogaway. Entity authentication and key distribution. In *Advances in Cryptology – CRYPTO'93*, volume 773 of *LNCS*, pages 232– 249. Springer, 1993. Full version: www-cse.ucsd.edu/users/mihir.

BR95.   M. Bellare and P. Rogaway. Provably secure session key distribution – the three party case. In *Proceedings of the 27th ACM Symposium on the Theory of Computing*, pages 57–66. ACM Press, 1995.

CBH05a.   K.-K. R. Choo, C. Boyd, and Y. Hitchcock. Errors in computational complexity proofs for protocols. In *Advances in Cryptology—Asiacrypt 2005*, volume 3788 of *LNCS*, pages 624–643. Springer, 2005.

CBH05b.   K.-K. R. Choo, C. Boyd, and Y. Hitchcock. Examining indistinguishability-based proof models for key establishment protocols.   In *Advances in Cryptology—Asiacrypt 2005*, volume 3788 of *LNCS*, pages 585–604. Springer, 2005.

CK01.   R. Canetti and H. Krawczyk.   Analysis of key-exchange protocols and their use for building secure channels.   In *Advances in Cryptology – Eurocrypt 2001*, volume 2045 of *LNCS*, pages 453–474. Springer, 2001. http://eprint.iacr.org/2001/040.ps.gz.

DGH+04.   Y. Dodis, R. Gennaro, J. Håstad, Krawczyk H., and T. Rabin. Randomness extraction and key derivation using the CBC, cascade and HMAC modes. In *Advances in Cryptology — CRYPTO 2004 Proceedings*, volume 3152 of *LNCS*, pages 494–510. Springer, 2004.

GHR04.   R. Gennaro, Krawczyk H., and T. Rabin. Secure hashed Diffie-Hellman over non-DDH groups. In *Advances in Cryptology — EUROCRYPT 2004 Proceedings*, volume 3027 of *LNCS*, pages 361–381. Springer, 2004. Full version in: Cryptology ePrint Archive (http://eprint.iacr.org/2004/099), Report 2004/099.

HBGN05.   Y. Hitchcock, C. Boyd, and J. M. González Nieto. Modular proofs for key exchange: rigorous optimizations in the Canetti-Krawczyk model. *Applicable Algebra in Engineering, Communication and Computing (AAECC) Journal*, 2005. Special issue on Mathematical Techniques in Cryptology; http://dx.doi.org/10.1007/s00200-005-0185-9.

HK99.   S. Halevi and H. Krawczyk. Public-key cryptography and password protocols. *ACM Trans. on Information and Systems Security*, 2(3):230–268, 1999.

HTB$^+$03.   Y. Hitchcock, Y. S. T. Tin, C. Boyd, J. M. González Nieto, and P. Montague. A password-based authenticator: Security proof and applications. In *4th International Conference on Cryptology in India – INDOCRYPT 2003*, volume 2904 of *LNCS*. Springer, 2003.

IEE06.   IEEE (Institute of Electrical and Electronics Engineers, Inc.). P1363.2: Standard specifications for password-based public-key cryptographic techniques (draft version d23), 2006.   http://grouper.ieee.org/groups/1363/passwdPK/draft.html.

KOY01.   J. Katz, R. Ostrovsky, and M. Yung. Efficient password-authenticated key exchange using human-memorable passwords. In *Advances in Cryptology— EUROCRYPT 2001*, volume 2045 of *LNCS*, pages 475–494. Springer, 2001.

Mac02.   P. MacKenzie.   The PAK suite: Protocols for password-authenticated key exchange.   Technical Report 2002-46, DIMACS, 2002.   ftp://dimacs.rutgers.edu/pub/dimacs/TechnicalReports/TechReports/2002/2002-46.ps.gz.

Secure Password-Based Authenticated Group Key Agreement for Data-Sharing Peer-to-Peer Networks

Qiang Tang[1,*] and Kim-Kwang Raymond Choo[2,**]

[1] Information Security Group, Royal Holloway,
University of London, Egham, Surrey TW20 0EX, UK
[2] Information Security Institute, Queensland University of Technology,
GPO Box 2434, Brisbane, QLD 4001, Australia
`qiang.tang@rhul.ac.uk, k.choo@qut.edu.au`

Abstract. We explore authenticated group key agreement in data-sharing Peer-to-Peer networks. We first propose a novel password-based authenticated group key agreement protocol with key confirmation. We present a formal statement of its security in a variant of the Bresson *et al.* security model adapted for the password-based setting. A discussion of the limitations of our protocol in the case where the group size becomes large is then presented. We conclude the paper with an enhanced version of the protocol, using a CAPTCHA technique, designed to make it more robust against online password guessing attacks.

Keywords: P2P network, key agreement, provable security, CAPTCHA.

1 Introduction

Data-sharing Peer-to-Peer (P2P) systems such as Napster[1] and Gnutella[2], are becoming increasingly popular for sharing large amounts of data, in particular music files. Because of the increasing popularity and the potential future applications of such systems, they have attracted much attention from the research community. We can broadly classify data-sharing P2P systems into two categories based on their system architecture. In the first category, the system has a central server that requires a one-time off registration by users prior to using the data-sharing service. However, all subsequent data transfers are conducted among the users without the involvement of the server. One typical example of a data-sharing P2P system in this category is Napster. In the second category, there is no central server and all operations are conducted in a self-organised manner. In such a framework, the precise specifications are dependent on the

* This research has been partially supported by a Thomas Holloway Studentship.
** This work was partially funded by the Australian Research Council Discovery Project Grant DP0345775.

[1] `http://www.napster.com/`
[2] `http://www.gnutella.com/`

J. Zhou, M. Yung, and F. Bao (Eds.): ACNS 2006, LNCS 3989, pp. 162–177, 2006.
© Springer-Verlag Berlin Heidelberg 2006

individual system, and an example of such a system is Gnutella. Systems in the first category are more easily monitored and controlled but not easily scalable whilst systems in the second category are scalable at the expense of management and security.. We refer the interested reader to recent work of Daswani, Garcia-Molina, and Yang [8] for a more comprehensive treatment of the open issues faced by existing data-sharing P2P systems.

In this paper, we primarily focus on the group key agreement issue in first category systems. Our results can be extended to second category systems if a trusted authentication server is added for the purpose of key establishment (i.e., authenticated key agreement) at the expense of the self-organised nature that defines category 2. However, authenticated key agreement allows the participants to authenticate each other when establishing a shared session key, and addresses some of the open issues in data-sharing P2P systems.

We first propose a novel password-based authenticated group key agreement protocol which provides key confirmation. This protocol is proven secure in an adapted version of the Bresson *et al.* model [4]. Like other password-based protocols in the literature, our protocol is vulnerable to online password guessing attacks when the group size becomes very large. As a counter-measure, we enhance our proposed protocol using a Completely Automated Public Turing Test to Tell Computers and Humans Apart (CAPTCHA) technique [2] and federated signature verification (both services are provided by the trusted authentication server).

The rest of this paper is organised as follows. We present our proposed password-based authenticated group key agreement protocol in Section 2. We then describe the security model in which we work in and present the security proof for our proposed protocol in Section 3. In Section 4, we describe the enhanced protocol and demonstrate its security against online password guessing attacks. We conclude this paper in Section 5.

2   A Novel Password-Based Group Key Agreement Protocol

2.1   Review of Password-Based Group Key Agreement

Since the seminal paper of Lomas, Gong, Saltzer, and Needham [12], many password-based key establishment schemes have been proposed. Some of the more recent password-based proposals include the group key agreement protocol of Bresson, Chevassut, and Pointcheval [4] derived from an earlier protocol [5]; the two-round key agreement protocol without key confirmation of Lee, Hwang, and Lee [11] and the group key agreement of Dutta and Barua [9][3]; and the Diffie-Hellman key exchange protocols of Byun and Lee [7][4]. However, to the best of our knowledge, much less attention has been devoted to password-based protocols

---

[3] Both protocols have recently been broken by Abdalla *et al.* [1].

[4] Tang and Chen [15] demonstrate that both protocols are vulnerable to several security problems.

in a group setting. In the next section, we present our proposed password-based authenticated group key agreement protocol.

2.2 Our Proposed Protocol

Let U_i $(1 \leq i \leq n, 3 \leq n)$ denote a set of participants sharing a secret password, π, selected from a password set, $\mathcal{PW}$. Each participant, U_i, possesses an associated identity, ID_i. We let ℓ be the security parameter. In our protocol, the following system parameters are public.

1. Two large prime numbers p and q, where $p = 2q + 1$.
2. Three collision-resistant one-way hash functions, $\mathcal{H}_0$, $\mathcal{H}_1$, and $\mathcal{H}_2$, where $\mathcal{H}_0 : \{0,1\}^* \to Z_p$, $\mathcal{H}_1 : \{0,1\}^* \to \{0,1\}^\ell$, $\mathcal{H}_2 : \{0,1\}^* \to \{0,1\}^\ell$.

We throughout assume that U_1 is the protocol initiator. Prior to the protocol execution, U_i $(1 \leq i \leq n)$ computes $g = \mathcal{H}_0(\pi||ID_u||x) \bmod p$, where $ID_u = ID_1||ID_2||\cdots||ID_n$ and $x \geq 0$ is the smallest integer that makes g a generator of a multiplicative subgroup G of order q in $GF(p)^*$.

In the protocol execution, the indices of the user names and the values exchanged between users are taken modulo n; and U_i $(1 \leq i \leq n)$ performs the following steps.

Stage 1: Message transfer and authentication.

1. U_i chooses a random s_i $(0 \leq s_i \leq q - 1)$, and broadcasts $Z_i = g^{s_i}$.
2. After receiving every Z_j $(1 \leq j \leq n, j \neq i)$, U_i verifies that none of them equals 1. If the check succeeds, U_i computes and broadcasts $A_{i,i-1}$ and $A_{i,i+1}$, where $Z = Z_1||Z_2||\cdots||Z_n$, $A_{i,i-1} = \mathcal{H}_1(i||i-1||Z||g^{s_{i-1}s_i}||g||ID_u)$, and $A_{i,i+1} = \mathcal{H}_1(i||i+1||Z||g^{s_{i+1}s_i}||g||ID_u)$.
3. After receiving every $A_{j,j-1}$ and $A_{j,j+1}$ $(1 \leq j \leq n, j \neq i)$, U_i verifies the received values of $A_{i-1,i}$ and $A_{i+1,i}$ by recomputing them using s_i, Z, and the stored values of Z_{i-1} and Z_{i+1}. If the checks succeed, then U_i continues with the next stage. Otherwise, the protocol execution is terminated and a notification of failure broadcasted.

Stage 2: Key agreement and key confirmation.

1. U_i computes and broadcasts $X_i = (\frac{Z_{i+1}}{Z_{i-1}})^{s_i}$.
2. After receiving every X_j $(1 \leq j \leq n, j \neq i)$, U_i computes the keying material M_i as:

$$M_i = (Z_{i-1})^{ns_i} \prod_{j=0}^{n-2} (X_{i+j})^{n-1-j} = g^{ns_{i-1}s_i} \prod_{j=0}^{n-2} \left(\frac{g^{s_{i+j}s_{i+j+1}}}{g^{s_{i+j-1}s_{i+j}}}\right)^{n-1-j}$$

$$= \prod_{j=1}^{n} g^{s_j s_{j+1}} = g^{\sum_{j=1}^{n} s_j s_{j+1}}$$

U_i then broadcasts its key confirmation message C_i, where

$$C_i = \mathcal{H}_1(i||ID_u||Z||A||X||M_i||g), \ X = X_1||X_2||\cdots||X_n, \text{ and}$$

$$A = A_{1,2}||A_{2,3}||\cdots||A_{n,1}||A_{1,n}||A_{2,1}||A_{3,2}||\cdots||A_{n,n-1}.$$

3. After receiving C_j $(1 \leq j \leq n, j \neq i)$, U_i checks whether the following equation holds:

$$C_j \stackrel{?}{=} \mathcal{H}_1(j||ID_u||Z||A||X||M_i||g).$$

If the check succeeds, U_i computes its session key as:

$$K_i = \mathcal{H}_2(ID_u||Z||A||X||M_i)$$

and concludes by computing a session identifier (SID). Note that the SID is defined to be the concatenation of the identities of all intended participants and the messages broadcast in every round of the ongoing protocol execution[5]. Otherwise, U_i terminates the protocol execution as a failure.

The above protocol is derived from the unauthenticated cyclic group key agreement protocol due to Burmester and Desmedt [6], which has been proven secure against a passive attacker under the Decisional diffie-Hellman (DDH) assumption. In our proposed protocol, the password is used to achieve authentication among participants. Note that U_i authenticates Z_{i-1} and Z_{i+1} in the first stage prior to computation and broadcasting of X_i. Without this authentication requirement, the protocol may be vulnerable to an offline dictionary attack.

3   Security Model and Security Analysis

We now describe the model in which we work, which is closely based on the model of Bresson et al. [4, 5]. The proposed model assumes that every protocol message will be broadcast to all the users. We then present a security proof for our proposed protocol in this security model.

3.1   Description of the Security Model

In the model, we denote the participants by U_i $(1 \leq i \leq n)$, each associated with a unique identity, ID_i. For any participant U_i, when the protocol is initiated, we say that a protocol instance of U_i is generated. In reality, when U_i starts a protocol execution, it knows some necessary information such as the identities of all the involved participants, the communication details, and the instance creation time. In this model, this necessary information is defined to be the participant instance identifier, which uniquely identifies the participant instance. If U_i is involved in an instance possessing an identifier id_i, we further define the participant instance to be an oracle $\Pi_i^{id_i}$, which is a probabilistic Turing machine processing the protocol messages on behalf of U_i. At any time, an oracle is in one of the following states:

---

[5] The SID is made public upon protocol completion, and the security of the protocol does not hinge on the difficulty of predicting a valid SID. In other words, anyone (including the attacker, $\mathcal{A}$) knows what a particular SID is.

- Active: the oracle is still waiting for inputs from other oracles, and the key agreement process has not finished.
- Accepted: the oracle has stopped and successfully generated the session key and a SID.
- Aborted: the oracle has stopped as a failure and has output an error message.

In the model, there exist a passive attacker and an active attacker. A passive attacker only eavesdrops on the communications, while an active attacker is allowed to intercept, delete, delay, and/or fabricate any messages at will. The security of a protocol is modelled by a series of games played between a challenger and the attacker. The challenger simulates the view of the attacker and answers all the queries of the following types asked by the attacker, $\mathcal{A}$.

- A Create query allows the attacker to initiate a new protocol instance.
- Upon receiving a Send query, the oracle will compute a response according to the protocol specification and a decision on whether to accept or reject, and return them to $\mathcal{A}$. If the oracle has either accepted with some session key or terminated, then this will be made known to $\mathcal{A}$.
- The Reveal query captures the notion of known key security. Upon receiving such a query, an oracle that has accepted and holds some session key, will return the session key to $\mathcal{A}$.
- The Test query is the only oracle query that does not correspond to any of $\mathcal{A}$'s abilities. If the oracle has accepted with some session key and is being asked a Test query, then, depending on a randomly chosen bit b, $\mathcal{A}$ is given either the actual session key or a session key drawn randomly from the session key distribution.

The definition of partnership is used in the definition of security to restrict the attacker's Reveal queries to accepted oracles that are not partners of the oracle whose key the attacker is trying to guess. Definition 1 describes the partnership definition.

Definition 1. *Two oracles, $\Pi_i^{id_i}$ and $\Pi_j^{id_j}$, for any $1 \leq i, j \leq n$ and $i \neq j$, are partners if and only if they accept and possess the same SID.*

We define a function Γ, which, on the input of an accepted oracle $\Pi_i^{id_i}$, returns $\Gamma(\Pi_i^{id_i}) = \sum_{j=1, j \neq i}^{n} \Psi_j(\Pi_i^{id_i})$, where $\Psi_j(\Pi_i^{id_i}) = 1$ if $\Pi_i^{id_i}$ has a partner oracle $(\Pi_j^{id_j})$, otherwise $\Psi_j(\Pi_i^{id_i}) = 0$. It is easy to see that the output of $\Gamma(\Pi_i^{id_i})$ equals the total number of participants that have at least one oracle partnered with $\Pi_i^{id_i}$.

Freshness is used to identify those session keys about which $\mathcal{A}$ ought not to know anything because $\mathcal{A}$ has not revealed any oracles that have accepted the key and has not corrupted any principals knowing the key. Definition 2 describes freshness, which depends on Definition 1.

Definition 2. *An oracle, $\Pi_i^{id_i}$, is said to be fresh if (1) $\Pi_i^{id_i}$ has accepted and has not been sent a Reveal query, and (2) no partner oracle of $\Pi_i^{id_i}$ (if such a partner exists) has been sent a Reveal query.*

3.1.1 Modelling Password Guessing Attacks

Without loss of generality, we assume that the password is chosen from the set $\mathcal{PW} = \{\pi_1, \pi_2, \cdots, \pi_m\}$, where π_i possesses the selection probability p_i and $p_i \leq p_j$ if $i > j$. It is easy to see that, after h tries and with no additional information, an attacker's advantage over the password (i.e. the largest probability the attacker can guess the correct password) is $\sum_{j=1}^{h+1} p_j$.

Password-based authenticated group key agreement protocols are designed to provide resilience against password guessing attacks, since passwords are usually of low entropy, and hence vulnerable to password guessing attacks. Password guessing attacks can be broadly categorised into online password guessing attacks and offline dictionary attacks. In an online password guessing attack, an attacker tries a guessed password by manipulating the inputs of one or more oracles. In an offline dictionary attack, an attacker exhaustively searches for the password by manipulating the inputs of one or more oracles. We remark that an offline dictionary attack presents a more subtle threat, as the adversary is able impersonate a legitimate party to initiate transactions without detection.

During the protocol execution, every oracle communicates with $n - 1$ oracles. Hence, an attacker may try $n - 1$ possible passwords by intervening in the inputs of only one oracle. Therefore, we regard a protocol to be secure if the attacker's advantage in guessing the "right" password is negligibly larger than the *evaluation probability* $\sum_{j=1}^{x(n-1)+1} p_j$ if x oracles aborted at the end of the following attack game. It should be noted that the *evaluation probability* $\sum_{j=1}^{x(n-1)+1} p_j$ can be replaced with any $\sum_{j=1}^{x(v)+1} p_j$ ($1 \leq v \leq n - 1$), where a smaller v means a stricter security requirement.

The attack game for modelling both kinds of password guessing attacks is carried out between the challenger and a polynomial-time attacker, $\mathcal{A}$, as follows:

Setup. The challenger generates a password, $\pi \in \mathcal{PW}$, and the public system parameters, *param*.

Challenge. The challenger runs $\mathcal{A}$ on the input of *param*. At some point, $\mathcal{A}$ terminates by outputting a guessed password π'. During its execution, $\mathcal{A}$ can make the following kinds of queries:

- Create(U), where U is any participant from the participant set.
- Send(Π, m), where Π is an active oracle and m is a message chosen by $\mathcal{A}$.
- Reveal(Π), where Π is an accepted oracle.

Suppose that there are x ($x < \frac{m}{n-1}$) aborted oracles at the end of the game. The attacker's advantage over the password in the game is defined to be $\mathsf{Adv}^{\mathcal{A}}(\pi) = \mathcal{F}(x, Pr(\pi = \pi'))$, where the function $\mathcal{F}$ is defined as follows: on the input of an integer a ($a < n$) and a value b ($0 \leq b \leq 1$), $\mathcal{F}(a, b)$ is computed as:

$$\mathcal{F}(a, b) = \begin{cases} 0, & \text{if } b \leq \sum_{j=1}^{a(n-1)+1} p_j \\ b - \sum_{j=1}^{a(n-1)+1} p_j, & \text{otherwise} \end{cases}$$

3.1.2 Modelling Attacks Against Key Authentication

The attack game against U_t $(1 \leq t \leq n)$ for key authentication is carried out between the challenger and a two-stage polynomial-time attacker $\mathcal{A} = (\mathcal{A}_1, \mathcal{A}_2)$ as follows:

Setup. The challenger generates a password $\pi \in \mathcal{PW}$ and the public system parameters *param*.

Phase 1. The attacker runs $\mathcal{A}_1$ on the input of *param*. $\mathcal{A}_1$ can make the following kinds of queries:

- Create(U), where U is any participant from the participant set.
- Send(Π, m), where Π is an active oracle and m is a message chosen by $\mathcal{A}_1$.
- Reveal(Π), where Π is an accepted oracle.

$\mathcal{A}_1$ terminates by making a Test($\Pi_t^{id_t}$) query, where $\Pi_t^{id_t}$ is a fresh oracle, and outputting some state information *state*.

Challenge. The challenger returns the output of Test($\Pi_t^{id_t}$).

Phase 2. The attacker runs $\mathcal{A}_2$ on the input of *state* and the output of the challenger. $\mathcal{A}_2$ can make the same kinds of query as those in Phase 1. But $\mathcal{A}_2$ is not allowed to make a Reveal query on the input of $\Pi_t^{id_t}$ or its partner oracle. $\mathcal{A}_2$ terminates by outputting a guess bit b'.

Suppose that there are x aborted oracles at the end of the game where $x < \frac{m}{n-1}$. The attacker's advantage in this game is defined to be $\mathsf{Adv}^\mathcal{A}(\mathsf{U}_t) = \mathcal{F}'(x, Pr(b = b'))$, where the function $\mathcal{F}'$ is defined as follows: on the input of an integer a $(a < n)$ and a value b $(0 \leq b \leq 1)$, $\mathcal{F}'(a, b)$ is computed as:

$$
\mathcal{F}'(a, b) = \begin{cases} 0, & \text{if } b \leq \frac{1 + \sum_{j=1}^{a(n-1)+1} p_j}{2} \\ b - \frac{1 + \sum_{j=1}^{a(n-1)+1} p_j}{2}, & \text{otherwise} \end{cases}
$$

3.1.3 Modelling Attacks Against Key Confirmation

The attack game against U_t $(1 \leq t \leq n)$ for key confirmation is carried out between the challenger and a two-stage polynomial-time attacker $\mathcal{A} = (\mathcal{A}_1, \mathcal{A}_2)$ as follows:

Setup. The challenger generates a password $\pi \in \mathcal{PW}$ and the public system parameters *param*.

Phase 1. The attacker runs $\mathcal{A}_1$ on the input of *param*. $\mathcal{A}_1$ can make the following kinds of queries:

- Create(U), where U is any participant from the participant set.
- Send(Π, m), where Π is an active oracle and m is a message chosen by $\mathcal{A}_1$.
- Reveal(Π), where Π is an accepted oracle.

$\mathcal{A}_1$ terminates by outputting an accepted oracle $\Pi_t^{id_t}$ and the state information *state*.

Challenge. The attacker continues running $\mathcal{A}_2$.

Phase 2. The attacker runs $\mathcal{A}_2$ on the input of *state*. $\mathcal{A}_2$ can make the same kinds of query as those in Phase 1. At some point, $\mathcal{A}_2$ terminates.

Suppose that, at the end of the game, there are x ($x < \frac{m}{n-1}$) aborted oracles and $\Pi_t^{id_t}$ has y partner oracles. The attacker's advantage in the game is defined to be $\mathsf{Adv}^{\mathcal{A}}(\mathsf{U}_t) = \mathcal{F}(x, Pr((y > n-1) \vee (\Gamma(\Pi_t^{id_t}) < n-1)))$.

Intuitively, if a protocol achieves key confirmation then it also guarantees mutual authentication which informally means that any legitimate accepted oracle confirms that the messages come from other legitimate oracles .

3.1.4 Security Definition

We first give a formal definition for negligible probability.

Definition 3. *The probability $P(\ell)$ is negligible if for any polynomial $f(\ell)$, where ℓ is the security parameter, there exists an integer N_f such that $P(\ell) \le \frac{1}{f(\ell)}$ for all $\ell \ge N_f$.*

Informally, a secure authenticated key agreement protocol with key confirmation guarantees that only the legitimate oracle can possibly compute the session key. Any oracle that accepts can confirm that it has $n-1$ partner oracles which compute the same session key. A formal statement is as follows.

Definition 4. *A password-based authenticated group key agreement protocol with key confirmation is secure, if it satisfies the following requirements:*

1. *When the protocol is run in the presence of a probabilistic, polynomial-time (PPT) attacker, all partnered oracles compute the same session key.*
2. *An oracle computes a uniformly distributed session key regardless of the inputs from other oracles.*
3. *An active PPT attacker only has negligible advantage in the attack game modelling password guessing attacks.*
4. *An active PPT attacker only has negligible advantage in the attack game against U_t ($1 \le t \le n$) for key authentication.*
5. *An active PPT attacker only has negligible advantage in the attack game against U_t ($1 \le t \le n$) for key confirmation.*

3.2 Security Analysis

We assume that the DDH problem is hard, i.e. given a finite cyclic group G of prime order, a generator α of G, and group elements α^a and α^b, distinguish α^{ab} and α^c, where α^c is a random element in G. In our proof, $\mathcal{H}_0$, $\mathcal{H}_1$, and $\mathcal{H}_2$ are modelled as random oracles.

Theorem 1. *The proposed authenticated password-based group key agreement protocol is secure in the sense of Definition 4 in the random oracle model under the DDH assumption.*

Proof Sketch for Theorem 1. It is straightforward to verify that the proposed protocol satisfies the first and second requirements of Definition 4. Next we prove that the proposed protocol satisfies the remaining (three) requirements.

Claim. In the attack game modelling password guessing attacks, the attacker's advantage is negligible.

Proof. The attack game is simulated by the challenger as follows.

Setup. Given a security parameter, ℓ, the challenger generates a password, $\pi \in \mathcal{PW}$, and the public system parameters, $param = \{p, q, \mathcal{H}_0, \mathcal{H}_1, \mathcal{H}_2, ID_i(1 \leq i \leq n)\}$. The attacker simulates $\mathcal{H}_0$, $\mathcal{H}_1$, and $\mathcal{H}_2$ as follows.

- $\mathcal{H}_0$ queries: The challenger maintains a list of request message and hash value pairs. When receiving the attacker's request message, the challenger first checks its list to see whether the hash value for the request message has been queried. If the check succeeds, the challenger sends the stored value to the attacker. Otherwise, the challenger generates a random value and sends it to the attacker. In the meantime, the challenger stores the request message and hash value pair to the existing list.
- $\mathcal{H}_1$ and $\mathcal{H}_2$ queries: These two kinds of queries are simulated in exactly the same way as the $\mathcal{H}_0$.

Challenge. The attacker runs $\mathcal{A}$ on the input of $param$. At some point, $\mathcal{A}$ terminates by outputting a guessed password π'. During its execution, $\mathcal{A}$ can make the following kinds of queries:

- Create(U), , where U is any participant from the participant set.
- Send(Π, m), where Π is an active oracle and m is a message chosen by A_1.
- Reveal(Π), where Π is an accepted oracle.

At the end of the game, suppose that there are x aborted oracles. We analyse the following different cases in which the attacker may try a guessed password:

1. Suppose $\mathcal{A}$ acts passively without manipulating any oracle's input. In this case, $\mathcal{A}$ needs to compute some $g^{s_i s_{i+1}}$ or M_i ($1 \leq i \leq n$), in order to test a guess. Computing $g^{s_i s_{i+1}}$ based on g^{s_i} and $g^{s_{i+1}}$ is equivalent to solving the Computational Diffie-Hellman (CDH) problem[6] and the probability of computing M_i is also negligible based on the DDH assumption [6]. Therefore, in this case $\mathcal{A}$ can only succeed with a negligible probability.
2. Suppose $\mathcal{A}$ has not manipulated the input of any oracle in the first stage during its execution. In this case, $\mathcal{A}$ can only succeed with a negligible probability for similar reasons as in the first case.
3. Suppose $\mathcal{A}$ has manipulated the input of an oracle in the first stage during its execution. Without loss of generality, suppose $\mathcal{A}$ replaces Z_{i+1} sent to $\Pi_i^{id_i}$ ($1 \leq i \leq n$) with Z'_{i+1}, where $Z'_{i+1} = (g')^s$, g' is computed based on a guessed password, and s is randomly chosen by $\mathcal{A}$. Then $\mathcal{A}$ postpones

---

[6] It is well known that CDH implies DDH.

forging $A_{i+1,i}$ until it obtains $A_{i,i+1}$. With $A_{i,i+1}$, $\mathcal{A}$ can test the guessed password by checking whether $A_{i,i+1} \stackrel{?}{=} h(i||i+1||Z'||(Z_i)^s||g'||ID_u)$ holds, where $Z' = Z_1||Z_2||\cdots||Z_i||Z'_{i+1}||Z_{i+2}||\cdots||Z_n$.
If $\pi' \neq \pi$, we can prove the following claims.

Claim. With the given information, $\mathcal{A}$ can only succeed in trying a different password with a negligible probability.

Proof. If $\mathcal{A}$ wishes to test another possible password, say π'', when its first guess is wrong ($\pi' \neq \pi$), then it must compute $(Z'_{i+1})^x$, where $x = \log_{g''}(Z_i)$ and g'' is computed based on π''. The computation can be abstracted as follows: Given $Z_i = (g'')^{x_1}$ and $Z'_{i+1} = (g'')^{x_2}$, where x_1 and x_2 are unknown, $\mathcal{A}$ computes $(g'')^{x_1 x_2}$. Based on the CDH assumption, $\mathcal{A}$ can only succeed with a negligible probability.   □

Claim. $\Pi_i^{id_i}$ accepts with a negligible probability.

Proof. To forge a key authentication message for $\Pi_i^{id_i}$, the attacker needs to compute the value, $(Z'_{i+1})^{s_i}$, where $Z'_{i+1} = (g')^s$, $Z_i = g^{s_i}$, and $g' \neq g$. The computation can be abstracted as follows: Given $Z_i = (g)^{x_1}$ and $Z'_{i+1} = (g)^{x_2}$, where x_1 and x_2 are unknown, $\mathcal{A}$ computes $g^{x_1 x_2}$. Based on the CDH assumption, $\mathcal{A}$ can only succeed in forging an authentication message with a negligible probability.   □

4. In order to exhaustively search for the password, $\mathcal{A}$ may also try to compute some M_i ($1 \leq i \leq n$), which is computed by some oracle, say $\Pi_i^{id_i}$, and then re-computes $\Pi_i^{id_i}$'s key confirmation message C_i. Suppose $\Pi_i^{id_i}$ receives the messages $X_1, X_2, \cdots, X_{i-1}, X_i, \cdots, X_{n-1}, X_n$, where X_i is computed by itself. Based on the discussions in the third case, it is easy to see that the probability, that any of these messages is computed by a legitimate oracle using at least one forged message (note that X_j ($1 \leq j \leq n$) is computed using two messages: Z_{j-1} and Z_{j+1}), is $\sum_{j=1}^{x+1} p_j$. As a result, the attacker can compute M_i with the probability $\sum_{j=1}^{x+1} p_j$ based on the results in [6].

Suppose that all the x aborted oracles resulting from the password guessing attacks, the attacker's advantage over the password is $\sum_{j=1}^{x+1} p_j + \mathcal{P}_1$, where $\mathcal{P}_1$ is negligible. As a result, in this game $\mathcal{A}$'s advantage $\mathsf{Adv}^{\mathcal{A}}(\pi) = \mathcal{F}(x, \sum_{j=1}^{x+1} p_j + \mathcal{P}_1)$ is also negligible and we have proved this claim.   □

Claim. In the attack game against U_t ($1 \leq t \leq n$) for key confirmation, the attacker's advantage is negligible.

Proof. The attack game is simulated by the challenger as follows.

Setup. Given a security parameter, ℓ, the challenger generates a password, $\pi \in \mathcal{PW}$, and the public system parameters, $param = \{p, q, \mathcal{H}_0, \mathcal{H}_1, \mathcal{H}_2, ID_i (1 \leq i \leq n)\}$. The attacker simulates $\mathcal{H}_0$, $\mathcal{H}_1$, and $\mathcal{H}_2$ as follows.

- $\mathcal{H}_0$ queries: The challenger maintains a list of request message and hash value pairs. When receiving the attacker's request message, the challenger first checks its list to see whether the hash value for the request message has been queried. If the check succeeds, the challenger sends the stored value to the attacker. Otherwise, the challenger generates a random value and sends it to the attacker. In the meantime, the challenger stores the request message and hash value pair to the existing list.
- $\mathcal{H}_1$ and $\mathcal{H}_2$ queries: These two kinds of queries are simulated in exactly the same way as the $\mathcal{H}_0$.

Phase 1. The attacker runs $\mathcal{A}_1$ on the input of *param*. $\mathcal{A}_1$ can make the following kinds of queries:
- Create(U), , where U is any participant from the participant set.
- Send(Π, m), where Π is an active oracle and m is a message chosen by $\mathcal{A}_1$.
- Reveal(Π), where Π is an accepted oracle.

$\mathcal{A}_1$ terminates by outputting an accepted oracle $\Pi_t^{id_t}$ and some state information *state*.

Challenge. The attacker continues running $\mathcal{A}_2$.

Phase 2. The attacker runs $\mathcal{A}_2$ on the input of *state*. $\mathcal{A}_2$ can make the same kinds of query as those in Phase 1. At some point, $\mathcal{A}_2$ terminates.

At the end of the game, suppose that $\Pi_t^{id_t}$ has y partner oracles and there are x aborted oracles. Next, we compute the probability of $y > n - 1$ and $\Gamma(\Pi_t^{id_t}) < n - 1$, respectively.

- In the proposed protocol, every participant U_i $(1 \le i \le n)$ generates and broadcasts $Z_i = g^{s_i}$, where s_i is a random number, outlined in the first stage. Hence, the probability that $y > n - 1$ happens is negligible because Z_i is part of the SID.
- As required by the protocol, $\Pi_t^{id_t}$ should have succeeded in verifying $n - 1$ key confirmation messages (which is computed based on SID and g (or π)) before it accepts in Phase 1. Suppose that $\Gamma(\Pi_t^{id_t}) < n-1$, then the attacker has forged at least one of the confirmation messages received by $\Pi_t^{id_t}$, which equivalently means the attacker has guessed the correct password. However, it is straightforward to verify that $\mathcal{F}(x, Pr(\Gamma(\Pi_t^{id_t}) < n - 1))$ is negligible based on the first claim.

Combining the above two possibilities, in this game the attacker's advantage $\mathcal{F}(x, Pr(\Gamma(\Pi_t^{id_t}) < n - 1) + Pr(y > n - 1))$ is negligible. As a result, we have proved this claim. □

Claim. In the attack game against U_t $(1 \le t \le n)$ for key authentication, the attacker's advantage is negligible.

Proof. The attack game is simulated by the challenger as follows.

Setup. Given a security parameter, ℓ, the challenger generates a password, $\pi \in \mathcal{PW}$, and the public system parameters, *param* $= \{p, q, \mathcal{H}_0, \mathcal{H}_1, \mathcal{H}_2, ID_i(1 \le i \le n)\}$. The attacker simulates $\mathcal{H}_0$, $\mathcal{H}_1$, and $\mathcal{H}_2$ as follows.

- $\mathcal{H}_0$ queries: The challenger maintains a list of request message and hash value pairs. When receiving the attacker's request message, the challenger first checks its list to see whether the hash value for the request message has been queried. If the check succeeds, the challenger sends the stored value to the attacker. Otherwise, the challenger generates a random value and sends it to the attacker. In the meantime, the challenger stores the request message and hash value pair to the existing list.
- $\mathcal{H}_1$ and $\mathcal{H}_2$ queries: These two kinds of queries are simulated in exactly the same way as the $\mathcal{H}_0$.

Phase 1. The attacker runs $\mathcal{A}_1$ on the input of $param$. $\mathcal{A}_1$ can make the following kinds of queries:

- Create(U), , where U is any participant from the participant set.
- Send(Π, m), where Π is an active oracle and m is a message chosen by $\mathcal{A}_1$.
- Reveal(Π), where Π is an accepted oracle.

$\mathcal{A}_1$ terminates by making a Test($\Pi_t^{id_t}$) query, where $\Pi_t^{id_t}$ is a fresh oracle, and outputting some state information $state$.

Challenge. The challenger returns the output of Test($\Pi_t^{id_t}$).

Phase 2. The attacker runs $\mathcal{A}_2$ on the input of $state$ and the output of the challenger. $\mathcal{A}_2$ can make the same queries as those in Phase 1. But $\mathcal{A}_2$ is not allowed to make a Reveal query on the input of $\Pi_t^{id_t}$ or its partner oracle. $\mathcal{A}_2$ terminates by outputting a guess bit b'.

At the end of the game, suppose that there are x aborted oracles. We have the following observations:

- Let $\mathcal{A}_S$, N_P, and $\overline{N_P}$ represent the events $\mathcal{A}$ succeeds, $\Gamma(\Pi_t^{id_t}) = n - 1$, and $\Gamma(\Pi_t^{id_t}) \neq n - 1$, the following equation holds:

$$Pr(\mathcal{A}_S) = Pr(b = b'|N_P)Pr(N_P) + Pr(b = b'|\overline{N_P})Pr(\overline{N_P})$$
$$\leq Pr(b = b'|N_P)Pr(N_P) + Pr(\overline{N_P})$$

- The attacker's advantage is computed as follows:

$$\mathsf{Adv}^{\mathcal{A}}(\mathsf{U}_t) = \begin{cases} 0, & \text{if } Pr(\mathcal{A}_S) \leq \frac{1+\sum_{j=1}^{x(n-1)+1} p_j}{2} \\ Pr(\mathcal{A}_S) - \frac{1+\sum_{j=1}^{x(n-1)+1} p_j}{2}, & \text{otherwise} \end{cases}$$

- Based on the second claim, we know that either $Pr(\overline{N_P}) \leq \sum_{j=1}^{x(n-1)+1} p_j$ holds or $Pr(\overline{N_P}) - \sum_{j=1}^{x(n-1)+1} p_j$ is negligible.

Suppose that the attacker's advantage $\mathsf{Adv}^{\mathcal{A}}(\mathsf{U}_t)$ in this game is non-negligible. Based on the above observations it is easy to see that $|Pr(b = b'|N_P) - \frac{1}{2}|$ is non-negligible, in contradiction of the security results in [6]. As a result, we have proved the claim. □

As a result, we have proved that the proposed protocol satisfies all the five security requirements so that it is secure under our definition. □

Conclusion of Proof for Theorem 1. As we have seen in the security proof, if n participants take part in the protocol execution $\mathcal{A}$ can try $2n$ possible passwords by simultaneously manipulating the messages sent to every participant. Moreover, $\mathcal{A}$ can mount the online password guessing attacks automatically by running a program. Consequently, an attacker can leverage this vulnerability, e.g., launches a successful online dictionary attack against the protocol when the group size n becomes very large. We remark that other password-based group key agreement protocols [5, 7, 11] also suffer from this security vulnerability.

4   Revisiting Online Password Guessing Attacks

As we have shown in the previous section, our proposed protocol suffers from automated online password guessing attacks (similar weaknesses can be found in other published password-based group key agreement protocols). In this section, we enhance the proposed protocol to make it more robust by using a CAPTCHA technique and federated verification provided by the server S.

4.1   CAPTCHA

Recent research on CAPTCHA techniques [2] suggests that CAPTCHA has many practical applications, e.g., sites such as Yahoo Mail and Hotmail use distorted image recognition to prevent automated account registration; online polls; search engine bots. CAPTCHA technique has also been deployed in combating spam and worms and preventing dictionary attacks [13]. Although distorted image recognition is most widely used, CAPTCHA means more than this – it is a test (any test) that can be automatically generated. Such tests generated are trivial to human but computationally hard for computer programs. Ahn *et al.* [2] studied two kinds of artificial intelligence (AI) problems and proposed several methods to construct CAPTCHA. However, we should note that the security of these AI problems, the foundation of the CAPTCHA, is based on the state of the art in pattern recognisation, and thus, heuristic. Several researchers have recently developed efficient methods to defeat some specific CAPTCHA. Despite this setback, CAPTCHA is still very popular.

4.2   Description of the Enhanced Protocol

In this enhanced protocol, we assume that S possesses a signature key pair (p_k, s_k) generated by a signature scheme (Gen, Sign, Vrfy) which is unforgeable under an adaptive chosen message attack (defined in [3]), and a public-key encryption key pair (p_k', s_k') generated by a IND-CCA2 secure public-key encryption scheme $(\mathcal{K}, \mathcal{E}, \mathcal{D})$ [14]. We also suppose that S can generate and verify CAPTCHA. Other parameters are generated in the same way as in the original protocol.

In a protocol execution, S and U_i $(1 \leq i \leq n)$ perform as follows.

Stage 0: Execution of CAPTCHA

1. U_i sends a random number, $r_i \in \{0, 1\}^\ell$, to S.
2. S sends a new CAPTCHA, pz, to U_1.

3. U_1 solves the CAPTCHA, pz, and sends the solution, sz, to S.
4. S checks whether sz is the correct solution of pz. If the check succeeds, S selects a random $s_{id} \in \{0, 1\}^{\ell}$, and then broadcasts s_{id}, $R = r_1||r_2||\cdots||r_n$, and a signature $\mathsf{Sig}_{s_k}(0||ID_u||R||s_{id})$.
5. After receiving the messages, U_i first verifies the signature. If the verification succeeds, U_i continues; otherwise, U_i aborts the protocol execution.

Stage 1: Message transfer and authentication

1. U_i chooses a random s_i $(0 \leq s_i \leq q - 1)$, and broadcasts $Z_i = g^{s_i}$.
2. After receiving every Z_j $(1 \leq j \leq n, j \neq i)$, U_i verifies that none of them equals 1. If the check succeeds, U_i selects two random number $r_i', r_i'' \in \{0, 1\}^{\ell}$, and sends

$$E_i = \mathsf{Enc}_{p_k'}(ID_i||A_{i,i-1}||A_{i,i+1}||A_{i-1,i}||A_{i+1,i}||r_i'||r_i''||s_{id})$$

   to S, where Z and $A_{i,i-1}, A_{i,i+1}, A_{i,i-1}, A_{i,i+1}$ $(1 \leq i \leq n)$ are defined in the same way as in the original protocol.
3. After receiving every E_i $(1 \leq i \leq n)$, S first decrypts them to check whether s_{id} is in its memory, and then checks whether $A_{i,i+1}$ (provided by U_i and U_{i+1}) and $A_{i,i-1}$ (provided by U_{i-1} and U_i) are correct, for all $1 \leq i \leq n$. If the checks succeed, S broadcasts a signature $\mathsf{Sig}_{s_k}(1||ID_u||R||R'||s_{id})$, where $R' = r_1'||r_2'||\cdots||r_n'$. Otherwise S broadcasts a failure message. Simultaneously, S deletes s_{id} and the related data.
4. If receiving a failure message, U_i aborts the protocol execution. Otherwise, after receiving R' and the signature from S, U_i verifies whether the signature is correct. If the verification succeeds, U_i continues the steps in next stage; otherwise it aborts the protocol execution.

Stage 2: Key agreement and key confirmation
This stage is similar to the original protocol presented in Section 2.2, except that the parameter A, used in the computation of key confirmation message and the session key, is substituted by $R||R'||s_{id}$.

4.3   Security Analysis of the Enhanced Protocol

Differences between our enhanced and our original versions include the following: (1) an additional stage 0 is added in our enhanced version, and (2) all the authentication messages in the first stage of our enhanced version are verified by the server, S. We now argue that these two features are effective countermeasures for online password guessing attacks, without compromising the overall security of our original protocol.

1. Assuming the hardness of the CAPTCHA, the possibilities of automated online password guessing attacks is now significantly reduced, since we assume that only a human being is intelligent enough to pass the CAPTCHA. In other words, we are assured that the initiator involved in every initialisation

of the protocol execution, is actually a human being and not some computer programs. Moreover, assuming the security of the underlying signature scheme, we can now verify that U_1 has successfully solved a CAPTCHA if, and only if, we receive a valid signature. Therefore, an automated program is prevening from mounting automated online password guessing attacks if the underlying CAPTCHA used is sufficiently strong.

Another alternative (without using the CAPTCHA) is to require the initiator to solve a computational puzzle [10] prior to the protocol execution with each individual protocol participant. However, such an approach is computationally intensive and it is difficult to adjust the hardness of the puzzles if the participants have very different computing power.

2. The federated verification ensures that $\mathcal{A}$ can only test at most one password in any single protocol execution. Assuming the security of the underlying public encryption scheme, $\mathcal{A}$ cannot simultaneously mount the attack by intervening in the protocol execution because $\mathcal{A}$ is unable to recover the encrypted messages or try its guess with the encrypted messages. Therefore, to test the guess, $\mathcal{A}$ must submit the forged messages to S for verification. However, S will definitely fail the verification and provide no other information about the failure if $\mathcal{A}$ attempts more than one guess at any one time.

The participants can indirectly verify the authentication messages by verifying the signature from S because of the presence of $r_i's$ in the signature but they cannot identify which authentication message goes wrong in the event that the verification fails.

5   Conclusions

We have proposed a password-based authenticated group key agreement protocol, and proved it secure in a variant of the model by Bresson *et al.* [4]. We then discussed the limitations of our protocol, followed by an enhanced version of the protocol using CAPTCHA. Consequently, our enhanced version is more robust against online password guessing attacks.

Acknowledgements. The authors would like to thank Chris J. Mitchell for his invaluable and constructive feedbacks, and the anonymous reviewers for their insightful comments.

References

1. M. Abdalla, E. Bresson, O. Chevassut, and D. Pointcheval. Password-based Group Key Exchange in a Constant Number of Rounds. In *PKC 2006*, LNCS. Springer-Verlag, 2006. To Appear.
2. L. Ahn, M. Blum, N. Hopper, and J. Langford. CAPTCHA: Using hard AI problems for security. In *EUROCRYPT 2003*, volume 2656 of *LNCS*, pages 294–311. Springer-Verlag, 2003.
3. M. Bellare and G. Neven. Transitive Signatures Based on Factoring and RSA. In *ASIACRYPT 2002*, volume 2501 of *LNCS*, pages 397–414. Springer-Verlag, 2002.

4. E. Bresson, O. Chevassut, and D. Pointcheval. Group Diffie–Hellman Key Exchange Secure Against Dictionary Attacks. In *ASIACRYPT 2002*, volume 2501 of *LNCS*, pages 497–514. Springer-Verlag, 2002.
5. E. Bresson, O. Chevassut, D. Pointcheval, and J.-J. Quisquater. Provably Authenticated Group Diffie–Hellman Key Exchange. In *ACM CCS 2001*, pages 255–264, 2001.
6. M. Burmester and Y. Desmedt. A Secure and Efficient Conference Key Distribution System. In A. D. Santis, editor, *Pre-Proceedings of EUROCRYPT '94*, LNCS, pages 279–290, 1994.
7. J. Byun and D. Lee. N-Party Encrypted Diffie–Hellman Key Exchange Using Different Passwords. In *ACNS 2005*, volume 3531 of *LNCS*, pages 75–90. Springer-Verlag, 2005.
8. N. Daswani, H. Garcia-Molina, and B. Yang. Open Problems in Data-Sharing Peer-to-Peer Systems. In *ICDT 2003*, volume 2572 of *LNCS*, pages 1–15. Springer-Verlag, 2002.
9. R. Dutta and R. Barua. Password-based Encrypted Group Key Agreement. *International Journal of Network Security*, 3(1):30–41, 2006.
10. A. Juels and J. Brainard. Client Puzzles: A Cryptographic Defense Against Connection Depletion. In *NDSS 1999*, pages 151–165, 1999.
11. S. M. Lee, J. Y. Hwang, and D. H. Lee. Efficient Password-Based Group Key Exchange. In *TrustBus 2004*, volume 3184 of *LNCS*, pages 191–199. Springer-Verlag, 2004.
12. T. Lomas, L. Gong, J. Saltzer, and R. Needham. Reducing Risks from Poorly Chosen Keys. *ACM SIGOPS Operating Systems Review*, 23(5):14–18, 1989.
13. B. Pinkas and T. Sander. Securing Passwords Against Dictionary Attacks. In *ACM CCS 2002*, pages 161–170. ACM Press, 2002.
14. C. Rackoff and D. R. Simon. Non-Interactive Zero-Knowledge Proof of Knowledge and Chosen Ciphertext Attack. In *CRYPTO 1991*, volume 576 of *LNCS*, pages 433–444. Springer-Verlag, 1991.
15. Q. Tang and L. Chen. Weaknesses in Two Group Diffie–Hellman Key Exchange Protocols. Cryptology ePrint Archive: Report 2005/197, 2005.

Stateful Subset Cover

Mattias Johansson[1], Gunnar Kreitz[2], and Fredrik Lindholm[1]

[1] Ericsson AB, SE-16480 Stockholm, Sweden
{mattias.a.johansson, fredrik.lindholm}@ericsson.com
[2] Royal Institute of Technology, Stockholm, Sweden
gkreitz@nada.kth.se

Abstract. This paper describes a method to convert stateless key revocation schemes based on the subset cover principle into stateful schemes. The main motivation is to reduce the bandwidth overhead to make broadcast encryption schemes more practical in network environments with limited bandwidth resources, such as cellular networks. This modification is not fully collusion-resistant.

A concrete new scheme based on the Subset Difference scheme [1] is presented, accomplishing a bandwidth overhead of $\Delta m + 2\Delta r + 1$ compared to e.g. Logical Key Hierarchy's $2(\Delta m + \Delta r) \log m$, where Δm and Δr is the number of members added and removed since the last stateful update and m is the number of current members.

Keywords: Broadcast encryption, key revocation, subset cover, Subset Difference, Logical Key Hierarchy, stateful, stateless.

1 Introduction

In this paper we show how a key server can establish a common group key K_g for a dynamically changing group (i.e., members can join and leave). One possible application area is the protection of broadcast streams (e.g., internet or mobile broadcasting of movies, music, or news), and the topic is therefore generally referred to as broadcast encryption. The group key which is to be distributed is often referred to as the media key, or session key.

This problem is well studied and is usually solved by using a key revocation scheme. One large class of key revocation schemes are the subset cover schemes, introduced in [1]. In this paper we present a general method for adding state to subset cover schemes, which reduces the bandwidth overhead greatly.

In the system setup stage, the key server gives each user u some key information K_u. This information can be thought of as a set of keys; in general it will be information from which keys can be derived. The size of K_u is called the *user storage*. Schemes where K_u is never updated are called *stateless*, whereas those where it is updated K_u are called *stateful*.

Every time a new group key is distributed, the key server will broadcast a *header*, using which all legitimate group members can calculate the new group key. The size of this header is called the *bandwidth overhead*, and the time it takes for a member to compute the group key from the header and her set of key information K_u is called the *computational overhead*.

J. Zhou, M. Yung, and F. Bao (Eds.): ACNS 2006, LNCS 3989, pp. 178–193, 2006.

1.1 Preliminaries

Broadcast encryption was first introduced by Berkovits in [2], and later Fiat and Naor started a more formal study of the subject [3]. The first practical broadcast encryption scheme was the stateful Logical Key Hierarchy (LKH) scheme proposed in [4, 5]. LKH accomplishes a worst case bandwidth overhead of $2(\Delta m + \Delta r) \log m$, where Δm and Δr are the number of added and removed members since the last stateful key update, and m is the number of current members.

Later, the class of schemes known as subset cover schemes, and the Subset Difference (SD) scheme were presented in [1]. Further variants of the SD scheme have been developed in [6, 7]. Other subset cover schemes include the Hierarchical Key Tree scheme [8], and the Punctured Interval scheme, π [9]. All of these schemes have bandwidth overhead which is linear in r.

Stateful or Stateless. The advantage of a stateless scheme compared to a stateful scheme is that a member does not have to receive all previous updates in order to decrypt the current broadcast. In many settings, this advantage is not as big as it first appears. Stateful schemes can be augmented with reliable multicast techniques or can make missed broadcasts available on request. Also, in e.g. a commercial settings where the group key is updated every five minutes, a stateless scheme would also need to use similar techniques, since missing five minutes of content due to a single packet lost would be unacceptable.

Notation. Let $\mathcal{M}$ be the set of members of the group, $\mathcal{R}$ be the set of revoked users and $\mathcal{U}$ be the total set of users, or potential members (i.e. the union of $\mathcal{M}$ and $\mathcal{R}$). Let m, r and u be the sizes of these sets. Let Δm and Δr be the number of users who have joined and left the group since the last *stateful* update. Let $E_K(M)$ be the encryption of message M under key K. In a binary tree, let $l(v)$ and $r(v)$ be the left and right child of node v. Let $par(v)$ and $sib(v)$ be the parent and sibling of node v.

1.2 Our Contribution

Subset cover schemes define a family of subsets of $\mathcal{U}$, where each subset is associated with a key. To distribute a new group key, the key server covers $\mathcal{M}$ (and avoids $\mathcal{R}$) with subsets from the family and encrypts the new group key K_g using the key of each subset used in the cover. We present a technique where a *state key*, K_S is added, which is held by current members of the group.

When distributing a new group key, the state key is used to transform all subset keys. Since only current members have access to the state key, the key server does not need to avoid covering all of $\mathcal{R}$, but only those who were recently removed (and thus have a current state key).

This technique can be applied to any scheme based on the subset cover principle. It is often beneficial to develop a new algorithm to calculate the cover, and this has been done for the SD scheme.

1.3   Organization of This Paper

In Section 2, a brief overview of subset cover schemes is given. In Section 3, our idea, Stateful Subset Cover, is presented in detail. In Section 4, we show practical performance results on some simulated datasets. In Section 5, we discuss the security of our proposed scheme. We give concluding remarks in Section 6. Algorithms for Stateful Subset Cover are given in Appendix A.

2   Subset Cover Schemes

A general class of stateless schemes are called subset cover schemes and were first introduced in [1]. In this class of revocation schemes, there is a preconfigured family of sets, $\mathcal{F} = \{f_1, f_2, \ldots\}, f_i \subseteq \mathcal{U}$. Each set $f_i \in \mathcal{F}$ has an associated key K_i such that each user belonging to f_i can compute K_i, but no user outside of f_i can compute K_i.

To distribute a new group key, the key server calculates an exact cover $\mathcal{F}'$ of $\mathcal{M}$, i.e. $\mathcal{F}' = \{f_{i_1}, f_{i_2}, \ldots\} \subseteq \mathcal{F}$ and $\bigcup \mathcal{F}' = f_{i_1} \cup f_{i_2} \cup \ldots = \mathcal{M}$. The key server then broadcasts the following message:

$$\mathcal{F}', E_{K_{i_1}}(K_g), E_{K_{i_2}}(K_g), \ldots$$

where $\mathcal{F}'$ here denotes some suitable representation of $\mathcal{F}'$ such that members can compute what part of the message to decrypt using what key. Since the sets $\mathcal{F}$ and the keys associated with the sets are fixed, this broadcast encryption scheme is stateless.

2.1   Subset Difference

In the Subset Difference (SD) scheme, which is a subset cover scheme, every user is associated with a leaf in a binary tree. For every node v in the tree, and every node w below v, we have $S_{v,w} \in \mathcal{F}$, where $S_{v,w}$ is the set of all leaves in the subtree rooted in v, except for those in the subtree rooted in w. In figure 1, two such sets are shown, the set $S_{2,10}$ and the set $S_{6,12}$. The corresponding broadcast from the key server would in this case be

$$\{S_{2,10}, S_{6,12}\}, E_{K_{S_{2,10}}}(K_g), E_{K_{S_{6,12}}}(K_g).$$

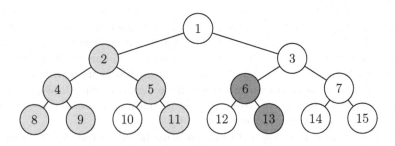

Fig. 1. The sets $S_{2,10}$ (light) and $S_{6,12}$ (dark) in an SD tree

A user is not given the keys $K_{S_{v,w}}$ she is entitled to directly, since that would consume too much user memory. Instead, she is given $\mathcal{O}(\log^2 u)$ values from which the keys she should have access to can be derived by $\mathcal{O}(\log u)$ applications of a pseudo-random number generator. For details on how the key derivation in SD works, see [1]. The SD scheme has a bandwidth overhead which is $\min(2r + 1, m)$.

2.2   The Punctured Interval Scheme π

In the punctured interval (π) scheme, users can be thought of as being on a line, each user indexed by an integer. The subsets used in the π scheme are of the form $S_{i,j;x_1,\ldots,x_q} = \{x | i \leq x \leq j, x \neq x_k, 1 \leq k \leq q\}$, i.e. all users between positions i and j (inclusive) except for the q users $x_1, \ldots, x_q$.

The scheme has two parameters, p and c affecting the performance of the system. The parameter c is the maximum length of the interval, e.g. $1 \leq j - i + 1 \leq c$, and the parameter p is how many users in the interval can at most be excluded, e.g. $0 \leq q \leq p$. Large p and c lower bandwidth requirements but increase user storage and computational overhead. The bandwidth overhead is about $\frac{r}{p+1} + \frac{u-r}{c}$ and the user storage is $\mathcal{O}(c^{p+1})$. For details on the π scheme, see [9].

3   Stateful Subset Cover

In this section, a general technique for transforming a subset cover scheme into a stateful scheme through the introduction of a *state key* is presented. This makes the bandwidth performance linear in $\Delta m + \Delta r$ instead of in r. As will be discussed further in Section 5, this weakens the security of the system somewhat in that it opens up the opportunity for collaboration. This risk can however be mitigated by periodically using the normal update mechanism of the underlying subset cover scheme, which is referred to as a *hard update*.

3.1   An Intuitive Description

Recall that, as presented in Section 2, a subset cover scheme by covering members using a static family of subsets of users. The subsets are created at startup-time and are constant throughout the life of the system. Each subset is associated with a key that only users in that subset have access to. To distribute a new group key, the key server broadcasts the new group key encrypted with the key for each subset in the cover.

We introduce a general extension to a subset cover scheme by adding a state key, which is distributed alongside with the group key to members. This state key is then used for distributing the next group key and state key. When the key server broadcasts a new group key (and state key) it will not encrypt the new group key directly with the keys of the selected subsets, instead it will use the key of the selected subset transformed by the current state key using some suitable function (e.g. xor). This means that to decrypt the new group key, a user must not only be in a selected subset, but must also have the current state key.

The key server, when it saves bandwidth doing so, is thus free to cover revoked users too, as long as they do not have access to the current state key. So, the key server need only avoid covering those who were revoked recently. To discourage cheating (see Section 5) the aim is to cover as few revoked users as possible, which is referred to as a *cheap* cover.

The alert reader may have noticed a problem with the system as described. If the state key is needed to decrypt the new group key and state key, how are recently joined members, who do not have the current state key, handled? The answer is that the state key is not used when covering joiners, and thus all of $\mathcal{R}$ must be avoided. However, the scheme is free to cover current members who have a state key, and it is preferable for it to cover as many of these as it can, since those covered here will not need to be covered in the cover using the state key. This is called a *generous* cover.

A variation of the above extension is to run the system in a *semi-stateless* mode. That means that the key server in each round is free to decide whether it wishes to update the state key or not. As long as the state key is not updated, the scheme will have the properties of a stateless scheme, but the bandwidth usage will gradually increase since Δm and Δr (membership changes since last *stateful* update, see Section 1.1) will increase. A group key update when the state key is changed is called a *stateful update* and one where the state key remains unchanged is called *stateless update*.

3.2   Generalized Stateful Subset Cover

For this type of scheme to work, a new cover function is needed. The traditional subset cover has two types of users: members and revoked, or blue and red. The new cover function has three types of users: must cover (MC), can cover (CC) and must not cover (NC). The output is a cover covering all users marked MC and not covering any NC users. Users marked as CC, can be either covered or not covered.

As discussed in Section 3.1, there are two versions of the cover algorithm for each scheme, *generous* and *cheap*. Both versions will primarily minimize the number of subsets used for the cover. The generous cover will attempt to cover as many CC users as possible and the cheap cover will cover as few as possible.

More formally, we have a new decision problem, OPTIONAL-SET-COVER($\mathcal{F}$, $\mathcal{M}$, $\mathcal{R}$, k, n), where $\mathcal{F}$ is a family of subsets of some finite set $\mathcal{U}$, $\mathcal{M}$ is subset of the same $\mathcal{U}$ and k and n are integers. The problem is: is there a subset $\mathcal{F}' \subseteq \mathcal{F}$ such that $\bigcup \mathcal{F}' \supseteq \mathcal{M}$, $|\mathcal{F}'| = n$, $|\bigcup \mathcal{F}'| = k$, and $(\bigcup \mathcal{F}') \cap \mathcal{R} = \emptyset$?

The two optimization problems, generous and cheap, both primarily want to minimize n, and then on the second hand either want to maximize or minimize k, respectively. The optimization problems are denoted GENEROUS-COVER($\mathcal{F}$, $\mathcal{M}$, $\mathcal{R}$) and CHEAP-COVER($\mathcal{F}$, $\mathcal{M}$, $\mathcal{R}$). The (optional) subset cover problem is in the general case NP complete, but subset cover schemes are designed in such a way that an efficient algorithm exists.

The Framework. The system is initialized exactly as the underlying subset cover scheme, with one exception. A state key, K_S, is generated by the key server and given to all initial members of the system. The key server also keeps track of the set of users to which it has given the current state key, the set S.

To update the group key, the key server first decides whether it is time to do a hard update or not. If a hard update is done, it uses the underlying scheme to distribute a new K'_g and K'_S and sets $S \leftarrow \mathcal{M}$.

If it was not time to do a hard update, it begins by calculating a cover $\mathcal{C}_1$ as $\mathcal{C}_1 \leftarrow$ GENEROUS-COVER$(\mathcal{F}, \mathcal{M} \backslash S, \mathcal{R})$. Note that this cover is empty if $\mathcal{M} \backslash S$ is empty, i.e. if no new members have been added since K_S was last updated.

After this, it checks if $\mathcal{R} \cap S = \emptyset$. If this is the case, i.e. no one has been removed since K_S was last updated, no one besides members has K_S, and thus K_S can be used to securely communicate with members. If $\mathcal{R} \cap S \neq \emptyset$, it instead calculates $\mathcal{C}_2 \leftarrow$ CHEAP-COVER$(\mathcal{F}, \mathcal{M} \backslash (\bigcup \mathcal{C}_1), \mathcal{R} \cap S)$.

The key server then first broadcasts a description of the covers $\mathcal{C}_1$, $\mathcal{C}_2$ in some form, so that members know what part of the broadcast to decrypt. The message will then consist of, firstly, for every $c \in \mathcal{C}_1$: $E_{K_c}(K_E)$, where K_c is the key associated with subset c. Secondly, if $\mathcal{R} \cap S \neq \emptyset$, the message will contain, for every $c \in \mathcal{C}_2$: $E_{K_c}(K_F)$, or if $\mathcal{R} \cap S = \emptyset$, $E_{K_S}(K_F)$. We let $K_E = f(K_F, K_S)$, where f is a suitable function, such as xor. Finally, the message will contain $E_{K_E}(K'_g, K_S)$ or $E_{K_E}(K'_g, K'_S)$ depending on if it was a stateless or stateful update, respectively. If the update was stateful, the key server sets $S \leftarrow \mathcal{M}$, otherwise S is left unchanged.

Generic Cover. A normal subset cover algorithm can be used to solve the optional subset cover problem, but generally not optimally. Since most subset cover schemes have bandwidth performance which linear in r, it is often beneficial to minimize $\mathcal{R}$.

So, for the optional subset cover problem, we can simply re-mark all CC users as members and then run the normal subset cover algorithm on the resulting set. Post-processing can be done to remove any sets covering only users who were labelled CC before the re-marking. Post-processing can also, in the cheap variant, attempt to narrow a set down (i.e. change the set so that fewer CC users are covered).

For a specific underlying scheme, it is often possible to make better use of the CC users than this rather naïve transformation. An optimal algorithm for the SD scheme will be discussed in the next section.

3.3   Stateful Subset Difference

For SD (Section 2.1), which is one of the most important subset cover schemes, a new cover algorithm has been developed. Pseudo-code for the algorithm can be found in Appendix A, but we describe and discuss it here.

The complexity of the algorithm has the same asymptotic complexity as the original. This algorithm could also be used in stateful variants of other subset cover schemes which use the SD cover method, such as LSD and SSD ([6, 7]).

Let each node v have three variables, two booleans, $v.\textbf{mc}$ and $v.\textbf{nc}$ and one integer, $v.\textbf{cc}$. The variable $v.\textbf{cc}$ counts the number of CC users which can be excluded under v. If $v.\textbf{mc}$ is true, it means that there are uncovered MC users (i.e., users which must be covered) below v. If $v.\textbf{nc}$ is true, it means that there are NC users (i.e., users which must not be covered) below v.

A basic observation is that a node v where both the left ($l(v)$) and the right child ($r(v)$) has a NC node below it cannot be used as a top node for a key. So, if any MC nodes are below such a node, the top node to use for the set cannot be higher up in the tree than $l(v)$ or $r(v)$.

For the algorithms given, we assume that the bottom nodes (i.e., the user nodes) have already been colored in the input. That means that for a MC user at node v, $v.\textbf{mc} = \textbf{true}$, $v.\textbf{nc} = \textbf{false}$ and $v.\textbf{cc} = 0$. Analogously for a NC user. For a CC user at node v, $v.\textbf{mc} = v.\textbf{nc} = \textbf{false}$ and $v.\textbf{cc} = 1$.

The algorithm consists of three functions. COVER() is the top-level function which is called to generate the entire cover, with a parameter telling it if a generous or cheap cover is wanted. COVER() "adds up" the marks of the child nodes, and call a helper-function to calculate the exact subset when it discovers that a subset has to be placed. When subsets are placed, they are guaranteed to cover all remaining MC users under the current node. This means that there is nothing left to be covered below that node, so the parent will be marked with only NC, instead of the usual "sum" of the child nodes.

The two functions, GENEROUS-FIND-SUBSET() and CHEAP-FIND-SUBSET() calculate a single subset, given a top node which is the highest place for the top node of the subset. Both versions use the markings placed by COVER() to calculate the subset. The generous version will just ensure that no NC users are covered, while the cheap version will both ensure that no NC users are covered and will attempt to exclude as many CC users as possible.

As an example, consider the tree shown in Figure 2. Let the letter 'N' denote $v.\textbf{nc} = \textbf{true}$, 'M' denote $v.\textbf{mc} = \textbf{true}$ and 'C' denote $v.\textbf{cc} = 1$. The bottom nodes have all been colored in the input to the algorithm. Going through the nodes in depth-first (left-to-right) order, in the first node, the NC and CC marks from the child nodes are combined into the parent. In its sibling, the CC and NC marks propagate up.

When we get to the left child of the root, then both children are marked with NC and at least one child is marked with MC. This will cause FIND-SUBSET() to be called. In both cases, FIND-SUBSET() will select the subset $S_{4,8}$, which covers the single MC node 9.

For the right subtree, marks will propagate upwards and the coloring will reach the right child of the root without FIND-SUBSET() being called. However, both children of the root are marked NC, and node 3 is marked MC, so one of the FIND-SUBSET() functions will be called again. In this case, the subset $S_{3,14}$ will be selected, which covers the two MC users 12 and 14 and the CC user 13.

This algorithm differs somewhat from the original cover algorithm for SD given in [1]. The original algorithm begins by calculating the Steiner tree of the revoked users and the root and then calculate the cover directly from the

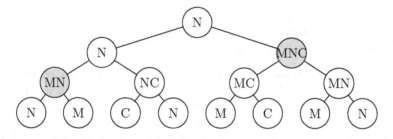

Fig. 2. A sample coloring of a stateful subset difference tree, gray nodes show on what nodes FIND-SUBSET() are called

properties of the Steiner tree. The algorithm presented here also works as a cover algorithm for the normal SD cover problem. Both algorithms have the same time complexity.

3.4   Stateful Punctured Interval

A very simple greedy (and suboptimal) cover algorithm has been tested with the π scheme. We do not present this algorithm here. Recall (Section 2.2) that this scheme has two parameters which can be tuned. Tests have been performed with four sets of parameters, $(c, p) = (1000, 1), (100, 2), (33, 3), (16, 4)$. These were selected such that user storage would be approximately 1 Mbyte, which we deemed reasonable for many scenarios. We present the results parameters giving the best results on our dataset, $(c, p) = (1000, 1)$. Further tuning may give even better performance.

3.5   Performance

The user storage will essentially be unchanged (a single extra key needs to be stored by members and the key server) by the addition of state, so they will be the same as those of the underlying scheme. Analogously for the computational overhead. The scheme will take on the negative properties of a stateful scheme in that packet loss becomes a more serious issue which will need to be handled, see the discussion in Section 1.1, where we argue that this is not as big a drawback as it first appears.

Bandwidth Impact. The bandwidth performance will in general improve. The bandwidth usage for the first cover calculated (for joining members, where the state key is not used) is at worst that of the underlying scheme with Δm members and r revoked users. For the second cover, where the state key is used, the performance is at worst that of the underlying scheme with m members and Δr revoked users. Inserting the values for SD, we get a worst-case bandwidth performance of $\min(2r+1, \Delta m)+\min(2\Delta r+1, m)$, which will, in most situations, be $\Delta m + 2\Delta r + 1$. This can be compared to for instance LKH, which has a performance of $2(\Delta m + \Delta r) \log m$.

The worst-case performance is better than previous protocols. A comparative performance evaluation in several usage scenarios has also been performed, and some of these results are presented in Section 4.

Computational Complexity for General Stateful Subset Cover. At most u users can be undecided, so at worst, u nodes must be re-labeled. The output of the cover will cover each undecided or cover node exactly once, so the cost of going through the sets is at most the number of such nodes, which is u. Thus, the added runtime for both the pre-processing and post-processing steps is $\mathcal{O}(u)$.

Computational Complexity for Stateful Subset Difference. The performance of the cover algorithm is $\mathcal{O}(u)$. On the way up, each node will be visited exactly once and the tree has $\mathcal{O}(u)$ nodes. When FIND-SUBSET() is called, the top node will only be colored red. All downward traversal in the FIND-SUBSET() functions will always stop at a node colored only red. This means that on the way down (i.e., in FIND-SUBSET()) each node can be visited at most twice.

3.6   Correctness

The framework is correct in that a member can recover the new key, as long as she has not missed the last stateful update. For a member there are two cases. Either, she is recently added and does not have the current state key, or she has the current state key.

If a member m does not have the current state key, then $\mathcal{M}\backslash\mathcal{S} \neq \emptyset$ since it must at least contain m. If so, the cover $\mathcal{C}_1 = $ GENEROUS-COVER($\mathcal{M}\backslash\mathcal{S}, \mathcal{R}$) will be calculated and the underlying scheme will be used to distribute the keys with the resulting cover. If the underlying scheme is correct, the member will be able to recover the key and the current state key.

If, on the other hand, m does have the current state key, there are three cases. If m is covered by $\mathcal{C}_1$ then she can discover that fact by looking at the information about the cover and recover the key, given that the underlying scheme was correct.

If $\mathcal{R} \cap \mathcal{S} = \emptyset$, then the new group key will be distributed as $E_{K_S}(K'_g)$ and since m has K_S, she can recover the new group key.

If $\mathcal{R} \cap \mathcal{S} \neq \emptyset$, then a second cover, $\mathcal{C}_2 = $ CHEAP-COVER($\mathcal{M}\backslash(\bigcup\mathcal{C}_1), \mathcal{S} \cap \mathcal{R}$) will be calculated. Since m has the state key and was not covered by $\mathcal{C}_1$, she will be covered by $\mathcal{C}_2$. Given that the underlying scheme is correct, she can then recover K_F, from which she can derive K_E since $K_E = f(K_F, K_S)$. She can then recover the new group key which is distributed as $E_{K_E}(K'_g)$.

4   Practical Results

For simulation purposes, two datasets have been used. In the first dataset, the number of users currently in the group follow a sinus-shaped form, and in the second dataset, the number of users go through (almost) the entire range of the system, from all users being members to almost all users being revoked.

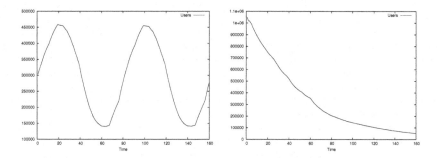

Fig. 3. The sinus-shaped and full-ranged dataset with 2^{20} users

Key updates occur only at discrete intervals (i.e., in batch mode), of which there were 160 in the simulation. To increase the dynamic of the system, except for the joins and leaves necessary to generate the proper form, a *base change* rate was added. The base change is a value between 0 and 1 signifying how large fraction of members that will be replaced by non-members during each round. Given that the scheme we present performs worse in a highly dynamic system, we have used simulations with a very high basechange of 2% to show that it still performs well under difficult conditions. The datasets are displayed in Figure 3. More simulation results are in [10].

The performance of the stateful subset cover schemes presented in this article were evaluated and compared to the performance of the popular LKH scheme, as well as the stateless subset schemes. Note that the stateless schemes do have significantly different performance characteristics, and will e.g. behave poorly when a majority of the population is revoked.

4.1   Performance in Stateful Subset Cover

The performance of the stateful SD and π schemes was evaluated using the scenarios presented in the previous section. As will be shown, the performance is significantly better than that of the LKH scheme, as could be expected from the theoretical analysis.

Figure 4 shows a comparison between two variations of stateful subset cover and LKH. The regular, stateless versions of the subset cover schemes were omitted from this figure for clarity. They do, in fact, have better performance than LKH in this scenario (due to the high base change rate), but the stateful variations still significantly outperform them.

Table 1 shows both the average number of sets used per key update and the maximum number of sets used for a single update. Both these measurements are important to minimize. Minimizing the average will keep total bandwidth usage down and minimizing the maximum will keep the latency for key refresh reasonably low. We show results without any hard updates in these tables. With periodic hard updates, the maximum for the stateful versions will be (about) the same as for the normal versions of the schemes.

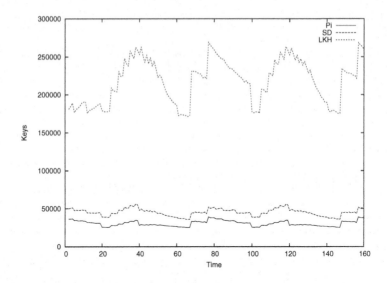

Fig. 4. Bandwidth performance in the sinus-shaped dataset

Table 1. Performance comparison between normal and stateful subset cover schemes (without hard updates), and LKH

Scheme	Sinus dataset		Full-range dataset	
	Avg. sets used	Max sets used	Avg. sets used	Max sets used
Stateful SD	45 136	55 983	43 214	59 798
Stateful π	30 549	39 067	28 153	33 980
LKH	218 046	269 284	241 362	393 758
Normal SD	222 409	295 778	170 175	305 225
Normal π	153 733	180 157	114 100	180 048

As the diagram and table shows, the stateful version acheives significantly lower bandwidth requirements compared to previous schemes. The worst-case performance (i.e., the maximum number of sets used) is reduced by a factor five and the average case is reduced by a factor four.

5   Security of Stateful Subset Cover

The scheme as presented is not fully collusion-resistant. Users can collaborate by one revoked user who has recently been removed sharing the current state key with a user who is covered, but who does not have the state key. In this section, techniques for mitigating this type of attacks will be discussed. Further, a model for this type of cheating will be given and, the expectancy for how long cheaters gain access will be analyzed using the same data as was used for performance evaluations.

5.1 Security Model

In a commercial setting, the concern is to make it cost-inefficient rather than impossible to illegally decrypt the broadcast. In this model it is assumed, that it is possible to make it expensive to extract state keys, by putting them in a protected area such as a smart card or other tamper resistant hardware. In addition, by using periodic hard updates, cheaters will also periodically be removed from the system. These two techniques can together be used to mitigate the effect of a collaborative behavior by dishonest users.

The major threat in a commercial setting would be the extraction of legitimate long-term keys, since that would allow for pirate decoders to be manufactured. This can be made hard by placing the long-term keys in protected hardware, and by using *traitor tracing* techniques, should the keys leak. Concerning this threat, the stateful subset cover schemes presented here have the same security properties as regular subset cover schemes, given that the long-term key structure is identical.

Another important threat would be redistribution of the group key by a member, i.e. every time a new group key is distributed, the dishonest (but paying) member sends the new group key to her friends. The group key is identical for all users in the group, so traitor tracing techniques are not applicable.

In the stateful schemes, another option would be for a dishonest user to instead redistribute the state key (along with the group key) to her friends. The advantage to the cheaters would be that this would not have to be done as frequently as the group key is to be distributed.

An important aspect to analyze is the expectancy of the time a user who illegally gets a state key can recover the group key. In our model, every user who is removed from the system is given the next round's state key and group key, so she can recover the group key for at least one more round. Then, as long as she is covered using the state key, she can keep decrypting, but as soon as she is not covered in a round, she will lose her ability to decrypt the broadcast. The larger this expectancy, the more seldom a traitor would need to redistribute the state key to keep enabling her friends to recover the group key.

This model of cheating simulates a user illegally receiving a state key. It is run over the same simulation data as the performance tests to give a real-world like cover. This also means that some users will be added again before they are successfully revoked by the system. These are ignored when calculating the average.

In the simulation, we measure the average number of rounds users who left in round r could watch the show, given that they were given one key. In the simulations, a hard update is always run immediately after the end of the simulation, i.e. it is assumed that after the last round, all current cheaters were revoked.

5.2 Subset Difference

In Figure 5, the average numbers of rounds a revoked user can watch if she receives that key is shown. The cheating model used is described in more detail in the previous section. As can be seen, even with hard updates done every 160:th round, a cheater can still at best expect to see approximately 10 rounds.

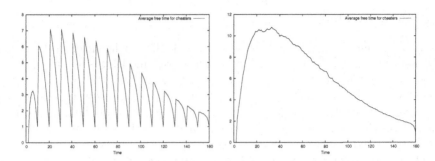

Fig. 5. Average free time for cheaters in stateful SD. 2^{20} users, full-range dataset, basechange 2%, hard updates every 10 (left) and 160 (right) rounds.

While this is worse than the normal schemes, where this number is constantly 1, it is still reasonably small.

At the cost of bandwidth, the frequency with which a traitor must redistribute the state key can be increased by doing hard updates more frequently.

6   Summary

This paper introduces the idea of adding state to a certain class of key revocation schemes, called subset cover schemes. Having state in a key revocation scheme has some drawbacks, like an increased vulnerability to packet loss. These drawbacks are not as bad as they first appear, as we argue for in Section 1.1.

The specific method used in this paper is not collusion-resistant by itself, but may need additional mitigation techniques, such as tamper resistant modules for acceptable security. This non-perfect security is however by practical examples shown to have a limited effect on the overall security from a commercial point of view, where the interest is more directed towards making illegal decryption cost-inefficient rather than impossible.

As a benefit, it is shown that the conversion of a stateless subset cover scheme may lead to greatly reduced bandwidth overhead. This is extremely important in network environments where the available bandwidth is a limited resource, like for example cellular networks. In particular, simulation results show a significant reduction of bandwidth compared to previous schemes.

The transformation presented in this paper is not very complex, with the addition of a global state key, common to all members. Could there be more advanced transformations of subset cover (or other broadcast encryption) schemes which further reduce bandwidth overhead or give better security properties?

References

1. D. Naor, M. Naor, and J. Lotspiech, "Revocation and tracing schemes for stateless receivers," *Lecture Notes in Computer Science*, vol. 2139, pp. 41–62, 2001.
2. S. Berkovits, "How to broadcast a secret," *Lecture Notes in Computer Science*, vol. 547, pp. 535–541, 1991.

3. A. Fiat and M. Naor, "Broadcast encryption," *Lecture Notes in Computer Science*, vol. 773, pp. 480–491, 1994.

4. D. M. Wallner, E. J. Harder, and R. C. Agee, "Key management for multicast: Issues and architectures," Internet Request for Comment RFC 2627, Internet Engineering Task Force, 1999.

5. C. K. Wong, M. Gouda, and S. S. Lam, "Secure group communications using key graphs," in *Proceedings of the ACM SIGCOMM '98 conference on Applications, technologies, architectures, and protocols for computer communication*, pp. 68–79, ACM Press, 1998.

6. D. Halevy and A. Shamir, "The LSD broadcast encryption scheme," *Lecture Notes in Computer Science*, vol. 2442, pp. 47–60, 2002.

7. M. T. Goodrich, J. Z. Sun, and R. Tamassia, "Efficient tree-based revocation in groups of low-state devices," *Lecture Notes in Computer Science*, vol. 3152, pp. 511–527, 2004.

8. T. Asano, "A revocation scheme with minimal storage at receivers," *Lecture Notes in Computer Science*, vol. 2501, pp. 433–450, 2002.

9. N.-S. Jho, J. Y. Hwang, J. H. Cheon, . M.-H. Kim, D. H. Lee, and E. S. Yoo, "One-way chain based broadcast encryption schemes," *Lecture Notes in Computer Science*, vol. 3494, pp. 559–574, 2005.

10. G. Kreitz, "Optimization of broadcast encryption schemes," Master's thesis, KTH – Royal Institute of Technology, 2005.

A   Algorithms

CHEAP-FIND-SUBSET(T, v)
Input: T is a stateful SD tree where all nodes up to v have been marked by FIND-COVER()
Output: A subset with top node in v or below, covering all uncovered MC users below v, and as few CC users as possible.

```
(1)      if not v.nc and not v.cc
(2)          if v = root
(3)              return S_{1,Φ} //(all users)
(4)          else
(5)              return S_{par(v),sib(v)}
(6)      if not l(v).mc
(7)          return CHEAP-FIND-SUBSET(T, r(v))
(8)      else if not r(v).mc
(9)          return CHEAP-FIND-SUBSET(T, l(v))
(10)     excl ← v
(11)     while excl.mc
(12)         if l(excl).nc
(13)             excl ← l(excl)
(14)         else if r(excl).nc
(15)             excl ← r(excl)
(16)         else if l(excl).cc > r(excl).cc
(17)             excl ← l(excl)
(18)         else
(19)             excl ← r(excl)
(20)     return S_{v,excl}
```

GENEROUS-FIND-SUBSET(T, v)
Input: T is a stateful SD tree where all nodes up to v have been marked by FIND-COVER()
Output: A subset with top node in v or below, covering all uncovered MC users below v, and as many CC users as possible.

```
(1)      if not v.nc
(2)          if v = root
(3)              return S_{1,Φ} //(all users)
(4)          else
(5)              return S_{par(v),sib(v)}
(6)      excl ← n
(7)      while not l(excl).nc or not r(excl).nc
(8)          if l(excl).nc
(9)              excl ← l(excl)
(10)         else
(11)             excl ← r(excl)
(12)     return S_{v,excl}
```

Find-Subset(T, v, *generous*)
Input: T is a stateful SD tree where all nodes up to v have been marked by Find-Cover()
Output: A generous or cheap subset with top node in v or below, covering all uncovered MC users below v.
(1)   **if** *generous* = **true**
(2)   **return** Generous-Find-Subset(T, v)
(3)   **else**
(4)   **return** Cheap-Find-Subset(T, v)

Find-Cover(T, *generous*)
Input: T is a stateful SD tree where the nodes representing users have been marked. *generous* is a boolean, true for generous cover, false for cheap
Output: A cover $\mathcal{C}$
(1) $\mathcal{C} \leftarrow \emptyset$
(2)   **foreach** node $v \in T$ in depth-first order
(3)   **if** $l(v).\mathbf{nc}$ and $r(v).\mathbf{nc}$ and $(l(v).\mathbf{mc}$ or $r(v).\mathbf{mc})$
(4)   **if** $r(v).\mathbf{mc}$
(5) $\mathcal{C} \leftarrow \mathcal{C} \cup$ Find-Subset($T, r(v), generous$)
(6)   **if** $l(v).\mathbf{mc}$
(7) $\mathcal{C} \leftarrow \mathcal{C} \cup$ Find-Subset($T, l(v), generous$)
(8) $v.\mathbf{nc} \leftarrow$ **true**
(9)   **else**
(10) $v.\mathbf{nc} \leftarrow l(v).\mathbf{nc} \mid r(v).\mathbf{nc}$
(11) $v.\mathbf{mc} \leftarrow l(v).\mathbf{mc} \mid r(v).\mathbf{mc}$
(12)   **if** $v.\mathbf{mc}$
(13) $v.\mathbf{cc} \leftarrow \max(l(v).\mathbf{cc}, r(v).\mathbf{cc})$
(14)   **else**
(15) $v.\mathbf{cc} \leftarrow l(v).\mathbf{cc} + r(v).\mathbf{cc}$
(16)   **if** root.$\mathbf{mc}$
(17) $\mathcal{C} \leftarrow \mathcal{C} \cup$ Find-Subset($T, root, generous$)
(18)   **return** $\mathcal{C}$

The Rainbow Attack on Stream Ciphers Based on Maiorana-McFarland Functions

Khoongming Khoo[1], Guang Gong[2], and Hian-Kiat Lee[1]

[1] DSO National Laboratories
20 Science Park Drive, Singapore 118230
[2] Department of Electrical and Computer Engineering
University of Waterloo, Waterloo, Ont. N2L 3G1, Canada
{kkhoongm, lhiankia}@dso.org.sg, ggong@calliope.uwaterloo.ca

Abstract. In this paper, we present the rainbow attack on stream ciphers filtered by Maiorana-McFarland functions. This can be considered as a generalization of the time-memory-data trade-off attack of Mihaljevic and Imai on Toyocrypt. First, we substitute the filter function in Toyocrypt (which has the same size as the LFSR) with a general Maiorana-McFarland function. This allows us to apply the attack to a wider class of stream ciphers. Moreover, our description replaces the time-memory-data trade-off attack with the rainbow attack of Oeshlin, which offers better performance and implementation advantages. Second, we highlight how the choice of different Maiorana-McFarland functions can affect the effectiveness of our attack. Third, we show that the attack can be modified to apply on filter functions which are smaller than the LFSR or on filter-combiner stream ciphers. This allows us to cryptanalyze other configurations commonly found in practice. Finally, filter functions with vector output are sometimes used in stream ciphers to improve the throughput. Therefore the case when the Maiorana-McFarland functions have vector output is investigated. We found that the extra speed comes at the price of additional weaknesses which make the attacks easier.

Keywords: Time-memory-data trade-off attack, Rainbow attack, Maiorana-McFarland functions.

1 Introduction

The construction of Boolean functions with good cryptographic properties has been a well studied area of research. Some of these properties include balance, high nonlinearity, high order of resiliency, high algebraic degree and high order of propagation criteria. These properties ensure the Boolean functions are resistant against various correlation attacks when used in stream ciphers [3, 17].

A well-known class of Boolean functions with good cryptographic properties are the Maiorana-McFarland class which ensures many of the above mentioned

J. Zhou, M. Yung, and F. Bao (Eds.): ACNS 2006, LNCS 3989, pp. 194–209, 2006.

properties. For example, when n is odd, we can construct t-resilient n-bit functions with nonlinearity achieving the quadratic bound $2^{n-1} - 2^{(n-1)/2}$. By concatenating such a function with its complement, we construct $(t + 1)$-resilient m-bit functions with nonlinearity satisfying the quadratic bound $2^{m-1} - 2^{m/2}$ for even $m = n + 1$. These nonlinearities are called the quadratic bounds because they are the maximum nonlinearities attainable for quadratic Boolean functions. When n is even, the Maiorana-McFarland also allows us to construct a large family of bent functions, i.e. Boolean functions with the highest nonlinearity $2^{n-1} - 2^{n/2-1}$. Finally, the saturated functions which achieve optimal order of resiliency $t = n - 1 - d$ and optimal nonlinearity $2^{n-1} - 2^{t+1}$ when the algebraic degree is d can be constructed by this method.

The Maiorana-McFarland class can be viewed as constructions based on concatenating linear functions. This is both an advantage and a weakness. It is an advantage because we can easily manipulate the distance between Maiorana-McFarland functions and linear functions to obtain resiliency and high nonlinearity. This helps to protect against correlation and fast correlation attacks [3, 17]. However, it also means the function becomes linear when we fix certain input bits. Mihaljevic and Imai were able to exploit this property to launch a search space reduction attack on Toyocrypt. Toyocrypt is a 128-bit stream cipher where a 128-bit modular linear feedback shift register (MLFSR) is filtered by a 128-bit Maiorana McFarland function. They were able to reduce the key space from 2^{128} to 2^{96} when 32 consecutive output bits are known. The attack works because for each guess on 96 bits of the 128-bit MLFSR, they were able to form 32 linear equations based on 32 consecutive output bits. This linear system can be solved to determine the remaining 32 bits in the MLFSR. Using the time-memory-data trade-off attack of Biryukov and Shamir, they further reduced the attack complexity to 2^{32} with 2^{80} pre-computation and 2^{64} memory based on 2^{48} keystream bits.

In Section 3, we generalize the time-memory-data trade-off attack on Toyocrypt by Mihaljevic and Imai [9] as follows:

1. We show that the search space reduction attack on Toyocrypt can be applied to a general Maiorana-McFarland function. Because linear feedback shift registers (LFSR's) are more commonly used in stream ciphers, we replace the MLFSR in Toyocrypt by an LFSR.

2. In [9], Mihaljevic and Imai describes how we can improve the search space reduction attack on Toyocrypt by applying the time-memory-data trade-off attack of Biryukov and Shamir [2, 7]. In this paper, we describe how we can improve the search space reduction attack on Maiorana-McFarland functions by applying the rainbow attack of Oeschlin [11]. The rainbow attack is twice as fast as the time-memory-data trade-off attack and offers various implementation advantages. We also incorporate an improvement of the rainbow attack by Mukhopadyay and Sarkar [10] in our attack.

3. We simplify the description of the time-memory-data trade-off attack of [9] by introducing a search function $F^{(c)}(x)$.

Based on our study, we characterize the performance of the attack for different Maiorana-McFarland functions. For n-bit Maiorana McFarland functions formed by concatenating $2^{n/2}$ linear functions of size $n/2$-bit, the search space is reduced from 2^n to $2^{3n/4}$. When we apply the rainbow attack, the search space is further reduced to $2^{n/4-1}$ with $2^{3n/8}$ consecutive keystream bits, $2^{5n/8}$ pre-computation and $2^{n/2}$ memory. This case correspond to the filter function in Toyocrypt with $n = 128$, $k = 64$ [9], the bent functions and the resilient functions whose nonlinearity satisfies the quadratic bound [4, 16].

For Maiorana-McFarland functions formed by concatenating a few large linear functions, we get a very effective reduction of the search space of an n-bit filter function generator from 2^n to $2^{n/2}$. In this case, the equivalent key length is only half of what is claimed. As shown by Gong and Khoo [6], this case corresponds to the degree-resiliency-nonlinearity optimized saturated functions introduced by Sarkar and Maitra at Crypto 2000 [14]. Thus although this class of functions has the best trade-off among important cryptographic properties like nonlinearity, resiliency and algebraic degree, they are weak against the search space reduction attack. When we apply the rainbow attack, the search space is further reduced to $2^{n/4-1}$ with $2^{n/2}$ consecutive keystream bits, $2^{n/2}$ pre-computation and $2^{3n/8}$ memory.

In Section 5, we extend our attack to the case where the Maiorana-McFarland function is of smaller size than the LFSR. This is a very common construction when the filtering function is implemented as a look-up-table (LUT). The LFSR may be 128-bit long and it is not possible to fit a LUT of size 2^{128} into the memory of the cipher. Thus a smaller filter function has to be used. In that case, the complexity of the search space reduction and rainbow attack depends on the width of the LFSR bits which are tapped to certain input bits of the filter function. These input bits have the property that when they are known, the Maiorana-McFarland function becomes linear.

In Section 6, we extend the attack to the filter combiner model. At each clock cycle, the Boolean function will extract several bits from each of s linear feedback shift registers $LFSR_i$, $i = 0, 1, \ldots, s - 1$, as input to produce a keystream bit. As analyzed by Sarkar [13], the filter combiner offers various advantages over the filter function and combinatorial generators. We show that in this case, the search space reduction and rainbow attack can also be applied effectively.

In Section 7, we extend the attack to the case where the filter function is a vectorial Maiorana-McFarland function. Vector output filter function generator has higher throughput for faster communication speed but it has an additional weakness. There is an exponential decrease in the complexity of search space reduction when compared to the single output case. This gives a very efficient attack even by a direct exhaustive search. This complexity can be further reduced by applying the rainbow attack.

In Sections 3 to 7, we simplified the attack scenarios to give a clearer explanation of the attack methods. In Section 8, we describe how these attacks can be easily adapted to apply to stream ciphers that use more general linear finite state machines, tap points and filter functions.

2   Preliminaries on Maiorana McFarland Functions

The *Hadamard Transform* of a Boolean function $f : GF(2)^n \to GF(2)$ is

$$\hat{f}(w) = \sum_{x \in GF(2)^n} (-1)^{w \cdot x + f(x)}.$$

The *nonlinearity* of a function $f : GF(2)^n \to GF(2)$ is defined as

$$N_f = 2^{n-1} - \frac{1}{2} \max_w |\hat{f}(w)|.$$

A high nonlinearity is desirable as it ensures linear approximation of f is ineffective. This offers protection against linear approximation based attacks [8, 17].

A Boolean function $f : GF(2)^n \to GF(2)$ is *t-th order correlation immune*, denoted $CI(t)$, if $\hat{f}(w) = 0$ for all $1 \le wt(w) \le t$ where $wt(w)$ is the number of ones in the binary representation of w. Correlation immunity ensure that f cannot be approximated by linear functions with too few terms, which offers protection against correlation attack [17]. Furthermore, if f is balanced and $CI(t)$, we say f is resilient of order t.

The Maiorana-McFarland functions is defined by the equation:

$$f(x_0, \ldots, x_{n-1}) = g(x_0, \ldots, x_{k-1}) + (x_k, \ldots, x_{n-1}) \cdot \phi(x_0, \ldots, x_{k-1}). \tag{1}$$

where $f : GF(2)^n \to GF(2)$, $g : GF(2)^k \to GF(2)$ and $\phi : GF(2)^k \to GF(2)^{n-k}$. ϕ is usually an injection or 2-to-1 map which would require $k \le n/2$ or $k \le n/2+1$ respectively.

The Maiorana-McFarland functions had been used extensively to construct Boolean functions with good cryptographic properties in the past decade (see [4] for a summary). Some notable examples are listed in the following two Propositions.

Proposition 1. *(extracted from [4, 16])*

1. *Let $f : GF(2)^n \to GF(2)$ be defined by equation (1). Let n be odd, $k = (n-1)/2$ and $\phi : GF(2)^{(n-1)/2} \to GF(2)^{(n+1)/2}$ be an injection such that*

$$wt(\phi(x_0, \ldots, x_{k-1})) \ge t+1 \text{ and } |\{z \in GF(2)^{(n+1)/2} | wt(z) \ge t+1\}| \ge 2^{(n-1)/2}.$$

   Then f is a t-resilient function with nonlinearity $2^{n-1} - 2^{(n-1)/2}$.
2. *Let $f(x_0, \ldots, x_{n-1})$, n odd, be a t-resilient function constructed as in part 1. Then*

$$g(x_0, \ldots, x_{n-1}, x_n) = f(x_0, \ldots, x_{n-1}) + x_n,$$

   is $t+1$-resilient and has nonlinearity $2^{m-1} - 2^{m/2}$ where $m = n+1$ is even.
3. *Let n be even, $k = n/2$ and $\phi(x_0, \ldots, x_{k-1})$ be a permutation in equation (1), then $f(x)$ is a bent function, i.e. it has the highest possible nonlinearity $2^{n-1} - 2^{n/2-1}$.*

The first construction is quite useful because a nonlinearity of $2^{n-1} - 2^{(n-1)/2}$ is considered high for functions with odd number of input bits. Furthermore, when $n \equiv 1 \pmod 4$, we can also obtain resiliency of order $(n-1)/4$ [4, page 555]. The second construction derives highly nonlinear resilient function with even number of input bits from the first construction. The third construction on bent functions are widely used in cryptography because of their high nonlinearity. Some examples include the ciphers CAST and Toyocrypt [1, 9]. The functions presented in Proposition 1 has the common property that $k \approx n/2$.

The saturated functions are functions which attain optimal trade-off between algebraic degree d, order of resiliency $t = n - d - 1$ and nonlinearity $2^{n-1} - 2^{t+1}$. Such functions were constructed by Sarkar and Maitra in [14]. It was shown by Gong and Khoo in [6] that the saturated functions correspond to n-bit Maiorana-McFarland functions as follows.

Proposition 2. *(Sarkar, Maitra [14, 6]) Fix $d \geq 2$ and let $n = 2^{d-1} + d - 2$. Define $f : GF(2)^n \to GF(2)$ by equation (1) where $k = d - 1$. Let $\phi : GF(2)^{d-1} \to GF(2)^{2^{d-1}-1}$ be an injection such that $wt(\phi(x_0, \ldots, x_{k-1})) \geq 2^{d-1} - 2$. Then $deg(f) = d$, f is t-resilient having nonlinearity $2^{n-1} - 2^{t+1}$ where $t = n - 1 - d$. In that case, the order of resiliency is optimal by Siegenthaler's inequality [17] and nonlinearity is optimal by Sarkar-Maitra inequality [14].*

The function in Proposition 2 has the property that $k \approx \log_2(n) << n$. Propositions 1 and 2 construct Boolean functions with optimal cryptographic properties by concatenating linear functions. But we shall show that their linear structures can be exploited to give efficient attacks on stream ciphers in Section 3.

3   The Rainbow Attack on Maiorana-McFarland Functions

In [9], Mihaljevic and Imai presented a time-memory-data trade-off attack on the stream cipher Toyocrypt. Toyocrypt is a filter function generator where we have an MLFSR of length 128 bit filtered by a 128-bit Boolean function of the form:

$$f(x_0, \ldots, x_{127}) = g(x_0, \ldots, x_{63}) + (x_{64}, \ldots, x_{127}) \cdot \pi(x_0, \ldots, x_{63}),$$

where g has 3 terms in its algebraic normal form (ANF) of degree $4, 17, 63$ and π permutes the bit positions of $(x_0, \ldots, x_{63})$. Mihaljevic and Imai showed that the effective key diversity of such a generator can be reduced from 128 bits to 96 bits when 32 consecutive output bits are known. Based on this observation, they modified the Biryukov-Shamir [2] time-memory-data tradeoff attack for improved cryptanalysis.

It is easy see that the filter function in Toyocrypt is a Maiorana-McFarland function with parameters $n = 128$, $k = 64$. Due to the wide usage of the Maiorana-McFarland construction, it will be useful to generalize the Mihaljevic-Imai attack to a general Maiorana-McFarland filter function generator. In this attack, we look at a stream cipher where an n-stage LFSR is filtered by a n-bit Maiorana-McFarland function defined by equation (1). We assume bit i of the LFSR is the i-th input of $f(x)$.

Suppose we know l consecutive output bits $y_0, \ldots, y_{l-1}$ and let $(x_i, \ldots, x_{i+n-1})$ be the LFSR state corresponding to y_i. Based on equation (1), we have:

$$y_i = g(x_i, \ldots, x_{i+k-1}) + (x_{i+k}, \ldots, x_{i+n-1}) \cdot \phi(x_i, \ldots, x_{i+k-1}), \ i = 0, \ldots, l-1. \tag{2}$$

Suppose we guess $k + l$ consecutive input bits $x_0, \ldots, x_{k+l-1}$. Then $g(x_i, \ldots, x_{i+k-1})$ and $\phi(x_i, \ldots, x_{i+k-1})$ will be known for $i = 0, \ldots, l-1$. In that case, the l equations in (2) will be linear and they will contain $n - (k+l)$ unknown variables $x_{k+l}, \ldots, x_{n-1}$. The variables $x_n, \ldots, x_{n+l-2}$ in equation (2) can be linearly expressed in terms of $x_0, \ldots, x_{n-1}$ using the LFSR feedback relation.

Thus we have l linear equations in $n - (k+l)$ variables. For this linear system to be solvable, we need:

$$l \geq n - (k+l) \Longrightarrow l \geq \frac{n-k}{2}.$$

Therefore, suppose we know $l = \lceil (n-k)/2 \rceil$ consecutive output bits $y_0, \ldots, y_{l-1}$ and we guess the $k+l = n-l = \lfloor (n+k)/2 \rfloor$ consecutive input bits $x_0, \ldots, x_{k+l-1}$. Then we can solve for the remaining l input bits $x_{k+l}, \ldots, x_{n-1}$ in equation (2) and counter check whether our guess is correct, by back-substitution and comparing with a sufficiently long keystream, e.g. of length $2n$ bits. Thus we have proven that:

Theorem 1. *Consider an n-bit LFSR filtered by equation (1) where bit i of the LFSR is the ith input of $f(x)$. The key space is reduced from 2^n to $2^{\lfloor (n+k)/2 \rfloor}$ bits when $\lceil (n-k)/2 \rceil$ consecutive output bits are known.*

Remark 1. For ease of notation, we assume that $(n+k)/2$, $(n-k)/2$ are integers from now on. The case when they are not integers can be handled by adding the appropriate ceiling $\lceil \ \rceil$ and floor $\lfloor \ \rfloor$ operations as in Theorem 1.

Next we improve the attack complexity of Theorem 1 by applying the rainbow attack [11]. The rainbow attack can be seen as an improvement of the time-memory-data trade-off attack [2, 7, 9] which is twice as fast and has various implementation advantages.

Let $f : GF(2)^n \to GF(2)$ be the filter function of an n-bit LFSR. Define $\tilde{f} : GF(2)^n \to GF(2)^n$ as:

$$\tilde{f}(\tilde{x}) = n\text{-bit output of filter function generator,}$$

when the LFSR is initialized by $\tilde{x} \in GF(2)^n$.

Let $c \in GF(2)^{(n-k)/2}$ be a fixed string. Given $x \in GF(2)^{(n+k)/2}$, we can use the proof of Theorem 1 to find $s \in GF(2)^{(n-k)/2}$ such that:

$$\tilde{f}(x||s) \text{ restricted to first } (n-k)/2 \text{ bits } = c,$$
$$\text{i.e. } \tilde{f}(x||s) = (c||y).$$

where '||' is concatenation of bit strings. Based on this computation, we introduce a *search function* $F^{(c)} : GF(2)^{(n+k)/2} \to GF(2)^{(n+k)/2}$ for the description of our attack. We define $F^{(c)}(x)$ to be the right most $(n+k)/2$ bits of $\tilde{f}(x||s)$, i.e.,

$$F^{(c)}(x) = y$$

The function $F^{(c)}$ will be the search function used in our description of the rainbow attack on Maiorana McFarland functions. We note that this function can also simplify the description of the attack in [9].

Setup:

1. Randomly choose a binary string $c \in GF(2)^{(n-k)/2}$ and define the function $F^{(c)}(x)$ as described above.
2. Define a chain of $t-1$ distinct functions $F_1(x), F_2(x), \ldots, F_{t-1}(x)$ which are slight variations of the search function $F^{(c)}(x)$ as follows. Randomly seed an $(n+k)/2$-bit LFSR (with maximum period) and generate a sequence of $(n+k)/2$-bit vectors $X_1, X_2, \ldots, X_{t-1}$. Let the variant functions be defined as $F_j(x) = F^{(c)}(x) \oplus X_j$ (Please see Remark 4 for further explanation on this step).
3. Let p and t be integers defined by $pt^2 = 2^{(n+k)/2}$. Form a $p \times t$ by 2 array as follows:
   For $i = 1 \ldots p \times t$, randomly choose a start point $y_{i,0}$ and compute the chain of values $y_{i,1} = F_1(y_{i,0}), y_{i,2} = F_2(y_{i,1}), \ldots, y_{i,t} = F_{t-1}(y_{i,t-1})$. Store the start and end points $(SP_i, EP_i) = (y_{i,0}, y_{i,t})$.

Attack:

1. We look among the keystream to find a n-bit string whose first $(n-k)/2$ bits matches the pattern c. Let the last $(n+k)/2$ bits of this string be y.
2. For $j = 2 \ldots t$, search among the endpoints EP_i in our table to check if

$$EP_i = F_{t-1}(\ldots (F_{t-j+1}(y) \ldots).$$

If there is a match, then $(x||s)$ is the secret initial state of the LFSR where

$$x = F_{t-j}(\ldots F_1(SP_i) \ldots),$$

and s is the $(n-k)/2$-bit string computed such that the leftmost $(n-k)/2$ bits of $\tilde{f}(x||s)$ is c. The string s can be found by solving linear equations as in the proof of Theorem 1.

Based on [2] and [11], the parameters in the attack satisfy the following constraint:

To look up the rainbow table, we need to compute $F_{t-1}(y)$, $F_{t-1}(F_{t-2}(y))$, $F_{t-1}(F_{t-2}(F_{t-3}(y)))$, ... The time taken is $T = \sum_{i=1}^{t-1} i = t(t-1)/2$ function computations. Let the amount of data collected be D. By [2], our table only need to cover $1/D$ of the whole search space $N = 2^{(n+k)/2} = pt^2$ because we just need one string out of D possible strings in the available keystream. Since we are only storing the end points, the memory M needed is pt/D. Thus we derive the relation:

$$TM^2D^2 = t(t-1)/2 \times (pt/D)^2 \times D^2$$
$$\approx p^2t^4/2 = N^2/2 \Longrightarrow T = N^2/(2M^2D^2).$$

Let the memory be $M = 2^{mem}$ and the number of strings of the form $(c\|x)$ (where $c \in GF(2)^{(n-k)/2}$ is fixed) in the collected data be $D = 2^d$. This means we need to sample $2^{(n-k)/2+d}$ consecutive keystream bits to collect this data. Thus the processing time is $N^2/(2M^2D^2) = 2^{n+k-2(d+mem)-1}$. The pre-processing time is $N/D = 2^{(n+k)/2-d}$. We state the result formally as:

Theorem 2. *Consider an n-bit LFSR filtered by equation (1) where bit i of the LFSR is the ith input of $f(x)$. The LFSR initial state can be found with complexity $2^{n+k-2(d+mem)-1}$ by using $2^{(n+k)/2-d}$ pre-processing and 2^{mem} memory when $2^{(n-k)/2+d}$ consecutive output bits are known.*

Remark 2. We note that in the time-memory-data trade-off attack of [9], the function chains in a table are derived from a constant function $F^{(c)}(x)$, thus they have a high chance of collision because the table (which have to cover the search space) is large. An alternative is suggested in [9] which uses multiple tables where the function for each table is a variant of $F^{(c)}(x)$. In that case, we let $N = 2^{(n+k)/2} = pt^2$ and construct t table of size $p \times t$. This set-up gives optimal performance by the "matrix stopping rule" [7]. Let the amount of data be D. Then the amount of memory needed is $M = pt/D$ because we are storing p end points in each of t tables and we only need to cover $1/D$ of the search space. The time to look up a table is t and the processing complexity which is the time to look up t table is $T = t^2$. We deduce that:

$$TM^2D^2 = t^2 \times (pt/D)^2 \times D^2$$
$$= p^2t^4 = N^2.$$

Thus the processing complexity is $T = N^2/(M^2D^2)$ which is twice as slow as in the rainbow attack.

Remark 3. The rainbow attack, besides being twice as fast as the time-memory-data trade-off attack, also has the following implementation advantages [11]. The number of table look up in the rainbow attack is reduced by a factor of t when compared to the time-memory-data trade-off (which uses t tables). Rainbow tables have no loops because each reduction function F_j is only used once. So we do not need to spend time to detect and reject loops when constructing the table. Merging chains in rainbow tables have identical endpoints. So it can be used to determine merging chains, just like distinguished points. In time-memory-data trade-off, distinguished points are used to detect merging chains and loops. However, the chains have variable lengths. In comparison, rainbow chains avoid merging chains and loops by using distinct reduction functions. Thus the rainbow chains have constant lengths. As explained in [11], this is more efficient and effective.

Remark 4. The method we use to generate the functions $F_j(x)$ from an LFSR is by Mukhopadyay and Sarkar [10]. The method suggested in [2, 9] (and originally by Hellman in [7]) is to generate $F_j(x)$ by permuting the output bits of $F^{(c)}(x)$. But it was shown by Fiat and Noar that there exist search functions which are polynomial time indistinguishable from a random function but for which the time-memory trade-off attack fails [5], when permutation of output bits are used. The advantage of the approach of [10] is that it is not possible to construct a Fiat-Noar type example for the LFSR-based rainbow method. Moreover, LFSR sequences are very efficient to compute.

Example 1. We apply Theorem 2 to Toyocrypt with the parameters $n = 128$, $k = 64$, $d = 16$ and $mem = 64$. The complexity of the time-memory-data trade-off attack is 2^{80} for pre-processing and 2^{31} for processing when we know 2^{48} consecutive output bits. This attack is twice as fast as the attack in [9].

Remark 5. To obtain 2^{16} 128-bit ciphertext blocks where the first 32 bits is a fixed pattern c in Example 1, we need to scan through 2^{48} keystream bits. This scanning complexity is not taken into account in the processing complexity 2^{31}, which only covers the search of the rainbow table. Part of the reason for not mixing the two complexities is that searching the rainbow table involves computing the function $F^{(c)}$ (by solving a linear system) which is more complex than scanning for a fixed pattern from the keystream. The same remark applies to Example 2 and 3 later in the paper.

4   On the Security of Different Maiorana-McFarland Functions against the Rainbow Attack

In general, the parameter k in the Maiorana-McFarland construction (equation 1) is in the range $1 \leq k \leq n/2$.

4.1   The Case When k Is Approximately $n/2$

Consider the extreme case $k \approx n/2$. There are many optimal functions belonging to this class as summarized in Proposition 1. In this case, $(n - k)/2 \approx n/4$ and the key diversity is reduced to $(n + k)/2 \approx 3n/4$ bits when $\approx n/4$ consecutive keystream bits are known. Suppose we collect $2^d = 2^{n/8}$ ciphertexts corresponding to a pre-computed $n/4$-bit pattern, i.e. $2^{3n/8}$ consecutive keystream bits. Then in a rainbow attack with 2^{mem} memory, the complexity is $2^{5n/8}$ for pre-processing and $2^{5n/4-2mem-1}$ for the actual attack by Theorem 2. If n is not too big, it is reasonable to use $2^{mem} = 2^{n/2}$ memory which means the attack complexity is $2^{n/4-1}$. If we can obtain more keystream bits, then the pre-computation and attack complexity can be reduced further.

4.2   The Case When k Is Much Smaller Than n

The other extreme is when $k << n$. This scenario may occur when we use a saturated function from Proposition 2. In this case, $(n + k)/2 \approx n/2$ and the key diversity is reduced to $\approx n/2$ bits when $\approx n/2$ consecutive output bits are known. Suppose we collect $2^d = 1$ (where $d = 0$) ciphertext corresponding to a pre-computed $n/2$-bit pattern, i.e. we need $2^{n/2}$ consecutive keystream bits. Then in a time-memory-data trade-off attack using 2^{mem} memory, the complexity is $2^{n/2}$ for pre-processing and $2^{n-2mem-1}$ for processing. Unlike the case $k \approx n/2$, we can use less memory here because the search space is smaller. If we use $2^{mem} = 2^{3n/8}$ memory, then the attack complexity is $2^{n/4-1}$.

From the above discussion, we see that as k decreases, the memory, pre-computation and attack complexity decreases but the number of consecutive keystream bits needed increases. Sometimes it is not possible to obtain so many keystream bits for time-memory-data trade-off attack on equation 2. It may be more feasible to use Theorem 1 directly and perform an exhaustive search with complexity $2^{(n+k)/2}$ based on $(n-k)/2$ consecutive output bits.

5 When the LFSR and Boolean Functions Have Different Sizes

As a generalization, we consider the above attack when an n-bit LFSR is filtered by a m-bit Maiorana McFarland function $f(x)$ where $m < n$. Let the function be of the form

$$f(x_0, \ldots, x_{m-1}) = g(x_0, \ldots, x_{r-1}) + (x_r, \ldots, x_{m-1}) \cdot \phi(x_0, \ldots, x_{r-1}). \quad (3)$$

where $f : GF(2)^m \rightarrow GF(2)$, $g : GF(2)^r \rightarrow GF(2)$ and $\phi : GF(2)^r \rightarrow GF(2)^{m-r}$.

Therefore the function $f(x)$ becomes linear when the first r input bits are fixed. Let these r input bits be tapped from the leftmost k bits of the LFSR, and the remaining $m - r$ input bits of $f(x)$ be tapped from the rightmost $n - k$ LFSR bits.

As before, assume l consecutive output bits of $f(x)$ are known and we guess $k + l$ leftmost LFSR bits. Then we can form l linear equations with $n - (k + l)$ unknown variables of the LFSR initial state. This system of equations can be solved when $l = \lceil (n-k)/2 \rceil$. So knowing $\lceil (n-k)/2 \rceil$ consecutive output bits will reduce the initial state space from n bits to $k + l = \lfloor (n+k)/2 \rfloor$ bits. It is easy to see that we can apply the rainbow attack as in Section 3 by using the same search function $F^{(c)}(x)$. The attack complexity for direct exhaustive search and rainbow attack is the same as before but now, the parameter k depends not just on $f(x)$ but also on the tap points from the LFSR. We summarize our discussion as a theorem:

Theorem 3. *Consider an n-bit LFSR which is filtered by a m-bit Maiorana-McFarland function defined by equation (3). Suppose the first r bits of $f(x)$ is tapped from the leftmost k bits of the LFSR, and the remaining $m - r$ input bits of $f(x)$ is tapped from the rightmost $n - k$ LFSR bits. Then the key space is reduced from 2^n to $2^{(n+k)/2}$ when $(n-k)/2$ consecutive output bits are known.*

Furthermore, the LFSR initial state can be found with $2^{n+k-2(d+mem)-1}$ processing, $2^{(n+k)/2-d}$ pre-processing and 2^{mem} memory when $2^{(n-k)/2+d}$ consecutive output bits are known.

6   Extending the Attack to Filter Combiner Model

In this section, we extend the search space reduction and rainbow attack on the filter combiner model. For ease of explanation, we consider the case of two linear feedback shift registers $LFSR_1$ and $LFSR_2$. The attacks on more LFSR's are similar. At each clock cycle, a Boolean function will take as input several state bits from each of $LFSR_1$ and $LFSR_2$ to output a keystream bit.

Let the length of $LFSR_1$ be n_1 and that of $LFSR_2$ be n_2. Let $f : GF(2)^m \rightarrow GF(2)$ be defined by:

$$f(x_0, \ldots, x_{m-1}) = (x_r, \ldots, x_{m-1}) \cdot \phi(x_0, \ldots, x_{r-1}) + g(x_0, \ldots, x_{r-1}). \quad (4)$$

Therefore when we fix the first r input bits, $f(x)$ becomes linear.

Let the first r input bits of $f(x)$, i.e. $(x_0, x_1, \ldots, x_{r-1})$ be tapped from among the leftmost k_1 and k_2 bits of $LFSR_1$ and $LFSR_2$. Let the rest of the $n - r$ input bits be tapped from the rightmost $n_1 - k_1$ and $n_2 - k_2$ bits of $LFSR_1$ and $LFSR_2$.

Suppose we know l consecutive output bits $y_0, y_1, \ldots, y_{l-1}$. Let us guess the leftmost $k_1 + l$ and $k_2 + l$ bits of $LFSR_1$ and $LFSR_2$. Then at time i, $\phi(x_i, \ldots, x_{i+r-1})$, $g(x_i, \ldots, x_{i+r-1})$ are known for all $i = 0, 1, \ldots, l - 1$. This means:

$$y_i = f(x_i, \ldots, x_{i+m-1}) = (x_{i+r}, \ldots, x_{i+m-1}) \cdot \phi(x_i, \ldots, x_{i+r-1}) + g(x_i, \ldots, x_{i+r-1}).$$

is a linear equation for $i = 0, 1, \ldots, l - 1$.

We have l equations in $n_1 - (k_1 + l) + n_2 - (k_2 + l)$ variables. For this linear system to be solvable, we need

$$n_1 - (k_1 + l) + n_2 - (k_2 + l) \le l$$
$$\Longrightarrow l \ge \lceil ((n_1 - k_1) + (n_2 - k_2))/3 \rceil.$$

We take $l = \lceil ((n_1 - k_1) + (n_2 - k_2))/3 \rceil$. Thus the search space is reduced from $2^{n_1 + n_2}$ to:

$$2^{(k_1+l)+(k_2+l)} \approx 2^{(2(n_1+n_2)+(k_1+k_2))/3}.$$

The rainbow attack can may be applied for our scenario as follows. Let $l = \lceil ((n_1 - k_1) + (n_2 - k_2))/3 \rceil$, we define a function $\tilde{f} : GF(2)^{n_1} \times GF(2)^{n_2} \rightarrow GF(2)^{k_1+k_2+3l}$ to be:

$$\tilde{f}(\tilde{x}_1, \tilde{x}_2) = \text{the } (k_1 + k_2 + 3l)\text{-bit output keystream},$$

when $(LFSR_1, LFSR_2)$ are initialized by $(\tilde{x}_1, \tilde{x}_2)$. For a fixed string $c \in GF(2)^l$ and $x_i \in GF(2)^{k_i+l}$, we can find $s_i \in GF(2)^{n_i-(k_i+l)}$ such that $\tilde{f}(x_1||s_1, x_2||s_2)=$

$(c||y)$ by the method described above. Based on this computation, we define a search function $F^{(c)} : GF(2)^{k_1+l} \times GF(2)^{k_2+l} \to GF(2)^{k_1+k_2+2l}$ to be the rightmost $k_1 + k_2 + 2l$ bits of $\tilde{f}(\tilde{x}_1, \tilde{x}_2)$, i.e.

$$F^{(c)}(x_1, x_2) = y$$

By using this search function, we can perform a rainbow attack as in Section 3. The search space is $N = 2^{k_1+k_2+2l}$. Assuming we have $M = 2^{mem}$ memory and we have 2^{l+d} consecutive keystream bits from which we can sample $D = 2^d$ ciphertext whose first l bits correspond to c. Then the preprocessing complexity is $N/D = 2^{k_1+k_2+2l-d}$ and processing complexity is $N^2/(2M^2D^2) = 2^{2(k_1+k_2+2l-(d+mem))-1}$.

Example 2. Let us consider a filter combiner generator where $LFSR_1$ and $LFSR_2$ have lengths $n_1 = 64 = n_2$. Let $f(x)$ be defined by equation (4) where $m = 64$ and $r = 32$. Let the first r bits of $f(x)$ be tapped from the leftmost k_1, k_2 bits of $LFSR_1$ and $LFSR_2$ where $k_1 = 16 = k_2$.

The complexity of direct search without applying rainbow attack is

$$2^{k_1+k_2+2l} = 2^{16+16+2\times32} = 2^{96}.$$

where $l = \lceil ((64 - 16) + (64 - 16))/3 \rceil = 32$. The complexity is less than the intended security of $2^{n_1+n_2} = 2^{128}$.

Assuming we have $2^{mem} = 2^{64}$ memory and $2^{l+d} = 2^{48}$ consecutive keystream bits where $d = 16$. The initial LFSR state can be recovered with 2^{80} preprocessing and 2^{31} processing. Thus the attack complexities are similar to Toyocrypt.

In a similar way, the search space reduction and rainbow attack of a filter combiner with s LFSR can be computed. We state this formally as:

Theorem 4. *Consider a filter combiner where equation (4) filters the content of $LFSR_1, LFSR_2, \ldots, LFSR_s$ of size $n_1, n_2, \ldots, n_s$ respectively. Let the first r bits of equation (4) be tapped from the leftmost k_i bits of $LFSR_i$. And let the remaining $m - r$ bits be tapped from the rightmost $n_i - k_i$ bits of $LFSR_i$, $i = 0, 1, \ldots, s - 1$.*

Let $l = ((n_1 - k_1) + \ldots + (n_s - k_s))/(s + 1)$. Then the key space of the filter combiner is reduced from $2^{n_1+\ldots+n_s}$ to $2^{k_1+\ldots+k_s+s\times l}$ when l consecutive output bits are known. Furthermore, the LFSR initial states can be found with $2^{2(k_1+\ldots+k_s+s\times l-(d+mem))-1}$ processing, $2^{k_1+\ldots+k_s+s\times l-d}$ pre-processing and 2^{mem} memory when 2^{l+d} consecutive keystream bits are known.

7   Extending the Attack to Vectorial Maiorana-McFarland Functions

In this section, we consider the case where an n-bit LFSR is filtered by a vectorial Maiorana-McFarland functions $F : GF(2)^n \to GF(2)^m$ defined by:

$$F(x_0, \ldots, x_{n-1}) = (f_0(x_0, \ldots, x_{n-1}), \ldots, f_{m-1}(x_0, \ldots, x_{n-1})) \qquad (5)$$

where each function $f_j : GF(2)^n \to GF(2)$ is defined by:

$$f_j(x_0, \ldots, x_{n-1}) = (x_k, \ldots, x_{n-1}) \cdot \phi_j(x_0, \ldots, x_{k-1}) + g_j(x_0, \ldots, x_{k-1}).$$

for $j = 0, 1, \ldots, m - 1$. This case may occur in practice because the encryption speed of a vector output generator is m times faster than a single bit filter function generator.

For good security, we want any linear combination of $f_j(x)$ to correspond to a t-resilient Maiorana-McFarland function with high nonlinearity. The usual method to construct $F(x)$ is to ensure that linear combinations of $f_j(x)$ correspond to concatenation of linear functions which are distinct and each linear function in the concatenation is an expression in $t + 1$ or more variables. This can be achieved by using linear codes as shown in [12].

We assume bit i of the LFSR is the i-th input of $F(x)$. Suppose we know l consecutive output words, i.e. $l \times m$ consecutive output bits.

$$\text{word 1: } y_{0,0}, y_{0,1}, \ldots, y_{0,m-1}$$
$$\text{word 2: } y_{1,0}, y_{1,1}, \ldots, y_{1,m-1}$$
$$\cdots$$
$$\text{word l: } y_{l-1,0}, y_{l-1,1}, \ldots, y_{l-1,m-1}$$

Let us guess the $k + l$ leftmost bits of the LFSR, i.e. $(x_0, x_1, \ldots, x_{k+l-1})$. Then $(x_i, x_{i+1}, \ldots, x_{i+k-1})$ is known at time $i = 0, 1, , \ldots, l - 1$ and the following equations are linear.

$$y_{i,0} = g_0(x_i, \ldots, x_{i+k-1}) + (x_{i+k}, \ldots, x_{i+n-1}) \cdot \phi_0(x_i, \ldots, x_{i+k-1})$$
$$y_{i,1} = g_1(x_i, \ldots, x_{i+k-1}) + (x_{i+k}, \ldots, x_{i+n-1}) \cdot \phi_1(x_i, \ldots, x_{i+k-1})$$
$$\cdots$$
$$y_{i,m-1} = g_{m-1}(x_i, \ldots, x_{i+k-1}) + (x_{i+k}, \ldots, x_{i+n-1}) \cdot \phi_{m-1}(x_i, \ldots, x_{i+k-1})$$

We have $l \times m$ equations in $n - (k + l)$ unknowns. For this linear system to be solvable, we need:

$$n - (k + l) \leq l \times m$$
$$\implies l \geq \lceil (n - k)/(m + 1) \rceil.$$

We take $l = \lceil (n - k)/(m + 1) \rceil$. Thus the search space is reduced from 2^n to $2^{k+l} = 2^{k+\lceil (n-k)/(m+1) \rceil}$.

The rainbow attack can may be applied for our scenario as follows. Let $l = \lceil (n - k)/(m + 1) \rceil$, we define a search function $\tilde{F} : GF(2)^n \to GF(2)^{k+(m+1)l}$ to be

$$\tilde{F}(\tilde{x}) = \text{the } (k + (m + 1)l)\text{-bit output keystream},$$

when the LFSR is initialized by $\tilde{x} \in GF(2)^n$. For a fixed string $c \in GF(2)^{ml}$ and $x \in GF(2)^{k+l}$, we can find $s \in GF(2)^{n-(k+l)}$ such that $\tilde{F}(x||s) = (c||y)$ by the method described above. Based on this computation, we define a search function $F^{(c)} : GF(2)^{k+l} \to GF(2)^{k+l}$ to be the rightmost $k + l$ bits of $\tilde{F}(x||s)$, i.e.,

$$F^{(c)}(x) = y$$

By using this search function, we can perform a rainbow attack as in Section 3. The search space is $N = 2^{k+l}$. Assume we have $M = 2^{mem}$ memory and 2^{ml+d} consecutive keystream bits (from which we can sample $D = 2^d$ ciphertext whose first l m-bit words correspond to c). Then the preprocessing complexity is $N/D = 2^{k+l-d}$ and processing complexity is $N^2/(2M^2D^2) = 2^{2(k+l-(d+mem))-1}$.

Theorem 5. *Let $l = \lceil (n - k)/(m + 1) \rceil$. Consider an n-bit LFSR filtered by equation (5) where bit i of the LFSR is the i-th input of $F(x)$. The key space is reduced from 2^n to 2^{k+l} when ml consecutive output bits are known.*

Furthermore, the LFSR initial states can be found with $2^{2(k+l-(d+mem))-1}$ processing, 2^{k+l-d} pre-processing and 2^{mem} memory when 2^{ml+d} consecutive keystream bits are known.

Remark 6. We may also consider the case where the vector Maiorana-McFarland function has different size as the LFSR as in Section 5.

Another extension is when the filter function in the filter combiner model is a vectorial Maiorana McFarland function. In that case, the result is a combination of Theorem 4 and 5.

Example 3. Consider the parameters in Toyocrypt where we have a 128-bit stream cipher filtered by a 128-bit vector Maiorana-McFarland function $F(x)$ with parameter $k = 64$ and m output bits. $F(x)$ may correspond to the vector function in Corollary 1 of [12] which is 1-resilient and has nonlinearity $2^{127} - 2^{64}$.

Then by Theorem 5, $l = \lceil 64/(m + 1) \rceil$ and the search space reduction is 2^{64+l}. Suppose we apply rainbow attack with 2^d ciphertext whose first $m \times l$ bits correspond to a fixed string c. Then we need a keystream of length 2^{ml+d}. If we have 2^{mem} memory, the pre-processing complexity is 2^{64+l-d} and the processing complexity is $2^{2(64+l-(d+mem))-1}$. These values are tabulated for different output size m in Table 1, 2.

In Table 1, we list the size of the reduced search space for different output size.

In Table 2, we list the pre-processing and processing complexities of rainbow attack for different amount of memory and keystream. Here we fix the attack complexity as 2^{31}, which is considered sufficiently fast in practice.

In this example, we see that as the number of output bits increases, the search space, memory, pre-processing and processing complexities decrease while the amount of consecutive keystream bits needed increases.

Table 1. Reduced Search Space for $n = 128$, $k = 64$ and Different Output Size m

Output Size m	1	2	3	4	5	6	8	16
Reduced Search Space	2^{96}	2^{86}	2^{80}	2^{77}	2^{75}	2^{74}	2^{72}	2^{68}

Table 2. Complexities of Rainbow Attack for $n = 128$, $k = 64$ and Different Output Size m where Attack Complexity is fixed as 2^{31}, this gives lower Memory and Keystream Requirements

Output Size m	1	2	3	4	5	6	8	16
Consecutive Keystream	2^{48}	2^{52}	2^{56}	2^{58}	2^{61}	2^{68}	2^{72}	2^{68}
Memory	2^{64}	2^{62}	2^{56}	2^{55}	2^{53}	2^{52}	2^{51}	2^{48}
Pre-processing Complexity	2^{80}	2^{78}	2^{72}	2^{71}	2^{69}	2^{68}	2^{67}	2^{64}
Processing Complexity	2^{31}	2^{31}	2^{31}	2^{31}	2^{31}	2^{31}	2^{31}	2^{31}
Number of Ciphertext	2^{16}	2^{8}	2^{8}	2^{6}	2^{6}	2^{6}	2^{5}	2^{4}

8   Further Generalizations

Some ways in which our attacks can be further generalized are as follows:

1. In Theorem 2 and 5, we have adopted the convention that the first k input bits of $f(x)$ are always tapped from the leftmost k bits of the LFSR. It is easy to see that the attacks have the same complexities if we tap any k consecutive bits of the LFSR.
2. Similarly, in Theorem 3, we can tap the first r input bits of $f(x)$ from any consecutive k bits of the LFSR. In Theorem 4, we can tap the r bits from any consecutive $k_1, \ldots, k_s$ bits of $LFSR_1, \ldots, LFSR_s$ respectively.
3. In our attacks, we have presented the rainbow attack on Maiorana McFarland functions because it is a well-known and common construction in the Boolean function literature. In that case, the function becomes linear when the leftmost k bits are known. To make the attack more general, we can look at any n-bit Boolean function which becomes linear when k (not necessarily consecutive) input bits are known.
4. In our attacks, we can replace the LFSR by any linear finite state machine like a modular linear feedback shift register (MLFSR), Galois linear feedback shift register (GLFSR) or linear cellular automata. This is because the attacks only make use of the property that any LFSR state bits at time i is a linear function of the initial state.

References

1. C. Adams, "The CAST-128 Encryption Algorithm", RFC 2144.
2. A. Biryukov and A. Shamir, "Cryptanalytic Time/Memory/Data Trade-offs for Stream Ciphers", LNCS 1976, *Asiacrypt 2000*, pp. 1-13, Springer-Verlag, 2000.
3. A. Canteaut and M. Trabbia, "Improved Fast Correlation Attack using Parity Check Equations of Weight 4 and 5", LNCS 1807, *Eurocrypt 2000*, pp. 573-588, Springer-Verlag, 2000.
4. C. Carlet, "A Larger Class of Cryptographic Boolean Functions via a Study of the Moriana-McFarland Construction", LNCS 2442, *Crypto'2002*, pp. 549-564, Springer-Verlag, 2002.

5. A. Fiat and M. Naor, "Rigorous Time/Space Tradeoffs for Inverting Functions", *STOC 1991*, pp. 534-541, 1991.
6. G. Gong and K. Khoo, "Additive Autocorrelation of Resilient Boolean Functions", LNCS 3006, *Selected Areas of Cryptography 2003*, pp. 275-290, Springer-Verlag, 2003.
7. M. Hellman, "A Cryptanalytic Time-Memory Trade-Off", *IEEE Trans. on Information Theory*, vol. 26, pp. 401-406, 1980.
8. M. Matsui, "Linear cryptanalysis method for DES cipher", LNCS 765, *Eurocrypt'93*, pp. 386-397, 1994.
9. M.J. Mihaljevic and H. Imai, "Cryptanalysis of Toyocrypt-HS1 Stream Cipher", IEICE Trans. Fundamentals, vol. E85-A no. 1, pp. 66-73, 2002.
10. S. Mukhopadyay and P. Sarkar, "Application of LFSRs in Time/Memory Trade-Off Cryptanalysis", Indian Statistical Institute Technical Report No. ASD/04/9 (Revised Version), 2005.
11. P. Oeschlin, "Making a Faster Cryptanalytic Time-Memory Trade-Off", LNCS 2729, *Crypto 2003*, Springer-Verlag, 2003.
12. E. Pasalic and S. Maitra, "Linear Codes in Constructing Resilient Functions with High Nonlinearity", LNCS 2259, *Selected Areas in Cryptography 2001*, pp. 60-74, Springer-Verlag, 2001.
13. P. Sarkar, "The Filter-Combiner Model for Memoryless Synchronous Stream Ciphers", LNCS 2442, *Crypto 2002*, pp. 533-548, Springer-Verlag, 2002.
14. P. Sarkar and S. Maitra, "Nonlinearity Bounds and Constructions of Resilient Boolean Functions", LNCS 1880, *Crypto 2000*, pp. 515-532, Springer-Verlag, 2000.
15. P. Sarkar and S. Maitra, "Construction of Boolean Functions with Important Cryptographic Properties", LNCS 1807, *Eurocrypt 2000*, pp. 485-506, Springer-Verlag, 2000.
16. J. Seberry, X.M. Zhang and Y. Zheng, "On Constructions and Nonlinearity of Correlation Immune Functions", LNCS 765, *Eurocrypt'93*, pp. 181-199, 1994.
17. T. Siegenthaler, "Decrypting a Class of Stream Ciphers using Ciphertexts only", *IEEE Transactions on Computers*, vol. C34, no. 1, pp. 81-85, 1985.

Breaking a New Instance of TTM Cryptosystems

Xuyun Nie[1,*], Lei Hu[1], Jianyu Li[1], Crystal Updegrove[2], and Jintai Ding[2]

[1] State Key Laboratory of Information Security,
Graduate School of Chinese Academy of Sciences,
Beijing 100049, China
[2] Department of Mathematical Sciences,
University of Cincinnati,
Cincinnati, OH, 45220, USA
nxy04b@mails.gucas.com.cn

Abstract. In 2004, the inventors of TTM cryptosystems proposed a new scheme that could resist the existing attacks, in particular, the Goubin-Courtois attack [GC00] and the Ding-Schmidt attack [DS03]. In this paper, we show the new version is still insecure, and we find that the polynomial components of the cipher (F_i) satisfy nontrivial equations of the special form

$$\sum_{i=0}^{n-1} a_i x_i + \sum_{0 \le j \le k \le m-1} b_{jk} F_j F_k + \sum_{j=0}^{m-1} c_j F_j + d = 0,$$

which could be found with 2^{38} computations. From these equations and consequently the linear equations we derive from these equations for any given ciphertext, we can eliminate some of the variables x_i by restricting the functions to an affine subspace, such that, on this subspace, we can trivialize the "lock" polynomials, which are the key structure to ensure its security in this new instance of TTM. Then with method similar to Ding-Schmidt [DS03], we can find the corresponding plaintext for any given ciphertext. The total computational complexity of the attack is less than 2^{39} operations over a finite field of size 2^8. Our results are further confirmed by computer experiments.

Keywords: Multivariate public key cryptography, TTM, quadratic polynomial.

1 Introduction

Public key cryptography is an important tool for our modern information society. Traditional public key cryptosystems such as RSA and ElGamal rely on hard number theory based problems such as factoring or discrete logarithms. However, techniques for factorization and solving discrete logarithm continually improve and polynomial time quantum algorithms can be used to solve both problems

---

* Corresponding author.

J. Zhou, M. Yung, and F. Bao (Eds.): ACNS 2006, LNCS 3989, pp. 210–225, 2006.
© Springer-Verlag Berlin Heidelberg 2006

efficiently [Sho97]. Hence, there is a need to search for alternatives which are based on other classes of problems.

Multivariate public key cryptosystem (MPKC) is one of the promising alternatives. The security of MPKC relies on the difficulty of solving systems of nonlinear polynomial equations with many variables, and the latter is a NP-hard problem in general. The public key of MPKC is mostly a set of quadratic polynomials. These polynomials are derived from composition of maps. Compared with RSA public key cryptosystems, the computation in MPKC can be very fast because it is operated on a small finite field. So MPKC may be suitable for even low-end devices.

The first promising construction of MPKC is the Matsumoto-Imai (MI) scheme [MI88] proposed in 1988. Unfortunately, it was defeated by Patarin in 1995 with the linearization method [Pat95].

Tame transformation method (TTM) schemes [Moh99] was proposed by Moh in 1999. The central map of TTM is the so-called tame transformations which is closely related to the famous Jacobian conjecture in algebraic geometry. The construction of TTM is very beautiful, and the decryption of TTM is very fast due to its special design.

But by now, all instances of TTM are insecure. In 2000, Goubin and Courtois claimed that they completely defeated all possible instances of TTM schemes using the Minrank method and demonstrated it by defeating one of the challenges set by the inventors of TTM [GC00]. However, the inventors of TTM refuted the claim, and they presented another construction to support their claim [CM01]. But this new scheme also had a defect common among all the existing TTM schemes at that time. Ding and Schmidt pointed out that there exist linearization equations satisfied by the components of the ciphers, and they extended linearization method to attack this new version [DS03]. In order to resist these attacks, the inventors of TTM proposed another new instance [MCY04] in 2004, and they claimed the security is 2^{148} against the Goubin-Courtois attack. To resist the Ding-Schmidt attack, they incorporated new lock polynomials which can not be trivialized by Ding-Schmidt attack.

Unfortunately, we find this new implementation of TTM also has a defect, that is, there exist nontrivial equations of the special form

$$\sum_{i=0}^{n-1} a_i x_i + \sum_{0 \leq j \leq k \leq m-1} b_{jk} F_j F_k + \sum_{j=0}^{m-1} c_j F_j + d = 0.$$

We call them **second order linearization equations**. We use these equations as a starting point to trivialize the lock polynomials in the TTM instance. In other words, for any given valid ciphertext, we can find an affine subspace W in the plaintext space such that all lock polynomials become constants on W. Then with method similar to Ding-Schmidt [DS03], we can recover the corresponding plaintext for a given ciphertext easily. This attack in principle is very similar to the attack of Ding and Hodges in [DH03]. The total computational complexity of our attack is less than 2^{39}.

The paper is organized as follows. We introduce the basic ideas and new instance of TTM schemes in Section 2. In Section 3, we describe how to attack this new TTM, present a practical attack procedure, and calculate the complexity of our attack. Finally, in Section 4, we conclude the paper.

2   TTM Cryptosystems

2.1   Basic Idea of TTM Schemes

Let $\mathbb{K}$ be a small finite field. The TTM systems is constructed as a composition of several maps $\phi_1, \phi_2, \cdots$, and ϕ_l, $F = \phi_l \circ \phi_{l-1} \circ \cdots \circ \phi_1$, where ϕ_i is a polynomial map from K^{n_i} to $K^{n_{i+1}}$ and $n = n_1 \leq n_2 \leq \cdots \leq n_{l+1} = m$, such that

1. The value of $F(x_0, \cdots, x_{n-1})$ at any given $(x_0, \cdots, x_{n-1})$ is easy to compute.
2. Each ϕ_i is easy to invert, and $F(x_0, \cdots, x_{n-1})$ is also easy to invert if one knows the composition factors of F, namely the ϕ_i. But it is hard to invert F if one does not know the factorization.
3. Some of the ϕ_i are linear polynomials, while F is a quadratic polynomial map.

The expression of $F(x_0, \cdots, x_{n-1})$ is taken as the public key in a TTM system and the linear ϕ_i as the secret key. $F : \mathbb{K}^n \to \mathbb{K}^m$ is a set of quadratic polynomials. In all known instances of TTM design, one uses the following two types of maps for the ϕ_i :

1. Linear affine maps of the form $f(X) = AX + b$, where $X, b \in \mathbb{K}^*$ are vectors and A is an invertible matrix.
2. Tame transformations. They are maps of the form

$$
\begin{aligned}
&(y_0, \cdots, y_{m-1}) \\
&= J(x_0, \cdots, x_{n-1}) \\
&= (x_0, x_1 + q_1(x_0), \cdots, x_{n-1} + q_{n-1}(x_0, \cdots, x_{n-2}), \\
&\quad q_n(x_0, \cdots, x_{n-1}), \cdots, q_{m-1}(x_0, \cdots, x_{n-1})).
\end{aligned}
$$

The inventor, an expert in algebraic geometry, uses the basic concept of tame transformation from algebraic geometry. The inverting process of a tame transformation is very simple and is also a tame transformation.

The key construction of TTM schemes is the so-called lock polynomials. In the new instance [MCY04], a set of new lock polynomial $G_j(x_0, \cdots, x_{n-1})$, $j = 0, \cdots, 6$, is constructed, where the central map becomes

$$
\begin{aligned}
&J(x_0, \cdots, x_{n-1}) \\
&= (x_0 + G_0, x_1 + q_1(x_0) + G_1, \cdots, x_6 + q_6(x_0, \cdots, x_5) + G_6, \\
&\quad x_7 + q_7(x_0, \cdots, x_6), \cdots, x_{n-1} + q_{n-1}(x_0, \cdots, x_{n-2}), \\
&\quad q_n(x_0, \cdots, x_{n-1}), \cdots, q_{m-1}(x_0, \cdots, x_{n-1})).
\end{aligned}
$$

A pure triangular system can be solved by Minrank method, therefore the lock polynomials are needed to resist this attack. Our attack uses a different method and we start from first trying to trivialize these lock polynomials.

2.2 New Instance of TTM

We use the same notation as in [MCY04]. Take $\mathbb{K}$ as the finite field with 2^8 elements and $m = 110$ and $n = 55$. The map $F : \mathbb{K}^{55} \to \mathbb{K}^{110}$ is a composition of 4 maps $\phi_1, \phi_2, \phi_3,$ and ϕ_4, namely $F = \phi_4 \circ \phi_3 \circ \phi_2 \circ \phi_1$:

$$F : \mathbb{K}^{55} \xrightarrow{\phi_1} \mathbb{K}^{55} \xrightarrow{\phi_2} \mathbb{K}^{110} \xrightarrow{\phi_3} \mathbb{K}^{110} \xrightarrow{\phi_4} \mathbb{K}^{110}.$$

ϕ_1 and ϕ_4 are invertible affine linear maps, ϕ_2 is a tame quadratic transformation, and ϕ_3 is a degree 8 map using lock polynomials.

The expressions of ϕ_2 and ϕ_3 are public information in the TTM system. ϕ_1 and ϕ_4 are taken as the private key, while the expression of the map $(y_0, \cdots, y_{109})$ $= F(x_0, ..., x_{54})$ is the public key. Each component polynomial $y_i = F_i(x_0, ...x_{54})$ of F is a quadratic polynomial. To encrypt a plaintext $(x_0, ..., x_{54})$ is to evaluate F at it.

Define

$$(\bar{x}_0, \cdots, \bar{x}_{54}) = \phi_1(x_0, \cdots, x_{54}), (\bar{y}_0, \cdots, \bar{y}_{110}) = \phi_2(\bar{x}_0, \cdots, \bar{x}_{54}),$$
$$(z_0, \cdots, z_{110}) = \phi_3(\bar{y}_0, \cdots, \bar{y}_{110}), (y_0, \cdots, y_{110}) = \phi_4((z_0, \cdots, z_{110}).$$

The exact description of ϕ_2 is given in appendix.

Seven lock polynomials, $G_j(\bar{x}_0, \cdots, \bar{x}_{n-1})$, $0 \leq j \leq 7$, are used to define ϕ_3 and they are defined as follows:

$R_1 := \bar{y}_{66}\bar{y}_{67} + \bar{y}_{68}\bar{y}_{69} + \bar{y}_{70}\bar{y}_{31} + \bar{y}_{71}\bar{y}_{32} + \bar{y}_{72}\bar{y}_{33} + \bar{y}_{73}\bar{y}_{34} + \bar{y}_{74}\bar{y}_{75} + \bar{y}_{76}\bar{y}_{35} + \bar{y}_{45};$

$R_2 := \bar{y}_{77}\bar{y}_{78} + \bar{y}_{79}\bar{y}_{80} + \bar{y}_{75}\bar{y}_{31} + \bar{y}_{36}\bar{y}_{81} + \bar{y}_{37}\bar{y}_{82} + \bar{y}_{38}\bar{y}_{83} + \bar{y}_{74}\bar{y}_{84} + \bar{y}_{39}\bar{y}_{85} + \bar{y}_{46};$

$R_3 := \bar{y}_{86}\bar{y}_{87} + \bar{y}_{88}\bar{y}_{89} + \bar{y}_{90}\bar{y}_{22} + \bar{y}_{91}\bar{y}_{23} + \bar{y}_{92}\bar{y}_{24} + \bar{y}_{93}\bar{y}_{25} + \bar{y}_{94}\bar{y}_{95} + \bar{y}_{96}\bar{y}_{26} + \bar{y}_{47};$

$R_4 := \bar{y}_{97}\bar{y}_{98} + \bar{y}_{99}\bar{y}_{100} + \bar{y}_{95}\bar{y}_{22} + \bar{y}_{27}\bar{y}_{101} + \bar{y}_{28}\bar{y}_{102} + \bar{y}_{29}\bar{y}_{103} + \bar{y}_{94}\bar{y}_{104} + \bar{y}_{30}\bar{y}_{105} + \bar{y}_{48};$

$R_5 := \bar{y}_{55}\bar{y}_{56} + \bar{y}_{57}\bar{y}_{58} + \bar{y}_{59}\bar{y}_{40} + \bar{y}_{60}\bar{y}_{41} + \bar{y}_{61}\bar{y}_{42} + \bar{y}_{62}\bar{y}_{43} + \bar{y}_{63}\bar{y}_{64} + \bar{y}_{65}\bar{y}_{44} + \bar{y}_{49};$

$S_1 := R_2R_4 + R_3R_5 + \bar{y}_{50} = \bar{x}_{50};$

$S_2 := R_1R_3 + R_4R_5 + \bar{y}_{51} = \bar{x}_{51};$

$S_3 := R_1R_4 + R_2R_5 + \bar{y}_{52} = \bar{x}_{52};$

$S_4 := R_1R_5 + R_2R_3 + \bar{y}_{53} = \bar{x}_{53};$

$S_5 := R_1R_2 + R_3R_4 + \bar{y}_{54} = \bar{x}_{54};$

$G_0 := S_2S_4 + S_3S_5 = \bar{x}_{51}\bar{x}_{53} + \bar{x}_{52}\bar{x}_{54};$

$G_1 := S_1S_3 + S_4S_5 = \bar{x}_{50}\bar{x}_{52} + \bar{x}_{53}\bar{x}_{54};$

$G_2 := S_1S_4 + S_2S_5 = \bar{x}_{50}\bar{x}_{53} + \bar{x}_{51}\bar{x}_{54};$

$G_3 := S_1S_5 + S_2S_3 = \bar{x}_{50}\bar{x}_{54} + \bar{x}_{51}\bar{x}_{52};$

$G_4 := S_1S_2 + S_3S_4 = \bar{x}_{50}\bar{x}_{51} + \bar{x}_{52}\bar{x}_{53};$

$G_5 := R_1S_1 + R_2S_2 + R_3S_3 + R_4S_4 + R_5S_5 = \bar{x}_{50}\bar{x}_{45} + \bar{x}_{51}\bar{x}_{46} + \bar{x}_{52}\bar{x}_{47} + \bar{x}_{53}\bar{x}_{48} + \bar{x}_{54}\bar{x}_{49};$

$G_6 := R_1S_2 + R_2S_3 + R_3S_4 + R_4S_5 + R_5S_1 = \bar{x}_{51}\bar{x}_{45} + \bar{x}_{52}\bar{x}_{46} + \bar{x}_{53}\bar{x}_{47} + \bar{x}_{54}\bar{x}_{48} + \bar{x}_{50}\bar{x}_{49}.$

ϕ_3 is defined as:

$$\phi_3(\bar{y}_0, \cdots, \bar{y}_{109}) = (\bar{y}_0 + G_0(\bar{y}_0, \cdots, \bar{y}_{109}), \cdots,$$
$$\bar{y}_6 + G_6(\bar{y}_0, \cdots, \bar{y}_{109}), \bar{y}_7, \cdots, \bar{y}_{109}).$$

Note that ϕ_3 is of degree 8 in terms of $\bar{y}_i$. Then

$$\phi_{32}(\bar{x}_0, \cdots, \bar{x}_{54}) = \phi_3 \circ \phi_2(\bar{x}_0, \cdots, \bar{x}_{54}) = (\bar{y}_0 + G_0(\bar{x}_0, \cdots, \bar{x}_{54}), \cdots,$$
$$\bar{y}_6 + G_6(\bar{x}_0, \cdots, \bar{x}_{54}), \bar{y}_7, \cdots, \bar{y}_{109}).$$

Note in the two formulas above, the functions G_i are seen differently, while in the first one they are functions of $\bar{y}_i$ with degree 8, in the second formula they are functions of $\bar{x}_i$ with degree 2. Denote by $\phi_{i,j}$ the j-th component function of ϕ_i. Similar notations $\phi_{32,j}$, $\phi_{1,j}^{-1}, \phi_{4,j}^{-1}$, and F_j are denoted for ϕ_{32}, ϕ_1^{-1}, ϕ_4^{-1}, and F, respectively. Obviously, each F_j is a quadratic polynomial, and $F(x_0, ..., x_{54}) = \phi_4 \circ \phi_{32} \circ \phi_1(x_0, ..., x_{54})$.

3   Cryptanalysis on New TTM Instance

Our attack is a ciphertext-only attack. We start from first finding all second order linearization equations. For any given ciphertext, we use them to trivialize the lock polynomials. Then, we derive the corresponding plaintext through the iteration of the process of first searching for linear relations in equations derived from the public key and the ciphertext and then substituting them into these equations.

3.1   Second Order Linearization Equations

We first observe that all the R_i ($1 \le i \le 5$) are linear on $\bar{x}_0, \cdots$, and $\bar{x}_{54}$. By a direct computation, we find that $R_1 = \bar{x}_{45}$, $R_2 = \bar{x}_{46}$, $R_3 = \bar{x}_{47}$, $R_4 = \bar{x}_{48}$, and $R_5 = \bar{x}_{49}$, namely,

$$\begin{cases} \bar{x}_{45} + \bar{y}_{66}\bar{y}_{67} + \bar{y}_{68}\bar{y}_{69} + \bar{y}_{70}\bar{y}_{31} + \bar{y}_{71}\bar{y}_{32} + \bar{y}_{72}\bar{y}_{33} + \bar{y}_{73}\bar{y}_{34} + \bar{y}_{74}\bar{y}_{75} + \bar{y}_{76}\bar{y}_{35} + \bar{y}_{45} = 0; \\ \bar{x}_{46} + \bar{y}_{77}\bar{y}_{78} + \bar{y}_{79}\bar{y}_{80} + \bar{y}_{75}\bar{y}_{31} + \bar{y}_{36}\bar{y}_{81} + \bar{y}_{37}\bar{y}_{82} + \bar{y}_{38}\bar{y}_{83} + \bar{y}_{74}\bar{y}_{84} + \bar{y}_{39}\bar{y}_{85} + \bar{y}_{46} = 0; \\ \bar{x}_{47} + \bar{y}_{86}\bar{y}_{87} + \bar{y}_{88}\bar{y}_{89} + \bar{y}_{90}\bar{y}_{22} + \bar{y}_{91}\bar{y}_{23} + \bar{y}_{92}\bar{y}_{24} + \bar{y}_{93}\bar{y}_{25} + \bar{y}_{94}\bar{y}_{95} + \bar{y}_{96}\bar{y}_{26} + \bar{y}_{47} = 0; \\ \bar{x}_{48} + \bar{y}_{97}\bar{y}_{98} + \bar{y}_{99}\bar{y}_{100} + \bar{y}_{95}\bar{y}_{22} + \bar{y}_{27}\bar{y}_{101} + \bar{y}_{28}\bar{y}_{102} + \bar{y}_{29}\bar{y}_{103} + \bar{y}_{94}\bar{y}_{104} + \bar{y}_{30}\bar{y}_{105} + \bar{y}_{48} = 0; \\ \bar{x}_{49} + \bar{y}_{55}\bar{y}_{56} + \bar{y}_{57}\bar{y}_{58} + \bar{y}_{59}\bar{y}_{40} + \bar{y}_{60}\bar{y}_{41} + \bar{y}_{61}\bar{y}_{42} + \bar{y}_{62}\bar{y}_{43} + \bar{y}_{63}\bar{y}_{64} + \bar{y}_{65}\bar{y}_{44} + \bar{y}_{49} = 0; \end{cases}$$

$$(3.1)$$

Since F is derived from ϕ_{32} by composing from the inner and outer sides by invertible linear maps ϕ_1 and ϕ_4, i.e., $\bar{x}_i = \phi_{1,i}(x_0, \cdots, x_{54})$ and $\bar{y}_j = \phi_{4,j}^{-1}(F_0, \cdots, F_{109})$ for $j > 21$, and $\bar{y}_0, \cdots, \bar{y}_{21}$ do not appear in equations (3.1), each of these equations can be changed into an identical equation of the form:

$$\sum_{i=0}^{54} a_i x_i + \sum_{0 \le j \le k \le 109} b_{jk} F_j F_k + \sum_{j=0}^{109} c_j F_j + d = 0, \qquad (3.2)$$

which is satisfied by any $(x_0, \cdots, x_{54}) \in \mathbb{K}^{55}$. Note that the coefficients a_i ($0 \le i \le 54$) are not all zero. Furthermore, there exist at least five equations of the above form such that their corresponding coefficient vectors $(a_0, \cdots, a_{54})$ are linearly independent since as linear combinations of $x_0, \cdots, x_{54}$, the coefficient vectors of $\bar{x}_{45}, \cdots, \bar{x}_{49}$ are linearly independent. Let V denote the $\mathbb{K}$-linear space composing of all second order linearization equations of the form (3.2), and let D be its dimension.

To find all equations in V is equivalent to find a basis of V. The equation (3.2) is equivalent to a system of equations on the coefficients a_i, b_{jk}, c_j, and d. It is well known that the number of monomials in n variables of degree $\leq D$ is $\binom{n+D}{D}$ ([CP03]), so the number of unknown coefficients in these equations is equal to

$$\binom{55}{1} + \binom{110+2}{2} = 6271.$$

To find a basis of V, we can randomly select slightly more than 6271, say 7000, plaintexts $(x_0, \cdots, x_{54})$ and substitute them in (3.2) to get a system of 7000 linear equations and then solve it. Let $\{(a_i^{(\rho)}, b_{jk}^{(\rho)}, c_j^{(\rho)}, d^{(\rho)}), 1 \leq \rho \leq D\}$ be the coefficient vectors corresponding to a basis of V, where i, (j,k), and j stand for $i = 0, \cdots, 54$, $0 \leq j \leq k \leq 109$, and $j = 0, \cdots, 109$, respectively.

Let V' be linear subspace which is consisting of the zero equation and all second order linearization equations with $(a_0, \cdots, a_{54}) \neq (0, \cdots, 0)$, and let $l = \dim V' \geq 5$. Without loss of generality, we assume $(a_0^{(1)}, \cdots, a_{54}^{(1)}), \cdots,$ $(a_0^{(l)}, \cdots, a_{54}^{(l)})$ are linearly independent and $(a_0^{(\rho)}, \cdots, a_{54}^{(\rho)}) = (0, \cdots, 0)$ for $l + 1 \leq \rho \leq D$. Let $E_\rho (1 \leq \rho \leq D)$ denote the equation

$$\sum_{i=0}^{54} a_i^{(\rho)} x_i + \sum_{0 \leq j \leq k \leq 109} b_{jk}^{(\rho)} F_j F_k + \sum_{j=0}^{109} c_j^{(\rho)} F_j + d^{(\rho)} = 0. \tag{3.3}$$

The work above depends only on any given public key, and it can be solved once for all cryptanalysis under that public key.

3.2   Deriving Linear Equations Satisfied by Plaintext

Let's assume we have a valid ciphertext $y' = (y'_0, \cdots, y'_{109})$. Our goal is to find its corresponding plaintext $x' = (x'_0, \cdots, x'_{54})$.

Substituting $(F_0, \cdots, F_{109}) = (y'_0, \cdots, y'_{109})$ into equations $E_1, \cdots, E_l$, we derive l linearly independent linear equations in $x_0, \cdots, x_{54}$, which are denoted by $E'_1, \cdots, E'_l$. These l equations are also satisfied by x'. Doing a simple Gaussian elimination, from these l equations we can represent l variables of $x_0, \cdots, x_{54}$ by linear combinations of other $55 - l$. That is, we can find two disjoint subsets of $\{0, \cdots, 54\}$, $A'_1 = \{v'_1, \cdots, v'_l\}$ and $A_1 = \{v_1, \cdots, v_{55-l}\}$, and linear expressions

$$x_{v'_j} = h_j(x_{v_1}, \cdots, x_{v_{55-l}}), 1 \leq j \leq l \tag{3.4}$$

such that $E'_1, \cdots, E'_l$ holds when (3.4) are substituted into them.

To put some calculations in one-time precomputation and make our attack more efficient, we can further refine the analysis about h_j. Clearly, only the constant term in h_j relies on y', the coefficients of the linear monomials in h_j rely on only the public key of the TTM scheme. Let W denote a $(55 - l)$-dimensional affine subspace of $\mathbb{K}^{55}$, the component $x_{v'_j}$ of any vector $(x_0, \cdots, x_{54})$ in W is $h_j(x_{v_1}, \cdots, x_{v_{55-l}})$. Each vector $x = (x_0, \cdots, x_{54})$ in W satisfies $\sum\limits_{i=0}^{54} a_i^{(\rho)} x_i = t_\rho$, $0 \le \rho \le l$, where

$$t_\rho = \sum_{0 \le j \le k \le 109} b_{jk}^{(\rho)} y'_j y'_k + \sum_{j=0}^{109} c_j^{(\rho)} y'_j + d^{(\rho)} \tag{3.5}$$

is a constant independent of $(x_0, \cdots, x_{54})$.

Since each equation in (3.1) is an element of V and hence a linear combination of $E_1, \cdots, E_D$, the linear part (i.e., excluding the constant term part of an affine function) of each $\bar{x}_i$ ($45 \le i \le 49$) at $x \in W$ is a linear combination of $\sum\limits_{i=0}^{54} a_i^{(\rho)} x_i$ ($1 \le \rho \le l$), that is, it is a linear combination of constants $t_1, \cdots, t_l$. Hence, as functions in $x_{v_1}, \cdots, x_{v_{55-l}}$, all $R_i = \bar{x}_{44+i}$ ($1 \le i \le 5$) are constants on W. Let they be $r_1, \cdots, r_5$, respectively.

Now substitute (3.4) into $F_j(x_0, \cdots, x_{54})$ and derive 110 new quadratic functions $\hat{F}_j(x_{v_1}, \cdots, x_{v_{55-l}})$ ($0 \le j \le 109$). The quadratic monomials of $\hat{F}_j$ rely on only the public key since so do the coefficients of the linear monomials of h_j.

3.3   Trivializing the Lock Polynomials

To continue the attack, we utilize the following equations stemming from the definition of the lock polynomials:

$$\begin{cases} \bar{y}_{50} + \bar{x}_{46}\bar{x}_{48} + \bar{x}_{47}\bar{x}_{49} + \bar{x}_{50} = \bar{y}_{50} + R_2 R_4 + R_3 R_5 + \bar{x}_{50} = 0; \\ \bar{y}_{51} + \bar{x}_{45}\bar{x}_{47} + \bar{x}_{48}\bar{x}_{49} + \bar{x}_{51} = \bar{y}_{51} + R_1 R_3 + R_4 R_5 + \bar{x}_{51} = 0; \\ \bar{y}_{52} + \bar{x}_{45}\bar{x}_{48} + \bar{x}_{46}\bar{x}_{49} + \bar{x}_{52} = \bar{y}_{52} + R_1 R_4 + R_2 R_5 + \bar{x}_{52} = 0; \\ \bar{y}_{53} + \bar{x}_{45}\bar{x}_{49} + \bar{x}_{46}\bar{x}_{47} + \bar{x}_{53} = \bar{y}_{53} + R_1 R_5 + R_2 R_3 + \bar{x}_{53} = 0; \\ \bar{y}_{54} + \bar{x}_{45}\bar{x}_{46} + \bar{x}_{47}\bar{x}_{48} + \bar{x}_{54} = \bar{y}_{54} + R_1 R_2 + R_3 R_4 + \bar{x}_{54} = 0. \end{cases} \tag{3.6}$$

On W, (3.6) is

$$\begin{cases} \bar{y}_{50} + \bar{x}_{50} + s_1 = 0; \\ \bar{y}_{51} + \bar{x}_{51} + s_2 = 0; \\ \bar{y}_{52} + \bar{x}_{52} + s_3 = 0; \\ \bar{y}_{53} + \bar{x}_{53} + s_4 = 0; \\ \bar{y}_{54} + \bar{x}_{54} + s_5 = 0, \end{cases} \tag{3.7}$$

where $s_1, \cdots, s_5$ are constants defined by $s_1 = r_2 r_4 + r_3 r_5$, $s_2 = r_1 r_3 + r_4 r_5$, $s_3 = r_1 r_4 + r_2 r_5$, $s_4 = r_1 r_5 + r_2 r_3$, and $s_5 = r_1 r_2 + r_3 r_4$. Through linear transformation ϕ_1 and ϕ_4^{-1}, equation (3.7) implies that there exist quadratic equations in $x_{v_1}, \cdots, x_{v_{55-l}}$ of the form

$$\sum_{i=1}^{55-l} \hat{a}_i x_{v_i} + \sum_{j=0}^{109} \hat{b}_j \hat{F}_j + \hat{d} = 0, \tag{3.8}$$

where $(\hat{b}_0, \cdots, \hat{b}_{109}) \neq (0, \cdots, 0)$.

To find all equations of the form (3.8), we can use the same method as the one used for equations (3.2). But the case is simpler and easier since far fewer unknowns are involved here.

To again improve efficiency by utilizing one-time precomputation, we use another alternative method, that is, we expand each $\hat{F}_j$ and compare the coefficients of quadratic monomials in $x_{v_1}, \cdots, x_{v_{55-l}}$ in the two sides of (3.8), we derive a system of linear equations in $\hat{b}_0, \cdots, \hat{b}_{109}$. Since quadratic monomials are of the form x_i^2 or $x_i x_j$ for $i \neq j$, this system has

$$\binom{55 - l}{1} + \binom{55 - l}{2} = (56 - l)(55 - l)/2$$

equations. It also depends on only the public key. Let $\hat{D}$ and $\{(\hat{b}_0^{(\rho)}, \cdots, \hat{b}_{109}^{(\rho)}) : 1 \leq \rho \leq \hat{D}\}$ be the dimension and a basis of the solution space of this system, respectively.

Substituting $(\hat{b}_0^{(\rho)}, \cdots, \hat{b}_{109}^{(\rho)})$ into (3.8) and comparing constant terms and coefficients of linear monomials in $x_{v_1}, \cdots, x_{v_{55-l}}$ in the two sides, we uniquely determine the other coefficients in (3.8), $\hat{a}_1^{(\rho)}, \cdots, \hat{a}_{55-l}^{(\rho)}$ and $\hat{d}^{(\rho)}$, because they are determined by the $\hat{b}_j^{(\rho)}$ ($0 \leq j \leq 109$) and the linear and constant terms of the $\hat{F}_j$ ($0 \leq j \leq 109$). These coefficients depend on specific values of the ciphertext y', since the linear and constant terms of the $\hat{F}_j$ depend on the constant terms of the h_j.

Let

$$\{(\hat{a}_1^{(\rho)}, \cdots, \hat{a}_{55-l}^{(\rho)}, \hat{b}_0^{(\rho)}, \cdots, \hat{b}_{109}^{(\rho)}, d^{(\rho)}), 1 \leq \rho \leq \hat{D}\}$$

be a basis of the space of the coefficient vectors of the equations of the form (3.8). Rearranging these basis vectors, we assume that $(\hat{a}_1^{(1)}, \cdots, \hat{a}_{55-l}^{(1)}), \cdots, (\hat{a}_1^{(k)}, \cdots, \hat{a}_{55-l}^{(k)})$ are linearly independent and the other vectors $(\hat{a}_1^{(i)}, \cdots, \hat{a}_{55-l}^{(i)})$ ($k + 1 \leq i \leq \hat{D}$) are their linear combinations. Let $\hat{E}_\rho$ denote the equation

$$\sum_{i=1}^{55-l} \hat{a}_i^{(\rho)} x_{v_i} + \sum_{j=0}^{109} \hat{b}_j^{(\rho)} \hat{F}_j + \hat{d}^{(\rho)} = 0, \tag{3.9}$$

$1 \leq \rho \leq k$. These k equations are satisfied by all $(x_{v_1}, \cdots, x_{v_{55-l}}) \in K^{55-l}$.

Substituting $(\hat{F}_0, \cdots, \hat{F}_{109})$ by y' into (3.9), we derive the equation $\hat{E}'_\rho$:

$$\sum_{i=1}^{55-l} \hat{a}_i^{(\rho)} x_{v_i} + \hat{r}_\rho = 0, \tag{3.10}$$

where $\hat{r}_\rho = \sum_{j=0}^{109} \hat{b}_j^{(\rho)} y'_j + \hat{d}^{(\rho)}$, $1 \leq \rho \leq k$. Doing a Gaussian elimination on $\hat{E}'_\rho$ ($1 \leq \rho \leq k$), we will find two disjoint subsets of $\{v_1, \cdots, v_{55-l}\}$: $A'_2 = \{w'_1, \cdots, w'_k\}$ and $A_2 = \{w_1, \cdots, w_{55-l-k}\}$, and linear functions in $x_{w_1}, \cdots, x_{w_{55-l-k}}$,

$$x_{w'_i} = \hat{h}_i(x_{w_1}, \cdots, x_{w_{55-l-k}}), 1 \leq i \leq k \tag{3.11}$$

such that (3.10) holds when (3.11) are substituted into it. We substitute (3.11) into $\hat{F}_j(x_{v_1}, \cdots, x_{v_{55-l}})$ to derive $\tilde{F}_j(x_{w_1}, \cdots, x_{w_{55-l-k}})$, $0 \le j \le 109$.

Let $\hat{W}$ denote a $(55 - l - k)$-dimensional affine subspace of W, where for each vector $(x_0, \cdots, x_{54})$ in $\hat{W}$, $x_{w_i'}$ is substituted by (3.11) for any $1 \le i \le k$. Thus, every vector $(x_0, \cdots, x_{54})$ in $\hat{W}$ satisfies (3.10).

Restricting on $\hat{W}$, each equation in (3.6) is a linear combination of $\hat{E}_1, \cdots, \hat{E}_{\hat{D}}$, and hence, the linear part of $\bar{x}_i$ ($50 \le i \le 54$) is a linear combination of

$$\sum_{i=1}^{55-l} \hat{a}_i^{(\rho)} x_{v_i}, \ (1 \le \rho \le k),$$ i.e., a linear combination of $\hat{r}_1, \cdots, \hat{r}_k$, which is a

constant independent of $x \in \hat{W}$. Therefore, $\bar{x}_{50}, \bar{x}_{51}, \bar{x}_{52}, \bar{x}_{53}$, and $\bar{x}_{54}$ are all constant on $\hat{W}$.

By the definitions of R_i, S_i, and G_i, they are all constants on $\hat{W}$ as functions in $x_0, \cdots, x_{54}$. Let G_i be g_i, $g_i \in K$, $i = 0, \cdots, 6$.

3.4   Finding the Plaintext

The analysis mentioned in the previous subsection is a step of trivializing lock polynomials. Although we do not know the concrete values of g_i, we know all G_i are constant on $\hat{W}$. This fact is used below to complete the remaining steps of our attack. We also use the fact that $\bar{y}_0 := \phi_{2,0}(\bar{x}_0, \cdots, \bar{x}_{54}) = \bar{x}_0$ and $\bar{y}_1 := \phi_{2,1}(\bar{x}_0, \cdots, \bar{x}_{54}) = f_1(\bar{x}_0) + \bar{x}_1$ for some quadratic f_1; please refer to the appendix.

Because ϕ_{32} is a tame triangular transformation on $\phi_1(\hat{W})$, set $\phi_{321} = \phi_{32} \circ \phi_1$. Since

$$\phi_{321,0}(x_0, \cdots, x_{54}) = \phi_{32,0}(\bar{x}_0, \cdots, \bar{x}_{54}) = (\bar{y}_0 + G_0(\bar{x}_0, \cdots, \bar{x}_{54})),$$

for $(x_0, \cdots, x_{54}) \in \hat{W}$, we have

$$\phi_{4,0}^{-1}(\tilde{F}) = \phi_{321,0}(x_0, \cdots, x_{54}) = \phi_{1,0}(x_0, \cdots, x_{54}) + g_0.$$

So there must exist identical equations of the form

$$\sum_{i=0}^{55-l-k} \tilde{a}_i x_{w_i} + \sum_{j=0}^{109} \tilde{b}_j \tilde{F}_j + \tilde{d} = 0, \tag{3.12}$$

which are satisfied by all $(x_{w_1}, \cdots, x_{w_{55-l-k}}) \in K^{55-l-k}$ and the coefficients $(\tilde{b}_0, \cdots, \tilde{b}_{109}) \ne (0, \cdots, 0)$.

Similarly to (3.8), we can derive a basis of linear space of all coefficient vectors $(\tilde{a}_1, \cdots, \tilde{a}_{55-l-k}, \tilde{b}_0, \cdots, \tilde{b}_{109}, \tilde{d})$ satisfying (3.12). Write these basis vectors as row vectors to get a matrix and change it into a top triangular matrix by row transformations. Substitute $\tilde{F}_i$ by y_i' in the equations (3.12) corresponding to each row of the matrix with $(\tilde{a}_1, \cdots, \tilde{a}_{55-l-k}) \ne (0, \cdots, 0)$, then we derive some, say p, linearly independent linear equations in $x_{w_1}, \cdots, x_{w_{55-l-k}}$. Therefore we can represent p variables of $x_{w_1}, \cdots, x_{w_{55-l-k}}$ as linear expressions of the remaining variables. We also derive a $(55 - l - k - p)$-dimensional affine subspace

$\tilde{W}$ of $\hat{W}$. Let $x_{u_1}, \cdots, x_{u_{55-l-k-p}}$ be the remaining variables. For the same reason as mentioned above, $\phi_{1,0}(x_0, \cdots, x_{54})$, and hence $f_1(\phi_{1,0}(x_0, \cdots, x_{54}))$, are constant on $\tilde{W}$.

Let $\tilde{F}_i(x_{u_1}, \cdots, x_{u_{55-l-k-p}})$ denote the p-variable-eliminated function $\bar{F}_i(x_{w_1}, \cdots, x_{w_{55-l-k}})$. Let $g_1' = g_1 + f_1(\phi_{1,0}(x_0, \cdots, x_{54}))$. Again, we have

$$\phi_{4,1}^{-1}(\tilde{F}) = \phi_{321,1}(x_0, \cdots, x_{54}) = \phi_{1,1}(x_0, \cdots, x_{54}) + g_1',$$

$(x_0, \cdots, x_{54}) \in \tilde{W}$, and we know there exist identical equations in $(x_{u_1}, \cdots, x_{u_{55-l-k-p}})$ of the form

$$\sum_{i=0}^{55-l-k-p} \tilde{\tilde{a}}_i x_{w_i} + \sum_{j=0}^{109} \tilde{\tilde{b}}_j \tilde{F}_j + \tilde{\tilde{d}} = 0 \tag{3.13}$$

with $(\tilde{\tilde{b}}_0, \cdots, \tilde{\tilde{b}}_{109}) \neq (0, \cdots, 0)$.

Repeating similar steps of eliminating and substituting variables, we derive in turn smaller and smaller affine subspaces of $\tilde{W}$. On these subspaces, we have in turn $\phi_{1,1}(x_0, \cdots, x_{54})$, $f_2(\phi_{1,0}, \phi_{1,1})$, $\cdots$, $\phi_{1,20}(x_0, \cdots, x_{54})$, $f_{21}(\phi_{1,0}, \cdots, \phi_{1,20})$, $\phi_{1,21}(x_0, \cdots, x_{54})$, $\cdots$, and $\phi_{1,54}(x_0, \cdots, x_{54})$ are constant. Since $\phi_{1,0}$ $(x_0, \cdots, x_{54})$, $\cdots$, and $\phi_{1,54}(x_0, \cdots, x_{54})$ are constants on the last subspace and ϕ_1 is an invertible map, $(x_0, \cdots, x_{54})$ is a constant vector on that subspace. This means that this affine subspace is a point (i.e., the 0-dimensional subspace). This point is exactly the plaintext.

Collecting all linear expressions between variables, we get the plaintext. Now the attack is accomplished.

3.5   A Practical Attack Procedure and Its Complexity

The attack in the previous subsections can be further divided into the following six steps. The first three steps are independent of the value of the ciphertext y' and can be done once for a given public key.

Step 1 of the attack. *Find a basis of the linear space of the coefficient vectors* (a_i, b_{jk}, c_j, d) *of the identical equations*

$$\sum_{i=0}^{54} a_i x_i + \sum_{0 \leq j \leq k \leq 109} b_{jk} F_j F_k + \sum_{j=0}^{109} c_j F_j + d = 0.$$

As mentioned in subsection 3.1, we randomly select 7000 plaintexts $(x_0, \cdots, x_{54})$ and substitute them into equation (3.2) to get a linear system of 7000 equations on 6271 unknowns. The computational complexity to solve it is $6271^2 \cdot 7000 \leq 2^{38}$ operations on the finite field $K = \mathbb{F}_{2^8}$. Reorder the resulting basis vectors such that $(a_0^{(\rho)}, \cdots, a_{54}^{(\rho)}) = (0, \cdots, 0)$ for $l+1 \leq \rho \leq D$, and that for the $l \times 55$ matrix with $(a_0^{(\rho)}, \cdots, a_{54}^{(\rho)})$ as its ρ-th row and its v_1'-,v_2'-, $\cdots$, v_l'-columns form an identity matrix of order l. (Let the columns are indexed by $0, 1, \cdots,$ and 54.)

Step 2 of the attack. *Let $\{v_1, \cdots, v_{55-l}\} = \{0, \cdots, 54\} \setminus \{v'_1, \cdots, v'_l\}$. Represent the variables $x_{v'_1}, x_{v'_2}, \cdots,$ and $x_{v'_l}$ as linear expressions of the form*

$$h_j(x_{v_1}, \cdots, x_{v_{55-l}}) = \sum_{i=1}^{55-l} h_{j,i} x_{v_i} + t_j,$$

respectively, $1 \leq j \leq l$, according to the system of l linear equations

$$\sum_{i=0}^{54} a_i^{(\rho)} x_i = t_\rho, 1 \leq \rho \leq l.$$

Substitute $x_{v'_j}$ by $h_j(x_{v_1}, \cdots, x_{v_{55-l}})$ $(1 \leq j \leq l)$ into the expressions $F_i(x_0, \cdots, x_{54})$ $(0 \leq i \leq 109)$ for the public key, and derive 110 new quadratic polynomials $\hat{F}_i(x_{v_1}, \cdots, x_{v_{55-l}})$, $0 \leq i \leq 109$. The coefficients of quadratic terms in $\hat{F}_i$ are independent of $t_1, \cdots, t_l$.

The first part of this step costs no computation. The second substitution part is of computational complexity about

$$55l(l+3)(55-l)(56-l) < 2^{23}.$$

Step 3 of the attack. *Comparing the coefficients of quadratic terms in the two sides of the equation*

$$\sum_{j=0}^{109} \hat{b}_j \hat{F}_j(x_{v_1}, \cdots, x_{v_{55-l}}) = 0$$

to derive a system of $(55-l)(56-l)/2$ linear equations on $\hat{b}_0, \cdots, \hat{b}_{109}$. Then use Gaussian elimination to find a basis of its solution space, $\{(\hat{b}_0^{(\rho)}, \cdots, \hat{b}_{109}^{(\rho)}), 1 \leq \rho \leq k\}$.

The computational complexity of this step is

$$110^2 \cdot (55-l)(56-l)/2 < 2^{13}(56-l)^2 < 2^{24}.$$

The above three steps can be precomputed for any given public key. The total complexity is less than 2^{38}. In what follows, we go to break the corresponding plaintext of a specific valid ciphertext $y' = (y'_0, \cdots, y'_{109})$.

Step 4 of the attack. *First, substitute $y' = (y'_0, \cdots, y'_{109})$ into (3.5) to obtain $t_1, \cdots, t_l$ and substitute $t_1, \cdots, t_l$ into $\hat{F}_i$ to get simplified $\hat{F}_i$. Then for each $(\hat{b}_0^{(\rho)}, \cdots, \hat{b}_{109}^{(\rho)})$, compare the coefficients of the linear and constant terms in the two sides of (3.9) to determine $\hat{a}_0^{(\rho)}, \cdots, \hat{a}_{54-l}^{(\rho)}$ and $d^{(\rho)}$.*

The computational complexity of substitution is

$$(2 \times (\binom{110}{1} + \binom{110}{2}) + \binom{110}{1}) \times l \approx 2^{14}l < 2^{17}.$$

The complexity of calculating $\hat{a}_0^{(\rho)}, \cdots, \hat{a}_{54-l}^{(\rho)}$ and $d^{(\rho)}$ is $(56-l)^2 \hat{D} < 2^{15}$.

Step 5 of the attack. *Do primary transformations (similar as primary row transformations on matrices) on the vectors*

$$(\hat{a}_1^{(\rho)}, \cdots, \hat{a}_{55-l}^{(\rho)}, \hat{b}_0^{(\rho)}, \cdots, \hat{b}_{109}^{(\rho)}, \hat{d}^{(\rho)}), 1 \le \rho \le \hat{D}$$

obtained in Step 4 to make $(\hat{a}_1^{(\rho)}, \cdots, \hat{a}_{55-l}^{(\rho)})$ *(1 ≤ ρ ≤ k) are linearly independent and* $(\hat{a}_1^{(\rho)}, \cdots, \hat{a}_{55-l}^{(\rho)}) = (0, \cdots, 0)$ *for* $k + 1 \le \rho \le \hat{D}$. *Calculate*

$$\hat{r}_\rho = \sum_{j=0}^{109} \hat{b}_j^{(\rho)} y_j' + \hat{d}^{(\rho)},$$

$1 \le \rho \le k$, *and do a Gaussian elimination on the system of linear equations*

$$\sum_{i=1}^{55-l} \hat{a}_i^{(\rho)} x_{v_i} + \hat{r}_\rho = 0, 1 \le \rho \le k$$

to eliminate k variables by expressing them as linear expressions in the remaining variables, $x_{w_j'} = \hat{h}_j(x_{w_1}, \cdots, x_{w_{55-l-k}})$, *where* $1 \le j \le k$ *and* $\{w_1', \cdots, w_k'\}$ *and* $\{w_1, \cdots, w_{55-l-k}\}$ *are two disjoint subsets of* $\{v_1, \cdots, v_{55-l}\}$. *Substitute* $x_{w_j'}$ *by* $\hat{h}_j(x_{w_1}, \cdots, x_{w_{55-l-k}})$ *(1 ≤ j ≤ k) into* $\hat{F}_i(x_{v_1}, \cdots, x_{v_{55}-l})$ *to derive 110 polynomials* $\tilde{F}_i(x_{w_1}, \cdots, x_{w_{55-l-k}})$, $0 \le i \le 109$.

The computational complexity of primary transformations on the vectors is

$$(55 - l + 110 + 1)^2 \hat{D} = (166 - l)^2 \hat{D} < 2^{18}.$$

To calculate $\hat{r}_\rho$, the complexity is $110k < 2^8 k < 2^{11}$, while the complexity of solving the system of linear equations (3.10) is $(55 - l)^2 k < 2^{14}$. Finally, the computational complexity of substituting $x_{w_j'} = \hat{h}_j(x_{w_1})$ into $\tilde{F}_i(x_{v_1}, \cdots, x_{54})$ $(0 \le i \le 109)$ is

$$55(k(k + 3)(55 - l - k)(56 - l - k)) < 2^{23}.$$

The total complexity of this step is less than $2^{18} + 2^{11} + 2^{14} + 2^{23} < 2^{24}$.

Step 6 of the attack. *Compare the coefficients of all terms in the two sides of the equation*

$$\sum_{i=0}^{55-l-k} \tilde{a}_i x_{w_i} + \sum_{j=0}^{109} \tilde{b}_j \tilde{F}_j + \tilde{d} = 0$$

to derive a system of linear equations in $(\tilde{a}_1, \cdots, \tilde{a}_{55-l-k}, \tilde{b}_0, \cdots, \tilde{b}_{109}, \tilde{d})$. *Solve it to find a basis of its solution space,* $(\tilde{a}_1^{(\rho)}, \cdots, \tilde{a}_{55-l-k}^{(\rho)}, \tilde{b}_0^{(\rho)}, \cdots, \tilde{b}_{109}^{(\rho)}, \tilde{d}^{(\rho)})$, $1 \le \rho \le \hat{p}$, *where* $\hat{p}$ *is its dimension. Among these vectors, select a set of vectors with maximal number, say p, such that for these p vectors,* $(\tilde{a}_1^{(\rho)}, \cdots, \tilde{a}_{55-l-k}^{(\rho)})$ *are linearly independent. Let* $\tilde{F}_i = y_i'$ *(0 ≤ i ≤ 109) in(3.12) and solve the resulting system of linear equations on* $x_{w_1}, \cdots, x_{w_{55-l-k}}$. *Again we will eliminate* *p variables by expressing them as linear functions of remaining variables. We substitute these linear functions into $\tilde{F}_i$ $(0 \leq i \leq 109)$ to derive 110 quadratic functions with smaller variables. Iterate the above process till all variables are eliminated. Then we collect all linear expressions between the variables and derive the plaintext $x' = (x'_0, \cdots, x'_{54})$.*

The number of iterations is less than $55 - l - k$ and the computation complexity of each iteration is less than $2^{24} + 2^{16} + 2^{24} < 2^{25}$. Hence the total complexity of this step is less than $2^{25}(55 - l - k) < 2^{31}$.

The largest computational complexity occurs in the first step with complexity less then 2^{38}; the complexity of other steps is minor in comparison. Hence, the total computation is less than 2^{39} $\mathbb{F}_{2^8}$-operations.

3.6   Experimental Results

We implement our attack on a Pentium IV 2.4Ghz PC with 256M memory, and we code the attack using VC++. We choose 100 different public keys, for each of which we give a ciphertext and try to find its corresponding plaintext. In TTM, each public key is a composition of ϕ_1, ϕ_{32}, and ϕ_4, and ϕ_{32} is determined by 25 randomly taken quadratic polynomials $f_i(x_0, \cdots, x_{i-1})$ $(i = 1, \cdots, 21)$ and $f_i(x_0, \cdots, x_{54})$ $(i = 106, \cdots, 109)$. We choose 10 different sets of the f_i, for each of which we choose 10 different pairs of ϕ_1 and ϕ_4 for experiments. The results are as follows:

1. For all 100 chosen ciphertexts, the attack successively finds their corresponding plaintexts. To find each plaintext, less than 1 hour and 37 minutes in total cost on the PC mentioned above, where 95 minutes cost on the execution of the step 1 in subsection (3.5), while about 1 minute and 20 seconds cost to execute the all remaining steps. Hence, the attack is very efficient. This timing data coincides with the analysis in the previous subsection: the remaining steps of the attack is about $2^{38}/2^{31} = 128$ times faster than the first.
2. For each chosen public key, the experiment finds $D = l = 5$ in step 1 and $\hat{D} = k = 5$ in step 3 and step 5. This means that we can eliminate 5 variables in step 2 and 5 variables in step 5. The experiment shows that if ϕ_1 is the identical map, we will find directly the values of $x'_{45}, \cdots, x'_{49}$ of the plaintext in step 1 and of $x'_{50}, \cdots, x'_{54}$ in step 5.
3. If we derive the systems of equations (3.8), (3.12) and (3.13) by taking sufficiently many (concretely, 200) plaintext/ciphertext pairs in the experiment, that is, not by comparing coefficients of monomials, then for each given ϕ_{32}, the number of total iterations of steps 4-6 and the numbers of the variables eliminated in each iteration in step 6 are respectively the same for the 10 chosen different pairs of ϕ_1 and ϕ_4. This can easily analyzed theoretically.

4   Conclusion and Discussion

In this paper, we present a very efficient attack on a new instance of TTM in [MCY04]. We need to do first precomputation, which takes 95 minutes on a PC with a 2.4Ghz Pentium IV processor. Our attack then can recover the corresponding plaintext of any valid ciphertext in less than 2 minutes. The computational complexity of the precomputation is 2^{38} $\mathbb{F}_{2^8}$-operations and the complexity for deriving a plaintext from a ciphertext is 2^{31}. Therefore the total complexity is less than 2^{39} and this new TTM instance is totally insecure. We think everyone should take our attack method into consideration when designing new MPKC.

The key point of the attack is finding the existence of certain quadratic relation (not linearization equations) on plaintexts and ciphertexts, which is used to trivialize the lock polynomials defined in TTM.

Like the previous ones, this instance of TTM has a very rigid structure and is not scalable, thus it is not possible to give a toy example to illustrate our attack and give the computation complexity in terms of a function of the dimensions of the plaintext and ciphertext space. We can only present the concrete complexity value for this instance.

Although the new instance of TTM is broken, TTM is still a very interesting idea, which could have great potential due to its high efficiency, if it can be made secure. We think, to make the TTM work, one must develop a systematic method to establish lock polynomials, which seems to require some deep insight from algebraic geometry.

References

[CM01] J.Chen and T.Moh. On the Goubin-Courtois attack on TTM. *Cryptology ePrint Archive*, 72, 2001. http://eprint.iacr.org/2001/072.

[CP03] N.Courtois and J.Patarin. About the XL algorithm over $GF(2)$. *CT-RSA'2003*,pages 141-157,2003.

[DH03] J.Ding and T.Hodges. Cryptanalysis of an Implementation Scheme of TTM. *J. Algebra Appl.*, pages 273-282, 2004. http://eprint.iacr.org/2003/084.

[DS03] J.Ding and D.Schmidt. The new TTM implementation is not secure. In H.Niederreiter K.Q.Feng and C.P. Xing, editors, *Proceedings of International Workshop on Coding, Cryptography and Combinatorics (CCC 2003)*, pages 106–121, 2003.

[GC00] L.Goubin and N.Courtois. Cryptanalysis of the TTM cryptosystem. *LNCS, Springer Verlag*, 1976:44–57, 2000.

[Moh99] T.Moh. A fast public key system with signature and master key functions. *Lecture Notes at EE department of Stanford University.*, May 1999. http://www.usdsi.com/ttm.html.

[MI88] T.Matsumoto and H.Imai. Public quadratic polynomial-tuples for efficient signature verification and message encryption. In C. G. Guenther, editor, *Advances in cryptology –EUROCRYPT'88, LNCS*, volume 330, pages 419–453. Springer, 1988.

[MCY04] T.Moh and J.Chen and B.Yang. Building Instances of TTM Immune to the Goubin-Courtois Attack andthe Ding-Schmidt Attack. IACR eprint 2004/168, http://eprint.iacr.org.

[Pat95] J.Patarin. Cryptanalysis of the Matsumoto and Imai public key scheme of Eurocrypt'88. In D.Coppersmith, editor, *Advances in Cryptology – Crypto'95, LNCS*, volume 963, pages 248–261, 1995.

[Sho97] P.Shor. Polynomial-time algorithms for prime factorization and discrete logarithms on a quantum computer. *SIAM Journal on Computing*, 26(5):1484-1509, October 1997.

Appendix: The Description of ϕ_2

The expressions of $(\bar{y}_0, \cdots, \bar{y}_{109}) = \phi_2(\bar{x}_0, \cdots, \bar{x}_{54})$ are listed as follows, where $f_i(\bar{x}_0, \cdots, \bar{x}_{i-1})$ $(1 \le i \le 21)$ and $f_i(\bar{x}_0, \cdots, \bar{x}_{54})$ $(106 \le i \le 109)$ are randomly chosen quadratic polynomials.

$\bar{y}_0 := \bar{x}_0;$

$\bar{y}_1 := f_1 + \bar{x}_1;$

$\bar{y}_2 := f_2 + \bar{x}_2;$

$\bar{y}_3 := f_3 + \bar{x}_3;$

$\bar{y}_4 := f_4 + \bar{x}_4;$

$\bar{y}_5 := f_5 + \bar{x}_5;$

$\bar{y}_6 := f_6 + \bar{x}_6;$

$\bar{y}_7 := f_7 + \bar{x}_7;$

$\bar{y}_8 := f_8 + \bar{x}_8;$

$\bar{y}_9 := f_9 + \bar{x}_9;$

$\bar{y}_{10} := f_{10} + \bar{x}_{10};$

$\bar{y}_{11} := f_{11} + \bar{x}_{11};$

$\bar{y}_{12} := f_{12} + \bar{x}_{12};$

$\bar{y}_{13} := f_{13} + \bar{x}_{13};$

$\bar{y}_{14} := f_{14} + \bar{x}_{14};$

$\bar{y}_{15} := f_{15} + \bar{x}_{15};$

$\bar{y}_{16} := f_{16} + \bar{x}_{16};$

$\bar{y}_{17} := f_{17} + \bar{x}_{17};$

$\bar{y}_{18} := f_{18} + \bar{x}_{18};$

$\bar{y}_{19} := f_{19} + \bar{x}_{19};$

$\bar{y}_{20} := f_{20} + \bar{x}_{20};$

$\bar{y}_{21} := f_{21} + \bar{x}_{21};$

$\bar{y}_{22} := \bar{x}_0\bar{x}_5 + \bar{x}_1\bar{x}_4 + \bar{x}_8 + \bar{x}_{22};$

$\bar{y}_{23} := \bar{x}_0\bar{x}_6 + \bar{x}_2\bar{x}_4 + \bar{x}_{23};$

$\bar{y}_{24} := \bar{x}_1\bar{x}_6 + \bar{x}_2\bar{x}_5 + \bar{x}_{24};$

$\bar{y}_{25} := \bar{x}_3\bar{x}_5 + \bar{x}_1\bar{x}_7 + \bar{x}_{25};$

$\bar{y}_{26} := \bar{x}_3\bar{x}_4 + \bar{x}_0\bar{x}_7 + \bar{x}_{26};$

$\bar{y}_{27} := \bar{x}_2\bar{x}_9 + \bar{x}_{22}\bar{x}_3 + \bar{x}_{27};$

$\bar{y}_{28} := \bar{x}_6\bar{x}_9 + \bar{x}_{22}\bar{x}_7 + \bar{x}_{28};$

$\bar{y}_{29} := \bar{x}_{10}\bar{x}_7 + \bar{x}_8\bar{x}_6 + \bar{x}_{29};$

$\bar{y}_{30} := \bar{x}_{10}\bar{x}_3 + \bar{x}_2\bar{x}_8 + \bar{x}_{30};$

$\bar{y}_{31} := \bar{x}_{11}\bar{x}_{16} + \bar{x}_{12}\bar{x}_{15} + \bar{x}_{19} + \bar{x}_{31};$

$\bar{y}_{32} := \bar{x}_{11}\bar{x}_{17} + \bar{x}_{13}\bar{x}_{15} + \bar{x}_{32};$

$\bar{y}_{33} := \bar{x}_{12}\bar{x}_{17} + \bar{x}_{13}\bar{x}_{16} + \bar{x}_{33};$

$\bar{y}_{34} := \bar{x}_{14}\bar{x}_{16} + \bar{x}_{12}\bar{x}_{18} + \bar{x}_{34};$

$\bar{y}_{35} := \bar{x}_{14}\bar{x}_{15} + \bar{x}_{11}\bar{x}_{18} + \bar{x}_{35};$

$\bar{y}_{36} := \bar{x}_{13}\bar{x}_{20} + \bar{x}_{31}\bar{x}_{14} + \bar{x}_{36};$

$\bar{y}_{37} := \bar{x}_{17}\bar{x}_{20} + \bar{x}_{31}\bar{x}_{18} + \bar{x}_{37};$

$\bar{y}_{38} := \bar{x}_{21}\bar{x}_{18} + \bar{x}_{19}\bar{x}_{17} + \bar{x}_{38};$

$\bar{y}_{39} := \bar{x}_{21}\bar{x}_{14} + \bar{x}_{13}\bar{x}_{19} + \bar{x}_{39};$

$\bar{y}_{40} := \bar{x}_{11}\bar{x}_{12} + \bar{x}_1\bar{x}_0 + \bar{x}_{39} + \bar{x}_{40};$

$\bar{y}_{41} := \bar{x}_{11}\bar{x}_2 + \bar{x}_{13}\bar{x}_0 + \bar{x}_{41};$

$\bar{y}_{42} := \bar{x}_1\bar{x}_2 + \bar{x}_{13}\bar{x}_{12} + \bar{x}_{42};$

$\bar{y}_{43} := \bar{x}_3\bar{x}_{12} + \bar{x}_1\bar{x}_{14} + \bar{x}_{43};$

$\bar{y}_{44} := \bar{x}_3\bar{x}_0 + \bar{x}_{11}\bar{x}_{14} + \bar{x}_{44};$

$\bar{y}_{45} := \bar{x}_{32}\bar{x}_{18} + \bar{x}_{14}\bar{x}_{33} + \bar{x}_{13}\bar{x}_{34} + \bar{x}_{17}\bar{x}_{35} + \bar{x}_{45};$

$\bar{y}_{46} := \bar{x}_{37}\bar{x}_{13} + \bar{x}_{39}\bar{x}_{18} + \bar{x}_{36}\bar{x}_{17} + \bar{x}_{38}\bar{x}_{14} + \bar{x}_{46};$

$\bar{y}_{47} := \bar{x}_{23}\bar{x}_7 + \bar{x}_3\bar{x}_{24} + \bar{x}_2\bar{x}_{25} + \bar{x}_6\bar{x}_{26} + \bar{x}_{47};$

$\bar{y}_{48} := \bar{x}_{28}\bar{x}_2 + \bar{x}_{30}\bar{x}_7 + \bar{x}_{27}\bar{x}_6 + \bar{x}_{29}\bar{x}_3 + \bar{x}_{48};$

$\bar{y}_{49} := \bar{x}_{14}\bar{x}_{41} + \bar{x}_3\bar{x}_{42} + \bar{x}_{13}\bar{x}_{43} + \bar{x}_2\bar{x}_{44} + \bar{x}_{49};$

$\bar{y}_{50} = \bar{x}_{46}\bar{x}_{48} + \bar{x}_{47}\bar{x}_{49} + \bar{x}_{50};$

$\bar{y}_{51} := \bar{x}_{45}\bar{x}_{47} + \bar{x}_{48}\bar{x}_{49} + \bar{x}_{51};$

$\bar{y}_{52} := \bar{x}_{45}\bar{x}_{48} + \bar{x}_{46}\bar{x}_{49} + \bar{x}_{52};$

$\bar{y}_{53} := \bar{x}_{45}\bar{x}_{49} + \bar{x}_{46}\bar{x}_{47} + \bar{x}_{53};$

$\bar{y}_{54} := \bar{x}_{45}\bar{x}_{46} + \bar{x}_{47}\bar{x}_{48} + \bar{x}_{54};$

$\bar{y}_{55} := \bar{x}_{11}\bar{x}_{42} + \bar{x}_1\bar{x}_{41} + \bar{x}_{13}\bar{x}_{39} + \bar{x}_3\bar{x}_{30};$

$\bar{y}_{56} := \bar{x}_0\bar{x}_{43} + \bar{x}_{12}\bar{x}_{44} + \bar{x}_2\bar{x}_{29} + \bar{x}_{14}\bar{x}_{40};$

$\bar{y}_{57} := \bar{x}_0\bar{x}_{42} + \bar{x}_{12}\bar{x}_{41} + \bar{x}_2\bar{x}_{39} + \bar{x}_{14}\bar{x}_{30} :$

$\bar{y}_{58} := \bar{x}_{11}\bar{x}_{43} + \bar{x}_1\bar{x}_{44} + \bar{x}_{13}\bar{x}_{29} + \bar{x}_3\bar{x}_{40};$

$\bar{y}_{59} := \bar{x}_{42}\bar{x}_{44} + \bar{x}_{41}\bar{x}_{43};$

$\bar{y}_{60} := \bar{x}_{42}\bar{x}_{29} + \bar{x}_{39}\bar{x}_{43} + \bar{x}_{14};$

$\bar{y}_{61} := \bar{x}_{41}\bar{x}_{29} + \bar{x}_{39}\bar{x}_{44} + \bar{x}_3;$

$\bar{y}_{62} := \bar{x}_{30}\bar{x}_{44} + \bar{x}_{41}\bar{x}_{40} + \bar{x}_{13};$

$\bar{y}_{63} := \bar{x}_{30}\bar{x}_{29} + \bar{x}_{39}\bar{x}_{40} + \bar{x}_1 + \bar{x}_0;$

$\bar{y}_{64} := \bar{x}_3\bar{x}_2 + \bar{x}_{13}\bar{x}_{14};$

$\bar{y}_{65} := \bar{x}_{30}\bar{x}_{43} + \bar{x}_{42}\bar{x}_{40} + \bar{x}_2;$

$\bar{y}_{66} := \bar{x}_{11}\bar{x}_{33} + \bar{x}_{12}\bar{x}_{32} + \bar{x}_{13}\bar{x}_{19} + \bar{x}_{14}\bar{x}_{21};$

$\bar{y}_{67} := \bar{x}_{15}\bar{x}_{34} + \bar{x}_{16}\bar{x}_{35} + \bar{x}_{17}\bar{x}_{20} + \bar{x}_{18}\bar{x}_{31};$

$\bar{y}_{68} := \bar{x}_{15}\bar{x}_{33} + \bar{x}_{16}\bar{x}_{32} + \bar{x}_{17}\bar{x}_{19} + \bar{x}_{18}\bar{x}_{21};$

$\bar{y}_{69} := \bar{x}_{11}\bar{x}_{34} + \bar{x}_{12}\bar{x}_{35} + \bar{x}_{13}\bar{x}_{20} + \bar{x}_{14}\bar{x}_{31};$

$\bar{y}_{70} := \bar{x}_{33}\bar{x}_{35} + \bar{x}_{32}\bar{x}_{34};$

$\bar{y}_{71} := \bar{x}_{33}\bar{x}_{20} + \bar{x}_{19}\bar{x}_{34} + \bar{x}_{18};$

$\bar{y}_{72} := \bar{x}_{32}\bar{x}_{20} + \bar{x}_{19}\bar{x}_{35} + \bar{x}_{14};$

$\bar{y}_{73} := \bar{x}_{21}\bar{x}_{35} + \bar{x}_{32}\bar{x}_{31} + \bar{x}_{13};$

$\bar{y}_{74} := \bar{x}_{21}\bar{x}_{20} + \bar{x}_{19}\bar{x}_{31} + \bar{x}_{12} + \bar{x}_{15};$

$\bar{y}_{75} := \bar{x}_{14}\bar{x}_{17} + \bar{x}_{13}\bar{x}_{18};$

$\bar{y}_{76} := \bar{x}_{21}\bar{x}_{34} + \bar{x}_{33}\bar{x}_{31} + \bar{x}_{17};$

$\bar{y}_{77} := \bar{x}_{11}\bar{x}_{13} + \bar{x}_{15}\bar{x}_{17} + \bar{x}_{38}\bar{x}_{31} + \bar{x}_{37}\bar{x}_{21};$

$\bar{y}_{78} := \bar{x}_{12}\bar{x}_{14} + \bar{x}_{16}\bar{x}_{18} + \bar{x}_{39}\bar{x}_{20} + \bar{x}_{36}\bar{x}_{19};$

$\bar{y}_{79} := \bar{x}_{12}\bar{x}_{13} + \bar{x}_{16}\bar{x}_{17} + \bar{x}_{39}\bar{x}_{31} + \bar{x}_{36}\bar{x}_{21};$

$\bar{y}_{80} := \bar{x}_{11}\bar{x}_{14} + \bar{x}_{15}\bar{x}_{18} + \bar{x}_{38}\bar{x}_{20} + \bar{x}_{37}\bar{x}_{19};$

$\bar{y}_{81} := \bar{x}_{11}\bar{x}_{39} + \bar{x}_{38}\bar{x}_{12} + \bar{x}_{17};$

$\bar{y}_{82} := \bar{x}_{15}\bar{x}_{39} + \bar{x}_{38}\bar{x}_{16} + \bar{x}_{13};$

$\bar{y}_{83} := \bar{x}_{37}\bar{x}_{16} + \bar{x}_{15}\bar{x}_{36} + \bar{x}_{14};$

$\bar{y}_{84} := \bar{x}_{37}\bar{x}_{39} + \bar{x}_{38}\bar{x}_{36};$

$\bar{y}_{85} := \bar{x}_{37}\bar{x}_{12} + \bar{x}_{11}\bar{x}_{36} + \bar{x}_{18};$

$\bar{y}_{86} := \bar{x}_0\bar{x}_{24} + \bar{x}_1\bar{x}_{23} + \bar{x}_2\bar{x}_8 + \bar{x}_3\bar{x}_{10};$

$\bar{y}_{87} := \bar{x}_4\bar{x}_{25} + \bar{x}_5\bar{x}_{26} + \bar{x}_6\bar{x}_9 + \bar{x}_7\bar{x}_{22};$

$\bar{y}_{88} := \bar{x}_4\bar{x}_{24} + \bar{x}_5\bar{x}_{23} + \bar{x}_6\bar{x}_8 + \bar{x}_7\bar{x}_{10};$

$\bar{y}_{89} := \bar{x}_0\bar{x}_{25} + \bar{x}_1\bar{x}_{26} + \bar{x}_2\bar{x}_9 + \bar{x}_3\bar{x}_{22};$

$\bar{y}_{90} := \bar{x}_{24}\bar{x}_{26} + \bar{x}_{23}\bar{x}_{25};$

$\bar{y}_{91} := \bar{x}_{24}\bar{x}_9 + \bar{x}_8\bar{x}_{25} + \bar{x}_7;$

$\bar{y}_{92} := \bar{x}_{23}\bar{x}_9 + \bar{x}_8\bar{x}_{26} + \bar{x}_3;$

$\bar{y}_{93} := \bar{x}_{10}\bar{x}_{26} + \bar{x}_{23}\bar{x}_{22} + \bar{x}_2;$

$\bar{y}_{94} := \bar{x}_{10}\bar{x}_9 + \bar{x}_8\bar{x}_{22} + \bar{x}_1 + \bar{x}_4;$

$\bar{y}_{95} := \bar{x}_3\bar{x}_6 + \bar{x}_2\bar{x}_7;$

$\bar{y}_{96} := \bar{x}_{10}\bar{x}_{25} + \bar{x}_{24}\bar{x}_{22} + \bar{x}_6;$

$\bar{y}_{97} := \bar{x}_0\bar{x}_2 + \bar{x}_4\bar{x}_6 + \bar{x}_{29}\bar{x}_{22} + \bar{x}_{28}\bar{x}_{10};$

$\bar{y}_{98} := \bar{x}_1\bar{x}_3 + \bar{x}_5\bar{x}_7 + \bar{x}_{30}\bar{x}_9 + \bar{x}_{27}\bar{x}_8;$

$\bar{y}_{99} := \bar{x}_1\bar{x}_2 + \bar{x}_5\bar{x}_6 + \bar{x}_{30}\bar{x}_{22} + \bar{x}_{27}\bar{x}_{10};$

$\bar{y}_{100} := \bar{x}_0\bar{x}_3 + \bar{x}_4\bar{x}_7 + \bar{x}_{29}\bar{x}_9 + \bar{x}_{28}\bar{x}_8;$

$\bar{y}_{101} := \bar{x}_0\bar{x}_{30} + \bar{x}_{29}\bar{x}_1 + \bar{x}_6;$

$\bar{y}_{102} := \bar{x}_4\bar{x}_{30} + \bar{x}_{29}\bar{x}_5 + \bar{x}_2;$

$\bar{y}_{103} := \bar{x}_{28}\bar{x}_5 + \bar{x}_4\bar{x}_{27} + \bar{x}_3;$

$\bar{y}_{104} := \bar{x}_{28}\bar{x}_{30} + \bar{x}_{29}\bar{x}_{27};$

$\bar{y}_{105} := \bar{x}_{28}\bar{x}_1 + \bar{x}_0\bar{x}_{27} + \bar{x}_7;$

$\bar{y}_{106} := f_{106};$

$\bar{y}_{107} := f_{107};$

$\bar{y}_{108} := f_{108};$

$\bar{y}_{109} := f_{109}.$

Cryptanalysis of the N-Party Encrypted Diffie-Hellman Key Exchange Using Different Passwords

Raphael C.-W. Phan[1] and Bok-Min Goi[2,*]

[1] Information Security Research (iSECURES) Lab,
Swinburne University of Technology (Sarawak Campus), 93576 Kuching, Malaysia
rphan@swinburne.edu.my
[2] Centre for Cryptography & Information Security (CCIS),
Faculty of Engineering, Multimedia University, 63100 Cyberjaya, Malaysia
bmgoi@mmu.edu.my

Abstract. We consider the security of the n-party EKE-U and EKE-M protocols proposed by Byun and Lee at ACNS '05. We show that EKE-U is vulnerable to an impersonation attack, offline dictionary attack and undetectable online dictionary attack. Surprisingly, even the strengthened variant recently proposed by the same designers to counter an insider offline dictionary attack by Tang and Chen, is equally vulnerable. We also show that both the original and strengthened EKE-M variants do not provide key privacy, a criterion desired by truly contributory key exchange schemes and recently formalized by Abdalla *et al.* We discuss ways to protect EKE-U against our attacks and argue that the strengthened EKE-U scheme shows the most potential as a provably secure n-party PAKE.

Keywords: Password-authenticated key exchange, n-party, cryptanalysis, dictionary attack, collusion, key privacy.

1 Introduction

Password authenticated key exchange (PAKE) protocols [1, 5, 7, 8, 13, 16, 17, 20] enable two or more parties to share a common secret key for securing (via secret-key cryptography) subsequent communications among them. For systems that depend on human interactions, using a password is more practical than a high-entropy secret key since the former is easier for a human to memorize by heart rather than be tempted to write it down somewhere [13].

One of the first PAKEs was the Encrypted Key Exchange (EKE) due to Bellovin and Merritt [5] for establishing a secret key between 2 parties. This was later extended to the 3-party case by Steiner *et al.* [20]. Further analysis and variants of the latter are found in [11, 16, 17, 1].

---

* The second author acknowledges the Malaysia IRPA grant (04-99-01-00003-EAR).

J. Zhou, M. Yung, and F. Bao (Eds.): ACNS 2006, LNCS 3989, pp. 226–238, 2006.

In extending from a 2-party PAKE to a 3-party one, the basic question raised is how the parties will share the password. Consequently, we can classify group-based (involving more than 2 parties) PAKEs into two broad types [7], namely those that use a single shared password among all parties (SPWA) [6] and those where each party shares a distinct password with a trusted server (DPWA) [20, 16, 17, 1].

DPWA-type PAKEs allow trust to be partitioned among all clients such that in the event of any client being compromised or corrupted, it will not affect the security of the entire group; e.g. only secrets (session keys shared with him, and his password) known to the affected client need to be changed, but other innocent clients can continue using their existing passwords. This also means that less trust needs to be put on each individual client since the compromise of any client is less devastating to the security of the group. In contrast, a compromise of any client in an SPWA-type PAKE would require that the password shared by all clients be updated and re-communicated to each of them. Further, DPWA-type PAKEs are very much suited for mobile and distributed computing networks which are increasingly becoming prevalent, where the parties (clients) come from diverse environments thus are less understood. Under such circumstances, one would not want to put too much trust on any client.

Abdalla *et al.* [1] presented a formal security model for 3-party DWPA-type PAKEs by combining the Bellare *et al.* model [3] for 2-party PAKEs with the Bellare-Rogaway model [4] for 3-party key distribution schemes generalized to the password case. They also formally defined the notion of *key privacy* to differentiate truly contributory key exchange protocols from key distribution protocols. This notion, first mentioned in [20], roughly means that even though a third-party server's help is required to establish a session key between two clients, the server is not able to obtain any information on the value of that established session key. The goal of key privacy is to limit the amount of trust put into the server, where it is assumed that the server is honest but curious [1], thus clients prefer to have their established session key known only to themselves. This appropriately models real-life situations where privacy of secret information is well guarded by individuals. In fact, some other work in related information security fields are also moving in this direction, e.g. protocols proposed without the use of trusted third parties (TTP) in [9, 22], and research showing the subtlety of putting too much trust on TTPs [19, 12]. To achieve key privacy, it is necessary [1] to have a 2-party authenticated key exchange (AKE) between the two clients.

In this paper, we are concerned with DPWA schemes for the *n-party* case. More specifically, at ACNS '05 Byun and Lee [7] presented two variants of an n-party EKE protocol, respectively called n-party EKE-U and EKE-M for unicast and multicast networks. These appear to be the first known *n-party* EKE protocols with provable security. Tang and Chen [21] subsequently showed that EKE-U is vulnerable to an offline dictionary attack, and that EKE-M is vulnerable to an undetectable online dictionary attack [11]. Byun and Lee [8] promptly countered with strengthened variants, which we will also discuss in Sections 3 and 4.

Although PAKEs have been extensively studied especially in the last few years [1, 3, 5, 6, 7, 8, 13, 16, 17, 20], most of them consider either the 2-party or 3-party case. And it was only very recently that the first provably secure PAKEs for the 3-party and n-party cases were presented in [1] and [7] respectively. Thus this field (that of provably secure group PAKEs) has potentially unexplored areas of future work, e.g. how to extend the existing provably secure 2-party or 3-party PAKEs to the n-party case in an efficient yet secure manner, i.e. without involving too many inter-client communications that would cause a bottleneck to the network especially when n is large.

We show attacks on both the original and strengthened EKE-U that exploit the server as an oracle to generate messages supposedly from an innocent client. Meanwhile for both the original and strengthened EKE-M, we point out that they do not achieve the key privacy property that is desired of contributory key exchange protocols.

In our concluding section, we discuss how to improve the *strengthened* EKE-U to resist our attacks and argue that it is a worthwhile candidate for a provably secure n-party PAKE.

2   The N-Party EKE Protocols

The n-party EKE protocols due to Byun and Lee [7] involve $n - 1$ clients and 1 server, and are specially designed to suit modern communication environments such as ad-hoc networks and ubiquitous computing, in particular EKE-U for unicast networks and EKE-M for multicast ones. *Unicast* networks allow for communication only between a single sender and a single receiver, while *multicast* networks allow for communication between a single sender and multiple receivers. For multicast networks, all messages from individual single senders can be sent in parallel during a single round to all receivers, thus more round-efficient group-based protocols can be designed in such networks.

Note that all arithmetic operations in this paper are performed under cyclic group $\mathbf{G} = \langle g \rangle$ of prime order.

2.1   N-Party EKE-U Protocol Variants

The EKE-U makes use of three types of functions which differ mainly in the number of elements produced at their respective outputs:

$$
\begin{aligned}
\pi(\alpha_1, \ldots, \alpha_{i-1}, \alpha_i) &= \{\alpha_1, \ldots, \alpha_{i-1}\}, \\
\phi(\{\alpha_1, \ldots, \alpha_{i-1}, \alpha_i\}, x) &= \{\alpha_1^x, \ldots, \alpha_{i-1}^x, \alpha_i, \alpha_i^x\}, \\
\xi(\{\alpha_1, \ldots, \alpha_{i-1}, \alpha_i\}, x) &= \{\alpha_1^x, \ldots, \alpha_{i-1}^x, \alpha_i^x\}.
\end{aligned}
$$

Note that π produces an output that is simply equal to its input less the last input element, and further π is only used by C_{n-1}. The functions ϕ and ξ take in the same number of input elements, and their outputs are similar except that ϕ has one more output element than ξ.

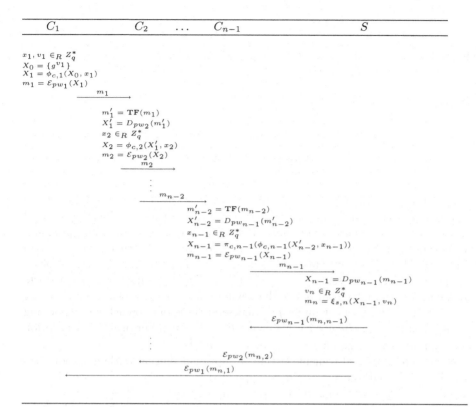

Fig. 1. Main protocol of n-party EKE-U

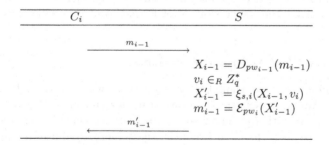

Fig. 2. TF protocol of n-party EKE-U

The main bulk of the EKE-U protocol is illustrated in Fig. 1, where clients $C_1, \ldots, C_{n-1}$ and the server S are arranged in a line. During the up-flow stage starting from C_1, each client C_i basically chooses its own secret x_i and calls the ϕ function to raise the intermediate value X'_{i-1} to the power of this x_i in order to generate the value X_i. This is encrypted with client C_i's password pw_i and sent to the next client C_{i+1} as the message m_i. Upon receipt of this,

	S	C_1	C_2	$\cdots$	C_{n-1}
Round 1	$s_i \in_R Z_q^*$	$x_1 \in_R Z_q^*$	$x_2 \in_R Z_q^*$	$\cdots$	$x_{n-1} \in_R Z_q^*$
	$\mathcal{E}_{pw_i}(g^{s_i})$	$\mathcal{E}_{pw_1}(g^{x_1})$	$\mathcal{E}_{pw_2}(g^{x_2})$	$\cdots$	$\mathcal{E}_{pw_{n-1}}(g^{x_{n-1}})$
Round 2	$N \in_R Z_q^*$				
	$sk_1 \oplus N\|\ldots\|sk_{n-1} \oplus N$				

Fig. 3. N-party EKE-M

C_{i+1} initiates an additional sub-protocol known as the **TF** protocol (see Fig. 2 and note that the function ξ is used here) with the server S so that the received message which was encrypted under client C_i's password could be decrypted and re-encrypted under client C_{i+1}'s password to form m_i'. This then allows C_{i+1} to access the decrypted contents of m_i', namely X_i' and the same process repeats until S receives the message m_{n-1} from C_{n-1}. The down-flow stage then starts by having S compute from m_{n-1} the keying material $m_{n,i}$ meant for client C_i ($i = 1, \ldots, n-1$), encrypt under pw_i and send these out to each corresponding client. Finally, each client with his own pw_i and x_i can perform the decryption and compute the session key $sk = (m_{n,i})^{x_i} = g^{v_n} \Pi_{i=1}^{n-1}(v_i x_i)$.

Byun and Lee [7] also mention that an optional mutual authentication step based on key confirmation could be appended to the scheme if it is desired to ensure that all other clients have really computed the agreed session key sk. In this case, each client computes an authenticator $\mathcal{H}(C_i\|sk)$, which is the hash value of client index (C_i) and new session key (sk), and sends this to all other clients for verification. Note however that even if this step is made compulsory, it does not protect EKE-U against our attacks in Sections 3.3 and 3.4.

There is a strengthened version [8] of EKE-U and this will be explained in Section 3.4.

2.2   N-Party EKE-M Protocol Variants

EKE-M is much simpler than EKE-U and is shown in Fig. 3. It consists of two rounds. Round 1 is basically a simultaneous run of a 2-party PAKE between each client with the server to set up a secure channel (in the confidentiality sense) between them. In Round 2, the server distributes a common keying message to all clients via the secure channel. This will be used to form the common secret session key sk among all clients. More precisely, denote $sk_i = \mathcal{H}_1(\mathcal{E}_{pw_1}(g^{x_1})\|\ldots\|\mathcal{E}_{pw_{n-1}}(g^{x_{n-1}})\|g^{x_i s_i})$ and $sk = \mathcal{H}_2(\mathcal{E}_{pw_1}(g^{x_1})\|\ldots\| \mathcal{E}_{pw_{n-1}}(g^{x_{n-1}})\|sk_1 \oplus N\|\ldots\|sk_{n-1} \oplus N\|N)$. Note that $\mathcal{H}_1$ and $\mathcal{H}_2$ are standard hash functions.

There is also a strengthened version of EKE-M proposed by Byun and Lee [8] to prevent the undetectable online dictionary attack in [21]. The basic idea is to add an extra step after Round 1 where an authenticator $\mathcal{H}(sk_i\|C_i)$ is broadcast by each client (or server) to be checked by all parties before Round 2 starts.

3   Cryptanalysis of the N-Party EKE-U Variants

In view of the low entropy password, the basic requirement for a PAKE is security against dictionary attacks on the password. Such attacks are typically online or offline, depending on whether or not the attacker needs to verify each guessed password by interacting online (being involved in a protocol run) with other parties. Another basic requirement of PAKEs is that they do not allow impersonation attacks where an attacker masquerades as any legitimate party because if this happens, there will be a non-achievement of mutual authentication.

3.1   Tang-Chen Attack

Before describing our attacks, we first briefly discuss an insider offline dictionary attack on EKE-U given by Tang and Chen [21]. See [15] for a formal treatment of insider attacks on group AKEs.

The basic idea behind this attack is that a malicious client C_j modifies the first two components (g_1, g_2) in the message X_j of $m_j = \mathcal{E}_{pw_j}(X_j)$ that it sends to C_{j+1} during the up-flow stage of the main protocol, such that they satisfy the relation $g_1^\alpha = g_2$. Then right at the end of the **TF** protocol when the server S returns $m'_j = \mathcal{E}_{pw_{j+1}}(X'_j)$ to C_{j+1}, this is intercepted by the malicious C_j who then guesses the value of pw_{j+1} and verifies his guess by checking if the first two components that he had initially modified satisfy the given relation.

At first glance, it seems that this attack requires having to modify the message $m_j = \mathcal{E}_{pw_j}(X_j)$. However, as later pointed out in the same paper [21], this attack could work without this requirement. Instead, it suffices to decrypt m'_j with the guessed password pw_{j+1} and check if the last two components (β, γ) of X'_j satisfy the relation $\beta^{x_j} = \gamma$.

Note however that even with this relaxation, the latter attack still limits the malicious C_j to attack only his next neighbour C_{j+1} but not on the other clients because the components within in his possessed X'_{j-1}, X_j do not allow him to verify any two components of these other clients' messages without having to guess the secrets of the server v_i, $i \in \{1, \ldots, n\}$ or the secrets of other clients x_t $(t \neq j)$.

3.2   By Any Outsider

Byun and Lee [7] have cleverly designed the EKE-U protocol such that the $m_{n,i}$ within each keying material message $\mathcal{E}_{pw_i}(m_{n,i})$ distributed by S to each client C_i in the down-flow stage does not have the random secret x_i chosen by client C_i in its exponent, thus only client C_i would be able to make use of its $m_{n,i}$ (i^{th} component of the message m_n) to generate the session key material $K = (m_{n,i})^{x_i} = (g^{x_1 \cdots x_{n-1}})^{v_1 \cdots v_n}$. Further, different functions (ϕ, π, ξ) are used in the main and **TF** protocols, e.g. each of the three functions produces an output having different number of elements, and ϕ is used in the main protocol while ξ is used in the **TF** protocol; thus it appears an attacker cannot exploit one protocol as an oracle for answering challenge-response-like queries in the other protocol.

However, note that this is only true for the communications during the up-flow stage of the main protocol from C_1 through C_{n-1}, but not true from C_{n-1} to S because for the latter there is an extra function π (see Fig. 1 in addition to the function ϕ that is used by C_{n-1}. Thus the output of the composition of the functions $\pi \circ \phi$ done by C_{n-1} during the main protocol results in the same number of elements as that of the output of the ξ function computed by S in the **TF** protocol; i.e. S can be exploited during the **TF** protocol as an oracle to generate messages supposedly generated by C_{n-1} during the main protocol when in fact C_{n-1} need not be present at all.

Our attack further exploits the fact that the messages transmitted during the **TF** protocol (Fig. 2) between a client and the server are similar in form to the messages transmitted during the up- or down-flow of the main unicast protocol (Fig. 1). In particular, message m_i and m'_{i-1} are both functions of $\mathcal{E}_{pw_i}(\cdot)$. Thus, the server S which is intended by the designers to act as an interpreter between two neighbouring clients, C_i and C_{i-1} could be used by the attacker as an oracle to generate messages m_i supposedly generated by the next neighbouring client C_i even when C_i is not present.

For ease of illustration, we take $n = 4$ (as in Fig. 4) though it similarly applies for any n. Note that in this case, $C_{n-1} = C_3$.

1. The attacker captures the message $m_2 = \mathcal{E}_{pw_2}(X_2)$ sent from C_2 to C_3 during the up-flow stage of the main protocol.
2. The attacker then initiates the **TF** protocol by forwarding this m_2 to S.
3. S thinks[1] this is from C_3 and decrypts it with pw_2 to obtain X_2. It then computes

$$X'_2 = \xi(X_2, v_3) = \{g^{v_1 v_2 x_2 v_3}, g^{v_1 x_1 v_2 v_3}, g^{v_1 x_1 v_2 x_2 v_3}\} \tag{1}$$

and encrypts this with pw_3 to get $m'_2 = \mathcal{E}_{pw_3}(X'_2)$ and returns this m'_2 thus completing the **TF** protocol.
4. The attacker now has m'_2 which he simply reuses as $m_3 = \mathcal{E}_{pw_3}(X_3) = \mathcal{E}_{pw_3}(X'_2)$ and then impersonates C_3 by sending this to S in the main protocol. This completes the up-flow stage.
5. To start the down-flow stage, S decrypts m_3 to obtain

$$X_3 = \{g^{v_1 v_2 x_2 v_3}, g^{v_1 x_1 v_2 v_3}, g^{v_1 x_1 v_2 x_2 v_3}\} \tag{2}$$

and then chooses v_4 to compute

$$m_4 = \xi(X_3, v_4) = \{g^{v_1 v_2 x_2 v_3 v_4}, g^{v_1 x_1 v_2 v_3 v_4}, g^{v_1 x_1 v_2 x_2 v_3 v_4}\}. \tag{3}$$

Each of these elements of m_4, denoted in turn as $m_{4,1}, m_{4,2}, m_{4,3}$ are then encrypted with the respective passwords pw_i of client C_i ($i = 1, \ldots, 3$) and sent to each client respectively as $\mathcal{E}_{pw_i}(m_{4,i})$ for ($i = 1, \ldots, 3$).

---

[1] Note that there is no explicit authentication of a client by S. An apparent way for S to properly keep in sequence is to track the number of **TF** sessions that have been initiated with it. The ith session would be taken to come from client C_{i+1} since C_1 does not initiated any **TF** with S.

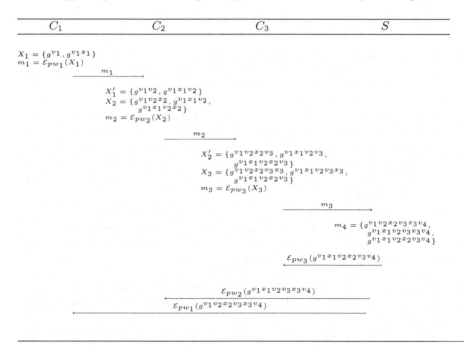

Fig. 4. An example of n-party EKE-U main protocol for $n=4$

6. Each client C_i ($i = 1, \ldots, 3$) can then decrypt $\mathcal{E}_{pw_i}(m_{4,i})$ and thus compute $sk = (m_{4,i})^{x_i} = (g^{x_1 x_2})^{v_1 v_2 v_3 v_4}$.

Note that though our attack can be used to attack only C_{n-1} and not any other client, the main plus is that it can be mounted by any outsider (in contrast to the attack in [21] which requires a malicious insider) and applies even without needing client C_{n-1} to be present. Having said that, C_{n-1}'s presence would pose no problem for the attacker either. Though the attacker is unable to recover the session key sk himself, he has successfully led all parties (except client C_{n-1} who is not present) to establish a totally new session key among them. This could also be viewed as a variant of the unknown key-share attack [10, 2, 14] in the n-party case since each client (except C_{n-1}) believes it is sharing a session key with all other clients including C_{n-1} which is true, but C_{n-1} is not present and does not know that such a key has been established. In contrast, recall that an unknown key-share attack on a 2-party case is where one party A believes it is sharing a session key with B which is rightly so, but B instead believes it is sharing a session key with $E \neq A$.

To prevent this attack, the mutual authentication step (e.g. via key confirmation [14]) must be made compulsory. Nevertheless, when performed by a malicious insider, the mutual authentication step is no longer effective to prevent this attack, and it further becomes an offline dictionary attack allowing him to retrieve the password of C_{n-1}, as will be explained next.

3.3   By a Malicious Insider

A malicious client C_i could launch a more devastating variant of the previous attack since he could exploit it to further obtain the password of the innocent client C_{n-1}. This offline dictionary attack works as follows:

1. The attacker, client C_i ($i \neq n-1$) performs steps 1 through 5 of Section 3.2.
2. Further, since the attacker is an insider, he could also decrypt the keying material intended for him $\mathcal{E}_{pw_i}(m_{4,i})$. We illustrate with an example. Consider C_1 is the malicious client. It can be similarly shown for all other clients C_i for ($i \neq n-1$). He can obtain $g^{v_1 v_2 x_2 v_3 v_4}$ from $\mathcal{E}_{pw_1}(m_{4,1}) = \mathcal{E}_{pw_1}(g^{v_1 v_2 x_2 v_3 v_4})$.
3. With his value of x_1, he can compute $y = (g^{v_1 v_2 x_2 v_3 v_4})^{x_1} = g^{v_1 x_1 v_2 x_2 v_3 v_4}$.
4. He intercepts $\mathcal{E}_{pw_3}(m_{4,3}) = \mathcal{E}_{pw_3}(g^{v_1 x_1 v_2 x_2 v_3 v_4})$ meant for client C_3, and makes guesses for all possible values of pw_3. For each guessed pw_3, he decrypts $\mathcal{E}_{pw_3}(m_{4,3})$ and obtains $z = g^{v_1 x_1 v_2 x_2 v_3 v_4}$. He then checks if z equals y. The correct pw_3 would satisfy this.

This attack can be mounted by any client C_i against C_{n-1}, thus it complements the attack in [21] where the attack is mounted by any client C_i against his neighbour C_{i+1}.

Note also that this attack works even with the mutual authentication step included since C_i has no problem in computing sk.

3.4   Attacking the Strengthened N-Party EKE-U

In [8], Byun and Lee suggested a strengthened n-party EKE-U protocol to counter the insider offline dictionary attack due to Tang and Chen [21].

Their basic idea to counter the attack is to use an ephemeral session key $sk_i = \mathcal{H}(C_i \| S \| g^{a_i} \| g^{b_i} \| g^{a_i b_i})$ instead of the password pw_i to encrypt keying material during both the up- and down-flow of the main protocol, where a_i and b_i are the random number chosen by C_i and S respectively.

Nevertheless, we first remark that this strengthened variant also falls to our attacks in the Sections 3.2 and 3.3 since it inherits from the original version the same properties we exploited, i.e. (1) the composition of functions $\pi \circ \phi$ produces an output with the same number of elements as that produced by ξ; (2) messages transmitted during the **TF** protocol are the same in form to messages transmitted during the main protocol.

More interestingly, we have a further undetectable online dictionary attack [11] on this strengthened variant as follows, again assuming for the purpose of illustration that $n = 4$ thus we have the parties C_1, C_2, C_3 and S:

1. All malicious clients except C_1 collude [18], meaning they share their secrets x_i.
2. They choose v and x, and for each guess of pw_1,
   (a) They compute $m_1 = \mathcal{E}_{pw_1}(X_1)$ where $X_1 = \{g^v, g^{vx}\}$.
   (b) Then C_2 starts the **TF** protocol with S, etc., and the rest of the up-flow proceeds as normal.

(c) Then during the down-flow, the keying material messages sent by S to C_1, C_2 and C_3 would be $\mathcal{E}_{pw_1}(g^{vv_2v_3v_4x_2x_3})$, $\mathcal{E}_{pw_2}(g^{vv_2v_3v_4xx_3})$ and $\mathcal{E}_{pw_3}(g^{vv_2v_3v_4xx_2})$.

(d) Now the colluding clients C_2 and C_3 can easily obtain $y = g^{vv_2v_3v_4}$ from $\mathcal{E}_{pw_2}(g^{vv_2v_3v_4xx_3})$ or $\mathcal{E}_{pw_3}(g^{vv_2v_3v_4xx_2})$, and their knowledge of x, x_2 and x_3.

(e) They then use their current guess of pw_1 to decrypt $\mathcal{E}_{pw_1}(g^{vv_2v_3v_4x_2x_3})$ to get z. They compare this z with $y^{x_2x_3}$, where y was computed in the previous step. A match means the guess of pw_1 is correct.

This is online because every time pw_1 is guessed, the attackers have to initiate a protocol run with S, but this is undetectable because S would not notice anything wrong while C_1 does not even have to be present.

The weakness exploited here is that the message from C_1 to C_2 is encrypted with a low-entropy password pw_1 instead of sk_1. Thus a direct fix is to use sk_1 in place of pw_1 similar to how sk_i (for $i \neq 1$) were used in place of pw_i for this strengthened EKE-U scheme.

4   N-Party EKE-M Does Not Provide Key Privacy

Byun and Lee [7] also proposed a multicast variant known as the n-party EKE-M protocol. It is illustrated in Fig. 3.

This variant does not exhibit the 'S-oracle' property of the U variant, i.e. the server S cannot be exploited as an oracle to generate messages that appear to be from a client, thus it does not appear to fall to our attacks on EKE-U. Nevertheless, there is one major problem with this M variant, namely that the server S is able to compute the session key sk established by the clients. This is quite unlike the U variant where even S is unable to know what sk is, and thus this M variant is undesirable in the sense that the privacy of the clients' communications cannot be safeguarded against a third-party server.

This *key privacy* property is important because it would mean less trust [12, 19] needs to be put on a third-party server, who may not always be malicious but could sometimes be curious [1]. The first known n-party (for n=3) EKE scheme to have this property is due to Steiner *et al.* [20] and this concept was later formally treated by Abdalla *et al.* [1]. Abdalla *et al.* argue that key privacy is the main difference between a key distribution protocol (for which the session key is known to the server) and a key exchange protocol (for which the session key remains unknown to the server). Thus, a true key exchange protocol where each party (in this case the client) contributes equal parts to the established session key, should have key privacy because the third-party server should not be able to listen in on future secret communications among the clients, and hence should not be able to know what this session key is.

Note that the strengthened EKE-M variant in [8] has the same problem even when mutual authentication via key confirmation is included, because the point here is that the server can compute sk even when C_i is not present, so mutual authentication is irrelevant.

We do not see any way to fix this with minor tweaks without destroying the basic structure of this M scheme, because essentially each client interacts only with the server, and never with each other, thus the keying material components that they contribute to the final establishment of the session key via a Diffie-Hellman way, can only be translated (decrypted with one password and re-encrypted with another) by the middleman S, thus S is able to view all communicated messages that it translates.

Alternatively, one could adopt the approach in [1] by appending one more phase where each client interacts directly with the other clients by contributing its secret part to jointly form the key but this would be infeasible for $n > 3$ parties. Unless one resorts to using the method used for EKE-U where each client in turn adds his secret to the key material accummulatively while forwarding from one client to the next until it reaches the server. However, this is then essentially EKE-U and thus we end up destroying the original EKE-M structure.

If it is desired that this key privacy against the server be upheld, then this variant should not be used.

5   Conclusion

We have illustrated attacks (impersonation, dictionary or collusion attacks) on the n-party EKE-U variants proposed by Byun and Lee [7,8].

EKE-U [7], even with strengthening [8], falls to our attacks in Sections 3.2 to 3.4, while EKE-M is not desirable as it does not provide key privacy. But to fix the key privacy problem requires clients to directly communicate with one another to contribute their secret key parts accummulatively, leading us therefore to EKE-U.

Thus it appears that *strengthened* EKE-U is the potential way to proceed for provably secure n-party PAKEs. Hence, to fix EKE-U, the mutual authentication step is compulsory in order to prevent the attack in Section 3.2, though attacks in Sections 3.3 and 3.4 still apply. A simple fix to prevent the attack in Section 3.3 is to require the server to check that $x_{n-1} \neq 1$ before replying so that it is not exploited as an oracle. To prevent the attack in Section 3.4, C_1 needs to also initiate the **TF** protocol to generate sk_1 with the server and use sk_1 instead of pw_1 in constructing m_1.

Acknowledgement

We thank the anonymous referees, especially for pointing out to explicitly differentiate between the basic unknown key-share attack applied to 2-party AKEs and our impersonation attack for the n-party case in Section 3.2. We thank IACR for maintaining the ePrint Archive which has become the de facto venue for publicly disseminating crypto documents (full versions, short notes etc.). We thank God for His many blessings. The first author dedicates this work to the memory of his grandmother MOK Kiaw (1907-1999), for being a constant inspiration.

References

1. M. Abdalla, P.-A. Fouque, and D. Pointcheval. Password-Based Authenticated Key Exchange in the Three-Party Setting. In *Proc. PKC '05*, LNCS 3386, pp. 65-84, Springer-Verlag, 2005.
2. J. Baek, and K. Kim. Remarks on the Unknown Key-share Attacks. In *IEICE Transactions on Fundamentals*, Vol. E83-A, No. 12, pp.2766-2769, 2000.
3. M. Bellare, D. Pointcheval, and P. Rogaway. Authenticated Key Exchange Secure against Dictionary Attacks. In *Advances in Cryptology - EUROCRYPT '00*, LNCS 1807, pp. 139-155, Springer-Verlag, 2000.
4. M. Bellare, and P. Rogaway. Provably Secure Key Distribution - the Three Party Case. In *Proc. ACM-SToC '96*, pp. 72-84, 1996.
5. S.M. Bellovin, and M. Merritt. Encrypted Key Exchange: Password-based Protocols Secure against Dictionary Attacks. In *Proc. IEEE S&P '92*, pp. 72-84, IEEE Press, 1992.
6. E. Bresson, O. Chevassut, and D. Pointcheval. Group Diffie Hellman Key Exchange Secure against Dictionary Attacks. In *Advances in Cryptology - ASIACRYPT '02*, LNCS 2501, pp. 497-514, Springer-Verlag, 2002.
7. J.W. Byun, and D.H. Lee. N-Party Encrypted Diffie-Hellman Key Exchange Using Different Passwords. In *Proc. ACNS '05*, LNCS 3531, pp. 75-90, Springer-Verlag, 2005.
8. J.W. Byun, and D.H. Lee. Comments on Weaknesses in Two Group Diffie-Hellman Key Exchange Protocols. IACR ePrint Archive, 2005/209, 2005.
9. J.G. Choi, K. Sakurai, and J.H. Park. Does It Need Trusted Third Party? Design of Buyer-Seller Watermarking Protocol without Trusted Third Party. In *Proc. ACNS '03*, LNCS 2846, pp. 265-279, Springer-Verlag, 2003.
10. W. Diffie, P. van Oorschot, and M. Wiener. Authentication and Authenticated Key Exchanges. In *Design, Codes and Cryptography*, Vol. 2, No. 2, pp.107-125, 1992.
11. Y. Ding, and P. Horster. Undetectable On-line Password Guessing Attacks. In *ACM Operating Systems Review*, Vol. 29, No. 4, pp.77-86, 1995.
12. M.K. Franklin, and M.K. Reiter. Fair Exchange with a Semi-trusted Third Party (Extended Abstract). In *Proc. ACM-CCS '97*, pp. 1-5, 1997.
13. D. Jablon. Strong Password-only Authenticated Key Exchange. In *ACM Computer Communications Review*, Vol. 20, No. 5, pp.5-26, 1996.
14. B.S. Kaliski, Jr. An Unknown Key-share Attack on the MQV Key Agreement Protocol. In *ACM Transactions on Information and System Security*, Vol. 4, No. 3, pp.275-288, 2001.
15. J. Katz, and J.S. Shin. Modeling Insider Attacks on Group Key-Exchange Protocols. In *Proc. ACM-CCS '05*, pp. 180-189, 2005.
16. C.-L. Lin, H.-M. Sun and T. Hwang. Three-Party Encrypted Key Exchange: Attacks and a Solution. In *ACM Operating Systems Review*, Vol. 34, No. 4, pp.12-20, 2000.
17. C.-L. Lin, H.-M. Sun, M. Steiner and T. Hwang. Three-Party Encrypted Key Exchange Without Server Public-Keys. In *IEEE Communication Letters*, Vol. 5, No. 12, pp.497-499, IEEE Press, 2001.
18. S. Saeednia, and R. Safavi-Naini. Efficient Identity-based Conference Key Distribution Protocols. In *Proc. ACISP '98*, LNCS 1438, pp. 320-331, Springer-Verlag, 1998.
19. V. Shmatikov, and J.C. Mitchell. Finite-state Analysis of Two Contract Signing Protocols. In *Theoretical Computer Science*, Vol. 283, No. 2, pp.419-450, Elsevier, 2002.

20. M. Steiner, G. Tsudik, and M. Waider. Refinement and Extension of Encrypted Key Exchange. In *ACM Operating Systems Review*, Vol. 29, No. 3, pp.22-30, 1995.
21. Q. Tang, and L. Chen. Weaknesses in Two Group Diffie-Hellman Key Exchange Protocols. IACR ePrint Archive, 2005/197, 2005.
22. J. Zhou, F. Bao, and R.H. Deng. Validating Digital Signatures without TTP's Time-Stamping and Certificate Revocation. In *Proc. ISC '03*, LNCS 2851, pp. 96-110, Springer-Verlag, 2003.

An AES Smart Card Implementation Resistant to Power Analysis Attacks*

Christoph Herbst, Elisabeth Oswald, and Stefan Mangard

Institute for Applied Information Processing and Communications (IAIK),
Graz University of Technology, Inffeldgasse 16a, A–8010 Graz, Austria
{christoph.herbst, elisabeth.oswald, stefan.mangard}@iaik.tugraz.at

Abstract. In this article we describe an efficient AES software implementation that is well suited for 8-bit smart cards and resistant against power analysis attacks. Our implementation masks the intermediate results and randomizes the sequence of operations at the beginning and the end of the AES execution. Because of the masking, it is secure against simple power analysis attacks, template attacks and first-order DPA attacks. Due to the combination of masking and randomization, it is resistant against higher-order DPA attacks. Resistant means that a large number of measurements is required for a successful attack. This expected number of measurements is tunable. The designer can choose the amount of randomization and thereby increase the number of measurements. This article also includes a practical evaluation of the countermeasures. The results prove the theoretical assessment of the countermeasures to be correct.

Keywords: AES, smart card, DPA resistance.

1 Introduction

Embedded processors have a large share in the processor market. Especially 8-bit processors are used in many smart cards. Smart cards play a crucial role in a lot of security systems. Due to the lack of secure PCs, smart cards are often used in order to store secret keys. In addition, smart cards are frequently used as authentication devices. For instance, in many ATM systems, users are authenticated not only via their PIN. In addition, the ATM card (the smart card) of the user authenticates itself to the ATM machine. In both scenarios it is imperative that the secret key never leaves the smart card. Consequently, the smart card not only stores the secret key, it is also capable of doing cryptographic operations with that key.

During the last six years, side-channel attacks in general, and power analysis attacks in particular, have shaken the believe in the security of smart cards.

---

* The work described in this paper has been supported in part by the European Commission through the IST Programme under Contract IST-2002-507270 SCARD and through the Austrian Science Fund (FWF) under grant number P16952.

J. Zhou, M. Yung, and F. Bao (Eds.): ACNS 2006, LNCS 3989, pp. 239–252, 2006.

Kocher showed in his pioneering article [KJJ99] that a smart card that is unprotected against power analysis attacks, can be broken easily. In a power analysis attack, the attacker records the power consumption of a smart card while it performs cryptographic operations with a fixed secret key. This secret key can subsequently be revealed based on the recorded data (the so called traces) and the corresponding plaintexts or ciphertexts. In the best case, such an attack requires no knowledge about the implementation details of the algorithm and no more than 100 traces [KJJ99].

The Advanced Encryption Standard (AES) [Nat01] is the most popular primitive for encryption today. It is a symmetric cipher and can be implemented efficiently on all kinds of platforms. It can also be used for authentication. Hence, it is an attractive algorithm for many security relevant applications. As we have pointed out already, the secure implementation of cryptographic primitives on smart cards is challenging. Nevertheless, implementations of the AES algorithm on smart cards that are resistance against power analysis attacks, are a primary interest of the industry. In addition, they are a challenging task for the research community: a smart card is a rather constraint device. It runs on a low clock frequency and is supposed to have a low power consumption. Furthermore, only a very limited amount of memory (program memory, RAM, ROM, etc.) is available that needs to be shared with the operating system.

In this article, we present an AES implementation that is highly resistant against power analysis attacks and that performs well on 8-bit processors (smart cards). We use a combination of countermeasures (masking and randomization of operations) to achieve resistance against power analysis attacks. A security analysis that includes a theoretical assessment and a practical evaluation accompanies this paper. The innovation in this work is the efficient combination of countermeasures, which is specifically tailored for AES implementations on 8-bit smart cards. This is the first work presenting an efficient implementation that offers resistance against power analysis attacks.

This article is organized as follows. In Sect. 2, we explain how masking and randomization work, how each of them can be attacked and how combining them increases the resistance against power analysis attacks. In Sect. 3, we explain how our masked and randomized AES implementation works. In Sect. 4, we analyze the security of our implementation and provide evidence on the soundness of our analysis by showing results of practical power analysis attacks. We conclude this article in Sect. 5. Throughout this article, we assume that the reader has a basic understanding of the working principle of differential power analysis (DPA) attacks.

2   Countermeasures Against DPA Attacks

In order to secure implementations of symmetric cryptographic algorithms against power analysis attacks, there are two approaches that are suitable for software implementations on smart cards. On the one hand, the intermediate values of the algorithm can be masked. On the other hand, the sequence of operations in the algorithm can be randomized. In this section, we briefly discuss these two methods.

2.1   Masking

In a masked implementation all intermediate values a are concealed by a random value m which is called mask. For every execution of the algorithm, new masks are generated on the smart card. Hence, the attacker does not know the masks. Most masking schemes use additive masking, *i.e.* the mask is exclusive-ored with the intermediate value. Thus, the masked intermediate value is $a_m = a \oplus m$. For AES, also multiplicative masking as been suggested [AG01]. Multiplicative masking means multiplying a mask value with an intermediate value: $b_m = b * m$. This multiplication is a modular multiplication. Hence, it is not suitable for most smart card implementations because a modular multiplier is not available on all smart cards. Consequently, we focus on additive masking schemes.

Masking prevents DPA attacks because the randomly masked intermediate values cause a power consumption that is not predictable by the attacker. The masks are added at the very beginning of the algorithm to the plaintext. During the execution of the algorithm, one needs to take care that every intermediate value stays masked. In addition, one needs to keep track how the masks are modified by the operations in the algorithm. For AES operations like ShiftRows and AddRoundKey this can be done with almost no effort. MixColumns requires some effort because it mixes bytes of different columns of the AES state. For the non-linear SubBytes operation, a more elaborated approach is required. In a typical software implementation the SubBytes operation is implemented as table look-up: $out = S(in)$ (S denotes the SubBytes table). The AES state consists of 16 bytes. Thus, we have to perform 16 table look-up operations. When we mask the SubBytes operation, we have to compute a masked SubBytes table S' such that $S'(a_m) = S'(a \oplus m) = S(a) \oplus m'$. At the very end of the algorithm, the masks are removed from the intermediate values.

Provably secure masking schemes for AES have recently been published in [BGK05] and [OMPR05]. Yet, these schemes have been mainly designed for hardware implementations. Nevertheless, also a first proposal for a software implementation of the scheme proposed in [OMPR05] has recently been published in [OS06]. This proposal is faster than the usual look-up table based scheme, if just one AES block needs to be encrypted using a fresh mask of 16 bytes. If several blocks are encrypted, the classical masking approach for AES (i.e. precomputing and storing masked S-Boxes in RAM) is more efficient. However, in an ideal masking scheme, where each intermediate value is masked with a different random value, one needs to keep track of 16 different masks. This leads to a serious decrease in performance and is unacceptable for most applications. In order to get a masked AES implementation with acceptable performance, tradeoffs between security and speed have to be made. Using fewer masks improves the performance but decreases the security against higher-order DPA attacks. Using only one mask leads to problems with MixColumns. If MixColumns needs to be computed efficiently, different masks for each row of the AES state have to be used. In most practical implementations, a small set of masks is used for all AES rounds. It is imperative for the security of a masked implementation that all intermediate values remain masked at all times.

Attacks on Masking Schemes. Masking schemes protect against fist-order DPA attacks. It is well known that, depending on the implementations, higher-order DPA attacks may succeed. In a higher-order DPA attack, several points of a power trace that correspond to several intermediate results, are combined in the statistical analysis. In particular, in a second-order DPA attack, one uses two intermediate points p_1 and p_2 of a trace that correspond to the processing of two values a_m and b_m. Typically the points are chosen such that they are concealed with the same mask m. Then, it holds that $|p_1 - p_2| \sim HW(a_m \oplus b_m)$. Because $a_m \oplus b_m = a \oplus b$ it is possible to predict the Hamming weight $HW(a_m \oplus b_m)$.

Only recently, the research community has picked up the topic of higher-order DPA attacks again, see [WW04], [SPQ05] and [JPS05]. The paper [OMHT06], that has been published only recently, provides theoretical discussions and practical results for second-order attacks on masked smart card implementation of AES. A conclusion from this paper is that second-order DPA attacks can be performed efficiently in practice with a low number of measurements. This means that masking alone does not lead to practically secure implementations if the masking scheme is supposed to be efficient. However, simply using more masks might not be the solution to the problem. This is because second-order DPA attacks work whenever two intermediate values are concealed by the same masks, or whenever the mask and the masked value occur at two moments in time. At some point in time, the masks have to be created, and at some point later, they are applied to some intermediate value. Hence, there are always two points in time that allow a second-order DPA attack.

As a consequence, it is better to combine a simple and efficient masking scheme with another countermeasure to achieve resistance against higher-order DPA attacks. For instance, the execution of the algorithm can be randomized.

2.2   Randomizing the Execution of the Algorithm

Randomizing the execution of the sequence of operations in an algorithm provides additional resistance against power analysis attacks. The goal of the randomization is to distribute the intermediate cipher operations (and thereby the intermediate values) over a given period of time. The distribution should neither be predictable nor be observable by the attacker.

Due to this distribution, the intermediate value that is used in the attack occurs only with a certain probability at a particular moment in time. Therefore, the correlation between this intermediate value and the power consumption is significantly reduced.

For this randomization approach, the insertion of random dummy operations or wait states has been proposed in the literature. The problem with wait states is that they can be easily identified and removed by analyzing a single power trace. When using random dummy operations, the programmer has to take care that dummy operations can not be distinguished from real operations of the algorithm.

We think that there are two efficient ways to introduce randomness in the execution of an algorithm. Either, one adds additional rounds (or parts of a round) to the encryption algorithm at the beginning and the end, or one randomly chooses the sequence of operations within the algorithm. The first method makes it impossible for the attacker to know when the real first round and the real last round takes place. The latter method provides an additional randomization within each round.

The statistical effects of randomization have been studied in [CCD00] and [Man04] in detail. Both papers come to the same conclusion. If the probability that the intermediate value occurs at a certain time is p, then the correlation coefficient decreases by a factor of p and the number of measurements needed for a successful attack increases by a factor of p^2.

3   A Power Analysis Resistant AES Smart Card Implementation

In our AES software implementation, we apply a combination of the countermeasures that we discussed in Sect. 2. The implementation is optimized for simple 8-bit smart cards. We make the common assumption that a random number generator is available.

All rounds of our implementation are masked. The first round and the last round are embedded in so-called randomization zones. Within a randomization zone, the sequence of masked AES operations is randomized and repeated a certain number of times. The number of repetitions in the first randomization zone defines the number of repetitions in the second randomization zone. The total number of repetitions is specified by the designer and is constant over multiple runs of the algorithm. The overall execution time stays therefore constant.

In principle, the masking scheme and the randomization scheme are designed independently from each other. However, we have changed the sequence of Mix-Columns and Shiftrows in order to facilitate the randomization. In the following subsections we first describe our masking scheme and afterwards the randomization of this scheme.

3.1   Efficiently Masking AES

In our masking scheme we use six different mask bytes. The first two bytes, M and M' are the input and output masks for the masked SubBytes operation. The remaining four bytes $M1$, $M2$, $M3$, and $M4$ are the input masks of the MixColumns operation. We take care that all intermediate values stay masked at all times.

Masking an AES round. At the start of each AES encryption, two precomputations take place. First we compute a masked SubBytes table S' such that $S'(x \oplus M) = S(x) \oplus M'$. Then we pre-compute the output masks for the MixColumns operation $(M1', M2', M3', M4') = \text{MixColumns}(M1, M2, M3, M4)$.

At the beginning of each round, the plaintext is masked with $M1'$, $M2'$, $M3'$, and $M4'$. Then, the AddRoundKey operation is performed. The round key is also masked (a detailed description is given in the subsequent section). Therefore, the masks change from $M1'$, $M2'$, $M3'$ and $M4'$ to the input mask M of the masked Subbytes table S'. Then, the table look-up with the table S' is performed. This changes the mask to M'. Before MixColumns, we change the mask from M' to $M1$ in the first row, to $M2$ in the second row, to $M3$ in the third row and to $M4$ in the fourth row. At the end of the round, MixColumns is performed which changes the masks Mi to Mi'. ShiftRows has no influence on the masks. At the end of the last encryption round, the masks are removed by the final AddRoundKey operation.

Masking the Key Schedule in Practice. Due to security reasons [Man03] the key schedule is also masked. In order to reuse the masked SubBytes table S', we decided to use the mask bytes M and M' also during calculation of the round keys. Furthermore, by applying the mask values Mi' to the round key bytes, we can save some remasking operations during the encryption round.

In the first step of the key schedule, the original cipherkey is masked. A byte of a word of the round key is masked with a value $Mi' \oplus M$. Figure 1 shows the masking scheme for all AES round keys, except for the one of the last round key. The masking scheme for the last round key is shown in Fig. 2. It differs because we want the last round key to remove the masks in order to obtain the ciphertext.

3.2   Randomizing the Masked AES

As explained in Sect. 2.2, there are two efficient possibilities to randomize the sequence of operations. Either, one adds additional rounds (or parts of a round) to the encryption algorithm at the beginning and the end, or one randomly chooses the sequence of operations within the algorithm.

In AES, several operations can be randomized. For instance, the AddRound-Key operation allows randomization. AddRoundKey adds each byte of the (masked) plaintext to the corresponding byte of the (masked) round key. The sequence of the processing can be randomized, because the 16 bytes of the state are processed independently. The same argument holds for the SubBytes operation. During MixColumns, the sequence of the processing of the columns can be randomized. Within each column, the processing of the rows can be randomized.

We also add parts of a round at the beginning and the end of each AES execution. The so-called dummy rounds work on a dummy state that lies in a different memory area in the smart card. In order to minimize information leakage about which state is used, we use base addresses for the dummy state and the real state that have the same Hamming weight. In Fig. 3, we depict the program flow of a randomized and masked AES encryption. The two randomization areas are called Randomization Zone 1 and Randomization Zone 2. Only in these zones,

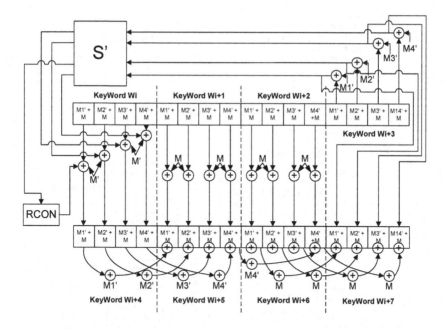

Fig. 1. Masking scheme for all but the last AES round keys

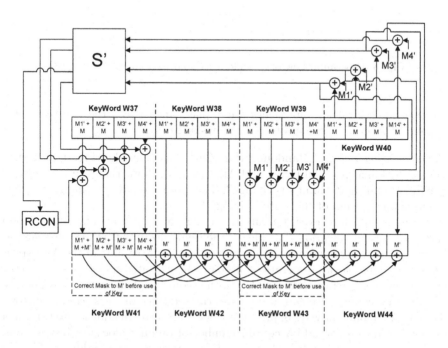

Fig. 2. Masking scheme for the last AES round key

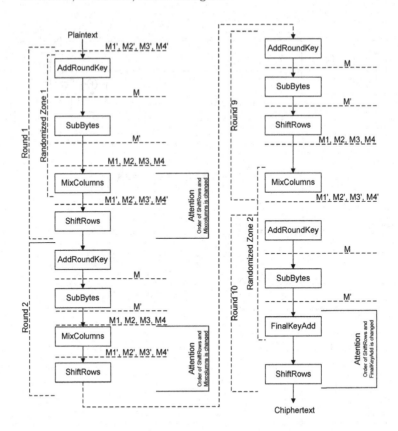

Fig. 3. Programm flow of a randomized and masked AES encryption

the two randomization approaches are applied. In between the two zones, the implementation of AES is protected by masking only.

Randomization Zone 1. Randomization Zone 1 includes the three transformations AddRoundKey, SubBytes and MixColumns. Note that the sequence of ShiftRows and MixColumns is changed. Therefore, we have to change the definition of one column of the state, see Fig. 4.

As discussed before, every operation that is included in Randomization Zone 1 allows some randomization. The idea of the randomization that we use is simple. We choose a block of operations that processes a single column of the AES state, see Fig. 5. This block of operations needs to be executed four times to process the complete AES state. We can choose the sequence of the columns randomly. Within each column, we can also choose the sequence of rows. Hence, in total there are 4×4 different ways of processing one AES state. In addition to this inner randomization we can add a certain number of dummy blocks of instructions, see Fig. 5. A variable called *Max_Ops* defines the amount of additional blocks added. If n blocks are added, then there are $16 + 4 \times n$ different ways of computing Randomization Zone 1.

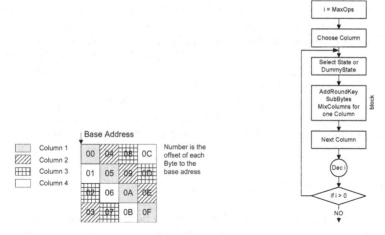

Fig. 4. The definition of a column of the state takes into account that Mix-Columns is performed before ShiftRows

Fig. 5. The Definition of Randomization Zone 1

Randomization Zone 2. Randomization Zone 2 includes the MixColumns operation of round nine, two AddRoundKey transformations, and a SubBytes transformation. In this randomized zone, the order of the final key addition and ShiftRows are changed. To compensate for this change, an InverseShiftRows transformation is applied to the last round key.

3.3   Performance Analysis

The implementation of countermeasures against power analysis attacks does not come for free. Additional memory and additional operations are necessary for masking and randomization. In Tab. 1, we compare the execution time in clock cycles (cc) of our implementation against several other protected and unprotected AES smart card implementations. We focus on implementations for AVR and 8051-based 8-bit microcontrollers. Compared are clock cycles for full 128-bit AES encryptions that include the key schedule. The first part of Tab. 1 compares different unprotected AES implementations and serves as a reference. There is a notable difference between the amount of clock cycles between the AVR-based and the 8051-based implementations. Implementations that use masking only

Table 1. Comparison of AES implementations for 8-bit smart card processors

Implementation Type	AVR	8051
AES	7498cc [Rö03]	90500cc [AG01]
	4427cc [Ins06]	46860cc [Ins06]
		38016cc [DR98]
masked AES	8420cc	293500cc [AG01]
masked & randomized AES	11845 + $n \times$ 240cc	

are compared in the second part of the table. Our implementation takes around 8420 clock cycles, which is roughly two times slower than the best unmasked implementation. In contrast, the multiplicative masking scheme [AG01], which was implemented for 8051-based smart cards, requires roughly 7 times more clock cycles than the best unmasked 8051-based implementation. The third part of the table shows the performance figure for our masked and randomized implementation. It takes 11845 clock cycles when no additional blocks are added. This increases the running time by a factor of 3 compared to the unmasked AVR-based implementation. When n blocks are added $11845 + n \times 240$ clock cycles are needed.

4   Security Analysis

The countermeasures that we have implemented are both well known and several papers on their effectiveness have been published. In this section we provide arguments why a combination of them provides resistance against power analysis attacks. First, we provide a theoretical assessment. Then, we report on the practical results that we have obtained.

4.1   Theoretical Analysis

We use a combination of masking and randomization to counteract various types of power analysis attacks. Our implementation is secure against simple power analysis attacks and template attacks because all intermediate values are masked. For the same reason, our implementation is secure against (first-order) DPA attacks. We are also resistant against second-order DPA attacks for the following reasons. Remember that in our implementation, the execution of AES starts and ends with a randomization zone. Within that zone, an operation occurs at a certain position only with probability $p = 1/(16 + 4 \times n)$, where n denotes the number of blocks and is defined by the designer. Consequently, a second-order DPA attack on operations within the randomization zone will produce a peak with height reduced by a factor of $p = 1/(16 + 4 \times n)$ and require $(16 + 4 \times n)^2$ more measurements than a standard second-order DPA attack. Consequently, n can be chosen such that an attack gets impractical. A second-order DPA attack outside the randomization zone requires either to predict two intermediate value that occurs after the MixColumns operation, or to predict one value that occurs after MixColumns and one that is in the randomization zone. Any intermediate value that occurs after MixColumns depends on 32 bits of the round key. Consequently, in order to make a second-order DPA attack on two bytes after MixColumns, the attacker has to guess at least 32 bits of the round key. This leads to a huge number guesses that need to be tested; we consider this to be impractical. For an attack on one value after MixColumns and one value in the randomization zone, the attacker needs to guess 32 bits of the key and needs $(16 + 4 \times n)^2$ times more traces than in a standard second-order DPA attack. We consider this to be impractical as well.

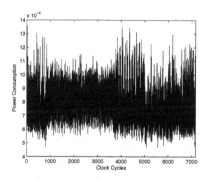

Fig. 6. Power trace of a masked AES encryption

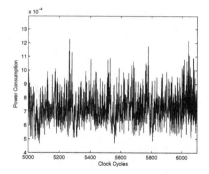

Fig. 7. Power trace showing the execution of the four columns only

4.2 Practical Analysis

We have applied first-order and second-order DPA attacks to a practical implementation of our secured AES. No first-order DPA attack has succeeded. In this section we report on one of the second-order DPA attacks that we have used to verify the theoretical estimates for the increase of the number of samples for a second-order DPA attack. Therefore, we have limited the amount of randomness that we introduce in the randomization zones to a factor of 4: no additional rounds are executed and there is no randomization of columns, only of rows.

Figure 6 shows the power consumption that we have acquired during the calculation of such an AES encryption. Each point in the trace represents one clock cycle. In the trace, several steps of the computation can be located. Between clock cycle 1000 and 3800 the pre-processing of the masked SubBytes table takes place. This calculation is followed by the masked key scheduling part of the algorithm which lasts approximately until clock cycle number 4900. Thereafter, until clock cycle 6100, Randomization Zone 1 is processed. We zoom into this part of the trace in Fig. 7. One can locate the four inner loops that correspond to the processing of the four columns. The first column is processed between clock cycle 5000 and 5200. Therefore, we have attacked this part of the trace with a second-order DPA attack.

Our attacked followed the scenario that has been described in Sect. 3.3 of [OMHT06]. In this scenario, one attacks two SubByte outputs. In [OMHT06], a theoretical estimate for the height of the correlation coefficient was given. The reported correlation coefficient was 0.24. This value can only be achieved under the assumption that the device leaks the Hamming weight of the processed data. Our smart card does not leak the Hamming weight. It leaks the Hamming distance of the data and the value that was manipulated before. Typically, the attacker does not know that value. Hence, the maximum correlation coefficient for our device is lower. We have assessed this height based on another unprotected AES implementation on the same device. It turned out, that the height is 0.7. We use this factor to scale the correlation coefficient

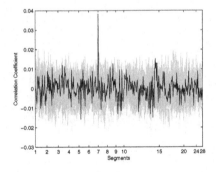

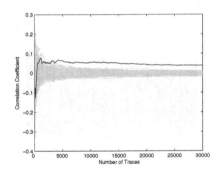

Fig. 8. The result of all key guesses in an attack

Fig. 9. Correlation coefficients for all keys depending on the number of power traces that are used in the attack

that was reported in [OMHT06]; the expected height of a second-order DPA on our implementation is therefore $0.24 * 0.7 = 0.168$. In the experiment that we performed, where only one column is randomized and no additional blocks are added, we expect a further decrease of the height by a factor of 4. Consequently, we expected to produce a peak of height 0.04 in a second-order DPA attack on the randomized AES. Figure 8 shows the result of the attack. It can be seen that for one of the segments (see [OMHT06] for a detailed explanation of the attack and the notation) we indeed produce a peak with a height that is roughly 0.04 for the correct key guess. Figure 9, shows the run of the correlation coefficient for an increasing number of samples. In both figures, the graphs for the incorrect key guesses are plotted in gray color and the graph for the correct key guess is plotted in black color. The results of this experiments confirm the theoretical estimates that we took from [CCD00] and [Man04].

5   Conclusion

In this article we have described an AES software implementation that is suited for 8-bit smart cards and that is resistant against power analysis attacks. Our implementation masks the intermediate results and introduces randomization at the beginning and the end of the execution. It is secure against simple power analysis attacks, template attacks and first-order DPA attacks because of masking. Due to the combination of masking and randomization, it is resistant against higher-order DPA attacks. Resistance means that a large amount of measurements has to be acquired for a successful attack. Our implementation compares well with other protected and unprotected AES software implementations for smart cards. The practical attacks that we have performed support our theoretical estimates about the security of the countermeasures.

References

[AG01]   Mehdi-Laurent Akkar and Christophe Giraud. An Implementation of DES
           and AES, Secure against Some Attacks. In Çetin Kaya Koç, David Nac-
           cache, and Christof Paar, editors, *Cryptographic Hardware and Embed-
           ded Systems – CHES 2001, Third International Workshop, Paris, France,
           May 14-16, 2001, Proceedings*, volume 2162 of *Lecture Notes in Computer
           Science*, pages 309–318. Springer, 2001.

[BGK05]   Johannes Blömer, Jorge Guajardo, and Volker Krummel. Provably Secure
           Masking of AES. In Helena Handschuh and M. Anwar Hasan, editors,
           *Selected Areas in Cryptography, 11th International Workshop, SAC 2004,
           Waterloo, Canada, August 9-10, 2004, Revised Selected Papers*, volume
           3357 of *Lecture Notes in Computer Science*, pages 69–83. Springer, 2005.

[CCD00]   Christophe Clavier, Jean-Sébastien Coron, and Nora Dabbous. Differ-
           ential Power Analysis in the Presence of Hardware Countermeasures.
           In Çetin Kaya Koç and Christof Paar, editors, *Cryptographic Hardware
           and Embedded Systems – CHES 2000, Second International Workshop,
           Worcester, MA, USA, August 17-18, 2000, Proceedings*, volume 1965 of
           Lecture Notes in Computer Science, pages 252–263. Springer, 2000.

[DR98]   Joan Daemen and Vincent Rijmen. AES proposal: Rijndael. First AES
           Conference, August 1998.

[Ins06]   Institute for Applied Information Processing and Communication,
           Graz University of Technology.   VLSI Products–Software Mod-
           ules.   http://www.iaik.tugraz.at/research/vlsi/02_products/index.php,
           January 2006.

[JPS05]   Marc Joye, Pascal Paillier, and Berry Schoenmakers. On Second-Order
           Differential Power Analysis. In Josyula R. Rao and Berk Sunar, editors,
           *Cryptographic Hardware and Embedded Systems – CHES 2005, 7th In-
           ternational Workshop, Edinburgh, UK, August 29 - September 1, 2005,
           Proceedings*, volume 3659 of *Lecture Notes in Computer Science*, pages
           293–308. Springer, 2005.

[KJJ99]   Paul C. Kocher, Joshua Jaffe, and Benjamin Jun. Differential Power Anal-
           ysis. In Michael Wiener, editor, *Advances in Cryptology - CRYPTO '99,
           19th Annual International Cryptology Conference, Santa Barbara, Cali-
           fornia, USA, August 15-19, 1999, Proceedings*, volume 1666 of *Lecture
           Notes in Computer Science*, pages 388–397. Springer, 1999.

[Man03]   Stefan Mangard. A Simple Power-Analysis (SPA) Attack on Implemen-
           tations of the AES Key Expansion. In Pil Joong Lee and Chae Hoon
           Lim, editors, *Information Security and Cryptology - ICISC 2002, 5th In-
           ternational Conference Seoul, Korea, November 28-29, 2002, Revised Pa-
           pers*, volume 2587 of *Lecture Notes in Computer Science*, pages 343–358.
           Springer, 2003.

[Man04]   Stefan Mangard. Hardware Countermeasures against DPA – A Statistical
           Analysis of Their Effectiveness. In Tatsuaki Okamoto, editor, *Topics in
           Cryptology - CT-RSA 2004, The Cryptographers' Track at the RSA Con-
           ference 2004, San Francisco, CA, USA, February 23-27, 2004, Proceed-
           ings*, volume 2964 of *Lecture Notes in Computer Science*, pages 222–235.
           Springer, 2004.

[Nat01]   National Institute of Standards and Technology (NIST).   FIPS-197:
           Advanced Encryption Standard, November 2001.   Available online at
           http://www.itl.nist.gov/fipspubs/.

[OMHT06] Elisabeth Oswald, Stefan Mangard, Christoph Herbst, and Stefan Tillich. Practical Second-Order DPA Attacks for Masked Smart Card Implementations of Block Ciphers. In David Pointcheval, editor, *Topics in Cryptology - CT-RSA 2006, The Cryptographers' Track at the RSA Conference 2006, San Jose, CA, USA, February 13-17, 2006, Proceedings*, volume 3860 of *Lecture Notes in Computer Science*, pages 192–207. Springer, 2006.

[OMPR05] Elisabeth Oswald, Stefan Mangard, Norbert Pramstaller, and Vincent Rijmen. A Side-Channel Analysis Resistant Description of the AES S-box. In Henri Gilbert and Helena Handschuh, editors, *Fast Software Encryption, 12th International Workshop, FSE 2005, Paris, France, February 21-23, 2005, Proceedings*, volume 3557 of *Lecture Notes in Computer Science*, pages 413–423. Springer, 2005.

[OS06]   Elisabeth Oswald and Kai Schramm. An Efficient Masking Scheme for AES Software Implementations. In J. Song, T. Kwon, and M. Yung, editors, *WISA 2005*, volume 3786 of *Lecture Notes in Computer Science*, pages 292–305. Springer, 2006.

[RÖ3]   Christian Röpke. Praktikum B:Embedded Smartcard Microcontrollers. http://www.christianroepke.de/studium_praktikumB.html, 2003.

[SPQ05]   Francois-Xavier Standaert, Eric Peeters, and Jean-Jacques Quisquater. On the Masking Countermeasure and Higher-Order Power Analysis Attacks. In *ITCC 2005*, 2005.

[WW04]   Jason Waddle and David Wagner. Towards Efficient Second-Order Power Analysis. In Marc Joye and Jean-Jacques Quisquater, editors, *Cryptographic Hardware and Embedded Systems – CHES 2004, 6th International Workshop, Cambridge, MA, USA, August 11-13, 2004, Proceedings*, volume 3156 of *Lecture Notes in Computer Science*, pages 1–15. Springer, 2004.

Physical Security Bounds Against Tampering[*]

Kerstin Lemke, Christof Paar, and Ahmad-Reza Sadeghi

Horst Görtz Institute for IT Security,
Ruhr University Bochum
44780 Bochum, Germany
{lemke, cpaar, sadeghi}@crypto.rub.de

Abstract. We consider the problem of an active adversary physically manipulating computations of a cryptographic device that is implemented in circuitry. Which kind of circuit based security can ever be guaranteed if *all* computations are vulnerable towards fault injection? In this paper, we define physical security parameters against tampering adversaries. Therefore, we present an adversarial model with a strong focus on fault injection techniques based on radiation and particle impact. Physical implementation strategies to counteract tampering attempts are discussed.

Keywords: Fault Analysis, Tamper-Proof Hardware, Physical Security, Implementation Attack, Adversarial Model, Fault Prevention, Error Detection, Fault Detection.

1 Introduction

Active implementation attacks can be classified as fault analysis, physical manipulations and modifications. *Fault analysis* aims to cause an interference with the physical implementation and to enforce an erroneous behavior that can result in a vulnerability of a security service or even a total break. The terms manipulation and modification stem from definitions of physical security, e.g., from ISO-13491-1 [1] and address similar attacks. *Physical manipulation* aims at changing the processing of the physical implementation so that it deviates from the specification. *Physical modification* is an active invasive attack targeting the internal construction of the cryptographic device.

If a cryptographic device is used in an hostile environment special properties for the device are required to ensure a certain level of physical security for the storage and processing of cryptographic keys. For the theoretical perspective we refer to the concepts on *Read-Proof Hardware* and *Tamper-Proof Hardware* as given in [11]. *Read-Proof Hardware* prevents an adversary from reading internal data stored and *Tamper-Proof Hardware* prevents the adversary from changing internal data. Moreover, we use the term of *Tamper-Resistant Hardware* as a

---

[*] The work described in this paper has been supported in part by the European Commission through the IST Programme under Contract IST-2002-507932 ECRYPT, the European Network of Excellence in Cryptology.

J. Zhou, M. Yung, and F. Bao (Eds.): ACNS 2006, LNCS 3989, pp. 253–267, 2006.

relaxed term of *Tamper-Proof Hardware*, e.g., the hardware is resistant to tampering to a certain extent. Such bounds are made more precise in this work.

In a tamper-proof implementation, fault injections are not feasible per definition. However, in real life, practical experiments have shown that approaches towards tamper resistance are hard. Many contributions (e.g., [16, 4, 24, 5, 23, 25]) have reported that semiconductor circuits are vulnerable against fault injections. Such findings are related to the development of devices for the use in aerospace and high-energy physics which have to tolerate particle radiation impact during operation [18, 19]. In contrast to applications developed for safety and reliability reasons, security applications have to withstand an active malicious adversary. Prior to the first scientific contribution [9] on fault analysis the FIPS-140 standard already required a cryptographic algorithm test ("known-answer test") [12] to be implemented in cryptographic modules during start-up. Moreover, in an error state, according to [12], the use of cryptographic algorithms shall be inhibited.

We recollect previous fault induction techniques to build an unified adversarial model based on [17] as first step towards bridging the gap between the theoretical framework of [11] and real-world experiences. In our model we cover fault analysis against physical cryptographic devices. We assume that each kind of data memory can be tampered with in a probabilistic sense and that the adversary is able to induce faults at any internal state and computation of the physical device. By doing so, we are able to model the manifold nature of faults as well as to include Differential Fault Analysis ([8, 22]) more adequately in case of physical devices.

As discussed in Section 1.1 the *Algorithmic Tamper-Proof (ATP)* security model [11] does only partly give a framework for existing attacks. In this paper we deal with the problem which kind of implementation based security can be guaranteed in an extended 'real-life' model against tampering. Therefore, we present a physical model with a strong focus on fault injection techniques based on radiation and particle impact. Physical security parameters are outlined and result in implementation strategies to prevent and detect tampering attempts.

1.1   Related Work: ATP Security

The model of *Algorithmic Tamper-Proof (ATP) Security* was introduced in [11]. It assumes that devices are built by using two different components; one being tamper-proof but readable, and the other being read-proof yet tamperable. Only data that is considered to be universally known (i.e., public data) is tamper-proof beyond the reach of the tampering adversary. Other data is subject to tampering, i.e., fault induction. ATP Security defines a powerful tampering adversary who is able to initiate three commands: Run(·), i.e., the cryptographic computation, Apply(·), i.e., the fault injection, and Setup(·). The adversary knows all construction details: especially, the adversary knows each bit-position in the device's memory. It is concluded in [11] that a component is needed which is both read-proof and tamper-proof to achieve general Algorithmic Tamper-Proof (ATP) Security.

The main limitation of [11] is caused by the fact that the command Run($\cdot$) itself is assumed to be not vulnerable to fault injection. In practice, there is no reason that the adversary does not attack Run($\cdot$) itself. Actually, standard scenarios of Differential Fault Analysis (DFA) apply faults *during* the cryptographic computation [8, 22]. Such a setting becomes especially important in case of tampering at memory-constrained devices as, e.g., a modification prior to Run($\cdot$) can hardly affect *only* the last round of DES. In [11], tamper-proofing a signature (or decryption) scheme is part of the command Run($\cdot$) which first checks whether the storage has integrity using a verification algorithm. If so, the signature (or decryption) algorithm is computed yielding an output as result. Otherwise, self-destruction of the device is invoked. In case the verification algorithm is subject to fault injection, too, the tamper-proofing solution of the ATP model does not hold anymore.

Reference [11] also discusses restrictions of the model assuming that the adversary is limited, for instance, it is only feasible for the adversary to perform a probabilistic flipping of bits in the device's memory. The type of DFA discussed in [11] requires the strong assumption that the memory type is significantly asymmetric. For this type of DFA, [11] argues that checking for faults can be sufficient for ATP security, even if the device is not equipped with a self-destruct capability. As recently shown, one can even precisely induce faults, e.g., by optical fault induction, as reported in a recent survey on hardware security analysis [25]. Therein, it is demonstrated that any individual bit of SRAM memory could be changed to a definitive state by light injection. Both the targeting state '0' and '1' could be set, just by a lateral adjustment of the light spot.

2   An Overview of Fault Analysis

Fault analysis against cryptographic primitives has become a new research area initiated by [9]. Besides targeting cryptographic primitives there are other applications of fault induction that target generic (non-cryptographic) building blocks.

2.1   Cryptographic Building Blocks

A recent survey on fault analysis against cryptographic primitives can be found in [26].

A Generic Attack: If the memory type used for key storage has the special property that flipping a bit from one state to the other is impossible (e.g., from state '1' to state '0'), all key bits finally accumulate in one state (e.g., state '1') after repetitive fault injections. Assuming the adversary owns cryptograms for each intermediate state, e.g., after each successive induced state transition, the adversary can iterate backwards recursively [7], starting at the known final state, yielding finally the original key value.

Block Ciphers (AES and DES): Fault attacks against block ciphers are differential attacks that require both a correct cryptogram and some faulty ones for the analysis. In [8] Differential Fault Analysis (DFA) has been introduced against DES. The original attack assumed that faults occur randomly in all rounds of DES and required about 50-200 faults in this model. If precise fault injection is possible, the number can be reduced to about three faults [26]. For AES, some scenarios are presented in [26]. Among them, the most promising one [22] requires two faults for recovering the AES key.

Stream ciphers: In [13] fault analysis techniques are presented targeting the linearity of LFSRs which are typical building blocks of stream ciphers. Another approach has been presented in [6] for the stream cipher RC4. This approach exploits the forced induction of impossible states.

Asymmetric primitives: Fault injection against an RSA-CRT implementation requires only one fault injection with very low requirements on the concrete fault occurrence [9]. Modular exponentiation which is used at RSA as well as ElGamal, Schnorr and DSA signature schemes can be also attacked by fault injection successively [9].

2.2   Non-cryptographic Building Blocks

Here, we use the notion of a *security service* as a general term for any security relevant or security enforcing building block of the cryptographic device.

Modification of Security States: For cryptographic devices, it is necessary to maintain security states by storing attributes, e.g., related to authorizations and privileges achieved. A fault injection against such a security state may end up in a more privileged state.

Modification of a Security Service: Modification of a security service itsself can be invoked by fault injection. By-passing checks of parameter bounds as presented by [3] is one example for this kind of threat.

Denial of Service: Fault injection can result in a permanent mal-function or destruction of circuit components used by a security service. For example, the destruction of a physical random generator might be attractive.

3   Adversary Model

The adversary model presented is an extended version of [17]. By assumption the physical device D is encapsulated. Especially, it does not offer a logical nor a physical interface to modify the internal memory or the internal construction of D. The set-up for fault analysis based attacks consists of i) the physical device D under test, ii) a reader device for the data communication interface, and iii) a fault injection set-up. Additionally, iv) a monitoring set-up can be used by the adversary to analyze the fault induction process and its effects, e.g., by measuring side channel leakage. The set-up as well as the information flow is illustrated in Fig. 1 and described in more detail below.

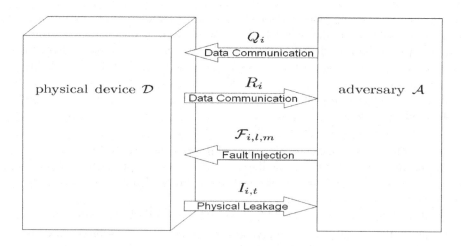

Fig. 1. Information Flow at a Fault Analysis Set-Up

We denote the adversary by $\mathcal{A}$. By assumption $\mathcal{A}$ has physical access to the physical device $\mathcal{D}$ under attack and can run a high number of instances of a security service $\mathcal{S}$. Each instance is initiated by a query Q_i of $\mathcal{A}$ and $\mathcal{D}$ finishes after some computational time at time T_i returning a response R_i where $i \in \{1, \ldots, N\}$. $\mathcal{A}$ applies a probabilistic physical interaction process aiming at disturbing the intended computation of $\mathcal{S}$. $\mathcal{A}$ may be able to monitor the effects caused by physical interaction using auxiliary means, e.g., by observing the instantaneous leakage $I_{i,t}$ of the implementation at a monitoring set-up at time t. If necessary, $\mathcal{A}$ applies cryptanalytical methods for a final analysis step.

Moreover, we assume that $\mathcal{A}$ is able to perform multiple fault injections at a fault injection set-up that are bounded by M, where M is a small number. Let L be a small number of spatially separated fault injection set-ups that can be operated in parallel. The distinct fault injections during one invocation of $\mathcal{S}$ are numbered as $\mathcal{F}_{i,l,m}$ with $l \in \{1, \ldots, L\}$ and $m \in \{1, \ldots, M\}$. These fault injections occur at the times $\{t_{i,1,1}, \ldots, t_{i,L,M}\}$ with $t_{i,1,1} \leq \cdots \leq t_{i,L,M} \leq T_i$.

$\mathcal{A}$ is an active adaptive adversary, i.e., both the queries Q_i as well as the parameters of $\mathcal{F}_{i,l,m}$ can be chosen adaptively. We point out that the leakage $I_{i,t}$ is typically not yet available for the configuration of $\mathcal{F}_{i,l,m}$ at the same instantiation of $\mathcal{S}$ unless a more demanding real-time analysis is applied.

For the physical device $\mathcal{D}$ we consider an implementation in circuitry. The target circuit $\mathcal{C}$ that is part of D consists of interconnecting Boolean gates and memory cells [1]. Each spatial position within $\mathcal{C}$ is uniquely represented in three dimensional co-ordinates $\boldsymbol{x} = (x, y, z)$. Processing of $\mathcal{C}$ is modelled by the transition states of the circuit at time t, i.e., by using four dimensional co-ordinates $(\boldsymbol{x}, t)$. The state of the circuit s_t at time t is given by the contents of the memory

---

[1] In a refined model one may distinguish different types of memory elements such as flip-flops, RAM, flash and EEPROM.

cells. Faults affecting Boolean gates cause computational faults by introducing glitches or short circuits. Such faults can result in erroneous states stored at memory cells. Faults affecting memory cells cause a direct transition from memory contents s_t to $f(s_t)$ with $s_t \neq f(s_t)$. Fault induction itsself is a probabilistic process with a certain success probability that depends on the circuit C, the underlying physical process P used for fault injection, and the configuration of the fault analysis set-up $F_{i,l,m}$.

Summarizing, the information channels are

1. the *Query Channel* modelling A sending the query Q_i to D,
2. the *Response Channel* modelling A receiving the response R_i of D,
3. the *Fault Channel* modelling A applying physical fault injection processes $F_{i,l,m}$ targeting D, and
4. the *Monitoring Channel* modelling A receiving physical leakage of D.

Informally speaking (we will give a more precise definition below in case of a digital signature scheme), an adversary A is *successful*, if the insertion of faults either i) yields access to a security service S without knowledge of the required secret or ii) yields partial information about the secret.

3.1   Objectives of the Adversary

As introduced in Section 2, manifold attack scenarios for fault analysis have been already proposed. At the core of all these scenarios there is a loop including both an instantiation of the security service S and a sequence of fault injection processes $F_{i,l,m}$. A classification into three main categories, namely Simple Fault Analysis (SFA), Successive Simple Fault Analysis (SSFA) and Differential Fault Analysis (DFA), can be found in [17].

For concreteness, we consider a digital signature scheme that is defined as a triple of algorithms (Gen, Sig, Ver) with key generation algorithm Gen, signing algorithm Sig and verifying algorithm Ver. Let (pk, sk) be public and secret key of the signing algorithm Sig that is implemented as security service S of D in the circuit C.

In our model, fault injection can both be done *prior* and *during* the computation of a digital signature. Fault injection may modify the computation of C (resulting in wrong intermediate data of the computation) as well as the actual memory contents of C. It is m_i included in Q_i the chosen message used for signature generation and s_i part of R_i such that $s_i \leftarrow Sig_{sk}(m_i)$. If $Ver_{pk}(m_i, s_i) =$ yes, the computation of the signature generation is correct, otherwise it is not.

As shown in Fig. 2, A invokes N instantiations of the signature computation. For each run, A configures $F_{i,l,m}$, chooses m_i and runs the signature computation $Sig_{sk}(m_i)$. Though configuration of $F_{i,l,m}$ may be done before the signature computation, fault injection of $F_{i,l,m}$ may also be effective during signature computation. A stores $(m_i, s_i, Ver_{pk}(m_i, s_i))$ for the analysis step. A is successful with N instantiations of $Sig_{sk}(m_i)$, if A succeeds in generating a valid signature s for a new message m which was not been used before during the training step. In practice, fault analysis against digital signature schemes may be even stronger: as result, A then outputs sk.

```
H ← {}; I ← {}; State ← ε;
for i = 1 ... N
        (State, F_{i,l,m}, m_i) ← A(State, pk, H)
        I ← I ∪ {(m_i)}
        (s_i) ← Sig_{sk}(m_i)
        H ← H ∪ {(m_i, s_i, Ver_{pk}(m_i, s_i))}
(m, s) ← A(pk, H)
m ∉ I and Ver_{pk}(m, s) = yes
```

Fig. 2. Tampering Attack against a Digital Signature Scheme based on adaptive chosen messages

3.2   Physical Means of the Adversary

In this Section we detail on the physical modelling of the circuit C and the physical interaction process P. Let assume a strong adversary A who is given a map of C including a behavioral simulation for each time t. A is then able to configure the setup $F_{i,l,m}$ for fault injection accordingly to the known circuit layout and processing times.

Interaction Range. According to FIPS 140-2 [2] we introduce the concept of the *cryptographic boundary* that encloses all security relevant and security enforcing parts of an implementation. Additionally, we define a second boundary that we call the *interaction boundary* that is specific for each physical interaction process. If the adversary does not pass the interaction boundary, the physical interaction is not effective at the cryptographic device. The interaction boundary can be an outer boundary of the cryptographic boundary, as, e.g., in case of temperature which affects the entire cryptographic module. Interaction with light is only feasible if a non-transparent encapsulation is partially removed, e.g., the chip is depackaged. Because of the limited range of the interaction, interaction processes using particles with non-zero mass may require the removal of the passivation and other layers which breaches the cryptographic boundary.

The means of A can be manifold. In our view the main limitations are caused by the technical equipment available. Because of this we distinguish the non-invasive adversary, the semi-invasive adversary, and the invasive adversary that are defined according to earlier work (e.g., [24, 17]) on fault induction.

Let A choose a physical interaction process P. A uses *non-invasive* means if the interaction boundary of P is an outer boundary of the cryptographic boundary. We denote the non-invasive adversary by $A_{non-inv}$. A uses *invasive* means if the interaction boundary of P is an inner boundary of the cryptographic boundary. We denote the invasive adversary by A_{inv}. A *semi-invasive* adversary $A_{semi-inv}$ uses light or electromagnetic fields as the interaction process and is a special case of $A_{non-inv}$.

In circuitry, modifications of charges, currents and voltage levels may cause faults of the implementation. Modification of charges can be invoked by injecting charged particles or photons. For example, the underlying physical process for optical fault induction is the photoelectric effect whereat injected photons are absorbed by the electronic semiconductor that in turn excites electrons from the valence band to the conduction band. Modification of currents can result from manipulating at the electrical circuit or by electromagnetic fields. Modifications of internal voltage levels within the cryptographic boundary are feasible by microprobing or the use of more sophisticated equipment, as focused ion beams. Note that often cumulative effects are needed to induce a fault, e.g., sufficient free carriers have to be generated or driven to load or unload a capacitance of the circuit. In the general case, multiple fault injections can not be considered as stochastically independent single fault injections, especially if their effects overlap in time or space.

Table 1. Physical Means according to the interaction range of an adversary

Adversary	Physical Means
$\mathcal{A}_{non-inv}$	glitches at external interfaces, changes of the environmental conditions
$\mathcal{A}_{semi-inv}$	light, electromagnetic radiation
$\mathcal{A}_{inv}$	active probes, charged particle beams

Spatial Resolution. If a special volume dV of the circuit $\mathcal{C}$ is targeted by the adversary then optimizing success rate requires that the physical interaction process needs to be injected into the cryptographic device with a good resolution in space. The following considerations are most suited for light, electromagnetic fields, and charged particles as interaction process.

We use $F(\boldsymbol{x}, E, t)$ to model the spatial, energetic and temporal density[2] of identical physical particles[3] as a function of a three-dimensional position vector $\boldsymbol{x} = (x, y, z)$, energy E and time t. Before impact on $\mathcal{C}$ the movement of the density is given by the three-dimensional velocity vector $\boldsymbol{v} = (v_x, v_y, v_z)$. For example, $F(\boldsymbol{x}, E, t)$ may describe a mono-energetic[4] light beam of photons that is injected into the circuit for a short amount of time.

Without loss of generality the circuit $\mathcal{C}$ is assumed to be in line with the two-dimensional $x - y$ plane (as seen in Fig. 3) at $z = 0$. The z-axis with $z \geq 0$ gives the penetration depth. An interaction process $\mathcal{P}$ of $F(\boldsymbol{x}, E, t)$ with the composition of electronic semiconductor material at position $\boldsymbol{x}$ is described by a differential cross section $d\sigma(\boldsymbol{x})$, defined as $d\sigma(\boldsymbol{x}) = \frac{dN(\boldsymbol{x})}{N(\boldsymbol{x})}$, wherein $dN(\boldsymbol{x})$ is the number of interacting particles per time unit dT and $N(\boldsymbol{x})$ is the number of particles that cross the area dA per time unit dT. Assuming that dA lies in a $x - y$ plane on the surface of $\mathcal{C}$ ($z = 0$), $N(\boldsymbol{x})$ is derived by $N(\boldsymbol{x}) = \int_0^{v_z \cdot dT} dz \int_{dA} dx \, dy \int_0^{\infty} dE \, F(\boldsymbol{x}, E, t)$.

Next, we consider the question of success probability to hit a target volume dV of $\mathcal{C}$ that is located at depth z with depth extension dz and spans an area

---

[2] The number of particles per space unit, per energy unit and per time unit.

[3] Correspondingly, one may consider a movement of a wave.

[4] The energy distribution can be modelled with the δ-function $\delta(E - E_0)$, i.e., all particles have energy E_0.

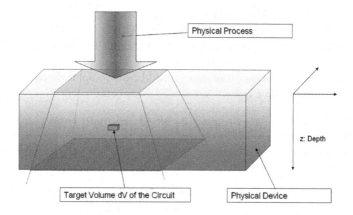

Fig. 3. Impact of the particle beam into the circuit

dA. During transfer through the circuit incident particles are partly absorbed, partly reflected and partly transmitted. Interaction processes with matter cause a decrease and spread of the energetic and spatial distribution of $F(\boldsymbol{x}, E, t)$ with increasing penetration range in $\mathcal{C}$. The interrelationship of $F(\boldsymbol{x}, E, t)$ as a function of penetration depth z is complex and does typically not solely depend on *one* interaction process. We assume that $F(\boldsymbol{x}, E, t)$ can be predicted for $z > 0$, e.g., by using a Monte-Carlo simulation of particles' movement by including the most important interaction processes as well as the circuit layout. The spatial spread of particles due to interactions shall be bounded by $\Delta A(z)$ in each $x - y$ plane within $\mathcal{C}$. Accordingly, the energetic spread shall be bounded by $\Delta E(z)$ in each $x - y$ plane within $\mathcal{C}$. In the general case, also the differential cross section depends on the energy E, so that we consider $d\sigma(\boldsymbol{x}, E)$ from now on.

Then, $N_{dV} = \int_z^{z+dz} dz' \int_{dA} dx' \, dy' \int_0^{\Delta E(z')} dE' \, F(\boldsymbol{x}', E', t) \, d\sigma(\boldsymbol{x}', E')$ is the number of interacting particles in $dV = dz \, dA$. Let ΔV of $\mathcal{C}$ be the overall volume that is affected by the physical interaction process. Accordingly, in the volume ΔV it is $N_{\Delta V} = \int_0^{\Delta z} dz' \int_{\Delta A(z')} dx' \, dy' \int_0^{\Delta E(z')} dE' \, F(\boldsymbol{x}', E', t) \, d\sigma(\boldsymbol{x}', E')$ with Δz being the thickness of $\mathcal{C}$. The probability to cause an interaction process within the volume dV that is located between depth z to $z + dz$ with area extension dA given the overall affected volume ΔV with $N_{\Delta V} \neq 0$ is

$$p_V = \frac{N_{dV}}{N_{\Delta V}} = \frac{\int_z^{z+dz} dz' \int_{dA} dx' \, dy' \int_0^{\Delta E(z')} dE' \, F(\boldsymbol{x}', E', t) \, d\sigma(\boldsymbol{x}', E')}{\int_0^{\Delta z} dz' \int_{\Delta A(z')} dx' \, dy' \int_0^{\Delta E(z')} dE' \, F(\boldsymbol{x}', E', t) \, d\sigma(\boldsymbol{x}', E')} \tag{1}$$

Example 1. Mono-energetic beam with exponential attenuation in homogeneous material: $F(\boldsymbol{x}', E', t) = F_0 \, \delta(E' - E_0) \, e^{-az'}$ with $a = (10\mu m)^{-1}$, $\Delta A(z') = 10\mu m^2$, $\Delta z = 100\mu m$, $dA = 0.02\mu m^2$, $dz = 0.1\mu m$, $z = 20\mu m$ and $\sigma(\boldsymbol{x}', E') = \sigma_0$. Then, it is $p_V = \frac{N_{dV}}{N_{\Delta V}} = \frac{dA \, e^{-a\,z}(1 - e^{-a\,dz})}{\Delta A \,(1 - e^{-a\,\Delta z})} \implies p_V \approx 2.69 \cdot 10^{-6}$.

Spatial and Timing Resolution. So far, we considered spatial resolution. Often additionally timing resolution is required, e.g., the physical interaction process has to be induced at a specific time frame dt of the computation of the implementation, i.e., within the time interval $[t, t + dt]$.

When considering timing resolution in addition to spatial resolution (1) the corresponding probability is

$$p_{VT} = \frac{\int_t^{t+dt} dt' \int_z^{z+dz} dz' \int_{dA} dx' \, dy' \int_0^{\Delta E(z')} dE' \, F(\boldsymbol{x}', E', t') \, d\sigma(\boldsymbol{x}', E')}{\int_{-\infty}^{\infty} dt' \int_0^{\Delta z} dz' \int_{\Delta A(z')} dx' \, dy' \int_0^{\Delta E(z')} dE' \, F(\boldsymbol{x}', E', t') \, d\sigma(\boldsymbol{x}', E')}. \quad (2)$$

Example 2. Continuing the previous example with

$$F(\boldsymbol{x}', E', t') = \begin{cases} F_0 \, \delta(E' - E_0) \, e^{-az'}, & \text{if } t \le t' \le t + \Delta T \\ 0, & \text{otherwise} \end{cases}$$

with $dt = 10ns$ and $\Delta T = 100ns \implies p_{VT} \approx 2.69 \cdot 10^{-7}$.

Immediate Consequences

- If $F(\boldsymbol{x}, E, t')$ does not reach the target area dV it is $p_{VT} = 0$.
- If $F(\boldsymbol{x}, E, t')$ is uniform in space and time and $\frac{dV}{\Delta V} \ll 1$ and $\frac{dt}{\Delta T} \ll 1$ then $p_{VT} \ll 1$ (e.g., in case of thermal radiation). It follows, that for $\mathcal{A}_{non-inv}$ it is $p_{VT} \ll 1$.

Sensitive and non-sensitive volumes of a circuit. We distinguish 'sensitive' and 'non-sensitive' volumes of the circuit $\mathcal{C}$ during computation of $\mathcal{S}$. A *sensitive volume* of the circuit at time t is composed of Boolean gates and memory cells that are used during computation of the security service $\mathcal{S}$ at the time t. The complementary set of volumes in $\mathcal{C}$ at time t is defined as *non-sensitive volume* of the circuit. As a consequence, physical interaction processes in non-sensitive volumes do not lead to a computational fault of $\mathcal{S}$, whereas physical interaction processes in sensitive volumes can have an impact on the computation of $\mathcal{S}$. In a refined version of (2) this fact can be included by neglecting non-sensitive volumes of the circuit at time t.

4   Physical Security Bounds

As already outlined, we assume a strong adversary $\mathcal{A}$ who is given a map of $\mathcal{C}$ including a behavioral simulation that also indicates sensitive and non-sensitive volumes of a circuit $\mathcal{C}$ for each time t. Given these means, $\mathcal{A}$ is able to perform a vulnerability analysis of $\mathcal{C}$ and to identify tampering attack paths of $\mathcal{C}$.

For security notions, metrics are needed to quantify physical properties of $\mathcal{C}$. Defining such quantities for a circuit $\mathcal{C}$ is strongly dependent on the concrete layout and has to consider all feasible attack paths, i.e. the set of all admissible events for $\mathcal{A}$. Suitable metrics of $\mathcal{C}$ could be, but are not limited to (i) the size of target gates, (ii) the attacking time frame for target gates, (iii) the smallest

Euclidean distance between target gates and the cryptographic boundary of $\mathcal{C}$, and (iv) the smallest Euclidean distance between target gates and other sensitive volumes of $\mathcal{C}$.

A circuit $\mathcal{C}$ implementing a security service S is said to be *statistically secure in the average case against an (N, L, M)-limited tampering adversary* if for all physical interaction processes $\mathcal{P}$ there exists a negligible function negl($\mathcal{C}, N, L, M$) such that the success probability of a fault analysis scenario is bounded by negl($\mathcal{C}, N, L, M$). For concreteness, if event E is the fault analysis scenario against a Digital Signature Scheme based on adaptive chosen messages of Fig. 2, then $\Pr(E) \leq$ negl($\mathcal{C}, N, L, M$) for the given circuit $\mathcal{C}$. As previously said, the function negl($\mathcal{C}, N, L, M$) depends on the concrete circuit layout. It is still an open question whether physical quantities can be formally tied to security notions in a realistic physical model for tampering.

4.1   Countermeasure Strategies

We consider generic passive and active physical defense strategies that result from physical means detailed in Section 3.2. Passive defense strategies aim at significantly reducing the success probability for fault injection (fault prevention). Active defense strategies require that $\mathcal{D}$ is capable to detect computational errors resulting from faults (error detection) or the presence of abnormal conditions that may lead to faults (fault detection). In any case, reliable defense strategies have to be part of the construction of $\mathcal{D}$. Combinations of these defense strategies are feasible, especially as most strategies have an impact on different parameters in (2). The decision whether or not the device shall enter a permanent non-responsive mode in case of error or fault detection depends on the concrete impact probability as well as the concrete security service. It is a matter of risk evaluation.

Table 2. Passive and Active Defense Strategies

Strategy	Impact on Parameter	Security Objective
Shrinking	dA, dz and N	fault prevention
Passive Encapsulation	z and $d\sigma(\boldsymbol{x}, E)$	fault prevention
Timing Modifications	t, dt and N	fault prevention
Error Detection Codes	L and N	error detection
Physical Duplication	L and N	error detection
Repeating Computations	M and N	error detection
Sensors	$\Delta A(z)$ and N	fault detection

Shrinking: Due to the shrinking process, integrated circuits become more and more compact. Shrinking decreases the target volume $dA \cdot dz$. Upcoming chip technology is based on 90 nm structures. For comparison, a focus of a laser beam on the chip surface of 1 μm was reported in [24] at an optical fault injection setup. Due to the limited spatial resolution, multiple faults at neighboring gates are much more likely to occur than single faults at the target resulting in an increase of N. Note that shrinking may enhance the sensitivity of the circuit so that less free carriers or currents are needed for fault injection.

Passive Encapsulation: Passive encapsulation aims that the interaction process is absorbed or reflected before its effects reach the target area, i.e., $F(x, E, t)$ should not reach the target area dV at depth z resulting in $p_{VT} = 0$ in (2). Such an encapsulation has to be constructed within the cryptographic boundary of the device to prevent it from the reach of $\mathcal{A}_{non-inv}$ and $\mathcal{A}_{semi-inv}$. One approach includes shields that are non-transparent in a broad light spectrum and prevent throughpassing of photons, i.e., aiming at high values of $d\sigma(x, E)$ within the shield. A simpler design aim is to place security critical parts in center of the chip to prevent both attacks from the front as well as from the back-end side of the chip. If considering different physical interaction processes $\mathcal{P}$, the range of $F(x, E, t)$ in semiconductor materials has to be evaluated, i.e., the average value of the depth to which a particle will penetrate in the course of slowing down to rest. This depth is measured along the initial direction of the particle. For high energy particles these data can be found at [21]. However, against invasive adversaries the effectiveness of passive encapsulation is quite limited.

Timing Modifications: This strategy can be useful if timing is crucial in a concrete fault analysis scenario. The objective is to randomly embed the relevant time interval dt within a larger time interval which leads to an enhancement of N. A possible realization includes delaying and interrupting the processing of $\mathcal{C}$, e.g., according to the value of a randomized internal counter. If the physical leakage of $\mathcal{C}$ can not be analyzed in real-time, an adversary is not able to adapt to the randomized timing. Instead, the source of randomness in the circuit may become an attractive target. Similarly, increasing the clock frequency of the circuits may help to increase N.

Error Detection Codes: Error detection codes of data items are well known for software implementations. For implementation in circuitry, [15] introduced parity based error detection at a substitution-permutation network based block cipher. In [20] error detection techniques based on multiple parity bits and nonlinear codes are evaluated. Among them, r-bit non-linear codes are the most promising, but at cost of an area overhead that is nearly comparable to duplication. As result, error detection codes lead to an enhancement of L which in turn typically increases N.

Physical Duplication: The objective is to duplicate critical target volumes of the circuit. In the context of asynchronous circuits, [10] has already proposed this idea to improve tamper resistance. These circuits make use of redundant data encoding, i.e., each bit is encoded onto two wires. Such dual-rail coding offers the opportunity to encode an alarm signal that can be used for error detection by the physical device. For memory cells, a 'dual flip-flop dual-rail' design is proposed. The main idea is that an error state on any gate input is always propagated to the gate output. In case of area duplication, the number of locations for fault injection is typically doubled, i.e., L is enhanced and precise control over the fault injection process is needed to prevent an error detection.

Repeating Computations: Repeating computations of the circuit and comparison of results is another strategy for error detection. However, this method is not reliable if a permanent fault is present in the circuit. In case of transient errors, repeating leads to an enhancement of M.

Sensors: Here, a network of short-distance sensors is spanned at critical parts of the circuit. The mean distance between sensors then gives an upper bound on the area $\Delta A(z)$ at which fault injection may not be detected by the sensors. It is aimed that an adversary has to precisely focus only on the target volume dV which establishes a hard problem for $\mathcal{A}_{non-inv}$ and $\mathcal{A}_{semi-inv}$. Alarm detection may be deployed at an active encapsulation within the cryptographic boundary of the device. Again, this encapsulation should be out of the reach of $\mathcal{A}_{non-inv}$ and $\mathcal{A}_{semi-inv}$. A different approach is given in reference [10]: the authors suggest to include small optical tamper sensors within each standard cell. These sensors consist of one or two transistors and enforce an error state if illuminated.

5   Conclusion

Implementation security is different from algorithmic security: for the assessment of implementation security, properties of the concrete layout and timing of the circuit are needed. In this contribution we initiate an approach towards the evaluation of physical security against tampering adversaries. We consider manipulating computations in circuitry and give a physical model on fault injection based on radiation and particle impact. We assume that fault injection can be both applied prior and during computations of a physical security service which is a realistic assumption that should be also included in provable security models. We hope that this framework is useful to both map concrete impact probabilities of a given circuit as well as to improve the circuits' layout.

References

1. ISO 13491-1:1998 Banking – Secure cryptographic devices (retail)– Part 1: Concepts, requirements and evaluation methods.
2. FIPS PUB 140-2, Security Requirements for Cryptographic Modules, 2001.
3. Ross Anderson and Markus Kuhn. Tamper Resistance — A Cautionary Note. In *The Second USENIX Workshop on Electronic Commerce Proocedings*, pages 1–11, 1996.
4. Christian Aumüller, Peter Bier, Wieland Fischer, Peter Hofreiter, and Jean-Pierre Seifert. Fault Attacks on RSA with CRT: Concrete Results and Practical Countermeasures. In Jr. et al. [14], pages 260–275.
5. Hagai Bar-El, Hamid Choukri, David Naccache, Michael Tunstall, and Claire Whelan. The Sorcerer's Apprenctice's Guide to Fault Attacks, available at http://eprint.iacr.org/2004/100. Technical report, 2004.
6. Eli Biham, Louis Granboulan, and Phong Q. Nguyen. Impossible Fault Analysis of RC4 and Differential Fault Analysis of RC4. In Henri Gilbert and Helena Handschuh, editors, *Fast Software Encryption: 12th International Workshop*, volume 3557 of *Lecture Notes in Computer Science*, pages 359–367. Springer, 2005.

7. Eli Biham and Adi Shamir. The Next Stage of Differential Fault Analysis: How to break completely unknown cryptosystems, available at http://jya.com/dfa.htm, 1996.
8. Eli Biham and Adi Shamir. Differential fault analysis of secret key cryptosystems. In Burton S. Kaliski Jr., editor, *CRYPTO*, volume 1294 of *Lecture Notes in Computer Science*, pages 513–525. Springer, 1997.
9. Dan Boneh, Richard A. DeMillo, and Richard J. Lipton. On the Importance of Checking Cryptographic Protocols for Faults (Extended Abstract). In Walter Fumy, editor, *Advances in Cryptology - EUROCRYPT '97*, volume 1233 of *Lecture Notes in Computer Science*, pages 37–51. Springer, 1997.
10. Jacques J. A. Fournier, Simon W. Moore, Huiyun Li, Robert D. Mullins, and George S. Taylor. Security evaluation of asynchronous circuits. In Walter et al. [27], pages 137–151.
11. Rosario Gennaro, Anna Lysyanskaya, Tal Malkin, Silvio Micali, and Tal Rabin. Algorithmic Tamper-Proof (ATP) Security: Theoretical Foundations for Security against Hardware Tampering. In Moni Naor, editor, *Theory of Cryptography*, volume 2951 of *Lecture Notes in Computer Science*, pages 258–277. Springer, 2004.
12. William N. Havener, Roberta J. Medlock, Lisa D. Mitchell, and Robert J. Walcott. Derived Test Requirements for FIPS PUB 140-1, Security Requirements for Cryptographic Modules, 1995.
13. Jonathan J. Hoch and Adi Shamir. Fault analysis of stream ciphers. In Marc Joye and Jean-Jacques Quisquater, editors, *Cryptographic Hardware and Embedded Systems - CHES 2004*, volume 3156 of *Lecture Notes in Computer Science*, pages 240–253. Springer, 2004.
14. Burton S. Kaliski Jr., Çetin Kaya Koç, and Christof Paar, editors. *Cryptographic Hardware and Embedded Systems - CHES 2002, 4th International Workshop, Redwood Shores, CA, USA, August 13-15, 2002, Revised Papers*, volume 2523 of *Lecture Notes in Computer Science*. Springer, 2003.
15. Ramesh Karri, Grigori Kuznetsov, and Michael Goessel. Parity-Based Concurrent Error Detection of Substitution-Permutation Network Block Ciphers. In Walter et al. [27], pages 113–124.
16. Oliver Kömmerling and Markus G. Kuhn. Design Principles for Tamper-Resistant Smartcard Processors. In *Proceedings of the USENIX Workshop on Smartcard Technology (Smartcard '99)*, pages 9–20, 1999.
17. Kerstin Lemke and Christof Paar. An Adversarial Model for Fault Analysis against Low-Cost Cryptographic Devices. In *Workshop on Fault Detection and Tolerance in Cryptography*, pages 82–94, 2005.
18. Regís Leveugle. Early Analysis of Fault Attack Effects for Cryptographic Hardware. In *Workshop on Fault Detection and Tolerance in Cryptography*, 2004.
19. P.-Y. Liardet and Y. Teglia. From Reliability to Safety. In *Workshop on Fault Detection and Tolerance in Cryptography*, 2004.
20. Tal G. Malkin, François-Xavier Standaert, and Moti Yung. A Comparative Cost/Security Analysis of Fault Attack Countermeasures. In *Workshop on Fault Detection and Tolerance in Cryptography*, pages 109–123, 2005.
21. National Institute of Standards and Technology (NIST). Physical Reference Data, available at http://physics.nist.gov/PhysRefData/contents.html.
22. Gilles Piret and Jean-Jacques Quisquater. A Differential Fault Attack Technique against SPN Structures, with Application to the AES and KHAZAD. In Walter et al. [27], pages 77–88.
23. David Samyde and Jean-Jacques Quisquater. Eddy Current for Magnetic Analysis with Active Sensor. In *Proceedings of ESmart 2002*, pages 185–194, 2002.

24. Sergei P. Skorobogatov and Ross J. Anderson. Optical Fault Induction Attacks. In Jr. et al. [14], pages 2–12.
25. Sergei S. Skorobogatov. Semi-invasive attacks — A new approach to hardware security analysis, available at http://www.cl.cam.ac.uk/techreports/ucam-cl-tr-630.pdf. Technical report, 2005.
26. F.-X. Standaert, L. Batina, E. de Mulder, K. Lemke, E. Oswald, and G. Piret. ECRYT D.VAM.4: Electromagnetic Analysis and Fault Attacks: State of the Art. Technical report, 2005.
27. Colin D. Walter, Çetin Kaya Koç, and Christof Paar, editors. *Cryptographic Hardware and Embedded Systems - CHES 2003, 5th International Workshop, Cologne, Germany, September 8-10, 2003, Proceedings*, volume 2779 of *Lecture Notes in Computer Science*. Springer, 2003.

Flexible Exponentiation with Resistance to Side Channel Attacks

Camille Vuillaume and Katsuyuki Okeya

Hitachi, Ltd., Systems Development Laboratory, Kawasaki, Japan
{camille, ka-okeya}@sdl.hitachi.co.jp

Abstract. We present a countermeasure for protecting modular exponentiations against side-channel attacks such as power, timing or cache
analysis. Our countermeasure is well-suited for tamper-resistant implementations of RSA or DSA, without significant penalty in terms of speed
compared to commonly implemented methods. Thanks to its high efficiency and flexibility, our method can be implemented on various platforms, from smartcards with low-end processors to high-performance
servers.

Keywords: RSA, side channel attacks, fractional width, simple power
analysis.

1 Introduction

With the rise of electronic communications, and in particular, electronic commerce, public-key cryptography has become an essential component in our daily
life. The de-facto standard for public-key encryption and digital signatures is
RSA, and with the development of miniaturization, RSA is now implemented
not only on high-performance servers, but also on various mobile devices such
as smartcards or mobile phones.

It is believed that with a bitlength of 1024 bits, RSA is secure for middle-term
applications, and with 2048 bits, for long-term applications. However, protecting against mathematical attacks is not sufficient in the real world. Indeed, it
has been shown that practical implementations of cryptosystems often suffer
from critical information leakage through side-channels: timings [6], power consumption [5] or cache usage [13], for instance. Such side-channel attacks are
no theoretical works that researchers secretly run in laboratories with expensive hardware, but practical threats to virtually any application where secrecy
matters.

On the one hand, there are numerous countermeasures for defeating side-
channel attacks on elliptic curve cryptosystems [4, 7, 9], but on the other hand,
there are few of them for RSA [15, 16]. At first sight, it seems that the keylength
of RSA is so long that even when side-channel information partially reveals the
secret, exhaustive searches often remain ineffective. However, when a sufficiently
large part of the secret key is known, RSA can be broken [3]. Thus, despite long
secret keys, RSA also needs a decent protection against side-channel attacks [13].

J. Zhou, M. Yung, and F. Bao (Eds.): ACNS 2006, LNCS 3989, pp. 268–283, 2006.

Unfortunately, many countermeasures that have been developed for elliptic curves cannot be transposed to the case of RSA: on elliptic curves, signed representations of the exponents are heavily used because they yield faster exponentiation algorithms when inversions are cheap. But unlike elliptic curves, RSA does not benefit from cheap inversions, and therefore, unsigned representations are the only option [16]. In other words, countermeasures which are efficient on elliptic curves are generally not practical at all in the case of RSA.

Our contribution is as follows: we show how to transform a countermeasure based on a signed representation [7] into a countermeasure based on an unsigned representation. Then, we improve the flexibility of our countermeasure with a fractional width technique [10]: with the improved method, the size of the precomputed table can be freely chosen. Our countermeasure is not only highly flexible, and therefore well-suited for a wide range of platforms, from constrained environments such as smartcards to high-performance servers, but in addition, can compete with the commonly implemented exponentiation techniques. In practical situations, our method is only about 5% slower than commonly used methods. And most importantly, our method thwarts several types of attacks, power analysis and cache attacks in particular. Finally, we refine attacks against fractional width techniques and introduce a new tool to evaluate the quality of our countermeasure in the sense of resistance to side channel attacks. We demonstrate that in the SPA model, our countermeasure can prevent information leakage.

2   Side Channel Attacks

Over the past few years, theoretical attacks against cryptosystems such as RSA or elliptic curves have shown little improvements. On the other hand, attacks based on physical information leakage, also known as side channel attacks, have revolutionized the definition of tamper-resistance.

2.1   Methodology of Side Channel Attacks

Side channel attacks take advantage of the correlation between secret values and physical emanations such as timings [6], power consumption [5] or even cache usage [13].

Power Analysis. On smartcards, which do not have any embedded power supply, the most powerful approach is probably to measure the power consumption of the device supplied from the outside [5]. One can classify power analysis attacks into two main classes: simple power analysis (SPA) and differential power analysis (DPA). The approach of SPA is to identify regions of a power trace which directly depend on the secret key. It is common for cryptographic algorithms to have conditional branches depending on the value of some secret bit, and typically, those branches are targets of choice for SPA. For example, in the frame of an RSA exponentiation computed with the binary method, the binary representation of the (secret) exponent is scanned; for the bit-value zero, a square is computed, whereas a square and a multiplication are calculated when the bit-value is one. Thus, it is easy to see that the knowledge of the operation sequence (square or square-multiplication) is equivalent to the knowledge of the secret exponent. In other words, by distinguishing squares from multiplications in power traces, one can reveal the secret exponent. A similar problem also exists in the case of elliptic curves, where the ability of distinguishing the two types of elliptic operations, namely point doublings and point additions, also leads to the secret scalar. DPA is more sophisticated: the idea is to guess the value of the secret bit-by-bit, and try to confirm or infirm the guess for each bit thanks to statistical analysis of several power traces.

Cache Attacks. Recently, cache attacks on public key cryptosystems have been investigated, and proof-of-concept attacks based on cache analysis confirmed that the cache should not be neglected as source of information leakage [13]. On computers, power analysis is extremely invasive, and although possible from a theoretical point of view, difficult to set up in practice. On the contrary, cache attacks are practical, because cryptographic algorithms leave characteristic footprints in the cache memory and other processes can spy on the cache. Using such techniques, it has been shown that on computers equipped with the hyperthreading technology, using one single RSA exponentiation, cache observation reveals the secret key [13].

2.2 Countermeasures

Countermeasures against side-channel attacks have been proposed on various cryptosystems and with various strategies. In particular, alternative representations of the secret are often used as countermeasures, on elliptic curves and on RSA.

Strategies and Requirements. It is not that difficult to protect cryptosystems against DPA. By definition, DPA requires that the same secret is used to perform several cryptographic operations with each time a different input value: decrypting or signing several messages, for instance. Signature schemes such as DSA and EC-DSA use a new random ephemeral as exponent for each new signature, and as a consequence, are naturally immune to DPA. In the case of RSA, a well-known technique to defeat DPA is to blind the secret exponent, that is, to add a random multiple of the group order to the secret. Because $c^{d+r\phi(n)} = c^d \bmod n$, blinding does not change the result of the exponentiation, but in the same time, changes the exponent itself. As a consequence, the side-channel information that arises from multiple power traces is not correlated. On the contrary, despite the relative simplicity of the idea behind SPA, it is not easy to design secure and efficient SPA countermeasures. However, SPA-resistance is always necessary, and is a prerequisite to DPA resistance. For instance, if only one random ephemeral exponent of DSA or EC-DSA is revealed, the secret key of the signature scheme can be easily inferred. Similarly, from the point of view of the attacker, a blinded RSA exponent $d + r\phi(n)$ is as good as the secret itself.

In the following, we explain how the *representation* of the secret exponent can be an effective countermeasure against side channel attacks, and especially against SPA. We call representation a function $\mathcal{R} : D^k \rightarrow \{0, 1, ..., 2^\mathcal{L} - 1\}$, where D is the *digit set* of the representation. For instance, the binary representation $\mathcal{R}_b(b_{\mathcal{L}-1} \ldots b_0) \in \{0,1\}^\mathcal{L} \mapsto \sum_{i=0}^{n-1} b_i 2^i \in \{0, 1, \ldots, 2^\mathcal{L} - 1\}$ utilizes base-2 digits (bits) to represent integers. Rather than $\{0, 1\}$, larger digit sets are sometimes preferred: in that case, pre-computations allow a faster execution of the cryptographic primitive. Finally, signed representations such as $\{0, \pm 1\}$ are advantageous when the computation of inverses is easy. In particular, this is attractive on elliptic curves where $-P$ can be computed from P for almost free. But the case of RSA is different: inversions are very expensive, and signed representations do not yield any interest in practice for RSA. Some representations are also valuable countermeasures against side channel attacks. Indeed, by changing the *representation* of the secret without changing its value, one can gain control on the operation sequence, and ultimately, on side-channel information leakage.

Möller's Countermeasure on Elliptic Curves. On elliptic curve cryptosystems, it is common to use representations with a large digit set and to pre-compute some small multiples of the base point in order to speed up the scalar multiplication. In particular, thanks to window methods with digit set $\{0, 1, 2, \ldots, 2^w - 1\}$, one can reduce the computational cost of the scalar multiplication given that small multiples of the base point P are pre-computed: $2P, 3P, \ldots, (2^w - 1)P$. Although standard window methods aim at greater efficiency only, they can also be enhanced to SPA-resistant scalar multiplication schemes, where the secret is recoded with a fixed pattern, using a signed representation with digit set $\{-2^w, 1, 2, \ldots 2^w - 1\}$, where 0 is absent [7]. More precisely, an additional conversion step is applied in each window in order to remove zero digits:

1. replace the digit 0 with -2^w, and add a carry of $+1$ to the next window when scanning the scalar from right to left,
2. replace the digit 2^w with -2^w, and add a carry of $+2$ to the next window,
3. replace the digit $2^w + 1$ with 1 and add a carry of $+1$ to the next window,
4. otherwise leave the digit as it is.

Thanks to this conversion technique, the scalar can be recoded with a fixed pattern: nonzero digits are always followed by exactly $w - 1$ zero digits. The advantage of this approach is that the operation pattern becomes regular as well: point additions are always followed by exactly w point doublings, which makes SPA impractical. Because the point $-2^w P$ must be readily available, the scheme requires that computing inversions in the group (in that case, elliptic point negative) is easy. Unfortunately, this is not the case for RSA.

Countermeasures on RSA. An obvious way to thwart SPA on RSA and other cryptosystems is to insert dummy operations in such a way that the operation sequence does not depend on the secret anymore. But this technique suffers from severe drawbacks: not only the computational cost is considerably increased, but the use of dummy operations is generally not recommended due to safe-error attacks, which can take advantage of such dummy operations [17]. Side-channel atomicity is a more sophisticated countermeasure, where side-channel information consists of the repetition of an atomic side-channel block [2]. However, on RSA, side-channel atomicity requires multiplications and squares to be indistinguishable. This is often not the case on high-speed implementations of RSA in software, where squares are implemented with a distinct procedure. Furthermore, side-channel atomicity does not address cache attacks.

In addition to that, there are some countermeasures for RSA which are based on randomized representations of the secret [15, 16]; their aim is to protect against SPA and in the same time to improve resistance to differential attacks. The principle of the MIST exponentiation algorithm [15] is to randomly change the basis (in other words, the digit set D) during the recoding. Rather than a pre-computed table, MIST utilizes efficient addition chains and is faster than the binary method. Following a different approach, Yen et al. utilize a large pre-computed table and randomize the representation of the secret [16]. Their exponentiation scheme is computed from left to right, without need for any inversion. With 14 pre-computed values, the efficiency of the countermeasure is about the same as the window method with $w = 2$. However, both of these methods suffer from a considerable overhead compared to high-speed techniques. For instance, compared to the sliding window method with $w = 5$, which is used in OpenSSL, these countermeasures yield more than 30% performance drop.

3   SPA-Resistant Unsigned Recoding Techniques

On elliptic curves, numerous recoding techniques have been proposed for means of defeating side-channel attacks. These representations are often based on signed digit sets. Unfortunately, this approach is not valid for RSA where computing inverses is too costly; hence our motivation to construct secure unsigned representations.

3.1   SPA-Resistant Unsigned Integral Width

Our approach is to extend Möller's recoding to the unsigned case. To obtain the unsigned digit set $\{1, 2, \ldots, 2^w\}$, the key idea of our method is to use *negative* carries rather than positive carries:

1. replace the digit 0 with 2^w, and add a carry of -1 to the next window when scanning the scalar from right to left,
2. replace the digit -1 with $2^w - 1$, and add a carry of -1 to the next window,
3. otherwise leave the digit as it is.

On the one hand, it is easy to see that Möller's algorithm terminates, and that if the original bitlength of the scalar was $\mathcal{L}$, the recoded scalar has at most

$\mathcal{L} + 1$ digits. On the other hand, in the case of the above rules for generating an unsigned representation with a fixed pattern, the situation is different: there is no guarantee that the algorithm will terminate because a carry can propagate indefinitely. To ensure a correct termination, we treat the case of the most significant bit separately: if a carry remains at the end of the recoding, we use the most significant bit to neutralize it, and reduce the length of the exponent. If instead of d, a blinded exponent $d + r\phi(n)$ with random r is used as DPA countermeasure, this approach is safe [1]. But if not, there is a direct information leakage, because the length of the recoded exponent depends on the value of some secret bits. To remove this leakage, we extend the bitlength of the exponent by 2, and fix the value of the 2 most significant bits $d_{\mathcal{L}+1} = 1$ and $d_{\mathcal{L}} = 0$. This is always possible because $c^{d+\phi(n)} = c^d \bmod n$: in other words, adding $\phi(n)$ to the exponent does not change the value of the exponentiation modulo n. By repeatedly adding $\phi(n)$, one can always set $d_{\mathcal{L}+1}$ to 1 and $d_{\mathcal{L}}$ to 0 (because $d < \phi(n) < n < 2^{\mathcal{L}}$). If the value of d and n are fixed (which is typically the case when d is a secret key), this calculation can be performed once for all at the key generation stage. Now, since $d_{\mathcal{L}} = 0$, independently from the value of the previous bits, the corresponding recoded digit is $u_{\mathcal{L}} \neq 0$ and a carry γ is generated. Finally, $u_{\mathcal{L}+1} = d_{\mathcal{L}+1} - 1 = 0$, therefore the length of the recoded expansion is *always* reduced by one.

Algorithm 1. Conversion to unsigned integral SPA-resistant representation

---

INPUT: $\mathcal{L} + 2$-bit exponent $d = (10d_{\mathcal{L}-1} \ldots d_0)_2$, width w;
OUTPUT: Recoded exponent $(u_{\mathcal{L}} \ldots u_0)$;

---

1. $i \leftarrow 0$; $\gamma \leftarrow 0$;
2. **while** $i \leq \mathcal{L} - w$ **do**
   (a) $u_i \leftarrow (d_{i+w-1} \ldots d_i)_2 - \gamma$;
   (b) **if** $u_i \leq 0$ **then** $u_i \leftarrow u_i + 2^w$; $\gamma \leftarrow 1$; **else** $\gamma \leftarrow 0$;
   (c) $u_{i+1} \leftarrow 0, \ldots, u_{i+w-1} \leftarrow 0$; $i \leftarrow i + w$;
3. **if** $i < \mathcal{L}$ **then**
   (a) $u_i \leftarrow (d_{\mathcal{L}-1} \ldots d_i)_2 - \gamma$;
   (b) **if** $u_i \leq 0$ **then** $u_i \leftarrow u_i + 2^{\mathcal{L}-i}$; $\gamma \leftarrow 1$; **else** $\gamma \leftarrow 0$;
   (c) $u_{i+1} \leftarrow 0, \ldots, u_{\mathcal{L}-1} \leftarrow 0$;
4. $u_{\mathcal{L}} \leftarrow 2 - \gamma$; **return** $(u_{\mathcal{L}} \ldots u_0)$;

Exponentiation With Integral Width Recoding. Algorithm 2 computes g^d with an unsigned SPA-resistant recoding of d. In fact, during the exponentiation, the operation pattern is fixed: w squares and 1 multiplication. Note that precomputations take advantage of faster squares.

---

[1] Blinding alone is not sufficient, because it protects only against DPA, not SPA, and should be used with an additional SPA countermeasure such as our recoding.

Algorithm 2. Integral width pre-computations and exponentiation

---

INPUT: $\mathcal{L} + 2$-bit exponent $d = (10d_{\mathcal{L}-1} \ldots d_0)_2$, width w, basis g;
OUTPUT: $c = g^d$;

---

1. $g[1] \leftarrow g$;
2. **for** i **from** 2 **to** 2^w **step** 2 **do** $g[i] \leftarrow g[i/2]^2$; $g[i+1] \leftarrow g[i] * g$;
3. recode d with Algorithm 1; $i \leftarrow \mathcal{L} - 1$; $c \leftarrow g[u_{\mathcal{L}}]$;
4. **while** $i \geq 0$ **do**
    (a) $c \leftarrow c^2$;
    (b) **if** $u_i > 0$ **then** $c \leftarrow c * g[u_i]$;
    (c) $i \leftarrow i - 1$;
5. **return** c;

3.2   SPA-Resistant Unsigned Fractional Width

A disadvantage of the previous method, and more generally, of table-based exponentiations, is that there are only limited choices for the table size. Since the table size and the cost of pre-computations grow exponentially with the width w, number of bits which are scanned simultaneously, large values of w become quickly impractical. However, it would be useful to be able to select *any* table size. Fractional width recodings make this possible, thanks to a degenerated width-w pre-computed table where some values are missing [8]. In addition, SPA-resistant fractional width methods exist in the case of elliptic curves, where it is advantageous to use signed representations [10]. We show that our unsigned (integral width) SPA-resistant recoding technique (Algorithm 1) can also be enhanced to an unsigned fractional width recoding.

Unsigned Fractional Width Recoding. The idea is the same as in the original signed SPA-resistant fractional width recoding: compute simultaneously the digits x and y, where x correspond to the width w and y to the width $w - 1$, and choose x or y depending on some criteria. The knowledge of the choice of x or y must not help attackers to gather information about the secret. To fulfill this requirement, the set of pre-computed values is randomized. More precisely, when the pre-computed table has k entries, define $w = \lceil \log_2(k) \rceil$. Then, the 2^{w-1} elements $\{c, c^2, \ldots, c^{2^{w-1}}\}$ are always pre-computed, but $k - 2^{w-1}$ additional pre-computed elements are randomly chosen in the set $\{c^{2^{w-1}+1}, c^{2^{w-1}+1}, \ldots, c^{2^w}\}$. In the following, we call B the set of the exponents of the chosen pre-computed elements.

The core idea in Algorithm 3 is that the choice of recoding a sequence of bits with the width w or $w - 1$ looks random to the attacker. The principle of the recoding is the same as in the signed fractional width algorithm [10]. Recall that B is the set of exponents of the pre-computed values, define the width $w = \lceil \log_2(k) \rceil$ and the probability $p = k/2^{w-1} - 1$. Then, for x computed with width w and y with width $w - 1$, we apply the following rules:

Algorithm 3. Conversion to unsigned fractional SPA-resistant representation

---

INPUT: $\mathcal{L} + 2$-bit exponent $d = (10d_{\mathcal{L}-1} \ldots d_0)_2$, table size k, index set B;
OUTPUT: Recoded exponent $(u_{\mathcal{L}} \ldots u_0)$;

---

1. $i \leftarrow 0$; $\gamma \leftarrow 0$; $w \leftarrow \lceil \log_2(k) \rceil$;
2. **while** $i \leq \mathcal{L} - w$ **do**
   (a) $x \leftarrow (d_{i+w-1} \ldots d_i)_2 - \gamma$;
   (b) $y \leftarrow (d_{i+w-2} \ldots d_i)_2 - \gamma$;
   (c) **if** $x \leq 0$ **then** $x \leftarrow x + 2^w$; $\gamma_x \leftarrow 1$; **else** $\gamma_x \leftarrow 0$;
   (d) **if** $y \leq 0$ **then** $y \leftarrow y + 2^{w-1}$; $\gamma_y \leftarrow 1$; **else** $\gamma_y \leftarrow 0$;
   (e) **if** $x \leq 2^{w-1}$ **then**
       i. $rnd \leftarrow$ generate $w - 1$ random bits;
       ii. **if** $rnd < k - 2^{w-1}$ **then** $u_i \leftarrow x$; $\gamma \leftarrow \gamma_x$; $r \leftarrow w$;
       iii. **else** $u_i \leftarrow y$; $\gamma \leftarrow \gamma_y$; $r \leftarrow w - 1$;
   (f) **else if** $x \in B$ **then** $u_i \leftarrow x$; $\gamma \leftarrow \gamma_x$; $r \leftarrow w$;
   (g) **else** $u_i \leftarrow y$; $\gamma \leftarrow \gamma_y$; $r \leftarrow w - 1$;
   (h) $u_{i+1} \leftarrow 0, \ldots, u_{i+r-1} \leftarrow 0$; $i \leftarrow i + r$;
3. **if** $i < \mathcal{L}$ **then**
   (a) $u_i \leftarrow (d_{\mathcal{L}-1} \ldots d_i)_2 - \gamma$;
   (b) **if** $u_i \leq 0$ **then** $u_i \leftarrow u_i + 2^{\mathcal{L}-i}$; $\gamma \leftarrow 1$; **else** $\gamma \leftarrow 0$;
   (c) $u_{i+1} \leftarrow 0, \ldots, u_{\mathcal{L}-1} \leftarrow 0$;
4. $u_{\mathcal{L}} \leftarrow 2 - \gamma$; **return** $(u_{\mathcal{L}} \ldots u_0)$;

---

1. if $x \leq 2^{w-1}$ then choose x with probability p or y with probability $1 - p$,
2. else if $x \in B$ (in other words, g^x is pre-computed), choose x (this occurs with probability p),
3. else choose y (in that case, g^x is not pre-computed, this happens with probability $1 - p$).

Therefore, for randomly chosen exponents, the width w is chosen with probability p and $w - 1$ with probability $1 - p$. Additionally, since the set B is randomized for each new recoding, the two patterns can actually appear for the same sequence of bits.

Exponentiation With Fractional Width Recoding. The technique for the exponentiation with a fractional SPA-resistant width is almost the same as in the integral case, with the exception of the pre-computation step. Indeed, since the pre-computed table is de-generated, the values in the upper half part of the table are computed with a special procedure. Since $g^i = g^{i-2^{w-1}} * g^{2^{w-1}}$, the pre-computations use the value $g^{2^{w-1}}$ which is already available in order to compute the upper half part of the table. Note that in Algorithm 4, for the sake of simplicity, the pre-computed table is indexed with the exponent of the pre-computed values. In reality, a look-up table should be used in order to save memory: such table could be indexed with the exponents of pre-computed values, and would additionally store a pointer to the actual location of the pre-computed value.

Algorithm 4. Fractional width pre-computations and exponentiation

---

INPUT: $\mathcal{L} + 2$-bit exponent $d = (10d_{\mathcal{L}-1} \ldots d_0)_2$, table length k, basis g;
OUTPUT: $c = g^d$;

---

1. $g[1] \leftarrow g$;
2. **for** i from 2 to 2^{w-1} step 2 **do** $g[i] \leftarrow g[i/2]^2$; $g[i+1] \leftarrow g[i] * g$;
3. **for all** $i > 2^{w-1}, i \in B$ **do** $g[i] \leftarrow g[i - 2^{w-1}] * g[2^{w-1}]$;
4. recode d with Algorithm 3; $i \leftarrow \mathcal{L} - 1$; $c \leftarrow g[u_{\mathcal{L}}]$;
5. **while** $i \geq 0$ **do**
    (a) $c \leftarrow c^2$;
    (b) **if** $u_i > 0$ **then** $c \leftarrow c * g[u_i]$;
    (c) $i \leftarrow i - 1$;
6. **return** c;

3.3 Efficiency of the Fractional Width Exponentiation

Next, we describe the advantages of our technique in terms of speed and memory, and compare its performances with that of commonly used exponentiation methods. For a table size k and a bitlength n, k elements of n bits (including the basis of the exponentiation g are pre-computed and stored in RAM. In contrary to other methods, which only allows $1, 2, 4, \ldots, 2^w, \ldots$ as table size, the fractional window method is much more flexible: any table size can be chosen. This is not only an advantage to fully occupy the available memory on constrained environments, but also means that the optimal table size k can be chosen on large-memory profiles: in that case, the fractional width method yields an exponentiation method which is faster than integral width techniques.

Efficiency. The cost of the pre-computations of the unsigned SPA-resistant technique is as follows: for the 2^{w-1} pre-computed values in the lower half table, 2^{w-2} squares and $2^{w-2} - 1$ multiplications, and for the upper half table, $k - 2^{w-1}$ multiplications. Recall that the upper width w is defined as $w = \lceil \log_2(k) \rceil$, and that probability of choosing the width w rather than $w - 1$ is $p = \frac{k}{2^{w-1}} - 1$. Multiplications occur only when there is a nonzero digit in the representation, therefore, for an n-bit exponent, there are on average $n/(w - 1 + p)$ multiplications. Then, the memory and average computational cost of exponentiations based on the unsigned fractional representations are as follows:

$$\begin{cases} \mathcal{M}_F = k \cdot \mathcal{L} \text{ bits} \\ \mathcal{C}_F = \left(2^{w-2} + \mathcal{L}\right) \cdot S + \left(k - 2^{w-2} - 1 + \frac{\mathcal{L}}{w-1+p}\right) \cdot M, \end{cases} \quad (1)$$

where S and M stand for the cost of squares and multiplications, respectively, $w = \lceil \log_2(k) \rceil$ and $p = \frac{k}{2^{w-1}} - 1$.

Comparison with the Sliding Window. The sliding window method is often utilized for practical implementations of exponentiations; for instance, OpenSSL

Table 1. Memory and cost of several exponentiation methods

512-bit exponentiation	Memory	Speed
Binary method	0 bytes	2.563 ms
Sliding window, $w = 5$	1,024 bytes	2.026 ms
Our technique, $k = 16$	1,024 bytes	2.173 ms
Our technique, $k = 33$	2,112 bytes	2.137 ms
1024-bit exponentiation	Memory	Speed
Binary method	0 bytes	15.05 ms
Sliding window, $w = 6$	4,096 bytes	11.49 ms
Our technique, $k = 32$	4,096 bytes	12.09 ms
Our technique, $k = 53$	6,784 bytes	12.05 ms

uses the sliding window with 16 pre-computed values $\{g, g^3, g^5, \ldots, g^{31}\}$ [12]. The cost of pre-computations for the sliding window method with width w, that is, 2^{w-1} pre-computed values, is one square and $2^{w-1} - 1$ multiplications. The idea of the sliding window is to consider odd pre-computed values only, reducing the size of the table and the number of multiplications.

$$\begin{cases} \mathcal{M}_{SW} = 2^{w-1} \cdot \mathcal{L} \text{ bits} \\ \mathcal{C}_{SW} = (\mathcal{L} + 1) \cdot S + \left(2^{w-1} - 1 + \frac{\mathcal{L}}{w+1}\right) \cdot M, \end{cases} \tag{2}$$

For the same memory, it is clear that the sliding window is faster than the SPA-resistant fractional window. However, thanks to its higher flexibility, the fractional window has a "better" optimal table size k. We implemented both techniques with the NTL library [14] and compared the algorithms running with their optimal parameters on our platform; Table 1 summarizes our implementation results. It comes out that, although the fractional width is slightly slower than the sliding window, the performance drop is very small in practice: only 5% for 512-bit and 1024-bit exponentiations and when the algorithms run in their optimal settings. For the same memory consumption, our method is 7% slower than the sliding window 512-bit exponentiation, and 5% than the 1024-bit exponentiation.

4   Security Analysis of the Unsigned Fractional Width

We now analyze the security of the unsigned SPA-resistant fractional width technique in the sense of SPA (and related attacks). We particularly study the distributions of digits in the representation, and introduce a tool to measure the quality of the countermeasure.

4.1   Non-uniform Digit Distribution

It has been shown that the signed fractional width recoding leaks some information about the secret [11]. The reason for this (relatively small) information leakage is the *degenerated* width w pre-computed table: the fact that some pre-computed values are missing in the table can be used to speed up attacks. Obviously, since it uses exactly the same principle for its recoding (but with a different digit set), the unsigned fractional width algorithm (Algorithm 3) can be targeted by this kind of attack as well. In the following, we refine the technique described in [11] by considering the influence of the degenerated table not only on blocks of bits recoded with the width w but also $w - 1$.

Non-uniformity when w is selected. The first point is that when the width w is selected rather than $w-1$, some digits do not appear in the recoding [11]. Indeed, to construct a length-k pre-computed table, one takes a length-2^w table and remove some values at random from its upper half part. Therefore, the exponents of the removed pre-computed values are absent from the representation. In other words, each time the width w is selected, there are only k possible digits instead of 2^w.

For instance, consider $k = 3$; from the length-4 table $\{g^1, g^2, g^3, g^4\}$, one value is chosen among g^3 and g^4, and removed from the table. In our example, we remove g^3. Then, our representation admits the following digit set: $B = \{1, 2, 4\}$.

Non-uniformity when $w-1$ is selected. The second point is that the distribution of digits recoded with the width $w - 1$ is not uniform. This problems occurs because when a missing digit is scanned in the secret (case where $x > 2^{w-1}$ and $x \notin B$), the width $w - 1$ is selected. But this event occurs only for some digits x, and as a consequence there are also constraints on the corresponding digits y. More precisely, $x = y + 2^{w-1} d_{i+w-1}$, and for a given value of $x \notin B$ there is only one possible value for y. Since there are only $2^w - k$ for $x \notin B$, there are also $2^w - k$ possible values for y (instead of 2^{w-1}). But when $x \leq 2^{w-1}$ and the width $w - 1$ is (randomly) chosen, the distributions of digits is uniform, therefore the case where $x > 2^{w-1}$ and $x \notin B$ introduces non-uniformity in the distribution of digits recoded with the width $w - 1$.

Assume for instance a table size $k = 5$ and digit set $B = \{1, 2, 3, 4, 5\}$. Suppose that during the recoding, $x = 6$ is computed. Now, there are two possibilities: either $(d_{i+2} d_{i+1} d_i)_2 = 6$ and the carry is zero ($\gamma = 0$), or $(d_{i+2} d_{i+1} d_i)_2 = 7$ and the carry is not zero ($\gamma = 1$). In both case, $(d_{i+1} d_i)_2 - \gamma = y = 2$. But when $x \leq 4$ and $w - 1 = 2$ is (randomly) selected, the distribution of the four digits $\{1, 2, 3, 4\}$ is uniform. Consequently, the digit 2 has a higher probability than 1, 3 and 4 when the width $w-1 = 2$ is selected. Note that although we concentrate on the case of the unsigned SPA-resistant fractional window in this paper, the signed technique shares similar properties.

4.2   Side-Channel Information and Entropy

Although the non-uniformity of the digit distribution is intuitively a problem, even when the bias is known, it is difficult to evaluate how serious the threat is. To explicitly evaluate SPA-resistance of the fractional width techniques, the calculation of the entropy of such representations is helpful.

Consider the following challenge: finding the secret integer $d \in \{0, 1, \ldots 2^{\mathcal{L}} - 1\}$. When performing side-channel analysis, attackers might be able to reveal a bias in the distribution of the candidates in $\{0, 1, \ldots 2^{\mathcal{L}} - 1\}$. The knowledge of this bias can help them find the secret integer by trying out the most probable candidates first.

Definition 1 (Side-Channel Information Entropy). *Let p be a probability function $p : \{0, 1, \ldots, 2^{\mathcal{L}} - 1\} \rightarrow 0..1$ with $\sum_{\delta \in \{0,1,\ldots,2^{\mathcal{L}}-1\}} p(\delta) = 1$, representing a bias in the seach space $\{0, 1, \ldots, 2^{\mathcal{L}} - 1\}$ obtained by side-channel analysis. We call side-channel information entropy the term:*

$$S = - \sum_{\delta \in \{0,1,\ldots,2^{\mathcal{L}}-1\}, p(\delta) \neq 0} p(\delta) \log_2(p(\delta)). \tag{3}$$

Assume for example that an attacker tries to find a secret $d \in \{0, 1, 2, 3\}$. Without the help of side-channel analysis, all candidates in the search space are equiprobable: $p(0) = p(1) = p(2) = p(3) = 1/4$ and the entropy is $S = 2$ bits. But imagine now that the attacker identified a feature in side-channel information which is more likely to occur for $\delta = 3$ than for the other candidates. For instance, $p(3) = 1/2$, and $p(0) = p(1) = p(2) = 1/6$. In that case, the entropy is reduced to $S = 1.79$ bits.

More generally, when all values for d are equiprobable even when SPA information is available, the entropy reaches its maxima, namely $S = \mathcal{L}$ bits. In that case, the representation is a perfect SPA countermeasure. When the values are not uniformly distributed (some values are forbidden or simply less probable), $S < \mathcal{L}$ bits. One interpretation of the entropy is the number of bits that remain secure (unknown to the attacker) despite side-channel information leakage. Note that the entropy does not necessarily represent the running time of the fastest attacks; in particular, on RSA, factoring the modulus is much faster than running an exhaustive search, even when the search space has been reduced by SPA. However, if too many bits of the secret key are revealed, factoring becomes easy [3]. But if the entropy is large enough so that there exist no practical attack on S bits, the countermeasure is secure against SPA. Thus, the entropy term S represents the quality of an SPA countermeasure.

Note that in the case of fractional window methods, the probabilistic recoding process is divided into two groups of events. First, the selection of the pre-computed table; in this case, we assume that the Ω_B possible choices for the pre-computed table are *equiprobable* and *indistinguishable* by SPA. And second, the recoding process itself, where some choices between the widths w and $w - 1$ are random. We call S_w and S_{w-1} the entropy of w-blocks (that is, a block of bits recoded with width w) and $w - 1$-blocks. Then, we abuse notations and call "entropy of the fractional width recoding" the term $S = \log_2 |\Omega_B| + \mathcal{L}_w S_w + \mathcal{L}_{w-1} S_{w-1}$, where $\mathcal{L}_w$ and $\mathcal{L}_{w-1}$ are the number of w-blocks and $w - 1$-blocks. In other words, we define the entropy of the fractional width recoding as the sum of the entropy of the pre-computed table and the entropy of each block. For an $\mathcal{L}$-bit secret key recoded with our fractional width method, the average entropy $\overline{S_F}$ and the worst entropy $\tilde{S_F}$ are:

$$\begin{cases} \overline{S_F} = \log_2 |\Omega_B| + \frac{\mathcal{L}}{w-1+p}\left(pS_w + (1-p)S_{w-1}\right) \\ \tilde{S_F} = \log_2 |\Omega_B| + \min\left(\frac{\mathcal{L}}{w}S_w, \frac{\mathcal{L}}{w-1}S_{w-1}\right) \end{cases} \tag{4}$$

Entropy of the pre-computed table. We first evaluate the contribution of the randomized pre-computed table to the entropy of the fractional width method. There are $k - 2^{w-1}$ exponents randomly chosen in the set of 2^{w-1} elements $\{2^{w-1} + 1, 2^{w-1} + 2, \ldots, 2^w\}$. Therefore, the entropy of the pre-computed table is:

$$\log_2 |\Omega_B| = \sum_{i=k-2^{w-1}}^{2^{w-1}} \log_2 i - \sum_{i=1}^{2^w-k} \log_2 i. \tag{5}$$

Entropy of a w-block. Then, we study the entropy of digits recoded with the width w. We consider the digits from the upper half table $x > 2^{w-1}$ first. If $x > 2^{w-1}$ (probability 1/2), since w has been chosen, $x \in B$: there are only $k - 2^{w-1}$ digits in the upper half table. Thus, when w is selected, the probability of a digit from the upper half table is $\frac{1}{2(k-2^{w-1})}$. Next, we consider digits from the lower half table ($x \leq 2^{w-1}$). When $x \leq 2^{w-1}$ (probability 1/2), since the lower half of the table is full, there are 2^{w-1} possible digits. Therefore, in the lower half table, the digits have a probability of $\frac{1}{2*2^{w-1}}$. Clearly, digits in the upper half table have a greater probability than digits in the lower half table. This difference is the origin of entropy loss when w is selected. More precisely, the entropy of a block of width w is:

$$S_w = \frac{w+1}{2} + \frac{1}{2}\log_2\left(k - 2^{w-1}\right) \tag{6}$$

Note that in the case of a perfect countermeasure, we have $S_w = w$ bits.

Entropy of a w − 1-block. The case of the width $w-1$ is slightly different. When $x \leq 2^{w-1}$ (probability 1/2), the choice among the 2^{w-1} digits is uniform. But when $x > 2^{w-1}$ (probability 1/2), among the 2^{w-1} possible digits, only $2^w - k$ can be selected (because $x \notin B$). Therefore, $k - 2^{w-1}$ digits have a probability of appearance of $\frac{1}{2}\frac{1}{2^{w-1}}$, whereas $2^w - k$ digits have a probability of appearance of $\frac{1}{2}(\frac{1}{2^{w-1}} + \frac{1}{2^w-k})$. As a consequence, the entropy of a block of width $w-1$ is:

$$S_{w-1} = \frac{k-2^{w-1}}{2^w}w - \left(\frac{2^w-k}{2^w} + \frac{1}{2}\right)\log_2\left(\frac{1}{2^w} + \frac{1}{2^{w+1}-2k}\right) \tag{7}$$

Again, a perfect countermeasure would have $S_{w-1} = w - 1$ bits.

4.3   Consequences on Security

Simple Power Analysis. Despite the entropy loss of the unsigned fractional window method, we claim that the representation is still a good SPA countermeasure. Indeed, one can interpret entropy as the equivalent bitlength of the secret when the SPA information can be fully utilized. Therefore, in practice, an SPA countermeasure is at least as strong as its SPA information entropy. As a consequence, if the worst-case entropy is large enough, we know for sure that the

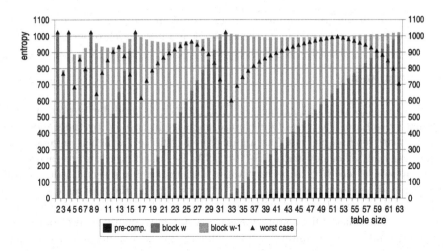

Fig. 1. Average and worst entropy, 1024-bit fractional width method

secret will be safe in any case. More precisely, if the table length k is carefully chosen, the entropy granted by the unsigned fractional width method is sufficient to thwart all known attacks against partially-compromised RSA secret keys. In particular, we remark that in Fig. 1, for from $k = 37$ to $k = 61$, the worst-case entropy is greater than 800 bits. Additionally, there is currently no attack on RSA or prime field cryptosystems which can take advantage of the bias of the fractional width technique: typically, to be effective, such attacks require the knowledge of the upper or lower bits, or consecutive bits. Thus, we argue that in practice, the security level of the unsigned fractional width technique is even higher than its SPA entropy.

Unfortunately, this is not the case for other exponentiation methods. The binary exponentiation has an entropy of 0 bits, because distinguishing squares from multiplications allows to fully revealing the secret key. In the case of the sliding window method, it is possible to distinguish blocks of consecutive zeros, where no multiplication occurs. Thus, the average entropy of the sliding window representation is $S_{SW} = \mathcal{L}/2$ bits. And in the worst case, the entropy can go as low as 0 bits. Even if the latter event is unlikely, situations where more than half of the bits are revealed can occur with a relatively high probability.

Cache Attacks. Cache analysis allows to distinguish not only different types of operations (such as squares and multiplications), but also reveals information about their operands (in particular, which pre-computed value is accessed by multiplications). On the one hand, standard SPA countermeasures have no effect against the latter type of leakage. On the other hand, thanks to its randomized pre-computed table, our countermeasure makes cache attacks less practical. For instance, with $k = 53$, there are more than 2^{26} possible pre-computed tables. And on the top of that, when considering practical cache attacks, one has to take other sources of noise into account: cache misses due to other non-cryptographic processes, multiple pre-computed values stored in the same cache line, same pre-computed value stored in consecutive cache lines among others.

5 Conclusion

We presented a new countermeasure for protecting modular exponentiations against side-channel attacks. Our countermeasure is inspired by the signed fractional width technique, but has an unsigned digit set, which is necessary for achieving high efficiency with RSA or DSA. Because the countermeasure produces a secure recoding of secret values, and because one secret value admits many recodings, our countermeasure protects exponentiations against several types of side-channel attacks: timing attacks, simple power analysis and cache attacks for instance. Our countermeasure is not only highly secure, but is also efficient; unlike other countermeasures which provoke a significant performance drop, thanks to its higher flexibility, our method is about as fast as commonly used exponentiation techniques such as the sliding window method. In fact, in optimal settings and in a practical situation, our method is only 5% slower than the sliding window exponentiation for 512-bit and 1024-bit moduli.

Acknowledgement

This work was partly supported by National Institute of Information and Communications Technology (NICT).

References

1. Boneh, D., DeMillo, R., Lipton, R.: On the Importance of Checking Cryptographic Protocols for Faults. In W. Fumy (Ed.): Advances in Cryptology–Eurocrypt'97. LNCS **1233**, pp.37-51. Springer-Verlag (1997).
2. Chevallier-Mames, B., Ciet, M., Joye, M.: Low-Cost Solutions for Preventing Simple Side-Channel Analysis: Side-Channel Atomicity. In IEEE Transactions on Computers, **53(6)**, pp.760-768. IEEE Computer Society (2004).
3. Coppersmith, D.: Finding a Small Root of a Bivariate Integer Equation; Factoring with High Bits Known. In U. Maurer (Ed.): Advances in Cryptology–Eurocrypt'96. LNCS **1070**, pp.178-189. Springer-Verlag (1996).
4. Coron, J.-S.: Resistance Against Differential Power Analysis for Elliptic Curve Cryptosystems. In Ç. Koç and C. Paar (Eds.): Cryptographic Hardware and Embedded Systems–CHES'99. LNCS **1717**, pp.292-302. Springer-Verlag (1999).
5. Kocher, P., Jaffe, J., Jun, B.: Differential Power Analysis. In M. Wiener (Ed.): Advances in Cryptology–Crypto'99. LNCS **1666**, pp.388-397. Springer-Verlag (1999).
6. Kocher, P.: Timing Attacks on Implementations of Diffie-Hellman, RSA, DSS, and Other Systems. In N. Koblitz (Ed.): Advances in Cryptology–Crypto'96. LNCS **1109**, pp.104-113. Springer-Verlag (1996).
7. Möller, B.: Securing Elliptic Curve Point Multiplication against Side-Channel Attacks. In G. Davida, Y. Frankel (Eds.): Information Security–ISC'01. LNCS **2200**, pp.324-334. Springer-Verlag (2001).

8. Möller, B.: Improved Techniques for Fast Exponentiation. In P.J. Lee, C.H. Lim (Eds.): Information Security and Cryptology–ICISC'02. LNCS **2587**, pp.298–312. Springer-Verlag (2003).

9. Okeya, K., Takagi, T.: The Width-w NAF Method Provides Small Memory and Fast Elliptic Scalar Multiplications Secure against Side Channel Attacks. In M. Joye (Ed.): Topics in Cryptology–CT-RSA'03. LNCS **2612**, pp.328-342. Springer-Verlag (2003).

10. Okeya, K., Takagi, T.: A More Flexible Countermeasure against Side Channel Attacks Using Window Method. In C. Walter, Ç. Koç, C. Paar (Eds.): Cryptographic Hardware and Embedded Systems–CHES'03. LNCS **2779**, pp.397–410. Springer-Verlag (2003).

11. Okeya, K., Takagi, T., Vuillaume, C.: On the Exact Flexibility of the Flexible Countermeasure Against Side Channel Attacks. In H. Wang, J. Pieprzyk, V. Varadharajan (Eds): Information Security and Privacy–ACISP'04. LNCS **3108**, pp.466-477. Springer-Verlag (2004).

12. OpenSSL: The Open Source Toolkit for SSL/TLS. www.openssl.org

13. Percival, C.: Cache Missing for Fun and Profit. Technical report, available at www.daemonology.net/papers/htt.pdf

14. Shoup, V.: NTL: A Library for Doing Number Theory. www.shoup.net/ntl/

15. Walter, C.: MIST, an Efficient, Randomized Exponentiation Algorithm for Resisting Power Analysis. In B. Preenel (Ed.): Topics in Cryptology – CT-RSA'02. LNCS **2271**, pp.53-66. Springer-Verlag (2002).

16. Yen, S.-M., Chen, C.-N., Moon, S.-J. , Ha, J.: Improvement on Ha-Moon Randomized Exponentiation Algorithm. In C. Park, S. Chee (Eds.): Information Security and Cryptology–ICISC'04. LNCS **3506**, pp.154-167. Springer-Verlag (2005).

17. Yen, S.-M., Joye, M.: Checking Before Output May Not Be Enough Against Fault-Based Cryptanalysis. In IEEE Transactions on Computers, **49(9)**, pp.967-970. IEEE Computer Society (2000).

An Improved Poly1305 MAC*

Dayin Wang, Dongdai Lin, and Wenling Wu

Key Laboratory of Information Security, Institute of Software,
Chinese Academy of Sciences, Beijing 100080, China
{wdy, ddlin, wwl}@is.iscas.ac.cn

Abstract. In this paper, we propose an improved Poly1305 MAC, called
IPMAC. IPMAC is a refinement of Poly1305 MAC shown by Bernstein.
We use only one 16-byte key and one 16-byte nonce for IPMAC while
Poly1305 MAC uses two 16-byte keys and one 16-byte nonce, 48-byte in
total. The cost of reducing the size of secret keys is almost negligible:
only one encryption. Similarly to Poly1305 MAC, our algorithm correctly
and efficiently handles messages of arbitrary bit length.

1   Introduction

BACKGROUND.In the private key setting, the primitive which provide data integrity is called a message authentication code. Unlike encryption schemes, whose encryption algorithms must be either randomized or stateful for the scheme to be secure, a deterministic, stateless tagging algorithm is not only possible, but common, and in that case we refer to the message authentication code as deterministic. While, in this paper, we mainly focus on stateful codes. The stateful codes specified by three algorithms: a key generation algorithm K; a tagging algorithm T and a verification algorithm V. The sender and receiver are assumed to be in possession of a key k generated via K and not known to the adversary. Meanwhile, the sender maintain a state, often a nonce or a counter, updating it as necessary. When the sender wants to send M in an authenticated way to B, she computes a tag σ for M as a function of M and a state non and the secret key k shared between the sender and receiver, in a manner specified by the tagging algorithm; namely, she sets $\sigma \leftarrow T_K(M, non)$. This tag accompanies the message and the state value in transmission; that is, S transmits (M, σ, non) to B. (Notice that the message is sent in the clear. Also notice the transmission is longer than the original message by the length of the tag σ and the length of the state non). Upon receiving a transmission (M', σ', non') purporting to be from S, the receiver B verifies the authenticity of the tag by using the verification algorithm $V_k(M', \sigma', non')$, which depends on the message, tag, state value and shared key. In fact, the verification algorithm uses the same algorithm with the tagging algorithm to get a tag and checks that the transmitted tag equals it or

* This research is supported by the National Natural Science Foundation of China under Grant No.60373047 and No.90204016; the National Basic Research 973 Program of China under Grant No.2004CB318004.

J. Zhou, M. Yung, and F. Bao (Eds.): ACNS 2006, LNCS 3989, pp. 284–292, 2006.

not. If they equal, $V_k(M', \sigma', non')$ return 1, else return 0. If this value is 1, it is read as saying the data is authentic, and so B accepts it as coming from S. Else it discards the data as unauthentic. Usually, a message authentication code is a 3-tuple $MA = (K, T, V)$ called the "key generator" algorithm, the "MAC generation"(or tagging) algorithm and the "MAC verification" algorithm. The MAC verification algorithm need not be explicitly specified, because it can be easily got from the MAC generation algorithm.

There are mainly two ways to construct MACs, one is using the block cipher completely, the other is using the combination of a universal hash family and a block cipher. In general, We call the MACs using the latter way to construct as Carter-Wegman MACs. The Carter-Wegman MACs are those which use a function from a Universal Hash Family to compress the message M to be MACed. The output of this hash function is then processed cryptographically to produce the tag. The Poly1305 MAC is a typical Carter-Wegman MAC.

Poly1305 MAC [1], proposed by Bernstein in 2005, computes a 16-byte authenticator of a variable-length message, using a 16-byte block-cipher key k, a 16-byte additional key r, and a 16-byte nonce n. While IPMAC proposed here only needs a 16-byte block-cipher key k and a 16-byte nonce.

Our contribution: In this paper, we present an improved Poly1305 MAC, called IPMAC, and prove its security. IPMAC takes only one key, k of a block cipher E, and a 16-byte nonce. IPMAC is obtained from Poly1305 by replacing r with $E_k(0)$, so the cost for reducing the size of secret keys is almost negligible: only one encryption. But this saving of the key length makes the security proof of IPMAC harder than that of Poly1305 MAC substantially as shown below.

2   Preliminaries

2.1   The Security of Message Authentication Code

The security of message authentication code is given by Goldwasser and Bellare in chapter 8 in [2], They give the definition through the following experiment.

> Experiment $\text{Exp}_{MA,A}^{uf-cma}$
> Let $k \xleftarrow{R} K$
> Let $(M, \sigma, non) \leftarrow A^{T_k(\cdot)}$
> If $V_k(M, \sigma, non) = 1$ and M was not a query of A to its oracle
> Then return 1 else return 0

In this experiment, the adversary A attempt forgery a new 3-tuple (M, σ, non) under chosen-message attack for this code and it is a valid forgery as long as $V_k(M, \sigma, non) = 1$ and M was never a query to the tagging oracle. From the experiment, we can see that the adversary's actions are divided into two phases. The first is a "learning" phase in which it is given oracle access to $T_k(\cdot)$, where k is a prior chosen at random according to K. It can query this oracle up to q times, in any manner it pleases, as long as all the queries are messages in the underlying message space associated to the code. After each query the state value is updated.

Once this phase is over, it enters a "forgery" phases, in which it outputs a 3-tuple (M, σ, non). The adversary is declared successful if $V_k(M, \sigma, non) = 1$ and M was never a query made by the adversary to the tagging oracle. Associated to any adversary A is thus a success probability. The insecurity of the code is the success probability of the "cleverest" possible adversary, amongst all adversaries restricted in their resources to some fixed amount. We choose as resources the running time of the adversary, the number of queries it makes, and the total bit-length of all queries combined plus the bit-length of the output message M in the forgery. Formally, we have the following definition.

Definition 1. *Let $MA = (K, T, V)$ be a message authentication code, and let A be an adversary that has access to an oracle. Let $\mathrm{Adv}_{MA,A}^{uf-cma}$ be the probability that experiment $\mathrm{Exp}_{MA,A}^{uf-cma}$ returns 1. Then for any t, q, μ let*

$$\mathrm{Adv}_{MA}^{uf-cma}(t, q, \mu) = \max_A \{\mathrm{Adv}_{MA,A}^{uf-cma}\}$$

where the maximum is over all A running in time t making at most q oracle queries, and such that the sum of the lengths of all oracle queries plus the length of the message M in the output forgery is at most μ bits. We say MA is secure if $\mathrm{Adv}_{MA}^{uf-cma}(t, q, \mu) \leq \epsilon$ and ϵ is negligible.

In the following, we will use this notion to prove the security of IPMAC.

2.2   Universal Hash Families

There are many different types of Universal Hash Families, and we now present three of them that will be used later.

In the following discussion and throughout the paper it is assumed that the domain and range of universal hash functions are finite sets of binary strings and that the range is smaller than the domain.

Definition 2. *[Carter and Wegman,1979] Fix a domain D and range R. A finite multiset of hash functions $H = \{h : D \longrightarrow R\}$ is said to be Universal if for every $x, y \in D$ where $x \neq y$, $\mathrm{Pr}_{h \in H}[h(x) = h(y)] = 1/|R|$*

If we slightly relax the requirement of the collision probability to be some $\epsilon \geq 1/|R|$, we will get the notion of Almost Universal Hash Families.

Definition 3. *[3, 4] Let $\epsilon \in R^+$ be a positive number. Fix a domain D and a range R. A finite multiset of hash functions $H = \{h : D \longrightarrow R\}$ is said to be ϵ-Almost Universal (ϵ-AU) if for every $x, y \in D$ where $x \neq y$, $\mathrm{Pr}_{h \in H}[h(x) = h(y)] \leq \epsilon$*

Definition 4. *[5, 6] Let $(B, +)$ be an Abelian group. A family H of hash functions that maps from a set A to the set B is said to be ϵ-almost Δ-universal (ϵ-AΔU)w.r.t.$(B, +)$, if for any distinct elements $x, y \in A$ and for all $g \in B$:*

$$\mathrm{Pr}_{h \in H}[h(x) - h(y) = g] \leq \epsilon$$

H is ΔU if $\epsilon = 1/|B|$.

Note that for the classes of hash function families defined in definitions 2-3, the latter are contained in the former, i.e. an ϵ-$A\Delta U$ family is also an ϵ-AU family.

3   Definition of IPMAC

Some of the content is the same as the content in the Ploy1305 MAC[1]. We include here for completeness.

Messages
A message is any sequence of bytes $m[0]$, $m[1]$, $\cdots$, $m[l-1]$; a byte is any element of $\{0, 1, \cdots, 255\}$. The length l can be any nonnegative integer, and can vary from one message to another.

Block cipher
IPMAC requires a block cipher $E : K \times \{0,1\}^{128} \to \{0,1\}^{128}$. Any block cipher that is pseudo-random permutation can be used here.

Key
IPMAC authenticates messages using a 16-byte secret key k shared by the message sender and the message receiver. Using this block cipher key k, we let $r = E_k(0)$. Here we represents this 128-bit integer r in unsigned little-endian form: i.e., $r = r[0] + 2^8 r[1] + \cdots + 2^{120} r[15]$.

In order to get better performance, after getting r, we need set certain bits of r to be 0: the top four bits of $r[3], r[7], r[11], r[15]$ (i.e., to be in $\{0, 1, \cdots, 15\}$), the bottom two bits of $r[4], r[8], r[12]$ (i.e., to be in $\{0, 4, 8, \cdots, 252\}$). Thus there are 2^{106} possibilities for r. In other words, r is required to have the form $r_0 + r_1 + r_2 + r_3$ where $r_0 \in \{0, 1, 2, 3, \cdots, 2^{28} - 1\}$, $r_1/2^{32} \in \{0, 4, 8, 12, \cdots, 2^{28} - 4\}$, $r_2/2^{64} \in \{0, 4, 8, 12, \cdots, 2^{28} - 4\}$, and $r_3/2^{96} \in \{0, 4, 8, 12, \cdots, 2^{28} - 4\}$. This process has no effects on the security proof of IPMAC. So we don't consider this process in the following proof.

Nonces
IPMAC requires each message to be accompanied by a non-zero 16-byte nonce, i.e., a unique message number. IPMAC feeds each nonce non through E_k to obtain the 16-byte string $E_k(non)$. Here the nonce can be any number except 0.

Conversion and padding
Let $m[0], m[1], \cdots, m[l-1]$ be a message. Write $p = \lceil l/16 \rceil$, Define integers $c_1, c_2, \cdots, c_p \in \{1, 2, 3, \cdots, 2^{129}\}$ as follows: if $1 \le i \le \lfloor l/16 \rfloor$ then

$$c_i = m[16i - 16] + 2^8 m[16i - 15] + 2^{16} m[16i - 14] + \cdots + 2^{120} m[16i - 1] + 2^{128}$$

if l is not a multiple of 16 then

$$c_p = m[16p - 16] + 2^8 m[16p - 15] + \cdots + 2^{8(l \bmod 16)-8} m[l - 1] + 2^{8(l \bmod 16)}$$

In other words: Pad each 16-byte chunk of a message to 17 bytes by appending a 1. If the message has a final chunk between 1 and 15 bytes, append 1 to the chunk, and then zero-pad the chunk to 17 bytes. Either way, treat the resulting 17-byte chunk as an unsigned little-endian integer.

Authenticators

The IPMAC authenticator of a message m under secret key k is defined as the 16-byte unsigned little-endian representation of

$$(((c_1 r^p + c_2 r^{p-1} + \cdots + c_p r^1) \bmod 2^{130} - 5) + E_k(non)) \bmod 2^{128}$$

Here the 16-byte string $E_k(non)$ is treated as an unsigned little-endian integer, and $c_1, c_2, \cdots, c_p$, block cipher E, r and non are defined above.

From above, we can see that the mainly difference between the Poly1305 MAC and IPMAC is the choice of r. IPMAC use the secret key k and the block cipher to generate r, while Poly1305 MAC randomly choose secret key r. This change makes the security proof of IPMAC much harder than that of Poly1305 MAC substantially as shown below.

4   Security of IPMAC

Firstly, we discuss the properties of Poly hash and the relation between PRP and PRF, and then we give two Theorems and prove them.

4.1   Properties of Poly Hash

Here we describe a hash family called "Poly hash". Let the hash domain $D = \{0, 1\}^*$. Let Poly hash H $= \{H_r : D \to \{0, 1\}^{128}\}$ be the family of functions where members are selected by the random choice of some r. For any message m, write $\overline{m}$ for the polynomial $c_1 x^p + c_2 x^{p-1} + \cdots + c_p x^1$, where $p, c_1, c_2, \cdots, c_p$ are defined in Section 3. Define $H_r(m)$, a member of Poly hash, as the 16-byte unsigned little-endian representation of $(\overline{m}(r) \bmod 2^{130} - 5) \bmod 2^{128}$. We now show that Poly hash has the properties that we need, in the next two straightforward lemmas.

Lemma 1 (Poly hash is ϵ-$A\Delta U$ family). *Fix $n \geq 1$. Let g be a 16-byte string. The function Poly hash is $8\lceil l/16 \rceil / 2^{128}$-almost Δ-universal ($A\Delta U$) when its inputs having at most l bytes.*

Proof. We consider two distinct input m and m', then analyze the probability of the event that

$$H_r(m) = H_r(m') + g$$

for some fixed 16-byte string g.

From the theorem 3.3 of [1], we know that there are at most $8\lceil l/16 \rceil$ integers $r \in \{0, \cdots, 2^{130} - 6\}$ such that this equation. If r is a uniform random element of $\{0, 1\}^{128}$, then $H_r(m) = H_r(m') + g$ with probability at most $8\lceil l/16 \rceil / 2^{128}$. Consequently, if r is a uniform random element of $\{0, 1\}^{106}$ as defined in Ploy1305 MAC, then this probability is at most $8\lceil l/16 \rceil / 2^{106}$. $\square$

4.2   A PRP Can Be a Good PRF

Perhaps the best-known cryptographic primitive is the block cipher. We use the alternate name "Finite Pseudorandom Permutation"(Finite PRP) since it is more descriptive. A finite PRP is a family of permutations where a single permutation from the family is selected by a finite string called the "key".

The security of a PRP is defined based on its "closeness" to a family of truly random permutation. If the adversary is unable to distinguish well between these two types of oracles, we say that the PRP is secure. The following two definitions come from section 2.2 of [7].

Definition 5. *Let D be a PRP adversary and let E be a PRP with block length l and key length n. Define the advantage of D as follows:*

$$\mathrm{Adv}_{E,D}^{prp} = \Pr[D^{E_k(\cdot)} = 1 | k \xleftarrow{R} \{0,1\}^n] - \Pr[D^{\pi(\cdot)} = 1 | \pi \xleftarrow{R} Perm^{l \to l}]$$

Pseudorandom Functions are another extremely useful building block used in cryptographic protocol. PRFs are a natural relaxation of PRPs: whereas PRPs were required to be permutations, PRFs need only be functions. The syntax and definition of security are completely analogous to the above but are given here for completeness.

Definition 6. *Let D be an adversary and let E be a PRF with input length l, output length L, and key length n. Define the advantage of D as follows:*

$$\mathrm{Adv}_{E,D}^{prf} = \Pr[D^{E_k(\cdot)} = 1 | k \xleftarrow{R} \{0,1\}^n] - \Pr[D^{\rho(\cdot)} = 1 | \rho \xleftarrow{R} Rand^{l \to L}]$$

It is often convenient to replace random permutations with random functions, or vice versa, in security proof. The following lemma lets us easily do this. For a proof see Proposition 2.5 in [8].

Lemma 2 (A PRP can be a good PRF). *The advantage $\mathrm{Adv}_{E,A}^{prf}$ of an adversary A in distinguishing a n-bit PRP E from a random function is bounded by*

$$\mathrm{Adv}_{E,A}^{prf} \le \mathrm{Adv}_{E,A}^{prp} + q(q-1)/2^{n+1}$$

where the value q is the number of queries to the function oracle.

4.3   Security Proof of IPMAC

We use the standard model for the security of a MAC in the presence of chosen-message attack, in which an adversary is given access to a tag generation oracle and a message/tag verification oracle. That is we defined in section 2.1. Formally we define the "experiment of running the adversary" A in an attack on IPMAC as following.

> Experiment $\mathrm{Exp}_{\mathrm{IPMAC_F},A}^{uf-cma}$
> let $F \xleftarrow{R} \mathrm{F}$
> $r = F(0)$
> Let $(M, \sigma, non) \leftarrow A^{H_r(\cdot)+F(non)}$
> If $V_k(M, \sigma, non) = 1$ and M was not a query of A to its oracle
> Then return 1 else return 0

We use IPMAC$_F$ to denote using the function family F to instance IPMAC. From the Definition 1 we know $\text{Adv}^{uf-cma}_{\text{IPMAC}_F,A}$ be the probability that experiment $\text{Exp}^{uf-cma}_{\text{IPMAC}_F,A}$ returns 1.

Firstly, we consider using random function family f = $Rand^{128\to128}$ to realize the IPMAC and give its security. Then we transfer it to complexity theoretic. In IPMAC$_f$, the sender maintain a nonce, non, which is an integer variable. Above all, the sender and receiver shared a random function f chosen randomly from f. To sign message M, the sender sends$(M, H_{f(0)}(M) + f(non), non)$. To verify a received message M with tag (σ, non), the receiver computer $H_{f(0)}(M) + f(non)$ and ensures it equals σ. We now state and prove a theorem on the security of this scheme.

Theorem 1. *Let $q, t \geq 1$ be integers. Then*

$$\text{Adv}^{uf-cma}_{\text{IPMAC}_f}(t, q, \mu) \leq 8\lceil l/16\rceil/2^{128} \tag{1}$$

Proof. Since the nonce cannot be 0, $f(0)$ is a uniformly-distributed random bit string. Then $H_{f(0)}$ is a random chosen function from H.

Recall the definition from Section 2.1: we must show that there cannot exist an adversary A which makes q queries $Q = (M_1, M_2, \cdots, M_q)$ of MAC, in sequence, receiving tags $T = (t_1, t_2, \cdots, t_q)$ and then outputs a new message $M^* \notin Q$ along with a tag t^* and a nonce non^* such that $H_{f(0)}(M^*) + f(non^*) = t^*$ with probability more than $8\lceil l/16\rceil/2^{128}$.

We compute the probability that A forges after making q queries. Since A outputs a nonce non^*, there are two possibilities: either non^* has been used or non^* hasn't been used. We consider the latter first. If non^* hasn't been used then $f(non^*)$ is a uniformly-distributed random bit string uncorrelated to any value yet seen, we know $H_{f(0)}(M^*) + f(non^*) = t^*$ is also uniformly distributed and independent of what has been seen. So $A's$ ability to guess t^* is exactly $1/2^{128}$.

Now consider the case that non^* has been used. In other words, A has chosen the value which has been used in the computation of a tag t_{i^*} for a message M_{i^*}. She has both of these values. Now she must produce $M^* \neq M_{i^*}$ and t^* such that $t^* = H_{f(0)}(M^*) + f(non^*)$. But this requires that $t^* - H_{f(0)}(M^*) = t_{i^*} - H_{f(0)}(M_{i^*})$, or that $H_{f(0)}(M^*) = H_{f(0)}(M_{i^*}) + (t^* - t_{i^*})$. But H is ϵ-$A\Delta U$ so the chance of this is at most ϵ.

Lemma 1 tells us that $\epsilon = 8\lceil l/16\rceil/2^{128} \geq 1/2^{128}$, so in either case A's chance of forging is at most ϵ.   □

The preceding is an "information theoretic" result. Now we consider the code IPMAC$_E$, where E is a block cipher. We now state and prove a theorem on the security of this code.

Theorem 2. *[IPMAC$_E$ is secure]Let $q, t \geq 1$ be integers, Let E be a 128-bit PRP and l_P be the total number of plaintext bits and $len(M) \leq l$ for each query. Then*

$$\text{Adv}^{uf-cma}_{\text{IPMAC}_E}(t, q, l_P) \leq \text{Adv}^{prp}_E(t', q') + \frac{q(q+1)}{2^{129}} + \frac{8\lceil l/16\rceil}{2^{128}} \tag{2}$$

where $q' = q + 1$ and $t' \approx t$.

Proof. Let A by any forger attacking the message authentication code IPMAC. Assume the oracle in Experiment $\text{Exp}_{\text{IPMAC},A}^{uf-cma}$ is invoked at most q times, and the "running time" of A is at most t. We design B_A, which is a distinguisher for PRP $E : \{0,1\}^{128} \times \{0,1\}^{128} \to \{0,1\}^{128}$ versus random function $Rand^{128 \to 128}$. B_A is given an oracle for a function $f : \{0,1\}^{128} \to \{0,1\}^{128}$. It will run A, providing it an environment in which A's oracle queries are answered by B_A. When A finally outputs its forgery, B_A checks whether it return 1, and if so bets that f must have been a block cipher rather than a random function.

By assumption the oracle in Experiment $\text{Exp}_{\text{IPMAC},A}^{uf-cma}$ is invoked at most q times, and for simplicity we assume it is exactly q. This means that the number of queries made by A to its oracle is $q-1$. Here now is the code implementing B_A.

Distinguisher B_A^f
$r = f(0)$
For $i = 1, \cdots, q-1$ do
    When A asks its oracle some query M_i,
        generate a nonce and answer with $(H_r(M_i) + f(non_i), non_i)$
End For
A outputs (M, σ, non)
$\sigma' \leftarrow H_r(M_i) + f(non)$
If $\sigma = \sigma'$ and M was not a query of A to its oracle
Then return 1 else return 0

At the very outset of the experiment, we query the function oracle with the input value 0, and set r to the value returned by the oracle. When A makes its first oracle query M_1, algorithm B_A pause and computes $H_r(M_1) + f(non_1)$ using its own oracle f and non_1 is the current state maintained by B_A. The value $H_r(M_1) + f(non_1)$ and non_1 are returned to A. B_A update its state. The execution of the latter continues in this way until all its oracle queries are answered. Now A will output its forgery (M, σ, non), B_A verifies the forgery, and if it is correct, return 1.

We now proceed to the analysis. From Definition 5, Definition 6 We claim that

$$\text{Adv}_{E,B_A}^{prf} = \Pr[B_A^f = 1 | f \xleftarrow{R} E] - \Pr[B_A^f = 1 | f \xleftarrow{R} Rand^{128 \to 128}]$$

$$= \text{Adv}_{\text{IPMAC}_E,A}^{uf-cma} - \text{Adv}_{\text{IPMAC}_f,A}^{uf-cma}$$

$$\geq \text{Adv}_{\text{IPMAC}_E,A}^{uf-cma} - 8\lceil l/16 \rceil / 2^{128}$$

Because B_A makes $q+1$ query to its oracle, using lemma 2 we get

$$\text{Adv}_{\text{IPMAC}_E,A}^{uf-cma} \leq \text{Adv}_{E,B_A}^{prp} + \frac{q(q+1)}{2^{129}} + \frac{8\lceil l/16 \rceil}{2^{128}} \tag{3}$$

We now proceed to the analysis. We claim that

$$\text{Adv}_{\text{IPMAC}_E}^{uf-cma}(t, q, l_P) = \max_A \{\text{Adv}_{\text{IPMAC}_E,A}^{uf-cma}\}$$

$$\leq \max_A \{\text{Adv}_{E,B_A}^{prp} + \frac{q(q+1)}{2^{129}} + \frac{8\lceil l/16 \rceil}{2^{128}}\}$$

$$\leq \max_A \{\mathrm{Adv}^{prp}_{E,B_A}\} + \frac{q(q+1)}{2^{129}} + \frac{8\lceil l/16 \rceil}{2^{128}}$$

$$\leq \max_B \{\mathrm{Adv}^{prp}_{E,B}\} + \frac{q(q+1)}{2^{129}} + \frac{8\lceil l/16 \rceil}{2^{128}}$$

$$\leq \mathrm{Adv}^{prp}_E(t', q') + \frac{q(q+1)}{2^{129}} + \frac{8\lceil l/16 \rceil}{2^{128}}$$

Above the first equality is by the Definition 1. The following inequality uses Equation 3. Next we simplify using properties of the maximum, and conclude by using the definition of the insecurity function as per Definition 5.5 of [2]. We can constrain r in $\{0,1\}^{106}$ as defined in Poly1305 MAC to accelerate implementations of "Poly hash" in various contexts. Thus the security bound will get a bit worse. $\square$

5   Conclusions

In this paper we present an improved Ploy1305 MAC(IPMAC) and prove its security. IPMAC takes only one key, k of a block cipher E, and a 16-byte nonce. The shorter key is very important for performance not only in the situation that one frequently changes the secret key but also in the situation that the resources are limited. For example, a wireless access point could be handling 1000 keys at any one time. In this situation, using 16-byte keys can save 16KB additional memory than using 32-byte keys. This is very important in small embedded devices.

References

1. D. J. Bernstein.: The Poly1305-AES message-authentication code. in Proceedings of FSE 2005.
2. S. Goldwasser and M.Bellare.: Lecture Notes on Cryptograhpy. http://www-cse.ucsd.edu/users/mihir.
3. J. Carter and M. Wegman.: Universal classes of hash functions. in Journal of Computer and System Sciences, vol.18, (1979)143-154.
4. D. Stinson.: Universal hashing and authentication codes. in Crypto'91, LNCS 576(1992)74-85.
5. H. Krawczyk.: LFSR-based hashing and authentication. in Crypto'94, LNCS 839(1994)129-139.
6. D. Stinson.: On the connection between universal hashing, combinatorial designs and error-correcting codes. In Proc. Congressus Numerantium 114(1996)7-27.
7. J. Black.: Message Authentication Codes. http://www.cs.colorado.edu/~jrblack.
8. M. Bellare, J. Kilian and P. Rogaway.: The security of the cipher block chaining message authentication code. http://www.cs.ucdavis.edu/~rogaway.

Certificateless Public-Key Signature: Security Model and Efficient Construction

Zhenfeng Zhang[1], Duncan S. Wong[2], Jing Xu[3], and Dengguo Feng[1]

[1] State Key Laboratory of Information Security, Institute of Software,
Chinese Academy of Sciences, Beijing 100080, China
[2] Department of Computer Science,
City University of Hong Kong, Hong Kong, China
[3] Graduate University of Chinese Academy of Sciences, Beijing 100039, China
zfzhang@is.iscas.ac.cn, duncan@cityu.edu.hk

Abstract. "Certificateless public-key cryptosystem" is a new and attractive paradigm, which avoids the inherent key escrow property in identity-based public-key cryptosystems, and does not need expensive certificates as in the public key infrastructure. A strong security model for certificateless public key encryption was established by Al-Riyami and Paterson in 2003. In this paper, we first present a security model for certificateless public-key signature schemes, and then propose an efficient construction based on bilinear pairings. The security of the proposed scheme can be proved to be equivalent to the computational Diffie-Hellman problem in the random oracle model with a tight reduction.

1 Introduction

In traditional certificate-based public key cryptosystems, a user's public-key is generated randomly and is uncorrelated to his identity. The key therefore needs to be certified by some trusted authority with respect to the user's identity. This approach takes the form of digital certificates generated by some trusted Certification Authorities (CAs), which aim at vouching for the fact that a given public-key actually belongs to its alleged owner. Any other user who wants to use the public-key must first verify the corresponding certificate for the validity of the key. Currently, PKI (Public Key Infrastructure) is an important mechanism to maintain certificates and disseminate trust information among users in a hierarchical manner. However, PKIs in practice is very costly to deploy and cumbersome to use.

In [17], Shamir introduced the notion of identity-based (ID-based) public-key cryptography (ID-PKC). This notion is to use a binary string which can uniquely identify a user (or an entity in general) as the user's public key. Examples of such a binary string include email address, IP address, social security number, etc. The motivation of ID-PKC is to simplify key management and remove the need of public key certificates as much as possible. Certificates are only needed for some trusted authorities called ID-based Private Key Generators (PKGs) [15]. These PKGs are responsible for generating private keys for users (unlike

J. Zhou, M. Yung, and F. Bao (Eds.): ACNS 2006, LNCS 3989, pp. 293–308, 2006.
© Springer-Verlag Berlin Heidelberg 2006

conventional public key schemes, users do not generate their own private keys). Although this does not completely remove the need of certificates, it drastically reduces the cost and complexity of the system as individual end users do not need to obtain certificates for their public keys.

An inherent problem of ID-based cryptography is the key escrow problem, i.e., the private key of a user is known to the PKG. The PKG can literally decrypt any ciphertext and forge signature on any message as any user. Therefore, it seems that ID-based cryptography may only be suitable for small private networks with low security requirements. To tackle this problem, several proposals have been made using multiple authority approach [5, 8]. If the master key of the PKG is distributed over several authorities and a private key is constructed in some threshold manner [5], key escrow problem may be alleviated. However, in many applications, multiple identifications for a user by multiple authorities can be quite a burden. Generating a new private key by adding multiple private keys [8] is another approach, but in this scheme, PKGs have no countermeasure against users' illegal usage. In [12], Gentry proposed an approach in which the private key is generated using some user-chosen secret information.

Independent of Gentry's work, in [1], Al-Riyami and Paterson successfully removed the necessity of certificates in a similar manner to that of user-chosen secrets, and they referred to it as certificateless public key cryptography (CL-PKC). Unlike ID-based cryptography, a user's private key in a CL-PKC scheme is not generated by the Key Generation Center (KGC) alone. Instead, it is a combination of some contribution of the KGC (called partial-private-key) and some user-chosen secret, in such a way that the key escrow problem can be solved. In particular, the KGC cannot obtain the user's private-key. Meanwhile, CL-PKC schemes are not purely ID-based, and there exists an additional public-key for each user. In order to encrypt a message, one has to know both the user's identity and this additional public key. Moreover and more importantly, this additional public key does not need to be certified by any trusted authority. The structure of the scheme ensures that the key can be verified without a certificate. In [1], a strong security model was established for certificateless public key encryption. The model has two types of adversaries. Type I adversary represents a malicious third party and Type II adversary represents a malicious KGC. More details of these two types of adversaries will be given in the later part of this paper. In [1, 2], efficient constructions of certificateless encryption based on bilinear pairings were proposed, and in [7], a scheme not using bilinear pairings was proposed.

Note that key escrow means that the KGC knows the key, not generates the key. In CL-PKC, the KGC can still generate keys but the KGC does not know the key if it is generated by the user. In ID-based cryptography, the user cannot generate a key for himself. Hence the key escrow problem is inherent. In certificate-based cryptography or CL-PKC, both the CA or the KGC, respectively, can generate the key. Therefore, we should assume the similar degree of trust on the CA to that of the KGC in this aspect. In other words, CL-PKC *retains* the beauty of PKI/CA that the KGC does not *know* the key generated by the user.

In conventional application of digital signature, no signer wants his signing key to be escrowed by others. So it seems to be more urgent to solve the key escrow problem as in ID-based setting. In [1], a certificateless public-key signature (CL-PKS) scheme was also proposed. However, a security model for analyzing the scheme's security in terms of unforgeability was not formalized. Also, the scheme was recently found to be vulnerable to key replacement attack [13]. The key replacement attack is launched by the malicious third party (i.e. Type I adversary) who replaces the additional public key of the targeting user with another key chosen by the adversary. By using this attack, the adversary can successfully forge signature on any message as the user. In [13], Huang et al. also proposed an improved scheme. In their security analysis, the Type I adversary can replace an entity's public-key, but is also required to provide a replacing secret value corresponding to the replacing public key. Hence the challenger (or game simulator) also learns the replaced secret. This restriction seems too strong to be reasonable. Due to the un-certified feature of user's public-key in the certificateless setting, a signer does not need to provide any proof about his knowledge of the corresponding secret value of the public-key. In addition, a signature verifier does not check whether a signer knows the secret either. The model in [18] did not deal with this either. We will discuss this further when presenting our security model..

Moreover, for a CL-PKS scheme, the validity of a certificateless signature and the validity of a un-certified public-key can be verified at the same time, which is different from certificateless public-key encryption, where the encryptor does not know whether the public-key used to encrypt is valid or not.

In this paper, we first develop a security model for CL-PKS schemes. The model captures the notion of existential unforgeability of certificateless signature against Type I and Type II adversaries. We then propose an efficient and simple certificateless public-key signature scheme and show its security in our model.

Paper organization. The rest of the paper is organized as follows. A security model for CL-PKS is given in Section 2. In Section 3, we propose a CL-PKS scheme based on bilinear pairings. Its security is analyzed in Section 4. We conclude the paper in Section 5.

2 Security Model for Certificateless Public-Key Signature

Definition 1 (CL-PKS). A CL-PKS (Certificateless Public Key Signature) scheme, Π, consists of the following probabilistic, polynomial-time algorithms:

- Setup: It takes as input a security parameter 1^k, and returns a list params of system parameters and a master private key masterKey.
  The parameter list params also defines message space $\mathcal{M}$, and is publicly known. The algorithm is assumed to be run by a Key Generation Center (KGC) for the initial setup of a certificateless system.
- Partial-Private-Key-Extract: It takes as inputs params, masterKey and a user identity $ID \in \{0,1\}^*$, and outputs a partial private key D_{ID}.

This algorithm is run by the KGC once for each user, and the partial private key generated is assumed to be distributed securely to the corresponding user.

- Set-Secret-Value: Taking as inputs params and a user's identity ID, this algorithm generates a secret value s_{ID}. This algorithm is supposed to be run by each user in the system.
- Set-Private-Key: This algorithm takes params, a user's partial private key D_{ID} and his secret value s_{ID}, and outputs the full private key SK_{ID}. This algorithm is run by each user.
- Set-Public-Key: It takes as inputs params and a user's secret value s_{ID}, and generates a public key PK_{ID} for that user. This algorithm is run by the user, and the resulting public key is assumed to be publicly known.
- CL-Sign: This is the certificateless signing algorithm. It takes as inputs params, a message m, a user's identity ID, and the user's full private key SK_{ID}, and outputs a signature σ.
- CL-Verify: This is the verification algorithm, a deterministic algorithm that takes as inputs params, a public key PK_{ID}, a message M, a user's identity ID, and a signature σ, and returns a bit b. $b = 1$ means that the signature is accepted, whereas $b = 0$ means rejected.

For security analysis of a CL-PKS, we extend the model for ID-based signature schemes so that the extension allows an adversary to extract partial private keys, or private keys, or both. We must also consider the ability of the adversary to replace the public key of any user with a value of his choice, because there is no certificate in a certificateless signature scheme.

Five oracles can be accessed by the adversary. The first is a partial private key exposure oracle that returns D_{ID} on input a user's identity ID. The second is a private key exposure oracle that returns SK_{ID} on input a user's identity ID if that user's public-key has not been replaced. The third is a public key request oracle that returns PK_{ID} on input an identity ID. The fourth is a public key replacement oracle that replaces the public key PK_{ID} with PK'_{ID} for a user with identity ID . The fifth is a signing oracle $O_{\text{CL-Sign}}(\cdot)$ that returns CL-Sign(params, m, ID, SK_{ID}) on input (m, ID).

Similar to Al-Riyami and Paterson's certificateless public-key encryption scheme [1], the security of a certificateless signature scheme can be analyzed by considering two types of adversaries. The first type of adversary (Type I) $\mathcal{A}^{\text{I}}$ is meant to represent third party attacks against the existential unforgeability of the scheme. Due to the uncertified nature of the public-keys generated by the users, we must assume that the adversary is able to replace users' public-keys at will. This represents the adversary's ability to fool a user on accepting a signature by using a public key that is supplied by the adversary.

Al-Riyami and Paterson's security model for certificateless encryption allows the adversary to make decryption queries, even for public keys which have already been replaced. This means that the challenger must be able to correctly answer decryption queries for public keys where the corresponding secret keys may not be known to the challenger. This is a very strong security requirement, and it is unclear how realistic this restriction is. In fact, several papers [4, 9, 11, 18] have chosen to weaken this requirement so that the challenger is not forced to provide correct decryption of ciphertexts after the corresponding public-key has been replaced. Instead, they only require that ciphertexts can be decrypted if the public key is replaced while the corresponding secret value is also supplied by the adversary.

As for a certificateless public-key signature scheme, a "weakened" security definition *requires that the adversary can only request signatures on identities for which if the public key has been replaced with some value that is not equal to its original value, then the corresponding secret information is also provided during the key replacement.* However, it is not compulsory for the adversary to provide the corresponding secret information when the adversary replaces a public key.

It seems that this weakened requirement is more reasonable, at least for a certificateless signature scheme. First, we can never expect that a signer will produce a valid signature for a public key that he does not know the corresponding private key in the real world. Second, the cost of obtaining a partial private key is much more expensive than generating a pair of secret value s_{ID} and public key PK_{ID} for a user. Therefore, a certificateless signature scheme may be implemented in such a way that the partial-private-key is kept invariant for a long period, while the pair (s_{ID}, PK_{ID}) can be changed arbitrarily by the user. Thus an attack is allowed to replace (s_{ID}, PK_{ID}) with a key pair of adversary's choice when it has access to the terminal-devices..

The second type of adversary (Type II) $\mathcal{A}^{II}$ for a certificateless signature scheme represents a malicious key generation center.. Here, the adversary is equipped with the key generation center's master key, but cannot replace any user's public key. In fact, if the Type II adversary is allowed to replace an user's public-key, then the adversary can definitely forge signatures of the user. This is the trivial case and is comparable to the damage caused by a malicious Certification Authority (CA) in the conventional certificate-based cryptosystem. Therefore, we do not consider this scenario in certificateless cryptography also.

Definition 2 (EUF-CMA of CL-PKS). Let $\mathcal{A}^{I}$ and $\mathcal{A}^{II}$ denote a Type I attacker and a Type II attacker, respectively. Let Π be a CL-PKS scheme. We consider two games "Game I" and "Game II" where $\mathcal{A}^{I}$ and $\mathcal{A}^{II}$ interact with their "Challenger" in these two games, respectively. We say that a CL-PKS scheme is existentially unforgeable against adaptive chosen message attacks, if the success probability of both $\mathcal{A}^{I}$ and $\mathcal{A}^{II}$ is negligible. Note that the Challenger keeps a history of "query-answer" while interacting with the attackers.

Game-I: This is the game in which $\mathcal{A}^{I}$ interacts with the "Challenger":

Phase I-1: The Challenger runs $\texttt{Setup}(1^k)$ for generating $\texttt{masterKey}$ and $\texttt{params}$. The Challenger then gives $\texttt{params}$ to $\mathcal{A}^{I}$ while keeping $\texttt{masterKey}$ secret.

Phase I-2: $\mathcal{A}^{I}$ performs the following oracle-query operations:

- **Extract Partial Private Key:** each of which is denoted by (ID, "partial key extract"). On receiving such a query, the Challenger computes $D_{ID} =$ Partial-Private-Key-Extract(params, masterKey, ID) and returns it to $\mathcal{A}^{\mathrm{I}}$.
- **Extract Private Key:** each of which is denoted by (ID, "private key extract"). Upon receiving such a query, the Challenger first computes $D_{ID} =$ Partial-Private-Key-Extract(params, masterKey, ID) and then $s_{ID} =$ Set-Secret-Value (params, ID) as well as $SK_{ID} =$ Set-Private-Key (params, D_{ID}, s_{ID}). It returns SK_{ID} to $\mathcal{A}^{\mathrm{I}}$.
- **Request Public Key:** each of which is denoted by (ID, "public key request").. Upon receiving such a query, the Challenger computes $D_{ID} =$ Partial-Private-Key-Extract(params, masterKey, ID), and $s_{ID}=$ Set-Secret-Value (params, ID). It then computes $PK_{ID}=$ Set-Public-Key (params, s_{ID}) and returns it to $\mathcal{A}^{\mathrm{I}}$.
- **Replace Public Key:** $\mathcal{A}^{\mathrm{I}}$ may replace a public key PK_{ID} with a value chosen by him. It is not required for $\mathcal{A}^{\mathrm{I}}$ to provide the corresponding secret value when making this query.
- **Signing Queries:** each of which is of the form (ID, M, "signature"). On receiving such a query, the Challenger finds SK_{ID} from its "query-answer" list, computes $\sigma=$CL-Sign(params, M, ID, SK_{ID}), and returns it to $\mathcal{A}^{\mathrm{I}}$. If the public key PK_{ID} has been replaced by $\mathcal{A}^{\mathrm{I}}$, then the Challenger cannot find SK_{ID} and thus the signing oracle's answer may be incorrect. In such case, we assume that $\mathcal{A}^{\mathrm{I}}$ *may additionally submit the secret information s_{ID} corresponding to the replaced public-key PK_{ID} to the signing oracle.*

Phase I-3: Finally, $\mathcal{A}^{\mathrm{I}}$ outputs a message M^*, and a signature σ^* corresponding to a target identity ID^* and a public key PK_{ID^*}. Note that ID^* cannot be an identity for which the private key has been extracted. Also, ID^* cannot be an identity for which both the public key has been replaced and the partial private key has been extracted. Moreover, M^* should not be queried to the signing oracle with respect to ID^* and PK_{ID^*}. However, *in case that the PK_{ID^*} is different from the original public key of the entity with identity ID^*, $\mathcal{A}^{\mathrm{I}}$ needs not to provide the corresponding secret value to the Challenger if it has not made signing queries for the identity ID^* and public key PK_{ID^*}.*

Game II: This is a game in which $\mathcal{A}^{\mathrm{II}}$ interacts with the "Challenger".

- **Phase II-1:** The challenger runs Setup($\cdot$) to generate masterKey and params. The challenger gives both params and masterKey to $\mathcal{A}^{\mathrm{II}}$.
- **Phase II-2:** $\mathcal{A}^{\mathrm{II}}$ performs the following operations:
  - Compute partial private key associated with ID: $\mathcal{A}^{\mathrm{II}}$ computes $D_{ID} =$ Partial-Private-Key-Extract(params, masterKey, ID). This can be done by $\mathcal{A}^{\mathrm{II}}$ since it holds the master key.
  - Make private key extraction queries: On receiving such a query, the Challenger computes $D_{ID} =$ Partial-Private-Key-Extract(params, masterKey, ID), $s_{ID} =$ Set-Secret-Value(params, ID), and $SK_{ID} =$ Set-Private-Key(params, D_{ID}, s_{ID}). It then returns SK_{ID} to $\mathcal{A}^{\mathrm{II}}$.

- Make public key request queries: On receiving such a query, the Challenger sets $D_{ID} =$ Partial-Private-Key-Extract(params, masterKey, ID), $s_{ID} =$ Set-Secret-Value(params, ID), and then computes PK_{ID} = Set-Public-Key(params, s_{ID}, ID). It returns PK_{ID} to $\mathcal{A}^{II}$.
- Make signing queries: On receiving such a query, the Challenger finds SK_{ID} from its "query-answer" list, computes $\sigma =$ CL-Sign(params, M, ID, SK_{ID}), and returns it to $\mathcal{A}^{II}$.
- **Phase II-3:** $\mathcal{A}^{II}$ outputs a message M^* and a signature σ^* corresponding to a target identity ID^* and a public key PK_{ID^*}. Note that ID^* has not been issued as a private key query. Moreover, M^* should not be queried to the signing oracle with respect to ID^* and PK_{ID^*}.

We say that an adversary $\mathcal{A}$ ($\mathcal{A}^{I}$ or $\mathcal{A}^{II}$) succeeds in the above games (Game I or Game II) if CL-Verify(params, PK_{ID^*}, M^*, ID^*, σ^*)=1. Denote the probability of $\mathcal{A}$'s success by $\mathrm{Succ}_{\mathcal{A}}(k)$. If for any probabilistic polynomial time (PPT) adversary $\mathcal{A}$, the success probability $\mathrm{Succ}_{\mathcal{A}}(k)$ is negligible, then we say that a CL-PKS scheme is existentially unforgeable against chosen message attacks.

Remark: The definition of security against a Type II adversary is as strong as Al-Riyami and Paterson's security notion for certificateless public-key encryption, where $\mathcal{A}^{II}$ can requesting for private-keys of its own choices. In fact, this is also a very strong security notion, and it is unclear how realistic it is. As $\mathcal{A}^{II}$ has the knowledge of the master key and hence can compute the partial private-key of any user, it gives the same degree of damage as a malicious KGC in the traditional certificate-based setting. Therefore, some authors [9] have chosen to weaken this notion and taken the security against $\mathcal{A}^{II}$ as the traditional public-key cryptosystems, i.e., the private-key extraction query is not allowed to make by a Type II adversary $\mathcal{A}^{II}$.

3   An Efficient CL-PKS Scheme Based on Bilinear Pairings

In this section, we propose an efficient certificateless public-key signature scheme based on bilinear pairings. Some definitions and properties of bilinear pairings are first reviewed in the following.

3.1   Preliminaries

Let $\mathcal{G}_1$ be a cyclic additive group generated by P, whose order is a prime q, and $\mathcal{G}_2$ be a cyclic multiplicative group of the same order. Let $e : \mathcal{G}_1 \times \mathcal{G}_1 \to \mathcal{G}_2$ be a pairing which satisfies the following conditions:

1. Bilinearity: For any $P, Q, R \in \mathcal{G}_1$, we have $e(P + Q, R) = e(P, R)\, e(Q, R)$ and $e(P, Q + R) = e(P, Q)e(P, R)$. In particular, for any $a, b \in \mathbf{Z}_q^*$,

$$e(aP, bP) = e(P, P)^{ab} = e(P, abP) = e(abP, P).$$

2. Non-degeneracy: There exists $P, Q \in \mathcal{G}_1$, such that $e(P, Q) \neq 1$.

3. Computability: There is an efficient algorithm to compute $e(P, Q)$ for all $P, Q \in \mathcal{G}_1$.

We write $\mathcal{G}_1$ with an additive notation and $\mathcal{G}_2$ with a multiplicative notation, since in general implementation $\mathcal{G}_1$ will be the group of points on an elliptic curve and $\mathcal{G}_2$ will denote a multiplicative subgroup of a finite field. Typically, the map e will be derived from either the Weil or Tate pairing on an elliptic curve over a finite field. We refer readers to [5, 3] for a more comprehensive description on how these groups, pairings and other parameters should be selected for efficiency and security. Interested readers may also refer to [16] for a comprehensive bibliography of cryptographic works based on pairings.

The computational Diffie-Hellman (CDH) problem in $\mathcal{G}_1$ states that, given P, aP, bP for randomly chosen $a, b \in \mathbf{Z}_q^*$, it is computationally infeasible to compute abP.

3.2   Our Construction

The proposed certificateless public-key signature scheme comprises the following seven algorithms.

Setup:

1. On input a security parameter 1^k where $k \in \mathbb{N}$, the algorithm first generates $\langle \mathcal{G}_1, \mathcal{G}_2, e \rangle$, where $(\mathcal{G}_1, +)$ and $(\mathcal{G}_2, \cdot)$ are cyclic groups of prime order q and $e :$ $\mathcal{G}_1 \times \mathcal{G}_1 \rightarrow \mathcal{G}_2$ is a bilinear pairing.

2. Arbitrarily choose a generator $P \in \mathcal{G}_1$.

3. Select a master-key $s \in_\mathcal{R} \mathbf{Z}_q^*$ uniformly and set $P_{pub} = sP$.

4. Choose three distinct hash functions H_1, H_2 and H_3, each of them maps from $\{0, 1\}^*$ to $\mathcal{G}_1$.

The system parameter list is $\mathtt{params} = \langle \mathcal{G}_1, \mathcal{G}_2, e, q, P, P_{pub}, H_1, H_2, H_3 \rangle$. The master-key is s.

Partial-Private-Key-Extract: This algorithm takes as inputs $\mathtt{params}$, master-key s, $ID_A \in \{0, 1\}^*$, and carries out the following for generating a partial private key D_A for a user A with identity ID_A.

1. Compute $Q_A = H_1(ID_A)$.

2. Output the partial private key $D_A = sQ_A$.

It is easy to see that D_A is actually a signature [6] on ID for the key pair (P_{pub}, s), and user A can check its correctness by checking whether $e(D_A, P) = e(Q_A, P_{pub})$.

Set-Secret-Value: This algorithm picks $x \in \mathbf{Z}_q^*$ at random and sets x as user A's secret value.

Set-Private-Key: This algorithm takes as inputs $\mathtt{params}$, A's partial private-key D_A and A's secret value x, and outputs a pair is A's full private key $SK_A = \langle D_A, x \rangle$. So, the private key for A is just the pair consisting of the partial private key and the secret value.

Set-Public-Key: This algorithm takes as inputs params and A's secret value x, and generates A's public-key as $PK_A = xP$.

CL-Sign. On inputs params, a message $m \in \{0,1\}^*$, signer A's identity ID_A and his private key $SK_A = \langle D_A, x \rangle$, the signer randomly picks $r \in \mathbf{Z}_q^*$, computes $U = rP$ and

$$V = D_A + rH_2(m, ID_A, PK_A, U) + xH_3(m, ID_A, PK_A),$$

where $PK_A = xP$. The signature is $\sigma = (U, V)$.

CL-Verify. Given params, PK_A, message m, ID_A and signature $\sigma = (U, V)$, the algorithm computes $Q_A = H_1(ID_A)$ and accepts the signature if the following equation holds:

$$e(V, P) = e(Q_A, P_{pub})e(H_2(m, ID_A, PK_A, U), U)e(H_3(m, ID_A, PK_A), PK_A) \tag{1}$$

The correctness of the scheme follows from the fact that $D_A = sQ_A$ and

$$
\begin{aligned}
e(V, P) &= e(sQ_A, P)e(rH_2(m, ID_A, PK_A, U), P)e(xH_3(m, ID_A, PK_A), P) \\
&= e(Q_A, sP)e(H_2(m, ID_A, PK_A, U), rP)e(H_3(m, ID_A, PK_A), xP) \\
&= e(Q_A, P_{pub})e(H_2(m, ID_A, PK_A, U), U)e(H_3(m, ID_A, PK_A), PK_A).
\end{aligned}
$$

The current set up of our construction allows a user to create more than one public key for the same partial private key. This can be a useful property in some applications, but may be not desirable in others. In the latter case, an alternative technique of [1] can be used to generate users' key. An entity A first generate its secret value x_A and public key $PK_A = x_A P$, and Q_A is defined as $Q_A = H_1(ID_A \| PK_A)$. The partial private key is still $D_A = sQ_A$ and the private key is $SK_A = (D_A, x_A)$. In this technique, Q_A binds a user's identifier ID_A and its public keyPK_A, and thus a user can only create one public key for which he knows the corresponding private key.

4   Security Proof

Theorem 1. *In the random oracle model, our certificateless public key signature scheme is existentially unforgeable against adaptive chosen-message attacks under the assumption that the CDH problem in $\mathcal{G}_1$ is intractable.*

The theorem follows at once from Lemmas 1 and 2, according to Definition 2.

Lemma 1. *If a probabilistic polynomial-time forger $\mathcal{A}^{\mathrm{I}}$ has an advantage ε in forging a signature in an attack modelled by **Game I** of Definition 2 after running in time t and making q_{H_i} queries to random oracles H_i for $i = 1, 2, 3$, q_{ParE} queries to the partial private-key extraction oracle, q_{PK} queries to the public-key request oracle, and q_{Sig} queries to the signing oracle, then the CDH problem can be solved with probability*

$$\varepsilon' > \left(\varepsilon - (q_S(q_{H_2} + q_S) + 2)/2^k\right)/e\left(q_{ParE} + 1\right),$$

within time $t' < t + (q_{H_1} + q_{H_2} + q_{H_3} + q_{ParE} + q_{PK} + q_{Sig})t_m + (2q_{Sig} + 1)t_{mm}$, *where* t_m *is the time to compute a scalar multiplication in* $\mathcal{G}_1$ *and* t_{mm} *is the time to perform a multi-exponentiation in* $\mathcal{G}_1$.

Proof. Let $\mathcal{A}^\mathrm{I}$ be a Type I adversary who can break our CL-PKS scheme. Suppose $\mathcal{A}^\mathrm{I}$ has a success probability ε and running time t. We show how $\mathcal{A}^\mathrm{I}$ can be used by a PPT algorithm $\mathcal{B}$ to solve the CDH problem in $\mathcal{G}_1$. It is interesting to note that the reductionist proof can be obtained without the requirement that $\mathcal{A}^\mathrm{I}$ should have submitted the secret information s_{ID} corresponding to the replaced public-key PK_{ID} when querying the signing oracle. And a tight security reduction similar to that of the ID-based signature scheme [14] can be obtained.

Let $(X = aP, Y = bP) \in \mathcal{G}_1 \times \mathcal{G}_1$ be a random instance of the CDH problem taken as input by $\mathcal{B}$. The algorithm $\mathcal{B}$ initializes $\mathcal{A}^\mathrm{I}$ with $P_{pub} = X$, and then starts performing oracle simulation. Without loss of generality, we assume that, for any key extraction query or signature query involving an identity, an $H_1(\cdot)$ oracle query has previously been made on that identity. And $\mathcal{B}$ maintains a list $L = \{(ID, D_{ID}, PK_{ID}, s_{ID})\}$ while $\mathcal{A}^\mathrm{I}$ is making queries throughout the game. $\mathcal{B}$ responds to $\mathcal{A}^\mathrm{I}$'s oracle queries as follows.

Queries on Oracle H_1: The proof technique of Coron [10] is used to answer such queries. When an identity ID is submitted to oracle H_1, $\mathcal{B}$ first flips a coin $T \in \{0, 1\}$ that yields 0 with probability ζ and 1 with probability $1 - \zeta$, and picks $t_1 \in \mathbf{Z}_q^*$ at random. If $T = 0$, then the hash value $H_1(ID)$ is defined as $t_1 P \in \mathcal{G}_1$. If $T = 1$, then $\mathcal{B}$ returns $t_1 Y \in \mathcal{G}_1$. In both cases, $\mathcal{B}$ inserts a tuple (ID, t_1, T) in a list $L_1 = \{(ID, t_1, T)\}$ to keep track the way it answered the queries.

Partial Private Key Queries: Suppose the request is on an identity ID. $\mathcal{B}$ recovers the corresponding (ID, t_1, T) from the list L_1 (recall that such a tuple must exist because of the aforementioned assumption).. If $T = 1$, then $\mathcal{B}$ outputs "failure" and halts because it is unable to coherently answer the query. Otherwise, $\mathcal{B}$ looks up the list L and performs as follows.

- If the list L contains $(ID, D_{ID}, PK_{ID}, s_{ID})$, $\mathcal{B}$ checks whether $D_{ID} = \perp$. If $D_{ID} \neq \perp$, $\mathcal{B}$ returns D_{ID} to $\mathcal{A}^\mathrm{I}$. If $D_{ID} = \perp$, $\mathcal{B}$ recovers the corresponding (ID, t_1, T) from the list L_1. Noting $T = 0$ means that $H_1(ID)$ was previously defined to be $t_1 P \in \mathcal{G}_1$ and $D_{ID} = t_1 P_{pub} = t_1 X \in \mathcal{G}_1$ is the partial private key associated to ID. Thus $\mathcal{B}$ returns D_{ID} to $\mathcal{A}^\mathrm{I}$ and writes D_{ID} in the list L.
- If the list L does not contain $(ID, D_{ID}, PK_{ID}, s_{ID})$, $\mathcal{B}$ recovers the corresponding (ID, t_1, T) from the list L_1, sets $D_{ID} = t_1 P_{pub} = t_1 X$ and returns D_{ID} to $\mathcal{A}^\mathrm{I}$. $\mathcal{B}$ also sets $PK_{ID} = s_{ID} = \perp$ and adds an element $(ID, D_{ID}, PK_{ID}, s_{ID})$ to the list L.

Public Key Queries: Suppose the query is made on an identity ID.

- If the list L contains $(ID, D_{ID}, PK_{ID}, s_{ID})$, $\mathcal{B}$ checks whether $PK_{ID} = \perp$. If $PK_{ID} \neq \perp$, $\mathcal{B}$ returns PK_{ID} to $\mathcal{A}^\mathrm{I}$. Otherwise, $\mathcal{B}$ randomly chooses $w \in \mathbf{Z}_q^*$

and sets $PK_{ID} = wP$ and $s_{ID} = w$. $\mathcal{B}$ returns PK_{ID} to $\mathcal{A}^I$ and saves (PK_{ID}, s_{ID}) into the list L.

- If the list L does not contain $(ID, D_{ID}, PK_{ID}, s_{ID})$, $\mathcal{B}$ sets $D_{ID} =\perp$, and then randomly chooses $w \in \mathbf{Z}_q^*$ and sets $PK_{ID} = wP$ and $s_{ID} = w$. $\mathcal{B}$ returns PK_{ID} to $\mathcal{A}^I$ and adds $(ID, D_{ID}, PK_{ID}, s_{ID})$ to the list L.

Private Key Extraction Queries: Suppose the query is made on an identity ID. $\mathcal{B}$ recovers the corresponding (ID, t_1, T) from the list L_1. If $T = 1$, then $\mathcal{B}$ outputs "failure" and halts because it is unable to coherently answer the query. Otherwise, $\mathcal{B}$ looks up the list L and performs as follows.

- If the list L contains $(ID, D_{ID}, PK_{ID}, s_{ID})$, $\mathcal{B}$ checks whether $D_{ID} =\perp$ and $PK_{ID} =\perp$. If $D_{ID} =\perp$, $\mathcal{B}$ makes a partial private key query itself to obtain D_{ID}. If $PK_{ID} =\perp$, $\mathcal{B}$ makes a public key query itself to generate $(PK_{ID} = wP, s_{ID} = w)$. Then $\mathcal{B}$ saves these values in the list L and returns $SK_{ID} = (D_{ID}, w)$ to $\mathcal{A}^I$.
- If the list L does not contain an item $\{(ID, D_{ID}, PK_{ID}, s_{ID})\}$, $\mathcal{B}$ makes a partial private key query and a public key query on ID itself, and then adds $(ID, D_{ID}, PK_{ID}, s_{ID})$ to the list L and returns $SK_{ID} = (D_{ID}, s_{ID})$.

Public Key Replacement Queries: Suppose $\mathcal{A}^I$ makes the query with an input (ID, PK'_{ID}).

- If the list L contains an element $(ID, D_{ID}, PK_{ID}, s_{ID})$, $\mathcal{B}$ sets $PK_{ID} = PK'_{ID}$ and $s_{ID} =\perp$.
- If the list L does not contain an item $(ID, D_{ID}, PK_{ID}, s_{ID})$, $\mathcal{B}$ sets $D_{ID} =\perp$, $PK_{ID} = PK'_{ID}$, $s_{ID} =\perp$, and adds an element $(ID, D_{ID}, PK_{ID}, s_{ID})$ to L.

Queries on Oracle H_2: Suppose (m, ID, PK_{ID}, U) is submitted to oracle $H_2(\cdot)$. $\mathcal{B}$ first scans a list $L_2 = \{(m, ID, PK_{ID}, U, H_2, t_2)\}$ to check whether H_2 has already been defined for that input. If so, the previously defined value is returned. Otherwise, $\mathcal{B}$ picks at random $t_2 \in \mathbf{Z}_q^*$, and returns $H_2 = t_2 P \in \mathcal{G}_1$ as a hash value of $H_2(m, ID, PK_{ID}, U)$ to $\mathcal{A}^I$ (we abuse the notation H_2 here), and also stores the values in the list L_2.

Queries on Oracle H_3: Suppose (m, ID, PK_{ID}) is submitted to oracle $H_3(\cdot)$. $\mathcal{B}$ first scans a list $L_3 = \{(m, ID, PK_{ID}, H_3, t_3)\}$ to check whether H_3 has already been defined for that input. If so, the previously defined value is returned. Otherwise, $\mathcal{B}$ picks at random $t_3 \in \mathbf{Z}_q^*$, and returns $H_3 = t_3 P \in \mathcal{G}_1$ as a hash value of $H_3(m, ID, PK_{ID})$ to $\mathcal{A}^I$ (we abuse the notation H_3 here), and also stores the values in the list L_3.

Signing Oracle Queries: Suppose that $\mathcal{A}^I$ queries the oracle with an input (m, ID). Without loss of generality, we assume that the list L contains an item $(ID, D_{ID}, PK_{ID}, s_{ID})$, and $PK_{ID} \neq\perp$. (If the list L does not contain such an item, or if $PK_{ID} =\perp$, $\mathcal{B}$ runs a public key query to get (PK_{ID}, s_{ID}).)

Then $\mathcal{B}$ picks at random two numbers $v, u \in \mathbf{Z}_q^*$, sets $U = vP_{pub}$, and defines the hash value of $H_2(m, ID, PK_{ID}, U)$ as $H_2 = v^{-1}(uP - Q_{ID}) \in \mathcal{G}_1$

($\mathcal{B}$ halts and outputs "failure" if H_2 turns out to have already been defined for (m, ID, PK_{ID}, U)). Then $\mathcal{B}$ looks up the list L_3 for $(m, ID, PK_{ID}, H_3, t_3)$ such that the hash value of $H_3(m, ID, PK_{ID})$ has been defined to $H_3 = t_3 P$ (If such an item does not exist, $\mathcal{B}$ makes a query on oracle H_3). Finally, $\mathcal{B}$ sets $V = uP_{pub} + t_3 PK_{ID}$. Now (U, V) is returned to $\mathcal{A}^I$, which appears to be a valid signature since

$$e(Q_{ID}, P_{pub})e(H_2, U)e(H_3, PK_{ID})$$
$$= e(Q_{ID}, P_{pub})e(v^{-1}(uP - Q_{ID}), vP_{pub})e(t_3 P, PK_{ID})$$
$$= e(Q_{ID}, P_{pub})e(uP - Q_{ID}, P_{pub})e(P, t_3 PK_{ID})$$
$$= e(Q_{ID}, P_{pub})e(P, uP_{pub})e(Q_{ID}, P_{pub})^{-1}e(P, t_3 PK_{ID})$$
$$= e(P, uP_{pub} + t_3 PK_{ID}) = e(V, P).$$

Note that, the above simulation for signing queries works even in the strong case that $\mathcal{B}$ does not know the secret value s_{ID} corresponding to the public key PK_{ID} of a user with identity ID.

Eventually, $\mathcal{A}^I$ outputs a forgery $\tilde{\sigma} = (\tilde{U}, \tilde{V})$ on a message $\tilde{m}$, for an identity $\tilde{ID}$ with public key $PK_{\tilde{ID}}$.[1] Now $\mathcal{B}$ recovers the triple $(\tilde{ID}, \tilde{t}_3, \tilde{T})$ from L_1. If $\tilde{T} = 0$, then $\mathcal{B}$ outputs "failure" and stops.. Otherwise, it goes on and finds out an item $(\tilde{m}, \tilde{ID}, PK_{\tilde{ID}}, \tilde{U}, \tilde{H}_2, \tilde{t}_2)$ in the list L_2, and an item $(\tilde{m}, \tilde{ID}, PK_{\tilde{ID}}, \tilde{H}_3, \tilde{t}_3)$ in the list L_3. Note that the list L_2 and L_3 must contain such entries with overwhelming probability (otherwise, $\mathcal{B}$ stops and outputs "failure"). Note that $\tilde{H}_2 = H_2(\tilde{m}, \tilde{ID}, PK_{\tilde{ID}}, \tilde{U})$ is $\tilde{t}_2 P \in \mathcal{G}_1$, and $\tilde{H}_3 = H_3(\tilde{m}, \tilde{ID}, PK_{\tilde{ID}})$ is $\tilde{t}_3 P \in \mathcal{G}_1$. If $\mathcal{A}^I$ succeeds in the game, then

$$e(\tilde{V}, P) = e(Q_{\tilde{ID}}, X)e(\tilde{H}_2, \tilde{U})e(\tilde{H}_3, PK_{\tilde{ID}})$$

with $\tilde{H}_2 = \tilde{t}_2 P$, $\tilde{H}_3 = \tilde{t}_3 P$ and $Q_{\tilde{ID}} = \tilde{t}_1 Y$ for known elements $\tilde{t}_1, \tilde{t}_2, \tilde{t}_3 \in \mathbf{Z}_q^*$. Therefore,

$$e(\tilde{V} - \tilde{t}_2 \tilde{U} - \tilde{t}_3 \tilde{PK}_{ID}, P) = e(\tilde{t}_1 Y, X),$$

and thus $\tilde{t}_1^{-1}(\tilde{V} - \tilde{t}_2 \tilde{U} - \tilde{t}_3 PK_{\tilde{ID}})$ is the solution to the target CDH instance $(X, Y) \in \mathcal{G}_1 \times \mathcal{G}_1$.

Now we evaluate $\mathcal{B}$'s probability of failure.. $\mathcal{B}$'s simulation of oracle H_3 is perfect. One can also readily check that the probability of failure in handling a signing query because of a conflict on H_2 is at most $q_S(q_{H_2} + q_S)/2^k$, as L_2 never has more than $q_{H_2} + q_S$ entries, while the probability for $\mathcal{A}^I$ to output a valid forgery $\tilde{\sigma}$ on a message $\tilde{m}$ for an identity $\tilde{ID}$ with public key $PK_{\tilde{ID}}$, without asking the corresponding $H_2(\tilde{m}, \tilde{ID}, PK_{\tilde{ID}}, \tilde{U})$ query or $H_3(\tilde{m}, \tilde{ID}, PK_{\tilde{ID}})$ query, is at most $2/2^k$. And, by an analysis similar to Coron's technique [10], the probability $\zeta^{q_{\text{ParE}}}(1 - \zeta)$ for $\mathcal{B}$ not to fail in key extraction queries or because $\mathcal{A}^I$ produces its forgery on a 'bad' identity $\tilde{ID}$ is greater than $1 - 1/e(q_{\text{ParE}} + 1)$ when the optimal probability $\zeta_{\text{opt}} = q_{\text{ParE}}/(q_{\text{ParE}} + 1)$ is taken. Therefore,

---

[1] We remark again that the Challenger $\mathcal{B}$ may not know the secret value $s_{\tilde{ID}}$ corresponding to $PK_{\tilde{ID}}$, while a reduction can be given even if $\mathcal{B}$ does not know $s_{\tilde{ID}}$.

it results that $\mathcal{B}$'s advantage in solving the CDH problem in $\mathcal{G}_1$ is at least $\big(\varepsilon - (q_S(q_{H_2} + q_S) + 2)/2^k\big)/e(q_{\text{ParE}} + 1)$.

Lemma 2. *If a PPT forger $\mathcal{A}^{\text{II}}$ has an advantage ε in forging a signature in an attack modelled by **Game II** of Definition 2 after running in time t and making q_{H_i} queries to random oracles H_i for $i = 2, 3$, q_E queries to the private-key extraction oracle, q_{PK} queries to the public-key request oracle, and q_{Sig} queries to the signing oracle, then the CDH problem can be solved with probability*

$$\varepsilon' > \big(\varepsilon - (q_S(q_{H_2} + q_S) + 2)/2^k\big)/e(q_E + 1),$$

within time $t' < t + (q_{H_2} + q_{H_3} + q_{PK} + q_{sig})t_m + (2q_{sig} + 1)t_{mm}$, where t_m is the time to compute a scalar multiplication in $\mathcal{G}_1$ and t_{mm} is the time to perform a multi-exponentiation in $\mathcal{G}_1$.

Proof. Suppose $\mathcal{A}^{\text{II}}$ is a Type II adversary that (t, ε)-breaks our certificateless signature scheme. We show how to construct a t'-time algorithm $\mathcal{B}$ that solves the CDH problem on $\mathcal{G}_1$ with probability at least ε'. Let $(X = aP, Y = bP) \in \mathcal{G}_1 \times \mathcal{G}_1$ be a random instance of the CDH problem taken as input by $\mathcal{B}$.

$\mathcal{B}$ randomly chooses $s \in \mathbf{Z}_q^*$ as the master key, and then initializes $\mathcal{A}^{\text{II}}$ with $P_{pub} = sP$ and also the master key s. The adversary $\mathcal{A}^{\text{II}}$ then starts making oracle queries such as those described in Definition 2. Note that the partial private key $D_{ID} = sH_1(ID)$ can be computed by both $\mathcal{B}$ and $\mathcal{A}^{\text{II}}$, thus the hash function $H_1(\cdot)$ is not modelled as a random oracle in this case.

$\mathcal{B}$ maintains a list $L = \{(ID, PK_{ID}, s_{ID}, T)\}$, which does not need to be made in advance and is populated when $\mathcal{A}^{\text{II}}$ makes certain queries specified below.

Public Key Queries: Suppose the query is make on an identity ID.

- If the list L contains (ID, PK_{ID}, s_{ID}, T), $\mathcal{B}$ returns PK_{ID} to $\mathcal{A}^{\text{II}}$.
- If the list L does not contain (ID, PK_{ID}, s_{ID}), as in Coron's proof [10], $\mathcal{B}$ flips a coin $T \in \{0, 1\}$ that yields 0 with probability ζ and 1 with probability $1 - \zeta$. $\mathcal{B}$ also picks a number $w \in \mathbf{Z}_q^*$ at random. If $T = 0$, the value of PK_{ID} is defined as $wP \in \mathcal{G}_1$. If $T = 1$, $\mathcal{B}$ returns $wY \in \mathcal{G}_1$. In both cases, $\mathcal{B}$ sets $s_{ID} = w$, and inserts a tuple (ID, PK_{ID}, s_{ID}, T) into a list $L_1 = \{(ID, PK_{ID}, s_{ID}, T)\}$ to keep track the way it answered the queries. $\mathcal{B}$ returns PK_{ID} to $\mathcal{A}^{\text{II}}$.

Private Key Extraction Queries: Suppose the query is made on an identity ID.

- If the list L contains (ID, PK_{ID}, s_{ID}, T), $\mathcal{B}$ returns $SK_{ID} = (D_{ID}, s_{ID})$ to $\mathcal{A}^{\text{II}}$ if $T = 0$, and halts otherwise.
- If the list L does not contain an item $\{(ID, PK_{ID}, s_{ID}, T)\}$, $\mathcal{B}$ makes a public key query on ID itself, and adds (ID, PK_{ID}, s_{ID}, T) to the list L. Then it returns $SK_{ID} = (D_{ID}, s_{ID})$ if $T = 0$, and halts otherwise.

Queries on Oracle H_2: When a tuple (m, ID, PK_{ID}, U) is submitted to oracle $H_2(\cdot)$, $\mathcal{B}$ first scans a list $L_2 = \{(m, ID, PK_{ID}, U, H_2, t_2)\}$ to check whether H_2

has already been defined for that input. If so, the existing value is returned. Otherwise, $\mathcal{B}$ picks a random number $t_2 \in \mathbf{Z}_q^*$, and returns $H_2 = t_2 P \in \mathcal{G}_1$ as the hash value of $H_2(m, ID, PK_{ID}, U)$ to $\mathcal{A}^{II}$, and also stores the values in the list L_2.

Queries on Oracle H_3: When a tuple (m, ID, PK_{ID}) is submitted to oracle $H_3(\cdot)$, $\mathcal{B}$ first scans a list $L_3 = \{(m, ID, PK_{ID}, H_3, t_3)\}$ to check whether H_3 has already been defined for that input. If so, the existing value is returned. Otherwise, $\mathcal{B}$ picks at random $t_3 \in \mathbf{Z}_q^*$, and returns $H_3 = t_3 Y \in \mathcal{G}_1$ as a hash value of $H_3(m, ID, PK_{ID})$ to $\mathcal{A}^{II}$, and also stores the values in the list L_3.

Signing Oracle Queries: Suppose $\mathcal{A}^{II}$ makes the query with an input (m, ID). Without loss of generality, we assume that there is an item $(ID, PK_{ID}, \cdot, \cdot)$ in the list L.

First, $\mathcal{B}$ picks $v, u \in \mathbf{Z}_q^*$ at random, sets $U = uPK_{ID}$, $V = vPK_{ID} + D_{ID}$ and defines the hash value of $H_2(ID, M, PK_{ID}, U)$ as $H_2 = u^{-1}(vP - H_3)$, where $H_3 = H_3(m, ID, PK_{ID})$ ($\mathcal{B}$ halts and outputs "failure" if H_2 turns out to have already been defined for (m, ID, PK_{ID}, U)). Now (U, V) is returned to $\mathcal{A}^{II}$, which appears to be a valid signature since

$$e(Q_{ID}, P_{pub})e(H_2, U)e(H_3, PK_{ID})$$
$$= e(Q_{ID}, P_{pub})e(u^{-1}(vP - H_3), uPK_{ID})e(H_3, PK_{ID})$$
$$= e(sQ_{ID}, P)e(vP, PK_{ID})e(-H_3, PK_{ID})e(H_3, PK_{ID})$$
$$= e(D_{ID}, P)e(vPK_{ID}, P)$$
$$= e(vPK_{ID} + D_{ID}, P) = e(V, P).$$

Eventually, $\mathcal{A}^{II}$ outputs a forgery $\tilde{\sigma} = (\tilde{U}, \tilde{V})$ on a message $\tilde{m}$, for an identity $\tilde{ID}$ with public key $PK_{\tilde{ID}}$. Then $\mathcal{B}$ recovers $(\tilde{ID}, PK_{\tilde{ID}}, s_{\tilde{ID}}, \tilde{T})$ from L_1 and evaluates $\tilde{T}$. If $\tilde{T} = 0$, then $\mathcal{B}$ outputs "failure" and stops. Otherwise, it looks up an item $(\tilde{m}, \tilde{ID}, PK_{\tilde{ID}}, \tilde{U}, \tilde{H}_2, \tilde{t}_2)$ in the list L_2 such that the value of $\tilde{H}_2 = H_2(\tilde{m}, \tilde{ID}, PK_{\tilde{ID}}, \tilde{U})$ has been defined to be $\tilde{t}_2 P$. $\mathcal{B}$ also looks up an item $(\tilde{m}, \tilde{ID}, PK_{\tilde{ID}}, \tilde{H}_3, \tilde{t}_3)$ in the list L_3 such that the value of $\tilde{H}_3 = H_3(\tilde{m}, \tilde{ID}, PK_{\tilde{ID}})$ has been defined to be $\tilde{t}_3 Y$. Note that the lists L_2 and L_3 must contain such entries with overwhelming probability. If $\mathcal{A}^{II}$ succeeds in the game, then

$$e(\tilde{V}, P) = e(Q_{\tilde{ID}}, P_{pub})e(\tilde{H}_2, \tilde{U})e(\tilde{H}_3, PK_{\tilde{ID}})$$

with $\tilde{H}_2 = \tilde{t}_2 P$, $\tilde{H}_3 = \tilde{t}_3 Y$, $P_{pub} = sP$ and $PK_{\tilde{ID}} = s_{\tilde{ID}} X$, for known elements $\tilde{t}_2, \tilde{t}_3, s, s_{\tilde{ID}} \in \mathbf{Z}_q^*$. Therefore,

$$e(\tilde{V} - sQ_{\tilde{ID}} - \tilde{t}_2 \tilde{U}, P) = e(\tilde{t}_3 Y, s_{\tilde{ID}} X),$$

and thus $(s_{\tilde{ID}} \tilde{t}_3)^{-1}(\tilde{V} - sQ_{\tilde{ID}} - \tilde{t}_2 \tilde{U})$ is the solution to the CDH instance (X, Y).

Now we evaluate the failure probability of $\mathcal{B}$. Our simulation for oracle H_3 is perfect. Also, the probability for $\mathcal{B}$ to fail in handling a signing query because of a conflict on H_2 is at most $q_S(q_{H_2} + q_S)/2^k$. The probability for $\mathcal{A}^{II}$ to output a valid forgery $\tilde{\sigma}$ on a message $\tilde{m}$ for identity $\tilde{ID}$ with public key $\tilde{PK}_{ID}$, without asking the corresponding $H_2(\tilde{m}, \tilde{ID}, \tilde{PK}_{ID}, \tilde{U})$ query or $H_3(\tilde{m}, \tilde{ID}, \tilde{PK}_{ID})$ query, is at most $2/2^k$. And, by an analysis similar to Coron's [10], we can see that the probability $\zeta^{q_E}(1 - \zeta)$ for $\mathcal{B}$ not to fail in a private key extraction query or because $\mathcal{A}^{II}$ produces its forgery on a 'bad' identity $\tilde{ID}$ is greater than $1 - 1/e(q_E + 1)$ when the optimal probability $\zeta_{opt} = q_E/(q_E + 1)$ is taken. Hence, $\mathcal{B}$'s advantage in solving the CDH problem in $\mathcal{G}_1$ is at least $\left(\varepsilon - (q_S(q_{H_2} + q_S) + 2)/2^k\right)/e(q_E + 1)$.

5   Conclusion

Al-Riyami and Paterson introduced the new paradigm of certificateless public key cryptography in 2003. They established a security model for certificateless public key encryption and proposed some efficient constructions. In this paper, we proposed a security model for certificateless public-key signature, and an efficient construction based on bilinear pairings. We also showed that the proposed scheme is tightly equivalent to the computational Diffie-Hellman problem in the random oracle model.

Acknowledgements

The work is supported by National Natural Science Foundation of China under Granted No. 60373039, 90604018, and National Grand Fundamental Research Project of China under Granted No.G1999035802. The second author was supported by a grant from CityU (Project No. 7001844).

References

1. S. Al-Riyami and K. Paterson, Certificateless public key cryptography, Advances in Cryptology-Asiacrypt'2003, *Lecture Notes in Computer Science*, vol. 2894, pages 452-473, Springer-Verlag, 2003.
2. S. Al-Riyami and K. Paterson, "CBE from CL-PKE: A generic construction and efficient schemes", Public Key Cryptography-PKC'05, *Lecture Notes in Computer Science*, vol. 3386, pages 398-415, Springer-Verlag, 2005.
3. P. Barreto, H. Kim, B. Lynn and M. Scott, Efficient algorithms for pairing-based cryptosystems, Advances in Cryptology-Crypto'2002, *Lecture Notes in Computer Science*, vol. 2442, pages 354-368, Springer-Verlag, 2002.
4. K. Bentahar, P. Farshim, J. Malone-Lee, and N.P. Smart, Generic constructions of identity-based and certificateless KEMs. IACR *Cryptology ePrint Archive*, Report 2005/058, 2005.
5. D. Boneh and F. Franklin, Identity-based encryption from the Weil pairing, Advances in Cryptology-Crypto'2001, *Lecture Notes in Computer Science*, vol. 2139, pages 213-229, Springer-Verlag, 2001; *SIAM J. COMPUT.*, 32(3): 586-615, 2003.
6. D. Boneh, B. Lynn and H. Shacham, Short signatures from the Weil pairing, Advances in Cryptology-Asiacrypt'2001, *Lecture Notes in Computer Science*, vol. 2248, pages 514-532, Springer-Verlag; *J. Cryptology*, 17(4): 297-319, 2004.

7. J. Baek, R. Safavi-Naini and W. Susilo, Certificateless public key encryption without pairing, Proc. of the 8th Information Security Conference (ISC 2005), *Lecture Notes in Computer Science*, vol. 3650, pages 134-148, Springer-Verlag, 2005.

8. L. Chen, K. Harrison, N. P. Smart, and D. Soldera, Applications of multiple trust authorities in pairing based cryptosystems, InfraSec 2002, *Lecture Notes in Computer Science*, vol. 2437, pages 260-275, Springer-Verlag, 2002.

9. Z.H. Cheng and R. Comley. Efficient certificateless public key encryption, IACR *Cryptology ePrint Archive*, Report 2005/012, 2005

10. J.S. Coron. On the exact security of Full Domain Hash. Advances in Cryptology-Crypto'00, *Lecture Notes in Computer Science*, vol.1880, pages 229-235, Springer-Verlag, 2000.

11. A.W. Dent and C. Kudla, On proofs of security for certificateless cryptosystems, IACR *Cryptology ePrint Archive*, Report 2005/348, 2005

12. C. Gentry, Certificate-based encryption and the certificate revocation problem, Advances in Cryptology-Eurocrypt'2003, *Lecture Notes in Computer Science*, vol. 2656, pages 272-293, Springer-Verlag, 2000.

13. X.Y. Huang, W. Susilo, Y.. Mu and F.T. Zhang, On the security of a certificateless signature scheme. Cryptology and Network Security: 4th International Conference, *Lecture Notes in Computer Science*, vol.3810, pages 13-25, Springer-Verlag, 2005

14. B. Libert and J.J. Quisquater. The exact security of an identity based signature and its applications, IACR *Cryptology ePrint Archive*, Report 2004/102, 2004.

15. B. Libert and J.J. Quisquater, What is possible with identity based cryptography for PKIs and what still must be improved, EuroPKI 2004, *Lecture Notes in Computer Science*, vol. 3093, pages 57-70, Springer-Verlag, 2004.

16. The pairing-Based Crypto Lounge.. Web page maintained by Paulo Barreto. Available at: http://planeta.terra.com.br/informatica/paulobarreto/pblounge.html

17. A.Shamir, Identity based cryptosystems and signature schemes, Advances in Cryptology-Crypto'84, *Lecture Notes in Computer Science*, vol.196, pages 47-53, Springer-Verlag, 1984.

18. D.H. Yum and P.J. Lee, Generic construction of certificateless signature. Proc. of Information Security and Privacy: 9th Australasian Conference, ACISP 2004, *Lecture Notes in Computer Science*, vol.3108, pages 200-211, Springer-Verlag, 2004

High Diffusion Cipher: Encryption and Error Correction in a Single Cryptographic Primitive

Chetan Nanjunda Mathur, Karthik Narayan, and K.P. Subbalakshmi

Department of Electrical and Computer Engineering,
Stevens Institute of Technology, Hoboken, NJ 07030, USA
cnanjund@stevens.edu

Abstract. In this paper we combine the error correction and encryption functionality into one block cipher, which we call High Diffusion (HD) cipher. The error correcting property of this cipher is due to the novel error correction code which we call High Diffusion code used in its diffusion layer. Theoretical bounds on the performance of the HD cipher in terms of security and error correction are derived. We show that the proposed HD cipher provides security equivalent to Rijndael cipher against linear and differential cryptanalysis. Experiments based on a four round HD cipher reveal that traditional concatenated systems using the Rijndael cipher followed by Reed Solomon codes require 89% more expansion to match the performance of HD cipher.

Keywords: Error correcting cipher, Joint error correction and encryption, Coding and cryptography, Block cipher, Error correcting code.

1   Introduction

In most cases, the very same properties that provide security to a cipher (e.g. avalanche effect) makes them sensitive to transmission errors. In block ciphers (which operates on a fixed block length of data at a time) a single bit flip in the encrypted data can cause a complete decryption failure. This sensitivity causes more retransmissions compared to unencrypted transmission, reducing the overall throughput [20]. Hence, transmitting encrypted data often requires the use of error correction codes to efficiently and reliably recover the information during decryption. Although, traditionally error correction and encryption are handled independently, some of the motivations to combine them into one primitive are a) both error correction and encryption are now performed in the same layer (e.g. link layer in wireless networks) b) error correction codes are already present in communication devices, therefore using codes as building blocks for a cipher is advisable from an implementation standpoint c) the increasing popularity of resource constrained devices in noisy media like the wireless networks could potentially benefit from a joint design of the error correction and encryption primitives in terms of achieving a better system level operating point than the traditional disjoint approach. Hence, designing ciphers to provide error correction functionality in addition to encryption is of significance in many applications.

J. Zhou, M. Yung, and F. Bao (Eds.): ACNS 2006, LNCS 3989, pp. 309–324, 2006.

Although mathematical relationships exist between error correction and encryption [24], there have been only a few attempts to build error correcting ciphers. Some of the notable results include the McEliece cipher [18], the Hwang and Rao cipher [13] and the Godoy-Pereira scheme [12]. Some of the issues with these ciphers are (a) these systems are not designed based on well known security principles (and hence are vulnerable to various attacks [2]) (b) they are not as efficient as traditional forward error correcting (FEC) codes in terms of error correction capability, as they trade error correction capacity to achieve security. In fact, in order to achieve meaningful error correction capacity, the parameters of the system have to be very large leading to high computational complexity. The difficulty in designing error correcting ciphers arise from the fact that error correction and encryption work at cross purposes to each other.

In this paper, we propose an error correcting block cipher called the High Diffusion (HD) cipher. The HD cipher, like standard block ciphers [23], is composed of several iterations of the round transformation and mixing with the secret key. The round transformation functions are composed of a non-linear substitution layer and a linear diffusion layer. The error correcting property of the HD cipher is due to the use of a novel class of codes that we call High Diffusion codes [16] [21] in the diffusion layer of a cipher. We show that HD ciphers are not vulnerable to known plaintext type of attacks described in [2] which were effective on previously known error correcting ciphers [13] [12] [18]. In fact, we show that the HD ciphers are as secure as the Rijndael cipher [10] against the well known differential, linear cryptanalysis [3][17] and Square attacks [14]. To assess the performance of our proposed cipher, we compare it with the traditional concatenated system that use Rijndael cipher followed by Reed Solomon codes [25]. We show that HD cipher outperforms the traditional mechanism both in terms of security and error correction.

2   Proposed High Diffusion Cipher (HD Cipher)

A block diagram of the High Diffusion cipher encryption is given in Fig. 1. The HD cipher is a Key-Alternating [8] block cipher, composed of several iterations of the round transformation and key mixing operation. The round transformation consists of three layers. The first one is the non linear substitution layer, this is followed by the symbol transposition layer and finally the High Diffusion encoding layer. Note that, HD encoding is not performed in the final round.

The key mixing layer follows every round transformation and is also performed once before the first round. The HD cipher decryption proceeds in the exact reverse order to that of the encryption process, however the HD encoding layer is replaced by the HD decoding layer.

Now, we introduce some notations that are used in the rest of this paper. The inputs to the HD cipher encryption are the plaintext (denoted by P) and the key (denoted by K). The output is the ciphertext (denoted by C). The total number of rounds in the cipher is denoted by R. The plaintext as it goes through each round of the cipher is referred to as the *cipher state*. The number of bits

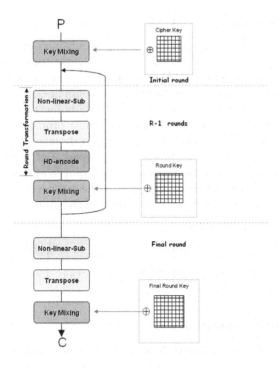

Fig. 1. Block Diagram of High Diffusion Cipher

in the cipher state after $r \in \{0...R\}$ rounds is denoted by n_b^r. Note that, n_b^0 is the number of bits in P and n_b^R is the number of bits in C. The total number of key bits, denoted by n_k, is equal to n_b^R. We propose to use the same key schedule algorithm as in Rijndael [10], which extends the n_k bit cipher key into $(R+1) \times n_k$ bits to produce $R+1$ round keys $\{k^0, k^1, ..., k^R\}$. All the operations in HD cipher are performed in the finite field of order 2^m, denoted by $\mathrm{GF}(2^m)$. Hence, the n_b^r bits are logically grouped into n_s^r symbols represented by m bits each. A detailed description of all the layers of HD cipher will follow.

2.1   Key Mixing Layer

The key mixing layer, which we denote by σ, is a bitwise XOR operation of the cipher state with the round key. Note that, the round keys are larger than the intermediate cipher states for all but the last round of the cipher. The input and output of σ at round r are denoted by x_σ^r and x_γ^r respectively. The σ transformation for round r can be expressed by,

$$\sigma^r : x_\gamma^{r+1} = \sigma(x_\sigma^r, k^r) \iff x_\gamma^{r+1} = (x_\sigma^r \oplus k^r). \tag{1}$$

Note that, the output of the key mixing layer forms the input to the next round. However, when $r = R$, the output of σ is the C.

2.2   Non-linear Substitution Layer

The substitution layer, denoted by γ, is the only non-linear step in the HD cipher. This layer uses an invertible local non-linear transformation called the S-box, S_γ. The construction of S_γ is similar to that in Rijndael [22], where the substitution box is generated by inverting elements in $GF(2^m)$ and applying an invertible affine transform (to prevent zeroes mapping to zero). The design of the S_γ minimizes large correlation and difference propagation (see Section 3) between input bits and output bits. The S_γ so designed, causes intra symbol avalanche [9] (that is every bit in the output symbol of the S-box flips with a probability of half for a single bit flip in the input symbol), which is essential for the security of the cipher. S_γ transforms the input vector $\boldsymbol{x}_\gamma^r$ to the output vector $\boldsymbol{x}_\pi^r$ by acting on each of the n_s^r symbols in the input vector independently.

The γ transformation can be expressed by,

$$\gamma^r : \boldsymbol{x}_\pi^r = \gamma(\boldsymbol{x}_\gamma^r) \Longleftrightarrow x_\pi^r(j) = S_\gamma(x_\gamma^r(j)) , \qquad (2)$$

where, $j \in \{1...n_s^r\}$. During HD cipher decryption, inverse substitution box, $s_{\gamma^{-1}}$, is used instead of s_γ.

2.3   Symbol Transposition Layer

The symbol transposition layer, denoted by π, is the first of the two diffusion operations used in the HD cipher. The aim of this layer is to permute the cipher state using a diffusion optimal transformation. It applies a matrix transposition type of permutation on the cipher state. With respect to π, the input state $\boldsymbol{x}_\pi^r$ is arranged into $n_u^r \times n_v^r$ matrix X_π^r (with n_u^r rows and n_v^r columns). This matrix is then transposed to obtain $n_v^r \times n_u^r$ matrix X_θ^r. This is then mapped to the vector representation $\boldsymbol{x}_\theta^r$. The π transformation can be expressed by,

$$\pi^r : \boldsymbol{x}_\theta^r = \pi(\boldsymbol{x}_\pi^r) \Leftrightarrow X_\theta^r = (X_\pi^r)^T \qquad (3)$$

In matrix transposition transformation, any two symbols appearing in the same column before the transformation appear in different columns after the transformation. Hence, this transformation is a diffusion optimal transformation [6].

2.4   High Diffusion Coding Layer

The High Diffusion coding layer is the second of the two diffusion operations used in the HD cipher. The aim of this layer is to diffuse the intra symbol avalanche caused by the substitution layer to a large number of symbols in the resulting cipher state. In HD cipher, this layer has an additional aim, which is to correct transmission errors during decryption. Hence, we need to use an error correcting code, with encoding operation θ, to perform this transformation.

In this section, we first introduce the criteria that channel codes to be used in this transformation should satisfy. We call the channel codes that satisfy these criteria as HD codes. Some techniques to construct HD codes are given. Finally, we define the HD coding and decoding transformations as applied in the HD cipher.

Design criteria for HD coding transformation: The aim of HD coding transformation is to design θ such that we attain the highest possible security (in terms of diffusion) and error correction. Therefore, we derive two criteria that θ codes must satisfy:

- *Security Criterion:* Since, the θ will be used in the diffusion layer it needs to spread the intra symbol avalanche caused by the substitution operation to a large number of output symbols. The spreading power, diffusion, is measured using the concept of *branch number* [8]. Let vectors a, b represent any two arbitrary k symbol input vectors and $\theta(a)$, $\theta(b)$ represent the corresponding n symbol output vectors. Then the branch number of the transformation θ is defined as,

$$B(\theta) = \min_{a,b \neq a} \{H_d(a, b) + H_d(\theta(a), \theta(b))\} \qquad (4)$$

Here, H_d denotes the symbol hamming distance. Since, the maximum output difference corresponding to a single non-zero symbol input difference is n. The upper bound for $B(\theta)$ is $n + 1$. To provide good security, θ must have the maximum possible branch number. Hence, we set

$$B(\theta) = n + 1 \qquad (5)$$

as the security criterion of θ.

- *Error Resilience Criterion:* The number of errors that can be corrected by a code is governed by the pairwise minimum distance between the codewords [25]. A large minimum distance would ensure good error resilience property. The minimum distance between two codewords in the code space is usually denoted by $d_{\min}$. The best possible $d_{\min}$ for a code is attained when the code satisfies the Singleton bound. That is,

$$d_{\min} = n - k + 1 \qquad (6)$$

where, n is the codeword length and k is the message length. Codes that satisfy Singleton bounds are referred to as Maximum Distance Separable (MDS) codes. Hence, we set θ to be an encoding function of an $[n, k, 2^m]$ MDS code as the error resilience criterion.

The following is an interesting property that connects the security criterion 5 to the error resilience criterion 6.

Theorem 1. *Any $[n, k, q]$ code C with encoding operation θ, that satisfies $B(\theta) = n + 1$ also satisfies $d_{\min} = n - k + 1$.*

Proof. Consider any two codewords c_i and c_j and m_i and m_j be the corresponding messages. Then,

$$H_d(c_i, c_j) + H_d(m_i, m_j) = n + 1$$
$$H_d(c_i, c_j) = n - H_d(m_i, m_j) + 1$$
$$H_d(c_i, c_j) \geq n - k + 1$$

Since, c_i and c_j are any two codewords. We have $d_{\min} = n - k + 1$.

However, the converse is not true. That is any code that satisfies 6 need not satisfy 5. To the best of our knowledge, there are no known channel codes that inherently satisfy both security and error resilience criteria.

The new codes that satisfy both the security and error resilience criterion are called as High Diffusion (HD) codes. The following is the definition of HD codes.

Definition 1. *High Diffusion codes are* $[n, k, q]$ *MDS codes that satisfy the branch number of* $n + 1$.

Construction of HD codes: Unlike usual error correcting codes, the branch number criterion for HD codes involves *pairs of messages* and their associated codewords. This makes deriving a closed form expression (or encoding transformation θ) for the construction of the codes tricky. A brute force search produces the complete mapping with the highest expected runtime. Then, the θ has to derived from these mappings. We have, so far developed some short-cut techniques to generate HD codes. A brief outline of these techniques follow:

- *Coset Based Search*: Cosets are formed such that the codewords are assigned to the coset leaders only. The codewords for the rest of the coset elements are related to each other, often they are rotations of each other. The coset based search makes use of cosets to reduce the complexity of the code assignment. This searching technique only needs to find codewords for the coset leaders. We then use the message to codeword mapping to derive θ.
- *Transformation from Reed Solomon Codes*: In this technique, we start with a known MDS code and transform the encoding transformation of this MDS code into an encoding transformation of the HD code. As Reed Solomon (RS) codes are an important subclass of MDS codes, we start with $[q-1, k, q]$ RS codes and transform them into $[q-1, k, q]$ HD codes using permutations of the message-codeword assignments that satisfy the branch number criterion. An example of this method is given in [16]. *Note that the traditional method to generate an RS code cannot be directly used to generate an HD code, because the HD codes have a second property to be satisfied viz., the branch number criterion.*
- *Puncturing Existing Codes:* This gives us an easy way to generate new HD codes from existing HD codes. The following Theorem 2 proves that Puncturing HD codes result in HD codes.

Theorem 2. *Punctured HD codes are HD codes.*

Proof. Let $\mathcal{C}$ be an $[n, k, q]$ HD code and $\mathcal{C}'$ be the punctured $[n-1, k, q]$ code obtained from $\mathcal{C}$. Let $\boldsymbol{m}_i$, $\boldsymbol{m}_j$ be any two messages with their corresponding codewords $\boldsymbol{c}_i$, $\boldsymbol{c}_j$ in $\mathcal{C}$ and $\boldsymbol{c}'_i, \boldsymbol{c}'_j$ in $\mathcal{C}'$. We know that $\mathcal{C}$ is an HD code, therefore $H_d(\boldsymbol{m}_i, \boldsymbol{m}_j) + H_d(\boldsymbol{c}_i, \boldsymbol{c}_j) \geq n+1$. We know that, $\boldsymbol{c}'_i$ and $\boldsymbol{c}'_j$ are obtained by puncturing $\boldsymbol{c}_i$ and $\boldsymbol{c}_j$ in one symbol position. This implies that $H_d(\boldsymbol{m}_i, \boldsymbol{m}_j) + H_d(\boldsymbol{c}'_i, \boldsymbol{c}'_j) \geq n$. Hence, $\mathcal{C}'$ is an HD code.

HD encoding operation (θ): The HD encoding operation, denoted by θ, uses HD codes. The cipher state, x_θ^r, at the input to the HD encoding operation, is arranged in the form of an $n_u^r \times n_v^r$ matrix X_θ^r. An $[n_{u'}^r, n_u^r, 2^m]$ HD code with encoding operation θ^r is used to encode each column of X_θ^r independently. The resulting output cipher state is now represented by a $n_{u'}^r \times n_v^r$ matrix X_σ^r which is then mapped to x_σ^r. The HD encoding operation θ can be represented as,

$$\theta^r : x_\sigma^r = \theta(x_\theta^r) \Leftrightarrow X_\sigma^r(j) = \theta^r(X_\theta^r(j)) , \tag{7}$$

where $X^r(j)$ represents the j-th column of the matrix. As the same θ^r is used on all the input columns, branch number $\mathcal{B}(\cdot)$ is lower bounded by:

$$\mathcal{B}(\theta^r) \geq n_{u'}^r + 1, \tag{8}$$
$$\geq n_u^r + d_{min}^r. \tag{9}$$

HD decoding operation ψ: HD decoding operation, denoted by ψ, is used during decryption. So far, we have generated HD codes by transforming the RS codes. Hence, we use the Berlekamp-Massey [1] algorithm, which is used to decode RS codes, to decode HD codes. For all valid cipher states, the branch number property of θ^r is also inherent in ψ^r. The bound on error correction capability, t^r, of ψ^r is derived from the minimum distance between codewords of the HD code θ^r as follows:

$$t^r = \lfloor \frac{d_{min}^r}{2} \rfloor$$
$$t^r = \lfloor \frac{n_{u'}^r - n_u^r + 1}{2} \rfloor$$
$$\therefore t^r = \lfloor \frac{\mathcal{B}(\theta^r) - n_u^r}{2} \rfloor \tag{10}$$

From 9 and 10 we can observe that the parameter d_{min} jointly controls the diffusion strength and error correction capacity in the HD cipher.

3   Security Analysis of HD Ciphers

Security of symmetric block ciphers is usually measured by their key lengths. This is because for an attacker, the complexity of the attack grows exponentially with the key length. Although the key length n_k used in HD cipher is n_b^R bits, we look at the existence of attacks with complexity lesser than $\mathcal{O}(2^{n_b^0})$, where n_b^0 is the length of plaintext. This is because, with $n_b^0 \leq n_b^R$, a dictionary attack will perform better than a brute force key search. However, a brute force attack is not the only possible attack. For example, shortcut attacks make use of the structure of the cipher to come up with a technique to break it (deduce the secret key) with complexity lesser than $\mathcal{O}(2^{n_b^0})$. In this section, we analyze the security of HD ciphers by looking at the resistance it offers against some well known cryptanalytic attacks.

3.1 Linear and Differential Cryptanalysis

In this section, we analyze the security of HD cipher in terms of linear and differential cryptanalysis. Differential cryptanalysis [3, 4] is a chosen plaintext-ciphertext attack that makes use of difference propagation property of a cipher to deduce the key bits. The difference propagation property of an S-box is the relative amount of all input pairs that for the given input difference results in a specific output difference and it is expressed as propagation ratio [5]. Let $x_{*_1}^r$ be any intermediate cipher state at round r resulting from the plaintext P_1. Similarly, let $x_{*_2}^r$ be the corresponding intermediate cipher state resulting from P_2. The non zero symbols in $x_{*_1}^r \oplus x_{*_2}^r$ are called active S-boxes or active symbols. The pattern that specifies the positions of the active symbols is called the (difference) activity pattern. The propagation ratio over all the rounds of a differential trail can be approximated by the product of the propagation ratios of the active symbols in its activity pattern. Differential cryptanalysis is possible if the maximum possible propagation ratio is significantly larger than $2^{1-n_b^0}$.

Linear cryptanalysis [17] is a known plaintext-ciphertext attack that makes use of linearity in the cipher to obtain the key bits. The substitution is the only non-linear step in most of the block ciphers including the proposed HD cipher. The linearity of an active symbol can be approximated to the maximum input-output correlation exhibited by it. The active symbols in a round are determined by the non zero symbols in the selection vectors at the input of the round. The pattern that specifies the positions of active symbols is called (correlation) activity pattern. The linearity of one round can be extended to multiple rounds to form a linear trail. The correlation (measure of linearity) of a linear trail (multiple rounds) can be approximated to the product of input-output correlations of its active symbols. Linear cryptanalysis is possible if the maximum possible correlation of any linear trail is significantly larger than $2^{-n_b^0/2}$, where n_b^0 is the size of the plaintext in bits.

The number of active symbols in an activity pattern, a_*^r, is called the *symbol weight*, denoted by $W_S(a_*^r)$. Let A_*^r be the matrix representation of a_*^r. Then any column $A_*^r(j)$ is said to be active if it contains at least one active symbol. The number of active columns in an activity pattern is called the *column weight*, denoted by $W_C(a_*^r)$. The difference and correlation activity patterns propagate through the transformations of different rounds of the cipher forming linear and differential trails. The number of active symbols in a trail is given by $\sum_{r=1}^{R}(W_S(a_\gamma^r))$. To defend a cipher against linear and differential cryptanalysis, the cipher design should ensure a large number of active symbols in any linear and difference trail. Hence, a lower bound on the number of active symbols in any linear or differential trail will give a lower bound on the resistance of the cipher to linear and differential cryptanalysis. In Theorem 4 we show that this lower bound for HD cipher is $\mathcal{B}(\theta^1) \times \mathcal{B}(\theta^2)$.

Lemma 1. *The total number of active columns of the function $\pi \circ \theta \circ \pi$ is lower bounded by the branch number of θ, $\mathcal{B}(\theta)$.*

This is true for any diffusion optimal π. Proof given in [7].

Theorem 3. *The number of active S-boxes or symbols for a two round trail of HD cipher is lower bounded by the branch number of the first round of HD code, $\mathcal{B}(\theta^1)$.*

Proof. Consider the first two rounds of HD cipher. Since γ and σ operate on the symbols locally, they do not affect the propagation pattern. Hence the number of active S-boxes or symbols for a two round trail, $W_S(a_\gamma^1) + W_S(a_\gamma^2)$, is bounded by the propagation property of θ^1. From the definition of HD codes and Equation 9 it follows that the sum of active S-boxes before and after θ^1 encoding of the first round is lower bounded by $\mathcal{B}(\theta^1)$.

Theorem 4. *The number of active S-boxes or symbols for a four round trail (starting with round 1) of HD cipher is lower bounded by $\mathcal{B}(\theta^1) \times \mathcal{B}(\theta^2)$.*

Proof. The sum of the number of active columns in a_γ^2 and a_θ^3 is lower bounded by $\mathcal{B}(\theta^2)$ (from Lemma 1). Hence we have,

$$W_C(a_\gamma^2) + W_C(a_\theta^3) \geq \mathcal{B}(\theta^2) \tag{11}$$

but, $W_C(a_\gamma^4) = W_C(a_\theta^3)$ (θ does not change the number of active columns). Therefore,

$$W_C(a_\gamma^2) + W_C(a_\gamma^4) \geq \mathcal{B}(\theta^2) \tag{12}$$

The total number of active S-boxes in a_θ^1 and a_γ^2 is given by,

$$W_S(a_\theta^1) + W_S(a_\gamma^2) \geq W_C(a_\gamma^2)\mathcal{B}(\theta^1) \tag{13}$$

Similarly, the total number of active S-boxes in a_θ^3 and a_γ^4 is given by,

$$W_S(a_\theta^3) + W_S(a_\gamma^4) \geq W_C(a_\gamma^4)\mathcal{B}(\theta^3) \tag{14}$$

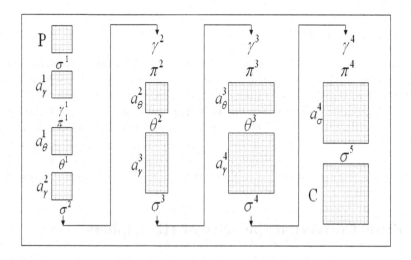

Fig. 2. Activity pattern propagation in four round HD cipher encryption

Combining 12 13 and 14 will give,

$$W_S(a_\theta^1) + W_S(a_\gamma^2) + W_S(a_\theta^3) + W_S(a_\gamma^4)$$
$$\geq W_C(a_\gamma^2)\mathcal{B}(\theta^1) + W_C(a_\gamma^4)\mathcal{B}(\theta^3)$$
$$\geq (W_C(a_\gamma^2) + W_C(a_\gamma^4))\mathcal{B}(\theta^1) +$$
$$W_C(a_\gamma^4)(d_{min}^2 + d_{min}^3 - 2)$$

Since, $W_C(a_\gamma^4)(d_{min}^2 + d_{min}^3 - 2)$ is non negative $(d_{min}^2, d_{min}^3 \geq 1)$ and $W_S(a_\theta^j) = W_S(a_\gamma^j)$ we get,

$$W_S(a_\gamma^1) + W_S(a_\gamma^2) + W_S(a_\gamma^3) + W_S(a_\gamma^4) \geq \mathcal{B}(\theta^1)\mathcal{B}(\theta^2) \tag{15}$$

The security of HD cipher against linear and differential cryptanalysis thus depends on the branch number of the HD coding operation at the diffusion layer.

Consider the Rijndael cipher and the HD cipher operating on the plaintext block length. Then, the design of HD cipher guarantees that the number of active S-boxes in any four round linear or differential trail of HD cipher is lower bounded by the number of active S-boxes in any four round linear or differential trail of Rijndael cipher. Also, the S-boxes used in the HD cipher are the same as the S-boxes used in the Rijndael cipher. Hence, we can conclude that HD cipher is as secure as the Rijndael with respect to linear and differential cryptanalysis. This also shows that, the error correction property of the HD code does not lead to information leakage or weakness in security with respect to linear and differential cryptanalysis. However, the HD ciphers use a larger key length ($n_k = n_b^R \geq n_b^0$) to achieve the same security level as that of Rijndael. The resistance to linear and differential cryptanalysis also shows that, the HD ciphers are not vulnerable to known plaintext type of attacks described in [2].

3.2 Square Attack

The square attack [6] (also known as Integral attack or the Saturation attack) makes use of the byte oriented nature of the Square block cipher which was the predecessor of Rijndael. As Rijndael is also a byte oriented cipher, this attack has been extended to reduced versions of Rijndael cipher [15, 11]. Although the attacks described applies directly to ciphers operating with symbol size in bytes, it can be easily extended to other symbol sizes. HD ciphers also comprise of symbol oriented operations which are loosely based on Rijndael, hence HD ciphers with fewer than seven rounds would be as weak as reduced versions of the Rijndael cipher.

4   Error Correction Capacity of HD Ciphers

In this section, we prove bounds on the error correction capacity of HD ciphers. After encryption the ciphertext of length n_s^R symbols (equivalently n_b^R bits) is

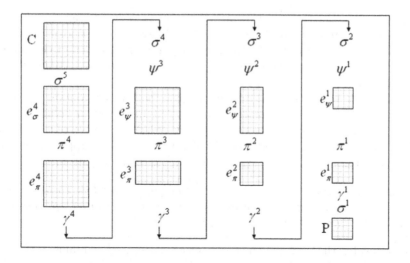

Fig. 3. Error pattern propagation in four round HD cipher decryption

transmitted across a noisy channel. Specifically, we consider a bursty channel
and use the term "full weight burst error" to denote an error burst where all the
symbols in the burst are in error. In order to formalize our analysis we introduce
the following assumptions, definitions and notations. Without loss of generality
we consider HD ciphers in which HD codes have equal error correcting capacity
in all rounds. That is, $t^r = t$; $\forall r \in \{1, .., R-1\}$. A symbol of the cipher state
that is in error (due to channel or propagation due to decryption) is referred
to as an *error symbol*. An *error pattern* is a vector whose non zero symbols
represent the error symbols. The error patterns for each round are denoted by,
e_*^r, $\forall r \in \{1, ..., R\}$. In the matrix representation of the error pattern (denoted
by E_*^r), a column (or row) in the error pattern is said to be in error if there
are at least $t + 1$ error symbols in the corresponding column (or row). We refer
to such columns and rows as *error column* and *error row* respectively. We say
that error correction is *complete* in round r if e_*^r is a zero vector, otherwise error
correction is said to be *incomplete*. Error correction capacity of a four round
HD cipher decryption is analysed in Theorem 5. An outline of a four round HD
cipher decryption is represented in the Fig. 3.

Lemma 2. *For a four round HD cipher, if there are at most t error columns
or rows in the ciphertext before decryption, the error correction will be complete
after at most three rounds of decryption. Here, t denotes the error correction
capacity of HD codes used in the HD cipher.*

Proof. Consider the first three rounds of HD cipher decryption in Fig. 3. Since
the inverse non-linear transform γ and round key addition σ operations do not
convert an error symbol to an error free symbol and vice versa, it can be excluded
from the analysis.

First, we consider the case in which the error pattern e_σ^4 contains at most t error columns. After π^4 transformation, we will have at most t error rows in e_π^4. Since, ψ^3 has an error correcting power of t, errors across each of the columns are corrected. Hence, the error pattern e_ψ^3 will contain all zeros, completing the error correction.

Consider the second case, in which the error pattern e_σ^4 contains at most t error rows. After π^4 transformation, we have at most t error columns in e_π^4. This is beyond the error correction capacity of ψ^3, hence we take the worst case scenario of having at most t error columns in e_ψ^3. Now, applying the same argument as the first case, the error pattern e_ψ^2 should have all zeros.

Lemma 3. *For a four round HD cipher, if there are at least $t+1$ error columns or rows in the ciphertext before decryption, the error correction will remain incomplete after three rounds of decryption.*

Proof. Consider the case in which the error pattern e_σ^4 contains $t+1$ error columns. After π^4 transformation, e_π^4 will contain at least $t+1$ error rows. This is beyond the error correction capacity of ψ^3. Hence e_ψ^3 will have all of its symbols in error and the decryption will remain incomplete even after ψ^2 in e_ψ^2. Similarly, when there are $t+1$ error rows in e_σ^4, there will be $t+1$ error columns in e_ψ^3 and every symbol will be in error in e_ψ^2. Hence the decryption will remain incomplete.

We now analyze the maximum full weight burst error length that is guaranteed to be corrected by a four round HD cipher. Our analysis is independent of the starting and ending locations of the burst with respect to the cipher state.

Theorem 5. *The full weight burst error correcting capacity of a four round HD cipher is $(t-1)(\mathcal{B}(\theta^3) - 1) + 2t + 1$.*

Proof. Without loss of generality we consider the row-wise transmission (with respect to matrix representation) of the ciphertext and hence full weight bursts that occur across the rows of the ciphertext. The following analysis can be trivially extended to column-wise transmission as well.

We know that a burst of $t+1$ errors in one row makes that an error row. The minimum full weight burst error length required to create two error rows is $2(t+1)$. Similarly, a full weight burst error of length $n_{u'}^3 + 2(t+1)$ can cause three error rows. Generalizing this result, we get that, a burst length of $(l-2)(n_{u'}^3) + 2(t+1)$ can cause l error rows. This is in fact the minimum length for a full weight error burst to cause l error rows. It follows that a full weight burst length of at least $(t-1)(n_{u'}^3) + 2(t+1)$ is required to generate $l = t+1$ error rows. This implies that a full weight burst of length $(t-1)(n_{u'}^3) + 2(t+1) - 1$ cannot generate $l \geq t+1$ error rows. From Lemma 2 a burst of length $(t-1)(n_{u'}^3) + 2(t+1) - 1$ is correctable and from Lemma 3 a burst of length $(t-1)(n_{u'}^3) + 2(t+1)$ is not correctable. Hence the minimum burst length that is guaranteed to be corrected by a 4 round HD cipher decryption is $(t-1)(n_{u'}^3) + 2(t+1) - 1$. Which is equal to $(t-1)(\mathcal{B}(\theta^3) - 1) + 2t + 1$ (from 8).

Although this gives the error correction capacity of the system, in some cases the system can correct longer burst errors. In other words, some longer bursts can be corrected, depending on their start and end positions. Theorem 6 gives the smallest burst length for which the probability of complete error correction in a four round HD cipher decryption is zero. Any full weight error burst that is smaller than this has some non zero probability of being correctable.

Theorem 6. *The smallest burst length of a full weight burst error, for which the probability of complete decoding is zero (by a four round HD cipher) is $t(\mathcal{B}(\theta^3) + 1) + 1$ symbols.*

Proof. We again assume row-wise transmission of the ciphertext and hence full weight burst errors occurring across rows. The maximum number of error rows for which error correction will be complete in three rounds is t (Lemma 2). The minimum length of a full weight burst that makes a row in error is $t + 1$, hence the maximum full weight burst length that can occur in an error free row is t. Therefore, the maximum full weight burst length that produces a error pattern with at most t error rows is $t n_{u'}^3 + 2t$. This is equal to $t(\mathcal{B}(\theta^3) + 1)$. Hence a burst length of $t(\mathcal{B}(\theta^3) + 1) + 1$ is the smallest burst length of a full weight burst, for which the probability of complete decoding is zero.

5 Simulation Results

To assess the performance of our proposed cipher, we compare it with a conventional, concatenated system that uses Rijndael for encryption and Reed-Solomon codes for error correction. As a proof of concept, we construct a four round HD cipher in the Gallois Field of order 8 ($\mathrm{GF}(2^3)$) and compare it against a system that uses the Rijndael in $\mathrm{GF}(2^3)$ concatenated with three RS codes, A, B and C with parameters $[7, 3, 8]$, $[15, 3, 16]$, $[31, 3, 32]$ respectively. We use three different RS codes, because there is no RS code with parameters that match the HD cipher performance exactly in terms of error correction. The selection here compares two systems which cause smaller data expansion (A and B) and one that causes more data expansion (C) compared to the HD cipher. Let us refer to the concatenated system produced by using RS code A, as "System A", and that produced by using RS code B and C, as "System B" and "System C" respectively. The HD cipher produces 147 bits of cipher text for every 27 bits of plaintext; System A, System B and System C produce 63, 135 and 279 bits of ciphertext for every 27 bits of plaintext respectively.

The parameters of the High Diffusion cipher in $\mathrm{GF}(2^3)$ is as follows: $n_b^0 = 27$ bits, $m = 3$, $R = 4$, HD code used for $\theta^1 = [3, 3, 2^3]$, $\theta^2 = \theta^3 = [7, 3, 2^3]$ (generated using RS code A) and $n_b^4 = 147$ bits. The parameters for Rijndael cipher in $\mathrm{GF}(2^3)$ are as follows: $n_b^0 = n_b^4 = 27$ bits, MixColumn transformation uses an invertible 3×3 matrix in $\mathrm{GF}(2^3)$ with branch number 4.

The sum of active S-boxes for a four round trail of HD cipher is $\mathcal{B}(\theta^1) \times \mathcal{B}(\theta^2) = 32$. The sum of active S-boxes for a four round trail of the Rijndael cipher

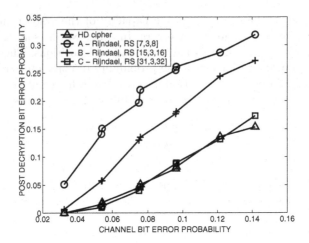

Fig. 4. Comparison of error resilience of HD cipher and Rijndael concatenated with Reed Solomon codes

is 16. The resistance to linear and differential cryptanalysis is lower bounded by the product of correlation and propagation ratio of the active S-boxes (see Section 3.1). This implies that *HD cipher is exponentially twice as resistant to linear and differential cryptanalysis as the Rijndael cipher.* However, HD cipher uses 147 bit key length to attain a security comparable to the 27 bit Rijndael cipher.

To simulate the bursty nature of wireless channel environment, we used the Gilbert-Elliott channel model with the following parameters [19], the transition probability from bad state to good state, $g = 0.1092$, the transition probability from good state to bad state, $b = 0.0308$, bit error probability in the bad state, $p_b = 0.5$ and bit error probability in the good state $p_g = 0.0128$. Fig. 4 plots the post decryption bit error rate of the proposed HD cipher and the concatenated Systems A, B and C against the channel bit error rate. It can be observed that the HD cipher performs significantly better than system A, B and matches the performance of System C. We can see that in order to match the HD cipher in terms of error correction performance, the conventional system will increase the data expansion by 89% when compared to the expansion in HD cipher.

We now compare HD cipher and Rijndael in terms of computational complexity. In Rijndael, the cipher state is multiplied with the MixColumn transformation matrix in every round. Whereas, in HD cipher encryption, the cipher state is multiplied with the generator matrix of HD code in every round. A large generator matrix will incur higher computational costs. The size of MixColumn used in our experiment is 3×3, whereas the size of generator matrix for HD code is 3×7. In HD cipher decryption, RS decoding algorithm is used, which requires higher computational complexity compared to the inverse MixColumn matrix multiplication. Since, the design of HD cipher is still in a theoretical stage, we have not done extensive analysis on its computational complexity.

6   Conclusions

Several motivating factors for the design of error correcting ciphers were discussed. The High Diffusion cipher, which combines a block cipher with a block error correcting code was proposed. A new class of Maximum Distance Separable (MDS) codes called High Diffusion codes were introduced. These codes were shown to achieve optimal diffusion and error resilience. Some techniques to construct HD codes were presented. The security of the four round HD cipher against linear and differential cryptanalysis was shown to be lower bounded by $\mathcal{B}(\theta^1)\mathcal{B}(\theta^2)$, where $\mathcal{B}(\cdot)$ is the branch number and θ^r is the rth round HD coding operation. We proved that the full weight burst error correction capacity of a four round HD cipher is $(t - 1)(\mathcal{B}(\theta^3) - 1) + 2t + 1$ symbols. Simulation results of a four round HD cipher operating in $GF(2^3)$ revealed that (a) HD cipher is as secure as Rijndael cipher with respect to linear and differential cryptanalysis (b) conventional, concatenated systems that independently perform encryption (using Rijndael) and error correction (using Reed Solomon codes) need to increase the data expansion by 89% to match the performance of HD cipher.

References

1. Berlekamp, E. R.: 1968, *Algorithmic Coding Theory*, Chapt. Ch. 7. New York: McGraw-Hill.
2. Berson, T. A.: 1997, 'Failure of the McEliece public-key cryptosystem under message-resend and related-message attack'. In: *Advances in Cryptology-CRYPTO '97, Lecture notes in computer science.*
3. Biham, E. and A. Shamir: 1991, 'Differential Cryptanalysis of Snefru, Khafre, REDOC-II, LOKI and Lucifer (Extended Abstract)'. *Lecture Notes in Computer Science* **576**, 156.
4. Biham, E. and A. Shamir: 1993, 'Differential Cryptanalysis of the Full 16-Round DES'. In: *CRYPTO '92: Proceedings of the 12th Annual International Cryptology Conference on Advances in Cryptology.* London, UK, pp. 487–496.
5. Daemen, J.: 1995, 'Cipher and hash function design strategies based on linear and differential cryptanalysis'. Ph.D. thesis, K.U.Leuven.
6. Daemen, J., L. R. Knudsen, and V. Rijmen: 1997, 'The Block Cipher Square'. In: *FSE '97: Proceedings of the 4th International Workshop on Fast Software Encryption.* London, UK, pp. 149–165.
7. Daemen, J. and V. Rijmen: 2001, 'The Wide Trail Design Strategy'. In: *Proceedings of the 8th IMA International Conference on Cryptography and Coding.* London, UK, pp. 222–238.
8. Daemen, J. and V. Rijmen: 2002, *The Design of Rijndael.* Secaucus, NJ, USA: Springer-Verlag New York, Inc.
9. Feistel, H.: 1973, 'Cryptography and Computer Privacy'. **228**(5), 15–23.
10. FIPS: 2001, 'Specification for the Advanced Encryption Standard (AES)'. Federal Information Processing Standards Publication 197.
11. Gilbert, H. and M. Minier: 2000, 'A Collision Attack on 7 Rounds of Rijndael.'. In: *AES Candidate Conference.* pp. 230–241.
12. Godoy, W. and D. Periera: 1997, 'A proposal of a cryptography algorithm with techniques of error correction'. *Computer Communications* **20**(15), 1374–1380.

13. Hwang, T. and T. Rao: 1988, 'Secret Error-Correcting Codes (SECC)'. In: *Advances in Cryptography - Crypto 1988*.
14. Kundsen, L. and D. Wagner: 2002, 'Integral Cryptanalysis'. *Lecture Notes in Computer Science* **2365**, 112.
15. Lucks, S.: 2000, 'Attacking Seven Rounds of Rijndael under 192-bit and 256-bit Keys.'. In: *AES Candidate Conference*. pp. 215–229.
16. Mathur, C. N., K. Narayan, and K. Subbalakshmi: 2005, 'High Diffusion Codes: A Class of Maximum Distance Separable Codes for Error Resilient Block Ciphers'. *2nd IEEE International Workshop on Adaptive Wireless Networks (AWiN), Globecom*.
17. Matsui, M.: 1993, 'Linear cryptanalysis method for DES cipher'. In: *Advances in cryptology -EUROCRYPT93, Lecture Notes in Computer Science*, Vol. 765. pp. 1–11.
18. McEliece, R.: 1978, 'A Publick Key Cryptosystem Based on Algebraic Codes'. *DNS Progress Reports 42-44, NASA Jet Propulsion Labaratory*.
19. Mushkin, M. and I. Bar-David, 'Capacity and coding for the Gilbert-Elliot channels'. *Information Theory, IEEE Transactions on* **35**, 1277–1290.
20. Nanjunda, C., M. Haleem, and R. Chandramouli: 2005, 'Robust Encryption for Secure Image Transmission over Wireless Channels'. In: *ICC' 2005, IEEE International Conference on Communications, May 16-20, 2005 - Seoul, Korea*.
21. Narayan, K.: 2005, 'On the Design of Secure Error Resilient Diffusion Layers for Block Ciphers'. Master's thesis, Steven Institute Of Technology, Hoboken, New Jersey.
22. Nyberg, K.: 1994, 'Differentially uniform mappings for cryptography'. In: *EUROCRYPT '93: Workshop on the theory and application of cryptographic techniques on Advances in cryptology*. Secaucus, NJ, USA, pp. 55–64.
23. Stinson, D.: 2002, *Cryptography: Theory and Practice,Second Edition*. CRC/C&H.
24. van Tilborg, H.: 1998, 'Coding theory at work in cryptology and vice versa'.
25. Wicker, S. B.: 1995, *Error control systems for digital communication and storage*. Upper Saddle River, NJ, USA: Prentice-Hall, Inc.

Authentication for Paranoids: Multi-party Secret Handshakes

Stanisław Jarecki, Jihye Kim, and Gene Tsudik

Computer Science Department,
University of California, Irvine
{stasio, jihyek, gts}@ics.uci.edu

Abstract. In a society increasingly concerned with the steady assault on electronic privacy, the need for privacy-preserving techniques is both natural and justified. This need extends to traditional security tools such as authentication and key distribution protocols. A secret handshake protocol allow members of the same group to authenticate each other *secretly*, meaning that a non-member cannot determine, even by engaging someone in a protocol, whether that party is a member of the group. Whereas, parties who *are* members of the same group recognize each other as members, and can establish authenticated secret keys with each other. Thus, a secret handshake protocol offers *privacy-preserving authentication* and can be used whenever group members need to identify and securely communicate with each other without being observed or detected.

Most prior work in secret handshake protocols considered 2-party scenarios. In this paper we propose formal definitions of *multi-party secret handshakes*, and we develop a practical and provably secure multi-party secret handshake scheme by blending Schnorr-signature based 2-party secret handshake protocol of Castelluccia et al. [5] with a group key agreement protocol of Burmester and Desmedt [4].

The resulting scheme achieves very strong privacy properties, is as efficient as the (non-private) authenticated version of the Burmester-Desmedt protocol [4, 6], but requires a supply of one-time certificates for each group member.

Keywords: privacy-preserving authentication, secret handshakes, group key agreement, anonymity, privacy, authentication protocols.

1 Introduction

Consider the following scenario: two undercover Interpol agents, Alice and Bob, are in a crowded public place, such as an airport or a city square. They are not aware of each others presence or affiliation. However, each wants to discover, and communicate with other Interpol agents. Interpol rules prohibit agents from revealing their affiliation to non-agents. Since the environment is potentially hostile, Alice would thus authenticate to Bob only if he is an agent, and vice versa. No one who is not an Interpol agent as well should be able to determine whether

J. Zhou, M. Yung, and F. Bao (Eds.): ACNS 2006, LNCS 3989, pp. 325–339, 2006.
© Springer-Verlag Berlin Heidelberg 2006

Alice (or Bob) is an agent, or even if Alice and Bob are members of any single organization. Likewise, if only one of the two (Alice or Bob) is a genuine agent, the other (the impostor) should learn nothing about the counterpart's affiliation. Furthermore, should anyone meet either Alice or Bob again, and engage them in an authentication protocol, they should not be able link the two encounters.

Traditional PKI-based authentication fails in the above scenario. Other intuitive approaches, such as key exchange followed by encrypted authentication, fail as well. Even more exotic cryptographic tools like group signatures and identity escrow are unsuitable since they protect anonymity of members within the same group, but are not designed to hide the *affiliation* of the group members.

1.1   Prior Work on Two-Party Secret Handshakes

To satisfy the security requirements for the secret agent example we need authentication schemes which are anonymous in the sense of hiding an affiliation of the participating parties. Such authentication schemes were named *secret handshakes* by Balfanz et al. in a paper [2] which introduced the notion of privacy (a.k.a. anonymity) for public-key two-party authentication schemes.[1] A (two-party) secret handshake (SH) scheme allows two group members (e.g. two entities certified by the same Certification Authority) to authenticate each other in an anonymous and unobservable manner in the sense that one party's membership is not revealed unless the other party's membership is also ensured. In other words, if party A who is a member of group G_1 engages in a (two-party) secret handshake protocol with party B who is a member of G_2, a secret handshake scheme guarantees the following [2]:

- A and B authenticate each other if and only if $G_1 = G_2$.
- If $G_1 \neq G_2$, both parties learn only the fact that $G_1 \neq G_2$.

A two-party secret handshake scheme can possess further desirable anonymity properties: (1) *Unobservability*: A non-group member cannot tell not only whether A or B belong to some given group but also whether A and B belong to any single group (and hence whether they accept or reject in the handshake protocol); (2) *Unlinkability*: Two occurrences of the same party cannot be linked with each other by anyone except the group manager; and (3) *Privacy against eavesdropping insiders*: Any *passive* observers, even including other group members, cannot learn anything from the protocol as well.

Balfanz, et al. [2] constructed the two-party SH scheme by adapting the key agreement protocol of Sakai, et al. [10]. Its security rests on the hardness of the Bilinear Diffie Hellman (BDH) problem. Subsequently, Castelluccia, et al. [5] developed a more efficient secret 2-party handshake scheme under more standard cryptographic assumption of Computational Diffie Hellman (CDH) problem. Both solutions are secure in the Random Oracle Model (ROM) for hash functions, and both attain properties (1) and (3) above, but attaining property (2), in both solutions, requires a supply of one-time certificates for each group member.

---

[1] Privacy for symmetric-key authentication schemes was considered before by Abadi [1].

1.2 Group Secret Handshakes: Prior Work and Our Contribution

Both aforementioned techniques are limited to 2-party settings. A natural next step is to explore the space of multi-party settings with similar security requirements. For example, we can re-consider our initial secret agent scenario but, this time, with four undercover Interpol agents. They are, as before, in certain proximity, and would like to discover each other and have a secure "conversation". However, each wants to authenticate to others if and only if all of them are similarly affiliated. The adversarial model is also similar. An adversary may eavesdrop or take part in the protocol in order to impersonate an agent or to detect others' affiliations. All properties of 2-party secret handshakes listed above can be adopted to *group* authentication and authenticated key agreement protocols. We will call authenticated group key agreement scheme which satisfies such privacy properties a *Group Secret Handshake* (GSH).

In a recent paper, Tsudik and Xu [12] presented the first group secret handshake (GSH) solution, which also supports reusable (sometimes called multi-show) certificates, instead of one-time certificates as in [2,5]. However, their scheme ensures successful authentication between group members only if each member holds the same most recently distributed group key, which requires a lot of real-time communication between group manager and the group members.

In this paper we give a more formal definition of the GSH scheme than that given in [12], and we provide a solution which fits the standard PKI setting, and in particular avoids having the group manager broadcast key-update messages to the group members. Our solution is based on commonly taken assumptions (Computational Diffie Hellman and the Random Oracle Model for hash functions), achieves very strong anonymity properties, and is as efficient as existing (non-private) two-round group key agreement protocol based on the same assumptions, i.e. the Burmester-Desmedt protocol [4,6]. On the negative side, our scheme requires a supply of one-time certificates for each group member, which implies more storage for group members, more computation for the group manager, and bigger sizes of the certificate revocation lists. However, such solution can still be practical for groups whose members do not engage in this authentication protocol all the time, e.g. no more than 100 times a month on the average.

1.3 Overview of Our GSH Construction

The idea of our scheme is to add affiliation-hiding authentication to the Burmester-Desmedt group key agreement protocol [4] via the signature-based affiliation-hiding encryption method which was given for the discrete-log setting by Castelluccia et al. [5].[2] In the signature-based encryption of [5], the certificate for member of a group G is a Schnorr signature (w, t), where $w = g^r$ and $t = r + x_G H(w, id)$ on a random ID strings id, under the public key $y_G = g^{x_G}$ of this group. The Schnorr signature can be thought of as a private key t and a public key $y = g^t$, which can be computed from the (w, id) pair as $y = w(y_G)^{H(e, id)}$.

---

[2] See section 1.4 below for a discussion of related works on signature-based encryption.

It was shown in [5] that, under the CDH assumption, if key y is computed from (w, id) as above then only the owner of a signature (t, w) on id under key y_G can decrypt ElGamal ciphertexts encrypted under y. Here we use the above "public key" $y = g^t$ not as an encryption key but as the contribution of a player to the Burmester-Desmedt group key agreement protocol, and we show that only the players who hold valid signatures (w, t) issued on some string id can contribute their values $y = g^t$ by sending (w, id) instead of y in the first round of the BD group key agreement protocol, and then recover the agreed-on key in the second round. We show that in this way only the certified group members can get the key that other certified members output, and moreover, that a non-certified player cannot tell what public key y_G the other players use, and hence that the scheme hides group membership of the authorized participants from the non-authorized.

The reason why this construction requires one-time certificates is that re-using a Schnorr certificate (w, t, id) in the protocol described above, corresponds to re-using the same contribution g^t in more than one instance of the Burmester-Desmedt key agreement protocol, which would yield that protocol insecure.

1.4   Other Related Work

In addition to the prior work described above, the work of Xu and Yung [13] constructed an interesting 2-party secret handshake scheme which achieves unlinkability with reusable credentials. However, this scheme requires each party to be aware of other groups (of which one is not a member) and offers weaker form of anonymity, referred to as k-anonymity.

The previously mentioned GSH scheme by Tsudik and Xu [12] achieves additional properties like self-distinction between players participating in the protocol, and traceability of the participating players by the group manager examining the transcript of the protocol. In our GSH protocol we achieve a weaker variant of the self-distinction property, called *counting* (see section 2.2).

Our GSH construction uses the signature-based encryption scheme based on the CDH problem given by [5]. Other signature-based encryption schemes, referred to as "oblivious signature-based envelopes" (OSBE), were developed for other cryptographic settings in [7] and [8]. We note that to satisfy the needs of private (group or two-party) authentication, the signature-based encryption scheme must have additional privacy property of affiliation-hiding[3] and it's an open problem to ensure this property for many OSBE schemes.

2   Definition of a Group Secret Handshake

In this section we describe the components of a GSH scheme and the security properties it should achieve.

A GSH scheme operates in an environment consisting of a set of players and a set of administrators who are responsible for creating groups, admitting chosen

---

[3] The same property was called "sender and receiver obliviousness" in [5].

players as group members, and possibly also revoking their membership. For simplicity's sake, we assume that each player is a member of exactly one group and that each group manager is responsible for a unique group, but our results can be easily generalized to the case when a player can be a member of many groups, and a manager can manage many groups as well. A GSH scheme is a tuple of algorithms (Setup, CreateGroup, AddPlayer, Handshake, RemovePlayer) described in figure 1.

Communication and Adversarial Model: We assume the existence of *anonymous* broadcast channels between all legitimates parties, where "anonymous" means that an outside attacker cannot determine identities of $\mathcal{GA}$, group members, as well as the dynamics and size of a group. Also, a malicious insider (group member) cannot determine identities of other honest group members as well as the dynamics and size of the group. This assumption is necessary in most privacy-preserving authentication schemes; otherwise, anonymity could be trivially compromised. However, we note that our requirement that SH protocols themselves must rely on anonymous channels does *not* necessarily present a problem. This is because a typical secret handshake application would be in a wireless LAN setting where *broadcast* – a natural source of anonymity – is a built-in feature. Additionally, we assume that participants' clocks are loosely synchronized. They specify when they start the protocol and how long they will wait for other player's messages in each protocol round. We stress that we do not assume any reliability properties of this broadcast medium, i.e. in our adversarial model the adversary can inject any messages into the protocol, delay, erase, and/or modify the messages sent between honest parties, and in particular deliver the broadcasted messages to arbitrarily selected players.

2.1 Basic Security Properties of GSH Scheme

A GSH scheme must be correct, authentic, and affiliation-hiding:

Correctness: For any group G managed by an honest GA, and any set Δ of honest players who are members of G, if the adversary forwards all messages between participants in a protocol GSH.Handshake(Δ), then all players in Δ output identical $(K, IDSet)$ pairs, where $IDSet$ has $|\Delta|$ elements, one per each player in Δ, uniquely identifying this player to the group manager GA.

Authenticity: The essence of this property is that if any honest player outputs a key in an instance of the GSH.Handshake scheme, then an attacker who can be an active participant in this protocol but who does not have a non-revoked certificate for that group, learns nothing about that key. Formally, we say that GSH.Handshake guarantees *authenticity*, if every polynomially-bounded adversary $\mathcal{A}$ has only negligible probability of winning of the following game:

1. GSH.Setup and GSH.CreateGroup algorithms are executed and resulting parameters params and public key $\mathcal{PK}_G$ are given to $\mathcal{A}$.
2. $\mathcal{A}$ triggers the GSH.AddMember algorithm under the public key $\mathcal{PK}_G$ polynomially many times. In each GSH.AddMember instance, $\mathcal{A}$ receives a mem-

GSH.Setup: This algorithm is executed publicly, on input of a sufficient security parameter k, to generate public parameters params common to all subsequently generated groups, e.g., k determines the size of the modulus used in cryptographic operations.

GSH.CreateGroup: This algorithm is executed by a group authority, GA to establish a group denoted G. It takes as input params, and outputs a the group public key $\mathcal{PK}_G$, the GA's private key $\mathcal{SK}_G$, and a certificate revocation list, $\mathcal{CRL}_G$, which is originally empty.

GSH.AddMember: This algorithm is executed between a player U and a GA who administers some group G. The input's are GA's private input $\mathcal{SK}_G$ and shared inputs params and $\mathcal{PK}_G$. The output is a membership cert for the player, which contains in particular a random bitstring id of fixed length, e.g. 160 bits. We say that a player who receives a cert in this protocol is a *member* of group G. We assume that GA admits members according to some admission policies, but specification and enforcement of such policies are outside the scope of this paper. The AddPlayer protocol can be executed between same GA and U many times, in which case U receives a set of certs as a result, each containing a different id string (except for negligible probability).

GSH.Handshake(Δ): This algorithm is executed by a set Δ of n players purporting to be members of a group G, where $\Delta = \{U_1, ..., U_n\}$ and $n \geq 2$. Each player U_i runs the protocol on inputs a public key $\mathcal{PK}_G$, a set of certs received from G's GA, and (U_i's current view of) $\mathcal{CRL}_G$. At the end of the protocol, each player outputs either $(K, IDSet)$, in which case we say that the player accepts, where K is an authenticated key for use in subsequent secure communication, and $IDSet$ is a set of id's, or REJECT, in which case we say that the player rejects.

GSH.RemoveMember:: This algorithm is executed by GA. On input of some player identity U, GA looks up the id's assigned to U in instances of the AddMember between this GA and U, and inserts them into $\mathcal{CRL}_G$. The updated $\mathcal{CRL}_G$ is assumed to be publicly available.

Fig. 1. GSH Scheme Components

bership cert from the $\mathcal{GA}$. Before the protocol starts, all certs $\mathcal{A}$ received are added to $\mathcal{CRL}_G$, which is sent to all honest players in G.

3. $\mathcal{A}$ chooses a set of player $\Delta = (V_1, ..., V_l)$ in G, triggers the execution of GSH.Handshake(Δ), and participates in this execution, i.e. hears all the messages, controls their delivery, and can any messages it wants to the participants.

4. If any honest player in Δ accepts, and outputs $(K, IDSet)$ pair, $\mathcal{A}$ wins if he has non-negligible advantage in distinguishing between the following two games: In game [A], $\mathcal{A}$ is given a key K output by some (randomly chosen) accepting player in Δ. In game [B], $\mathcal{A}$ is given a random bitstring of the same length.

Note: The above definition of is a simplified form of the security requirement of an authenticated group key agreement scheme (AGKA). In particular, it does not model security under concurrent execution of multiple instances of the GSH protocol. However, the emphasis of our contribution is on the *anonymity* properties of a group key agreement, so we examine the *security* of the protocol we propose only under the restricted notion above. The full analysis of the security of the group key agreement protocol involves modeling it as an ideal functionality, as in the Katz-Yung [6], and is out of the scope of this current paper.

Affiliation-hiding:[4] A GSH scheme is affiliation-hiding if all messages from an honest player in the entire protocol do not leak the identity of the GA which certified that player, even if this player is engaged in a group handshake protocol involving malicious participants. Formally, we call a GSH scheme *affiliation hiding* if there exists a probabilistic polynomial-time algorithm SIM, such that no polynomially-bounded adversary $\mathcal{A}$ has a non-negligible advantage in distinguishing between the following two games:

1-2. Steps 1-2 are the same as in the *authenticity* property.
  3. $\mathcal{A}$ picks any set of players $\Delta = (V_1, ..., V_l)$, not necessarily belonging to one group, and then:
3.1 In game 1, $\mathcal{A}$ interacts with players in Δ executing protocol GSH. Handshake(Δ).
3.2 In game 2, $\mathcal{A}$ interacts with SIM which runs only on input $l = |\Delta|$ and params.

Note: This definition implies that an adversary $\mathcal{A}$ cannot tell not only if the other participating players are members of some group G (for which $\mathcal{A}$ does not have non-revoked certs), but also if the other players belong to any single group at all. Thus the above definition implies the property of GSH scheme which can be called **unobservability**. This definition also implies the **unlinkability** property, which says that even an active adversary cannot link two instances of the handshake protocol in which the same player participates. These strong anonymity properties are implied by the above definition because the simulator's only input is the *size* of the set Δ, and not the identities of the individual players, nor their group membership(s). We remark that our GSH protocol achieves the unlinkability property in a rather trivial way by using one-time certificates which are discarded after a single use.

2.2   Other Security Properties of a GSH Scheme

We also specify two less central but potentially useful security properties for GSH schemes, *counting* and *affiliation-hiding against eavesdropping insiders*:

Counting: The counting property says that the set of *id*'s, *IDSet*, output by an honest player that accepts in a handshake protocol, has some correspondence to the number of players who are group members among the participants. Namely, as long as no malicious group member participates in the protocol, the size of the *IDSet* is no larger than the set of group members participating in this protocol. (We cannot require $|IDSet|$ is *equal* to the number of participating group members, because the adversary controls the communication network, and hence can always not deliver some players' messages.) Formally, we say that a GSH scheme accomplishes the *counting* property if every polynomially bounded adversary $\mathcal{A}$ has negligible probability of winning in the following game:

---

[4] The *affiliation-hiding* property we define here implies what was called *detection-resistance* in previous secret-handshake papers [2, 5, 12].

1. GSH.Setup and GSH.CreateGroup algorithms are executed and resulting parameters params and public key $\mathcal{PK}_G$ are given to $\mathcal{A}$.
2. $\mathcal{A}$ triggers the GSH.AddMember algorithm under the public key $\mathcal{PK}_G$ polynomially many times. In each GSH.AddMember instance, $\mathcal{A}$ receives a membership cert from the GA for this group G. Before the protocol starts, all secrets $\mathcal{A}$ received are added to $\mathcal{CRL}_G$, which is sent to all players in G.
3. $\mathcal{A}$ runs GSH.Handshake with any group Δ of honest members in G.
4. $\mathcal{A}$ wins if any honest player in Δ outputs $(K, IDSet)$, where $IDSet$ includes more id's than the size of set Δ.

Affiliation-hiding against eavesdropping insiders: Note that the affiliation-hiding property implies security against both passive (i.e. only eavesdropping) and active *outsiders*, i.e. adversaries that have no current non-revoked certificates for an attacked group. However, a GSH scheme could also offer affiliation-hiding protection (which, as we pointed out above, implies unobservability and unlinkability) against an adversary who does have non-revoked certificates (i.e. an adversary who is a valid member of the attacked group) but who is only eavesdropping on the handshake protocol. (Note furthermore that this is the best we can ask for, because if such adversary is active, he can learn everything by just participating in the handshake protocol using his non-revoked cert.) We do not formally define this property, since it is very similar to the security against active attackers which we already defined for the properties of authenticity and affiliation-hiding.

3   Construction of a Group Secret Handshake Scheme

We now construct a practical GSH scheme achieving authenticity and affiliation-hiding under the CDH assumption in ROM. As mentioned in section 1.3, it is based on the Burmester-Desmedt (unauthenticated) group key agreement scheme [4] (see figure 4 in the appendix).

We point out from the outset that we modify the Burmester-Desmedt protocol in the process, by adding an extra layer of hashing into the key derivation (see the form of our session key shown in Lemma 1). The reason is that our authentication method is highly non-standard; hence, the security argument for the resulting authenticated group key agreement (AGKA) scheme becomes easier once the components of the session key related to each player are put through a hash function modeled as a random oracle. Our GSH scheme is shown in figure 2.

Lemma 1. *Protocol* AGKA *in figure 2 is a correct group key agreement scheme. That is, if all parties adhere to the protocol then each will compute the same key:*
$$K = F(g^{t_1 t_2})F(g^{t_2 t_3}) \cdots F(g^{t_n t_1}) \pmod{p}$$

Proof. Let
$$B_{i-1} \equiv F(z_{i-1}^{t_i}) \equiv F(g^{t_{i-1} t_i}) \pmod{p},$$
$$B_i \equiv F(z_{i-1}^{t_i}) \cdot X_i \equiv F(g^{t_i t_{i+1}}) \pmod{p},$$
$$B_{i+1} \equiv F(z_{i-1}^{t_i}) \cdot X_i \cdot X_{i+1} \equiv F(g^{t_{i+1} t_{i+2}}) \pmod{p},$$
$$\cdots$$

Setup: This algorithm outputs the standard discrete logarithm parameters (p, q, g) of security k, i.e., primes p, q of size polynomial in k, s.t. g is a generator of a subgroup in Z_p^* of order q. $\mathcal{GA}$ also defines hash functions $H : \{0,1\}^* \to Z_q$, $F : \{0,1\}^* \to Z_p$. The hash functions are modeled as random oracles.

CreateGroup: $\mathcal{GA}$ sets the group secret $\mathcal{SK}_G$ to be a random number $x \in Z_q$ and the group public key $\mathcal{PK}_G$ to be $y = g^x \pmod{p}$.

AddMember: To add a player U to the group G, $\mathcal{GA}$ does the following: First, it generates a list of random "pseudonyms" $id_1, ..., id_f \in \{0,1\}^{160}$, where f is chosen to be larger than the number of handshakes U will execute before receiving new player secrets. Then, $\mathcal{GA}$ computes a corresponding list of Schnorr signatures $(w_1, t_1), ..., (w_f, t_f) \in (Z_p^*, Z_q)$ on all ids picked above under the key y as [11], i.e., a pair (w_k, t_k) where $w_k = g^{r_k} \pmod{p}$, and $t_k = r_k + xH(w_k, id_k) \pmod{q}$, for random $r_k \leftarrow Z_q$. A signature pair (w_k, t_k) on id_k satisfies that $g^{t_k} = w_k y^{H(w_k, id_k)} \pmod{p}$. The player's outputs are the list of $certs$ $((t_1, id_1, w_1), ..., (t_f, id_f, w_f))$. Sometimes we will refer to a t_i value as a "trapdoor" for the (id_i, w_i) pair.

RemoveMember: To remove a player U from the group G, $\mathcal{GA}$ looks up pseudonyms $(id_1, ..., id_f)$ it has issued to U, adds the pseudonyms to the current $\mathcal{CRL}$ and outputs an updated $\mathcal{CRL}$.

AGKA(Δ): This is a group key agreement algorithm for some set $\Delta = \{U_1, ..., U_n\}$ of the honest players, where each player $U_i \in \Delta$ receives a signal to start the protocol. Each player U_i *removes* a single cert (t_i, id_i, w_i) from its list of certs. (Note that this cert will be removed from the list whether the subsequent protocol succeeds or not.) The protocol consists of two rounds:

  [Round 1]: Each player U_i broadcasts (id_i, w_i).

    • If there are collisions between id's, U_i just abandons the protocol. If U_i receives any id's on $\mathcal{CRL}$, he broadcasts a random value as X_i in Round 2 and outputs REJECT.

    • If there are neither id collisions nor revoked id's, U_i determines the order between players based on id's. We assume that the order of players is determined by their pseudonyms, e.g., increasing order of hash images of pseudonyms. For simplicity of description, wlog, we assume that the ordered result is $(U_1, U_2, ..., U_n)$ and the indices are taken in a cycle modulo n, i.e. $U_{n+1} = U_1$.

      * U_i computes $z_{i+1} = w_{i+1}y^{H(w_{i+1}, id_{i+1})} (= g^{t_{i+1}})$ and $z_{i-1} = w_{i-1}y^{H(w_{i-1}, id_{i-1})} (= g^{t_{i-1}})$.

      * U_i computes $X_i = F(z_{i+1}^{t_i})/F(z_{i-1}^{t_i}) \pmod{p}$

  [Round 2]: Each player U_i broadcasts X_i.

    • U_i computes $K_i = F(z_{i-1}^{t_i})^n \cdot X_i^{n-1} \cdot X_{i+1}^{n-2} \cdots X_{i-2} \pmod{p}$.

    • U_i outputs $(K_i, IDSet_i)$, where $IDSet_i = \{id_1, ..., id_n\}$.

Fig. 2. GSH: A Group Secret Handshake Scheme

$$B_{i-2} \equiv F(z_{i-1}^{t_i}) \cdot X_i \cdot X_{i+1} \cdot X_{i+2} \cdots X_{i-2} \equiv F(g^{t_i - 2t_{i-1}}) \pmod{p}.$$
Then $K_i \equiv B_{i-1}B_iB_{i+1} \cdots B_{i-2} \equiv F(z_{i-1}^{t_i})^n \cdot X_i^{n-1} \cdot X_{i+1}^{n-2} \cdots X_{i-2} \pmod{p}$.

$\square$

Note on Performance: We compare the performance of the GSH scheme in figure 2 with the original (non-authenticated) Burmester-Desmedt scheme, shown in figure 4 of the appendix. Communication cost is the same since both schemes require two communication rounds. When we consider the on-the-fly computation, BD requires two modular exponentiations and GSH involves two modular multi-exponentiations, respectively. Thus, the efficiency of the GSH scheme is comparable to the original BD scheme. Therefore, the GSH scheme not only provides an authentication to the BD protocol almost for free, but also provides an authentication with very strong privacy property of affiliation-hiding. On the other hand, we note that our GSH scheme requires use of one-time certificates, which compared to standard PKI authentication creates additional storage requirements for the group members, increases the computation cost for the group manager, who needs to create a list of certificates for each group member, and increases the size of the CRL list.

Theorem 2. *The GSH scheme in figure 2 is* **affiliation-hiding** *under the CDH assumption in the Random Oracle model.*

Proof. The simulator required to prove the affiliation-hiding property is very simple: It sends random values on behalf of all the honest players $(V_1, ..., V_l)$ participating in the protocol: It picks random id_i's, w_i's chosen at random in the subgroup generated by g, and random values X_i's in Z_p^*. It is easy to see that neither id_i nor w_i values sent by the honest players in the first round of the protocol reveal any information about the $\mathcal{GA}$ in the first round: Since each w is created as $w = g^r$ for random r, it is independent from $\mathcal{GA}$'s public key y, and id's are randomly chosen as well.

The only values which can reveal something about the group membership of the honest players are the X_i values sent in the second round. However, the only way an adversary can distinguish between a conversation with honest players and a conversation with the above simulator sending random X_i's is if the adversary queries the random oracle F on one of the two inputs, $z_{i+1}^{t_i}$ or $z_{i-1}^{t_i}$, used to compute the X_i value used by any honest player V_i. We will argue that if such adversary exists then this adversarial algorithm can be used to break the Computational Diffie-Hellman assumption, i.e. on input a random pair (y, c) in the subgroup generated by g in Z_p^*, the simulator will output c^x s.t. $y = g^x$ with a non-negligible probability. First, in the initialization procedure the adversary is given the y part of this CDH challenge as the public key of the $\mathcal{GA}$ of the group it is attacking. The simulator then uses the c value in its simulation, and extracts the c^x from one of the queries the adversary makes to the F oracle, as follows.

Without loss of generality, we can assume the adversary queries F on one of the $z_{i+1}^{t_i}$ values, since the argument is the same in the other case. Also, if the adversary has a non-negligible probability of querying F on any such value, then there exists an index $i \in \{1, ..., l\}$ s.t. the adversary has a non-negligible probability of querying F on a value with this particular index i. Moreover, since the adversary makes polynomial number of queries to F, there is an index j of his queries to F and a non-negligible probability ϵ s.t. value $z_{i+1}^{t_i}$ appears as j-th query to F.

For that index i, the simulator in round one sends (w_i, id_i) pair chosen in a special way. Namely, it picks random id_i as before, but it picks also a random value e_i in the range of F, computes $w_i = c * y^{-e_i}$ and sets $H(w_i, id_i)$ to e_i. In this way, we will have $z_i = w_i * y^{H(w_i, id_i)} = w_i * y^{e_i} = c$. (The distribution created by the simulator in this way is correct because c is random in the group generated by g.) Now, note that $z_{i+1}^{t_i} = z_i^{t_{i+1}}$, and since $z_i = c$, it follows that one of the queries the adversary makes to F is equal to $c^{t_{i+1}}$. Now, without loss of generality we can assume that index $i + 1$ corresponds to a corrupt player A_{i+1}, and therefore the value t_{i+1} is defined as a value s.t. $g^{t_{i+1}} = w_{i+1}y^{e_{i+1}}$ where $e_{i+1} = H(w_{i+1}, id_{i+i})$. If we can rewind the adversary and witness two of its executions which run on the same random inputs until the adversary queries H on pair (w_{i+1}, id_{i+1}), but feed the adversary different challenges, $e_{i+1}^{(1)}$ and $e_{i+1}^{(2)}$, as F's responses in these two executions, then by the forking lemma of Pointcheval-Stern [9], it follows that with probability $O(q_H/\epsilon)$, where q_H is the number of queries the adversary makes to H, we see two executions, for $r = 1$ and $r = 2$, s.t. the adversary's j-th query to oracle F is equal to value $\alpha^{(r)} = c^{t_{i+1}^{(r)}}$, where $g^{t_{i+1}^{(r)}} = w_{i+1}y^{e_{i+1}^{(r)}}$. Since it follows from the last constraint that $t_{i+1}^{(r)} = k_{i+1} + x * e_{i+1}^{(r)}$ where $g^{k_{i+1}} = w_{i+1}$, the simulator can extract c^x from these two values $\alpha^{(1)}$ and $\alpha^{(2)}$, by outputting $(\alpha^{(1)}/\alpha^{(2)})^{1/\delta e}$ where $\delta e = e_{i+1}^{(1)} - e_{i+1}^{(2)}$. $\qquad\square$

Theorem 3. *The GSH scheme in figure 2 is* **authentic** *under the CDH assumption in the Random Oracle Model.*

Proof. The proof is almost identical to the one above. The only way the adversary can distinguish key K_i output by any honest player V_i is if the adversary queries oracle F at point $z_{i-1}^{t_i}$. The proof above shows that the adversary who can compute *either* $z_{i+1}^{t_i}$ or $z_{i-1}^{t_i}$ for any index i of an honest player, can be reduced to breaking CDH. Therefore the authenticity of our AGKA holds under the same assumption.

4   Group Secret Handshake Scheme with Counting

In this section we add explicit mutual authentication to the GSH scheme from the previous section, which allows us to support the counting property.

Bresson et al. [3] show how to accomplish explicit authentication for any group key agreement protocol with minimal extra computation. We adopt their method, which consists of MAC-ing the transcript using the agreed-upon key, and we show that this simple mechanism enables the counting property, and that the resulting protocol still maintains the properties of authenticity or affiliation-hiding. Note that the extra cost due to generation and verification of hash-based MACs is negligible.

Given a hash function $H_3 : \{0, 1\}^* \rightarrow \{0, 1\}^k$ modeled as a random oracle, we modify the Handshake protocol in our GSH scheme, as shown in figure 3. We denote the GSH scheme resulting from this modification of the Handshake protocol GSH+MAC.

Theorem 4. *The* GSH+MAC *construction in figure 3 is an authentic and affiliation hiding GSH scheme, which additionally provides the* counting *property.*

Proof of Authenticity (sketch). The authenticity property is very clear since the GSH scheme provides authenticity by theorem 3 and the message in Round 3 does not reveal any information of the agreed key the Random Oracle Model.

GSH+MAC.Handshake(Δ): The protocol proceeds as the GSH.Handshake(Δ) protocol
(see figure 2 on page 9), with the following modification:

[**Run** GSH.Handshake(Δ)]

- If U_i computes $(K_i, IDSet_i)$ in round 2 of the GSH.Handshake protocol, it does not output it, but computes $M_i = H_3(K_i, id_i)$. If U_i was to reject in the GSH.Handshake protocol, it picks M_i as a random bitstring of appropriate length.

[**Round 3**]: Each player U_i broadcasts M_i.

- U_i computes $M'_j = H(K_i, id_j)$ and checks if $M_j = M'_j$ for $1 \leq j \leq n$. If U_i verifies all M_j's, then U_i outputs $(K_i, IDSet_i = \{id_1, ..., id_n\})$, in which case we say that U_i accepts. Otherwise it rejects and outputs REJECT.

Fig. 3. GSH+MAC: A GSH Scheme with MAC-based Authentication

Proof of Affiliation-hiding (sketch). We will show a simulator SIM s.t. if $\mathcal{A}$ distinguishes between interactions with SIM and interactions with a group member, we can break the authenticity property. Since the underlying AGKA achieves affiliation-hiding property there exist simulators $SIM_{(AGKA)}$ which satisfy the affiliation-hiding criteria. We define a simulator SIM, running on inputs (params), as follows: (1) To simulate U_i's messages in AGKA, we use $SIM_{(AGKA)}$. (2) To simulate U_i's message in the third round, SIM sends random $M_i \leftarrow \{0,1\}^k$. If $\mathcal{A}$ can distinguish a conversation with such SIM from a conversation with a true group member U_i, since the $SIM_{(AGKA)}$ simulator produces messages which are indistinguishable from the message of an honest U_i, it must be that $\mathcal{A}$ distinguishes random values M_i chosen by SIM from values $M_i = H(K_i, id_i)$, In ROM, it can happen only if $\mathcal{A}$ makes an oracle query on the input (K_i, id_i). In this case, since $\mathcal{A}$ can make only polynomially-many queries to H, we pick one such query at random. And we will have a non-negligible chance of outputting K_i. This contradicts to authenticity property in AGKA. Therefore $\mathcal{A}$ can distinguish a conversation with SIM from a conversation with a group group member with only negligible probability.

Proof of Counting (sketch). The counting property follows immediately from the authenticity property: Since by the latter property, the adversary cannot distinguish a key K_i, for any player U_i in Δ, from a random string. Therefore the adversary also cannot forge a proper MAC M_i on any string, and hence the size of the set $IDSet_i$ output by any honest accepting player U_i in Δ, is at most equal to the size of set Δ.

5   Privacy Issues Involved in Revocation

Every $\mathcal{GA}$ that issues certificates will also need to revoke them. There can be many reasons for this. One reason is that the private keys corresponding to the certificate have been lost or compromised. Then the certificate holder contacts the $\mathcal{GA}$ and asks that the certificate be revoked. A $\mathcal{GA}$ may also decide to revoke a certificate. For example, the certificate holder may violate the issuing agreement, or there can be promotions or retirement. Whatever the reason, the revoked group member's pseudonyms appears on the CRL of the issuing $\mathcal{GA}$, and anyone who receives the CRL knows which pseudonyms are revoked from the particular $\mathcal{GA}$. Since the CRL is generally public, we should examine whether there is any loss of privacy in the context of secret handshakes. Especially, we recognized that forward secrecy can be subverted if we depend on the normal revocation method, the CRL.

The CRL destroys the forward secrecy property against affiliation hiding and unlinkability. When non-group members receives the CRL, they may detect some group members by comparing pseudonyms on the CRL and pseudonyms they have seen in other protocol executions. In the case that the same group members get the CRL, they may link the same party from the previous protocol runs by looking at the difference in the update CRL. This is because all pseudonyms assigned to one group member are treated atomically in the revocation process.

One solution to mitigate the CRL problem is to issue time-based certificates, which are used only at a specified time and automatically expires after the time. When a group member needs to be revoked, the $\mathcal{GA}$ places only un-expired pseudonyms to the CRL. Since the used pseudonyms expire implicitly, this method is free from leaking any information regarding to the earlier protocol runs. The main disadvantage of this approach is that each group member needs to have lots of pseudonyms more than they use. For example, if a player participates a protocol at least once a week and each certificate expires every day, the player will be given seven certificates only for the one protocol execution. If the certificate expires every minute, the problem will be even worse. This approach may be practical in a very limited setting where players know when and how many times they will execute the protocol.

Another solution is to distribute the CRL only to the non-revoked group members. This can be done, for example, by keeping a group key among the current group members and publish the encrypted CRL using the group key. In this case, the issue will be how to update the group key efficiently. We may need a cryptographic tool such as broadcast encryption. However, security properties should be considered again, while we integrate other cryptographic tools. For example, we should check if updating messages in broadcast encryption reveal affiliation information of the group.

Instead of using the CRL, the $\mathcal{GA}$ can invalidate all the issued certificates by changing its public key. Whenever the public key is updated, non-revoked members synchronize their new pseudonyms lists with their $\mathcal{GA}$. This approach easily solves the revocation problem without revealing any further information. However, each player's burden will not be negligible if the revocation happens frequently.

We briefly mentioned three possible approaches for the private-preserving revocation technique. It is our future work to efficiently implement the proposed methods.

References

1. M. Abadi. Private authentication. In *Workshop on Privacy-Enhancing Technologies (PET)*, 2002.
2. D. Balfanz, G. Durfee, N. Shankar, D. Smetters, J. Staddon, and H. Wong. Secret handshakes from pairing-based key agreements. In *24th IEEE Symposium on Security and Privacy*, Oakland, CA, May 2003.
3. E. Bresson, O. Chevassut, D. Pointcheval, and J.-J. Quisquater. Provably Authenticated Group Diffie-Hellman Key Exchange. In *ACM CCS*, 2001.
4. M. Burmester and Y. Desmedt. A secure and efficient conference key distribution system. In A. D. Santis, editor, *Proc. EUROCRYPT 94*, pages 275–286. Springer, 1994. Lecture Notes in Computer Science No. 950.
5. C. Castelluccia, S. Jarecki, and G. Tsudik. Secret handshakes from ca-oblivious encryption. In *Advances in Cryptology - ASIACRYPT 2004*, volume 3329 of *Lecture Notes in Computer Science*, pages 293–307. Springer, 2004.
6. J. Katz and M. Yung, Scalable Protocols for Authenticated Group Key Exchange. In Proceedings of CRYPTO 2003, LNCS 2729, pp. 110–125. Springer-Verlag, 2002.
7. N. Li, W. Du, and D. Boneh. Oblivious signature-based envelope. *In Proceedings of 22nd ACM Symposium on Principles of Distributed Computing (PODC 2003)*, Boston, Massachusetts, July 13-16 2003.
8. S. Nasserian and G. Tsudik, Revisiting Oblivious Signature-Based Envelopes. In Proceedings of Financial Cryptography 2006 (FC'06), February 2006.
9. D. Pointcheval and J. Stern. Security proofs for signatures. *Advances in Cryptology - EUROCRYPT 1996*, pages 387–398, Springer, 1996.
10. R. Sakai, K. Ohgishi, and M. Kasahara. Cryptosystems based on pairing. In *Proceedings of the Symposium on Cryptography and Information Security (SCIS)*, 2002.
11. C. Schnorr. Efficient identification and signatures for smart cards. In *Advances in Cryptology - CRYPTO 1989*, Santa Barbara, CA, August 1989.
12. G. Tsudik and S. Xu. A Flexible Framework for Secret Handshakes. In *ACM Conference on Principles of Distributed Computing (PODC'05)*, August 2005.
13. S. Xu and M. Yung. k-anonymous secret handshakes with reusable credentials. In *Proceedings of the 11th ACM conference on Computer and communications security (CCS'04)*, pages 158–167. ACM Press, 2004.

Appendix A: Burmester-Desmedt Group Key Agreement

Figure 4 shows the Burmester-Desmedt group key agreement protocol. Note that this protocol is not an *authenticated* group key agreement.

$\mathsf{GKA}(\Delta)$: This is a group key agreement algorithm for $\Delta = \{U_1, ..., U_n\}$, where U_i's are members of a group G that want to generate a group key. g is a generator in Z_p^*.

   [**Round 1**]: Each player U_i picks a random $t_i \in Z_q$ and broadcasts $z_i = g^{t_i}$. U_i computes $X_i = (z_{i+1}/z_{i-1})^{t_i} \pmod{p}$, where the indices are taken in a cycle.

   [**Round 2**]: Each player U_i broadcasts X_i

   U_i computes the key: $K_i = (z_{i-1})^{nt_i} \cdot X_i^{n-1} \cdot X_{i+1}^{n-2} \cdots X_{i-2} \pmod{p}$

(It may be easily verified that all players compute that same key $K = g^{t_1 t_2 + t_2 t_3 + ... + t_n t_1}$.)

Fig. 4. Burmester-Desmedt's Group Key Agreement Protocol

On the Security of the Authentication Module of Chinese WLAN Standard Implementation Plan*

Xinghua Li[1,2], SangJae Moon[2], and Jianfeng Ma[1,3]

[1] Key Laboratory of Computer Networks and Information
Security (Ministry of Education), Xidian University, Xi'an 710071, China
flame168@sohu.com
[2] Mobile Network Security Technology Research Center,
Kyungpook National University, Sankyuk-dong, Buk-ku, Daegu 702-701, Korea
sjmoon@ee.knu.ac.kr
[3] School of Computing and Automatization,
Tianjin Polytechnic University, Tianjin 300160, China
jfma@mail.xidian.edu.cn

Abstract. Compared with the original standard, the greatest change that WAPI (Chinese WLAN security standard) implementation plan made lies in the key-agreement protocol in WAI (Wireless Authentication Infrastructure). This contribution presents a security analysis of the WAI module in the implementation plan with the Canetti-Krawczyk (CK) model. The results indicate that if the elliptic curve encryption scheme ECES adopted is secure against adaptive chosen ciphertext attack (CCA2 attack), then its key-agreement protocol is secure in the CK model, and it realizes the mutual identity authentication between STA (station) and AP (access point).

1 Introduction

The Chinese WLAN standard GB 15629.11-2003 [1], the first issued Chinese standard in the field of WLAN, has been formally implemented since November 1, 2003. Its security mechanism WAPI (WLAN Authentication and Privacy Infrastructure) consists of two parts: WAI and WPI (Wireless Privacy Infrastructure). They realize the identity authentication and data encryption respectively. In March of 2004, China Broadband Wireless IP Standard Group of National IT Standardization Technical Committee drafted out WAPI Implementation Plan [2], which improves the original standard and fixes its some security weaknesses. Compared with the original standard, the greatest change the implementation plan made lies in the key-agreement protocol in the WAI module. Currently, it is said that the Chinese National Administration for Cryptography would open

---

* Research supported by the National Natural Science Foundation of China (Grant No. 90204012), the National "863" High-tech Project of China (Grant No. 2002AA143021), the Excellent Young Teachers Program of Chinese Ministry of Education, the Key Project of Chinese Ministry of Education, and the University IT Research Center Project of Korea.

J. Zhou, M. Yung, and F. Bao (Eds.): ACNS 2006, LNCS 3989, pp. 340–348, 2006.

the cryptography algorithms in WAPI before long. In January 2006, the related national departments stated that the high priority would be given to the wireless products that meet national wireless standards when they purchase the related products for the government.

So, it is significant to evaluate the security of the WAPI implementation plan. However, as far as we know there are no articles that systemically analyze the security of WAI in the implementation plan, especially in a rigorous formal method. This contribution analyzes the security of WAI in the implementation plan with the CK model [3]. The results indicate that: (1) its key-agreement protocol is secure in the CK model if the elliptic curve encryption scheme ECES adopted is secure against CCA2 attack; (2) it realizes the mutual identity authentication between STA and AP.

The rest of the paper is organized as follows. In Section 2, we give an overview of the CK model. In Section 3, WAI in the implementation plan is given. We analyze it in Section 4. This paper is concluded in Section 5.

2   The CK Model

At present, the CK model is a very popular formal methodology for the analysis of key-agreement protocols [4]. In this section, we give a brief description of the CK model.

A key-exchange (KE) protocol is run in a network of interconnected parties where each party can be activated to run an instance of the protocol called a session. A KE session is a quadruple (A, B, X, Y) where A is the identity of the holder of the session, B the peer, X the outgoing messages in the session, and Y the incoming messages. The session (B, A, Y, X) (if it exists) is said to be matching to the session (A, B, X, Y). Matching sessions play a fundamental role in the definition of security.

2.1   Attacker Model

The attacker is modeled to capture realistic attack capabilities in open networks, including the control of communication links and the access to some of the secret information used or generated in the protocol. The attacker, denoted $\mathcal{M}$, is an active "man-in-the-middle" adversary with full control of the communication links between parties. $\mathcal{M}$ can intercept and modify messages sent over these links, it can delay or prevent their delivery, inject its own messages, interleave messages from different sessions, etc. (Formally, it is $\mathcal{M}$ to whom parties hand their outgoing messages for delivery.) $\mathcal{M}$ also schedules all session activations and session-message delivery. In addition, in order to model potential disclosure of secret information, the attacker is allowed access to secret information via session exposure attacks of three types: state-reveal queries, session-key queries, and party corruption.

State-reveal query. A state-reveal query is directed at a single session while still incomplete (i.e., before outputting the session key) and its result is that the attacker learns the session state for that particular session (which may include, for example, the secret exponent of an ephemeral DH value but not the long-term private key used across all sessions at the party).

Session-key query. A session-key query can be performed against an individual session after completion and the result is that the attacker learns the corresponding session key.

Party corruption. Party corruption means that the attacker learns all information in the memory of that party (including the long-term private key of the party as well all session states and session keys stored at the party); in addition, from the moment a party is corrupted all its actions may be controlled by the attacker. Indeed, note that the knowledge of the private key allows the attacker to impersonate the party at will.

2.2   Definition of Session-Key Security

In addition to the regular actions of the attacker $\mathcal{M}$ against a key-exchange protocol, he can perform a *test session query*. That is, at any time during its run, $\mathcal{M}$ is able to choose, a test session among the sessions that are completed, unexpired and unexposed at the time. Let k be the value of the corresponding session key. We toss a coin b, $b \xleftarrow{R} \{0,1\}$. If $b=0$ we provide $\mathcal{M}$ with the value k. Otherwise we provide $\mathcal{M}$ with a value r randomly chosen from the probability distribution of keys generated by this protocol. The attacker $\mathcal{M}$ is not allowed state-reveal queries, session-key queries, or party corruptions on the test session or its matching session. At the end of its run, $\mathcal{M}$ outputs a bit b' (as its guess for b).

An attacker that is allowed test session queries is referred to as a KE-adversary.

Definition 1. *Session-key Security: A key-exchange protocol is called Session-key secure (or SK-secure) if the following properties hold for any KE-adversary.*

1. *The protocol satisfies the property that if two uncorrupted parties complete matching sessions then they both output the same key; and*
2. *the probability that $\mathcal{M}$ guesses correctly the bit b(i.e., outputs $b'=b$) is no more than 1/2 plus a negligible fraction ε in the security parameter. ε is called "advantage".*

3   WAI in the Implementation Plan

WAI adopts port-based authentication architecture that is identical with IEEE 802.1X. The whole system is composed of STA, AP, and Authentication Service Unit (ASU). In WAI, digital certificate is used as the identity credential. The interaction procedure of WAI in the implementation plan is shown in Fig.1. From this figure, we can see that WAI consists of two parts: certificate authentication and key agreement.

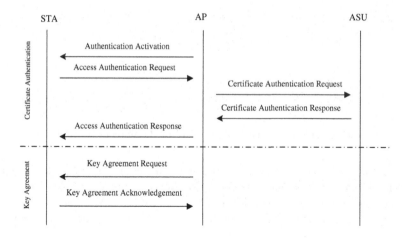

Fig. 1. WAI in the implementation plan

In WAI of the implementation plan, certificate authentication maintains same as that of the original standard. In this process, STA sends its public key certificate and access request time to AP in the access authentication request. AP sends its certificate, STA's certificate, access request time and AP's signature on them to ASU in the certificate authentication request. After ASU validates the AP's signature and the two certificates, it sends the certificates validation result, STA's access request time and its signature on them to STA and AP.

Compared with the original standard, the implementation plan made rather big improvement in the key-agreement protocol. In this plan, the key agreement request has to be initiated by AP in which its signature is required, and a message authentication code by STA is needed in the key agreement acknowledgement. The following is the key agreement process in the implementation plan which is shown in Fig.2.

1. **AP sends key agreement request to STA.** AP generates a random value r_1 and encrypts it using PK_{STA} (the public key of STA) with the elliptic curve encryption scheme ECES. This request also includes the security parameter index SPI and an AP's signature on the message. The signature algorithm is the elliptic curve digital signature algorithm ECDSA.
2. **STA replies to AP with the key agreement acknowledgement.** Upon receipt the key agreement request, STA decrypts $PK_{STA}(r_1)$ to get r_1. It also generates its random value r_2 and computes the unicast host key $k = r_1 \oplus r_2$. Then STA extends k with KD-HMAC-SHA256 algorithm to get the session key k_d, the integration check key and message authentication key k_a. STA encrypts r_2 using PK_{AP} (the public key of AP) with the ECES algorithm. Thereafter, STA computes the message authentication code of this acknowledgement message with k_a through HMAC-SHA256 algorithm.
3. **AP processes the key agreement acknowledgement message.** Upon receipt the key agreement acknowledgement, AP decrypts the $PK_{AP}(r_2)$ to

STA **AP**

$$\overleftarrow{\quad SPI, ENC(PK_{STA}, r_1), Sig_{AP}(SPI, ENC(PK_{STA}, r_1)) \quad}$$

$$\overrightarrow{\quad SPI, ENC(PK_{AP}, r_2), HMAC-SHA256_{k_a}(SPI, ENC(PK_{AP}, r_2)) \quad}$$

SPI=the MAC of the STA‖the BSSID of the AP‖STA's access request time

Fig. 2. The key agreement protocol in the implementation plan

get r_2. It also computes the host key k, the session key k_d, the integration check key and message authentication key k_a. Thereafter AP validates the message authentication code from STA. If valid, STA is permitted to access the networks; otherwise AP discards this acknowledgement message.

4 The Security Analysis of WAI in the Implementation Plan

In the certificate authentication, AP makes signature on the certificate authentication request, and ASU makes signature on the certificate authentication response. Both these messages include STA's access authentication time which ensures the freshness of the signatures. Therefore ASU can authenticate AP's identity and STA can authenticate ASU's identity. In addition, STA trusts ASU. So STA can authenticate the identity of AP indirectly after the certificate authentication. That is, STA binds the MAC address of AP with its identity. And it just accepts the key agreement request from the AP. At the same time, AP authenticates the certificate provided by STA.

The key-agreement protocol in the implementation plan is denoted by π. In the following, we will prove that π is SK-secure without PFS [5]. That is, the protocol is SK-secure, but does not provide forward secrecy of the session keys. In order to prove that π is SK-secure, we define a "game" as follows.

4.1 The Design of an Encryption Game

Let (G, ENC, DEC) be a key-generation, encryption and decryption algorithm, respectively, of a public-key encryption scheme that is secure against CCA2 attack [6]. Let K be the security parameter. STA and AP have invoked $G(K)$ to get their public and private key pairs.

This game integrates the CCA2-security of ENC with the key-agreement protocol [3, 6]. We will proceed to show that if an attacker can break the SK-security of π, then he can win the game, i.e., he can break the CCA2-security of ENC.

The two participants in the game are $\mathcal{G}$ and $\mathcal{B}$. $\mathcal{G}$ is the party against which $\mathcal{B}$ plays the game. $\mathcal{G}$ acts as a decryption Oracle. $\mathcal{B}$ is the attacker of protocol π. He leverages the abilities he gets in the attack of π to take part in this game. The game is shown in Fig.3.

The Encryption Game

The parties to the game are $\mathcal{G}$ and $\mathcal{B}$ (for good and bad). $\mathcal{G}$ possesses a pair of public and private keys, PK_{STA} and SK_{STA} (generated via the key generation algorithm G). $\mathcal{B}$ knows PK_{STA} but not SK_{STA}.

Phase 0: $\mathcal{G}$ provides $\mathcal{B}$ with a challenge ciphertext $c^* = ENC$ (PK_{STA}, r_1) for $r_1 \xleftarrow{R} \{0,1\}^K$.

Phase 1: $\mathcal{B}$ sends a triple (c, r, t) to $\mathcal{G}$ who responds with HMAC-SHA256$_{k'_a}(t)$. ($k'_a = last$(KD-HMAC-SHA256(k')), $k' = r \oplus r', r' = DEC(SK_{STA}, c)$. The $last($) is a function that extract out the last sixteen bytes from a bit string.) This is repeated a polynomial number of times with each triple being chosen adaptively by $\mathcal{B}$ (i.e., after seeing $\mathcal{G}$'s response to previous triple), but he keeps r unchanged in every triple.

Phase 2: $\mathcal{B}$ sends a test string $t^* = (SPI \| PK_{AP}(r))$ to $\mathcal{G}$. Then $\mathcal{G}$ chooses a random bit $b \xleftarrow{R} \{0,1\}$. If $b=0$ then $\mathcal{G}$ responds with HMAC-SHA256$_{k''_a}(t^*)$ where $k''_a = last$(KD-HMAC-SHA256(k'')), $k'' = r_1 \oplus r$, r_1 is the value encrypted by $\mathcal{G}$ in phase 0. If $b=1$ then $\mathcal{G}$ responds with a random string s^* of the same length as HMAC-SHA256$_{k''_a}(t^*)$.

Phase 3: Same as Phase 1.

Phase 4: $\mathcal{B}$ outputs a bit b' as the guess of b.

And the winner is... $\mathcal{B}$ if and only if $b=b'$.

Fig. 3. A game that captures the CCA2-security of the encryption function ENC

The following notes are made about the game. The challenging ciphertext c^* in phase 0 is also the ciphertext sent by AP in the key agreement request of π . In phase 1, $\mathcal{B}$ randomly chooses a test ciphertext c, random value r and string t, and sends them to $\mathcal{G}$ for process. It should be noticed that $\mathcal{B}$ cannot simultaneously chooses c^* and t^* as the input of $\mathcal{G}$. $\mathcal{B}$ keeps r unchanged in every triple in order to reduce the difficulty of the attack.

4.2   Security Analysis of the Key-Agreement Protocol in WAI

According to Definition 1, in order to prove that π is SK-secure, we have to argue that it can meet two requirements. The first one is that STA and AP can get a same session key after they complete matching sessions. The second one is that $\mathcal{B}$ cannot distinguish the session key k_d from a random value with a non-negligible advantage. In the following, we will prove that π can meet these two requirements.

Lemma 1. *If the encryption scheme ECES is secure against the CCA2 attack, then at the end of protocol π, STA and AP will complete matching sessions and get a same session key.*

Proof. Since the signature algorithm ECDSA is secure against existential forgery by adaptive chosen-message attack [7], in addition, SPI in the key agreement request can guarantee the freshness of this message, and bind this message with the two communication parties, the attacker cannot forge or modify the request message.

In addition, the attacker $\mathcal{B}$ cannot forge a key agreement acknowledgment message. Let's prove this with the reduction to absurdity. It is assumed that the attacker can forge an acknowledgment message with a non-negligible probability during the run of the protocol π. That is, he can choose a random value (say r_3) and forge a message authentication code that AP can validate. Then $\mathcal{B}$ takes advantage of this ability to run the game above. In Phase 1, he also chooses r_3 as the random value r in the triple, while selects c and t randomly. Then, in Phase 2, he can work out HMAC-SHA256$_{k_a''}(t^*)$ because this value is same as the forged message authentication code in the key agreement acknowledgment. Therefore the attacker can distinguish HMAC-SHA256$_{k_a''}(t^*)$ from s^* and guess correctly b in Phase 4, thus wins the game, which indicates that the encryption scheme is not CCA2-secure. This contradicts with the presupposition. So during the run of protocol π, the attacker cannot forge a key agreement acknowledgment with a non-negligible probability.

Therefore STA and AP will complete matching sessions and get a same session key at the end of protocol π, if ECES is CCA2-secure. □

Lemma 2. *If the encryption scheme ECES is secure against the CCA2 attack, the attacker cannot distinguish the session key k_d from a random value with a non-negligible advantage.*

Proof. It is assumed that the attacker $\mathcal{B}$ can distinguish the session key k_d from a random value with a non-negligible advantage η_1. In the CK model, the KE-attacker is not permitted to corrupt the test session or its matching session, so the attacker $\mathcal{B}$ cannot directly get the session key k_d from the attack of π. While $k_d = first(\text{KD-HMAC-SHA256}(k))$ (The $first(\ )$ is a function that extracts out the first sixteen bytes from a bit string), so the attacker $\mathcal{B}$ has only two possible methods to distinguish k_d from a random value. The first one: $\mathcal{B}$ learns k. The second one: $\mathcal{B}$ succeeds in forcing the establishment of a session (other than the test session or its matching session) that has the same session key as the test session. In this case $\mathcal{B}$ can learn the test session key by simply querying the session with the same key, and without having to learn the value k. In the following, we prove that neither of these two methods is feasible.

The first method means that, from the attack of π, the attacker can distinguish $k = r_1 \oplus r_2$ from a random value with a non-negligible advantage. Based on this ability, $\mathcal{B}$ also can distinguish $k'' = r_1 \oplus r$ from a random value with a non-negligible advantage. This is because r in the k'' is selected by the attacker himself, which makes the difficulty that he distinguishes k'' from a random value no bigger than that he distinguishes k from a random value. It is assumed that the advantage that $\mathcal{B}$ distinguishes k'' from a random value is η_2, then $\eta_2 \geq \eta_1$. And because $k_a'' = last(\text{KD-HMAC-SHA256}(k''))$, $\mathcal{B}$ can get k_a''. Further, he can work out HMAC-SHA256$_{k''_a}(t^*)$ with a non-negligible probability, which enables the attacker to win the encryption game. That means that the encryption scheme is not secure against CCA2 attack. This contradicts the presupposition. So the attacker $\mathcal{B}$ can not get k with a non-negligible probability. Then this method is not practical.

As for the second method, there are two strategies that the attacker can take. (1) After STA and AP complete the matching sessions, the attacker $\mathcal{B}$ establishes a new session with AP or STA. But the session key of this session will not be k_d, because the encrypted random value is chosen randomly by AP or STA. (2) When AP and STA perform the key agreement, $\mathcal{B}$ intervene this negations, and makes them get a same session key without the completion of the matching sessions. That is, under the attack of $\mathcal{B}$, STA and AP cannot complete matching sessions but get a same session key. But from Lemma 1, we know that if the encryption scheme ECES is secure against the CCA2 attack, $\mathcal{B}$ cannot succeed in this intervention. So this method is not feasible either.

Let us sum up the analysis above. The attacker $\mathcal{B}$ neither can get the host key k, nor can he force to establish a new session with STA or AP that has the same session key as the test session. So the attacker cannot distinguish the session key k_d from a random value with a non-negligible advantage.   □

Theorem 1. *If the encryption scheme ECES adopted is secure against CCA2 attack, then π is SK-secure without PFS.*

Proof. According to Lemma 1 and Lemma 2, we know that STA and AP will get a same session key after the completion of matching sessions and the attacker cannot distinguish the session key from a random value with a non-negligible advantage. Then in accordance with Definition 1, protocol π is SK-secure. In addition, if the private keys of STA and AP are compromised, the attacker can get the random values exchanged and can work out all the session keys that have been agreed about. Thus this protocol cannot provide PFS. So we can get that the key-agreement protocol is SK-secure without PFS.   □

In addition, for AP, this is an explicit key authentication protocol [8] , and it is SK-secure, therefore AP can authenticate the identity of STA at the end of this protocol. At the same time, in the key agreement request, AP's signature includes STA's access request time, therefore STA also can authenticate AP's identity. So, AP and STA can authenticate each other's identity through the WAI module.

5   Conclusion

We analyze the WAI module in the implementation plan with the CK model. The results show that if the encryption scheme ECES adopted is secure against the CCA2 attack, then its key-agreement protocol is SK-secure without PFS; in addition, through this module, STA and AP authenticate each other's identity.

References

1. National Standard of the People's Republic of China. GB 15629.11-2003 ≪ Information technology–Telecommunications and information exchange between systems–Local and metropolitan area networks–Specific requirements–Part 11: Wireless LAN Medium Access Control (MAC) and Physical Layer (PHY) Specifications≫. 2003.
2. National Standard of the People's Republic of China. Guide for GB 15629.11-2003 ≪Information technology–Telecommunications and information exchange between systems-Local and metropolitan area networks–Specific requirements–Part 11: Wireless LAN Medium Access Control (MAC) and Physical Layer (PHY) Specifications≫ and GB 15629.1102-2003≪Information technology–Telecommunications and information exchange between systems–Local and metropolitan area networks–Specific requirements-Part 11: Wireless LAN Medium access control (MAC) and physical layer(PHY) Specifications: Higher-Speed Physical layer Extension in the 2.4 GHz Band≫. 2004.3
3. Canetti, R., Krawczyk, H.: Analysis of Key-Exchange Protocols and Their Use for Building Secure Channel. Eurocrypt 2001, Lecture Notes in Computer Science, Springer-Verlag, Vol. 2045. (2001) 453-474
4. Boyd, C., Mao, W., Paterson, K.: Key Agreement using Statically Keyed Authenticators. Applied Cryptography and Network Security 2004. 2004: Lecture Notes in Computer Science, Springer-verlag, Vol. 3089 (2004) 248 - 262
5. Güther, C.G.: An identity-based key-exchange protocol. Advances in Cryptology-EUROCRYPT'89, Lecture Notes in Computer Science, Springer-Verlag, Vol.434 (1990) 29-37
6. Mao,W.: Modern CryptographyTheory and Practice. Hewlett-Packard Company. Publisher: Prentice Hall PTR (2003)
7. Brown, D.R.L.: The Exact Security of ECDSA. IEEE 1363 (2001).
8. Menezes, A., van Oorschot, P., Vanstone, S.: Handbook of Applied Cryptography. CRC Press (1996)

W3Bcrypt: Encryption as a Stylesheet

Angelos Stavrou, Michael E. Locasto, and Angelos D. Keromytis

Department of Computer Science
Columbia University
1214 Amsterdam Avenue
Mailcode 0401
New York, NY 10027
{angel, locasto, angelos}@cs.columbia.edu

Abstract. While web-based communications (*e.g.,* webmail or web cha-trooms) are increasingly protected by transport-layer cryptographic mechanisms, such as the SSL/TLS protocol, there are many situations where even the web server (or its operator) cannot be trusted. The end-to-end (E2E) encryption of data becomes increasingly important in these trust models to protect the confidentiality and integrity of the data against snooping and modification.

We introduce W3Bcrypt, an extension to the Mozilla Firefox platform that enables application-level cryptographic protection for web content. In effect, we view cryptographic operations as a type of style to be applied to web content, similar to and along with layout and coloring operations. Among the main benefits of using encryption as a stylesheet are (*a*) reduced workload on the web server, (*b*) targeted content publication, and (*c*) greatly increased privacy. This paper discusses our implementation for Firefox, although the core ideas are applicable to most current browsers.

Keywords: E2E cryptography, web security, cryptographic applications.

1 Introduction

The growth in popularity of hosted web services (including online merchants, blogging, and webmail) offers new possibilities for commerce and communication. Unfortunately, most of these services are hosted by third parties that should not be trusted with the content of the messages that are passed between content publisher and the reader. As a simple example, users of popular webmail services like MSN Hotmail or Google's Gmail must trust that MSN or Google will respect the confidentiality of their mail messages. Of course, the user could employ PGP or S/MIME for email messages, but this presupposes that the webmail service can be accessed by a trusted mail client. The webmail interfaces of these services do not provide such a trustworthy client. Even if these interfaces supported client-side PGP operations (via ActiveX, Flash, or a Java applet), users cannot trust these components with their private key or passphrase.

Our goal is to build a trustworthy client-side environment into web browsers that is independent of the service provider. This environment need not be limited

J. Zhou, M. Yung, and F. Bao (Eds.): ACNS 2006, LNCS 3989, pp. 349–364, 2006.

to webmail services, but it should support treating any web-service provider as a transit conduit for an opaque block of encrypted and integrity–protected data.

1.1   E2E Security for Web Content

Traditional methods for confidentiality and integrity involve the use of cryptography in the middle of a communications pathway. Communications involving web content can be protected at several layers in the network stack. Connections between client and server could be secured at the network level using IPsec. General-purpose web servers typically employ transport layer encryption.

To the casual observer, these techniques may seem identical. Each can protect the confidentiality and integrity of the content in transit. In reality, these approaches are orthogonal to each other and have fundamental differences. They operate at different levels in the network and protect different notions of "content." Most importantly, neither can protect from a compromised or malicious application server because their confidentiality and integrity[1] protections do not reach up through the application layer.

The privacy and security of web content has usually been addressed by TLS/SSL. Encryption at this layer presumes that the application provider is trustworthy, just as encryption at the network level (*e.g.,* IPsec) assumes that the endpoints are trustworthy. In a growing number of scenarios, it is undesirable, if not unreasonable, for users to trust the communications provider with the confidentiality and integrity of their data. For example, a blogger (Bob) may not trust his hosting provider, or a customer (Alice) may not trust a commercial webmail service with her banking information. Currently, the blogger is forced to trust the blog hosting service and has no expectation of confidentiality between himself and his readers. Likewise, a customer purchasing items from an online store has to divulge sensitive personal and financial information to the merchant. Revealing such information to an online store is an unacceptable risk, especially since such entities cannot guarantee the security of their systems against electronic (or physical) theft leading to identity theft.

For situations where we cannot trust the service provider, we advocate the use of end-to-end (E2E) encryption where the endpoints are the actual users (or as close to them as possible). Not only is E2E encryption good for the privacy and security of the end user, but it is unexpectedly beneficial for service providers as well. A recent example is AOL's decision to allow users of its AIM instant messaging service to encrypt their conversations E2E. The alternative would have been for AOL to set up SSL connections for each conversation taking place on their network. Not only does the latter choice insert AOL's servers as *de facto* men-in-the-middle (and thus violate the users' expectation of privacy for an encrypted conversation), it places an unreasonable performance demand on AOL's servers. Assuming that AOL's business model does not require examining

---

[1] We specifically choose not to address availability in this paper, as it would be trivial for the service provider to impose a DoS on the user. Such an occurrence is anathema to the concept of being a useful provider of services.

AIM traffic, the use of E2E cryptography avoids performance issues and the associated cost of hardware, systems, and management.

1.2 Contributions

A better system would allow both the blogger and customer to treat the service providers as a mere communications pipe through which they can tunnel confidential information to their target audience (in Bob's case, his readers or subscribers; in Alice's, her financial institution).

We present W3Bcrypt, a system for transparent E2E encryption of web content that uses public-key cryptography (*e.g.,* PGP). W3Bcrypt can be thought of as another layer of HTML rendering; in effect, we treat encryption as another style applied to content. W3Bcrypt makes three major contributions:

- **An E2E privacy-enhancing browser extension:** W3Bcrypt provides confidentiality and integrity to content producers who wish to publish to a set of readers. The system also supports the ability for customers of web merchants to communicate with their financial institution, and a way for users of webmail systems to employ PGP even if the interface does not support it.
- **The offload of cryptographic processing:** from the server to clients. SSL has typically been used to protect web communications. However, SSL places a burden on servers that only increases with the number of clients. With W3Bcrypt, the burden of cryptographic operations is placed mostly on the client – content only has to be encrypted once in the server data store. While W3Bcrypt is not meant to replace SSL, it can complement SSL to provide a net gain in security (defense in depth) against multiple threats.
- **The concept of cryptographic processing as another phase of styling web content:** Just as content is rendered by the browser for placement, size, and coloring, so too can the content be decoded into something the user is authorized to view.

The remainder of this paper discusses the design and implementation of W3Bcrypt as well as background work on SSL, web spoofing attacks, and browser security. We also provide a security analysis of the system and present a performance evaluation.

2   Approach

The W3Bcrypt package is an extension to Firefox that permits a publisher to securely convey content to a consumer at the application level in an end-to-end fashion. The core functionality is the ability to perform PGP (or similar) cryptographic operations on blocks of web content. To support these features, the extension includes changes affecting layout operations, small additions to the UI and the ability to invoke PGP. Since one major goal is to refrain from modifying the source code of the browser, the new features are packaged as an extension for easy installation, upgrade, and removal. Adding encryption as a style takes advantage of the power of CSS, because no new tags need to be added to the HTML grammar. Work is being done in that vein on XML encryption [9].

This section discusses our primary use cases, presents a security analysis of the system (including the threat model, attacks, and potential countermeasures), and talks about some of our limitations. Section 3 discusses the actual implementation of the Firefox extension. We provide an analysis of the system's performance in Section 4.

2.1 Use Cases

We are motivated to build and analyze W3Bcrypt to enhance the amount of privacy provided by the current web infrastructure. Privacy, in this case, refers to the confidentiality and integrity of web content – the system is not used to obfuscate referrer headers or similar information, although it could be leveraged for this purpose. Below, we offer three situations we have personally encountered as motivating examples and use cases.

1. Web *peers* may wish to exchange information through a public email service such as Google's Gmail or Microsoft's Hotmail. Currently, these services are at liberty to scan, data mine, and store the content of the peers' messages. While PGP has traditionally been used to protect email communications, the use of a webmail client makes it difficult to use PGP because the browser has no built-in application-level key handling, and any code (ActiveX, Java, Javascript) from the webmail provider cannot be trusted to not divulge the private key or user passphrase. W3Bcrypt solves this problem by providing such a trustworthy client-side environment.
2. A *customer* of an online merchant may wish to use the merchant as a transit network or information conduit by passing an opaque block of data (encompassing the customer's account number and billing address) to the customer's financial institution via the merchant. The bank or credit card company then authorizes payment to the merchant without the merchant knowing the customer's account number(s). In addition, the customer could encode her shipping address such that the merchant does not know where items are shipped, but the transportation agent (*e.g.*, the USPS, UPS, or FedEx) can decode the address and deliver goods as appropriate. We discuss a possible attack on this protection scheme in Section 2.3.
3. A web content *publisher* may wish to forgo *or* supplement traditional authentication and authorization services by publishing content under a specific "audience" key (or series of such keys). Publishers can include bloggers and other content producers like news organizations or media companies.

2.2 Security Analysis

We present a security analysis for our major use cases, including the threat model for each, attacks on the system, and countermeasures that the system provides or could provide with additional implementation or support from the browser.

Threat Model. In all of our proposed use cases, our threat model is based on the concept of an untrustworthy service provider as the attacker. In the *publisher* use case, the attacker is the blog-hosting provider or media-content-hosting network. In the *customer* use case, the attacker is the online merchant. In the *peer* use case, the attacker is the webmail provider. The service provider could be merely curious, compromised, or actively malicious. We are not primarily interested in defending against passive or active attackers who attempt to sniff or otherwise control the communications links between the service provider and the client. These traditional attacks can be addressed by using SSL, but SSL cannot protect against a service provider because the provider controls the application level and has access to the data after it has been processed by SSL.

Except for a special case (the Hitchhiker attack), we do not consider any defense against client-side attacks such as trojan horses, viruses, spyware, or other malware on the user's host. In all cases, the attacker is interested in violating the confidentiality and/or integrity of the user's content. We believe that for most situations the availability of content is not an issue; a service provider that denies service is not a very effective service provider, and it is trivial to cause DoS by changing the server to interrupt connections containing PGP content.

Yet, it is a very real possibility that the service provider has defined the ability to examine user content as a core competency or central business need. This type of service provider will therefore be satisfied with imposing a denial of service on users that violate an agreement stating that users are not allowed to obfuscate, encrypt, or otherwise hide their content from the service provider. We consider the existence of W3Bcrypt problematic for such service providers and demonstrate an attack that they could carry out to get around the protections afforded by W3Bcrypt (the aforementioned special case).

We also exclude attacks on the content after it has left W3Bcrypt's purview. For example, a news provider may wish to employ W3Bcrypt as part of a type of DRM scheme where content is targeted to a specific consumer or group of consumers. After the consumer's W3Bcrypt system has decrypted the content, the consumer is free to copy the content and pass it on. Since the content is out of W3Bcrypt's control at this point, we do not consider this part of our threat model. We note that this type of attack exists for all DRM or content distribution schemes. Furthermore, the threat model in these situations is different from ours – we assume that the receiver is free to do whatever they want with content directed at them.

Attacks. There are two major types of attacks against W3Bcrypt: the brute force attack and the Hitchhiker attack. We discuss the possibility of replay attacks in section 2.3. The brute force attack is carried out by a service provider that attempts to discover the private key being used to sign or decrypt content. We assume that W3Bcrypt is no stronger against this attack than PGP itself. The attacker could also attempt to gain the key through coercion or economic incentives, an attack that is effective against any cryptographic scheme.

The Hitchhiker attack is very interesting in that the attacker does not try to directly subvert or control the cryptosystem. Instead, the service provider attempts to piggyback code that bypasses the cryptographic controls on the content and accesses the content either before or after it has passed through the cryptosystem. Additionally, the attacker can attempt to insert web content that is meant to masquerade or blend in with the encoded or decoded web content. This attack is a type of spoofing attack. If the attacker has not discovered the private key, he or she cannot forge a signature for such content.

For example, a webmail provider may include, as part of their webmail client, Javascript that captures a user's keystrokes. If the user later uses W3Bcrypt to encode the mail message, the webmail provider still has a log of the plaintext by virtue of the keystroke monitoring. Such monitoring is already done to support automatic spell-check and automatic saving functionality in some webmail applications. On the receiving side, the attacker could include Javascript that attempts to read the contents of a message once it has been decrypted by W3Bcrypt.

Countermeasures. In order to overcome the Hitchhiker attack, the browser would ideally support a policy-driven mandatory access control on a fine-grained namespace framework for the browser objects, like SELinux does for the Linux operating system. Lacking such controls, we can attempt to perform input operations in a transparent overlay frame, encrypt the content in this overlay frame, and then transfer it to the target element in encrypted form. Likewise, encrypted content can be transferred to a new overlay frame and decrypted in that context with "external" Javascript disabled or unable to read or write to that frame.

This solution still leaves open the question of a user that unknowingly includes malicious Javascript in the content they have encrypted. The solution to this problem is an open area of research. One potential (but unappealing) solution is to employ some form of model or proof-carrying code [16] combined with a policy mechanism like the Java Policy and Permissions framework.

2.3   Limitations and Discussion

W3Bcrypt currently depends on the presence of the GnuPG software package and invokes an *xterm* to call the *gpg* tool. We plan to improve W3Bcrypt so that it can detect and use other PGP packages. We are also investigating the use of the appropriate command shell tool so that W3Bcrypt can be used on the Windows version of Firefox.

We note that W3Bcrypt alone does not support the *customer* use case. Merchants and financial institutions would need to modify their systems to expect PGP encoded data and process it properly. In particular, the online merchant would need to alter input validation routines for the protected data.

Key Management. As with all systems that employ a form of public key cryptography, the issue of key management is important. We refrain from dealing with key management or revocation. W3Bcrypt's design avoids the use of a large scale PKI and employs the peer-to-peer "web of trust" approach implicit with user-managed PGP keys. Key creation, sharing, signing, and revocation are explicitly not handled by the current tool. Instead, these operations are deferred to the underlying PGP package. We plan to include GUI entry points (*e.g.*, a "buddy" list) to this functionality in later releases.

Privacy Preferences. While our goal is to enhance privacy, W3Bcrypt does not take advantage of or interface with the Platform for Privacy Preferences (P3P) initiative [6], nor is it meant to directly support other browser-based privacy-enhancing mechanisms like referrer header rewriting or blanking, although it could be used to do so. Determining if the use of W3Bcrypt can benefit these areas is an open problem.

Integration Complexity. In the customer use case, the customer needs to communicate with at least three entities: the merchant, to select goods and create the order; her financial institution, to arrange payment of the final sum; and a shipping agent, to arrange a particular type of shipping. The merchant, in order to make online shopping attractive to the customer, must integrate the latter two communications into its online shopping process. Since merchants currently expect to at least parse the customer information for sanity, a customer using W3Bcrypt would require the merchant to partially rewrite their web application and modify their database.

While the system provides the basis for a number of use cases, Schneier reminds us that security is a process, not a product. In many use cases, W3Bcrypt handily fills an immediate need. In other situations, such as those involving complex, multi-party protocols, W3Bcrypt alone does not provide adequate privacy against higher-level attacks. As a simple example, the merchant use case assumes that the customer wants to hide both her financial credentials and shipping address from the merchant. However, the shipping agent usually prices service according to location and delivery method. If the shipping agent returns this information in a plaintext format to the merchant, the merchant could potentially guess the location of the customer (especially if the information is correlated with information gleaned from IP address geo-location services).

In theory, these problems are not difficult to solve. The customer should merely set up a key pair with the chosen shipping agent, financial institution, *etc.* In practice, this key management may prove difficult, and leaves open the large question of how this sort of information integration actually occurs in the merchant's web application.

Furthermore, any of the use cases could suffer from replay attacks, although such an attack would be more noticeable and presumably not as harmful in the *peer* and *publisher* use cases. Duplicate blog postings or emails will probably be recognized as such and ignored (even if their content were relatively dire – for example, an inflammatory news bulletin or letter of dismissal). More care must be taken in the *customer* use case. The customer should include some randomness in the data to be communicated to their financial institution. A timestamp, sequence number, or randomly generated ticket prepended to the account number would serve to identify duplicate transactions submitted by the merchant. W3Bcrypt does not currently support transparently concatenating a timestamp to all encrypted fields, but this capability is straightforward to add.

Even with these limitations, we believe our system is immediately useful, and we employ it almost daily. We look forward to incorporating some of the countermeasures and solutions to the limitations in our ongoing development of the Firefox extension, which we describe next.

3   Implementation

We have implemented W3Bcrypt as an extension to version 1.5.x of the Mozilla Firefox web browser, although the core ideas are browser-agnostic. W3Bcrypt could easily be implemented in other popular browsers like Opera, Safari, and Microsoft Internet Explorer, or even a text-based browser like *wget* or *lynx*. Our extension is available at our website[2]. The major features of the W3Bcrypt system include the ability to transform chunks of HTML content from and to PGP-encrypted, ASCII-armored blocks of data. In addition, the system supports the ability for the browser to automatically decrypt div's marked with a special CSS class id. The most immediately useful feature is the ability to select free text in form objects like textareas and textboxes, access the context menu, and utilize one of the basic PGP functions from a menu of six: encrypt, sign, encrypt and sign, decrypt, verify, and decrypt and verify.

3.1   Package Layout

Our prototype adheres to the packaging conventions for Firefox 1.5.x extensions. The system is comprised of four files: *install.rdf, chrome.manifest, overlay.js*, and *overlay.xul*. The first two files are used during installation of the extension and contain the metadata that describe the package and its capabilities. In particular, the *chrome.manifest* file contains directives that overlay our new widgets on the standard browser GUI components.

The latter two files contain the bulk of our implementation, and they are located in the *chrome/content/* subdirectory of the extension XPI file. They reflect a clean split between the new GUI components and the raw functionality for invoking GPG. The XUL file defines a new sub-menu for the context menu. The JS file contains Javascript functions that invoke the GPG functionality via an *xterm*, and it supplies a function to automatically decrypt marked div's.

3.2   Integration with GPG

One of the design goals of W3Bcrypt was to provide a quick manual method for invoking the extension functionality. To simplify implementation, we made a design decision to leverage any PGP software already installed on the host. We currently use GPG, which is available for both Windows and Linux (and a number of other platforms). We decided to implement the six major cryptographic operations as choices in the context menu. These choices are gathered into a submenu to avoid crowding the regular context menu. The various functions in

---

[2] http://nsl.cs.columbia.edu/projects/w3bcypt/

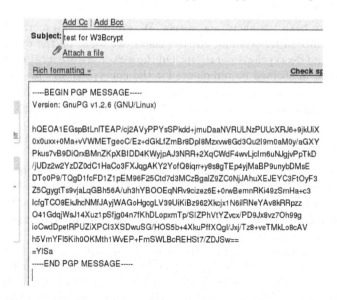

Fig. 1. *Encrypted Data.* After the text is selected and W3Bcrypt is invoked via the context menu, the selected text is replaced with ASCII-armored data. This data can be decrypted by the receiver either manually or automatically.

overlay.js are accessible via this context menu. These functions do some setup work (gathering content, setting up temporary files, creating an *xterm*) and then delegate to *gpg*. The result is gathered and written into the HTML element it originated from, via the `innerHTML` attribute.

3.3   Auto-rendering of Encrypted DIVs

One of our primary goals is to treat cryptographic content as another type of style. To this end, the prototype recognizes specially marked `div` elements (those with the class attribute set to "w3bcrypt" as follows) and automatically decrypts them.

```
<div class="w3bcrypt">
...encrypted content here...
</div>
```

When Firefox finishes loading the DOM for a page, the extension requests a list of all `div` elements marked with the *w3bcrypt* class and proceeds to decrypt them, prompting the user for his passphrase. Only the decrypt and verify operations are automated for marked `div`'s, as this arrangement alleviates the burden of manually selecting some text and decrypting it via the context menu.

4   System Evaluation

In order to make sure that the cost of employing W3Bcrypt is justifiable, we need to quantify the impact of the system on the resources (*i.e.,* space and time) used by both the client and server. We employed two metrics to evaluate the performance of the system. For the client, we focus on the overhead due to encryption and decryption operations. On the server, we are most concerned with the difference in storage requirements for the encrypted and plain content. We classify objects as text or binary to differentiate between two cases: the content stored in a database, which is mostly text, and the content served by a web server (likely a mixture of both text and binary objects). We ignore the initial cost of the encryption of the server's web or database content since it happens only once and it is not repeated for any of the subsequent client requests.

For these experiments, we used a machine with a 2.7 GHz Intel Pentium 4 processor with 1GB of RAM running a Debian Linux distribution. Cryptographic operations were provided by GPG version 1.4.2 with the ASCII armored output option enabled. All of the results presented are the computed averages of multiple experimental runs with tight confidence intervals.

We used two different types of datasets in our experiment: a text repository containing the American Constitution[3] and three commercial web sites[4]. For the web sites, we stored and used all the data returned when accessing their first page, including the index page and any other pop-up, overlay, or roll-over objects that appeared as a result of scripting. This type of capture results in slightly larger web content sizes than what we usually expect.

4.1   Encrypted Versus Plaintext Content Size

The pure text experiments use parts of the plaintext version of the American Constitution. Figure 3 shows that for small text sizes there is a significant increase in the space required for the generated ciphertext. For text sizes above a threshold (about 2KB), we observe the opposite effect: a significant drop in the space requirements. This is because GPG uses GNU ZLIB compression library to compress, aiming to effectively increase the entropy of the files, before encrypting them. For smaller text sizes, this compression does not work very well, and we can observe the opposite effect – the produced ciphertext file increases in size. Of course, GPG supports other, more sophisticated, compression algorithms which can possibly improve the encrypted file sizes for all file types.

We conducted experiments involving real web content. Figure 4 depicts our results. In general, binary objects like images (high entropy) demonstrate size inflation whereas pure textual objects (*e.g.,* HTML and Javascript) undergo a size decrease. However, the images are usually of bigger cumulative size and the overall result is a rise in storage requirements for the encrypted files. This rise is proportional to the initial content size, and it is almost always no more than twice the size of the original unencrypted web content.

4.2   Overhead of Encryption and Decryption Operations

W3Bcrypt employs two types of actions: manual operations requiring user intervention (encryption), and the decryption operation, which happens automat-

---

[3] http://www.house.gov/Constitution/Constitution.html

[4] http://www.cnn.com, www.nytimes.com and www.chase.com

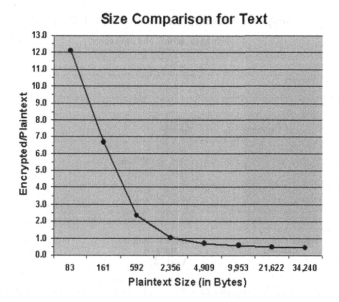

Fig. 2. *Comparison of Size for Encrypted vs Plaintext.* Small plaintext size have a significant increase in the generated encrypted text size. This size drops sharply to values below 1 for plaintext sizes of more than 2KB.

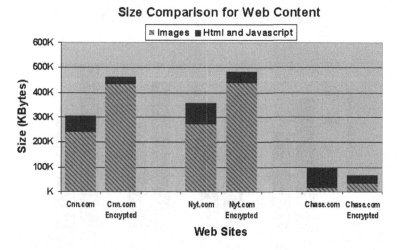

Fig. 3. *Web Content Size Comparison.* There is an increase in size for the produced encrypted text which is proportional to the initial size of the site. This increase comes solely from the encryption of the binary images (lower portion of the bars). HTML and Javascript files decrease in size (upper portion of the bars).

ically when the browser detects an encrypted object. We measure the latency overhead from the automatic execution of an encryption or decryption of an object or set of objects. This penalty is what really matters to the end user. When

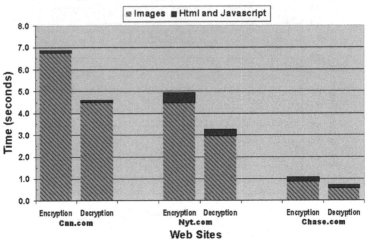

Fig. 4. *Encryption and Decryption Overhead.* The bars display the cumulative time for different operations and for different site content. The lower portion of the bar indicates the time required for the binary and the upper portion for the textual content. The latency overhead depends on the size of the site and the number of object that it contains.

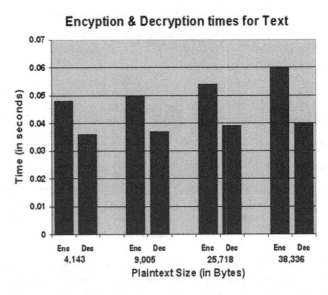

Fig. 5. *Latency overhead for text.* For text objects the latency overhead is just few milliseconds. Such a delay is unnoticeable to the end user.

downloading an encrypted page, the user wants to see how much longer it will take for the page to complete. This type of measurement avoids any comparison

Table 1. Web sites: size and number of objects

Site name	Total Size(Bytes)	# objects
cnn.com	305,586	137
nyt.com	357,378	88
chase.com	99,504	22

between a manual and an automated operation and thus avoids the need to take user-browser interaction into account.

Figure 4 displays the results of both operations on different web sites. Decryption takes less time than encryption both for HTML and for images. For sites that offer content of smaller size, such as the chase.com website, the decryption process requires just over half second to complete. We note that the latency overhead depends both on the size of the site and the number of objects that it contains. This dependency is an artifact of our implementation. We use a different call to GPG for cryptographic operations on each object. This organization generates extra overhead for the system since a page might contain multiple objects. The impact is clear if we compare the encryption and decryption time for the first two sites, in Figure 5. Although both sites have similar content size, the first (cnn.com) has many more objects than the second (nyt.com) (see Table 1) resulting in almost double the amount of time required.

On the other hand, all pure text operations are almost instantaneous, only taking a few milliseconds even for large chunks of text, as shown in Figure 5. Our tool excels when it is used for textual objects. Performance drops when the tool is used on binary objects, but the observed times can be improved by an implementation that first loads the page and then operates on all the encrypted objects with just one call to the necessary library function.

5   Related Work

Our work on E2E confidentiality and integrity protection for web content draws naturally on a number of related efforts in cryptography and web engineering. In particular, work on XML encryption faces many of the same technical challenges. Recent work on encrypting RSS feeds provides extra motivation, while the performance and security analysis of SSL provides some insight into how W3Bcrypt can enhance security while decreasing (or at least not significantly adding to) the performance burden for servers. Finally, work on trusted paths for browsers and more secure browser architectures is of interest because W3Bcrypt can provide some level of visual disambiguation. Since non-decodable PGP blocks are rendered poorly (or not at all) by the extension, they provide visual cues that the content was not meant for the viewer (or represents untrustable content most probably injected by a phisher). The work on more secure browser architectures is of use for cases where the service provider attempts the Hitchhiker attack by including Javascript code that tries to discover the encrypted content. During our research, we were alerted to a parallel suggestion by Gregorio [7] to use

GreaseMonkey for encrypting RSS feeds. We take this as an encouraging sign that the problem we are working on is a current and meaningful one.

XML Encryption. Some work has been done on content encryption using XSLT and XML. Work suggesting the element-level encryption of XML content appeared as early as April of 2000 [13]. This work, and efforts related to it [9, 10], are complementary to W3Bcrypt. W3Bcrypt currently treats the contents of a `div` element as a single-level block of content. The results are undefined if the content includes HTML markup, although our tests show that Firefox *does* successfully render the HTML markup in the auto-decrypted content. In addition, the goals of the XML encryption projects are quite similar to some of our use cases, especially the *customer* scenario.

SSL Encryption. SSL is widely used to secure transport layer communication, by providing confidentiality and integrity for sessions between a web server and a web client. However, SSL is not immune to attacks [5, 2], and since it operates at the transport layer its use assumes at least a trusted server application. We do not argue for replacing SSL; rather, we advocate for augmenting security at another layer.

The use of SSL imposes a hefty performance penalty on servers, and much work has been done to decrease this performance hit. Coarfa *et al.* [4] provide an analysis of the bottlenecks for SSL processing and propose some adjustments to alleviate them. Various other mechanisms for speeding up SSL by both distributing the work [12, 14] and speeding up the underlying cryptographic operations [8] have been proposed.

Other Work. Phishing is an attack that has grown in popularity. Both the Spoofguard [3] system and Ye and Smith [17] discuss various methods of creating a trusted path from the server to the user. Both of these systems extend the browser to accomplish client-side protection. While W3Bcrypt is not explicitly built to counter phishing or spoofing attacks, it could be leveraged to display trusted content by decrypting the entire page. Injected content would not decrypt properly (assuming that the attacker does not know the encryption key).

Ross *et al.* [15] implement a browser extension to generate passwords on a per-website basis. This work is complimentary in that it explores ways to protect multiple secrets against malicious websites. It also transparently addresses the tendency to use the same password across multiple sites.

One of the more interesting attacks against W3Bcrypt is the Hitchhiker attack. This attack is a type of cross-site scripting attack, enabled by the ability of the attacker to piggyback Javascript code onto the page. If the browser does not provide namespace separation and access controls (as suggested by Anupam and Mayer [1]), then this Javascript can read content that is meant to be protected by our system. There has been some work on providing a secure browsing environment [11] using sub-process sandboxing and privilege separation. Finally, trusted path techniques (such as randomizing elements of the extension's dialog components) can help in the case of Hitchhiker code that attempts to steal the user's passphrase by displaying a fake dialog. In addition, we can store the user's passphrase so they only have to enter it once per session (identical approaches are taken by *ssh-agent* and desktop mail clients).

6   Conclusions

The growth of hosted web services introduces new methods of communication, collaboration, and commerce. In many of these situations, the client cannot trust the service provider with the confidentiality and integrity of the client's data. W3Bcrypt is a practical and effective mechanism that supports the E2E confidentiality and integrity of web content. Our implementation is an extension to the Firefox web platform and supplies a trustworthy client-side environment for performing cryptographic operations on web content.

Measurements show that HTML content size does not increase significantly; rather, there is a reduction in size for text greater than 2KB. Cryptographic operations take only a few milliseconds to complete, and web content that contains both text and binary objects incurs a processing overhead that is less than 1 second for small sites and only a few seconds for larger sites.

We are motivated to work on this problem because we want to use webmail services without forfeiting the privacy of our messages, communicate with our financial institutions without having an intermediary learn our account information, and publish blogs with only a selected audience knowing what the content is. The protection offered by E2E cryptography at the application level is the correct model for these situations. W3Bcrypt is a step in the right direction for the privacy of end users.

References

1. V. Anupam and A. Mayer. Security of Web Browser Scripting Languages: Vulnerabilities, Attacks, and Remedies. In *Proceedings of the 7th USENIX Security Symposium*, January 1998.
2. D. Brumley and D. Boneh. Remote Timing Attacks Are Practical. In *Proceedings of the 12th USENIX Security Symposium*, August 2003.
3. N. Chou, R. Ledesma, Y. Teraguchi, and J. C. Mitchell. Client–side Defense Against Web–based Identity Theft. In 11th *Annual Network and Distributed System Security Symposium (NDSS 2004)*, February 2004.
4. C. Coarfa, P. Druschel, and D. S. Wallach. Performance Analysis of TLS Web Servers. In 9th *Annual Network and Distributed System Security Symposium (NDSS 2002)*, February 2002.
5. D. Dean and A. Stubblefield. Using Client Puzzles to Protect TLS. In *Proceedings of the 10th USENIX Security Symposium*, August 2001.
6. R. W. et al. Platform for Privacy Preferences (P3P) Project. http://www.w3.org/P3P/, September 2005.
7. J. Gregorio. Secure RSS Syndication. http://www.xml.com/pub/a/2005/07/13/secure-rss.html, July 2005.
8. V. Gupta, D. Stebila, S. Fung, S. C. Shantz, N. Gura, and H. Eberle. Speeding Up Secure Web Transactions Using Elliptic Curve Cryptography. In 11th *Annual Network and Distributed System Security Symposium (NDSS 2004)*, August 2004.

9. T. Imamura, B. Dillaway, and E. Simon. XML Encryption Syntax and Processing. http://www.w3.org/TR/xmlenc-core/, 2002.

10. T. Imamura and H. Maruyama. Specification of Element-wise XML Encryption. http://lists.w3.org/Archives/Public/xml-encryption/2000Aug/att-0005/xmlenc-spec.html, 2000.

11. S. Ioannidis and S. M. Bellovin. Building a Secure Web Browser. In *Freenix Annual Technical Conference (USENIX 2001)*, June 2001.

12. C. Lesniewski-Laas and M. F. Kaashoek. SSL Splitting: Securely Serving Data From Untrusted Caches. In *Proceedings of the 12th USENIX Security Symposium*, August 2003.

13. H. Maruyama and T. Imamura. Element-Wise XML Encryption. http://lists.w3.org/Archives/Public/xml-encryption/2000Apr/att-0005/01-xmlenc, 2000.

14. E. Rescorla, A. Cain, and B. Korver. SSLACC: A Clustered SSL Accelerator. In *Proceedings of the 11th USENIX Security Symposium*, August 2002.

15. B. Ross, C. Jackson, N. Miyake, D. Boneh, and J. C. Mitchell. Stronger Password Authentication Using Browser Extensions. In *Proceedings of the 14th USENIX Security Symposium.*, pages 17–32, August 2005.

16. R. Sekar, C. Ramakrishnan, I. Ramakrishnan, and S. Smolka. Model-Carrying Code (MCC): A New Paradigm for Mobile-Code Security. In *Proceedings of the New Security Paradigms Workshop (NSPW)*, September 2001.

17. Z. Ye and S. Smith. Trusted Paths for Browsers. In *Proceedings of the 11th USENIX Security Symposium*, August 2002.

Combinatorial Structures for Design of Wireless Sensor Networks

Dibyendu Chakrabarti and Jennifer Seberry

Applied Statistics Unit, Indian Statistical Institute,
203 B T Road, Kolkata 700 108
University of Wollongong, Northfields Av.,
NSW 2522, Australia
dibyendu_r@isical.ac.in, jennie@uow.edu.au

Abstract. Combinatorial designs are very effective tools for managing keys in an infrastructure where power and memory are two major constraints. None of the present day wireless technologies takes the advantage of combinatorial designs. In this paper, we have proposed a general framework using combinatorial designs which will enable the participating devices to communicate securely among themselves with little memory and power overhead. The scheme caters for different kinds of user requirements and allows the designer to choose different combinatorial designs for different parts or levels of the network. This general framework will find application in all wireless radio technologies, typically WPANs and WLANs. This is a hitherto unexplored technique in wireless technologies.

Keywords: Combinatorial Design, Sensor Network, Key Pre-distribution, Projective Plane, Transversal Design.

1 Introduction

Combinatorial designs are very effective tools for managing keys in an infrastructure where power and memory are two major constraints. None of the present day wireless technologies takes the advantage of combinatorial designs. In this paper, we have proposed a general framework using combinatorial designs which will enable the participating devices to communicate securely among themselves with little memory and power overhead. The scheme caters to different kinds of user requirements and allows the designer to choose different combinatorial designs for different parts or levels of the network. A few examples of WLAN technologies are IEEE 802.11a/b/e/g/h/i, HiperLAN/2, HomeRF etc. and on the other hand, Bluetooth, ZigBee, UWB etc. are examples of WPAN technologies.

Very recently it is reported that two researchers have been successful in cracking the Bluetooth PIN [18]. The other wireless LAN technology protocol 802.11x also suffers from several security loopholes: insertion attacks, interception and monitoring wireless traffic, misconfiguration, jamming and client to client attacks are a few of the important ones. For more details, one may refer to [7]. In the following, we shall introduce the desiderata of wireless technologies.

J. Zhou, M. Yung, and F. Bao (Eds.): ACNS 2006, LNCS 3989, pp. 365–374, 2006.

1.1   Wireless Technologies: How the Properties of Radio Waves Affect Networking Capabilities

An ideal radio wave for wireless technologies should have high speed, travel far distances and consume little energy. Had such radio waves existed, it would have been possible for us to transfer information very rapidly at any distance using little battery power. Unfortunately, real radio waves do not behave like that. The high speed and long range of a radio wave demands more energy. That is why the designers of the wireless technologies try to optimise certain parameters under a given condition. As a direct consequence, we find wireless area networks of different orders (e.g., personal, local, metropolitan, global, etc.) and each of them is suitable to a particular application or usage.

As an example, in wireless local area network (WLAN), the power consumption is less important compared to range/speed whereas the design of a wireless personal area network (WPAN) demands low power in preference to high speed or long range.

For more details on wireless technologies, refer to [17].

1.2   Our Proposal: An Uncharted Territory

However, an unexplored area in the security of wireless technologies is the use of combinatorial designs. Our proposal is an endeavour to propose the security solutions in a wireless network using combinatorial designs. The method is not restricted to smart homes only and may also find application in Hierarchical Sensor Networks where the deployment of the sensor nodes may be made in a more or less controlled manner. One can even think of other situation where a hierarchical structure may be deemed fit. As an extreme example, suppose the different countries of the world are divided into a few groups (possibly based on their geographical locations), and a multinational company operates globally, setting up branches in different countries. However, the management may decide to delegate the authority to each of the branch offices in an hierarchical structure. That structure may easily be translated to our model. In the following, we shall talk about two specific application areas viz., smart homes and sensor networks, though we have a common set of objectives in mind:

1. The entire communication in the network will take place securely.
2. The protocol will be as simple as possible.
3. The network will comprise of several logical parts. The network will be resilient to such an extent that the other parts will continue to function even if one/more parts of the network are compromised.

1.3   Smart Homes

A smart home or building is a home or building, usually a new one, that is equipped with special structured wiring to enable occupants to remotely control or program an array of automated home electronic devices by entering a single command. For example, a homeowner on vacation can use a Touchtone phone to arm a home security system, control temperature gauges, switch appliances on or off, control lighting, program a home theater or entertainment system, and perform many other tasks. The field of home automation is expanding rapidly as electronic technologies converge. The home network encompasses communications, entertainment, security, convenience, and information systems. For more details, refer to [22].

Suppose we want to install the network in such a building. Naturally each of the rooms of the building forms a "logical part" of the network. The natural user requirement would be that the devices in one room should function independently of the devices of any other room. If one room has to be cut off from the network, still the other parts of the building should be able to function unhindered. One can use same/different combinatorial designs to model the different parts of the network.

1.4   Sensor Networks: A Brief Introduction

Secure communication among sensor nodes has become an active area of research [2, 6, 9, 14, 15, 16, 10]. One may refer to [12] for broader perspective in the area of sensor networks. Based on the architectural consideration, wireless sensor networks may be broadly classified into two categories viz.(i) Hierarchical Wireless Sensor Networks (HWSN) and (ii) Distributed Wireless Sensor Networks (DWSN). In HWSN, there is a pre-defined hierarchy among the participating nodes. There are three types of nodes in the descending order of capabilities: (a) base stations, (b) cluster heads, and (c) sensor nodes. The sensor nodes are usually placed in the neighbourhood of the base station. Sometimes the network traffic (data) is collected by the cluster heads which in turn forward the traffic to the base station.

There may be three different modes of data flow as follows: Unicast (sensor to sensor), multicast (group wise), broadcast(base station to sensor). However, it may be pointed out that the HWSN is best suited for applications where the network topology is known prior to deployment. On the other hand, there is no fixed infrastructure in the case of a DWSN and the network topology is unknown before the deployment. Once the nodes are scattered over the target area, the nodes scan their radio coverage area and find their neighbours. In this case also, the data flow may be divided into three categories (as discussed above) with the only difference that the broadcast might take place between any two nodes.

In this paper, we shall talk about wireless sensor networks in general, possibly with the exception of some special nodes with higher memory and/or computational capacity. Also we shall assume that the deployment is more or less controlled.

The size of the sensor network is usually very large (say, of size N). The sensor nodes are usually memory-constrained and that is why it is not possible to maintain $N - 1$ keys in each sensor node so that ultimately different secret keys are maintained for each of the pairs. The nodes often do not have much computational capacity to implement public key framework (though very recently implementations of ECC and RSA on 8-bit CPUs have been proposed [11]). Still key pre-distribution solutions are bound to be much faster since they are less computation intensive.

One usually faces a few problems in key pre-distribution. Often two nodes are not directly connected and communicate through one or more hops. Also the compromise of a few node results in the failure of a large part of the network since the keys revealed were also shared between the other nodes. For a more detailed account of these, please refer to [3, 4, 5, 1, 9, 14, 10, 15, 2].

1.5   Key Pre-distribution in General: Our Proposal

One possible solution is to have a situation where every node is guaranteed to have a common key with every other node that it needs to communicate with. For a very large network, this is not possible, as explained earlier. We propose to divide the network into certain logical sub networks. Intra sub network nodes always share keys with each other. For each sub network, we earmark a particular node as a special node. Inter sub network communication takes place by the communication between the special nodes of the respective sub networks.

The issues at this point are as follows:

1. One has to have some control over the deployment of the nodes.
2. For the special nodes, the number of keys to be stored in each node will clearly increase. So one needs to decide the availability of storage space. In [15, Page 4], it has been commented that storing 150 keys in a sensor node may not be practical. On the other hand, in [9, Page 47], [14, Section 5.2], scenarios have been described with 200 keys. If one considers 4 Kbytes of memory space for storing keys in a sensor node, then choosing 128-bit key (16 byte), it is possible to accommodate 256 keys.

Thus the goal in this paper is to present a scheme that aims at failsafe connectivity all-over the network. We differ from the existing works where it is considered that any two nodes will have either 0 or 1 common key all over the network. Our motivation is to have a design strategy where the entire network is divided into a number of subnetworks. Any two nodes of a particular subnetwork share a common key. The special nodes of different subnetworks share more than one common keys. This is important from resiliency consideration in an adversarial framework since even if a certain subnetwork is compromised, the other parts of the network, i.e., the other subnetworks may function without any disturbance. Moreover, even if one or more special nodes are compromised, the other special nodes can still communicate among themselves. In other words, the connectivity of the network is not disturbed at all.

The rest of the paper is organised as follows: We begin with a preliminary introduction to combinatorial designs. In the next section, we use a detailed example to explain the problem and discuss the solution. The paper concludes with the future research proposals.

2   Preliminaries

2.1   Basics of Combinatorial Design

For a ready reference to *set system, block design, BIBD, group-divisible design, projective planes* and *transversal design*, refer to [8, 20, 19, 21].

Projective Plane
A finite projective plane of order n is formally defined as a set of points with the properties that:

1. Any two points determine a line,
2. Any two lines determine a point,
3. Every point has $n + 1$ lines through it, and
4. Every line contains $n + 1$ points.

(Note that some of these properties are redundant.) A projective plane is therefore a symmetric $(n^2 + n + 1, n + 1, 1)$ block design.

A finite projective plane exists when the order n is a power of a prime, i.e., for $n = p^a$. It is conjectured that these are the only possible projective planes, but proving this remains one of the most important unsolved problems in combinatorics.

The smallest finite projective plane is of order $n = 2$, and consists of the configuration known as the Fano plane. The remarkable Bruck-Ryser-Chowla theorem says that if a projective plane of order n exists, and $n = 1$ *or* $2 (\mathrm{mod}\, 4)$, then n is the sum of two squares. This rules out $n = 6$. Even before that, Tarry ruled out projective planes of order 6 by hand calculations. Lam [13] showed, using massive computer calculations on top of some mathematics, that there are no finite projective planes of order 10. The status of the order 12 projective plane remains open.

The projective plane of order 2, also known as the Fano plane, is denoted

PG(2, 2). It has incidence matrix
$$
\begin{pmatrix}
1 & 1 & 1 & 0 & 0 & 0 & 0 \\
1 & 0 & 0 & 1 & 1 & 0 & 0 \\
1 & 0 & 0 & 0 & 0 & 1 & 1 \\
0 & 1 & 0 & 1 & 0 & 1 & 0 \\
0 & 1 & 0 & 0 & 1 & 0 & 1 \\
0 & 0 & 1 & 1 & 0 & 0 & 1 \\
0 & 0 & 1 & 0 & 1 & 1 & 0
\end{pmatrix}
$$

Every row and column contains three 1s, and any pair of rows/columns has a single 1 in common.

3   Key Predistribution in General: Our Approach

3.1   The Correspondence Between a Combinatorial Design and a Sensor Network

The blocks of the combinatorial design corresponds to a sensor node and the elements present in a block represent the keys present in a sensor node.

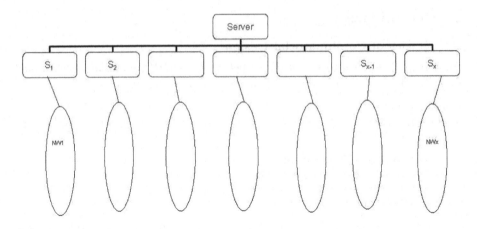

Fig. 1. The Network

3.2   The Method

In [15], it has been shown that using a transversal design, there is direct connectivity between two nodes in 60% of the cases. Overall, any two nodes can communicate either directly or through an intermediate node (i.e., a two-hop path) with almost certainty. For a large network, the compromise of even 10 nodes will render 18% of the nodes unusable.

Our approach is very different from the approach of [15]. In the diagram, we have shown a network with only two levels of hierarchy. There may be more levels depending on the user requirements. Our proposal is perfectly general and fits into networks of any size. The root of the hierarchy tree is assumed to be a central server, S. At the next level, x special nodes $S_1, S_2, \cdots, S_x$ are placed. The leaf level comprises of the subnetworks $NW_1, NW_2, \cdots, NW_x$.

One has the freedom to choose different combinatorial designs for different parts of the network. Again, that depends on the specific requirements of the user. For example, if the sub networks are required to form a totally connected network graph, one can choose projective planes. This may be applicable in case of a smart home. If the subnetworks are very large in size and total connectivity is not a requirement (i.e., if single/multi-hop connectivity is permissible), transversal designs might be a reasonable choice.

Let us assume that we are using only projective planes in all the parts of the network. We know that a projective plane of order n (n is a prime power) has $n^2 + n + 1$ number of blocks and each block contains $n + 1$ keys. If we use a projective plane of order n, we can accommodate a network of $n^2 + n + 1$ nodes with $n + 1$ keys per node.

Let us assume that $max_i|NW_i| = \alpha$ (for $i = 1, 2, \cdots, x$), i.e., the subnetwork size is at most α, so that a projective plane of order $\geq \left\lceil \sqrt{\alpha - \frac{3}{4}} - \frac{1}{2} \right\rceil$ may be used to model the subnetwork.

In fact, we should choose the sub network size $n^2 + n$ instead of $n^2 + n + 1$ because we shall have to include the special node S_i (at the next higher level) corresponding to each sub network NW_i. The corresponding projective plane is of order $\left\lceil \sqrt{\alpha + \frac{1}{4}} - \frac{1}{2} \right\rceil$.

If we have x such sub networks, we have also x corresponding projective planes. They may or may not be of the same order depending on the same / different sizes of the various sub networks. One can use different projective planes for different sub networks NW_i simple by replacing α by NW_i in the above expression.

Note that each of the subnetworks NW_i including the special node S_i, i.e., $S_i \bigcup NW_i$ (for $i = 1, 2, \cdots, x$) forms a complete network graph. Since we are using a projective plane to distribute the keys in the underlying nodes, this property is guaranteed. In other words, any two nodes of $NW_i \bigcup S_i$ for $i = 1, 2, \cdots, x$ share a common key with each other.

Had we used a transversal design $TD(k, r)$ instead of a projective plane, every pair of nodes would not have been connected. However, a constant fraction of the total number of pairs would have been connected (i.e., would have shared a common key). It is easy to see that the value of the fraction is $\frac{k}{r+1}$. Out of r^2 blocks of the $TD(k, r)$, a particular block shares keys with $kr - k = k(r - 1)$ blocks. Excepting that particular block, there are $r^2 - 1$ blocks in the $TD(k, r)$. So the fraction is $\frac{k(r-1)}{r^2-1} = \frac{k}{r+1}$.

At the next stage, we would like to have several common keys between any two special nodes S_j and S_k. In order to achieve that, we may again choose projective planes. A projective plane of order $m \geq \left\lceil \sqrt{x + \frac{1}{4}} - \frac{1}{2} \right\rceil$ will suffice to connect all the S_is for $i = 1, 2, \cdots, x$ and also the root server S may be included as the $(x + 1)$-th node. Using multiple copies (say t copies) of the projective plane of order m, and labelling them differently, we easily obtain t common keys between any two nodes of $\left(\bigcup_{i=1}^{x} S_i \right) \bigcup S$.

The special nodes/devices (which may be the cluster head in the case of a sensor network) should have more storage capacity in comparison with the other nodes in order to accommodate $t(m + 1)$ keys.

3.3   An Example Using Projective Planes

Let us continue our discussion apropos of the previous network diagram, i.e., a network with only two levels of hierarchy. The root of the hierarchy tree is the central server, S. At the next level, $x = 18$ special nodes $S_1, S_2, \cdots, S_{18}$ are placed.

The leaf level comprises of the subnetworks $NW_1, NW_2, \cdots, NW_{18}$. Let us use only projective planes all over the network.

Let us assume that $max_i |NW_i| = 900$, i.e., the subnetwork size is at most 900, or, $\alpha = 900$.

The corresponding projective plane is of order $\geq \left\lceil \sqrt{900 + \frac{1}{4}} - \frac{1}{2} \right\rceil \geq 30$.

The next highest prime being 31, let us choose a projective plane of order 31.

Since we have 18 such sub networks, we have also 18 corresponding projective planes. They may or may not be of the same order depending on the same/different sizes of the various sub networks. One can use different projective planes for different sub networks NW_i simply by replacing 900 by $|NW_i|$ in the above expression.

Note that each of the subnetworks NW_i including the special node S_i, i.e., $S_i \bigcup NW_i$ forms a complete network graph. Since we are using a projective plane to distribute the keys in the underlying nodes, this property is guaranteed. In other words, any two nodes of $NW_i \bigcup S_i$ share a common key with each other.

At the next stage, we would like to have several common keys between any two special nodes S_j and S_k. In order to achieve that, we may again choose projective planes. A projective plane of order $m \geq \left\lceil \sqrt{18 + \frac{1}{4}} - \frac{1}{2} \right\rceil \geq 4$ will suffice to connect all the S_is (for $i = 1, 2, \cdots, 18$) and also the root server S may be included as the 19-th node. Let us choose $m = 4$. Using multiple copies (say 4 copies) of the projective plane of order m, and labelling them differently, we readily have 4 common keys between any two nodes of $\left(\bigcup_{i=1}^{x} S_i \right) \bigcup S$.

The special nodes/devices (which may be the cluster head in the case of a sensor network) should have more storage capacity in comparison with the other nodes in order to accommodate $4(4 + 1) = 20$ keys.

3.4   Another Example Using Projective Planes and Transversal Designs

Suppose we have a different kind of requirement. The sub networks are very large, say each subnetwork may be of size 2500 and hence multi-hop communication is permissible.

Again let us assume that the network has only two levels of hierarchy, the root of the hierarchy tree is the central server, S. At the next level, $x = 25$ special nodes $S_1, S_2, \cdots, S_{25}$ are placed. The leaf level comprises of the subnetworks $NW_1, NW_2, \cdots, NW_{25}$.

At the sub network level, we do not have the requirement that any two nodes should be able to communicate directly. So we may use transversal designs at this level. However, since all the special nodes should be able to communicate directly among themselves and need an enhanced level of security by having multiple keys shared between any two nodes, we prefer to use projective planes at this level.

Since the sub network may have 2500 nodes, we should choose a transversal design accordingly. We know that a $TD(k, r)$ has r^2 blocks. We also know that if r is prime, and $2 \leq k \leq r$, then there exists a $TD(k, r)$ [3].

Since $\sqrt{2500} = 50$, we choose the next highest prime 53 as our r. Now we can choose k according to our convenience. We choose $k = 36$.

As mentioned earlier, the key sharing probability between any two nodes of the sub network $= \frac{k}{r+1} = \frac{36}{53+1} = 0.667$.

Note that each of the subnetworks NW_i including the special node S_i, i.e., $S_i \bigcup NW_i$ (for $i = 1, 2, \cdots, 25$) does not form a complete network graph. Since we are using a transversal design to distribute the keys in the underlying nodes, any two nodes of $NW_i \bigcup S_i$ share a common key with each other with probability 0.667.

At the next stage, we would like to have several common keys between any two special nodes S_j and S_k. In order to achieve that, we may again choose projective planes. A projective plane of order $m \geq \left\lceil \sqrt{25 + \frac{1}{4}} - \frac{1}{2} \right\rceil \geq 5$ will suffice to connect all the S_is for $i = 1, 2, \cdots, 25$ and also the root server S may be included as the 26-th node. Let us choose $m = 5$. Using multiple copies (say 4 copies) of the projective plane of order m, and labelling them differently, we readily have 4 many common keys between any two nodes of $\left(\bigcup_{i=1}^{x} S_i \right) \bigcup S$.

The special nodes/devices (which may be the cluster head in the case of a sensor network) should have more storage capacity in comparison with the other nodes in order to accommodate $4(5 + 1) = 24$ keys.

4   Conclusion and Future Research

We shall further investigate networks where "users" have differing resources and capacity requirements. One case involves a large network with large, mostly self-contained sub-networks. Another case involves networks which need more robustness at different levels of application. For example, at the second level of hierarchy (i.e., the level containing the special nodes), one may need to have different number of common keys shared between two given nodes. It will be an interesting combinatorial problem to find out a design having such a property. One may even look for better alternatives compared to the use of copies of projective planes at this level.

References

1. R. Blom. An optimal class of symmetric key generation systems. *Advances in Cryptology –Eurocrypt 84, LNCS,* vol 209, Springer Verlag, 1985, pp 335–338.
2. S. A. Camtepe and B. Yener. Combinatorial design of key distribution mechanisms for wireless sensor networks. *Computer Security – Esorics 2004, LNCS,* vol 3193, Springer Verlag, 2004.
3. D. Chakrabarti, S. Maitra and B. Roy. A key pre-distribution scheme for wireless sensor networks: merging blocks in combinatorial design. *8th Information Security Conference, ISC'05, LNCS,* vol 3650, Springer Verlag, pp 89–103.
4. D. Chakrabarti, S. Maitra and B. Roy. A hybrid design of key pre-distribution scheme for wireless sensor networks. *1st International Conference on Information Systems Security, ICISS 2005, LNCS,* vol 3803, Springer Verlag, 2005, pp 228–238.
5. D. Chakrabarti, S. Maitra and B. Roy. Clique size in sensor ketworks with key pre-distribution based on transversal design. *7th International Workshop on Distributed Computing, IWDC 2005, LNCS,* vol 3741, Springer Verlag, 2005, pp 329–337.

6. H. Chan, A. Perrig, and D. Song. Random key predistribution schemes for sensor networks. *IEEE Symposium on Research in Security and Privacy*, 2003, pp 197–213.

7. Christopher W. Klaus,Internet Security Systems (ISS). Wireless LAN Security FAQ. URL:http://www.iss.net/wireless/WLAN_FAQ.php [accessed on:17th January, 2006]

8. C. J. Colbourn, J. H. Dinitz. *The CRC Handbook of Combinatorial Designs*. CRC Press, Boca Raton, 1996.

9. W. Du, J. Ding, Y. S. Han, and P. K. Varshney. A pairwise key pre-distribution scheme for wireles sensor networks. *Proceedings of the 10th ACM conference on Computer and Communications Security, ACM CCS 2003*, pp 42–51.

10. L. Eschenauer and V. B. Gligor. A key-management scheme for distributed sensor networks. *Proceedings of the 9th ACM conference on Computer and Communications Security, ACM CCS 2002*, pp 41–47.

11. N. Gura, A. Patel, A. Wander, H. Eberle, S. C. Shantz. Comparing elliptic curve cryptography and RSA on 8-bit CPUs. *CHES 2004, LNCS*, vol 3156, Springer Verlag, 2004, pp 119–132.

12. J. M. Kahn, R. H. Katz and K. S. J. Pister. Next century challenges: Mobile networking for smart dust. *Proceedings of the 5th annual ACM/IEEE international conference on mobile computing and networking*, 1999, pp 483–492.

13. Lam, C.W.H. The search for a finite projective plane of order 10. *Amer. Math. Monthly 98, 1991*, pp 305–318.

14. J. Lee and D. Stinson. Deterministic key predistribution schemes for distributed sensor networks. *SAC 2004, LNCS*, vol 3357, Springer Verlag, 2004, pp 294–307.

15. J. Lee and D. Stinson. A combinatorial approach to key predistribution for distributed sensor networks. *IEEE Wireless Computing and Networking Conference (WCNC 2005)*,13–17 March, 2005, New Orleans, LA, USA.

16. D. Liu, and P. Ning. Establishing pairwise keys in distributed sensor networks. *Proceedings of the 10th ACM conference on Computer and Communications Security, ACM CCS 2003*.

17. Michelle Man. Bluetooth and Wi-Fi: Understanding these two technologies and how they can benefit you URL: www.socketcom.com/pdf/TechBriefWireless.pdf [accessed on 17th January, 2006]

18. Y. Shaked and A. Wool. Cracking the Bluetooth PIN. *In Proc. 3rd USENIX/ACM Conf. Mobile Systems, Applications, and Services (MobiSys), Seattle, WA, June 2005*, pp 39–50.

19. D. R. Stinson. *Combinatorial Designs: Constructions and Analysis*. Springer, New York, 2003.

20. A. P. Street and D. J. Street. *Combinatorics of Experimental Design*. Clarendon Press, Oxford, 1987.

21. Projective Plane URL: http://mathworld.wolfram.com/ProjectivePlane.html [accessed on: 17th January, 2006]

22. URL:http://searchsmb.techtarget.com/sDefinition/0,,sid44_gci540859,00.html [accessed on 17th January, 2006]

Public Key Cryptography Sans Certificates in Ad Hoc Networks

Nitesh Saxena

School of Information and Computer Science,
University of California, Irvine
nitesh@ics.uci.edu

Abstract. Several researchers have proposed the use of threshold cryptographic model to enable secure communication in ad hoc networks without the need of a trusted center. In this model, the system remains secure even in the presence of a certain threshold t of corrupted/malicious nodes.

In this paper, we show how to perform necessary public key operations without node-specific certificates in ad hoc networks. These operations include pair-wise key establishment, signing, and encryption. We achieve this by using Feldman's verifiable polynomial secret sharing (VSS) as a key distribution scheme and treating the *secret shares as the private keys*. Unlike in the standard public key cryptography, where entities have independent private/public key pairs, in the proposed scheme the private keys are *related* (they are points on a polynomial of degree t) and each public key can be computed from the public VSS information and node identifier. We show that such related keys can still be securely used for standard signature and encryption operations (using resp. Schnorr signatures and ElGamal encryption) and for pairwise key establishment, as long as there are no more that t collusions/corruptions in the system.

The proposed usage of shares as private keys can also be viewed as a threshold-tolerant identity-based cryptosystem under standard (discrete logarithm based) assumptions.

1 Introduction

Securing communication in so-called ad hoc networks, such as mobile ad hoc networks and sensor networks, is a challenging problem due to the lack of a trusted centralized authority. Starting with the seminal proposal by Zhou and Haas [1], several researchers have proposed the use of a threshold cryptographic model to distribute trust among the nodes of the network (see [2, 3, 4, 5, 6, 7, 8, 9]), towards solving this problem. Such a model tolerates a threshold t of corruptions/collusions in the network, and at the same time, allows any set of $t+1$ nodes to make distributed decisions (for example, regarding admission of new nodes to the network). This is achieved by (t, n) polynomial secret sharing scheme of Shamir [10] that splits up the network-wide secret among n nodes using a polynomial of degree t. More specifically, if p, q be large primes s.t. q divides $p - 1$

J. Zhou, M. Yung, and F. Bao (Eds.): ACNS 2006, LNCS 3989, pp. 375–389, 2006.

then each player/node P_i receives a secret share x_i equal to a value $f(i) \bmod q$ of some t-degree polynomial f. In order to ensure the robustness of the secret sharing and secret reconstruction protocols in the presence of malicious nodes, Feldman's verifiable secret sharing (VSS) [11] is employed. Additionally, Feldman's VSS creates an $O(t * |p|)$-size public file (which is nothing but the commitments to the polynomial coefficients) from which everyone can compute and verify $y_i = g^{x_i} \bmod p$ for every $i = 1, \ldots, n$.

The above-mentioned proposals on ad hoc network security required that each node be issued a certificate and also a secret share in a distributed manner. Most recently, [12] shows that as long as each node is able to obtain an updated VSS information, there is no need for node-specific certificates. However, [12] focuses mainly on how to efficiently admit new nodes, i.e., how to create new secret shares in a distributed manner. In this work, we are concerned with the problem of how to enable secure communication among the nodes once they have been admitted. In particular, we show that the secret shares created by Feldman's VSS can be securely and efficiently used as private keys in many standard discrete-log based public-key cryptosystems, namely in a Schnorr signature scheme, in an ElGamal encryption, and in a non-interactive version of the Diffie-Hellman pairwise key establishment protocol. Note that if the VSS share x_i is treated as P_i's private key, the Feldman's VSS public information allows everyone to compute the corresponding public key y_i.

Motivation. The motivation for establishing pairwise keys is straight-forward – it is needed to secure communication between any pair of nodes, e.g., as required in various secure routing protocols, such as Ariadne [13]. Signing is required in cases when *non-repudiation* is needed, e.g., as in ARAN secure routing protocol [14]. Encryption is suitable for scenarios where an authorized node outside the network needs to send a *private* query to a node inside. An example scenario is in a wireless sensor network, where a base station sends a maintenance query to a particular sensor node (e.g., to obtain its reading of nuclear activity in the environment). However, sending the query in clear would leak critical information to an adversary who might be interested in knowing what the sensor network is installed for (e.g., for detecting a nuclear attack [15]).

Related vs. Independent Keys. It is not obvious whether the proposed usage of secret shares as private keys is safe. The reason is simple – unlike in the standard public-key cryptosystems where every user gets an *independently created* private/public key pair, here the private keys of all parties are related by being values of a t-degree polynomial (Note, for example, that any set of $t + 1$ such values determines all the others). Recall, for example, that the "text-book RSA" is not secure when public keys of two users are related [16].

Our Contributions. We show that indeed such use of the *secret shares as private keys* is just as secure as the standard discrete-log based signatures, encryption, and key establishment, as long as no more than t of the players in the group collude or are corrupted by an attacker. Note that this is the best that one can hope for because if the private keys are shares in a secret sharing with t-degree privacy threshold, any collection of $t + 1$ such keys enables reconstruction of the whole secret-sharing and hence also all the other private keys. Our proposal renders necessary public key operations efficiently feasible in ad hoc networks, without the need of certificates.

Threshold-tolerant ID-based Cryptography. The proposed scheme is essentially equivalent to an identity-based cryptosystem that tolerates upto a threshold of corruptions/collusions. However, as compared to well-known ID-based cryptographic mechanisms, such as IBE [17] and other related schemes, our approach is more efficient and is also based on standard cryptographic assumptions.

Paper Organization. Section 2 describes some preliminaries followed by Section 3, which presents our new scheme. Finally, in Section 4, we compare our proposal to prior identity-based cryptosystems. In the rest of the paper, we use the terms group/network/system and member/node/player/user interchangeably.

2   Preliminaries

2.1   Computation, Communication and Adversarial Model

We work in the standard model of threshold cryptography and distributed algorithms known as synchronous, reliable broadcast, static adversary model. This model involves nodes equipped with synchronized clocks. We assume some nomenclature system that provides each node in the network with a unique identifier, and also that it's computationally hard for an adversary to forge identities.

We assume the existence of an on-line trusted public repository where the network-wide or group public key is published. The nodes (both within and outside the network) are connected by weakly synchronous communication network offering point-to-point channels and a reliable broadcast. To interact with a node in the network, an outsider must first be able to retrieve the group public key from the repository.

We consider the presence of the so-called "static" adversary, modeled by a probabilistic polynomial time algorithm, who can *statically*, i.e., at the beginning of the life time of the scheme, schedule up to $t < n/2$ arbitrarily malicious faults among n users in the group. Such an adversary is said to break our scheme if it is able to break the underlying key establishment, signature and encryption schemes against the standard notions of security.

2.2   Discrete Logarithm Setting and Underlying Assumptions

In this paper, we work in the standard discrete logarithm setting: p, q are large primes s.t. q divides $p - 1$ and g denotes a generator of subgroup G_q of order q in $\mathbb{Z}_p^*$. For definitional convenience we'll denote by $DL\text{-}INST(k)$ any set of instances of this discrete-log setting, i.e. of triples (p, q, g) which satisfy the above constraints, but where q is a k-bit prime and p is $poly(k)$-bit prime, long enough to fend off known attacks on the discrete logarithm.

We call function f *negligible* if for every polynomial $P(.)$, $f(k) \leq 1/P(k)$ for all sufficiently large k. We say that some event occurs with a negligible probability if the probability of this event is a negligible function of the security parameter k.

Assumption 1 (Discrete Logarithm (DL) Assumption). For every probabilistic polynomial time algorithm I, for every (p, q, g) in $DL\text{-}INST(k)$, probability $Pr[x \leftarrow \mathbb{Z}_q; I(p, q, g, g^x) = x]$ is negligible.

Assumption 2 (Computational Diffie-Hellman (CDH) Assumption). For every probabilistic polynomial time algorithm I, for every (p, q, g) in $DL\text{-}INST(k)$, probability $Pr[x \leftarrow \mathbb{Z}_q; y \leftarrow \mathbb{Z}_q; I(p, q, g, g^x, g^y) = g^{xy}]$ is negligible.

Assumption 3 (Square Computational Diffie-Hellman (SCDH) Assumption). For every probabilistic polynomial time algorithm I, for every (p, q, g) in $DL\text{-}INST(k)$, probability $Pr[x \leftarrow \mathbb{Z}_q; I(p, q, g, g^x) = g^{x^2}]$ is negligible.

2.3 Random Oracle Model (ROM)

Our proofs of security are in the so-called Random Oracle Model [19], i.e. we model hash functions like MD5 or SHA1 as ideal random oracles. Doing security analysis in the ROM model effectively means that our proofs will consider only such attacks on the cryptographic schemes we propose whose success does not change if the fixed hash function like MD5 or SHA in these schemes are replaced with truly random functions. Of course, since functions like MD5 or SHA are not truly random functions, the security analysis in the ROM model provides only a heuristic argument for the security of the actual scheme. However, such heuristic seems the best we can currently hope for. Indeed, the ROM heuristic arguments are currently the only security arguments for most practical cryptographic schemes including OAEP RSA encryption [19] and full-domain hash RSA signatures [20], as well as the two fundamental discrete-log-based cryptosystems, the hashed ElGamal encryption [21] and Schnorr signature scheme [22, 23], the two schemes which we extend to a threshold setting in this paper.

2.4 Feldman's Verifiable Secret Sharing (VSS)

The idea of secret sharing [16] is to divide a secret x into pieces or *shares* which are distributed among n players such that pooled shares of a threshold $t + 1$ number players allow reconstruction of the secret x. We use Shamir's secret sharing scheme [10] which is based on polynomial interpolation. To distribute shares among n users, a trusted dealer chooses a large prime q, and selects a polynomial $f(z)$ over $\mathbb{Z}_q$ of degree t such that $f(0) = x$. The dealer computes each user's share x_i such that $x_i = f(id_i) \mod q$, and securely transfers x_i to user M_i. Then, any group G of $t + 1$ players who have their shares can recover the secret using the Lagrange interpolation formula:

$$x = \sum_{i \in G} x_i \, l_i^G(0) \pmod{q}$$

where $l_i^G(0) = \prod_{j \in G, j \neq i} \frac{-j}{i-j} \pmod{q}$.

Feldman's *Verifiable Secret Sharing* (VSS) [11] allows players to validate the correctness of the received shares. VSS setup involves two large primes p and q, and an element $g \in \mathbb{Z}_p^*$ chosen in a way that q divides $p-1$ and g is an element of $\mathbb{Z}_p^*$ which has order q. The dealer computes commitment to the coefficients a_i $(i = 0, \cdots, t)$ of the secret sharing polynomial in the form of witnesses w_i $(i = 0, \cdots, t)$, such that $w_i = g^{a_i} \pmod{p}$, and publishes these w_i-s in some public domain (e.g., a directory server). The secret share x_i can be validated by checking that

$$g^{x_i} \stackrel{?}{=} \prod_{j=0}^{t}(w_j)^{id_i{}^j} \pmod{p}$$

2.5 Schnorr's Signature

The private key is x, chosen at random in $\mathbb{Z}_q$. The public key is $y = g^x \pmod{p}$. A Schnorr's signature [22] on message m is computed as follows. The signer picks a one-time secret k at random in $\mathbb{Z}q$, and computes the signature on m as a pair (c, s) where $s = k + cx \pmod{q}, c = H(m, r)$, and $r = g^k \pmod{p}$. Signature (c, s) can be publicly verified by computing $r = g^s y^{-c} \pmod{p}$ and then checking if $c = H(m, r)$. The Schnorr's signature scheme is proven secure against chosen message attack [24, 25] in ROM [23].

2.6 ElGamal Encryption

We use a variant of ElGamal Encryption scheme, called *Hashed* ElGamal [21], which is semantically secure under the CDH assumption in ROM. For a private key, public key pair $(x, y = g^x)$, the encryptor chooses a random $r \in \mathbb{Z}_q$ and computes the ciphertext (c_1, c_2) where $c_1 = g^r \pmod{p}$ a $c_2 = m \oplus H(y_i{}^r)$ ($\oplus$ denotes the bit-wise XOR operator). The plaintext can be obtained by computing $c_2 \oplus H(c_1^{x_i})$ from the ciphertext (c_1, c_2).

3 Our Proposal: "Secret-Shares-as-Private-Keys"

In this section we present our proposal on using secret VSS shares as private keys that renders public key operations efficiently feasible in ad hoc networks. We begin by providing a brief overview of the scheme.

3.1 Overview

The idea of the scheme is very simple. Basically, we use Feldman's VSS (summarized in Section 2.4), to build our scheme. A dealer (or a set of founding nodes in an ad hoc network) chooses a secret sharing polynomial $f(z) = a_0 + a_1 z + \cdots a_t z^t$

in $\mathbb{Z}_q$, where a_0 (also denoted as x) is the group secret key. The dealer also publishes commitments to the coefficients of the polynomial, as $w_i = g^{a_i} \pmod{p}$, for $i = 0, \cdots, t$. These witnesses constitute the public key of the group. To join the group, a user M_i with a unique identifier (such as an email address) id_i, receives from the dealer (or a set of $t + 1$ or more nodes distributedly [12]) a secret share $x_i = f(id_i) \pmod{q}$ over a secure channel. The public key $y_i = g^{x_i} \pmod{p}$ of M_i can be computed using the public key of the group and its identifier id_i as

$$y_i = \prod_{j=0}^{t} (w_j)^{id_i{}^j} \pmod{p}$$

Now, any user (within or outside) the group, can send encrypted messages to M_i using its public key y_i, which M_i can decrypt using its secret key x_i. Similarly, M_i can use x_i to sign messages, which can be publicly verified using y_i. Moreover, any two users M_i and M_j can establish pairwise keys in a non-interactive manner: M_i and M_j compute $k_{ij} = (y_j)^{x_i} \pmod{p}$, and $k_{ji} = y_i{}^{x_j} \pmod{p}$, respectively. Since $K_{ij} = k_{ij} = k_{ji}$, a hash of K_{ij} can be used as session keys for secure communication between M_i and M_j.

We call these secret sharing based pairwise key establishment, signature and encryption procedures as *SS-KE*, *SS-Sig* and *SS-Enc*, respectively. *SS-Sig* is realized using the Schnorr's signature scheme, and *SS-Enc* using ElGamal encryption.

3.2   Setup and Joining

In order to setup the system, a dealer (or a set of co-founding members) first chooses appropriate parameters (p, q, g) for the group, and selects a polynomial $f(z) = a_0 + a_1 z + \cdots + a_t z^t$ in $\mathbb{Z}_q$, where a_0 (also denoted as x) is the group secret. The dealer keeps the polynomial secret and publishes commitments to the coefficients of the polynomial, as $w_i = g^{a_i} \pmod{p}$, for $i = 0, \cdots, t$. These witnesses constitute the public key of the group.

To join the group, a user M_i sends its unique identifier id_i to the dealer, who issues it its secret share $x_i = f(id_i) \pmod{q}$. (We assume there exists some kind of a unique nomenclature system for the users in the group, and that its computationally hard for anyone to forge the identities.) In an ad hoc network, the setup and joining are performed in a distributed manner. Refer to [12] for these decentralized setup and admission processes.

3.3   SS-KE: Secret Sharing Based Pairwise Key Establishment

Any pair of users M_i and M_j in the group can establish shared keys with each other using their secret keys and the group public key. M_i computes the public key y_j of M_j (knowing its identifier id_j only) as

$$y_j = \prod_{i=0}^{t} (w_i)^{id_j{}^i} \pmod{p}$$

M_i then exponentiates y_j to its own secret key x_i, to get $k_{ij} = y_j{}^{x_i} = g^{x_j x_i}$ (mod p). Similarly, M_j computes public key y_i of M_i as

$$y_i = \prod_{j=0}^{t} (w_j)^{id_i{}^j} \quad (\text{mod } p),$$

and exponentiates it to its own secret key x_j, to get $k_{ji} = y_i{}^{x_j} = g^{x_i x_j}$ (mod p). Since, k_{ij} equals k_{ji}, M_i and M_j can use $K_{ij} = H(k_{ij}) = H(k_{ji})$, as a session key for secure communication with each other.

Computational Complexity. Each party needs to compute the other party's public key via interpolation, and one exponentiation only. Using the well-known scheme of multi-exponentiation (or Shamir's trick) [26], the cost of interpolation is $O(log(n^t))$ squarings and $O(log(n^t))$ multiplications, where n denotes the total number of parties. For reasonable threshold values and network sizes, the interpolation is fairly efficient.

Next, we present the security argument for the above *SS-KE* procedure. Basically we show that an adversary, who corrupts t users, can not distinguish a key K_{IJ} for some uncorrupted user pair (M_I, M_J) from random *even* if he learns all other session keys K_{ij} for $(i, j) \neq (I, J)$.

Theorem 1 (Security of SS-KE). *Under the CDH Assumption in ROM, there exists no probabilistic polynomial time adversary A, which on inputs of secret keys of t corrupted users, and shared keys K_{ij} between every user pair except K_{IJ} $\{(i, j) \neq (I, J)\}$, is able to distinguish with a non-negligible probability K_{IJ} from a random value.*

Proof. We prove the above claim by contradiction, i.e, we prove that if a polynomial time adversarial algorithm A, which on inputs of secret keys of t corrupted users, and shared keys K_{ij} between every user pair except K_{IJ} $\{(i, j) \neq (I, J)\}$, is able to distinguish with a non-negligible probability K_{IJ} from a random value, then there exists a polynomial time algorithm B, which is able to break the CDH assumption in the random oracle model.

In order to construct the algorithm B which breaks the CDH assumption, we first construct a polynomial time algorithm C, which breaks the SCDH assumption. The algorithm C runs on input of an SCDH instance $y = g^x$ (mod p), and would translate the adversarial algorithm A into outputting g^{x^2} (mod p).

Without loss of generality, we first assume that the adversary A corrupts t players denoted by $M_1, M_2, \cdots, M_t$. Now, the algorithm C runs as follows:

As in the simulation of Feldman's VSS, C picks $x_1, x_2, \cdots, x_t$ values corresponding to the secret keys of corrupted users, uniformly at random from $\mathbb{Z}_q$. It then sets $x_i = F(id_i)$, and employs appropriate Lagrange interpolation coefficients in the exponent to compute the public witnesses $g^{A_1}, \cdots, g^{A_t}$ (mod p), where $F(z) = x + A_1 z + \cdots + A_t z^t$ (mod q).

Corresponding to the shared keys K_{ij} between every user pair, C picks a random value R_{ij}, and runs the algorithm A on $x_1, \cdots, x_t$ and $R_{i,j}$ values. Note that the values $x_1, \cdots, x_t$ and the witnesses have an identical distribution to an actual run of the Feldman's secret sharing protocol, and therefore A can not see the difference between C's inputs and actual protocol run. Also, since the K_{ij} values for $(i, j) \neq (I, J)$ are obtained by hashing $g^{x_i x_j}$, the only way A can tell the difference, except with negligible probability, between $K_{i,j}$ and $R_{i,j}$ for $(i, j) \neq (I, J)$, is by querying the random oracle on at least one appropriate $g^{x_i x_j}$ value. If A does tell the difference, then C records $R = g^{x_i x_j}$, and use the following equations to compute g^{x^2},

$$x = \sum_{k=1}^{t} x_k l_k^i + x_i l_i^i \pmod{q}$$

$$x = \sum_{k=1}^{t} x_k l_k^j + x_j l_j^j \pmod{q}$$

(l_k^i denotes the lagrange coefficient $l_k^G(0)$, where $G = \{1, \cdots, t, i\}$). Multiplying above two equations, we get

$$x^2 = (\sum_{k=1}^{t} x_k l_k^i)(\sum_{k=1}^{t} x_k l_k^j) + x_i x_j l_i^i l_j^j \pmod{q}$$

This implies,

$$g^{x^2} = g^{(\sum_{k=1}^{t} x_k l_k^i)(\sum_{k=1}^{t} x_k l_k^j)} R^{l_i^i l_j^j} \pmod{p}$$

If A doesn't tell the difference between $K_{i,j}$ and $R_{i,j}$ for $(i, j) \neq (I, J)$, then it must tell the difference between $K_{I,J}$ and $R_{I,J}$. However, as above, this is only possible, except with negligible probability, if A queries $g^{x_I x_J}$ to the random oracle. Them C records this value (say K) and computes g^{x^2} similarly as above, using the following equation

$$g^{x^2} = g^{(\sum_{k=1}^{t} x_k l_k^I)(\sum_{k=1}^{t} x_k l_k^J)} K^{l_I^I l_J^J} \pmod{p}$$

Now, we will use C to construct B to break a CDH instance (g^u, g^v). This is very simple as outlined in [27]: B runs C on input g^u, then on g^v, and finally on $g^{u+v} = g^u g^v$, and receives $g^{u^2}, g^{v^2}, g^{(u+v)^2}$, respectively. Now, since $(u + v)^2 = u^2 + v^2 + 2uv \pmod{q}$, B can easily compute g^{uv} from the outputs of C.

Clearly, $Pr(B) = Pr(C)^3$, where $Pr(B), Pr(C)$, denote the probabilities of success of B and C respectively.

3.4   SS-Sig: Secret Sharing Based Signatures

As mentioned previously, we realize *SS-Sig* using the Schnorr's signature scheme.

Signing. To sign a message m, M_i (having secret key x_i), picks a random secret $k \in Z_q$ and computes $r = g^k \pmod{p}$. It then outputs the signature as a pair (c, s), where $c = H(m, r)$ and $s = k + r x_i \pmod{q}$.

Verification. In order to verify the above signature (c, s), a recipient first computes the public key y_i of the signer M_i using its identity id_i as $y_i = \prod_{j=0}^{t}(w_j)^{id_i^j}$ (mod p), and then verifies whether $c = H(m, r)$, where $r = g^s y_i^{-c}$ (mod p).

Computational Complexity. The signer needs to compute only one exponentiation, while the verifier requires one interpolation operation, two exponentiations and and two multiplications.

In the following theorem, we argue the security of *SS-Sig*. More precisely, we argue that *SS-Sig* remains secure against existential forgery under chosen message attack (CMA) [24] in ROM as long as the discrete logarithm assumption holds. Notice that *SS-Sig* is different from regular signatures in the sense that the users generate signatures with related (and not independent) secret keys, and the adversary knows at most t of these secret keys.

For clarity of our argument, we first recall the argument for security of the underlying Schnorr's signature scheme against CMA attack in ROM and discrete logarithm assumption; the simulator algorithm, on input $y = g^x$, can produce Schnorr's signatures on any m by picking s and c at random in $\mathbb{Z}_q$, computing $r = g^s y^{-c}$ (mod p) and setting $H(m, r) = c$. This simulator can also translate the adversary's forgery into computing $dlog_g y$ as follows. It runs the adversary until the adversary outputs a forgery (c, s) on some message m. Note that because H is a random function, except for negligible probability, the adversary must ask to H a query (m, r) where $r = g^s y^{-c}$ (mod p), because otherwise it could not have guessed the value of $c = H(m, r)$. The simulator then rewinds the adversary, runs it again by giving the same answers to queries to H until the query (m, r), which it now answers with new randomness c'. If the adversary forges a signature on m in this run, then, except for negligible probability, it produces s' s.t. $r = g^{s'} y^{-c'}$ (mod p), and hence the simulator can now compute $dlog_g y = (s - s')/(c' - c)$ (mod q). One can show that if the adversary's probability of forgery is ϵ, this simulation succeeds with probability $\epsilon^2/4q$: $O(\epsilon)$ probability that the adversary forges in the first run times the $O(\epsilon/qH)$ probability that it will forge on the second run and that it will choose to forge on the same (m, r) query out of its q queries to H. We refer to [23] for the full proof.

Theorem 2 (Security of *SS-Sig*). *Under the DL assumption in ROM, as long as the adversary corrupts no more than t users, SS-Sig is secure against the chosen-message attack for every remaining uncorrupted user*

Proof. We prove the following claim: if there exists a polynomial time algorithm A, which on inputs the secret keys of t corrupted users, is able to create an existential forgery in CMA model corresponding to an uncorrupted user, then there exists a polynomial time algorithm B, which can break the DL assumption in ROM.

We construct an algorithm B, which runs on input of a DL instance $y = g^x$ (mod p), and would translate the adversarial algorithm A into outputting x. We first assume that the adversary A corrupts t players denoted by $M_1, M_2, \cdots, M_t$, w.l.o.g.

Note that in our multiple user scenario, the adversary A can request the signature oracle to sign chosen messages corresponding to any honest player. In other words, when A sends (m, id_i) to the signature oracle, the oracle responds with a signature on message m signed with x_i.

B picks $x_1, x_2, \cdots, x_t$ values corresponding to the secret keys of corrupted users, uniformly at random from $\mathbb{Z}_q$. It then sets $x_i = F(id_i)$, and employs appropriate Lagrange interpolation coefficients in the exponent to compute the public witnesses $g^{A_1}, \cdots, g^{A_t} \pmod{p}$, where $F(z) = x + A_1 z + \cdots + A_t z^t \pmod{q}$. Since, $x = \sum_{k=1}^{t} x_k l_k^i + x_i l_i^i \pmod{q}$, B can compute the public key y_i, corresponding to an honest player M_i $(i \geq t+1)$ as

$$y_i = (y/g^{\sum_{k=1}^{t} x_k l_k^i})^{1/l_i^i} \pmod{p} \tag{1}$$

B now runs A on inputs $x_1, x_2, \cdots, x_t$ and simulates the signature oracle on A's query (m, id_i), by picking s and c at random in $\mathbb{Z}_q$, computing $r = g^s y_i^{-c} \pmod{p}$ and setting $H(m, r) = c$. A then outputs a forgery (C, S) on some message M corresponding to user M_i. Note that because H is a random function, except for negligible probability, A must have asked to H a query (M, R) where $R = g^S y_i^{-C} \pmod{p}$, because otherwise it could not have guessed the value of $C = H(M, R)$. B then reruns A by giving the same answers to queries to H until the query (M, R), which it now answers with new randomness C'. If A outputs the forgery on the same message M, but this time for a different user M_j $(i \neq j)$ then, except for negligible probability, it produces S' s.t. $R = g^{S'} y_j^{-C'} \pmod{p}$. B can now (using equation 1) compute

$$x = (S - S' + (C/l_i^i) \sum_{k=1}^{t} x_k l_k^i - (C'/l_j^j) \sum_{k=1}^{t} x_k l_k^j)/(C/l_i^i - C'/l_j^j) \pmod{q}$$

As in the security proof of Schnorr's Signatures, the probability of success of B would be $\epsilon^2/4q$, where ϵ represents the success probability of A and q is the total number of queries to $H()$.

3.5   SS-Enc: Secret Sharing Based Encryption

We use Hashed ElGamal encryption scheme in the SS-Enc procedure.

Encryption. In order to encrypt a message m for a user M_i in the group, the encryptor computes the public key of M_i as $y_i = \prod_{j=0}^{t} (w_j)^{id_i^j} \pmod{p}$, chooses a random $r \in \mathbb{Z}_q$ and then sends a pair (c_1, c_2) to M_i, where $c_1 = g^r \pmod{p}$ and $c_2 = m \oplus H(y_i^r)$ ($\oplus$ denotes the bit-wise XOR operator).

Decryption. M_i recovers the message by computing $c_2 \oplus H(c_1^{x_i})$ from the ciphertext (c_1, c_2).

Computational Complexity. In the above procedure, the encryptor performs one interpolation and two exponentiation. The decryptor, on the other hand, needs to compute only a single exponentiation.

Before presenting the security argument for *SS-Enc*, we briefly discuss the indistinguishability notion [28]. Indistinguishability is defined as the following game: the adversary is first run on input of the public key and outputs two messages to be challenged upon. Next, one of these messages is encrypted and given to the adversary. The adversary is said to win this game if he can output which message was encrypted with non-negligible probability greater than half.

The above notion of indistinguishability was designed for a single user scenario, where multiple messages are being encrypted for one user. However, to capture the security of *SS-Enc*, where there are multiple users in the group and the messages are encrypted using *related* keys, we adopt the *multi-user* indistinguishability notion of Baudron et al. [29] and Bellare et al. [30]. In this notion, the adversarial game is as follows: first the adversary is given as input n public keys $(pk_1, \cdots, pk_n)$ of all the users. The adversary then outputs two vectors of n messages $M_0 = \{m_{01}, \cdots, m_{0n}\}$ and $M_1 = \{m_{11}, \cdots, m_{1n}\}$, which might be related or same, to be challenged upon. One of the message vectors M_b (b is 0 or 1) is then encrypted with n public keys (the order of the encryption is preserved, i.e., m_{bi} is encrypted with pk_i). The adversary is said to win the game if he can, with probability non-negligibly greater than half, output which message was encrypted. It has been shown in [30, 29] that an encryption scheme secure in the sense of single-user indistinguishabilty is also secure in the sense of multi-user indistinguishability.

Following is the security argument for *SS-Enc* based on a slightly modified multi-user indistinguishability notion, as described above (Basically, the adversary is only challenged for the encryptions of $n - t$ honest users in the group).

Theorem 3 (Security of *SS-Enc*). *Under the CDH assumption in ROM, as long as the adversary corrupts no more than t users, SS-Enc is secure in the sense of multi-user indistinguishability notion.*

Proof. As usual, the proof goes by contradiction, i.e., we proof that if there exists a polynomial time algorithm A, which on inputs the secret keys of t corrupted users, is able to break the multi-user indistinguishability notion, then there exists a polynomial time algorithm B, which can break the CDH assumption in ROM.

We construct an algorithm B, which running on input of a CDH instance $U = g^u, V = g^v$, translates the algorithm A into outputting g^{uv}. As usual, we first assume that the adversary A corrupts t players denoted by $M_1, M_2, \cdots, M_t$, w.l.o.g.

As in the security proof of *SS-Sig*, B picks $x_1, x_2, \cdots, x_t$ values corresponding to the secret keys of corrupted users, uniformly at random from $\mathbb{Z}_q$. It then sets $x_i = F(id_i)$, and employs appropriate Lagrange interpolation coefficients in the exponent to compute the public witnesses $g^{A_1}, \cdots, g^{A_t} \pmod{p}$, where $F(z) = u + A_1 z + \cdots + A_t z^t \pmod{q}$. Since, $u = \sum_{k=1}^{t} x_k l_k^i + x_i l_i^i \pmod{q}$, B can compute the public key y_i, corresponding to an honest player M_i ($i \geq t+1$) using Equation 1.

To help the reader understand the construction of our translator algorithm B, we first recall the how the translator works in the security proof (under CDH and ROM) of single-user hashed ElGamal. The translator works as follows: on input of a CDH instance $(U = g^u, V = g^v)$, it first runs the adversary on input g^u. The adversary outputs two messages m_0, m_1. The translator picks one message m_b ($b = 0$ or 1) at random, and sends the encryption (c_1, c_2) to the adversary, where $c_1 = V * g^r \pmod{p}$ and $c_2 = R$ (r is a random value in $\mathbb{Z}_q$ and R is a random pad of same length as the message). In the random oracle model, the only way the adversary can distinguish this encryption is by querying the random oracle on value $O = c_1^u = U^{r+v}$, which will be recorded by the translator, and used to compute $g^{uv} = OU^{-r}$. If there are a total of q queries being made to the oracle, this means that the probability of success of translator would be $1/q$ times the probability of success of the adversary.

Now, we are ready to describe the translation based on our multi-user setting: B runs A on inputs the secret keys $x_1, \cdots, x_t$ corresponding to the corrupted users, and the public keys $y_{t+1}, \cdots, y_n$ of all honest ones. A outputs two vectors of $n - t$ messages $M_0 = \{m_{0i}\}$ and $M_1 = \{m_{1i}\}$, where $i = t + 1, \cdots, n$, to be challenged upon. B then picks M_b (b is 0 or 1) and sends to A the vector $\{(V * g^{r_i}, R_i)\}$, where r_i is a random value in $\mathbb{Z}_q$, and R_i is a random pad equally long as the message m_{bi}, for $i = t+1, \cdots, n$. The only possibility for A to win this game, is by querying the random oracle on at least one of the value $O = (V * g^{r_j})^{x_j}$, for some $j \in \{t+1, \cdots, n\}$. B records this value, and assuming that it corresponds to M_j, it computes g^{uv} as follows:

$$u = \sum_{k=1}^{t} x_k l_k^j + x_j l_j^j \pmod{q}$$

This implies that

$$g^{uv} = g^{v \sum_{k=1}^{t} x_k l_k^j} g^{v x_j l_j^j} \pmod{q}$$

and

$$g^{uv} = V^{\sum_{k=1}^{t} x_k l_k^j} V^{x_j l_j^j} \pmod{p}$$

Since, $O = (V * g^{r_j})^{x_j}$, this means $V^{x_j} = O y_j^{-r_j}$, and therefore,

$$g^{uv} = V^{\sum_{k=1}^{t} x_k l_k^j} O y_j^{-r_j l_j^j} \pmod{p}$$

Given that there are a total of q queries to the random oracle, the probability of success of B would be probability of success of A times $1/q(n - t)$, as only one query will yield correct g^{uv} value and each query might correspond to one j value in $\{t + 1, n\}$.

Remark: *Extension to Chosen Ciphertext Security.* The hybrid encryption techniques for extending standard hashed ElGamal to chosen ciphertext security (refer to [31], [32]) can be used to achieve chosen ciphertext security for the *SS-Enc* scheme.

4   Comparison with ID-Based Cryptography

As previously pointed out in the introduction section, our proposed scheme can be viewed as an identity-based cryptosystem based on threshold assumption. Basically, a trusted center provides each user with a secret value (VSS share in our case) derived from the unique identifier of the user, and publishes the VSS information as its public key. Knowing the identifier of a particular user and also the public key of the trusted center, one can send encrypted messages and verify signatures. This is equivalent to IBE [17], and ID-based signatures [33], apart from the fact that our scheme becomes insecure if there are more than a threshold of collusions or corruptions. However, unlike other ID-based schemes, our proposal is based on standard (discrete logarithm) assumptions. Moreover, for reasonable group sizes and threshold values, our scheme is much more efficient than these prior ID-based schemes, which require costly computations (such as scalar point multiplications, map-to-point operations and bilinear mappings [17]) in elliptic-curves. For example, for a group size of around 100, and threshold of 10 (10% of group size), the encryption in our scheme would require less than 70 squarings, less than 70 modular multiplications, and only 2 modular exponentiations. The decryption would just require 1 exponentiation. On the other hand, IBE requires 1 map-to-point operation, 2 scalar point multiplications, and 1 bilinear mapping, for encryption, and 1 bilinear mapping for decryption. It is well-known that for appropriate security parameters, the IBE computations are extremely costly (e.g., a bilinear mapping takes around 80ms, scalar point multiplication costs around 30 ms, while a single modular exponentiation is only a few milliseconds on fast processors). Refer to, e.g., [8] for details regarding these cost comparisons.

Acknowledgments

The author is thankful to Stanisław Jarecki for his help with the paper, and anonymous reviewers for their useful comments.

References

1. Zhou, L., Haas, Z.J.: Securing Ad Hoc Networks. IEEE Network Magazine **13** (1999) 24–30
2. Luo, H., Lu, S.: Ubiquitous and Robust Authentication Services for Ad Hoc Wireless Networks. Technical Report TR-200030, Dept. of Computer Science, UCLA (2000) Available online at http://citeseer.ist.psu.edu/luo00ubiquitous.html.
3. Kong, J., Zerfos, P., Luo, H., Lu, S., Zhang, L.: Providing Robust and Ubiquitous Security Support for MANET. In: IEEE 9th International Conference on Network Protocols (ICNP). (2001) 251–260
4. Kong, J., Luo, H., Xu, K., Gu, D.L., Gerla, M., Lu, S.: Adaptive Security for Multi-level Ad-hoc Networks. In: Journal of Wireless Communications and Mobile Computing (WCMC). Volume 2. (2002) 533–547

5. Luo, H., Zerfos, P., Kong, J., Lu, S., Zhang, L.: Self-securing Ad Hoc Wireless Networks. In: Seventh IEEE Symposium on Computers and Communications (ISCC '02). (2002)

6. Narasimha, M., Tsudik, G., Yi, J.H.: On the Utility of Distributed Cryptography in P2P and MANETs: The Case of Membership Control. In: IEEE International Conference on Network Protocol (ICNP). (2003) 336–345

7. Saxena, N., Tsudik, G., Yi, J.H.: Admission Control in Peer-to-Peer: Design and Performance Evaluation. In: ACM Workshop on Security of Ad Hoc and Sensor Networks (SASN). (2003) 104–114

8. Saxena, N., Tsudik, G., Yi, J.H.: Identity-based Access Control for Ad-Hoc Groups. In: International Conference on Information Security and Cryptology (ICISC). (2004)

9. Liu, D., Ning, P.: Establishing Pairwise Keys in Distributed Sensor Networks. In: ACM Conference on Computers and Communication Security. (2003) 52–61

10. Shamir, A.: How to Share a Secret. Communications of the ACM **22** (1979) 612–613

11. Feldman, P.: A Practical Scheme for Non-interactive Verifiable Secret Sharing. In: 28th Symposium on Foundations of Computer Science (FOCS). (1987) 427–437

12. Saxena, N., Tsudik, G., Yi, J.H.: Efficient node admission for short-lived mobile ad hoc networks. In: International Conference on Networking Protocols (ICNP). (2005)

13. Hu, Y.C., Perrig, A., Johnson, D.B.: Ariadne: A secure on-demand routing protocol for ad hoc networks. In: Proceedings of the Eighth ACM International Conference on Mobile Computing and Networking (Mobicom 2002). (2002)

14. Dahill, B., Levine, B., Royer, E., Shields, C.: A secure routing protocol for ad hoc networks. Technical Report UM-CS-2001-037, University of Massachusetts (2001)

15. Hills, R.: Sensing for danger. Science Technology Report (2001) Available at http://www.llnl.gov/str/JulAug01/Hills.html.

16. Menezes, A.J., van Oorschot, P.C., Vanstone, S.A.: Handbook of applied cryptography. CRC Press series on discrete mathematics and its applications. (1997) ISBN 0-8493-8523-7.

17. Boneh, D., Franklin, M.K.: Identity-based encryption from the weil pairing. In: CRYPTO. (2001) 213–229

18. Bazzi, R.A., Konjevod, G.: On the establishment of distinct identities in overlay networks. In: Principles of Distributed Computing (PODC). (2005)

19. Bellare, M., Rogaway, P.: Random Oracles are Practical: A Paradigm for Designing Efficient Protocols. In: ACM Conference on Computer and Communications Security. (1993) 62–73

20. Bellare, M., Rogaway, P.: The exact security of digital signatures — how to sign with RSA and Rabin. In: EUROCRYPT'96. Volume 1070 of LNCS. (1996) 399–416

21. ElGamal: A public-key cryptosystem and a signature scheme based on discrete logarithms. In: IEEE Transactions in Information Theory (IT-31). (1999) 469–472

22. Schnorr, C.P.: Efficient Signature Generation by Smart Cards. Journal of Cryptology **4** (1991) 161–174

23. Pointcheval, D., Stern, J.: Security proofs for signature schemes. In: EUROCRYPT'96. Volume 1070 of LNCS. (1996) 387–398

24. Goldwasser, S., Micali, S., Rivest, R.L.: A "paradoxical" solution to the signature problem. In: IEEE Annual Symposium of Foundations of Computer Science (FOCS'84). (1984) 441–448

25. Goldwasser, S., Micali, S., Rivest, R.L.: A digital signature scheme secure against adaptive chosen-message attacks. SIAM Journal on Computing **17** (1988) 281–308

26. Möller, B.: Algorithms for multi-exponentiation. In: Selected Areas in Cryptography. (2001) 165–180
27. Maurer, U.M., Wolf, S.: Diffie-Hellman oracles. In: CRYPTO'96. Volume 1109 of LNCS. (1996) 268–282
28. Goldwasser, S., Micali, S.: Probabilistic encryption. Journal of Computer and System Sciences, **28** (1989) 270–299
29. Baudron, O., Pointcheval, D., Stern, J.: Extended notions of security for multicast public key cryptosystems. In: International Colloquium on Automata, Languages and Programming (ICALP'00). Volume 1853 of LNCS. (2000) 499–511
30. Bellare, M., Boldyreva, A., Micali, S.: Public-key encryption in a multi-user setting: Security proofs and improvements. In: EUROCRYPT'00. Volume 1807 of LNCS. (2000) 259–274
31. Bellare, M., Boldyreva, A., Palacio, A.: An uninstantiable random-oracle-model scheme for a hybrid encryption problem. In: EUROCRYPT'04. Volume 3027 of LNCS. (2004) 171–188
32. Fujisaki, E., Okamoto, T.: Secure integration of asymmetric and symmetric encryption schemes. In: CRYPTO'99. Volume 1666 of LNCS. (1999) 537–554
33. Cha, J., Cheon, J.: An ID-based signature from Gap-Diffie-Hellman Groups. In: Proceedings of International Workshop on Practice and Theory in Public Key Cryptography. Volume 2567 of LNCS. (2003) 18–30

Location-Aware Key Management Using Multi-layer Grids for Wireless Sensor Networks

JongHyup Lee[1], Taekyoung Kwon[2], and Jooseok Song[1]

[1] Dept. of Computer Science,
Yonsei University, Seoul, 120-749, Korea
{jhlee, jssong}@emerald.yonsei.ac.kr
[2] Dept. of Computer Engineering,
Sejong University, Seoul, 143-747, Korea
tkwon@sejong.ac.kr*

Abstract. Since small low-powered sensor nodes are constrained in their computation, communication, and storage capabilities, it is not easy to achieve secure key establishment in a wireless sensor network where a number of such sensor nodes are spread over. There are many previous studies in the area of secure key establishment without public key cryptography for the wireless sensor networks. Among them, location-aware key management is a considerable approach for easy management and security enhancement. In this paper, we propose a new key establishment scheme by utilizing both the rough sensor location information and the multi-layer grids. As for the multi-layer grids, we devise an extended grid group which covers all nodes deployed in two adjacent basic grids and overlaps each other. With regard to communication and power consumption overhead, our approach shows better performance than the previously proposed schemes without losing its security.

1 Introduction

Sensor nodes are small low-powered devices which are constrained severely in their computation, communication, and storage capabilities. They may sense around themselves and communicate over wireless channels, but within very short ranges. A wireless sensor network is composed of a large number of sensor nodes for covering wider area through multi-hop connections, and has various kinds of applications including environmental monitoring, industrial monitoring, safety and security services, military system, health-care services, etc. The mission critical applications of wireless sensor networks make security and privacy functions required, while secure key establishment is the most fundamental part of them.

* This research was supported by the MIC (Ministry of Information and Communication), Korea, under the ITRC (Information Technology Research Center) support program supervised by the IITA (Institute of Information Technology Assessment).

J. Zhou, M. Yung, and F. Bao (Eds.): ACNS 2006, LNCS 3989, pp. 390–404, 2006.
© Springer-Verlag Berlin Heidelberg 2006

It is widely recognized that the secure key establishment is not easy for wireless sensor networks due to the limited capabilities of sensor nodes that restricts the use of public key cryptography. Another major obstacle to secure key establishment for wireless sensor networks is the high risk of physical attacks to sensor nodes which are deployed in unattended or even hostile environments. Thus, the key management schemes devised for the existing computer networks are not well-suited to the wireless sensor network, and the need for new schemes has arisen indefinitely. Note that symmetric key cryptography is preferred in the wireless sensor network unless there is a significant hardware improvement of the economically-viable sensor nodes in the near future.

Lately, a number of studies have been done in the area of secure key establishment without public key cryptography for the wireless sensor network [3, 4, 5, 6, 7]. Among them, we are interested in the location-aware key management schemes [6, 7]. Though exact positions of the sensor nodes cannot be controlled, it should be a reasonable attempt to partition a sensor deployment area into multiple square areas in a large dense wireless sensor network for easier management and security enhancement. There are three notable schemes in which the sensor location information is utilized for secure key establishment. They are based on the famous Blom scheme [1] and can be found from [3], [7], and [6]. However, two of them [3, 7] are vulnerable to selective node capture attacks allowing the key exposure of non-compromised nodes or introduce additional complexity owing to the uneven distribution of sensors within a given area. The other scheme [6] resists the so-called selective node capture attack and the node fabrication attack, but introduces new problems resulting from the heterogeneity of internal key establishment schemes. The heterogeneity may affect security as well as performance of the entire network. We will discuss this problem in more detail in the following section.

In this paper, we propose a new key establishment scheme utilizing the rough sensor location information but resolving the aforementioned problems. Following the Du-Deng scheme [3], we assume the whole deployment space is divided into multiple small areas, *grids*, where a group of sensor nodes are deployed. Our basic idea is to consider multi-layer grid groups where the grid implies a partitioned square area. As for the multi-layer grids, we devise an extended grid group which covers all nodes deployed in two adjacent basic grids and overlaps each other. In each grid, the key establishment scheme based on the Blom scheme is consistently operated. Our scheme improves the previous schemes in that the the amount of power consumption and communication overheads are reduced, the key connectivity in adjacent grids goes high significantly, and the node replication attack is defeated in the realm of an extended grid.

The rest of this paper is organized as follows. In Section 2, we introduce the heterogeneity problems arising from the grid-group deployment after reviewing the previous key management schemes briefly. In Section 3, we propose a new grid-group deployment scheme in which the aforementioned problems are resolved effectively. Key connectivity, area coverage, and security analysis are manipulated in Section 4, while the performance is evaluated in Section 5 with regard to communication overhead, power consumption, and storage overhead. This paper is concluded in Section 6.

2   Background: Location-Aware Key Management Scheme

2.1   Key Management in Wireless Sensor Networks

There have been many studies in the area of key establishment without public key cryptography for wireless sensor networks, specifically for pairwise keys. They can be classified into two basic categories, one is a deterministic scheme such as LEAP [8], while the other a probabilistic scheme that includes a number of random-key schemes [5, 2]. Among them, we only focus on probabilistic schemes in this paper.

Random key pre-distribution. In [5], Eschenauer and Gligor proposed a random key pre-distribution scheme for wireless sensor networks. There are three main phases in this scheme. First, from a large random key pool, a random subset of keys are selected for each node. Second, after the deployment of sensor nodes, if two adjacent nodes have any common key in the respective sub-key pools, they can use it as a shared key and further establish a new pairwise key using the shared key. Third, for the case that those neighbors do not share the same sub-key in their pools, a path key establishment step is proceeded. The procedure has been a standard in the probabilistic key establishment scheme for wireless sensor networks.

Blom scheme with multiple spaces. In [4], Du et al. combines the Blom scheme [1] with the random key pre-distribution. The Blom scheme is actually a key matrix based scheme and guarantees any pair of nodes to compute a secret shared key in the whole key matrix. The multiple space scheme allows the key computation when nodes share at least one key space. As a result, the multiple key space can improve the scalability and the physical capture resistance of the original scheme.

Key graph. Each node could maintain its key graph , $G = (V, E)$, where V is the vertices set and E is the edges set. The set V consists of the neighbor nodes. When two nodes of V share a required number of keys, an edge between those nodes are added.

2.2   Grid-Group Deployment Scheme

In [6], Huang et al. proposed a grid-group deployment scheme that is one of the location-aware key pre-distribution schemes. In this scheme, the sensor deployment area are partitioned into grids. Then two different pre-distribution schemes are used for a single grid and adjacent grids, respectively. In a single grid, they use *I-scheme* in which the multi space Blom scheme is utilized,

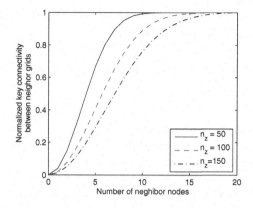

Fig. 1. Degradations of the normalized key connectivity

while *E-scheme* is used for adjacent grids. Note that those two schemes such as I-scheme and E-scheme are different. This disharmony causes the following heterogeneity problems. Readers are referred to [6] for the details of the grid-group deployment scheme.

2.3 Heterogeneity Problems

The grid-group deployment scheme [6] uses two different schemes for key pre-distribution, *I-scheme* based on the multi-space Blom scheme for nodes within the same grids and *E-scheme* based on the random key pre-distribution scheme for nodes between adjacent grids. Therefore, two phases are necessary for both key pre-distribution and key establishment. The key graph connectivity of *I-scheme* should depend on the number of selected key spaces while the total number of nodes in a grid, n_z, affects the key connectivity of *E-scheme*. Figure 1 depicts that, when n_z grows high (from 50 to 150), the key connectivity between adjacent grids (in Y-axis) decreases as the coverage area or communication range becomes smaller due to the number of neighboring nodes (in X-axis). The decrement appears more drastically than that of nodes within a single grid. This unbalanced key connectivity can make the *isolated grid* problem, saying that a node cannot connect with any of adjacent grids even it can communicate within the same grid, in the high n_z environments.

Additionally, since each node should maintain two types of keys for I and E schemes, and the key of each type is used independently to the other in [6], the reusability of keys are limited and two separate stages of key establishment for the same grid and adjacent grids are needed. This may cause needs for additional storage maintenance and extra control messages.

As for security, *I-scheme* and *E-scheme* do not provide the same degree. For example, if a node i located in an angular point of a grid is captured while its *E-scheme* pair j is located in the opposite side of the other diagonal grid, saying they may not detect each other, then the replicated node of i can be added to the diagonal grid of the grid of j by *E-scheme* in spite that *I-scheme* resists it.

This scenario shows the heterogeneity of key establishment affects security of the entire network as well as its performance.

3   Multi-layer Grid-Group Deployment Scheme

3.1   Basic Idea

We assume the deployment area of sensor nodes is divided into two-dimensional squares which called '*grids*'. Each grid has fixed size, $a \times a$ and the whole deployment area is covered by $N_G \times N_G$ squares. Figure 2 shows the grid structure for the sensor deployment. The groups of sensor nodes deployed in the grid located at i^{th} row and j^{th} column of the deployment area is named '*grid groups*' and denoted by $G(i, j)$. We assume sensor nodes are uniformly distributed over the deployment area. We set the total number of sensor node as N and each group has the same number of sensor nodes n_z.

In our scheme, we define an *extended grid group* for key predistribution and discovery. An extended group has twice size of a square, $a \times 2a$ or $2a \times a$. That is, one extended grid group covers two grid groups. Then, there are 4 overlaid layers of extended grid groups which overlap each other. This forms multilayer grids. Figure 3 and 4 depict the architecture of multilayer grid and the positioning of extended grid groups. Each extended grid group can be identified by a tuple, (*row, column, layer_number*) as shown in Fig 4. Then $EG(i_E, j_E, l)$ is an identifer for the extended grid group located in i_E^{th} row, j_E^{th} column and l^{th} layer.

The process for Multilayer Grid Group schemes is divided into 4 phases, *Key predistribution, Sensor deployment, Key discovery, Pairwise key establishment*. The detailed processes are described in following sections.

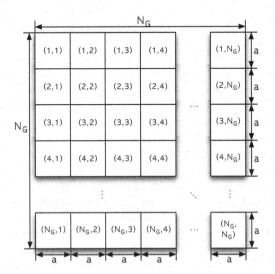

Fig. 2. Grid structure

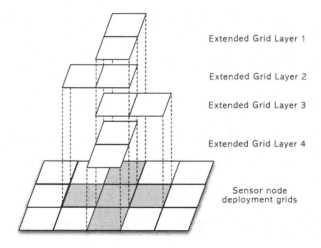

Fig. 3. Multi-layer grid

3.2 Key Predistribution

Before key-predistribution, some constraints are required to guarantee the security of multi-layer grid group scheme. Due to the λ-secure property of Blom scheme and multiple key spaces of [4], we have to limit the upper bound of the number of sensor nodes in a grid. In the λ-secure property, for a given key space, less than λ sensor nodes are allowed. In other words, n_z should be smaller than $\lambda\omega/\tau$. However, an extended grid group covers twice area of grids and twice number of sensor nodes, $2n_z$, when the uniform distribution is assumed for the sensor deployment. Therefore, to satisfy the condition of $2n_z \leq \lambda\omega/\tau_E$ for the extended grid group, we select the τ_E as $\tau_E \leq \frac{\lambda\omega}{2n_z}$ which is a half of τ.

1. Partition N sensor nodes for $N_G \times N_G$ grid groups by the deploy location. Then, according to the configuration of the overlapped extended grid group in Fig 3 and 4, assign sensor nodes to extended grid groups of each layer, $EG(i_E, j_E, l)$. Due to the overlapped nature of extended grid groups, sensor nodes within the same grid share 4 extended grid groups but nodes between adjacent grids share only one extended grid group.

2. The whole key pool P is divided into a number of sub-key pools to assign each sub-key pool to an extended grid group. Additionally, each key pool has ω sub-key spaces, $P(i_E, j_E, l)$ where $i_E = 1, ..., N_{Ei,l}$, $j_E = 1, ..., N_{Ej,l}$ and $l = 1, ..., 4$. From [4], a sub-key space has $N \times (\lambda + 1)$ key matrix A where $A = (D \cdot G)^T$.

3. For each extended grid group, unique IDs within $EG(i_E, j_E, l)$ are given to the nodes. Then, randomly select τ_E sub-key spaces from ω sub-key spaces $P(i_E, j_E, l)$ and allocate keys to each sensor node in $EG(i_E, j_E, l)$.

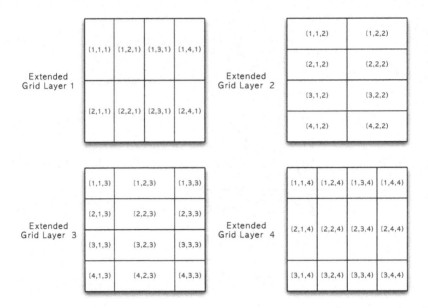

Fig. 4. The configuration of extended grid groups

4. After the key assignment, the sensor node stores pairs of its extended grid group ID and the selected key spaces for the extended group, which will be used in the Key discovery phase.

3.3   Sensor Node Deployment

In the deployment phase, sensor nodes are deployed according to the position of its grid group. Because we assume the uniform distribution of sensor nodes' location, the density of deployed nodes is easily calculated from n_z/a^2. Additionally, a unique identifier, ID_u, is assigned to each sensor node in advance of the deployment.

3.4   Key Discovery and Pairwise Key Establishment

After the deployment of sensor nodes, sensor nodes try to discover neighbor sensor nodes who belong to the same extended grid group and share the same key spaces.

1. (*Key discovery phase*) Each sensor node broadcasts a key list which includes its identifier and series of pairs of an extended grid group ID and key spaces identifiers for the extended grid group. For example, a sensor node u broadcasts $[ID_u, (ID_{EG}^{(1)}, \tau_1^{(1)}, \cdots), (ID_{EG}^{(2)}, \tau_1^{(2)}, \cdots), (ID_{EG}^{(3)}, \tau_1^{(3)}, \cdots), (ID_{EG}^{(4)}, \tau_1^{(4)}, \cdots)]$ where ID_u is the identifier of the node u, $ID_{EG}^{(l)}$ and $\tau^{(l)}$ indicate the identifier of node u's extended grid group of layer l and the selected key space identifiers for the extend grid group, respectively.

2. The node u compares its pair of the extended grid group ID and key spaces with the received key list from neighbor nodes. If there are one or more matching pairs between two nodes, node u creates a key graph which has all neighbor nodes of u as vertices and adds edges to each neighbor-node vertex of the matching pairs.

3. (*Pairwise key establishment phase*) For the key graph connected neighbor nodes, node u sends connection requests. Because the nodes share the same $ID_{EG}^{(l)}$ and $\tau^{(l)}$ pair, they can generate a pairwise key using the key agreement method of [4] in a secure way.

4. If there are unconnected neighbor nodes in the key graph, the node u broadcast the ID list of the unconnected nodes. Then the node u sends a connection request by relaying of the node who shares keys with the unconnected nodes and carries out a pairwise key agreement process. Subsequently, the node u adds edges to the newly key established node in its key graph. This process is repeated until all the neighbor nodes are connected or no connectable node is found anymore.

In the key discovery and pairwise key establishment phases, the process is the same for nodes within the same grid and nodes in the adjacent grid. However, the nodes within the same grid have higher possibilities to connect each other directly since they have all the extended grid group in common while the nodes between adjacent grids share only one extended grid group.

4   Analysis

4.1   Key Graph Connectivity Analysis

Since we use the key predistribution based on [4], we start the probability, p_1, that given two sensor nodes share at least one key space in common. With given ω and τ, the p_1 is

$$p_1 = 1 - \frac{\binom{\omega}{\tau}\binom{\omega - \tau}{\tau}}{\binom{\omega}{\tau}^2}$$

However, in the key discovery phase of the proposed scheme, more than one extended grid groups are overlapped. We use the τ_E for the extended grid group instead of τ. Thus the probability, p_c, that given two sensor nodes are connected without helping of neighbor nodes is

$$p_{c,l} = 1 - \left(\frac{\binom{\omega}{\tau_E}\binom{\omega - \tau_E}{\tau_E}}{\binom{\omega}{\tau_E}^2} \right)^l$$

where l is the number of the sharing extended grid group for given two sensor nodes.

$$l = \begin{cases} 4 & \text{within the same grid} \\ 1 & \text{between adjacent grids} \\ 0 & \text{otherwise} \end{cases}$$

Key Graph Connectivity within the Same Grid. In order to connect a neighbor node within the same grid, a sensor node can connect directly (1 hop) or with relaying of neighbor nodes (more than 1 hop). Let $N_u(i, j, R)$ be the number of neighbor nodes within the same grid of a node u with its communication range R and $N_u(i\pm, j\pm, R)$ be the number of neighbor nodes between horizontally and vertically adjacent grids. When a node u connects to a node v, the probability of the former case is $P_{u,v}[1 \text{ hop}] = p_{c,4}$ and that of the later case is

$$P_{u,v}[2 \text{ hop}] = 1 - (1 - p_{c,4})^{p_{c,4} \cdot N_u(i,j,R)} \cdot (1 - p_{c,1})^{p_{c,1} \cdot N_u(i\pm,j\pm,R)}$$

where $(1 - p_{c,4})^{p_{c,4} \cdot N_u(i,j,R)}$ is the probability of that all the neighbor nodes within the same grid are not connected to the node v and $p_{c,4} \cdot N_u(i, j, R)$ is the average number of connected neighbor nodes. Likewise, $(1 - p_{c,1})^{p_{c,4} \cdot N_u(i\pm,j\pm,R)}$ means the unconnecting probability of all the neighbor nodes in the horizontally and vertically adjacent grids to the node v. Therefore, when we consider the connectivity within 2 hops, the probability of key graph connectivity between nodes within the same grid is

$$\begin{aligned} P_{u,v} &= P_{u,v}[1 \text{ hop}] + (1 - P_{u,v}[1 \text{ hop}])P_{u,v}[2 \text{ hop}] \\ &= p_{c,4} + (1 - p_{c,4})\{1 - (1 - p_{c,4})^{p_{c,4} \cdot N_u(i,j,R)} \cdot (1 - p_{c,1})^{p_{c,1} \cdot N_u(i\pm,j\pm,R)}\} \end{aligned}$$
(1)

Key Graph Connectivity between Horizontally and Vertically Adjacent Grids. In a similar way to the connectivity within grids, $P_{u,v\pm}$ is the probability that given two nodes between adjacent grids connect each other with the help of all neighbor nodes.

$$\begin{aligned} P_{u,v\pm} &= P_{u,v\pm}[1 \text{ hop}] + (1 - P_{u,v\pm}[1 \text{ hop}])P_{u,v\pm}[2 \text{ hop}] \\ &= p_{c,1} + (1 - p_{c,1})\{1 - (1 - p_{c,1})^{p_{c,4} \cdot N_u(i,j,R)} \cdot (1 - p_{c,4})^{p_{c,1} \cdot N_u(i\pm,j\pm,R)}\} \end{aligned}$$
(2)

where $(1 - p_{c,1})^{p_{c,4} \cdot N_u(i,j,R)}$ and $(1 - p_{c,4})^{p_{c,1} \cdot N_u(i\pm,j\pm,R)}$ are probabilities for the help of nodes in the same grid and in the adjacent grid respectively. From Eq. 2, we can derive the probability that a sensor node u can connect to the horizontally and vertically adjacent grid with the help of all its neighbor nodes.

$$P_{u\pm} = 1 - \{(1 - p_{c,1})^{N_u(i\pm,j\pm,R)}\}^{p_{c,4} \cdot N_u(i,j,R)}$$
(3)

Key Graph Connectivity between Diagonally Adjacent Grids. Since extended grids do overlay each other only in horizontal and vertical directions, we consider neighbor nodes in diagonally neighboring grid separately. Let $N_u(i\pm, j\mp, R)$ be the number of neighbor nodes in diagonally adjacent grid of a node u. In order to connect to the diagonally adjacent grid, the help of neighbor

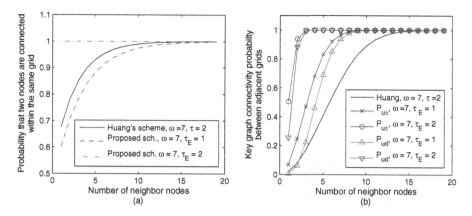

Fig. 5. The key graph connectivity within the same grid and between the adjacent grids

nodes in horizontally and vertically adjacent grids is required. In other words, the connection request must be relayed to the diagonally adjacent grid by the neighbor nodes. Therefore, the P_{ud} is probability that a sensor node u can connect to the diagonally adjacent grid.

$$P_{ud} = P_{u\pm} \cdot [1 - \{(1 - p_{c,1})^{N_u(i\pm,j\mp,R)}\}^{p_{c,4} \cdot N_u(i\pm,j\pm,R)}] \tag{4}$$

Using the system configuration of Huang scheme[6], Figure 5 depicts the probability of key graph connectivity for the change of the number of neighbors($n_z = 100$). Figure 5 (a) is for the probability within the same grid. In case of $\tau_E = 1$, the connectivity of two nodes is 7% lower than Huang scheme of $\tau = 2$ as the maximum, but the difference decreases under 2% when the number of neighbor nodes is more than 10. Figure 5 (b) shows the probability that a sensor node can connect to adjacent grids. The proposed scheme has 3.4 times higher key graph connectivity between adjacent grids as the maximum. In case of $\tau_E = 2$, the proposed scheme outperforms in both cases drastically.

4.2 Area Coverage vs. Key Graph Connectivity Analysis

The number of neighbor nodes is determined by the communication range, R, and the density of the deployed sensor nodes, ρ. For accurate calculation of the key connectivity, the coverage area should be considered separately by 3 cases: within the same grid, in horizontally and vertically adjacent grids and in diagonally adjacent grids. The value of ρ can be calculated by $\frac{n_z}{a^2}$ since the assumption of the uniform distribution.

We use the coverage analysis of [6]. For a given R, the number of neighbor nodes are like as followings:

$$
\begin{aligned}
N(i,j,R) &= \lfloor \rho \cdot C_b(i,j,R)|_{(x,y)} \rfloor \\
N(i\pm,j\pm,R) &= \lfloor \rho \cdot (C_b(i,j^-)|_{(x,y)} + C_b(i^+,j)|_{(x,y)}) \rfloor \\
N(i\pm,j\mp,R) &= \lfloor \rho \cdot C_b(i^+,j^-)|_{(x,y)} \rfloor
\end{aligned}
$$

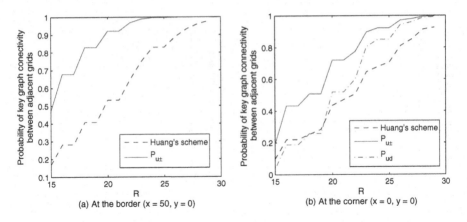

(a) At the border (x = 50, y = 0)   (b) At the corner (x = 0, y = 0)

Fig. 6. Area Coverage vs. Key graph connectivity($\omega = 7, \tau = 2, \tau_E = 1$)

where $C_b(i, j, R)|_{(x,y)}$ is the coverage within the same grids. $C_b(i, j^-)|_{(x,y)}$ and $C_b(i^+, j)|_{(x,y)}$ are the coverages for horizontally and vertically adjacent grids, respectively, and that of diagonal adjacent grids is $C_b(i^+, j^-)|_{(x,y)}$. Please refer the appendix of [6] about $C_b(\cdot)$.

Figure 6 shows the probability of key graph connectivity as the increase of R. In Figure 6 (a), the node locates at the border between grids. The connectivity to the neighboring grid increases as the coverage area becomes wider and our proposed scheme shows the higher connectivity at the same coverage area. In case of Figure 6 (b) that the node is at the corner of the grid, the diagonally adjacent grids are also concerned. The connectivity to the diagonally adjacent grid are a bit lower than Huang scheme under $R = 19$ but the connectivity to the horizontally and vertically adjacent grids are higher than Huang scheme at any case.

4.3   Security Analysis

Security of the proposed scheme is mainly dependent upon that of Blom's scheme [1] and that of Huang's grid scheme [6]. The λ-secure property of the key matrix is preserved in overlaid grids by allowing more efficient key computation than [3, 4], saying that pairwise keys are secure if no more than λ nodes are compromised in each extended grid while the restricted number of nodes within an extended grid reduces the number of modular multiplication operations for deriving a pairwise key, due to $n_z = \lambda\omega/\tau$. As for the Huang's grid scheme, however, we already mentioned that the heterogeneity of key establishment in *I-scheme* and *E-scheme* may affect security of the entire network in Section 2.3. Say, a node replication attack is possible by adding the replicated node to the network through *E-scheme*. Our scheme solves this problem and resists the node replication attack as well. We discuss the resistance against three attacks below.

Node capture attack. Since we restrict n_z under $\lambda\omega/\tau$ and the number of nodes in an extended grid group under $\lambda\omega/\tau_E$ at the key predistribution phase, the secret key matrix is not revealed without regard to the number of captured sensor nodes by the λ-secure property. The security of our scheme against the random node capture attack and selective node capture attack can be observed from the same perspectives of Huang's scheme. The resistance against the node capture attack is discussed well in [6].

Node fabrication attack. The attacker who captured a sensor node can modify and use the information from the captured node, such as the secret keys pre-installed in that node, for fabricating a new node with new identity. When random key pre-distribution scheme is used improperly without identification method, this kind of attack can cause severe problems with regard to security of the entire network. For example, if an adversary captures two nodes containing m keys respectively, (s)he can fabricate $\binom{2m}{m}$ new nodes over the network. However, since our scheme follows the multiple space Blom scheme by using the node's id as identification of the row of matrix A, the node fabrication attack could easily be defeated.

Node replication attack. As we mentioned already, the heterogeneity of key establishment in Huang's scheme may allow a node replication attack in which *E-scheme* is only exploited. If a node i located in an angular point of a grid is captured while its *E-scheme* pair j is located in the opposite side of the other diagonal grid, then the replicated node of i can be added to the diagonal grid of the grid of j by *E-scheme*. Note that *I-scheme* which follows the multiple space Blom scheme resists the replication attack by restricting it in a single grid only where a replicated node could be excluded more easily. In our scheme, the multiple space Blom scheme is only used in an extended grid along with path key establishment, and the node replication attack is defeated in that sense.

5   Performance Evaluations

5.1   Communication Overhead

When the two nodes are not directly connected, extra communications between neighbor nodes are required. This makes more communication overhead in a sensor node. Figure 7 depicts the probability of connectivity directly (1 hop) and with the help of neighbor nodes (2 hop), separately. The result shows the portion of direct connection grows larger as the number of neighbor nodes. In other words, the communication overhead to connect adjacent grids goes lower as the number of neighbor nodes increases.

Further, due to the unified key establishment scheme for both case of same grid and adjacent grids, there is no need to have separate stages of key establishment. Therefore, the total control messages for the key establishment of nodes at the border of grid can decrease by a half.

5.2   Power Consumption

Based on free-space propagation model, the power density p_t is given by $p_t = \frac{P_T}{4\pi d^2}$ where P_T and d are transmitted signal power and distance, respectively.

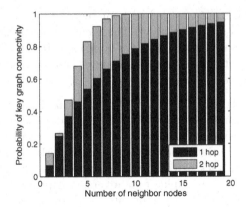

Fig. 7. Communication overhead for the probability of the key graph connectivity between adjacent grids

In other words, to widen the communication range twice, 2^2 times of transmission power is required. Using on the result of Section 4.2, Figure 8 depicts required transmission power to achieve the given probability of key graph connectivity between adjacent grids. Because the proposed scheme has higher key graph connectivity between adjacent grids than that of Huang scheme, the required transmission power of the proposed scheme is only 36% of Huang scheme for achieving the same connectivity. Therefore, our proposed scheme can reduce power consumption of a sensor node with guaranteeing the equal connectivity. With considering the lower communication overhead of the proposed scheme, the effect of power saving can be amplified.

5.3   Storage Overhead

The number of nodes in a grid should not exceed $\lambda w / \tau$ to preserve λ-secure property of [4]. Additionally the area of a extended grid group is twice of that of a grid and each node belongs to 4 extended grid group. Therefore, in our scheme, each node has to store $m = 4(\lambda + 1)\tau$ keys and it is restricted by $n_z = \lambda w / \tau$. In other words, $\lambda = 2n_z \tau_E / w$ where $\tau_E = \tau/2$.

The total number of keys that to be preinstalled in a sensor node is:

$$m = 4(\lceil \frac{2n_z \tau_E}{w} \rceil + 1)\tau_E \qquad (5)$$

From the required number of keys in a sensor node from Huang scheme, $m_h = (\lceil \frac{n_z \tau}{w} \rceil + 1)\tau + \gamma \alpha$, the value of m is slightly lower than the twice of m_h by the amount of $2\gamma \alpha$.

$$
\begin{aligned}
m &= 4(\lceil \frac{2n_z \tau_E}{w} \rceil + 1)\tau_E \\
&= 2(\lceil \frac{2n_z \tau}{2w} \rceil + 1)\tau \\
&= 2(\lceil \frac{n_z \tau}{w} \rceil + 1)\tau
\end{aligned}
$$

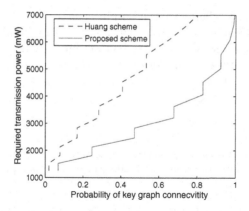

Fig. 8. Required transmission power for the probability of key graph connectivity between adjacent grids ($n_z = 100$, $a = 100$m, $\omega = 7$, $\tau_E = 1$, $\tau = 2$ and $p_t = 0.001$)

Table 1. Required key storage

n_z	ω	τ_E	Key size(bits)	Storage(bytes)
50	7	1	64	512
100	7	1	64	960
200	7	1	64	1888
50	7	1	128	1024
100	7	1	128	1920
200	7	1	128	3776
50	7	2	64	1920
100	7	2	64	3776
200	7	2	64	7424

Table 1 shows the key storage overhead on various configurations. Based on configurations of [4] and [6], in which they use $\omega = 7$, $\tau = 2$ ($\tau_E = 1$) and 64-bit (8 byte) key, the required key storage for the proposed scheme is under 1 kbytes. Even in the cases of 128-bit key and $\tau_E = 2$, the key storage does not exceed several kbytes. Hence, keys are small enough to be pre-installed to the memory of sensor nodes because MICAz sensor nodes usually have a 128-kbyte program memory and a 512-kbyte secondary memory.

6   Conclusion

We propose a new location-aware key management scheme using multi-layer grids. Our approach is simple and efficient on the basis of configuration of the overlaid grids. We extend the multi-space Blom scheme to both within the same grid and between adjacent grids. We pointed out the heterogeneity problems such as an isolated grid problem from the previous location-aware key management scheme [6]. Our scheme resolves those problems intrinsically because the same key establishment scheme is used within or between the grid groups. The improved key graph connectivity between adjacent grids resolves the isolated grid problem and guarantees the better connectivity of grids. With regard to communication and power consumption overhead, our approach shows better performance than the previously proposed schemes without losing its security.

References

1. R. Blom, "An optimal class of symmetric key generation system," in *Eurocrypt'84*, Lecture Notes in Computer Science, vol. 209, Springer-Verlag, pp. 335-338, 1985.
2. H. Chan, A. Perrig, and D. Song, "Random key predistribution schemes for sensor networks," in *Proc. of IEEE Syposium on Security and Privacy*, pp. 197-215, 2003.
3. W. Du, J. Deng, Y. S. Han, S. Chen and P. Varshney, "A Key Management Scheme for Wireless Sensor Networks Using Deployment Knowledge," in *Proc. of IEEE INFOCOM*, March 2004.
4. W. Du, J. Deng, Y. Han, P. Varshney, J. Katz and A. Khalili, "A Pairwise Key Predistribution Scheme for Wireless Sensor Networks," *ACM Trans. on Information and System Security*, vol. 8, no. 2, pp. 228-258, 2005.
5. L. Eschenauer and V. D. Gligor, "A Key-management Scheme for Distributed Sensor Networks," in *Proc. of the 9th ACM Conference on Computer and Communication Security (CCS'02)*, pp. 41-47, Nov. 2002.
6. D. Huang, M. Mehta, D. Medhi and L. Harn, "Location-aware Key Management Scheme for Wireless Sensor Networks," in *Proc. of the 1st ACM workshop on Security of ad-hoc and sensor networks (SASN'04)*, pp. 29-42, Oct. 2004.
7. D. Liu and P. Ning, "Location-based pairwise key establishments for static sensor networks," in *Proc. of the 1st ACM workshop on Security of ad-hoc and sensor networks (SASN'03)*, pp. 72-82, Nov. 2003.
8. S. Zhu, S. Setia, and S. Jajodia, "LEAP: Efficient security mechanisms for large-scale distributed sensor networks," in *Proc. of the 10th ACM Conference on Computer and Communication Security (CCS'03)*, Nov. 2003.

A General Methodology for Pipelining the Point Multiplication Operation in Curve Based Cryptography
(Extended Abstract)

Kishan Chand Gupta[1], Pradeep Kumar Mishra[2], and Pinakpani Pal[3]

[1] CACR, University of Waterloo, Waterloo, ON, N2L 3G1, Canada
[2] CISC, University of Calgary, Calgary, Alberta, T2N 1N4, Canada
[3] ECSU, Indian Statistical Institute, 203, B T Road, Kolkata - 700108, India
kgupta@math.uwaterloo.ca, pradeep@math.ucalgary.ca, pinak@isical.ac.in

Abstract. Pipelining is a well-known performance enhancing technique in computer science. Point multiplication is the computationally dominant operation in curve based cryptography. It is generally computed by repeatedly invoking some curve (group) operation like doubling, tripling, halving, addition of group elements. Such a computational procedure may be efficiently computed in a pipeline. More generally, let Π be a computational procedure, which computes its output by repeatedly invoking processes from a set of *similar* processes. Employing pipelining technique may speed up the running time of the computational procedure. To find pipeline sequence by trial and error method is a nontrivial task. In the current work, we present a general methodology, which given any such computational procedure Π can find a pipelined version with improved computational speed. To our knowledge, this is the first such attempt in curve based cryptography, where it can be used to speed up the point multiplication methods using inversion-free explicit formula for curves over prime fields. As an example, we employ the proposed general methodology to derive a pipelined version of the hyperelliptic curve binary algorithm for point multiplication and obtain a performance gain of 32% against the ideal theoretical value of 50%.

1 Introduction

Public Key Cryptography can now be broadly divided into two classes: first, the ones based on algebraic curves and secondly the others based on other algebraic structures. The curve based cryptography was jointly pioneered by Koblitz [13] and Miller [24] in 1985 with their path breaking independent works introducing elliptic curve cryptosystems (ECC). In 1987, Koblitz [14] again proposed hyperelliptic curve cryptography (HECC). Since then many other algebraic curves (like super-elliptic curves [8] and its particular case Picard curves [7]) have been considered for devising newer cryptosystems. In curve based cryptography the curve is used for constructing a group. The cryptosystem is built over the strength of the discrete logarithm problem (DLP) over this group.

J. Zhou, M. Yung, and F. Bao (Eds.): ACNS 2006, LNCS 3989, pp. 405–420, 2006.
© Springer-Verlag Berlin Heidelberg 2006

In case of elliptic curves, the group is the set of all the points on the elliptic curve. In case of hyperelliptic or Picard curves the group is the Jacobian of the curves. The reason for looking for newer curves has been two fold: firstly, to find curves for which the underlying group operations may be easier to implement and secondly, the DLP over the underlying group may be harder than the ones known so far. The hyperelliptic curves of lower genus (2 or 3) or Picard curves do not provide groups over which DLP is stronger than elliptic curve discrete logarithm problem, but they can be implemented over smaller base fields.

The most fundamental operation in implementation of any curve based cryptographic primitive is the point multiplication. In the current work by a point we mean an element of the group. Let P be any point in the group provided by the curve and let m be an integer. The operation of computing $m \times P$ is called the operation of point multiplication. The efficiency of an implementation depends upon the efficiency of performing this operation. So tremendous effort has been put in by the research community to compute this operation efficiently. Another important issue is the resistance against side-channel attacks. Side-channel attacks ([16,17]) find out the secret key of a user by sampling and analyzing the side-channel information like timing, power consumption and electromagnetic radiation traces etc.

If a system admits two multipliers, then the best method to compute the scalar multiplication in ECC is the pipelining scheme introduced in [25]. It performs better than all known parallel schemes. If cost of a squaring and a multiplication in the underlying field is taken to be the same (which is true if the squaring is computed using the multiplication hardware) then cost of a point doubling is 10 and that of a mixed addition is 11 multiplications. Using the pipelining technique one can compute these operations in the computation time of 6 multiplications only. To implement pipelining one needs one extra multiplier and some additional memory. In case of ECC this extra hardware demand is worth allowing for a faster and secure implementation. However, the scheme proposed in [25] is very restricted one. It applies to elliptic curves point multiplication algorithm using double and add approaches only in Jacobian coordinates. In the current work we look at the most general set up. We consider the any point multiplication algorithm over any algebraic curve and check if the pipelining technique can lead to a significant speed up.

The simplest methods to compute point multiplication are the binary algorithms. These methods compute it by a series of point doublings and additions. These operations are applied based on the binary representation of the integer m. The number of addition required is Hamming weight of the representation. To reduce the number of additions, sparser representations like NAF, w-NAF [28] and various window based methods have been proposed. The same techniques can be implemented representing the multiplier m in base 3 and using point tripling [22] and addition/subtraction algorithms. Some other methods involve point halving [27] and some others use efficiently computable endomorphisms like Frobenius map [15].

Here the computation is speeded up by reducing the number of costlier operations like addition, doubling etc. and instead computing the images of the base point under repeated application of the efficiently computable endomorphism.

The point multiplication methods described above can be generalized as follows: Let Σ be a set of operations like point doubling, addition, point halving, tripling etc. The point multiplication algorithm is a computational procedure which computes its output by applying some of the operations in Σ to the initial input (the base point) one after another. The order of these invocations is dependent on a specific representation of the scalar m.

Pipelining of point multiplication is based on the following simple observation: while computing the point multiplication one can speedup the computation by cascading the operations, i.e. starting an operation as soon as some partial inputs are available to it from its predecessor operation.

In case of elliptic curves where the group operations are cheaper, it is simpler to devise a pipelined version of the point multiplication procedure. The number of inputs and outputs are small, i.e. 3 only (X, Y, Z in Jacobian coordinates). Hence if the participating group operations (e.g. ECADD and ECDBL) compute their outputs in the specific order (e.g. Z, X, Y) and the corresponding algorithms are reformulated so that they can make use of the partial inputs available to them, a perfect pipelining with very good throughput can be achieved.

However, in case of curves of higher genera, the number of field operations per group operation is much higher than those in ECC. Also there are many more inputs and outputs. Hence it is quite difficult to determine the specific input sequence which is most suitable to pipelining. Even after determining the optimal input/output sequences, it is not a simple task to reformulate the various group operations to implement them in a pipelined manner.

Here we provide a general methodology to automate this reformulation process. Given any set of group operation and a point multiplication method, the proposed methodology reformulates it to make it suitable for pipelining. Of course all computational procedure may not be suitable for pipelining. Some will have less attractive throughput. Given any point multiplication method, our algorithm can automatically design the most efficient pipelined version of it and compute the throughput. The implementer can then decide whether the speedup obtained is worth the extra hardware requirement that a pipelined implementation would demand.

To settle the pipeline issue systematically, we take up an even more general problem. Let Π be any computational procedure, which computes its output by repeatedly applying some operations to the initial inputs by invoking processes from a set Σ of *similar* processes depending upon a scheduling rule Λ. If the pipelining technique is applied to execute the procedure Π, what is the *optimal* expected throughput? Needless to mention the point multiplication is a special case of the procedure Π. The proposed methodology may be of importance to computer scientists working on various other field. For example hardware designers employ some adhoc methods for the purpose. Our methodology may have some overlapping with those adhoc methods. However, our method is more formal and can be automated to deal with any kind and any size of the individual processes. To our knowledge, it is first such attempt to design a pipelined version of such a general procedure.

We have proposed an algorithm, which given any such computational procedure can reformulate it for pipelining and also give the expected throughput. We have applied the proposed methodology to genus 2 hyperelliptic curve binary point multiplication using the best available explicit formulae. The throughput of the pipeline in case of hyperelliptic curve case is not as high as the ECC. The pipelined version of binary algorithm (with or without NAF representation of the scalar) is 32% faster than the sequential version. It should be noted that, as the pipeline scheme uses two multipliers, in the ideal case the performance gain can be at most 50%.

To apply our technique to hyperelliptic curve point multiplication we use curves of genus 2. For general curves of genus 2, the explicit formulae proposed by Lange are the most efficient ones. The latest version with an extensive comparison of coordinate systems is available in [21]. We refer to that paper for further details and notations.

2   The Problem

The pipelined computation of point multiplication is a simple technique, which provides significant speed up with slightly more hardware support. The idea is – start a new curve operation as soon as some of its inputs are available to it. Successive curve operations are streamlined into the pipe and gets executed in an overlapped fashion at the subtask (arithmetic operations) level. Pipelining may be achieved even if the curve operations are strictly sequential in nature.

Let a computational procedure Π is computed by invoking a sequence of processes $\Pi_{i_1}, \Pi_{i_2}, \cdots, \Pi_{i_t}$ where, each of these processes are elements of the set $\Sigma = \{\Pi_1, \Pi_2, \cdots, \Pi_k\}$ of processes. The processes are invoked according to some scheduling criteria, Λ. Initially all the inputs to the first process Π_{i_1} are provided to it. Then each process uses the outputs of its predecessor process as its input. We have the following assumptions on the processes:

1. The processes are straight line programs (If there are loops in them, these have been unrolled).
2. All the processes have the same number (say, l) of inputs and outputs.
3. Types of inputs and outputs are also the same.
4. Some processes may use some constants besides the inputs mentioned above.

Note that all point multiplication algorithms follow the assumptions mentioned above. For example, in case of binary algorithm, Σ consists of only two processes DBL and ADD. The scheduling criterion Λ is : Represent the multiplier in binary, DBL for every bit of the multiplier and ADD the base point if the corresponding bit is 1. For other point multiplication algorithms, the processes constituting Σ and the scheduling criterion Λ change.

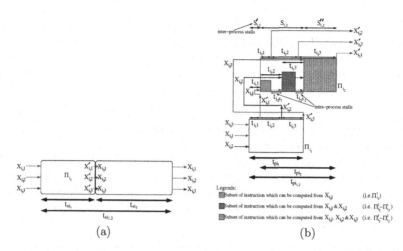

Fig. 1. (a) A sequential version (b) a pipeline version — of execution of two processes

We will use the following notation to explain sequential/pipelined execution: Let Π_{i_α} be any process, $\Pi_{i_\alpha} \in \Sigma$. We will refer $\{x_{i_\alpha 1}, x_{i_\alpha 2}, \cdots, x_{i_\alpha l}\}$ and $\{x'_{i_\alpha 1}, x'_{i_\alpha 2}, \cdots, x'_{i_\alpha l}\}$ as its inputs and outputs respectively and the time difference to generate the jth output as $t_{i_\alpha j}$. If Π_{i_α} is invoked followed by Π_{i_β}. In that case Π_{i_β} gets its input from Π_{i_α} i.e. $x_{i_\beta j} \leftarrow x'_{i_\alpha j}, \forall j, 1 \leq j \leq l$.

In a sequential execution of the computational procedure Π, the processes are executed in a batch processing manner (refer Figure 1(a)):

The initial process Π_{i_1} is called, based on the determining criteria Λ with all its inputs (say $x_{i_1 1}$, $x_{i_1 2}$ and $x_{i_1 3}$). After successful execution, it produces outputs (say $x'_{i_1 1}$, $x'_{i_1 2}$ and $x'_{i_1 3}$ after time t_{si_1} and exits. Then the next process Π_{i_2} is called with the outputs of Π_{i_1} as its inputs (i.e. $x_{i_2 j} \leftarrow x'_{i_1 j}, \forall j, 1 \leq j \leq 3$). Additionally it may have some constants also. At the exit of each process, its successor is invoked which uses its output as its (successor) input. It continues till the determining criteria Λ dictates the end of the process Π.

A pipelined Π will compute in the following manner (refer Figure 1(b)):

The initial process Π_{i_1} will start execution in the same manner as described in the sequential version above. But, as soon as it produces some partial output (say $x'_{i_1 1}$ after time $t_{i_1 1}$), the next process Π_{i_2} enters the pipeline (after some delay $S'_{1,2}$, which is in this case the time $t_{i_1 1}$; we shall call such delay as inter-process stall). Π_{i_2} based on these partial output of Π_{i_1} ($x'_{i_1 1}$), as its input ($x_{i_2 1}$), continues to run in parallel with Π_{i_1}. Actually Π_{i_2} executes only that subset of its instruction which can be computed from those partial input ($x_{i_2 1}$). In an ideal situation Π_{i_2} get its next input (computed as an output by process Π_{i_1}) as soon as Π_{i_2} completes executing this subset of instructions. In such case, Π_{i_2} will run in parallel with Π_{i_1} without waiting for its input, resulting in maximum throughput. But it may happen that the process Π_{i_1} may take more time (say $t_{i_1 2}$) to compute its next output (say $x'_{i_1 2}$). Then Π_{i_2} will have to wait (say for a time $t_{i_2s_1}$, we shall refer such 'wait' as intra-process stall) till Π_{i_1} produces the next output $(x'_{i_1 2})$. Thus the two processes in the pipeline continue to execute themselves in a *producer-consumer* relation.

While Π_{i_1} and Π_{i_2} are in pipeline running in parallel and interdependently, one of the following situation can occur:

1. Π_{i_2} produces partial output based on partial input it receives. Next process Π_{i_3} may enter the pipeline and run in parallel with Π_{i_1} and Π_{i_2}, there by increasing the pipestages to three.

2. Π_{i_1} produces all its output and exits. If Π_{i_2} has already produced its first output, the next process Π_{i_3} can enter the pipe to execute as a consumer process. Otherwise Π_{i_2} will continue to run alone till it produces enough output and the next process Π_{i_3} enters the pipeline. In such a situation we say some *inter-process stalls* have occurred.

It may happen (due to case 1) at some point of time several processes are in pipeline resulting in several pipestages or cores. However, it has been seen that a curve based crypto coprocessor can be optimal if it has only two cores (see [3]). Since we are interested in applying our methodology to point multiplication in curve base cryptography, we restrict ourselves on two pipestages only. In a two-core situation:

Inter-process stall appears whenever a core/process is running alone to produce enough output for the next process to start running in parallel. It is the delay for the next process to enter the pipeline. Only one process is live, the later process is waiting to start.

Intra-process stall appears when two core/process have started running, the producer process is still running to produce some output, but the consumer process is waiting for inputs for further computation. Two processes are live, but only the producer is running.

If we consider any two successive processes Π_{i_1} and Π_{i_2} (refer Figure 1(b)), inter-process stall appears only in the portion marked $S'_{1,2}$; intra-process stall may appear only in the portion marked $S_{1,2}$.

These stalls may vary for even two processes appearing in the same order. Say two processes Π_{i_1} and Π_{i_2} are in the order $\{\Pi_{i_1}, \Pi_{i_2}\}$. If Π_{i_1} is the initial process based on the determining criteria Λ, it has all its inputs. It might produce the first output much earlier than in case Π_{i_1} is not the initial process and is getting its input one by one from the previous process in the pipeline. As a result, duration of inter-process stalls vary. Depending upon Π_{i_1} has all its input or not, t_{i_1j} $\forall j$ may differ and Π_{i_2} will receive inputs in different time interval. As a result, intra-process stall may also vary. If Π_{i_2} is the last process, after Π_{i_1} completes its execution, Π_{i_2} has to run alone for a longer period (i.e. the entire portion marked $S''_{1,2}$).

All computational procedure may not be suitable for pipelining. If the consumer process spends more time in waiting for an input from the producer process (i.e. higher value of inter-process and intra-process stalls) and computes for lesser time then clearly the throughput of the pipeline will be less attractive (at least when $t_{pi_1} + t_{pi_2} - (t_{i_2s_1} + t_{i_2s_2}) \leq t_{pi_{1,2}}$ in Figure 1(b)).

We have ignored the time required to call a process, assuming execution time of each process is much higher. Also note that pipelining a procedure does not change its scheduling criterion Λ.

Thus the problem is: *Let Π be a procedure of the type described above. Is it possible to have an efficient pipelined Π? What is the throughput of such a pipeline? Also, what will be the best sequence of computation of the processes in Σ for such an efficient pipelined version of Π?*

2.1   A Closer Look at the Problem

Let Π_{i_τ} be any of the processes, $\Pi_{i_\tau} \in \Sigma$. By an *input sequence* we mean an ordering of its inputs. Based on an input sequence we can divide Π_{i_τ} into l parts as follows: Let $\Pi_{i_\tau}^1$ be the set of all instructions in Π_{i_τ}, which can be computed with input $x_{i_\tau 1}$ only. Let $\Pi_{i_\tau}^2$ be the set of all instructions in Π_{i_τ}, which can be computed with $x_{i_\tau 1}, x_{i_\tau 2}$ only. Similarly, let $\Pi_{i_\tau}^j$ be the set of all instructions in Π_{i_τ} which can be computed with the inputs $x_{i_\tau 1}, \cdots, x_{i_\tau j}$. Thus $\Pi_{i_\tau j}, 1 \leq j \leq l$ form an increasing sequence of sets of instructions bounded above by Π_{i_τ} itself. We can order the instructions in Π_{i_τ} as $\Pi_{i_\tau}^1, \Pi_{i_\tau}^2 - \Pi_{i_\tau}^1, \cdots, \Pi_{i_\tau}^l - \Pi_{i_\tau}^{l-1}$.

Thus given any permutation of the inputs $x_1, \cdots, x_l$, we can rearrange the instructions in each of the process Π_{i_τ} such that the first portion can be computed with the first input only, the next part can be computed with the first two inputs only and so on (refer Figure 1(b)).

Note that, by an instruction, we mean some unit of computation. Instructions may not be of same complexity. For simplicity, we may assume one instruction is one arithmetic operation in a specific algebraic structure. For example, if the processes represent curve operations as in the case of point multiplication, the instructions are various operations $\{+, -, /, \times\}$ in the underlying field. They are three address codes in the form $Id_r : LHS_r = operand_r^1 \ op_r \ operand_r^2$, where Id_r is an identifier of this operation, $operand_r^1$ and $operand_r^2$ are two operands, $op_r \in \{+, -, /, \times\}$ is an operation and LHS_r is the result of the operation. For a unary operation we can take one of the operand to be a suitable constant to conform to this form. Thus each process is a sequence of such three address codes.

We restrict our attention to the case two pipestages only. Therefore at any point of time there will be at most two processes in the pipeline. We call them a *couple*. The process which has entered the pipeline first will be computing its outputs and the later process will be accepting these as its inputs. Once the former process has produced all its output, it will exit. Either of the two situation may occur now. If the later process has already computed its first output a new process can enter the pipeline. Else, the later process has to run alone leading to some inter-process stalls and produce output for the next process to come into the pipeline. Thus, after a delay (which may be zero as in the former case), the next process will enter the pipeline. This will create the next couple. In the new couple, the process that acted as a consumer earlier will act as a producer and the newly joined process will act as a consumer. Therefore a couple is a listing of two processes in a pipelined manner.

Given any two processes Π_{i_1} and Π_{i_2} we make two couples: Π_{i_1,i_2} and Π_{i_2,i_1}. The processes may be same or different. But instructions of a process may be ordered in various way while coupling it with another process, resulting in different inter-process and intra-process stalls. Thus any couples may have various versions with varying inter-process and intra-process stalls. Our aim is to form, for any ordered pair (say $\{\Pi_i, \Pi_j\}$) of processes, the most *suitable* couple ($\Pi_{i,j}$) among all its versions. In the most suitable couple, the sum of intra-process and inter-process stalls should be minimum.

Let $\Pi_{i_{1,2}}$ be the first couple of a computational procedure Π, which lists the instructions of Π_{i_1} and Π_{i_2} (as mentioned in Section 2, refer Figure 1(b)). The first process of the first couple will have all its input ready. Π_{i_1} has all its inputs, and can start. Π_{i_2} enters the pipeline after a delay. It computes $\Pi_{i_2}^1$ in parallel with Π_{i_1}. Then Π_{i_2} may have to wait for Π_{i_1} to produce the next output. Again Π_{i_2} starts to compute $\Pi_{i_2}^2 - \Pi_{i_2}^1$ in parallel with Π_{i_1}. The process Π_{i_2} which has entered the pipeline may run in parallel or wait depending upon if Π_{i_1} has produced suitable output as its inputs. After producing all its outputs Π_{i_1} exits. Now Π_{i_2} runs smoothly as now it has all its input ready. When process Π_{i_2} has produced enough output process Π_{i_3} enters the pipeline, forming the second couple and so on. There may be some inter-process stalls if the process Π_{i_2} has not produced adequate outputs for the next process (Π_{i_3}) to enter the pipeline. If the computational procedure Π is a path, the couples are the mosaics for creating the path. The procedure Π can now be computed by joining the couples.

3 General Methodology

The problem of pipelining now boils down to finding the most suitable couple: the couple with minimum inter-process and intra-process stalls. These stalls are mainly dependent on the order in which the processes generate the outputs.

Since we are more interested in the order in which a process generates its outputs, we call such an ordered list of outputs of a process a *valid output sequence*. Note that any permutation of the set of outputs is not an valid output sequence. For example, in the (mixed) addition and doubling operation of elliptic curves, there are three inputs/outputs, X, Y, Z (we treat the coordinates of the base point as constants used by mixed addition). Hence there are six (3!) output sequences. However, the computation of Y coordinates requires X. So Y cannot be computed before X. Thus the output sequences in which Y precedes X (i.e. (Z, Y, X), (Y, Z, X) and (Y, X, Z)) are invalid. That is because, the producer process cannot produce outputs in those orders. So there are only three valid output sequences.

For each ordered pair $\{\Pi_i, \Pi_j\}$ of processes we need to form the couple $\Pi_{i,j}$. Since for each output sequence of Π_i, at least one couple $\Pi_{i,j}$ can be formed (for each valid output sequence of Π_i, corresponding input order that Π_j accepts may have one or more valid operation sequence), we first find the set of all valid output sequences of Π_i. Let us call this set $VOutSeq_i$. Now for each valid output sequence in $VOutSeq_i$, we generate all the Π_{ij} couples. Then we have to choose the most suitable one of them. For each of these couples we calculate the corresponding intra-process and inter-process stalls. The one for which the sum of intra-process and inter-process stalls is minimum will be the most suitable $\Pi_{i,j}$ couple. We will refer to this couple plainly as *suitable* $\Pi_{i,j}$ couple.

Note that, in the ideal situation, the output sequence of the processes remains the same in all the couples. This is the situation in the pipelining scheme proposed for ECC in [25]. Both the processes DBL and ADD in every couple produce their outputs in the order Z, X, Y. The second process in each couple consume their inputs in the same order. This has several advantages too. The processes can be rewritten to facilitate this input and output order, so that the scheduling of various arithmetic operations of the processes becomes static. This may have some advantage in an implementation in hardware. However, the hyperelliptic curve processes do not lead to this easy scenario automatically. For an hardware implementation, this condition can be imposed as an restriction while creating the couples. However, the throughput of the pipeline will be adversely affected. In the current work we do not impose such restriction on the processes while creating the couples in order to keep the discussion more general.

Thus, we choose an ordered set $\{\Pi_i, \Pi_j\}$ of two processes from Σ and make the couple $\Pi_{i,j}$. We calculate the total intra-process s_{ij} stalls and total inter-process stalls (in $s'_{1,2}$ as shown in Figure 1(b)) s'_{ij} for this each $\Pi_{i,j}$ couple. We repeat this process for every valid pair of processes Π_i and Π_j.

GenerateSuitableCouple (Algorithm 1) calls GenerateAllCouples (Algorithm 2) to create all possible couples for $\Pi_{i,j}$ corresponding to every valid output sequence of Π_i from the set O_i, and then chooses the most suitable among these couples as the couple $\Pi_{i,j}$.

GenerateAllCouples (Algorithm 2) creates every valid output sequence of Π_i and for each such valid sequence it calls CreateACouple (Algorithm 3) to form all possible Π_{ij} couple and return the most suitable one.

Thus the three nested algorithms produce all the necessary couples for a given computational procedure. Note that, although the couples are the building blocks of the computational procedure, their optimal creation leads to an efficient implementation. That is because we have taken care of intra-process stalls during their creation process. So they seamlessly join to each other to form the optimal computational path. Of course there will be stalls even for the most efficient set of couples, but that will be to the minimal level.

Algorithm 1. GenerateSuitableCouple(l, Π_i, Π_j)

Input Number of inputs/outputs (l) of the processes and two processes Π_i and Π_j in three address codes. Let O_i be the set of all outputs of the process Π_i.
Output Suitable couple $\Pi_{i,j}$.
  1: read l;
  2: call Algorithm GenerateAllCouples(O_i, Π_i, Π_j);
  3: read s_{ij} and s'_{ij} for all couples and return the couple with minimum $s_{ij} + s'_{ij}$.

Algorithm 2. GenerateAllCouples(O_i, Π_i, Π_j)

Input O_i, Π_i, Π_j.
Output All possible couples $\Pi_{i,j}$ (through Algorithm CreateACouple()).
    while $\mathcal{O} \neq \emptyset$ **do**
2:    let $O_{i_r} \in \mathcal{O}$;
    if $(O_{i_r} \in VOutSeq_i)$;
4:    call Algorithm CreateACouple(Π_i, Π_j, O_{i_r});
    $\mathcal{O} \leftarrow \mathcal{O} - \{O_{i_r}\}$;

Algorithm 3. CreateACouple(Π_i, Π_j, O_{i_r})

Input Π_i, Π_j and O_{i_r}.
Output All possible couple $\Pi_{i,j}$ corresponding to the output sequence O_{i_r} and the
    respective stalls.
    read all operations of Π_i and Π_j;
2: $r \leftarrow 1$;
    while $r \leq l$ **do**
4:    list the subset of operations from Π_i required to generate the rth output in
    sequence from O_{i_r} of Π_i;
    list further sub-set of operations in Π_j that can be executed with the first r
    variables of the sequence O_{i_r};
6:    $r \leftarrow r + 1$;
    let s_{ij} = intra-process and s'_{ij} = inter-process stalls in the couple;
8: tune the subset of operations for minimum s_{ij} and s'_{ij};
    return the couple and s_{ij}, s'_{ij}.

3.1   Analysis of the Pipelined Procedure

In the current section we will analyze the expected speedup that can be obtained
in pipelining. Let the involved processes be $\Pi_1, \Pi_2, \cdots, \Pi_k$. Let $t_i^{(s)}$ be the computation time of the process Π_i, $1 \leq i \leq k$. Let N be the number of processes
invoked by the procedure Π. Let f_i be the frequency of the process Π_i, $1 \leq i \leq k$
among these N invocations. Then the cost (or time) of a sequential execution of
the procedure Π is $L_s = \Sigma_{i=1}^{k} f_i \times t_i^{(p)}$.

Let $t_i^{(p)}$ be the computation time of the process Π_i, $1 \leq i \leq k$ in the pipelined
scenario. It has been reported in [25] that in pipelined ECC scalar multiplication,
$t_{ADD}^{(p)} = t_{DBL}^{(p)} = 6$. where one unit of time is computation time of one atomic
block, which is almost equal to computation time of one field multiplication
([m]). In the present work, it is found (see Table 1) that in HECC scalar multiplication, each DBL except the first one takes 35[m] and each ADD takes 28[m].
In sequential execution, these processes take 50[m] and 44[m] of computation
time respectively. In some cases it may happen that in pipelined computation,
various invocation of the same process may take different unit of time. In that
case $t_i^{(p)}$ may be taken to be the average of all these observed values for the
process Π_i.

Let us calculate the computation time for pipelined version of the process Π. Let Π_j be the first process invoked by Π. This first invocation of Π_j will take $t_j^{(s)}$ amount of time. After this every invoked process Π_i (including Π_j) will take $t_i^{(p)}$ amount of computation time. Hence, the whole procedure will require

$$L_p = 1 \times t_j^{(s)} + f_1 \times t_1^{(p)} + \cdots + f_{j-1} \times t_{j-1}^{(p)} + (f_j - 1) \times t_j^{(p)} + f_{j+1} \times t_{j+1}^{(p)} + \cdots + f_k \times t_k^{(p)}$$

amount of time. Hence expected speedup is $(1 - L_s/L_p) \times 100$ percent.

In case of hyperelliptic curve, $t_{ADD}^{(s)} = 44[m]$, $t_{ADD}^{(p)} = 28[m]$, $t_{DBL}^{(s)} = 50[m]$ and $t_{DBL}^{(p)} = 35[m]$. In Section 5, detailed analysis for pipelined HECC point multiplication using binary and NAF methods have been presented.

4   Implementation

The methodology formulated above was programmed and extensive experimentation was carried out using various addition and doubling formulae for both elliptic and hyperelliptic curve. We used elliptic curve formulae for two reasons. Elliptic curve formulae are simpler and hence were used to test the correctness of the employed methodology. Again we experimented using various ECC formulae using various point representations to determine which set of formulae best suited for pipelining. We found that the formulae based on Jacobian coordinates are the best suited ones for pipelining. Due to space constraints the presentation of details of ECC formulae are beyond the scope of the current paper. A case study on genus 2 hyperelliptic curves using projective coordinates is provided in the next section.

5   A Case Study

For HECC, very efficient arithmetic has been proposed in [18, 19, 20] for genus 2 curves. We concentrate on [19], where a formulae in "projective" coordinates has been proposed.

The inversion-free versions of explicit formulae trade inversions for several multiplication. Hence inversion-free arithmetic is not suitable for fields where I/M ratio is lesser (for example binary fields). Hence we concentrate on fields of odd characteristic only.

The point multiplication method we tried to pipeline is the ordinary binary algorithm using binary or NAF representation of the scalar m. These methods use two curve operations, doubling and mixed addition (see [6]). We will refer to the doubling and mixed addition formulae proposed in [19] as HCDBL and mHCADD respectively.

In the scheme under consideration, Σ consists of two operation only, HCDBL and mHCADD. We require three couples, HCDBL-mHCADD, HCDBL-HCDBL, mHCADD-HCDBL. That is because two consecutive additions are not required by the point multiplication algorithm. Thus we run our program with these process pair (HCDBL, HCDBL), (HCDBL, mHCADD) and (mHCADD, HCDBL) and obtained the couples $\Pi_{D,D}$, $\Pi_{D,A}$ and $\Pi_{A,D}$.

To measure the efficiency we count the number of field operations needed; we use [m], [s], [a], to denote a multiplication, a squaring or an addition respectively. We will use the following notations (refer Figure 1(b)): Given any couple $\Pi_{i,j}$, let $S'_{i,j}$ denote the inter-process stall and $S_{i,j}$ denote the number of parallel rounds (i.e. Π_i and Π_j are running in parallel, with some intra-process stall). For initial couple $\Pi_{i,j}$, we denote them as $^{ic}S'_{i,j}$ and $^{ic}S_{i,j}$ respectively. If $\Pi_{i,j}$ is the last couple, $S''_{i,j}$ be the portion where Π_i is running alone to complete the procedure. Let $L()$ denote the number of instruction in the process or (portion of the process). Therefore $L(\Pi_i)$ be the number of instruction in the process Π_i. $L(S'_{i,j})$, $L(S_{i,j})$, $L(^{ic}S'_{i,j})$, $L(^{ic}S_{i,j})$, and $L(S''_{i,j})$ represents the number of instruction in the portion of $\Pi_{i,j}$ mentioned as $S'_{i,j}$, $S_{i,j}$, $^{ic}S'_{i,j}$, $^{ic}S_{i,j}$ and $S''_{i,j}$ respectively.

We have $L(HCDBL) = 50[m]$ and $L(mHCADD) = 44[m]$ (in projective representation), neglecting additions/subtractions and taking $[m] = [s]$.

5.1   Hardware Requirement

Let the number of registers required for sequential execution of HCDBL and mH-CADD be $R_{s_{HCDBL}}$ and $R_{s_{mHCADD}}$ respectively. For pipeline execution the register requirement will be $\max(R_{HCDBL}, R_{mHCADD})$ + additional registers required to execute the operations of the second process, when two processes are in pipeline. The additional registers varies from couple to couple It is observed that maximum additional registers will be $\sim 35\%$ of $\max(R_{HCDBL}, R_{mHCADD})$. Therefore for pipeline execution the register requirement will be $R_p = 1.35 \times \max$ (R_{HCDBL}, R_{mHCADD}). Since two process may be in pipeline, additional adder, inverters and multiplier are also required. But, the computation of point multiplication in projective coordinates requires only one inversion at the end. So one inverter suffices and no extra inverter is required. Also, addition being a very cheap operation, both the pipestages can share one adder (using it sequentially). If side-channel atomicity [5] is employed to resist side-channel attacks, squaring are to be done by the multiplication hardware. Hence the scheme does not require any hardware for squaring. However, the scheme requires separate multipliers for both the pipestages as multiplications are carried out in parallel. Thus, the hardware overhead of the proposed scheme is 35% extra registers and one extra multiplier.

5.2   Synchronization

There might be chances of *collision* since two processes running in parallel are sharing the same memory. A collision may arise if:

1. Two processes running in the two pipestages are trying to write at a location simultaneously.
2. One process is writing one location the other is trying to read the same location.

The second process starts generating its output only after the first process has generated all its output. Hence the collision of the first type cannot occur. The second type of synchronization is handled through intra-process stall. Intra-process stall takes care so that the second process will start reading only after the first process has written its output.

5.3 Side-Channel Resistance

The pipeline scheme proposed in [25] has been immunized against side-channel attacks by using side-channel atomicity (proposed in [5]) and other DPA countermeasures. The same trick can be applied here as well. The processes can be divided into small atomic blocks. DPA can be resisted by using the curve randomization countermeasure proposed in [12, 1]. We avoid these trivialities to save space.

5.4 Performance

The HECC formulae in projective coordinates do not lead to pipelining as naturally as ECC formulae in Jacobian coordinates. There are many intra-process stalls in each of the couples. In case of ECC, a process exits the pipeline in every 6 multiplication/squaring time. Let us consider the pipeline of point multiplication for a very small scalar $m = 27$, $(11011)_2$. The computation involves the following sequence of ADD (mHCADD) and DBL (HCDBL) operations: DBL ADD DBL DBL ADD DBL ADD. Then, for every DBL operation except the first one takes 35[m] computation and every ADD takes 28[m]. Since the frequency of the operations depends upon the representation of the scalar (binary or NAF), the throughput will depend upon the representation. Using the notation of Section 3.1, we have $t_{ADD}^{(s)} = 44[m]$, $t_{DBL}^{(s)} = 50[m]$, $t_{ADD}^{(p)} = 28[m]$ and $t_{DBL}^{(p)} = 35[m]$. For a n bit scalar, the binary algorithm computes the point multiplication by invoking HCDBL $(n-1)$ times and mHCADD $\frac{n}{2}$ times on the average. Hence $f_{ADD} = n-1$ and $f_{DBL} = \frac{n}{2}$. So cost of a sequential implementation is $L_s = (n-1) \times 50 + \frac{n}{2} \times 44 = 72n - 50$. As the first process is a doubling, the cost of a pipelined execution will be, $L_p = 50 + (n-2) \times 35 + \frac{n}{2} \times 28 = 49n - 20$. In case the scalar is represented in NAF, the scheme requires $(n-1)$ doubling and $\frac{n}{3}$ additions on the average. Hence, $f_{DBL} = (n-1)$ and $f_{ADD} = \frac{n}{3}$ and cost of a sequential implementation is $L_s = (n-1) \times 50 + \frac{n}{3} \times 44 = (64.67n - 50)[m]$. Pipelined implementation of NAF scheme has complexity $L_p = 50 + (n-2) \times 35 + \frac{n}{3} \times 28 = (44.33n - 20)[m]$. For adequate medium term security, n is generally taken to be a 160 bit integer. In Table 2, we compare performance of proposed pipelined scheme vis-a-vis sequential ones. Note that in either case (binary or NAF) we get a performance enhancement of around 32%. As there are two pipestages, the maximum speedup one can achieve is ideally 50%.

In case of binary representation, for a n bit scalar there will be $\frac{n}{2}$ mHCADD on average and $n - 1$ HCDBL. Hence cost of pipelined computation $L_p = L(HCDBL) + \frac{n}{2} \times 28 + (n-1) \times 35 = 50 + 14 \times n + 35 \times (n-1) - 35 = (15 + 49 \times n)$ [m]. Cost of sequential cost is $L_s = (n-1) \times 50 + \frac{n}{2} \times 44 = (72 \times n - 50)$ [m]. In case of NAF, there will be $n/3$ mHCADD and n HCDBL. Hence, $L_p = L(HCDBL) + \frac{n}{3} \times 28 + (n-2) \times 35 = 50 + 9.3333 \times n + 35 \times n - 70 = (44.3333 \times n - 20)$ [m] and $L_s = (n-1) \times 50 + \frac{n}{3} \times 44 = (64.66 \times n - 50)$ [m]. For a typical value of

Table 1. Table showing the number of instructions in the processes or various portions of different couples. Process A and D refers to $mHCADD$ and $HCDBL$ respectively.

Process	$L(\Pi_i)$	Couple	$L(S'_{i,j})$	$L(S_{i,j})$	IPS	$L(S''_{i,j})$	$L(^{ic}S'_{i,j})$	$L(^{ic}S_{i,j})$	IPS
Π_A	44	$\Pi_{D,D}$	14	21 (34)	6	35	24	26 (34)	11
Π_D	50	$\Pi_{D,A}$	14	21 (29)	5	28	24	26 (29)	10
		$\Pi_{A,D}$	4	24 (33)	9	35			

The intra-process stalls (IPS) are included in part $L(S_{i,j})$ of each couple. The number in the brackets indicates the total number of instructions.

Table 2. Comparison of performance of proposed pipelined scheme and corresponding sequential schemes for point multiplication by a 160 bit multiplier

	Sequential	Pipelined
Binary	11470[m]	7820[m]
NAF	10298[m]	7072[m]

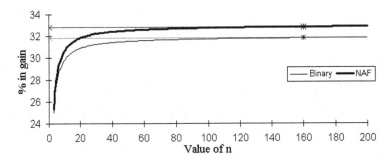

Fig. 2. Percentage of gain in pipeline of HECC for various values of n in binary and NAF representation

$n = 160$, performance of gain for binary and NAF representation for becomes 31.81% and 32.84% respectively. Figure 2 shows percentage of gain for binary and NAF representation for different values of n.

6   Conclusion

In the present work we present a general methodology for pipelining the point multiplication operation in curve based cryptography. Our method applies to any point multiplication algorithm. Moreover, the method can also be applied to any point-multiplication-like computational procedure occurring in any other branch of computer science. The pipelined version so obtained is optimal in the sense that the occurrence of stalls (both inter-process and intra-process) is minimum. We have applied the methodology to binary or NAF based point multiplication in hyperelliptic curves of genus 2 and have shown that the pipelined computation can lead to a speedup of 32%.

References

1. R. M. Avanzi. Countermeasures Against Differential Power Analysis for Hyperelliptic Curve Cryptosystems. *Cryptographic Hardware and Embedded Systems - CHES 2003, 5th International Workshop, Cologne, Germany, September 8-10, 2003, Proceedings*, LNCS 2779, pp. 366–381, Springer-Verlag, 2004.
2. R. Avanzi, H. Cohen, C. Doche, G. Frey, T. Lange, K. Nguyen, F. Vercauteren. Editors G. Frey and H. Cohen; *Handbook of Elliptic and Hyperelliptic Curve Cryptography*. CRC Press 2005.
3. G. Bertoni, L. Breveglieri, T. Wollinger and C. Paar. Finding Optimum Parallel Coprocessor Design for Genus 2 Hyperelliptic Curve Cryptosystems. *Cryptology ePrint Archive*, http://eprint.iacr.org/, Report 2004/29, 2004.
4. D. G. Cantor. Computing in the Jacobian of a Hyperelliptic curve. In *Mathematics of Computation*, 48:95–101, 1987.
5. B. Chevallier-Mames, M. Ciet and M. Joye. Low-cost Solutions for Preventing Simple Side-Channel Analysis: Side-Channel Atomicity. *IEEE Trans. on Computers*, 53:760–768, 2004.
6. H. Cohen, A. Miyaji, and T. Ono. Efficient Elliptic Curve Exponentiation Using Mixed coordinates. *Advances in Cryptology - ASIACRYPT'98 International Conference on the Theory and Application of Cryptology and Information Security, Beijing, China, October 18-22, 1998, Proceedings Series*, LNCS 1514, pp. 51–65, Springer-Verlag, 1998.
7. S. Flon and R. Oyono. Fast Arithmetic on Jacobian of Picard curves. *Public Key Cryptography – PKC 2004 7th International Workshop on Theory and Practice in Public Key Cryptography, Singapore, March 1-4, 2004*, LNCS 2947, pp. 55-68, Springer-Verlag, 2004.
8. S. D. Galbraith, S. M. Paulus, N. P. Smart. Arithmatic on Superelliptic Curves, *Mathematics of Computations*, 71(237):393–405, 2002
9. P. Gaudry and R. Harley. Counting Points on Hyperelliptic Curves over Finite Fields. In *ANTS IV*, LNCS 1838, pp. 297–312, Springer-Verlag, 2000.
10. D. Hankerson, A. Menezes and S. Vanstone. *Guide to Elliptic Curve Cryptography*, Springer-Verlag Professional Computing Series, ISBN: 0-387-95273-X, 2004.
11. R. Harley. Fast Arithmetic on Genus 2 Curves. Available at http://cristal.inria.fr/ harley/hyper/adding.txt.
12. M. Joye and C. Tymen. Protection against differential attacks for elliptic curve cryptography. *Cryptographic Hardware and Embedded Systems - CHES 2001, Third International Workshop, Paris, France, May 14-16, 2001, Proceedings* LNCS 2162, pp. 402–410, Springer-Verlag, 2001.
13. N. Koblitz. Elliptic Curve Cryptosystems. *Mathematics of Computations*, 48:203–209, 1987.
14. N. Koblitz. Hyperelliptic Cryptosystems. In *Journal of Cryptology*, 1(3):139–150, 1989.
15. N. Koblitz. CM Curves with Good Cryptographic Properties. *Advances in Cryptology - CRYPTO '91, 11th Annual International Cryptology Conference, Santa Barbara, California, USA, August 11-15, 1991, Proceedings*, LNCS 576, pp. 279–287, Springer Verlag, 1992.
16. P. Kocher. Timing Attacks on Implementations of Diffie-Hellman, RSA, DSS and Other Systems. *Advances in Cryptology - CRYPTO '96, 16th Annual International Cryptology Conference, Santa Barbara, California, USA, August 18-22, 1996, Proceedings*, LNCS 1109, pp. 104–113, Springer-Verlag, 1996.

17. P. Kocher, J. Jaffe and B, Jun. Differential Power Analysis. *Advances in Cryptology - CRYPTO '99, 19th Annual International Cryptology Conference, Santa Barbara, California, USA, August 15-19, 1999, Proceedings*, LNCS 1666, pp. 388–397, Springer-Verlag, 1999.

18. T. Lange. Efficient Arithmetic on Genus 2 Curves over Finite Fields via Explicit Formulae. *Cryptology ePrint Archive*, `http://eprint.iacr.org/`, Report 2002/121, 2002.

19. T. Lange. Inversion-free Arithmetic on Genus 2 Hyperelliptic Curves. *Cryptology ePrint Archive*, `http://eprint.iacr.org/`, Report 2002/147, 2002.

20. T. Lange. Weighted Co-ordinates on Genus 2 Hyperelliptic Curves. *Cryptology ePrint Archive*, `http://eprint.iacr.org/`, Report 2002/153, 2002.

21. T. Lange. Formulae for Arithmetic on Genus 2 Hyperelliptic Curves. `http://www.itsc.ruhr-uni-bochum.de/tanja/preprints.html`, 2004 (to appear in J. AAECC).

22. A. J. Menezes, S. Vanstone Elliptic curve cryptosystems and their implementation. *Journal of Cryptology*, 6:209–224, 1993.

23. A. Menezes, Y. Wu, R. Zuccherato. An Elementary Introduction to Hyperelliptic Curves. *Technical Report*, CORR 96-19, University of Waterloo, Canada, 1996. Available at `http://www.cacr.math.uwaterloo.ca`.

24. V. S. Miller. Use of Elliptic Curves in Cryptography. *Advances in Cryptology - CRYPTO '85, Santa Barbara, California, USA, August 18-22, 1985, Proceedings*, LNCS 218, pp. 417-426, Springer-Verlag, 1985.

25. P. K. Mishra. Pipelined Computation of the Scalar Multiplication in Elliptic Curve Cryptosystems. *Title: Cryptographic Hardware and Embedded Systems - CHES 2004: 6th International Workshop Cambridge, MA, USA, August 11-13, 2004. Proceedings*, LNCS 3156, pp 328-342, Springer-Verlag, 2004. (Full version to appear in *IEEE Trans on Computers*).

26. P. K. Mishra and P. Sarkar. Parallelizing Explicit Formula for Arithmetic in the Jacobian of Hyperelliptic Curves. *Advances in Cryptology - ASIACRYPT 2003, 9th International Conference on the Theory and Application of Cryptology and Information Security*, LNCS 2894, pp. 93–110, Springer-Verlag, 2003.

27. R. Schroeppel. Elliptic curve point halving wins big. *Second Midwest Arithmetical Geometry in Cryptography Workshop*. Urbana, Illinois, November 2000.

28. J. Solinas. An improved Algorithm on a Family of Elliptic Curves. *Advances in Cryptology - CRYPTO '97, 17th Annual International Cryptology Conference, Santa Barbara, California, USA, August 17-21, 1997, Proceedings*, LNCS 1294, pp.357–371, Springer-Verlag, 1997.

29. A. M. Spallek. Kurven vom Geschletch 2 und irhe Anwendung in Public-Key-Kryptosystemen. *PhD Thesis*, Universität Gesamthochschule, Essen, 1994.

Results on Almost Resilient Functions

Pinhui Ke[1,3], Jie Zhang[1,2], and Qiaoyan Wen[1]

[1] School of Science, Beijing University of Posts and Telecommunications,
Beijing, 100876, P.R. China
keph@eyou.com
[2] State Key Laboratory of Information Security,
Chinese Academy of Sciences, Beijing 100039, P.R. China
[3] School of Mathematics and Computer Science,
Fujian Normal University, Fujian 350007, P.R. China

Abstract. Almost resilient function is the generalization of resilient function and has important applications in multiple authenticate codes and almost security cryptographic Boolean functions. In this paper, some constructions are provided. In particular, the Theorem 3 in [7] is improved. As ε-almost $(n, 1, k)$-resilient functions play an important role in the secondary constructions, we concluded some properties and constructions. Specially we presented a spectral characterization of almost $(n, 1, k)$-resilient functions, which can be used to identify an almost $(n, 1, k)$-resilient function by computing its walsh spectra.

Keywords: Almost resilient Function, Resilient function, Almost correlation immune function.

1 Introduction

A Boolean functions is a map from F_2^n to F_2 and by a multi-output Boolean functions we mean a map from F_2^n to F_2^m. They are used as basic primitives for designing ciphers. In order to resist known attacks, several criteria of Boolean functions have been developed. However there are some tradeoffs between these criteria. Strict fulfillment in one criterion may lead to weaken another one. For example, bent functions have the best nonlinearity, but they are never balanced or correlation immune. So we may relax the definition's conditions and functions with better parameters can be obtained.

The concept of a resilient function was first introduced by Chor et al. [1], which have been found to be applicable in fault-tolerant distribute computing, quantum cryptographic key distribution and so on. K.Kurosawa et al. [2] generalized the concept and introduced the definition of almost resilient function. An ε-almost(n, m, k)-resilient function is an n-input m-output function f with the property that the deviation of output's distribution from uniform distribution is not great than ε when k arbitrary inputs are fixed and the remaining $n - k$ inputs run through all the 2^{n-k} input tuples. It was showed to have parameters superior to resilient function. As pointed out in [4], one important task of

J. Zhou, M. Yung, and F. Bao (Eds.): ACNS 2006, LNCS 3989, pp. 421–432, 2006.
© Springer-Verlag Berlin Heidelberg 2006

construction of vector resilient functions is to construct (n, m, k)-resilient functions with degree $d > m$ and high nonlinearity. It have been shown that we are able to improve the degree of the constructed functions with a small trade-off in the nonlinearity and resiliency. The notations of independent sample space was introduced by Naor and Naor [3], which had been proved to have many cryptographic applications, such as multiple authentication codes [5], almost security cryptographic Boolean functions [6] and so on. In [2], the relations between the almost resilient functions and the large sets of almost independent sample spaces were established. Recently, the relation between almost resilient function and its component functions was investigated in [7]. They proved that if each nonzero linear combination of $f_1, f_2, \cdots, f_m$ is an ε-almost $(n, 1, k)$-resilient function, then $F = (f_1, f_2, \cdots, f_m)$ is a $\frac{2^m-1}{2^m-1}\varepsilon$-almost (n, m, k)-resilient function. However up to the present, the known constructions of almost resilient functions are by using almost independent sample space [2] and a constructions of almost $(3n, 2, 2k+1)$-resilient function based on a balanced resilient function[7]. In Section 3, more constructions will be presented.

Because the close relation between almost resilient function and large set of almost independent sample space, the constructions of balanced almost resilient function are concerned. Balanced almost CI function plays an important role in the secondary construction of balanced almost resilient function. On the other hand by Siegenthalar's inequality, correlation immune order and algebraic degree are shown to be two contradictory criteria. Almost CI function was then proposed to solve this problem. Walsh Spectrum is useful tool in the characterization of CI function, which is known as Xiao-Massey theorem. But in the almost case, there is not such an efficient characterization. In Section 4, we will investigate this problem.

This paper is organized as follows. Some definitions and preliminaries that will be used later in the paper are described in Section 2. In Section 3, more constructions of almost resilient functions are provided. In section 4, we conclude some construction methods and properties of almost $(n, 1, k)$-resilient functions. Especially we present a spectral characterization of almost $(n, 1, k)$-resilient functions and prove it is feasible to determine an almost $(n, 1, k)$-resilient function by computing its walsh spectra, which can be regarded as the generalization of Xiao-Massey theorem in the almost case to a certain extent.

2   Preliminaries

The vector spaces of n-tuples of elements from GF(2) is denoted by F_2^n. Let F be a function from F_2^n to F_2^m.

Definition 1. *The function F is called an (n, m, k)-resilient function if*

$$Pr[F(x_1, \cdots, x_n) = (y_1, \cdots, y_m)|x_{i_1}x_{i_2}\cdots_{i_k} = \alpha] = 2^{-m}$$

for any k positions $i_1 < i_2 < \cdots < i_k$, for any k-bit string $\alpha \in F_2^k$, and for any $(y_1, \cdots, y_m) \in F_2^m$, where the values x_j ($j \notin \{i_1, i_2, \cdots, i_k\}$) are chosen independently at random.

Following propositions are well-known and useful in understanding the relationship between a resilient functions and its component functions. It has appeared in many references (see, for example, [9]).

Proposition 1. *Let $F = (f_1, \cdots, f_m)$ be a function from F_2^n to F_2^m, where n and m are integers with $n \geq m \geq 1$, and each f_i is a function on F_2^n. Then F is an (n, m, k)-resilient function if and only if every nonzero combination of $f_1, \cdots, f_m$*

$$f(x) = \bigoplus_{i=1}^{m} c_i f_i(x)$$

is a $(n, 1, k)$-resilient function, where $c = (c_1, \cdots, c_n) \in F_2^n$.

K.Kurosawa et al. introduced a notation of ε-almost(n, m, k)-resilient function [2].

Definition 2. *The function F is called a ε-almost (n, m, k)-resilient function if*

$$|Pr[F(x_1, \cdots, x_n) = (y_1, \cdots, y_m)|x_{i_1} x_{i_2} \cdots_{i_k} = \alpha] - 2^{-m}| \leq \varepsilon$$

for any k positions $i_1 < i_2 < \cdots < i_k$, for any k-bit string $\alpha \in F_2^k$, and for any $(y_1, \cdots, y_m) \in F_2^m$, where the values x_j ($j \notin \{i_1, i_2, \cdots, i_k\}$) are chosen independently at random.

By the definition, it is easy to prove following lemma.

Lemma 1. *If F is an ε-almost (n, m, k)-resilient function, then F is also an ε-almost (n, m, r)-resilient function for any $r \leq k$.*

An almost k-wise independent sample space is probability space on n-bit tuples such that any k-bits are almost independent. A large set of (ε, k)-independent sample spaces, denoted by $LS(\varepsilon, k, n, t)$, is a set of $2^{m-t}(\varepsilon, k)$-independent sample spaces, each of size 2^t, such their union contains all 2^n binary vectors of length n. For details about k-wise independent sample spaces and $LS(\varepsilon, k, n, t)$, we refer to [2, 3].

The relation between $LS(\varepsilon, k, n, t)$ and almost resilient function is revealed in [2].

Proposition 2. *If there exists an $LS(\varepsilon, k, n, t)$, then there exists a δ-almost $(n, n - t, k)$-resilient function, where $\delta = \frac{\varepsilon}{2^{n-t-k}}$.*

A (n, m)-function F is called balanced if

$$Pr[F(x_1, \cdots, x_n) = (y_1, \cdots, y_m)] = 2^{-m}$$

for all $(y_1, \cdots, y_m) \in F_2^m$.

Proposition 3. *If there exists a balanced ε-almost (n, m, k)-resilient function, then there exists a $LS(\delta, k, n, n - m)$, where $\delta = \frac{\varepsilon}{2^{k-m}}$.*

Using Weil-Carlitz-Uchiyama bound, K.Kurosawa et al. [2] present a construction of t-systematic (ε, k)-independent sample spaces and then extended to large set of almost independent sample spaces. So by Proposition 2, some almost resilient functions are obtained.

Let $F(X) = (f_1, f_2, \cdots, f_m)$ be an (n, m)-function, the *nonlinearity* of F is defined to be $nl(F) = min\{nl(l \circ f) : l$ is a non-constant m-variable linear function$\}$, where $nl(f)$ is the least hamming distance between Boolean function f and all affine functions. And the *degree* of F defined to be the minimum of the degree of $l \circ f$, where l ranges over all non-constant m-variable linear function.

Similar to the resilient function, correlation immune function can also be generalized. K. Kurosawa et al. [2] called it the almost correlation immune function. In fact, an earlier generalization version of the single output case has been introduced by Yixian Yan [11].

Definition 3. *The function F is called an ε-almost (n, m, k)-correlation immune function if*

$$|Pr[F(x_1, \cdots, x_n) = (y_1, \cdots, y_m)|x_{i_1} x_{i_2} \cdots {}_{i_k} = \alpha] - Pr[F(x_1, \cdots, x_n) = (y_1,$$

$$\cdots, y_m)]| \leq \varepsilon$$

for any k positions $i_1 < i_2 < \cdots < i_k$, for any k-bit string $\alpha \in F_2^k$, and for any $(y_1, \cdots, y_m) \in F_2^m$, where the values x_j $(j \notin \{i_1, i_2, \cdots, i_k\})$ are chosen independently at random.

The relation between almost CI function and nonuniform $LS(\varepsilon, k, n, t)$ is given in [2]. It is easy to see that an ε-almost (n, m, k)-resilient function is equivalent to an balanced ε-almost (n, m, k)-CI function.

Let f be a function from F_2^n to F_2, then

$$S_f(w) = \sum_{x \in F_2^n} (-1)^{f(x) \oplus w \cdot x}$$

is called a *Walsh transformation* of f. Walsh transform is a useful tool and many cryptographic criteria of a Boolean function can be characterized by it.

3   Construction of Almost Resilient Functions

In the following, if h is a functions from F_2^n to F_2^m or F_2, denote

$$L(h(X) = Y) = \{(x_1, x_2, \cdots, x_n) : h(x_1, x_2, \cdots, x_n) = Y\}. \tag{1}$$

Let $X_i, 1 \leq i \leq m$, be m independent random variables on F_2. The number of nonzero combination of $X_1, X_2, \cdots, X_m$ is $C_m^1 + C_m^2 + \cdots + C_m^m = 2^m - 1$. We divide it into two parts, each contains 2^{m-1} and $2^{m-1} - 1$ elements respectively. Denote them as A_1 and A_2. For a fixed $(y_1, y_2, \cdots, y_m) \in F_2^m$ and a nonzero linear combination of $X_1, X_2, \cdots, X_m$, it determine a set $L(\oplus_{i=1}^m c_i X_i = $

$\oplus_{i=1}^m c_i y_i)$. We call the set *determined* by $(y_1, y_2, \cdots, y_m)$. Furthermore we call the set $L(\oplus_{i=1}^m c_i X_i = \oplus_{i=1}^m c_i y_i \oplus 1)$ the *determined complement* set induced by $(y_1, y_2, \cdots, y_m)$. For each nonzero m-bit string $(c_1, c_2, \cdots, c_m) \in F_2^m$ and $a \in F_2$, by (1) it is obvious that

$$|L(\oplus_{i=1}^m c_i X_i = a)| = 2^{m-1}, L(\oplus_{i=1}^m c_i X_i = 0) \cup L(\oplus_{i=1}^m c_i X_i = 1) = F_2^m. \quad (2)$$

Lemma 2. *[7] Let notations defined as above. For an arbitrary m-bit string $Y = (y_1, y_2, \cdots, y_m) \in F_2^m$, then the collection of determined sets of A_1 equals to the collection of determined complement sets of A_2 added $2^{m-1}Y$. Note again that we call the two collections are equal if and only if the elements and its multiplicity in the two collections are identical.*

In [7], relations between almost resilient function and its component functions were presented.

Theorem 1. *Let $F = (f_1, \cdots, f_m)$ be a function from F_2^n to F_2^m, where n and m are integers with $n \geq m \geq 1$, and each f_i is a function on F_2^n. If F is an ε-almost (n, m, k)-resilient function, then each nonzero combination of $f_1, \cdots, f_m$*

$$f(x) = \bigoplus_{i=1}^m c_i f_i(x)$$

is a $2^{m-1}\varepsilon$-almost $(n, 1, k)$-resilient function.

Theorem 2. *Let $F = (f_1, \cdots, f_m)$ be a function from F_2^n to F_2^m, where n and m are integers with $n \geq m \geq 1$, and each f_i is a function on F_2^n. If each nonzero combination of $f_1, \cdots, f_m$*

$$f(x) = \bigoplus_{i=1}^m c_i f_i(x)$$

is an ε-almost $(n, 1, k)$-resilient function, then F is a $\frac{2^m-1}{2^m-1}\varepsilon$-almost (n, m, k)-resilient function , where $x = (x_1, \cdots, x_n) \in F_2^n$.

Remark. By Theorem 1 for any ε-almost (n, m, k)-resilient function $F=(f_1,..., f_m)$ every nonzero linear combination of f_i is an $2^{m-1}\varepsilon$-almost $(n, 1, k)$-resilient function. But by Theorem 2 if every nonzero linear combination is an $2^{m-1}\varepsilon$-almost $(n, 1, k)$-resilient function then $(f_1, ..., f_m)$ is $(2^m - 1)\varepsilon$-almost (n, m, k)-resilient function. Thus starting from ε-almost (n, m, k)-resilient function one can obtain an $(2^m - 1)\varepsilon$-almost (n, m, k)-resilient function. This gap between ε and $(2^m - 1)\varepsilon$ implies that both statements are not equally strong. Compared with Proposition 1 we could see although the almost resilient function only bias ε from resilient function in definition it is difficult for us to prove the same proposition of resilient function in almost case.

A construction based on a balanced almost $(n, 1, k)$-resilient function was presented in [7].

Theorem 3. *Let f be a balanced ε-almost $(n, 1, k)$-resilient function, then*

$$g(X, Y, Z) = (f(X) \oplus f(Y), f(Y) \oplus f(Z))$$

is a balanced $\frac{9}{2}\varepsilon$-almost $(3n, 2, 2k + 1)$-resilient function.

But the proof of the theorem is tedious. Here we present a direct proof and improve the result.

Theorem 4. *Let f be a balanced ε-almost $(n, 1, k)$-resilient function, then*

$$g(X, Y, Z) = (f(X) \oplus f(Y), f(Y) \oplus f(Z))$$

is a balanced $\frac{3}{2}\varepsilon$-almost $(3n, 2, 2k + 1)$-resilient function.

Proof. Denote $h(X, Y) = f(X) \oplus f(Y)$. It is obvious that $h(X, Y)$ is balanced. We first prove that

$$|Pr(h(X, Y) = 1 | x_{i_1} \cdots x_{i_r} y_{i_{r+1}} \cdots y_{i_{2k+1}}) - \frac{1}{2}| \le \varepsilon$$

for any $2k + 1$ positions $x_i, 1 \le i \le r$ and $y_j, r + 1 \le j \le 2k + 1$.

Without loss of generality, we may assume $r \le k$. Then by Lemma 1, for any $a \in F_2$,

$$|Pr(f(X) = a | x_{i_1} \cdots x_{i_r}) - \frac{1}{2}| \le \varepsilon.$$

By notation (1), for any $a \in F_2$, we have

$$2^{n-r-1} - 2^{n-r}\varepsilon \le |L(f(X) = a | x_{i_1} \cdots x_{i_r})| \le 2^{n-r-1} + 2^{n-r}\varepsilon.$$

Because we are taking a direct sum of $f(X)$ and $f(Y)$, therefore we can deduce the bounds for the $|L(f(X) \oplus f(Y) = 1 | x_{i_1} \cdots x_{i_r} y_{i_{r+1}} \cdots y_{i_{2k+1}})|$ by multiplying the previous inequality for $|L(f(X) = a | x_{i_1} \cdots x_{i_r})|$ with the weight of $\{f(Y) | y_{i_{r+1}} \cdots y_{i_{2k+1}}\}$. That is

$$2^{n-(2k+1-r)}(2^{n-r-1} - 2^{n-r}\varepsilon) \le |L(f(X) \oplus f(Y) = 1 | x_{i_1} \cdots x_{i_r} y_{i_{r+1}} \cdots y_{i_{2k+1}})|$$

$$\le 2^{n-(2k+1-r)}(2^{n-r-1} + 2^{n-r}\varepsilon).$$

i.e.

$$|Pr(h(X, Y) = 1 | x_{i_1} \cdots x_{i_r} y_{i_{r+1}} \cdots y_{i_{2k+1}}) - \frac{1}{2}| \le \varepsilon.$$

So $h(X, Y)$ is a balanced ε-almost $(2n, 1, 2k + 1)$ resilient function. The case $f(Y) \oplus f(Z)$ and $f(X) \oplus f(Z)$ can be similarly proved. And each of them is balanced, so g is also balanced. By Theorem 2, the proof is completed.

We can generalize above result as follows.

Theorem 5. *Let f_i be a balanced ε_i-almost $(n_i, 1, k_i)$-resilient function, $1 \le i \le l$, G be a $[l, m, d]$ linear code. Then*

$$F(X_1, X_2, \cdots, X_l) = (f_1(X_1), f_2(X_2), \cdots, f_l(X_l))G^T$$

is a balanced $\frac{2^m - 1}{2^m - 1}\varepsilon$-almost $(\sum_{i=1}^{l} n_i, m, dk + d - 1)$-resilient function, where $k = min_{1 \le i \le l} k_i$ and $\varepsilon = max_{1 \le i \le l} \varepsilon_i$.

Proof. Assume that $G = [a_{ij}], 1 \leq i \leq m, 1 \leq j \leq l$. Then

$$F = (\oplus_{i=1}^{l} a_{1i} f_i, \oplus_{i=1}^{l} a_{2i} f_i, \cdots, \oplus_{i=1}^{l} a_{mi} f_i).$$

For any nonzero linear combination of its component functions of F, we have

$$\oplus_{j=1}^{m} c_j (\oplus_{i=1}^{l} a_{ji} f_i) = \oplus_{i=1}^{l} f_i (\oplus_{j=1}^{m} c_j a_{ji}).$$

where $c = (c_1, \cdots, c_m) \in F_2^m$ is a nonzero vector. And note that minimum weight of code of G is d. So at least d functions of $f_1, \cdots, f_l$ appear in above formulation. Similar to the proof in Theorem 4, we known that any nonzero linear combination of its component functions of F is ε-almost $(\sum_{i=1}^{l} n_i, 1, dk + d - 1)$-resilient function. By Theorem 2, we complete the proof.

Corollary 1. *If there exit an $[l, m, d]$ linear code and ε-almost $(n, 1, k)$-resilient function, then an $\frac{2^m - 1}{2^{m-1}} \varepsilon$-almost $(ln, m, dk + d - 1)$-resilient function must exist.*

If we take $f_1 = f_2 = f_3 = f$ and

$$G = \begin{bmatrix} 1 & 1 & 0 \\ 0 & 1 & 1 \end{bmatrix},$$

then Theorem 4 may be regarded as a corollary of Theorem 5.

Theorem 6. *Let $F = (f_1, \cdots, f_m)$ be ε_1-almost (n_1, m, t_1)-resilient function and $G = (g_1, \cdots, g_m)$ be ε_2-almost (n_2, m, t_2)-resilient function. Then $F(X) \oplus G(Y) = (f_1(x) \oplus g_1(y), \cdots, f_m(x) \oplus g_m(y))$ is ε-almost $(n_1 + n_2, m, t_1 + t_2 + 1)$-resilient function, where $\varepsilon = max(\varepsilon_1, \varepsilon_2)$.*

Proof. By definition, we need to prove that

$$|Pr(F(X) \oplus G(Y) = \eta | x_{i_1} \cdots x_{i_r} y_{i_{r+1}} \cdots y_{i_{t_1+t_2+1}}) - \frac{1}{2^m}| \leq \varepsilon$$

holds for arbitrary chosen $\eta \in F_2^m$ and for any $t_1 + t_2 + 1$ positions $x_i, 1 \leq i \leq r$ and $y_i, r + 1 \leq i \leq t_1 + t_2 + 1$.

Without loss of generality, assume that $r \leq t_1$. Then for arbitrary $G(Y) = \alpha$, there exist exactly one $\beta \in F_2^m$ such that $F(X) = \beta$ and $F(X) + \alpha = \eta$. For $r \leq t_1$, we have

$$|Pr(F(X) = \beta | x_{i_1} \cdots x_{i_r}) - \frac{1}{2^m}| \leq \varepsilon.$$

i.e.

$$2^{n_1-r-m} - 2^{n_1-r} \varepsilon \leq |L(F(X) = \beta | x_{i_1} \cdots x_{i_r})| \leq 2^{n_1-r-m} + 2^{n_1-r} \varepsilon.$$

So we have

$$2^{n_2-(t_1+t_2+1-r)}(2^{n_1-r-m} - 2^{n_1-r} \varepsilon) \leq |L(F(X) \oplus G(Y) = \eta | x_{i_1} \cdots x_{i_r}$$

$$y_{i_{r+1}} \cdots y_{i_{t_1+t_2+1}})| \leq 2^{n_2-(t_1+t_2+1-r)}(2^{n_1-r-m} + 2^{n_1-r} \varepsilon).$$

That is

$$2^{n_1+n_2-(t_1+t_2+1)-m} - 2^{n_1+n_2-(t_1+t_2+1)}\varepsilon \leq |L(F(X) \oplus G(Y) = \eta|x_{i_1} \cdots x_{i_r}$$

$$y_{i_{r+1}} \cdots y_{i_{t_1+t_2+1}})| \leq 2^{n_1+n_2-(t_1+t_2+1)-m} + 2^{n_1+n_2-(t_1+t_2+1)}\varepsilon.$$

Thus we know that $F \oplus G$ is ε-almost $(n_1 + n_2, m, t_1 + t_2 + 1)$-resilient function. The conclusion of Theorem 6 can be slightly generalized with a similar proof.

Theorem 7. *Let* $F_i(X)$, $1 \leq i \leq l$, *be* ε_i-*almost* (n_i, m, t_i)-*resilient function. Then* $\oplus F_i(X_i)$ *is an* ε-*almost* $(\sum_{i=1}^{l} n_i, m, \sum_{i=1}^{l} t_i + l - 1)$*resilient function,where* $\varepsilon = max_{1 \leq i \leq l}\varepsilon_i$.

The Theorem 4.1 in [8] could be generalized to almost case.

Theorem 8. *Let* $F(X)$ *be an* ε-*almost* (n, m, t) -*resilient function and* G *be a* $[N, k, d]$ *linear code. Then*

$$H(X_1, X_2, \cdots, X_N) = (F(X_1), F(X_2), \cdots, F(X_N))G^T$$

is an $\frac{2^{km}-1}{2^{km-m}}\varepsilon$-*almost* $(nN, mk, d(t+1) - 1)$-*resilient function.*

Proof. The proof is similar to that of [8]. The only difference is that any nonzero linear combination of component functions of $F(X)$ is an $2^{m-1}\varepsilon$-almost $(n, 1, t)$ -resilient function by Theorem 1. By Theorem 2 again, the proof is completed.

Just as we point out in the above remark , the gap between Theorem 1 and 2 is responsible for the increasing of ε in former secondary constructions. So although Theorem 5 may be seemed as a special case of Theorem 8 (let m=1), we would prefer to Theorem 5 in secondary construction of almost resilient function under the present condition.

4   Spectral Characterization of ε-Almost $(n, 1, k)$-Resilient Functions

As we have described in the last paragraph of Section 3 and Proposition 3, we are interest in balanced ε-almost $(n, 1, k)$-CI functions , i.e. ε-almost $(n, 1, k)$-resilient functions. Furthermore as we have known that the algebraic degree and correlation immune order is incompatible, almost CI function is also proposed to avoid this dilemma when it was used as combination or filter function in stream cipher.

Some constructions of almost CI functions had been presented in [11].

Theorem 9. *[11] Let* f *be a* k *order CI function and* g *be a functions such that* $wt(g)$ *is a little number. Then* $h = f \oplus g$ *is a* $\frac{3+2^{k+1}}{2^n}wt(g)$-*almost* $(n,1,k)$-*CI function.*

Theorem 10. *[11] Let* f_1 *be a balanced* ε_1-*almost* $(n, 1, k)$-*CI function and* f_2 *be a balanced* ε_2-*almost* $(n, 1, k)$-*CI function. Then* $f(x_1, \cdots, x_n, x_{n+1}) = x_{n+1}f_1 \oplus (1 \oplus x_{n+1})f_2$ *is a balanced* ε-*almost* $(n + 1, 1, k)$-*CI function,where* $\varepsilon = max(\varepsilon_1, \varepsilon_2)$.

We could see that it is easy to obtain an almost balanced CI function by modifying a CI function slightly. In this way we may derive many constructions.

It is well known that f is a $(n, 1, k)$-CI function if and only if each $f \bigoplus \oplus_{i=1}^{n} a_i x_i$ is a balanced function for all $1 \leq wt(\alpha) \leq k$, $\alpha = (a_1, a_2, \cdots, a_n) \in F_2^n$. It can be restated in the word of walsh transform, which is the well-known Xiao-Massey theorem. In the almost case, Yixian Yan [11] presented the following result.

Theorem 11. *Let f be an ε -almost $(n, 1, k)$-CI function, then*

$$|Pr(f(X) \bigoplus \oplus_{i=1}^{n} a_i x_i = 1) - \frac{1}{2}| \leq \varepsilon$$

for any $1 \leq wt(\alpha) \leq k$, $\alpha = (a_1, a_2, \cdots, a_n) \in F_2^n$.

It means that for an ε -almost $(n, 1, k)$-CI function the function $f \bigoplus \oplus_{i=1}^{n} a_i x_i$ should be almost balanced for all α, $1 \leq wt(\alpha) \leq k$. Now Let us consider the opposite direction, i.e. if a function f such that $f \bigoplus \oplus_{i=1}^{n} a_i x_i$ is almost balanced for all $\alpha, 1 \leq wt(\alpha) \leq k$, is the function f an almost $(n, 1, k)$-CI function? It is an interesting problem because if it holds we will be able to identify an almost CI function by computing its walsh spectra. Firstly in the case $k = 1$ and f is balanced, we have the following lemma.

Lemma 3. *Let f be a function from F_2^n to F_2 . If f is balanced and*

$$|Pr(f(X) \oplus x_i = 1) - \frac{1}{2}| \leq \varepsilon$$

holds for any $1 \leq i \leq n$ if and only if f is an ε -almost $(n, 1, 1)$-CI function.

Proof. By Theorem 11, the sufficiency is obvious. Let us prove the necessity. Without lost of generality, we assume $i = 1$. Denote $P_{ij} = Pr(f(X) = i | x_1 = j), 0 \leq i, j \leq 1$. It is easy to verify that

$$P_{00} + P_{01} = 2Pr(f(x) = 0), P_{10} + P_{11} = 2Pr(f(x) = 1), \tag{3}$$

$$P_{00} + P_{10} = P_{01} + P_{11} = 1. \tag{4}$$

By the condition of the lemma, we have

$$|Pr(f(X) \oplus x_1 = 1) - \frac{1}{2}| \leq \varepsilon.$$

Furthermore,

$$Pr(f(X) \oplus x_1 = 1) = Pr(f(X) = 1, x_1 = 0) + Pr(f(X) = 0, x_1 = 1) = \frac{1}{2}(P_{10} + P_{01}).$$

Hence,

$$1 - 2\varepsilon \leq P_{10} + P_{01} \leq 1 + 2\varepsilon. \tag{5}$$

From (3) and (5), we have

$$1 - 2\varepsilon + 2Pr(f(X) = 1) \leq P_{10} + P_{01} + P_{10} + P_{11} \leq 1 + 2\varepsilon + 2Pr(f(X) = 1),$$

$$1 - 2\varepsilon + 2Pr(f(X) = 1) \leq 2P_{10} + P_{01} + P_{11} \leq 1 + 2\varepsilon + 2Pr(f(X) = 1).$$

By (4),
$$-\varepsilon \le P_{10} - Pr(f(X) = 1) \le \varepsilon.$$
Thus,
$$|Pr(f(X) = 1|x_1 = 0) - Pr(f(x) = 1)| \le \varepsilon.$$
Similarly we can prove
$$|Pr(f(X) = 1|x_i = a) - Pr(f(x) = 1)| \le \varepsilon, \text{for any } 1 \le i \le n, a \in F_2. \quad (6)$$
For f is balanced,
$$|Pr(f(X) = 1|x_i = a) - \frac{1}{2}| \le \varepsilon.$$

Thus the proof is completed.

Now we prove the main result.

Theorem 12. *Let f be a function from F_2^n to F_2 . If f is balanced and*
$$|Pr(f(X) \bigoplus \oplus c_i x_i = 1) - \frac{1}{2}| \le \varepsilon$$
holds for any $c = (c_1, c_2, \cdots, c_n) \in F_2^n$ and $1 \le wt(c) \le k$. Then f is an $(2^k - 1)\varepsilon$-almost $(n, 1, k)$-resilient function.

Proof. We prove the theorem in three steps.

1. For a fixed nonzero vector $c \in F_2^n$,
$$|Pr(f(X) \bigoplus \oplus c_i x_i = 1) - \frac{1}{2}| \le \varepsilon,$$
then we have
$$|Pr(\oplus c_i x_i = 1|f(X)) - \frac{1}{2}| \le \varepsilon. \quad (7)$$

Note that $c \ne (0, 0, \cdots, 0)$ and f is balanced. The proof of step 1 is similar to that of Lemma 3.

2. If
$$|Pr(\oplus_{i=1}^k c_i x_i|f(X)) - \frac{1}{2}| \le \varepsilon,$$
then we have
$$|Pr(x_1 \cdots x_k|f(X)) - \frac{1}{2^k}| \le \frac{2^k - 1}{2^{k-1}}\varepsilon. \quad (8)$$

Divide all the nonzero linear combinations of $x_1, \cdots, x_k$ into two part A_1 and A_2, such that $|A_1| = 2^{k-1}$ and $|A_2| = 2^{k-1} - 1$. For any fixed $\alpha = (a_1, \cdots, a_k) \in F_2^k$, by Lemma 2, we have
$$\sum_{c \in A_1} |L(\oplus c_i x_i = c_i a_i|f(X))| = \sum_{c' \in A_2} |L(\oplus c_i' x_i = c_i' a_i \oplus 1|f(X))|$$
$$+ 2^{k-1}|L((x_1, \cdots, x_k) = (a_1, \cdots, a_k)|f(X))|. \quad (9)$$

By the condition of theorem and step 1, we know (7) holds for any nonzero vector $c = (c_1, c_2, \cdots, c_n) \in F_2^n$ and $1 \leq wt(c) \leq k$. So (7) holds for any nonzero vector $c \in F_2^k$.

By

$$2^{k-1}(\frac{1}{2} - \varepsilon) \leq \sum_{c \in A_1} Pr(\oplus c_i x_i | f(X)) \leq 2^{k-1}(\frac{1}{2} + \varepsilon),$$

$$(2^{k-1} - 1)(\frac{1}{2} - \varepsilon) \leq \sum_{c' \in A_2} Pr(\oplus c_i' x_i | f(X)) \leq (2^{k-1} - 1)(\frac{1}{2} + \varepsilon),$$

and (9), we have

$$\frac{1}{2} - (2^k - 1)\varepsilon \leq 2^{k-1} Pr((x_1, \cdots, x_k) = (a_1, \cdots, a_k) | f(X)) \leq \frac{1}{2} + (2^k - 1)\varepsilon.$$

That is

$$|Pr((x_1, \cdots, x_k) = (a_1, \cdots, a_k) | f(X)) - \frac{1}{2^k}| \leq \frac{2^k - 1}{2^{k-1}}\varepsilon.$$

3. It is easy to verified that

$$Pr(f(X) | x_1 \cdots x_k) = 2^{k-1} Pr(x_1 \cdots x_k | f(X)).$$

So by (8) we have

$$|Pr(f(X) | x_1 \cdots x_k) - \frac{1}{2}| = 2^{k-1}|Pr(x_1 \cdots x_k | f(X)) - \frac{1}{2^k}| \leq (2^k - 1)\varepsilon.$$

Thus we have done.

Corollary 2. *Let f be a function from F_2^n to F_2. If $S_f(0) = 0$ and $|S_f(w)| \leq 2^{n+1}\varepsilon$ for any $w \in F_2^n, 1 \leq wt(w) \leq k$, then f is an $(2^k - 1)\varepsilon$-almost $(n, 1, k)$-resilient function.*

Proof. Note that $|Pr(f(X) \bigoplus \oplus w_i x_i = 1) - \frac{1}{2}| \leq \varepsilon$ holds if and only if $-2^n \varepsilon + 2^{n-1} \leq wt(f(X) \oplus w \cdot X) \leq 2^n \varepsilon + 2^{n-1}$. And f is balanced if and only if $S_f(0) = 0$. By $S_f(w) = \sum_{x \in F_2^n} (-1)^{f(x) \oplus w \cdot x} = 2^n - 2wt(f(x) \oplus w \cdot x)$ and Theorem 12, the result is obtained.

By Corollary 2, it is convenient for us to identify an almost $(n, 1, k)$-resilient function by computing its walsh spectra.

5   Conclusion

In this paper, some constructions of almost resilient function are presented. For the relation between almost resilient function and large set of almost independent sample space, the constructions of balanced almost resilient function are concerned. As almost $(n, 1, k)$-resilient function play an important role in the secondary construction, we conclude some constructions methods. Especially we prove it is feasible to determine weather a function is an almost $(n, 1, k)$-resilient function by computing its walsh spectra, which can be regard as the generalization of Xiao-Massey theorem in the almost case to a certain extent.

Acknowledgements

The authors wish to thank the referees for their comments and suggestions that helped to improved the correspondence. This work was supported by the National Natural Science Foundation of China (No.60373059), the National Research Foundation for the Doctoral Program of Higher Education of China (No.20040013007) and the Major Research Plan of the National Natural Science Foundation of China(Grant No. 90604023).

References

1. B.Chor, O.Goldreich, J.Håstad, J.Friedman, S.Rudich, and R.Smoledsky. The bit extraction problem or t-resilient functions. *IEEE Symp. on Foundations of Computer Science*, 1985, Vol.26, pp.396-407.
2. K.Kurosawa, T.Johansson,D.Stinson. Almost k-wise independent sample spaces and their applications. *J.Cryptology*, 2001, Vol.14, no.4, pp.231-253.
3. J.Naor, M.Naor. Small bias probality spaces:efficient constructions and applications. *SIAM Journal on Computing* 1993, Vol.22, pp.838-856.
4. K.C.Gupta, P.Sarkar. Improved construction of nonlinear resilient S - Boxes. *IEEE Tran. on Info. Theory*, 2005, Jan., Vol.51, No.1, pp.339-348.
5. M.N.Wegman, J.L.Carter. New hash functions and their use in authentication and set equality. *Journal of Computer and System Sciences* ,1981, Vol.22, PP.265-279.
6. K.Kurosawa, R.Matsumoto. Almost security of cryptographic Boolean functions,*IEEE Tran. on Info. Theory*, 2004, Vol.50, No.11, PP.2752-2761.
7. Pinhui Ke, Tailin Liu, Qiaoyan Wen. Construction of almost resilient functions. *Cryptology and Network Security: 4th International Conference, CANS 2005*,Yvo G. Desmedt et al. ed. LNCS 3810, Springer-Verlag 2005, pp.236-246.
8. Chuankun Wu, Ed Dawson. On construction of resilient functions. *Information Security and Privacy,Proceedings of First Australasian Conference*, LNCS 1172, Springer-Verlag 1996, pp.79-86.
9. Xianmo Zhang, Yuliang Zheng. Cryptographically resilient functions. *IEEE Tran. on Info. theory*, 1997, Vol.43. No.5, PP.1740-1747.
10. Guozhen Xiao, J.Massey. A special characterization of correlation immune combining functions,*IEEE Tran. on Info. theory*,1988, Vol.34, PP.569-571.
11. Yixian Yan, Xuduan Lin. Coding theory and cryptography. People post and telecomunication publisher, 1992. (in chinese).

Real Perfect Contrast Visual Secret Sharing Schemes with Reversing

Ching-Nung Yang, Chung-Chun Wang, and Tse-Shih Chen

Department of Computer Science and Information Engineering,
National Dong Hwa University
#1, Sec. 2, Da Hsueh Rd., Hualien, Taiwan
cnyang@mail.ndhu.edu.tw

Abstract. The visual secret sharing (VSS for short) scheme is a secret image sharing scheme. A secret image is visually revealed from overlapping shadow images without additional computations. However, the contrast of reconstructed image is much lost. By means of the reversing operation (reverse black and white), Viet and Kurosawa used the traditional VSS scheme to design a VSS scheme which the secret image is almost perfectly reconstructed. Two drawbacks of the Viet-Kurosawa scheme are: (1) one can only reconstruct an almost ideal-contrast image but not an ideal-contrast image (2) the used traditional VSS scheme must be a perfect black scheme. This paper shows a real perfect contrast VSS scheme such that black and white pixels are all perfectly reconstructed within finite runs, no matter what type (perfect black or non-perfect black) of the traditional VSS scheme is.

Keywords: Visual secret sharing scheme, secret sharing scheme, ideal contrast.

1 Introduction

Naor-Shamir (k, n) VSS scheme [1] is to share the secret image into n shadow images (shadows) by dividing a pixel in the secret image to m black(B)/white(W) sub pixels in each shadow. When decrypting, any k out of n participants can reconstruct the secret image by stacking their shadows. In the reconstructed image, the '$m-h$'B'h'W and '$m-l$'B'l'W sub pixels are used to represent the white and black secret pixels, respectively, where h and l are the whiteness of the white and black secret pixel and $m > h > l \geq 0$. For a perfect black VSS (PBVSS) scheme ($l=0$), the black pixel is perfectly reconstructed but the white pixel is not. For the specific h and l, Eisen and Stinson [2] had found the minimum m to achieve the better contrast. However, since $m > h > 0$, '$m-h$'B'h'W is impossibly changed into 'm'W anyway and thus we cannot reconstruct an ideal-contrast image, i.e., all black and white pixels are perfectly reconstructed.

   Consider another totally different approach to improve the contrast, by more runs of stacking shadows and reversing operation (a non-cryptographic operation), Viet and Kurosawa used the PBVSS scheme to design an almost ideal VSS scheme [3]. Note that, in fact, many copy machines have the reversing operation that the black (white) color is changed into the white (black) color. For the Viet-Kurosawa scheme,

J. Zhou, M. Yung, and F. Bao (Eds.): ACNS 2006, LNCS 3989, pp. 433–447, 2006.
© Springer-Verlag Berlin Heidelberg 2006

'm'B sub pixels are reconstructed for the black secret pixel and 'm'W sub pixels are reconstructed for almost all white secret pixels. The more runs the more 'm'W sub pixels for the white secret pixels. However, the ideal whiteness cannot be achieved even for large number of runs. So we call the Viet-Kurosawa scheme an almost contrast VSS scheme. Afterwards, Cimato et al. [4] achieved the ideal-contrast image within m finite runs. In this paper, a cyclic shift operation of sub pixels in the shadow image is used to design a real perfect contrast VSS (RPCVSS) with an ideal-contrast image when finishing ($m-h+1$) finite runs. Moreover, for even m and $h=m/2$ the number of runs is reduced to two. Besides, the shift operation can also be applied to design a RPCVSS scheme based on the non-perfect black VSS (NPBVSS) scheme with odd '$h-l$'.

The rest of this paper is organized as follows. Section 2 reviews the previous works. In Section 3 we describe the proposed RPCVSS schemes based on the PBVSS and NPBVSS schemes, respectively. Experimental results, discussion and comparison are given in Section 4, and we draw our conclusion in Section 5.

2 Previous Works

2.1 Naor-Shamir VSS Scheme

Suppose that B_1 and B_0 are the black and white $n \times m$ basis Boolean matrices $A = [a_{ij}]$, where $a_{ij} = 1$ if and only if the jth sub pixel in the ith shadow is black, otherwise $a_{ij} = 0$ for the (k, n) VSS with the pixel expansion m. C_1 and C_0 are their corresponding black and white sets including all matrices obtained by permuting the columns of B_1 and B_0. The dealer randomly chooses one row of the matrix in the set C_1 (resp. C_0) to a relative shadow for sharing a black (resp. white) pixel. The chosen matrix defines the gray level of the m sub pixels in the reconstructed image.

When any k or more shadows are stacked, we view a reconstructed image whose black sub pixels are represented by the Boolean 'OR' of the corresponding rows in A.

The gray level of this reconstructed image is proportional to the Hamming weight of the ORed m-vector V. If $H(V) \geq (m-l)$, this gray level is interpreted by the user's visual system as black, and if $H(V) \leq (m-h)$, the result is interpreted as white. For example, in a (2, 2) VSS scheme, let black and white matrices be $B_1 = \begin{bmatrix} 0 & 1 \\ 1 & 0 \end{bmatrix}$, $B_0 = \begin{bmatrix} 0 & 1 \\ 0 & 1 \end{bmatrix}$ and then their corresponding sets are $C_1 = \left\{ \begin{bmatrix} 0 & 1 \\ 1 & 0 \end{bmatrix}, \begin{bmatrix} 1 & 0 \\ 0 & 1 \end{bmatrix} \right\}$, $C_0 = \left\{ \begin{bmatrix} 0 & 1 \\ 0 & 1 \end{bmatrix}, \begin{bmatrix} 1 & 0 \\ 1 & 0 \end{bmatrix} \right\}$. For sharing a black secret pixel in the recovered image, the dealer may randomly choose the first matrix or second matrix in the black set C_1. Suppose choosing the first matrix $\begin{bmatrix} 0 & 1 \\ 1 & 0 \end{bmatrix}$, we then use 1W1B in the first shadow and 1B1W in the second shadow. The stacked result of the black secret pixel is 2B, but otherwise it is observed that the stacked result of white secret pixel is 1B1W or 1W1B. Therefore, we can view the recovered secret due to the different contrast, while we cannot get any information from any one shadow because every pixel is represented as 1B1W or 1W1B sub pixels in shadows.

Formal contrast and security conditions for (k, n) VSS schemes are shown below [1]:

(1) Contrast condition:

For any r ($\geq k$) shadows, $s_{i_1}, \ldots, s_{i_r}$, the ORed V of rows $i_1, i_2, \ldots, i_r$ of matrices in C_1 (resp. C_0) satisfies $H(V) \geq (m-l)$ (resp. $H(V) \leq (m-h)$).

(2) Security condition:

For any r ($<k$) shadows, $s_{i_1}, \ldots, s_{i_r}$, the two collections of $r \times m$ matrices obtained by restricting each $n \times m$ matrices in C_1 and C_0 to rows $i_1, i_2, \ldots, i_r$ are not visual in the sense that they contain the same matrices with the same frequencies.

For $l=0$, we call a VSS scheme the PBVSS scheme because the black secret pixel is all reconstructed by m black sub pixels; otherwise we call it the NPBVSS scheme. In this paper, we use (k, n, h, l, m)-VSS scheme to denote a (k, n) VSS scheme with the whiteness h, l and the pixel expansion m. Example 1 shows (k, n, h, l, m)-PBVSS and (k, n, h, l, m)-NPBVSS schemes, respectively.

Example 1. For a $(2, 2, 1, 0, 2)$-PBVSS scheme with the black and white matrices $B_1 = \begin{bmatrix} 0 & 1 \\ 1 & 0 \end{bmatrix}$ and $B_0 = \begin{bmatrix} 0 & 1 \\ 0 & 1 \end{bmatrix}$, the black secret pixel is represented as 2B sub pixels and the white pixel is 1B1W sub pixels in the reconstructed image. For a $(2, 3, 2, 1, 3)$-NPBVSS with $B_1 = \begin{bmatrix} 1 & 0 & 0 \\ 0 & 1 & 0 \\ 0 & 0 & 1 \end{bmatrix}$ and $B_0 = \begin{bmatrix} 1 & 0 & 0 \\ 1 & 0 & 0 \\ 1 & 0 & 0 \end{bmatrix}$, the black secret pixel is 2B1W sub pixels and the white secret pixel is 1B2W sub pixels in the reconstructed image. Table 1 shows the diagrammatic representation for the stacked results of $(2, 2, 1, 0, 2)$-PBVSS scheme and the $(2, 3, 2, 1, 3)$-NPBVSS scheme. The whiteness percentage P_W means the whiteness percentage in all the white (or black) secret pixels for a reconstructed image.   □

Table 1. The $(2, 2, 1, 0, 2)$-PBVSS scheme and the $(2, 3, 2, 1, 3)$-NPBVSS scheme

(k, n, h, l, m)-VSS schemes	Secret pixel	Probability	Reconstructed pixel	Whiteness percentage P_W
(2, 2, 1, 0, 2)-PBVSS scheme	□	1/2		50%
		1/2		
	■	1/2		0%
		1/2		
(2, 3, 2, 1, 3)-NPBVSS scheme	□	1/3		67%
		1/3		
		1/3		
	■	1/3		33%
		1/3		
		1/3		

2.2 Almost Ideal VSS Scheme: The Viet-Kurosawa Scheme

By using the reversing operation of copy machines, Viet-Kurosawa scheme shows a novel idea to achieve the perfect reconstruction of white pixel by using a (k, n)-PBVSS scheme [3]. The sharing phase includes two steps: (1) distribution (2) reconstruction. A brief description for the Viet-Kurosawa scheme is shown as follow.

Distribution phase

Perform a (k, n)-PBVSS scheme R times independently. These n shadows, $s_1^i, \ldots, s_n^i$, are used for the ith run, $i \in [1, R]$. Finally, Participant j gets R shadows $s_j^1, \ldots, s_j^R$.

Reconstruction phase

For ith run, we first reconstruct the image T_i by stacking any k ore more shadows, $T_i = s_{i_1}^i + \ldots + s_{i_r}^i$, $i \in [1, R]$. Note that each T_i is a reconstructed image of the PBVSS scheme. To improve the contrast we perform the following operations: reverse the reconstructed image in each round and then stack them; finally reverse the stacked image again. The reconstructed image of the ith run is $\overline{\overline{T}_1 + \overline{T}_2 + \ldots + \overline{T}_i}$; for example, the final run is $\overline{\overline{T}_1 + \overline{T}_2 + \ldots + \overline{T}_R}$.

Doing more runs, the whiteness of the white secret pixel is increased. Table 2 shows a $(2, 2, 1, 0, 2)$-PBVSS scheme with reversing for two runs. The whiteness percentage of the white secret pixel is increased from 50% to 75 % and the whiteness percentage of the black secret pixel is still 0 %. The average P_W of the white secret pixel when finishing R runs is $\left(1 - (1 - h/m)^R\right)$ [3]. To achieve the percentage $\left(1 - (1 - h/m)^R\right) \approx 100\%$ (ideal contrast), the R value needs to be infinite. So there is a loss of resolution for the Viet-Kurosawa scheme within finite runs. Also, for the higher resolution, a participant needs to store more shadows.

Table 2. An almost ideal contrast VSS scheme based on $(2, 2, 1, 0, 2)$-PBVSS scheme for two runs

Secret Pixel	Probability	T_1	T_2	$U = \overline{T}_1 + \overline{T}_2$	$\overline{U}$	Whiteness percentage P_W
□	1/4					
	1/4					75%
	1/4					
	1/4					
■	1					0%

2.3 Ideal VSS Scheme: Cimato et al's Scheme

Cimato et al. [4] used reversing operation to propose an ideal contrast VSS scheme based on (n, k, h, l, m)-PBVSS scheme which the whiteness percentage of the white secret pixel P_W=100% (ideal contrast) can be achieved within m finite runs. Meantime the shadow size is not expanded. The sharing process is described below.

Distribution phase

When sharing a black (resp. white) pixel, the dealer randomly chooses one matrix form C_1 (resp. C_0) and delivers a pixel p_i, where $(p_1, \ldots, p_m)$ is located in ith row of matrix, to the s_j^i shadow for participant j. Finally, participant j gets m shadows $s_j^1, \ldots, s_j^m$ for m runs. Note that a secret pixel is represented by a pixel in the shadow, and hence the shadow size is same to the original image.

Reconstruction phase

For ith run, we first reconstruct the image α_i by stacking any k ore more shadows, $\alpha_i = s_{i_1}^i + \ldots + s_{i_r}^i$, $i \in [1, m]$. Using reversing and stacking to get $\beta = \overline{\alpha_1} + \overline{\alpha_2} + \ldots + \overline{\alpha_i}$, the reconstructed image is then obtained by reversing again, i.e, $\overline{\beta}$.

Table 3 shows the whiteness percentage of the white secret pixel can be improved to 100% within two runs. It is evident that the whiteness percentage of the black secret pixel is still 0% because we use the PBVSS scheme. So it is a really ideal contrast VSS scheme when finishing m runs.

Table 3. The ideal contrast VSS scheme based on (2, 2, 1, 0, 2)-PBVSS scheme for two runs

Secret Pixel	Probability	α_1	α_2	$\beta = \overline{\alpha_1} + \overline{\alpha_2}$	$\overline{\beta}$	Whiteness percentage P_W
☐	1/2	☐	■	■	☐	100%
	1/2	■	☐	■	☐	
■	1	■	■	☐	■	0%

3 The Proposed RPCVSS Schemes

In this section, two RPVCC schemes based on PBVSS scheme and one RPVCC scheme based on NPBVSS scheme are proposed. All schemes achieve the real perfect contrast, i.e., the whiteness percentage of white and black secret pixels are 100% and 0%, respectively, within finite runs.

3.1 RPCVSS Scheme Based on Perfect Black VSS Scheme

For the description of the construction, we first define a matrix operation $\Gamma(\cdot)$ that cyclically shifts right one sub pixel in every m sub pixels (for a secret pixel) in the shadow image.

Let the shadow image s be represented as a matrix $[s_{ijk}]$ as follows, where s_{ijk} means the secret pixel s_{ij} in the $(W \times H)$-pixel secret image replaced by m sub pixels $(s_{ij1}, s_{ij2}, \ldots, s_{ijm})$, where $i \in [1, H]$, $j \in [1, W]$, $k \in [1, m]$. Then the matrix operation $\Gamma([s_{ijk}]) = [\gamma(s_{ijk})]$, where $\gamma(s_{ij1}, s_{ij2}, \ldots, s_{ijm}) = (s_{ijm}, s_{ij1}, \ldots, s_{ijm-1})$.

Method A:
Distribution phase
Perform a $(n, k, h, l=0, m)$-PBVSS scheme to generate n shadows, $s_1^1, ..., s_n^1$ to n participants, for the first run. For ith run, Participant j gets the shadows $s_j^i = \Gamma(s_j^{i-1})$, $i \in [2, (m-h+1)]$. Finally a participant has $(m-h+1)$ shadows.

Reconstruction phase
Same to the Viet-Kurosawa scheme.

Theorem 1. The whiteness percentages P_W for the white and black secret pixels of the RPCVSS scheme based on Method A are 100% and 0%, respectively, when finishing $(m-h+1)$ runs.

Proof. here are '$m-h$'B'h'W sub pixels for the white secret pixel. The maximum interval between two "0" is $(m-h)$ an thus when shifting right one bit $(m-h)$ times, there is at least a white sub pixel in a same position in a white secret pixel block for these T_i images, $i=\in [1, (m-h+1)]$. Reversing and stacking will result in all black sub pixels and finally reverse again to get the pure white color. It is evident that the whiteness percentage of the black secret pixel is $P_W=0\%$ because we use the PBVSS scheme and other shadows are obtained from the shadows in the first run by shifting operation. The proof is completed.   □

For even m and $h=m/2$, the number of runs can be substantially reduced to two. From observation of the proof for Theorem 1, it is evident that if only assure a same position of at least a white sub pixel, we can reconstruct the ideal-contrast image using the same decoding way.

Method B:
Distribution phase
Perform a $(n, k, h=m/2, 0, m$: even)-PBVSS scheme to generate n shadows, $s_1^1, ..., s_n^1$ to n participants, for the first run. For the second run, Participant j gets the shadows $s_j^2 = \overline{s_j^1}$, $j \in [1, n]$. Finally a participant has only two shadows.

Reconstruction phase
Same to the Viet-Kurosawa scheme.

Theorem 2. The whiteness percentages P_w for the white and black secret pixels of the RPCVSS scheme based on Method B are 100% and 0%, respectively, when finishing two runs.

Proof. Because the two shadows for these two runs are complemented, the sub pixel in a in a white secret pixel block for T_1 and T_2 are mutually complemented. So, reversing and stacking will result in all black sub pixels in the white secret pixel and finally reverse again to get the pure white color. Same as the poof in Theorem 1, the whiteness percentage of the black secret pixel is $P_W=0\%$. The proof is completed.   □

Using the (2, 2, 1, 0, 2)-PBVSS scheme, we can design a RPCVSS scheme (Method A) with two runs (since $(m-h+1)= 2$). Table 4 shows that our RPCVSS scheme has the whiteness percentage of the white (resp. black) secret pixel $P_W=100\%$ (resp. 0%) when finishing two runs.

Table 4. The RPCVSS scheme based on (2, 2, 1, 0, 2)-PBVSS scheme for two runs

Secret Pixel	Probability	T_1	T_2	$U = \bar{T_1} + \bar{T_2}$	$\bar{U}$	Percentage of whiteness P_W
□	1/2	■□	□■	■	□□	100%
	1/2	□■	■□	■	□□	
■	1	■	■	□□	■	0%

3.2 RPCVSS Scheme Based on Non-perfect Black VSS Scheme

Both the almost ideal VSS scheme and the ideal VSS scheme [3, 4] are based on PBVSS scheme. The shift operation used in Section 3.1 can also be used to design a RPCVSS scheme based on the NPBVSS scheme. However, the difference of whiteness '$h-l$' needs to be odd number and the exclusive or (XOR) operation is required for decoding.

Generally, copy machines support reversing operation (i.e. NOT) and OR can be done by stacking shadows. By Boolean reduction, the XOR($\oplus$) operation can be reduced as $A \oplus B = \overline{(A+\bar{B})} + \overline{(\bar{A}+B)}$. Thus XOR operation can be implemented by four NOTs and three ORs.

Method C:
Distribution phase
Perform a $(n, k, h, l\neq 0, m)$-NPBVSS scheme, where '$h-l$' is odd number, to generate n shadows, $s_1^1,\ldots,s_n^1$, for the first run. For ith run, Participant j gets the shadows $s_j^i = \Gamma(s_j^{i-1})$, $i \in [2, m]$. Finally a participant has m shadows.

Reconstruction phase
Reconstruct T_i image for i-th run, $i \in [1, m]$. Use XOR operation to reconstruct $U' = T_1 \oplus \ldots \oplus T_m$. If '$m-h$' is even (i.e., '$m-l$' is odd) then the reconstructed image is U'; otherwise the reconstructed image is $\overline{U'}$.

Theorem 3. The whiteness percentages P_W for the whie and black secret pixels of the RPCVSS scheme based on Method C are 100% and 0%, respectively, when finishing m runs.

Proof. There are '$m-h$'B'h'W (resp. '$m-l$'B'l'W) sub pixels for the white (resp. black) secret pixel. When shifting right one bit m times, there is $m-h$ (resp. $m-l$) black sub pixels for the white (resp. black) secret pixels in U'. Suppose '$m-h$' is even (resp. odd), then XORing will result in all white sub pixels for the white pixels in U' (resp. $\overline{U'}$). Thus, P_W for the white secret pixel is 100%. On the other hand, even (resp. odd) 'm–h' means odd (resp. even) 'm–l' since 'h–l' is odd. It is evident that XORing operation will result in all black sub pixels for the black pixels in U' (resp. $\overline{U'}$), i.e., P_W for the black secret pixel is 0%. The proof is completed.   □

Example 2. Using a (2, 3, 2, 1, 3)-NPBVSS with $B_1 = \begin{bmatrix} 1 & 0 & 0 \\ 0 & 1 & 0 \\ 0 & 0 & 1 \end{bmatrix}$ and $B_0 = \begin{bmatrix} 1 & 0 & 0 \\ 1 & 0 & 0 \\ 1 & 0 & 0 \end{bmatrix}$ to

design our RPCVSS scheme (Method C), we show the patterns of black and white pixels for these three runs.

Suppose three sub pixels for the white secret pixel in the 1st-run shadow s_1^1 is (010) for Participant #1, where 1 and 0 denote black and white colors, so Participant #2 and Participant #3 also have the pattern (010) on s_2^1 and s_3^1. Then the patterns of sub pixels for other shadows s_1^2, s_1^3, s_2^2, s_2^3, s_3^2 and s_3^3 are determined from the following.

The patter in s_i^2 is γ(the pattern in s_i^1) = γ(010) = (001), i=1, 2, 3;

the patter in s_i^3 is γ(the pattern in s_i^2) = γ(001) = (100), i=1, 2, 3.

Suppose three sub pixels for the black secret pixel in the 1st-run shadow s_1^1 is also (010) for Participant #1, so Participant #2 and Participant #3 have the patterns (100) and (001) on s_2^1 and s_3^1, respectively. Then the patterns of sub pixels for other shadows s_1^2, s_1^3, s_2^2, s_2^3, s_3^2 and s_3^3 are determined from the following.

The patter in s_1^2 is γ(the pattern in s_1^1) = γ(010) = (001);

the patter in s_1^3 is γ(the pattern in s_1^2) = γ(001) = (100);

the patter in s_2^2 is γ(the pattern in s_2^1) = γ(100) = (010);

the patter in s_2^3 is γ(the pattern in s_2^2) = γ(010) = (001);

the patter in s_3^2 is γ(the pattern in s_3^1) = γ(001) = (100);

the patter in s_3^3 is γ(the pattern in s_3^2) = γ(100) = (010).

Table 5 shows that our RPCVSS scheme has the whiteness percentages of the white and black secret pixels are P_W=100% and 0%, respectively, when finishing three runs. We successfully implement a real perfect contrast VSS scheme from a NPBVSS scheme.   □

Note that as the Method C uses the XOR operation. For obtaining the ideal-contrast secret image it can not be implemented just by superimposing the shadows but need using XOR operations among shadows, i.e., $U' = T_1 \oplus ... \oplus T_m$. As the above description, one XOR can be implemented by 4 NOTs and 3 ORs. For example, to get $T_1 \oplus T_2$, one needs to first superimpose separately (T_1 and $\overline{T_2}$) and ($\overline{T_1}$ and T_2). Then will have to process (T_1 and $\overline{T_2}$) (resp. $\overline{T_1}$ and T_2) to get ($\overline{T_1 + \overline{T_2}}$) (resp.

$\overline{T_1+T_2}$) and then superimpose them. So, although it does not follow the traditional VSS scheme where just superimposes shadows and no additional computation is required, it still can be implemented using the copy machine with reversing function to achieve the XORed result step by step according the above procedure. Even if we do not have the copy machine with reversing function, like the Viet-Kurosawa scheme, Method C can reconstruct the secret image by stacking the shadows directly in the same way as the traditional VSS scheme. The reason is that for the same round our shadows are just obtained from the first shadow by cyclically shifting right a creation position.

Table 5. The RPCVSS scheme based on (2, 3, 2, 1, 3)-NPBVSS scheme for three runs

Secret Pixel	Probability	T_1	T_2	T_3	$U' = T_1 \oplus T_2 \oplus T_3$	$\bar{U}'$	Whiteness percentage P_W
☐	1/3	■☐☐	☐■☐	☐☐■	■■	☐☐☐	
	1/3	☐■☐	☐☐■	■☐☐	■■	☐☐☐	100%
	1/3	☐☐■	■☐☐	☐■☐	■■	☐☐☐	
■	1/3	■■☐	☐■■	■■☐	☐☐☐	■■	
	1/3	■■☐	■■☐	☐■■	☐☐☐	■■	0%
	1/3	☐■■	■☐■	■■☐	☐☐☐	■■	

4 Experimental Results and Comparison

We show experimental results of the (2, 2, 1, 0, 2)-PBVSS scheme, the (2, 2, 2, 0, 4)-PBVSS scheme and the (2, 3, 2, 1, 3)-NPBVSS scheme among the Viet-Kurosawa scheme [3], Cimato et al's scheme [4] and our proposed RPCVSS schemes. The first twos show the case of different h, and the third shows the case of NPBVSS scheme. Also, discussion and comparison for these schemes are given.

4.1 Experimental Results

Fig. 1 is the original secret image (a school badge of National Dong Hwa University). Fig. 2 (a) is our RPCVSS scheme, Fig. 2(b) is the almost ideal contrast scheme (the Viet-Kurosawa scheme) and Fig. 2(c) is the ideal contrast scheme (Cimato et al's scheme) based on the (2, 2, 1, 0, 2)-PBVSS scheme. For viewing convenience, we

Fig. 1. The original secret image

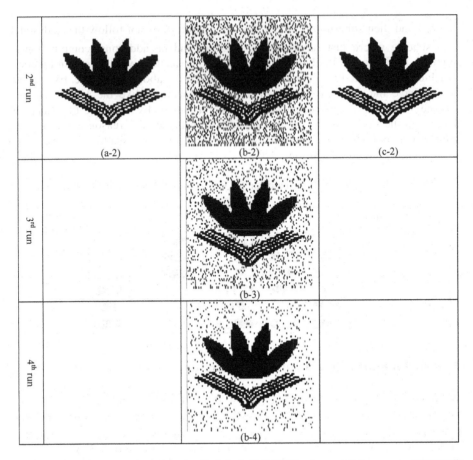

Fig. 2. Different schemes based on the (2, 2, 1, 0, 2)-PBVSS scheme (a) the proposed RPCVSS scheme (Method A) (b) the Viet-Kurosawa scheme (c) Cimato et al's scheme

arrange the reconstructed images to the same original image size without expansion. From Fig. 2(b), the reconstructed images by the Viet-Kurosawa scheme of 1, 2, 3, 4-run, it is shown that the whiteness of the white secret pixel is increased gradually. There are still noise-like random dots on the reconstructed image in Fig. 2(b-4). On the contrary, Figs. 2(a) and (c) show that the proposed scheme (Method A) and Cimato et al's scheme achieve 100% whiteness of the white secret pixel within two runs. The pixel expansion of our RPCVSS scheme is 2; however there is no pixel expansion for Cimato et al's scheme because it uses the construction nature of the probabilistic VSS schemes [5, 6].

When using (2, 2, 2, 0, 4)-PBVSS scheme, do the same experiment like Fig. 2. The results are given in Fig.3. Our scheme (Method B) still achieves 100% whiteness of the white secret pixel within two runs. According Cimato et al's construction in [4], they prepared four shadows for each participant but, in fact, only three runs are required to achieve 100% whiteness. This is due to the using of 2B2W for a white

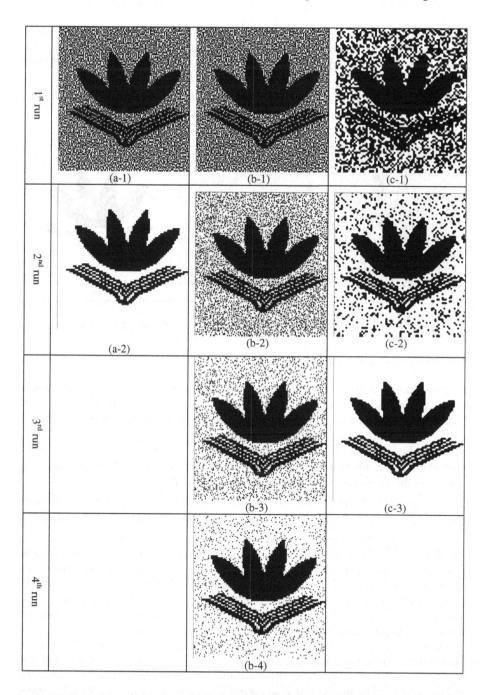

Fig. 3. Different schemes based on the (2, 2, 2, 0, 4)-PBVSS scheme (a) the proposed RPCVSS scheme (Method B) (b) the Viet-Kurosawa scheme (c) Cimato et al's scheme

secret pixel and there is at least one white sub pixel in a same position when finishing three runs. Thus, the number of runs for Cimato et al's scheme should be modified to $(m-h+1)$. In Fig. 4, we show a RPCVSS scheme based on the (2, 3, 2, 1, 2)-NPBVSS scheme (Method C). We have the perfect whiteness of the white secret pixel and perfect blackness of the black secret pixel when finishing three runs. However, we see nothing in other runs except the first and last runs due to the XOR operation.

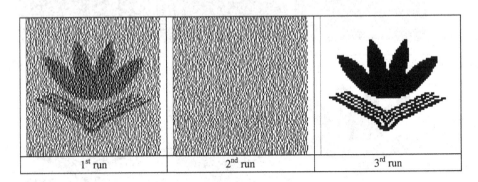

Fig. 4. The RPCVSS scheme based on the (2, 3, 2, 1, 2)-NPBVSS scheme (Method C)

4.2 Discussion and Comparison

In this section, we discuss about the security, compatibility, complexity and contrast for the R-run VSS schemes. Besides, the comparison is given for three schemes: the RPCVSS schemes, the almost ideal contrast scheme and the ideal contrast scheme.

Security: For the R-run (k, n) VSS schemes, as examples, the participants store more than one shadow for improving the contrast of the reconstructed image, e.g., the dealer needs to prepare $n \times R$ shadows, s_j^i, $i \in [1, R]$ and $j \in [1, n]$. Considering security, the first concern is that one should not get any secret information from his own shadows, $s_j^1, \ldots, s_j^R$. The Viet-Kurosawa scheme performs the VSS scheme R times independently. Cimato et al's scheme uses the concept of probabilistic scheme and delivers the elements in one row to the shadows of different runs. In the same position of m different shadows, the frequencies of black and white sub pixels are same and thus one cannot obtain any information from his own shadows. The proposed RPCVSS schemes only perform the shift operation on the first shadow to generate other shadows. Therefore, all three schemes satisfy the first security concern, i.e., there is no any mutual information among their own shadows.

The second concern is that whether stacking any k or more shadows of the different run from the different participants, the secret information should be kept secret or not. For this scenario, the leak of secret information does not affect the secrecy of secret sharing scheme. The reason is that when one discloses the shadow, in fact, he agrees to share the secret. So, at this time, if one can see the secret image it does not compromise the secrecy. Unlike the Viet-Kurosawa scheme performing the VSS scheme R times independently, Cimato et al's scheme and the RPCVSS schemes may have the secret image when stacking shadows of different runs. Considering these two schemes constructed from (2, 2, 1, 0, 2)-PBVSS scheme, our cyclic shift operation and Cimato et al's delivering elements of one row to different shadows are just right changing the black and white color in the stacking result. For example, for the RPCVSS scheme, when stacking the shadows of different runs the black and white matrices in the stacked result are $B_1' = \begin{bmatrix} 0 & 1 \\ 0 & 1 \end{bmatrix}$ and $B_0' = \begin{bmatrix} 0 & 1 \\ 1 & 0 \end{bmatrix}$ which same to the white and black matrices $B_0 = \begin{bmatrix} 0 & 1 \\ 0 & 1 \end{bmatrix}$ and $B_1 = \begin{bmatrix} 0 & 1 \\ 1 & 0 \end{bmatrix}$ in a (2, 2, 1, 0, 2)-PBVSS scheme. Fig. 5 shows this situation. Both schemes are secure even though Figs. 5(a) and (b) reveal the secret.

Compatibility: Even if we do not have the copy machine with reversing operation, the Viet-Kurosawa scheme could reconstruct the image by stacking the shadows directly. We call the Viet-Kurosawa scheme fully compatible to the traditional VSS scheme. It is evident that the proposed RPCVSS schemes and Cimato et al's scheme also have the compatibility (see Fig. 2 ~ Fig. 4). However, in [4], another construction method based on binary secret sharing scheme and Boolean function method [7, 8] was proposed for reducing the number of shadows to $\lfloor \log(n-k+2) \rfloor + 1$ (lower bound). The scheme does not hold the compatibility. For example an ideal contrast (k, k) VSS scheme in [4] only needs one shadow and one run to achieve the ideal contrast by XORing these shadows but get nothing when stacking them directly. Although our Method C for NPBVSS scheme also uses XOR operation but we can reconstruct the image by direct stacking.

Complexity: Operations of stacking any k shadows equal $(k-1)$ ORs. When finishing R runs of the Viet-Kurosawa scheme, we require R NOTs to reverse T_i and $(R-1)$ ORs to stack them and finally a NOT to reverse the image. So, the total operations are $(R(k-1) + (R-1)) = (Rk-1)$ ORs, $(R+1)$ NOTs. Instead of R by $(m-h+1)$ and 2, the operations are $((m-h+1)k-1)$ ORs, $(m-h+2)$ NOTs (Method A and Cimato et al's scheme), and $(mk-1)$ ORs, 3 NOTs (Method B). For the RPCVSS scheme (Method C) based on NPBVSS scheme, except the operations of stackind shadows, we require $(k-1)$ XORs and one NOT when finishing m runs. So, the total operations are $(m(k-1) + 3(m-1)) = (mk + 2m - 3)$ ORs and $(4(m-1)+1) = (4m-3)$ NOTs. (Note: 1 XOR = 3 ORs + 4 NOTs).

Contrast: The Viet-Kurosawa scheme is an almost ideal contrast scheme but our proposed RPCVSS scheme and Cimato et al's scheme are really ideal contrast scheme. So the reconstructed images of the last two schemes are better than the first scheme. Actually, our scheme is the deterministic VSS scheme with the pixel expansion m and Cimato et al's scheme is the probabilistic VSS scheme with no pixel expansion. The disadvantage of the probabilistic VSS scheme is that details of the

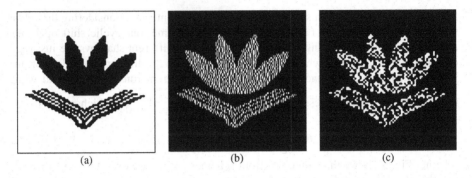

| (a) | (b) | (c) |

Fig. 5. Stacking $s_1^1 + s_2^2$ for the RPCVSS scheme and Cimato et al's scheme based on the (2, 2, 1, 0, 2)-PBVSS scheme (a) the original secret image: white background color (b) the RPCVSS scheme: black background color (c) Cimato et al's scheme: black background color

Table 6. Comparison of VSS schemes with reversing

		RPCVSS scheme			Viet-Kurosawa scheme	Cimato et al's scheme
		Method A	Method B	Method C		
Number of runs		$m-h+1$	2	m	$R: 1\to\infty$	$m-h+1$
Shadow expansion		m	m	m	m	1
Operation complexity	OR	$(m-h+1)k-1$	$2k-1$	$mk+2m-3$	$(m-h+1)k-1$	$mk-1$
	NOT	$m-h+2$	3	$4m-3$	$m-h+2$	$m+1$
Compatibility		YES	YES	YES	YES	YES (or NO for XOR based scheme)
Available to NPBVSS scheme		NO	NO	YES	NO	NO
Contrast		The best among these three schemes			the random dots due to the almost ideal contrast	the loss of clarity due to th probabilstc nature

picture are not recognizable if they do not consist of enough pixels. When comparing these two schemes, our reconsructed image is better than Cimato et al's scheme. From the above description, our contrast is the best among these three schemes.

The comparison among the proposed RPCVSS schemes and the schemes in [3, 4] are summarized in Table 6. The RPCVSS schemes based on PBVSS scheme has less runs and operations than other two schemes and the RPCVSS scheme based on NPBVSS is the first R-run scheme available to the NPBVSS scheme.

5   Conclusion

We first use the cyclic shift operation of the sub pixels to design a real perfect contrast VSS scheme based on the PBVSS scheme with simple reversing operation within less finite runs. Using the same strategy and the XOR operation (also a no-cryptographic operation), we next propose the scheme based on the NPBVSS scheme. It will be interesting to further design the real perfect contrast scheme based on the NPBVSS scheme for even $(h - l)$ by means of other simple operations.

References

[1] M. Naor and A. Shamir, "Visual cryptography," Advances in *Cryptology-EUROCRYPT'94*, pp.1-12, 1994.

[2] P.A. Eisen and D.R. Stinson, "Threshold visual cryptography schemes with specified whiteness levels of reconstructed pixels," *Designs, Codes and Cryptography*, Vol.25, No.1, pp. 15-61, 2002.

[3] D.Q. Viet and K. Kurosawa, "Almost ideal contrast visual cryptography with reversing," in Proceeding of Topics in Cryptology—CT-RSA2004. *Lecture note in Computer Science*, vol. 2964, pp. 353-365, 2004.

[4] S. Cimato, A. De Santis, A.L. Ferrara and B. Masucci, "Ideal contrast visual cryptography schemes with reversing," *Information Processing Letters*, vol. 93, issue 4, pp. 199-206, 2005.

[5] C.N. Yang, "New Visual Secret Sharing Schemes Using Probabilistic Method," *Pattern Recognition Letters*, vol. 25, issue 4, pp. 481-494, 2004.

[6] R. Ito, H. Kuwakado and H. Tanaka, "Image size invariant visual cryptography," *IEICE Trans. Fundamentals*, vol. E82-A, no. 10, pp. 2172-2177, Oct. 1999.

[7] A. De Bonis and A. De Santis, "Randomness in secret sharing and visual cryptography schemes," *Theoretical Computer Science*, vol. 314, issue 3, pp. 351-374, 2004.

[8] P. Tuyls, H.D.L. Hollmann, J.H. Van Lint and L. Tolhuizen, "XOR-based Visual Cryptography Schemes," *Designs, Codes and Cryptography*, vol. 37, pp. 169-186, 2005.

On Optimizing the Security-Throughput Trade-Off in Wireless Networks with Adversaries

Mohamed A. Haleem, Chetan Nanjunda Mathur, R. Chandramouli, and K.P. Subbalakshmi

Department of Electrical and Computer Engineering,
Stevens Institute of Technology, Hoboken, NJ 07030, USA
mhaleem@stevens.edu

Abstract. In this paper, we model the adversary (eavesdropper) present in the wireless communication medium using probabilistic models. We precisely formulate the security-throughput optimization and derive analytical solutions. The effect of different adversary models, and single and multi-rate modulation schemes (BPSK and MQAM) are studied. Simulation results are given to show that significant throughput gain can be achieved by using link (channel) adaptive and adversary adaptive encryption techniques compared to fixed block length encryption.

Keywords: Opportunistic, Tradeoff, Optimization, Encryption, Wireless, Security.

1 Introduction

Traditionally, design of encryption algorithms and their parameters has used only the security against an adversary attack as the main criterion. To achieve this goal, the cipher is made to satisfy several properties including the *avalanche* effect [1][2].

The avalanche effect principle requires that a minor change to the plain text or the key must result in significant and random-looking changes to the cipher text. For a given transformation to exhibit the avalanche effect, an average of one half of the output bits should change whenever a single input bit is complemented. This implies that there should not be any noticeable resemblance between two ciphertexts obtained by applying two neighboring keys for encrypting the same plain text. Otherwise, there would be considerable reduction of the keyspace search by the cryptanalyst.

We note that block ciphers that satisfy the avalanche property are very sensitive to bit errors induced by the wireless link. This means that a single bit error in the received encrypted block could lead to about half the decrypted block to be in error (error propagation), resulting in throughput loss when the channel introduces errors. Hence, there is a fundamental trade-off between security and throughput in encryption based wireless networks. We explore this trade-off in this paper and investigate methods to optimize it.

J. Zhou, M. Yung, and F. Bao (Eds.): ACNS 2006, LNCS 3989, pp. 448–458, 2006.

It is customary to measure the level of security in encrypted data against cryptanalysis, as the amount of work (computation) required by the adversary to crack the ciphertext (encrypted information). Computationally secure encryption is achieved if the cost of cracking the information is higher than the value of the information and if the time required to crack the informaiton exceeds the useful time period of the information being sent [1]. Meanwhile, it is reasonable to say that the level of security can only be quantified relative to the strength of the adversary present in the environment. For mobile wireless environment, the adversary's strength also varies with the location and time, and cannot be predicted deterministically. In other words, the adversary's "strength" to crack a cipher is a random parameter that could be modeled using a probability distribution. It is reasonable to assume that the ability of the adversary to crack the cipher text becomes less probable as the computational complexity of attack increases.

In this work, we propose to model the adversary strength probabilistically. The model assumes a finite set of discrete values for the maximum possible block lengths an adversary can crack. Note that the strength of a block cipher is decided by the minimum of the length of key and the length of plaintext, the set of block lengths represent the minima of the lengths of planitext/key pairs. If the adversary is capable of cracking a cipher with a block length of N bits then (s)he is capable of cracking any block length less than or equal to N bits. We associate a probability to each possible attack strength of the adversary. In particular, we consider two probability distributions namely uniform leading to the *linear model* and exponential leading to the *exponential model*. It is reasonable to assume that in a typical communication medium, the probability of the presence of an adversary with certain strength decreases as the strength increases. Such a model is justified from the following fact. In the absence of a shortcut attack (*e.g.* linear and differential cryptanalysis [1]), the computational strength required by the attacker to crack the cipher increases exponentially with the block length. For example, it is exponentially harder to crack 128 bit AES [3] compared to a 64 bit DES [4]. Thus an exponential model is deemed an appropriate one. Nevertheless, the linear model can be considered as the representation of the worst case scenario where we assume that the presence of adversary with a given strength has the same probability for all values of strength. In this case, we assume that the probability of the adversary reduces to zero beyond a maximum defined block length.

The wireless communication channel quality is a highly time varying parameter due to the environmental noise and fading [5]. Traditionally, encryption designs do not consider the effect of bit errors occurring during the transmission of information through the channel and this issue is considered to be an orthogonal problem that should be handled by efficient coding and modulation techniques. In contrast, it is seen in recent work [6] that present and future wireless communication systems and networks can greatly benefit from an encryption design that considers the channel quality. Such an approach makes it possible to achieve a desirable tradeoff between the security and performance. However, security cannot be merely reduced to increase throughput. The presence of adversaries play a crucial role in security throughput tradeoff.

In the optimization problems formulated in this paper, we make the assumption that the channel states are known for the extent of the message being transmitted. The solution derived with such an assumption provides us an upper bound on the performance. Further, the study presented in this work considers block encryption.

In Section 2 we discuss the measure of security based on the probabilistic models of adversary strength. In Section 3 we present the discussion on the tradeoff between the security and the throughput performance. The optimization problems are formulated and the solutions are derived. Sample numerical results are given in Section 4.

2   Channel Model and Security Measure

In a typical packet mode communication, frames consisting of fixed length of bit stream (with fixed modulation schemes) or symbol stream (variable modulation schemes) are formed. The frame lengths are in general much larger than the encryption block lengths and may consist of multiple encrypted blocks. Let a message be sent by forming n frames of lengths L_i bits for $i = 1, \cdots, n$ and transmitted in distinct time intervals using encryption block lengths $N_i, i = 1, \cdots, n$. N_i is selected by the optimization procedure based on the channel condition. With the block fading [7] assumption on the wireless channel, all the information bits in a frame are encrypted using the same encryption block length as the quality of the channel is assumed to be fixed over the frame duration.

We define the *vulnerability* (which increases as the encryption block length is decreased) $0 \leqslant \Phi \leqslant 1$ of a message as the expected fraction of the total message being successfully decrypted by the adversary. Let the frames be arranged in the ascending order of the respective encryption block lengths. If the adversary's attack strength is α bits, then the adversary can successfully crack all the data frames with encryption block length less than or equal to α. Assume that there are $K(\leqslant n)$ distinct encryption block lengths being used and m_k be the number of frames with encryption block length less than or equal to $M_k, k = 1, \cdots, K$, and $Pr(\alpha = M_k)$ be the probability that the attacker's strength α is M_k. Note that $Pr(\alpha = M_k)$ also is the probability with which the m_k frames (in the ordered list) would be cracked by the adversary resulting in the leakage of a fraction $x_k = \sum_{i=1}^{m_k} l_i$ of the total message, where l_i is the frame length normalized by message length $(l_i = \frac{L_i}{\sum_{j=1}^{n} L_j})$. Thus we can define the vulnerability Φ of the message as the expected leakage given by,

$$\Phi = \sum_{k=1}^{K} x_k P(x_k) \tag{1}$$

where $P(x_k) = Pr(\alpha = M_k)$ is the probability of exposing a fraction x_k of the total message. From a known result in probability theory, this is equivalent to

$$\Phi = \sum_{k=1}^{K} Pr(x \geqslant x_k). \tag{2}$$

Further, if each frame is encrypted with a distinct block length we have $K = n$ and the above equation reduces to

$$\Phi = \sum_{i=1}^{n} Pr(\alpha \geqslant N_i) \tag{3}$$

3 Security-Throughput Tradeoff Optimization

For the discussion in this section, we consider two probability distributions, namely uniform and exponential to model the adversary strength leading to respectively the *linear* and *exponential* adversary strength models. We show in the sequel that with linear model, the optimization problem is equivalent to "fractional knapsack" problem and therefore the optimum algorithm has linear execution time [8]. With the exponential model, the optimal solution resembles "water-filling" algorithm [9], which also has a linear execution time. As discussed in the introduction we assume that a single bit error during the decryption process would cause the loss of entire block of encrypted information. The throughput per block is given by $R_i(1 - P_i)^{N_i} \approx R_i(1 - P_i N_i)$ where R_i and P_i are respectively the transmission rate selected for the frame and the channel bit error probability. The approximation is valid when the channel bit error probability is sufficiently small. If there is any bit error in an encrypted block within a frame, the avalanche effect would cause propagation of the error to the entire block leading to discarding of such a block of N_i bits. However, blocks of data with no bit errors can be decrypted without any errors and can be accumulated in the receiver as useful data. With such an approach, the throughput of the message (sequence of frames) can be expressed by,

$$T = \sum_{i=1}^{n} R_i(1 - P_i N_i) \tag{4}$$

In the sequel we present the optimization process to compute the optimum values of N_i for a known sequence of channel instantiations. The procedures are presented for the two different adversary models.

3.1 Linear Adversary Strength Model

Let the probability mass function of the attacker strength be a uniform distribution *i.e.*, $Pr(\alpha = N_i) = \frac{1}{N_{max} - N_{min}}$ for $i = 1, \cdots, n$ where N_{min} and N_{max} are the minimum and maximum block length used in the encryption system. Then for the linear model we have,

$$\phi_i = Pr(\alpha \geqslant N_i) = \frac{N_{max} - N_i}{N_{max} - N_{min}}, i = 1, \cdots, n \tag{5}$$

We maximize the throughput given by,

$$T = \sum_{i=1}^{n} R_i(1 - P_i(N_{\max} - (N_{\max} - N_{\min})\phi_i)) \tag{6}$$

subject to the conditions

$$\phi_{\min} \leqslant \phi_i \leqslant \phi_{\max}, i = 1, \cdots, n \tag{7}$$

$$\frac{1}{n}\sum_{i=1}^{n}\phi_i \leqslant \varPhi_0 \tag{8}$$

Here, $\varPhi_0$ is the maximum allowable average vulnerability level, and $\phi_{\min}$ and $\phi_{\max}$ are the minimum and maximum allowable values of the vulnerability of a frame corresponding to a maximum and a minimum encryption block length, respectively. Under the assumption of continuous values for ϕ_i, the optimal solution is achieved with the equality in the condition $\frac{1}{n}\sum_{i=1}^{n}\phi_i \leqslant \varPhi_0$. By expanding (6) and omitting the terms that are independent of $\phi_i, \forall i$, the problem reduces to the maximization of the following cost function over $\{N_i\}$:

$$T' = \sum_{i=1}^{n} w_i\phi_i \tag{9}$$

where, $w_i = P_iR_i$. This problem is a special case of *fractional knapsack problem* which is solvable in polynomial time. Selecting ϕ_is in the non-increasing order of maximum w_i maximizes T' and hence T [8]. As any data frame in the message should be assigned at least the minimum vulnerability level, $\phi_{\min}$ corresponding to the maximum encryption block length, $N_{\max}$, the formulation can be modified such that the optimization problem is

$$\max_{\phi_1,\cdots,\phi_n} \sum_{i=1}^{n} w_i\phi_i \text{ such that}$$

$$\frac{1}{n}\sum_{i=1}^{n}\phi_i \leqslant \varPhi_0'; 0 \leqslant \phi_i \leqslant \phi_{\max} - \phi_{\min} \tag{10}$$

where $\varPhi_0' = \varPhi_0 - n\phi_{\min}$. The following greedy algorithm optimally solves the problem. The proof of this claim follows along the lines discussed in [10].

1. *Initialization*: Allocate a vulnerability level of $\phi_{\min}$ for all frames $i, i = 1, \cdots, n$.
2. Sort the frames in the non-increasing order of $w_i = P_iR_i, i = 1, \cdots, n$.
3. Allocate the additional maximum allowed vulnerability level of less than or equal to $\phi_{\max} - \phi_{\min}$ for each frame i in the sorted order, i.e., $w_i > w_{i+1}$. That is, allocate $\phi_{\max} - \phi_{\min}$ units to frames $i = 1, \cdots, j^* - 1$ for some j^*, fewer than $\phi_{\max} - \phi_{\min}$ or 0 for frame j^* and 0 for $i = j^* + 1, \cdots, n$ with the sum total of the additional allocation is $\varPhi_0'$.

3.2   Exponential Adversary Strength Model

Let the attacker strength be given by:

$$\phi_i = \Pr(\alpha \geqslant N_i) = e^{-kN_i} \tag{11}$$

where $k > 0$ is a constant. We are required to maximize the throughput given by

$$T = \sum_{i=1}^{n} R_i(1 + \frac{P_i}{k} \log_e \phi_i) \tag{12}$$

subject to the conditions

$$\phi_i - \phi_{\min} \geqslant 0, i = 1, \cdots, n \tag{13}$$

$$\phi_{\max} - \phi_i \geqslant 0, i = 1, \cdots, n \tag{14}$$

$$\Phi_0 - \frac{1}{n} \sum_{i=1}^{n} \phi_i = 0 \tag{15}$$

where Φ_0 is the maximum allowable overall vulnerability level, and $\phi_{\min}$ and $\phi_{\max}$ are the minimum and maximum values of the vulnerability of a frame corresponding to a maximum and a minimum encryption block length respectively. The equality in (15) results from the observation that maximum of T is achieved by using the maximum allowed overall vulnerability. The augmented objective function can be written as,

$$C = \sum_{i=1}^{n} R_i(1 + \frac{P_i}{k} \log_e \phi_i) + \nu(n\Phi_0 - \sum_{i=1}^{n} \phi_i)$$

$$+ \sum_{i=1}^{n} \lambda_i(\phi_i - \phi_{\min}) + \sum_{i=1}^{n} \mu_i(\phi_{\max} - \phi_i) \tag{16}$$

where $\nu, \lambda_i, \mu_i, i = 1, \cdots, n$ are constants (Lagrange multipliers). The Karush Kuhn-Tucker Conditions (KKC) [11] for this problem are obtained by considering the vanishing point of the first order derivative of C w.r.t. ϕ_i and also from the complimentary slackness. Thus we have,

$$\phi_i = \frac{R_i P_i}{k(\mu_i + \nu - \lambda_i)}$$

$$\lambda_i(\phi_i - \phi_{\min}) = 0$$

$$\mu_i(\phi_{\max} - \phi_i) = 0$$

$$\lambda_i \geqslant 0$$

$$\mu_i \geqslant 0$$

$$n\Phi_0 - \sum_{i=1}^{n} \phi_i = 0$$

$$\nu \geqslant 0 \tag{17}$$

for $i = 1, \cdots, n$. Therefore the optimal value of ϕ_i is found from one of the following three cases.

Case 1: $\lambda_i = 0, \mu_i = 0 \Rightarrow \phi_{min} < \phi_i < \phi_{max}$ and we have $\phi_i = \alpha w_i$ with $\alpha = \frac{1}{k\nu}, \nu > 0$ and $w_i = R_i P_i$

Case 2: $\lambda_i = 0, \mu_i \neq 0 \Rightarrow \phi_i = \phi_{max}$

Case 3: $\lambda_i \neq 0, \mu_i = 0 \Rightarrow \phi_i = \phi_{min}$

The following iterative algorithm provides the optimal solution. Any value of ϕ_i computed complies with one of the three cases above.

1. Sort the channels in the non-increasing order of $w_i, i = 1, \cdots, n$; let $j = 1$
2. Compute $\alpha = \frac{\phi_{min}}{w_j}$
3. Compute $\phi_i = \alpha w_i$ for $i = 1, \cdots, n$; if $\phi_i < \phi_{min}$ set $\phi_i = \phi_{min}$; if $\phi_i > \phi_{max}$ set $\phi_i = \phi_{max}$
4. If $n\Phi_0 > \sum_{k=1}^{n} \phi_i$ set $j = j + 1$ and goto step 2); else goto step 5)
5. If $n\Phi_0 = \sum_{k=1}^{n} \phi_i$ the current set of $\phi_i, i = 1, \cdots, n$ are optimal; else goto step 6)
6. The optimum α is in between the two values say α_j and α_{j-1} computed in the last two iterations. Fine tune as follows. Default to the allocation corresponding to $\alpha = \alpha_{j-1}$. Let l be the index of the largest $w_i, i = 1, \cdots, n$ such that $\phi_i < \phi_{max}$, and i_{min} is the index of smallest w_i such that $\phi_i > \phi_{min}$
7. Set $\alpha = \frac{\phi_{max}}{w_l}$; if $\alpha < \frac{\phi_{min}}{w_{i_{min}+1}}$ set $\phi_i = \alpha w_i, i = 1, \cdots, n$; $\phi_i(\phi_i < \phi_{min}) = \phi_{min}$; $\phi_i(\phi_i > \phi_{max}) = \phi_{max}$; goto the step (8); else set $l = l - 1$ and goto step (9)
8. If $\sum_{i=1}^{n} \phi_i = n\Phi_0$ optimal values are found; else if $\sum_{i=1}^{n} \phi_i < n\Phi_0$ set $l = l+1$ and goto step (7); else set $l = l - 1$; goto step (9)
9. The optimal α is found from $\alpha = \frac{1}{\sum_{i=i_{min}}^{l} w_i}(n\Phi_0 - (n - i_{min})\phi_{min} + (l - 1)\phi_{max})$; set $\phi_i = \alpha w_i, i = 1, \cdots, n$, $\phi_i(\phi_i < \phi_{min}) = \phi_{min}$, and $\phi_i(\phi_i > \phi_{max}) = \phi_{max}$

The following discussion establishes that this algorithm is indeed optimal. Consider the quantity to be maximized namely $T = \sum_{i=1}^{n} R_i(1 + \frac{P_i}{k} \log_e \phi_i)$ subject to the constraints as in (13)-(15). This is equivalent to maximizing $S = \sum_{i=1}^{n} w_i \log_e \phi_i$ where $w_i = R_i P_i$ with the set of constraints. Each of the terms in the summation expression of S is concave and therefore the optimum allocation of ϕ_i resembles "water-filling" solution. Let $y_i = w_i \log_e \phi_i$. The marginal gain of additional allocation to the ith channel is given by $\frac{\partial y_i}{\partial \phi_i} = \frac{w_i}{\phi_i}$. Let the channels be ordered such that $w_1 \geqslant w_2 \geqslant \cdots \geqslant w_n$. The optimal allocation procedure should first allocate $\phi_i = \phi_{min}$ for $i = 1, \cdots, n$. Next, starting with the first channel in the ordered list, ϕ_1 should be increased from the initial value of ϕ_{min} until the condition $\frac{\partial y_1}{\partial \phi_1} = \frac{\partial y_2}{\partial \phi_2}$ is reached which is equivalent to $\frac{\phi_1}{w_1} = \frac{\phi_2}{w_2}$ with $\phi_2 = \phi_{min}$. From this point onward both ϕ_1 and ϕ_2 should be increased such that $\frac{\phi_1}{w_1} = \frac{\phi_2}{w_2}$ until the common ratio is equal to $\frac{\phi_3}{w_{min}}$. The procedure continues including more and more channels while maintaining equal marginal gains for all channels under consideration. Due to the upper limit of ϕ_{max} on ϕ_i, they may be capped at ϕ_{max}. The procedure continues until the condition $n\Phi_0 = \sum_{i=1}^{n} \phi_i$ is met. Our formulation of the algorithm is to carry out this allocation process in discrete values for computational efficiency.

The algorithm starts by allocating $\phi_i = \phi_{\min}, i = 1, \cdots, n$ and proceeds with the iteration by selecting increasing values for α so that to assign $\phi_i > \phi_{\min}$ to more and more channels in the increasing order of w_i until the condition $n\Phi_0 \geqslant \sum_{k=1}^{n} \phi_i$ is achieved. If the equality of constraint is not achieved, the subsequent steps performs fine tuning to achieve the optimal solution.

4   Numerical Illustrations

We carried out computations of sample performance curves with parameter settings as follows. Cases with fixed transmission rate namely BPSK and multi-rates namely MQAM were considered. Block length equivalents of the target, minimum, and maximum security levels for these computations were respectively 128, 16 and 1024 bits. For the exponential adversary model, the decay constant k_i was set to 0.0001 for all $i = 1, \cdots, n$. It was assumed that the channel gain remains fixed during the transmission of a frame. For the optimization, $n = 5000$ channel samples were drawn from Rayleigh distribution with each setting of average signal to noise ratio (SNR). The optimum encryption block lengths were assigned based on the algorithm for each of the adversary models. The throughput was computed with optimum allocation of block lengths and with fixed block length of 128 bits. The gain in throughput was computed as $\frac{T_{\mathrm{opt}} - T_{\mathrm{fixed}}}{T_{\mathrm{fixed}}}$, where T_{opt} and T_{fixed} are throughput with respectively the optimum and fixed block length allocations.

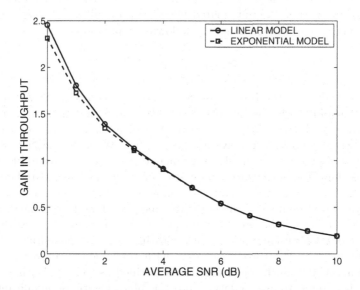

Fig. 1. Throughput gain of proposed channel adaptive encryption compared to fixed block length encryption for single rate (BPSK) transmisision. Linear and exponential adversary attack models are compared.

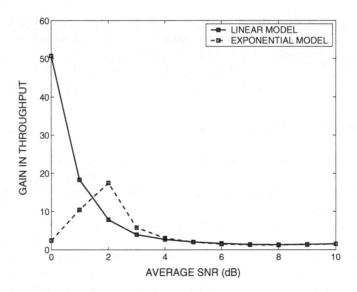

Fig. 2. Throughput gain of proposed channel adaptive encryption compared to fixed block length encryption for multi- rate (MQAM) transmisision. Linear and exponential adversary attack models are compared.

Fig. 1 shows the throughput gains of proposed adaptive encryption with respect to fixed block length encryption for single rate (BPSK) signaling. For the optimization process, the anticipated bit error probabilities during channel instantiations were evaluated using the following expression.

$$P_i(\gamma_i) = \frac{1}{2}\text{erfc}(\sqrt{\gamma_i})^1 \qquad (18)$$

Here γ_i and $\bar{\gamma}$ are the frame-wise SNR and the average SNR. A throughput gain of 2.5 fold is observable with $\bar{\gamma} = 0dB$. Note that in this example the performance with exponential adversary model is slightly inferior to that of linear adversary model at low average SNR values. With exponential model, the probability of presence of an adversary increases as the encryption block length decreases. Thus the optimization process has a tendency to allocate larger block lengths to a larger fraction of frames compared to the case with linear model. Therefore, throughput loss is higher with exponential model compared to linear model. Nevertheless, the optimization process has its advantage with respect to fixed block length encryption, both with linear and exponential models. As the SNR increases the throughput gain with both models approaches a fixed value of about 0.2. Such a convergence is justified as follows. With large SNR values it is possible to use the largest possible block length for significantly large fraction of frames without causing much performance degradation. However, as we are interested in achieving a level of security equivalent to that with fixed

---

[1] $\text{erfc}(x) = \frac{2}{\sqrt{\pi}} \int_x^\infty e^{-t^2} dt$

block length encryption, the optimization algorithm is constrained to maintain the allocation of large block lengths within a limit. Therefore the achievable throughput gain with respect to fixed block length encryption saturates at large SNR values.

Fig. 2 shows the performance with multi-rate (MQAM) transmission. The bit error probability of M-arry QAM is given by the well known approximation

$$P_i(\gamma) \approx \frac{\sqrt{M} - 1}{\sqrt{M} log_2 \sqrt{M}} \text{erfc} \left[\sqrt{\frac{3 log_2 M}{2(M - 1)} \gamma} \right] \quad (19)$$

where M is the constellation size. In this computation we include BPSK and $M = 4, 16$, and 64 with which we have the set of transmission rates $R = 1, 2, 4$, and 6 bits/symbol. Rate and block length allocation in this case was performed in two steps. The maximum feasible rate R_i was selected from this set such that $R_i \leqslant log_2(1 + \gamma)$. The block length allocation followed with the optimization algorithms. Gain of 50 fold is observable at low SNR with linear models. However, with exponential model, the gain is maximized at moderate values of SNR around 2 dB, but decreases both at smaller and larger SNR values. The fact that transmission rates are optimally selected for the prevailing channel conditions by the channel adaptive rate selection procedure reduces the room for further optimization of throughput. In addition, the fact that the flexible encryption algorithm for exponential model has the tendency to select larger block lengths for a larger fraction of channel instantiations compared to the case with linear model, brings the throughput performance close to that of fixed block length encryption. However for a range of intermediate SNR values, the optimization process shows significant performance improvement. As in the case of fixed rate transmission, the throughput gain converges to a fixed value of about 2 with both adversary models.

5   Conclusions

In this paper, we proposed and studied probabilistic models for adversary strength to crack a cipher. Based on these models, we formulated techniques where the encryption strength is a variable matched to the time varying channel, thereby improvement was brought to the throughput performance of wireless link with data encryption compared to using a fixed encryption block length. We presented optimal block length allocation algorithms with uniform and exponential distributions for the attacker strength leading to respectively the linear adversary model and the exponential adversary model. With linear model, the optimal allocation process uses fractional knapsack algorithm. We developed an algorithm resembling "water-filling" process for the case with exponential model. Numerical results were presented showing significant gains in throughput for a range of practical average SNR values. Results were presented for single rate (BPSK) transmission and channel adaptive multi-rate (MQAM) transmission. Different trends in throughput gains were observable with the two different adversary models and the associated optimization algorithms. This work shows the advantage of a channel adaptive flexible block length encryption scheme which is achievable with probabilistic models for adversary strength.

References

1. Stinson, D.R.: Cryptography: Theory and Practices. Discrete Mathematics and its Applications. CRC Press Inc., 2000 Corporate Blvd., N.W., Boca Raton, Florida 33431 (1995)
2. Schneier, B.: Applied cryptography: protocols, algorithms, and source code in C. 2nd edn. Wiley, New York (1996)
3. FIPS: Specification for the advanced encryption standard (AES). Federal Information Processing Standards Publication 197 (2001)
4. FIPS: Specification for the data encryption standard (DES). Federal Information Processing Standards Publication 46-2 (1988)
5. Stein, S.: Fading channel issues in systems engineering. IEEE Journal on Selected Areas in Communications $5(2)$ (1987) 68–89
6. Y.Xaio, Guizani, M.: Optimal stream-based cipher feedback mode in error channel. IEEE Globecom Conference (Globecom 2005) (2005)
7. Ozarow, L.H., Shamai, S., Wyner, A.D.: Information theoretic considerations for cellular mobile radio. IEEE Trans. Veh. Tech. $43(2)$ (1994) 359 – 378
8. Cormen, T.H., Leiserson, C.E., Rivest, R.L., Stein, C.: Introduction to Algorithms. Second edition edn. The MIT Press,, Cambridge, MA, (2003)
9. Cover, T.M., Thomas, J.A.: Elements of Information Theory. Wiley Series in Telecommunicatons. Wiley-Interscience, New York (1991)
10. Bapatla, S., Chandramouli, R.: Battery power optimized encryption. IEEE International Conference on Communications $27(1)$ (2004) 3802–3806
11. Boyd, S., Vandenberghe, L.: Convex Optimization. Cambridge University Press (2004)

Improving the Randomized Initial Point Countermeasure Against DPA

Kouichi Itoh, Tetsuya Izu, and Masahiko Takenaka

FUJITSU LABORATORIES Ltd.
4-1-1, Kamikodanaka, Nakahara-ku, Kawasaki, 211-8588, Japan
{kito, izu, takenaka}@labs.fujitsu.com

Abstract. DPA-countermeasures are one of the essential technology for implementing elliptic curve cryptosystems (ECC) on smart cards. Not only standard DPA but also recently proposed refined power analysis (RPA) and zero value analysis (ZVA) should be considered. Itoh, Izu and Takenaka proposed a secure and efficient countermeasure (the randomized initial point countermeasure, RIP) in order to resist these attacks. Then, Mamiya, Miyaji and Morimoto improved the efficiency. This paper also aims at improving RIP in another direction. As a result, compared to the original RIP, about 28% improvement can be established. In other words, the proposed countermeasure has almost no penalty from a non DPA-resistant scalar multiplication.

Keywords: Smart card, Elliptic Curve Cryptosystems (ECC), DPA, RPA, ZVA, countermeasure, RIP.

1 Introduction

Smart cards are a new infrastructure in the coming ubiquitous society because of its plenty of applications such as SIM card, ID card, and driving licence. However, side channel attacks are real threats for such applications. When a cryptographic procedure is computed in a smart card with a secret key hidden in the device, the card leaks side channel information such as power consumption. In the side channel attacks, an adversary analyzes the information and tries to detect the secret key. The attacks will be successful if there is a connection between the information and the secret. Among these attacks, the differential power analysis (DPA) [KJJ99, MDS99] is a very strong attack, in which the adversary statistically analyzes the side channel information from some thousands of observations. DPA-countermeasures are essential for smart cards.

Elliptic curve cryptosystems (ECC) are considered as a suitable choice for smart card applications because they achieve high security with shorter key compared to other public-key cryptosystems such as RSA or ElGamal. In 2003, a new variant of DPA, the refined power analysis (RPA), was proposed by Goubin [Gou03]. Soon it is extended to the zero value analysis (ZVA) by Akishita and Takagi [AT03]. Thus ECC requires not only secure against these DPA-attacks but efficient countermeasures. In CARDIS 2004, Itoh, Izu and Takenaka proposed

J. Zhou, M. Yung, and F. Bao (Eds.): ACNS 2006, LNCS 3989, pp. 459–469, 2006.
© Springer-Verlag Berlin Heidelberg 2006

an efficient countermeasure, the randomized initial point countermeasure (RIP) [IIT04]. Then, in the same year, Mamiya, Miyaji and Morimoto applied RIP to the binary method from the most significant bit (MSB) and window-based methods, and improved the efficiency significantly [MMM04]. However, this approach requires a look-up table. Generally, there is a time-memory trade-off between efficiency of scalar multiplications and available memory. Although recent smart cards have enough memory, it is desirable to compute scalar multiplications with less memory in an efficient way.

This paper is also aimed at applying RIP to the binary method from MSB in a different way, namely by checking effects of changing initial points in some algorithms for scalar multiplications. Especially, we apply RIP to the Montgomery Ladder, a variant of the binary method from MSB, which is known as an efficient algorithm when it is combined to the x-coordinate-only addition formula [IT02], about 28% improvement compared to the original RIP, or reduction of the efficiency or the number of registers can be established.

A rest of the paper is organized as follows: we briefly introduce elliptic curve cryptosystems (ECC) and side channel attacks for ECC in section 2. Then, in section 3, we propose the extended RIP as a DPA-countermeasure. Section 4 compares some secure countermeasures in detail.

2   Preliminaries

This section briefly introduces elliptic curve cryptosystems (ECC). Power analysis attacks and countermeasures for ECC are also reviewed.

2.1   Elliptic Curve Cryptosystems

In this paper, we assume that the characteristic of a definition finite field K is greater than 3 (however, most countermeasures can be applied to finite fields with characteristics 2 or 3).

Elliptic Curve. An elliptic curve over a definition field K is given by an equation

$$E : y^2 = x^3 + ax + b \ (a, b \in K, \ 4a^3 + 27b^2 \neq 0).$$

A set of K-rational points on E is defined by

$$E(K) = \{(x, y) \in E \mid x, y \in K\} \cup \{\mathcal{O}\},$$

where the special point $\mathcal{O}$ is called the *point at infinity*, which is the only point that can not be represented as a pair of two K-elements like (x, y) (conversely, other points can be represented as a pair of K-elements). In this paper, we identify an elliptic curve E and its K-rational point $E(K)$ for simplicity.

Standard Addition Formula. An elliptic curve $E(K)$ has an additive group structure by the following rules: a neutral element of the group is the point at infinity $\mathcal{O}$. Inversion of the neutral point is itself ($-\mathcal{O} = \mathcal{O}$). For a point

$P = (x, y) \in E(K) \backslash \{\mathcal{O}\}$, inversion is defined by $-P = (x, -y) \in E(K) \backslash \{\mathcal{O}\}$. For the point at infinity $\mathcal{O}$ and an arbitrary point $P \in E(K)$, we define their addition as $\mathcal{O} + P = P + \mathcal{O} = P$. We also define $P + (-P) = \mathcal{O}$. If two arbitrary points $P_1 = (x_1, y_1)$, $P_2 = (x_2, y_2) \in E(K) \backslash \{\mathcal{O}\}$, $P_1 \neq -P_2$ are given, their addition $P_3 = P_1 + P_2 = (x_3, y_3)$ is defined by

$$x_3 = \lambda^2 - x_1 - x_2, \; y_3 = \lambda(x_1 - x_3) - y_1, \qquad (1)$$

where

$$\lambda = \begin{cases} (y_2 - y_1)/(x_2 - x_1) & \text{if } P_1 \neq P_2 \\ (3x_1^2 + a)/(2y_1) & \text{if } P_1 = P_2. \end{cases}$$

The above formula is called the *addition formula*, an addition $P_1 + P_2$ $(P_1 \neq P_2)$ is called an *elliptic curve addition* (ECADD), and a doubling $P_1 + P_1 = 2P_1$ is called an *elliptic curve doubling* (ECDBL). Note that ECADD and ECDBL are computed by a sequence of fundamental operations in the definition field K such as additions, subtractions, multiplications and divisions. However, the sequences differs for ECADD and ECDBL.

x-coordinate-only Addition Formula. In the standard addition formula (1), both x_3, y_3 are functions on x_1, x_2, y_1 and y_2. The x-coordinate-only addition formula, in which x_3 is computed from x-coordinates, are as follows [Mon87, BJ02, IT02], where $P_3 = (x_3, y_3)$, $P_3' = P_1 - P_2 = (x_3', y_3')$, $P_4 = 2P_1 = (x_4, y_4)$:

$$x_3 = \frac{2(x_1 + x_2)(x_1 x_2 + a) + 4b}{(x_1 - x_2)^2} - x_3',$$

$$x_3 = \frac{1}{x_3'} \frac{(x_1 x_2 - a)^2 - 4b(x_1 + x_2)}{(x_1 - x_2)^2},$$

$$x_4 = \frac{(x_1^2 - a)^2 - 8bx_1}{4(x_1^3 + ax_1 + b)}.$$

We denote an elliptic addition (doubling) by the x-coordinate-only formula as xECADD (xECDBL), respectively. Note that, x_3' is required to compute xECADD. Also note that there is 2 formulas for xECADD; we may distinguish them by using xECADD^{add} (additive xECADD) and xECADD^{mul} (multiplicative xECADD).

Scalar Multiplication. When a point $P \in E(K)$ and a scalar $d \in \mathbb{Z}_{>0}$ are given, a *scalar multiplication* of P by d is to compute $dP = P + \cdots + P$. Here, P is called a *base point*. Computing dP from d, P is easy (as described later), while computing d from dP, P is known to be hard in general. This problem is called the *elliptic curve discrete logarithm problem* (ECDLP) and no efficient algorithms are known. In ECC, a base point P and a scalar multiplied point dP are public, while the scalar d is secret. The hardness of ECDLP assures the security of ECC.

Algorithm 1. Montgomery Ladder

```
INPUT: d, P
OUTPUT: d*P
1: T[0] = P, T[1] = 2*P
2: for i=n-2 downto 0 {
3:    T[2] = 2*T[d[i]]
4:    T[1] = T[0]+T[1]
5:    T[0] = T[2-d[i]]
6:    T[1] = T[1+d[i]]
7:    }
8: return T[0]
```

Algorithm 2. ADA(from LSB)

```
INPUT: d, P
OUTPUT: d*P
1: T[0] = 0, T[2] = P
2: for i=0 upto n-1 {
3:    T[1] = T[0]+T[2]
4:    T[2] = 2*T[2]
5:    T[0] = T[d[i]]
6: }
7: return T[0]
```

Since a scalar multiplication is the most time consuming part in ECC, various techniques for speeding-up has been proposed. On the other hand, this computation is a main target of side channel attacks .

Addition Chain. Let $d = d_{n-1}2^{n-1} + \cdots + d_1 2^1 + d_0$ $(d_i \in \{0,1\}, d_{n-1} = 1)$ be a binary representation of an n-bit scalar d. Then the binary method from the least significant bit (LSB), the binary method from the most significant bit (MSB), and the Montgomery Ladder (Algorithm 1) computes scalar multiplications efficiently. Standard addition formula can be combined with all of the methods, while the x-coordinate-only formula can be combined only to the Montgomery Ladder.

Note that some algorithms use precomputed tables in order to improve the efficiency. Since such methods require rather a large amount of registers and are expensive for low-end smart cards, we do not consider such strategies in the followings.

Coordinate System. In the previous section, an elliptic curve is given by the affine coordinate system, in which addition formulas require inversions in K. In most environments (especially, in our supposed environments), computing inversions is sometimes a hard task. Thus following coordinate systems are widely used to avoid inversions. In the projective coordinate system, a point on an elliptic curve is represented as a tuple of K-elements (X, Y, Z), and two points (X, Y, Z) and $(\lambda X, \lambda Y, \lambda Z)$ $(\lambda \in K \backslash \{0\})$ are identified. The elliptic curve equation is obtained by substituting $x = X/Z$, $y = Y/Z$ into the affine equation. The point at infinity is represented as points whose Z-coordinate value being 0.

Table 1. Computing amounts of ECADD/ECDBL

	Coordinate	ECADD		ECDBL
	System	$Z \neq 1$	$Z = 1$	$a \neq -3$
Standard	$\mathcal{P}$	$12M + 2S$	$9M + 2S$	$7M + 5S$
Formula	$\mathcal{J}$	$12M + 4S$	$8M + 3S$	$4M + 6S$
x-coordinate	$\mathcal{P}$	$8M + 2S$	$8M + 3S$	$6M + 3S$
Formula			$13M + 4S$	

The Jacobian coordinate system is also used. However, a detailed description is omitted here (see [CMO98]).

Table 1 summarizes amounts of computations of ECADD and ECDBL in the projective coordinate system $\mathcal{P}$ and the Jacobian system $\mathcal{J}$, where M, S, I denote the computing times of a multiplication, a squaring and an inversion in the definition field K, respectively. The last row of Table 1 describes amounts of computations of a merged function xECADDDBL, which computes xECADD and xECDBL together [IT02].

2.2 Power Analysis

Power analysis attack is a powerful side channel attack in which power traces of smart cards are observed and analyzed. The following SPA and DPA are typical examples of the power analysis. For elliptic curve cryptosystems, the following RPA and ZVA, variants of DPA, should be also considered.

Simple Power Analysis (SPA). Binary methods compute an ECADD when d_i, the i-th bit of d, equals to 1. Since power traces of ECADD and ECDBL have different patterns, an adversary easily detect the corresponding value of d_i by analyzing power traces. This is a main idea of the simple power analysis (SPA) proposed by Kocher [Koc96], which can be applied to other exponentiation-based cryptosystems such as RSA.

The simplest way to resist SPA is the add-and-double-always method (ADA) proposed by Coron [Cor99], in which an ECADD and an ECDBL are computed for every bit independent from a value d_i (Algorithm 2, 3). Since power traces of these algorithm become fixed, the adversary cannot detect d_i any more. However, the efficiency of a scalar multiplication is reduced because of dummy operations. On the other hand, the Montgomery Ladder substantially resists SPA since it computes ECADD and ECDBL for each bit.

Differential Power Analysis (DPA). Patterns of power traces depend on not only operations but operands. Assume an adversary is able to simulate the target computation and obtain arbitrary intermediate status. By assuming $d_i = 1$ (for example), the adversary can collect simulated power traces and classify them into two groups depending on the hamming weight of intermediate values. If the assumptions is correct, there appears some differences between these power traces, and the adversary can confirm the correctness of his/her assumption. This is a basic strategy of the differential power analysis (DPA) [KJJ99, MDS99]. DPA can be applied to ECC and RSA.

Refined Power Analysis (RPA) and Zero Value Analysis (ZVA). Goubin enhanced DPA to the refined power analysis (RPA) applicable to ECC only [Gou03]. Points with 0-coordinate values are called the *special points*. These points are easily observed by DPA since power traces with regard to the special points are so characteristic. In RPA, an adversary adaptively chooses the base point and tries to detect such characteristic patterns in power traces. RPA can be applied to all of described addition chains.

Algorithm 3. ADA (from MSB)

INPUT: d, P
OUTPUT: d*P
1: T[0] = 0, T[1] = P
2: for i=n-1 downto 0
3:    T[0] = 2*T[0]
4:    T[1] = T[0]+T[2]
5:    T[0] = T[d[i]]
6: }
7: return T[0]

Algorithm 4. MMM method

INPUT: d, P
OUTPUT: d*P
1: T[0] = randompoint()
2: T[1] = -T[0]
3: T[2] = P+T[1]
4: for i=n-1 downto 0 {
5:    T[0] = 2*T[0]
6:    T[0] = T[0]+T[1+d[i]]
7: }
8: return T[0]

Akishita and Takagi extended RPA to the zero value analysis (ZVA) [AT03], in which an adversary detects 0-values in ECADD and ECDBL, rather than 0-values in intermediate points. ZVA is also applicable to ECC only.

Countermeasures. Since SPA and DPA are independent attacks, the Montgomery Ladder (Algorithm 1) or add-and-double-always methods (Algorithm 2,3) are required to resist SPA. We assume to use these algorithms in the followings.

In order to resist DPA, RPA and ZVA, randomization is a common technique [Cor99]. Clavier and Joye split a scalar randomly, in which dP is computed by $dP = rP + (d - r)P$ for a random integer r (exponent splitting, ES) [CJ01]. ES requires at least twice amount of computation than without it. Ciet and Joye proposed another splitting method, in which dP is computed by $\lfloor d/r \rfloor (rP) + (d \bmod r)P$ for a random integer r (improved exponent splitting, iES) [CJ03]. The size of r can be as long as half of the size of d, and, with the Shamir's trick, it provides an efficient computation without reducing the security.

On the other hand, the randomized linearly-transformed coordinates countermeasure (RLC) [IIT04] is an extension of Coron's randomized projective coordinates countermeasure (RPC) [Cor99]. While RPC is vulnerable to RPA/ZVA, RLC resists all of DPA/RPA/ZVA. Itoh et al. also proposed the randomized initial point countermeasure (RIP) in the same paper [IIT04]. Since RIP is a main topic of this paper, we proceed to the next section.

3   Randomized Initial Point Countermeasure (RIP)

The randomized initial point countermeasure (RIP), which is a main topic of this paper, is a DPA/RPA/ZVA-countermeasure proposed by Itoh et al. [IIT04]. When a scalar multiplication is computed by the binary method from LSB, or the add-and-double-always method from LSB, compute $R + dP$ for a randomly generated point R in the addition chain and output dP by subtracting R from the above result. RIP is very similar to Coron's 2nd countermeasure [Cor99] which computes a scalar multiplication dP by $d(P + Q) - R$ for $R = dQ$. Since R should be equal to dQ, R is not a random point. In fact, Okeya and Sakurai showed the security problem of the Coron's 2nd countermeasure [OS00]. In a sense, RIP is an extension of the Coron's 2nd countermeasure.

In the proposal paper, Itoh et al. claimed that RIP can be combined only to LSB methods [IIT04] (in spite of the naming). However, a principle of RIP, namely

Add a random point to initial points in the beginning. After finishing a main scalar multiplication, exclude an unnecessary point from the result

is not dependent from addition chains. Thus, in the followings, we discuss the possibility of the application of this principle to add-and-double-always method from LSB (Algorithm 2), add-and-double-always method from MSB (Algorithm 3), and the Montgomery Ladder (Algorithm 1).

3.1 Binary Methods from LSB

Algorithm 2 uses 3 registers T[0], T[1], T[2]. When an initial point of a register T[0] is replaced from $\mathcal{O}$ to an arbitrary (random) point R, since the algorithm outputs $R + dP$, desired dP is obtained by subtracting R from the above output. This is the original RIP proposed by Itoh et al. [IIT04]. We denote this algorithm as RIP(LSB,0). For generating a random point R, Itoh et al. proposed some concrete algorithms. For example, R can be kept inside of a smart card (as a global register).

Since a register T[1] is initialized in step 3, changing an initial point has no effect on a scalar multiplication.

On the other hand, when an initial point of a register T[2] is replaced from P to $P + R$, (and if an initial point of T[0] is not changed) since the algorithm outputs $d(P + R)$, desired dP is contained by subtracting dR from the above output. This is the randomized base-point countermeasure by Coron [Cor99] (RIP(LSB,2)), however, there requires to compute dR in turn. In addition, a security problem is pointed out in [OS00].

It is possible to replace initial points of registers T[0], T[2] at the same time (RIP(LSB,0+2)). However, the efficiency is not competitive since it requires another scalar multiplication.

3.2 Binary Methods from MSB

Algorithm 3 uses 3 registers T[0], T[1], T[2]. When an initial point of a variable T[0] is replaced from $\mathcal{O}$ to a random point R (and if an initial point of a register T[2] is not changed), the algorithm outputs $dP + 2^n R$ (RIP(MSB,0)). By subtracting $2^n R$ from the output, we obtain a desired dP. If we update R by $R \leftarrow 2R$ after step 5, $2^n R$ is obtained when step 6 finishes. Or keeping a pair $(R, 2^n R)$ inside a smart card would be another solution. Since 2^n is independent from the secret d, there are no leakage of d in the computation of $2^n R$.

Since a register T[1] is initialized in step 4, changing an initial point has no effect on a scalar multiplication.

On the other hand, when an initial point of a register T[2] is replaced from P to $P + R$ (and if an initial point of a register T[0] is not changed), the algorithm outputs $d(P + R)$ (RIP(MSB,2)). This is again identical to Coron's countermeasure. Similar to the LSB case, it is possible to replace initial points of registers T[0], T[2] at the same time (RIP(MSB,0+2)).

Let us denote -1 as $\bar{1}$. Using a fact that an arbitrary point R is represented as $R = (1\bar{1}\ldots\bar{1})_2 R$, Mamiya et al. proposed a countermeasure (Algorithm 4, RIP(MSB,MMM)) [MMM04], which is a variant of RIP(MSB,0+2). Here a function randompoint() generates a random point on an elliptic curve. See [IIT04] for concrete constructions.

3.3   Montgomery Ladder

Algorithm 1 uses 3 registers T[0], T[1], T[2]. Since a register T[2] is initialized in step 3, changing an initial point has no effect on a scalar multiplication.

When an initial point of one of registers T[0], T[1] is added by a random point R, Algorithm 1 outputs $dP + d'R$ (RIP(Mon,0), RIP(Mon,1)). Then computing $d'P$ is required in turn. Since a scalar d' is dependent on d, computing $d'R$ might introduce the leakage of the secret d. This strategy is not suitable as a countermeasure.

On the other hand, when initial points of both of T[0], T[1] are added by a random point R, Algorithm 1 outputs $dP + 2^{n-1}R$ (RIP(Mon,0+1)). Here computing $2^{n-1}R$ is required again, but it is obtained easily similar to RIP(MSB,0). Since 2^{n-1} is independent form the secret d, there are no leakage of d in the computation of $2^{n-1}R$.

Strongly note that in step 6 of the Montgomery Ladder (Algorithm 1), a difference of two registers T[0] and T[1] is kept always to be P. Therefore, the x-coordinate-only method can be applied to the algorithm and the efficiency will be considerably improved.

4   Comparison

In this section, we compare amounts of computation for a scalar multiplication and of intermediate registers of the exponent splitting countermeasure (ES) [CJ01], the improved exponent splitting countermeasure (iES) [CJ03], the randomized linearly-transformed coordinates countermeasure (RLC) [IIT04] and the randomized initial point countermeasure (RIP) [IIT04] discussed in this paper. Note that all of above algorithms resist all of DPA, RPA, ZVA. A comparison is summarized in Table 2.

Assumption. In each countermeasure, add-and-double-always method (including the Montgomery Ladder) is used as an SPA-countermeasure. The projective or Jacobian coordinates is used. We assumed $a \neq 3$ and $1S = 0.8M$ in the estimation, here M, S denotes computing times for a multiplication and a squaring in the definition field. In addition, we assumed that pre-computations and post-computations of a scalar multiplication are negligible. Especially, we assumed

Table 2. A comparison of SPA/DPA/RPA/ZVA/ADPA-resistant countermeasures

Countermeasure	# of global reg.	# of local reg.	Computing time per bit
ES + ADA (from MSB)	–	5	$24M + 18S$ $(38.4M)$
iES + ADA (from MSB) + Shamir's trick	–	4	$12M + 9S$ $(19.2M)$
RLC + ADA (from MSB) + RA	–	3	$20M + 10S$ $(28.0M)$
RLC + ADA (from LSB) + RA	–	4	$17M + 10S$ $(25.0M)$
RLC + ADA (from LSB) + iECDBL + RA	–	4	$17M + 8S$ $(23.4M)$
RIP + ADA (from MSB) + RA	0/1	5/4	$16M + 10S$ $(24.0M)$
RIP + ADA (from MSB) + SSM($t = 2$) + RA	0/1	7/6	$10.3M + 8.1S$ $(16.8M)$
RIP + ADA (from MSB) + SSM($t = 3$) + RA	0/1	11/10	$8.7M + 7.6S$ $(14.7M)$
RIP + ADA (from MSB) + SSM($t = 4$) + RA	0/1	19/18	$8.2M + 7.4S$ $(14.1M)$
RIP(LSB,0) + RA	0/1	4/3	$16M + 10S$ $(24.0M)$
RIP(LSB,0) + iECDBL + RA	0/1	–[1]	$16M + 8S$ $(22.4M)$
RIP(LSB,0+2) + RA	0/1	5/4	$32M + 20S$ $(48.0M)$
RIP(MSB,0) + RA	0/1	4/3	$16M + 15S$ $(28.0M)$
	2	3	$12M + 9S$ $(19.2M)$
RIP(MSB,0+2) + RA	0/1	5/4	$32M + 30S$ $(56.0M)$
	2	4	$24M + 18S$ $(38.4M)$
RIP(Mon,0+1) + RA	0/1	4/3	$13M + 4S$ $(16.2M)$
	2	3	$13M + 4S$ $(16.2M)$

a processing time for the function `randompoint()`. We used the estimation in [IIT04] for ES, iES, RLC, ADA (from MSB)+RIP. Here RIP (from MSB) is identical to a countermeasure proposed by Mamiya et al. [MMM04] and SSM denotes a simultaneous scalar multiplication.

Address-bit DPA. In addition to SPA/DPA/RPA/ZVA, we also consider the address-bit DPA (ADPA) proposed by Itoh et al. [IIT02], since RLC and RIP are vulnerable to this attack. However, the randomized addressing countermeasure (RA) [IIT03] is an efficient countermeasure for these algorithms.

The Number of Intermediate Registers. For a random point generation in RIP, we used methods described in [IIT04]. Since the number of intermediate (global or local) registers vary from the generating algorithms, we list up the possible values. Here we assumed that 1 register holds coordinate for 1 point.

In Table 2, registers outside a scalar multiplication are called as the *global*, registers inside are as *local*. For example, for RIP(LSB,0), there is a description 0/1 for global registers and 4/3 for local registers. This means that 0 global registers are required if 4 local registers are used, and 1 global register is required if 3 local registers are used.

Discussion. As in Table 2, the most efficient countermeasure is a combination of RIP (from MSB) and a simultaneous scalar multiplication (ADA(from

---

[1] Since iterated ECDBL (iECDBL) computes ECDBLs in the addition chain layer, rather than as the function, the number of (apparently) required registers grows larger. Thus we omit the number because this situation is quite different from others.

MSB)+RIP +SSM($t = 4$)+RA). On the other hand, when we consider the number of local registers, a combination of RIP and the Montgomery Ladder (RIP(Mon,0+1)+RA) provides relatively efficient countermeasure. Especially, this method establishes about 28% improvement from the original RIP countermeasure [IIT04]. Thus this countermeasures can be regarded as a leading alternative for low-end smart card applications.

5   Concluding Remarks

This paper discussed the randomized initial point method (RIP) as a DPA/RPA/ZVA-countermeasure, and propose some countermeasures. Especially, a combination of RIP and the Montgomery Ladder establishes about 28% improvement on the original countermeasure.

It is taken for granted that there is no choice to sacrifice the efficiency for implementing power analysis countermeasures. However, RIP countermeasure has almost no penalty from scalar multiplication algorithms without such countermeasures. [2]. On this point, RIP randomizes without sacrifice the efficiency. But RIP even requires dummy operations for SPA-resistance. Reducing dummy operations without reducing the security will be the future work.

Acknowledgements

The authors would like to thank Naoya Torii and anonymous reviewers for their helpful comments.

References

[AT03]   T. Akishita, T. Takagi, "Zero-value Point Attacks on Elliptic Curve Cryptosystem", *ISC 2003*, LNCS 2851, pp.218-233, Springer-Verlag, 2003.

[BJ02]   E. Brier, M. Joye, "Weierstraß Elliptic Curvs and Side-Channel Attacks", *PKC 2002*, LNCS 2274, pp.335-345, Springer-Verlag, 2002.

[Cor99]   J. Coron, "Resistance against differential power analysis for elliptic curve cryptosystem", *CHES'99*, LNCS 1717, pp.292-302, Springer-Verlag, 1999.

[CJ01]   C. Clavier, M. Joye, "Universal exponentiation algorithm – A first step towards provable SPA-resistance –", *CHES 2001*, LNCS 2162, pp. 300-308, Springer-Verlag, 2001.

[CJ03]   M. Ciet, M. Joye, "(Virtually) Free Randomization Technique for Elliptic Curve Cryptography", *ICICS 2003*, LNCS 2836, pp. 348-359, Springer-Verlag, 2003.

[CMO98]   H. Cohen, A. Miyaji, T. Ono, "Efficient Elliptic Curve Exponentiation using Mixed Coordinates", *Asiacrypt'98*, LNCS 1514, pp.51-65, Springer-Verlag, 1998.

[Gou03]   L. Goubin, "A Refined Power-Analysis Attack on Elliptic Curve Cryptosystems", *PKC 2003*, LNCS 2567, pp.199-210, Springer-Verlag, 2003.

---

[2] Of course some overheads are required for pre-computations and post-computations. However, these computations can be negligible from a total computation.

[IIT02]   K. Itoh, T. Izu, M. Takenaka, "Address-bit Differential Power Analysis of Cryptographic Schemes OK-ECDH and OK-ECDSA", *CHES 2002*, LNCS 2523, pp.129-143, Springer-Verlag, 2003.

[IIT03]   K. Itoh, T. Izu, M. Takenaka, "A Practical Countermeasure against Address-bit Differential Power Analysis", *CHES 2003*, LNCS 2779, pp. 382-396, Springer-Verlag, 2003.

[IIT04]   K. Itoh, T. Izu, M. Takenaka, "Efficient Countermeasure against Power Analysis for Elliptic Curve Cryptosystems", *CARDIS 2004*, pp.99-114, Kluwer, 2004.

[IT02]   T. Izu and T. Takagi, "A Fast Parallel Elliptic Curve Multiplication Resisntant against Elliptic Curve Cryptosystems", *PKC 2002*, LNCS 2274, pp.280-296, Springer-Verlag, 2002.

[Koc96]   C. Kocher, "Timing attacks on Implementations of Diffie-Hellman, RSA, DSS, and other systems", *Crypto'96*, LNCS 1109, pp.104-113, Springer-Verlag, 1996.

[KJJ99]   C. Kocher, J. Jaffe, B. Jun, "Differential Power Analysis", *Crypto'99*, LNCS 1666, pp.388-397, Springer-Verlag, 1999.

[Mon87]   P. Montgomery, "Speeding the Pollard and Elliptic Curve Methods for Factorizations", *Mathematics of Computation*, vol.48, pp.243-264, 1987.

[MDS99]   T. Messerges, E. Dabbish, R. Sloan, "Power Analysis Attacks of Modular Exponentiation in Smartcards", *CHES'99*, LNCS 1717, pp. 144-157, Springer-Verlag, 1999.

[MMM04]   H. Mamiya, A. Miyaji, H. Morimoto, "Efficient Countermeasures against RPA, DPA, and SPA", *CHES 2004*, LNCS 3156, pp. 343-356, Springer-Verlag, 2004.

[OS00]   K. Okeya, K. Sakurai, "Power Analysis Breaks Elliptic Curve Cryptosystems even Secure Against the Timing Attack", *Indocrypt 2000*, LNCS 1977, pp.178-190, Springer-Verlag, 2000.

Syntax-Driven Private Evaluation of Quantified Membership Queries

Aggelos Kiayias[1] and Antonina Mitrofanova[2]

[1] Computer Science and Engineering,
University of Connecticut Storrs, CT, USA
aggelos@cse.uconn.edu
[2] Computer Science, Rutgers University,
New Brunswick, NJ, USA
amitrofa@cs.rutgers.edu

Abstract. Membership queries are basic predicate operations that apply to datasets. Quantifications of such queries express global properties between datasets, including subset inclusion and disjointness. These operations are basic tools in set-theoretic data-mining procedures such as frequent-itemset-mining. In this work we formalize a family of such queries syntactically and we consider how they can be evaluated in a *privacy-preserving* fashion. We present a syntax-driven compiler that produces a protocol for each query and we show that semantically such queries correspond to basic set operation predicates between datasets. Using our compiler and based on the fact that it is syntax-driven, two parties can generate various privacy-preserving protocols with different complexity behavior that allow them to efficiently and securely evaluate the predicate of interest without sharing information about the datasets they possess. Our compiler sheds new light on the complexity of privacy-preserving evaluation of predicates such as disjointness and subset-inclusion and achieves substantial complexity improvements compared to previous works in terms of round as well as communication complexity. In particular, among others, we present protocols for both predicates that require one-round of interaction and have communication less than the size of the universe, while previously the only one round protocols known had communication proportional to the size of the universe.

1 Introduction

While data sharing and processing across organizations becomes more and more common, the transfer of data of an organization to an extrinsic data-processing entity raises serious issues from the data privacy point of view. For this reason privacy preserving data processing has recently become an area of crucial importance. The goal of any privacy-preserving data processing operation is to allow the processing of data without revealing it to the processing entity. Moreover, privacy concerns frequently cut both ways as the processing entity may also wish to protect the privacy of its local data that relates to the computation.

A common general setting is the following: two entities, dubbed Alice and Bob, possess two datasets A and B respectively that are subsets of a publicly known universe of elements. Either Alice or Bob wishes to calculate a set theoretic function on the

J. Zhou, M. Yung, and F. Bao (Eds.): ACNS 2006, LNCS 3989, pp. 470–485, 2006.

two datasets without sharing any information with the other player. Depending on the application domain and the function of interest, a number of recent previous works has appeared exploring this problem; for example, the work of [16] for equality tests, the work of [17] for intersection and the cardinality of the intersection, the work of [20] for the disjointness predicate, the work of [14] for multiset operations, the work of [15] for subset inclusion, and others.

Our Results. In this paper, we investigate a new efficient way to evaluate *quantified membership queries* in a privacy preserving fashion. An example of a quantified membership query (or QMQ for short) is $\forall x \in A : x \in B$; this query has a set theoretic semantic interpretation which corresponds to the predicate $A \subseteq B$. All QMQ's we consider have a semantic set-theoretic predicate interpretation. Moreover, various queries correspond to the same semantic interpretation. We take a unique advantage of this fact as will be seen below. Our syntactic definition for QMQ's corresponds to all possible set theoretic predicates that one can express for two sets A, B and their complements using the intersection and subset operations. Two particular application domains for privacy preserving QMQ evaluation operations are testing disjointness and subset inclusion.

Our main result is a compiler that processes a QMQ and generates a specific protocol according to the syntax of the query. The main idea behind our compiler design is the algebraic interpretation of a QMQ that maps a universal quantification to a summation between polynomial evaluations and an existential quantification to a product between polynomial evaluations.

Our compiler is in fact *syntax-driven* in the sense that the resulting protocol is dependent on the syntax of the query (and not only on the query's semantic set-theoretic interpretation). It turns out that the construction of such a mechanism is extremely beneficial as the communication, round and time complexity of semantically equivalent protocols that result from our compiler vary, and the two players may choose the one that suits them best, depending on the certain application domain (and we do provide a full analysis on which variant to use). Depending on the relative sizes of $A, B, [n]$, where $[n]$ is the universe from which A, B are drawn, the two parties should follow a different protocol in order to optimize their privacy-preserving operation.

We apply our compiler to solve two known set-theoretic predicates whose privacy-preserving evaluation has been considered before, namely disjointness and subset inclusion. In particular, using our compiler for different QMQ's that correspond to disjointness and subset inclusion, we obtain 8 distinct protocols for each predicate. The resulting protocols advance the state of the art of these two problems w.r.t. communication and round complexity as shown in figure 1. In particular, among others, our compiler produces protocols for both predicates that require one-round of interaction and have communication less than the size of the universe, while previously the only single round protocols had communication proportional to the size of the universe. Moreover, our compiler offers flexibility in choosing the best protocol for a given application domain depending on the relative sizes of the involved sets (cf. section 5).

Our constructions employ variants of the ElGamal encryption function [12] and are proven secure under the Decisional Diffie Hellman assumption. Our compiler descrip-

	Subset-Inclusion $C \subseteq S$	Intersection $C \cap S \neq \emptyset$
[20] 1st Scheme		$O(n)$, 1 round
[20] 2nd Scheme		$O(c \cdot s)$, c rounds
[15]	$O(n)$, 1 round	-
Present paper	$O(c \cdot s)$, 1 round	$O(c \cdot s)$, s rounds
based on the compiler	$O(s)$, 1.5 rounds	$O(\bar{c})$, 1 round
for various QMQ's	$O(\bar{c})$, 1 round	$O(\bar{s})$, 1.5 rounds
	etc. (cf. section 5)	etc. (cf. section 5)

Fig. 1. An example of the results from our compiler for privacy-preserving evaluation of two predicates by a client and a server. Note $C, S \subseteq [n]$, with $|C| = c$ and $|S| = s$, $\bar{c} = n - c$, $\bar{s} = n - s$. The table shows the communication and round complexity.

tion is suited to the so called semi-honest setting [19], but we also present all necessary modifications that are required to transform each protocol generated by our compiler to the general malicious adversary setting. For dealing with such adversaries we employ zero-knowledge proofs [18] that are efficient [7] and universally composable commitments, [3, 10]. It should be noted that all our applications can also be solved by generic protocols of [24, 21] operating over circuits; nevertheless, the communication, time and round complexity of such protocols is typically much inferior to application specific protocols such as the ones presented in this work.

Applications to Privacy-Preserving FIM. Privacy-preserving evaluation of set theoretic predicates has many applications in frequent-itemset-mining (or FIM) operations, see e.g., [13]. In the FIM setting, a server has a database of transactions $t_1, \ldots, t_m$; each transaction t_j is a subset of a given set of n items (which is the universe in our terminology, i.e., $t_j \subseteq [n] = \{1, \ldots, n\}$). For example a transaction may correspond to the items that were bought from a provider's inventory. Consider now the following challenge: a client (that performs a data-processing operation on the database owned by the server) possesses a challenge set of items c and wants to process the transactions in the database that contain c (e.g., for the purpose of counting them or performing other statistics). It follows that the client wishes to evaluate the predicate $c \subseteq t_j$ for $j = 1, \ldots, m$, i.e., perform a privacy preserving subset-inclusion operation. Consider also the following scenario: the client has a *transaction* t and wants to count how many transactions from the database share some common item with t. In this case the client wishes to evaluate the predicate $c \cap t_j$ for $j = 1, \ldots, m$.

While the above problems have received a lot of attention in the data-mining community (see e.g., [13]), it was only recently that such problems were considered from a privacy-preserving point of view (in particular the subset-inclusion variant as above). In [15] the privacy-preserving scenario for FIM was discussed and a protocol was presented that required communication complexity proportional to n for each predicate evaluation. Note that n is the size of the universe of all possible items and in most settings it is substantially larger than the size of each transaction t_j. Our results, as evidenced in table 1 achieve substantial improvements for various special cases, e.g., when $c, t_j < \sqrt{n}$, when $t_j \ll n$, when t is large etc.

2   Cryptographic Tools

Homomorphic Encryption. An encryption scheme is a triple $\langle K, E, D \rangle$ of algorithms defined as follows: the key generation algorithm K on input 1^ℓ (where ℓ is the key length) outputs a public key pk and a secret key sk. The encryption function E_{pk} uses the public key pk for its operation $E_{pk} : R \times P \to C$. In this case, P is the plaintext space, C is the ciphertext space and R is the randomness space (all parameterized by ℓ). At the same time, the decryption function $D_{sk} : C \to P$ uses the secret key sk so that for any plaintext $p \in P$, if $E_{pk}(r, p) = c$, then $D_{sk}(c) = p$ for any $r \in R$. Homomorphic encryption adds to the above the following requirements: there exist binary operations $+, \oplus, \odot$ defined over the spaces P, R, C so that $\langle P, + \rangle, \langle R, \oplus \rangle$ are the groups written additively and $\langle C, \odot \rangle$ multiplicatively. We say that an encryption scheme is homomorphic if for all $r_1, r_2 \in R$ and all $x_1, x_2 \in P$ it holds that $E_{pk}(r_1, x_1) \odot E_{pk}(r_2, x_2) = E_{pk}(r_1 \oplus r_2, x_1 + x_2)$.

Informally, this means that if we want to "add" plaintexts that are encrypted, we may "multiply" their corresponding ciphertexts. Moreover, we can multiply an encrypted plaintext by an integer constant, by raising its corresponding ciphertext to the power that is equal to the integer constant — which is essentially multiplying a ciphertext by itself a number of times; note that this can be done efficiently by using standard repeated squaring (squaring under the operation $\odot$).

ElGamal Homomorphic Encryption. We will employ a standard variant of ElGamal encryption [12]. This variant of ElGamal has been employed numerous times in the past (e.g., in the context of e-voting [8]). This public-key encryption scheme is a triple $\langle K, E, D \rangle$ defined as follows:

- Key-generation K. Given a security parameter ℓ, the probabilistic algorithm $K(1^\ell)$ outputs a public-key $pk := \langle p, q, g, h \rangle$ and the corresponding secret-key x so that the following are satisfied: (i) p is a ℓ-bit prime number so that $q \mid (p - 1)$ and q is also a prime number of length $s(\ell)$ where $s(\cdot)$ is a publicly known parameter function (e.g., $s : \mathbb{N} \to \mathbb{N}$ with $s(\ell) = \lfloor \ell/2 \rfloor$). (ii) g is an element of order q in $\mathbb{Z}_p^*$. (iii) $h \in \langle g \rangle$ are randomly selected. (iv) $x = \log_g h$.
- Encryption E. Given public-key $pk = \langle p, q, g, h \rangle$ and a plaintext $m \in \mathbb{Z}_q$, E samples $r \leftarrow_R \mathbb{Z}_q$ and returns $\langle g^r, h^r g^m \rangle$.
- Decryption D. Given secret-key x and a ciphertext $\langle G, H \rangle$ the decryption algorithm returns the value $G^{-x} H \bmod p$. Note that this will only return g^m, nevertheless this would be sufficient for our setting as, given a ciphertext $\langle g^r, h^r g^m \rangle$ we will only be interested in testing the predicate $\mathsf{Zero}(m)$ which is true if and only if $m = 0$. Note that this predicate is easily computable given $g^m \bmod p$ by simply testing whether $G^{-x} H \equiv_p 1$).

Observe that the above encryption scheme is homomorphic: indeed, the randomness space R, the plaintext space P and the ciphertext space C satisfy the following: (i) $R = P = \mathbb{Z}_q$ and $(R, \oplus), (P, +)$ are additive groups by setting the operations $\oplus, +$ to be addition modulo q. (ii) $C \subseteq \mathbb{Z}_p^* \times \mathbb{Z}_p^*$ and it holds that $(C, \odot)$ is a multiplicative group when $\odot$ is defined as pointwise multiplication modulo p. (iii) it holds that for any $r_1, r_2 \in R, x_1, x_2$, and $pk = \langle p, g, h, f \rangle$, $E_{pk}(r_1, x_1) \odot E_{pk}(r_2, x_2) = \langle g^{r_1}, h^{r_1} f^{x_1} \rangle \odot \langle g^{r_2}, h^{r_2} f^{x_2} \rangle = \langle g^{r_1 + r_2}, h^{r_1 + r_2} f^{x_1 + x_2} \rangle$.

Superposed Encryption. A superposed encryption scheme is an encryption scheme between two-players that is homomorphic and allows a player to transform a ciphertext that is generated by the other player into a "superposed" ciphertext that contains the encryption of a product of the two plaintexts, the original plaintext and one selected by the party doing the superposing operation. Superposed ciphertexts are *doubly encrypted* ciphertexts that neither player can decrypt. Nevertheless, given a superposed ciphertext any player can remove his/her encryption from the superposed ciphertext and reduce it to a regular ciphertext that the other player can subsequently decrypt.

More precisely, given a ciphertext c that is encrypting m according to the key of player A, a player that possesses m' can transform c to a superposed ciphertext that no player alone can decrypt and contains the encryption of $m \cdot m'$. The superposed ciphertext can be subsequently reduced to a player-A-ciphertext that encrypts $m \cdot m'$ by player B, or to a player-B-ciphertext that encrypts $m \cdot m'$ by player A. Superposed encryption was introduced in [20] and as a notion subsumes $(2, 2)$-threshold encryption which was also demonstrated to have a number of applications in two party secure computations (see e.g., [23]). Formally, superposed encryption is a sequence of procedures $\langle K, K', E, E^{\text{ext}}, D, D^{\text{sup}} \rangle$ defined as follows:

- The key generation algorithm K is comprised by an initial key generation step that produces the public parameter *param*, as well as K' that produces the public-key and secret-key for each user (given the parameter *param*).

  Below we fix *param* $\leftarrow K(\ell)$ and

$$(pk_A, sk_A), (pk_B, sk_B) \leftarrow K'(param)$$

- The two encryption functions are defined as follows: $E_{pk_X} : P \to C$ and $E_{pk_A, pk_B}^{\text{sup}, X} : P \times C \to C^{\text{sup}}$ for each player $X \in \{A, B\}$.
- The encryption function E_{pk_X} is homomorphic for the plaintext $(P, +)$, randomness $(R, \oplus)$ and ciphertext group $(C, \odot)$. Moreover, $(P, +, \cdot)$ is a ring.
- The superposed encryption: $E_{pk_A, pk_B, sk_X}^{\text{sup}, X}(m, E_{pk_{\overline{X}}}(m'))$ as well as the one with the plaintexts in reverse order: $E_{pk_A, pk_B, sk_X}^{\text{sup}, X}(m', E_{pk_{\overline{X}}}(m))$ are indistinguishable for any fixed m, m', where X is a player, $X \in \{A, B\}$, and $\overline{X}$ is the other player, $\overline{X} \in \{A, B\} - \{X\}$.
- The decryption functions satisfy the following conditions:
  - $D_{sk_X}(E_{pk_X}(m)) = m$ if $X \in \{A, B\}$, for all $m \in P$.
  - For any fixed $c \in E_{pk_X}(m')$, it holds that if c' is distributed according to

$$D_{sk_X}^{\text{sup}}(E_{pk_A, pk_B, sk_{\overline{X}}}^{\text{sup}, \overline{X}}(m, c))$$

  then c' is uniformly distributed over $E_{pk_{\overline{X}}}(m \cdot m')$.
  where $X \in \{A, B\}$ and $\overline{X}$ is the single element of $\{A, B\} - \{X\}$.

Implementation. It is possible to build a superposed encryption scheme based on ElGamal encryption as follows:

Parameter Generation. Two primes p, q such that q dividing $p - 1$ are selected as well as an element g of order q inside $\mathbb{Z}_p^*$. The public-parameters *param* are set to $\langle p, q, g \rangle$.

Key Generation. Each player X samples sk_X at random from $\mathbb{Z}_q$ and sets $pk_X = h_X = g^{sk_X}$.

Encryption. The encryption function using $param$ and pk_X, given $m \in \mathbb{Z}_q$ it samples r from $\mathbb{Z}_q$ and returns $\langle g^r, h_X^r g^m \rangle$.

Decryption. The decryption function using param and sk_X, given $\langle G, H \rangle$ it returns HG^{-sk_X} [note again that this does not reveal the value of m but this does not affect our constructions that require the extraction of only a single bit from m; in particular we will only be interested in the predicate $\mathsf{Zero}(D_{sk_X}(\langle G, H \rangle)) = 1$.

Superposed Encryption. Given a ciphertext $\langle G, H \rangle$ that was sampled from $E_{pk_{\overline{X}}}(m')$ the superposed encryption operates as follows:

$$E^{\mathsf{sup},X}_{pk_A, pk_B, sk_X}(m, \langle G, H \rangle) = \langle G^{m'} g^{r'}, H^{m'} G^{m' \cdot sk_X}(h_A \cdot h_B)^{r'} \rangle$$

Observe that

$$E^{\mathsf{sup},X}_{pk_A, pk_B, sk_X}(m, \langle g^r, (h_{\overline{X}})^r g^m \rangle) = \langle g^{rm' + r'}, (h_{\overline{X}})^{m' r} g^{mm'}(h_X)^{m' r}(h_A \cdot h_B)^{r'} \rangle$$

$$= \langle g^{r^*}, (h_A \cdot h_B)^{r^*} g^{m \cdot m'} \rangle$$

where $r^* = rm' + r'$ and r' is sampled at random from $\mathbb{Z}_q$, i.e., r^* is also uniformly distributed over $\mathbb{Z}_q$ for any fixed value of r, m'.

A player $X \in \{A, B\}$ removes his decryption from the superposed ciphertext $\langle G_{\mathsf{sup}}, H_{\mathsf{sup}} \rangle$ using his secret-key sk_X as follows $\langle G_{\mathsf{sup}}, H_{\mathsf{sup}} G_{\mathsf{sup}}^{-sk_X} \rangle$. Observe that this is equal to $\langle g^{r^*}, (h_A \cdot h_B)^{r^*} g^{-r^* \cdot sk_X} g^{m \cdot m'} \rangle = \langle g^{r^*}, (h_{\overline{X}})^{r^*} g^{m \cdot m'} \rangle$ i.e., it results in a ciphertext under the public-key of player $\overline{X}$.

Additional cryptographic tools, including interactive protocols, semi-honest security, zero-knowledge proofs of knowledge and universally composable commitments can be found in the appendix.

3   Quantified Membership Queries

Suppose that there are two parties, Client and Server, each one possessing a non-empty set of objects, C and S respectively. Without loss of generality we assume that $C, S \subseteq [n] \stackrel{\text{def}}{=} \{1, \ldots, n\}$. Note that for any $M \subseteq [n]$, we will denote by $\overline{M}$ the complement of M inside $[n]$.

The client wants to evaluate the truth-value of a predicate over the two sets C and S which is expressed as a "quantified membership query" that has the following syntactic definition:

Definition 1. *A* quantified membership query *(QMQ) is a predicate which has the following syntactic form:*

$$\nu(Qx \in A : x \in B)$$

where Q is a quantifier s.t. $Q \in \{\forall, \exists\}$, ν is either $\neg$ or the empty string, $A \in \{C, S, \overline{C}, \overline{S}\}$ and $B \in \{C, S, \overline{C}, \overline{S}\} - \{A, \overline{A}\}$.

When talking about a general QMQ as above, instead of client and server we will use Alice and Bob to signify the owners of the sets A and B respectively (and Alice and Bob may be either the client or the server depending on the particular choice of the sets A, B).

Given a QMQ ϕ and the actual values of the subsets C, S, we can define the truth valuation of ϕ as follows: the QMQ "$\forall x \in C : x \in S$" is to be interpreted as $\forall x \, (x \in C) \to (x \in S)$ and the QMQ "$\exists x \in C : x \in S$" is to be interpreted as $\exists x \, (x \in C) \land (x \in S)$. Similarly for other choices of $A, B \in \{C, S, \overline{C}, \overline{S}\}$. The valuation of ϕ would be equal to the truth value of the corresponding predicate as defined above. We will denote this truth value as $\mathsf{t}_{C,S}(\phi) \in \{\mathrm{T}, \mathrm{F}\}$.

Definition 2. *A protocol for evaluating a QMQ ϕ is a two-party interactive protocol $\mathcal{P}_\phi$ between two-players, the client and the server, each one possessing a set, C, S respectively, which are both subsets of $[n]$. Either party may perform the first move of the protocol $\mathcal{P}_\phi$, but only the client receives output. The protocol computes the functionality $\mathsf{t}_{C,S}(\phi)$, i.e., upon termination of the protocol the client's output matches the valuation of ϕ on the two sets C, S.*

Given the definition above, the problem that the present work is focused on is as follows: given a QMQ ϕ, design a protocol that evaluates ϕ so that the inputs of the client and the server are private, in the semi-honest privacy model as well as in the malicious model. With respect to security, we assume that the values $|C|$ and $|S|$ are publicly known.

$$
\begin{array}{lll}
C \cap S \neq 0 & \exists x \in C : x \in S & \neg \forall x \in C : x \in \overline{S} \\
& \exists x \in S : x \in C & \neg \forall x \in S : x \in \overline{C} \\
\overline{C} \cap S \neq 0 & \exists x \in \overline{C} : x \in S & \neg \forall x \in \overline{C} : x \in \overline{S} \\
& \exists x \in S : x \in \overline{C} & \neg \forall x \in S : x \in C \\
C \cap \overline{S} \neq 0 & \exists x \in C : x \in \overline{S} & \neg \forall x \in C : x \in S \\
& \exists x \in \overline{S} : x \in C & \neg \forall x \in \overline{S} : x \in \overline{C} \\
\overline{C} \cap \overline{S} \neq 0 & \exists x \in \overline{C} : x \in \overline{S} & \neg \forall x \in \overline{C} : x \in S \\
& \exists x \in \overline{S} : x \in \overline{C} & \neg \forall x \in \overline{S} : x \in C \\
C \subseteq S \neq 0 & \forall x \in C : x \in S & \neg \exists x \in \overline{S} : x \in C \\
& \forall x \in \overline{S} : x \in \overline{C} & \neg \exists x \in C : x \in \overline{S} \\
\overline{C} \subseteq S \neq 0 & \forall x \in \overline{C} : x \in S & \neg \exists x \in \overline{S} : x \in \overline{C} \\
& \forall x \in \overline{S} : x \in C & \neg \exists x \in \overline{C} : x \in \overline{S} \\
C \subseteq \overline{S} \neq 0 & \forall x \in S : x \in \overline{C} & \neg \exists x \in S : x \in C \\
& \forall x \in C : x \in \overline{S} & \neg \exists x \in C : x \in S \\
S \subseteq C \neq 0 & \forall x \in S : x \in C & \neg \exists x \in \overline{C} : x \in S \\
& \forall x \in \overline{C} : x \in \overline{S} & \neg \exists x \in S : x \in \overline{C}
\end{array}
$$

Fig. 2. QMQ's and their set theoretic semantics

Semantic Interpretation of QMQ's. Each QMQ ϕ in the semantic sense corresponds to one of eight possible relations (cf. figures 2,3) that two sets may have with respect to each other, considering intersection and inclusion operations. A list of QMQ's together with their semantic interpretation as set relations using intersection and inclusions is

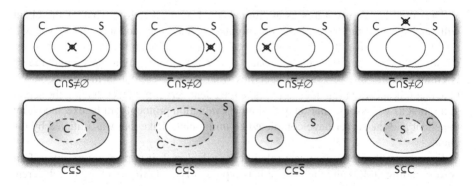

Fig. 3. The eight possible dataset predicate relations based on intersection and inclusion operators

presented in figure 2. As shown in figure 2, each of the relations of figure 3 can be expressed by four different QMQ's. Moreover for each QMQ two different protocols are possible, depending on which party will send the first message in the protocol (this will produce quite different protocols as we will see in our compiler construction below).

4 Syntax-Driven Compiler for QMQ's

In this section we describe a syntax-driven compiler for QMQ's. For uniformity we think of the protocols as interactions between two players, Alice and Bob, that may be interchangeably either the server or the client depending on the given QMQ.

The main idea. The main idea of the compiler is the following: Bob selects a polynomial f so that the roots of f are the elements of the private set of Bob. Then, depending on the quantifier of the QMQ, Alice and Bob will engage in an interaction that will compute either $\sum_{a \in A} r_a \cdot f(a)$ (case $\forall$) or $\prod_{a \in A} f(a)$ (case $\exists$). Observe that the sum is zero if and only if *all* values $f(a)$ equal 0 (with high probability) and that the product is zero if and only if *there exists* a value $f(a)$ that equals 0. Based on this algebraic interpretation of a QMQ (and additional fine tuning steps, see below) the semantics are achieved.

In more detail. The input to the compiler is ϕ, a QMQ in the form of definition 1, i.e., a string $\nu(Qx \in A : x \in B)$. The compiler reads QMQ ϕ and assigns set A to Alice who is either the client or the server depending on A, and assigns the set B to Bob who is either the client or the server depending on B. In each protocol, Bob defines a polynomial $f \in \mathbb{Z}_q[x]$ where q is a large prime so that $f(i) = 0$ iff $i \in B$. This polynomial is evaluated with all elements of Alice's set A. The final result of the protocol is obtained as follows: If $Q = \forall$, the protocol allows the two parties to calculate $\sum_{a_i \in A} r_i \cdot f(a_i)$ (in encrypted form) where each r_i is randomly sampled from $\mathbb{Z}_q$. Observe that $\sum_{a_i \in A} r_i \cdot f(a_i) = 0$ (with high probability) if and only if all $f(a_i) = 0$ for all $a_i \in A$. On the other hand, if $Q = \exists$, the protocol allows the two parties to calculate $\prod_{a \in A} f(a)$ (in encrypted form). Observe that $\prod_{a \in A} f(a) = 0$ iff at least one of $f(a) = 0$. It follows that the output of the protocol can be obtained by checking whether a ciphertext decrypts to 0.

The compiler also requires as additional input a specification: whether the client will send the first message of the polynomial evaluation protocol or the server will send the first message; this choice will produce two different protocols. In other words, the input to the compiler will be a pair $\langle \phi, \mathtt{first} \rangle$ where ϕ is a QMQ, and $\mathtt{first}$ is either $\mathtt{client}$ or $\mathtt{server}$ and specifies what party goes first in the protocol. We note that this specification does not violate the client-server model by having the server going first as we assume that the polynomial evaluation protocol will be executed after the client and the server have completed an initial handshake that was initiated by the client.

For any set-theoretic predicate relation described in 3, it is possible to obtain four corresponding QMQs and then generate two protocols per QMQ resulting in 8 different protocols in total. While these protocols will correspond to the same functionality, they will have different constructions as well as communication and round complexities. In fact, the communication complexity of the generated protocols follows these general rules: If $Q = \forall$ and Alice starts the protocol, complexity is $O(|A| \times |B|)$; if Bob starts, the complexity will be $O(|B|)$. If $Q = \exists$, regardless who sends the first message, the communication complexity is $O(|A| \times |B|)$ and the protocol is performed in $O(|A|)$ rounds. As a result, players can choose what is best depending on their application domain. The construction of the compiler is as follows:

Compiler. Given $\langle \nu(Qx \in A : x \in B), \mathtt{first} \rangle$, If $A \in \{C, \overline{C}\}$ then the compiler specifies Alice to be the client and Bob to be the server; otherwise Alice is the server and Bob is the client. If $\mathtt{first} = \mathtt{client}$ and Alice is the client, Alice starts the protocol; otherwise, Bob starts the protocol. If Alice is the client, we say that Alice receives output; otherwise, Bob receives output.

The compiler produces the protocol for the given input by traversing a path of the directed acyclic graph of figure 4 to obtain the steps that are required for the output protocol. The directed acyclic graph is traversed based on: whether Alice or Bob starts the protocol, the quantifier Q, whether Alice or Bob receives the output and whether the QMQ starts with the negation sign $\neg$. After a path of the graph is determined, the compiler produces the protocol by substituting each step with the specifications that are given below. Note that all occurrences of Alice and Bob will be substituted with either client or server depending on the input to the compiler as explained above.

Step 0. The public parameters $param$ for a superposed encryptions scheme are sampled using the procedure K. Alice and Bob execute the procedure K' to obtain their public-keys pk_A, pk_B and secret-keys sk_A, sk_B.

Step 1. Bob defines a polynomial $f \in \mathbb{Z}_q[x]$ such that $f(b) = 0$ if and only if $b \in B$. The degree of the polynomial is m and $f(x) = t_0 + t_1 x + \ldots t_{|B|} x^{|B|}$.

Step 2A∀A. Alice prepares the encryptions of the elements $a, a^2, \ldots, a^{|B|}$ for each $a \in A = \{a_1, \ldots, a_{|A|}\}$. In particular Alice computes $C_{i,j} = E_{pk_A}(a_i^j)$ for $j = 1, \ldots, |B|$ and $i = 1, \ldots, |A|$ and $j = 1, \ldots, |B|$. Alice transmits the ciphertexts $\langle C_{i,j} \rangle_{i=1,\ldots,|A|, j=1,\ldots,|B|}$.
Communication: $|A| \cdot |B|$

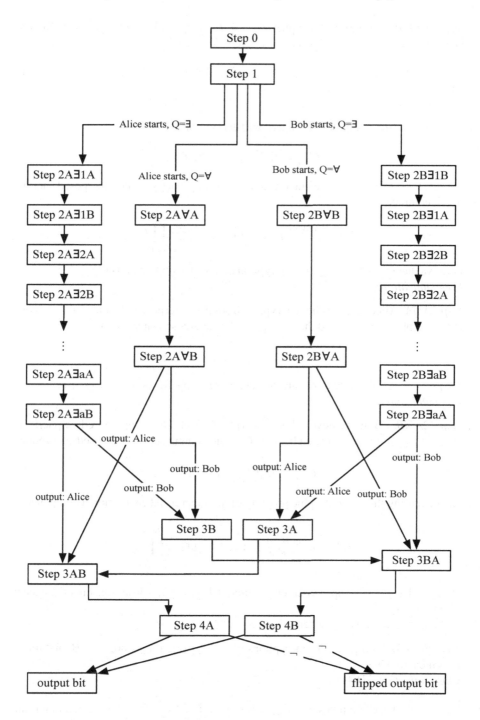

Fig. 4. Compiler protocol overview. Note that **a** $= |A|$.

Step 2A∀B. Bob computes the ciphertext $c = E_{pk_A}(t_0) \cdot \prod_{i=1}^{|A|}(\prod_{j=1}^{|B|} c_{i,j}^{t_j})^{r_i}$. Observe that $c = E_{pk_A}(\sum_{i=1...|A|} r_i \times f(a_i))$ where r_i is a random number drawn from Z_q.

Step 2A∃1A. Alice computes $C_{1,j} = E_{pk_A}(a_1^j)$ for $j = 1, \ldots, |B|$ and transmits the ciphertexts $\langle C_{1,j}\rangle_{j=1,\ldots,|B|}$.
Communication: $|B|$

Step 2A∃1B. Bob computes the superposed encryptions

$$C_{1,j}^* = E_{pk_A,pk_B,sk_B}^{\mathsf{sup},B}(t_j, C_{1,j})$$

for $j = 1, \ldots, |B|$ and then using the homomorphic property of the superposed encryption it computes

$$C_1^* = E_{pk_A,pk_B,sk_B}^{\mathsf{sup},B}(t_0, E_{pk_A}(1)) \cdot \prod_{j=1}^{|B|} C_{1,j}^*$$

Observe that C_1^* is a superposed encryption of $f(a_1)$. Bob transmits C_1^*.
Communication: 1

Step 2A∃iA. Alice removes her encryption from the superposed ciphertext C_{i-1}^* to obtain the ciphertext C_{i-1} and then computes the superposed encryptions

$$C_{i,j}' = E_{pk_A,pk_B,sk_A}^{\mathsf{sup},A}(a_i^j, C_{i-1})$$

for $j = 1, \ldots, |B|$. Alice transmits the superposed ciphertexts $\langle C_{i,j}'\rangle_{j=1,\ldots,|B|}$.
Communication: $|B|$

Step 2A∃iB. Bob removes his encryption from the superposed ciphertexts $\langle C_{i,j}'\rangle_{j=1,\ldots,|B|}$ to obtain the ciphertexts $C_{i,j}$ and computes the superposed encryptions

$$C_{i,j}^* = E_{pk_A,pk_B,sk_B}^{\mathsf{sup},B}(t_j, C_{i,j})$$

and then using the homomorphic property of the superposed encryption it computes

$$C_i^* = E_{pk_A,pk_B,sk_B}^{\mathsf{sup},B}(t_0, E_{pk_A}(1)) \cdot \prod_{j=1}^{|B|} C_{i,j}^*$$

Observe that C_i^* is a superposed encryption of $\prod_{\ell=1}^{i} f(a_\ell)$. Bob transmits C_i^* except when $i = |A|$.
Communication: 1 except when $i = |A|$.

Step 2B∀B. Bob prepares the encryptions $c_j = E_{pk_B}(t_j)$ for $j = 0, \ldots, |B|$ and transmits them to Alice.
Communication: $|B + 1|$

Step 2B∀A. Alice computes $c = E_{pk_A}(0) \cdot \prod_{i=1}^{|A|}(\prod_{j=0}^{|B|} c_j^{a_i^j})^{r_i}$ using the homomorphic property. Observe that $c = E_{pk_A}(\sum_{i=1...|A|} r_i \times f(a_i))$ where r_i is a random variable drawn from Z_q.

Step 2B∃1B. Bob prepares the encryptions $c_j = E_{pk_B}(t_j)$ for $j = 0, \ldots, |B|$ and transmits them to Alice.
Communication: $|B| + 1$

Step 2B∃1A. Alice computes the superposed encryptions

$$C^*_{1,j} = E^{\mathsf{sup},A}_{pk_A,pk_B,sk_A}(a^j_1, c_j)$$

for $j = 0, \ldots, |B|$. Using the homomorphic property of superposed encryptions it computes $C^*_1 = \prod^{|B|}_{j=0} C^*_{1,j}$. Observe that C^*_1 is a superposed ciphertext that encrypts $f(a_1)$. Alice transmits C^*_1.
Communication: 1

Step 2B∃iB. Bob removes his encryption from C^*_{i-1} to obtain the ciphertext C_{i-1} and then computes the superposed ciphertexts

$$C'_{i,j} = E^{\mathsf{sup},B}_{pk_A,pk_B,sk_B}(t_j, C_{i-1})$$

for $j = 0, \ldots, |B|$. Bob transmits to Alice the ciphertexts $C'_{i,0}, \ldots, C'_{i,|B|}$.
Communication: $|B| + 1$

Step 2B∃iA. Alice removes her encryption from $C'_{i,j}$, $j = 0, \ldots, |B|$ to obtain the ciphertexts $C_{i,j}$ and computes the superposed encryptions

$$C^*_{i,j} = E^{\mathsf{sup},A}_{pk_A,pk_B,sk_A}(a^j_i, c_{i,j})$$

for $j = 0, \ldots, |B|$. Using the homomorphic property of superposed encryptions it computes $C^*_i = \prod^{|B|}_{j=0} C^*_{i,j}$. Observe that C^*_i is a superposed ciphertext that encrypts $\prod^i_{\ell=1} f(a_\ell)$. Alice transmits C^*_i except when $i = |A|$.
Communication: 1 except when $i = |A|$.

Step 3A. Alice sends the superposed ciphertext C^* to Bob.
Communication: 1

Step 3B. Bob sends the superposed ciphertext C^* to Alice.
Communication: 1

Step 3AB. Bob removes his encryption from C^* to obtain the ciphertext C and transmits to Alice.
Communication: 1

Step 3BA. Alice removes her encryption from C^* to obtain the ciphertext C and transmits C to Bob.
Communication: 1

Step 4A. Alice tests whether C encrypts 0 and returns 1 in this case, otherwise 0. If $\nu = \neg$ it flips her answer.

Step 4B. Bob tests whether C encrypts 0 and returns 1 in this case, otherwise 0. If $\nu = \neg$ it flips his answer.
This completes the description of the compiler.

Theorem 1. *For each* $\langle\phi,\texttt{first}\rangle$, $\texttt{first} \in \{client, server\}$, *the syntax-driven compiler described above produces a protocol* $\mathcal{P}$ *between two parties, the client and the server, that evaluates the QMQ* ϕ *correctly with overwhelming probability so that the party* $\texttt{first}$ *sends the first message in the protocol.*

Note that "overwhelming probability" is interpreted as $1 - 2^{-\nu}$ where ν is a security parameter.

4.1 Security

In this section we will argue about the security of the protocols that are generated by the compiler. The theorem below is based on the fact that the view of either player, Alice or Bob, in all the protocols that are possible outputs of the compiler as described in figure 4 can be simulated without having access to the private input of either player. This is also based on the fact that ciphertexts, regular and superposed, using the implementation of encryption of section 2, are semantically secure under the Decisional Diffie Hellman assumption.

Theorem 2. *For all QMQ* ϕ *and* $\texttt{first}$ *that belongs to* $\{\texttt{client}, \texttt{server}\}$ *the protocol generated by the compiler on input* $\langle\phi,\texttt{first}\rangle$ *is secure with respect to semi-honest behavior under the Decisional Diffie Hellman assumption.*

Security against malicious behavior will require additional modifications to the compiler construction. Note that the general structure of the compiler will remain the same; nevertheless, additional actions will be required to be taken by the players in each step. In this extended abstract we will only provide a brief overview of the set of modifications that are required for the malicious adversarial setting.

Let us consider the step $2A\forall A$, where Alice sends the encryption of the elements $a, a^2, \ldots, a^{|B|}$. Since this is the first time that Alice communicates with Bob, in addition to whatever actions Alice does at this step she will provide a sequence of universally composable commitments to all her private values. For example for each value $a \in A$, Alice will provide the commitment $\langle\psi, C_a\rangle$ where C_a is of the form $\gamma_1^a \gamma_2^r$ and ψ is a ciphertext that encrypts a. Note that the ciphertext ψ is encrypted with a public-key that is part of a common reference string that the two players can employ in their interaction and is assumed to be securely generated. Alice subsequently will prove in zero-knowledge that all encryptions she publishes are consistent with the the UC-commitments C_a, for $a \in A$. In particular, recall that $C_{1,1} = E_{pk_A}(a_1) = \langle G_1, H_1\rangle = \langle g^{r_1}, (h_A)^{r_1}g^{a_1}\rangle$. Alice will prove the following statement in zero-knowledge to Bob: $\mathsf{PK}(x_1, x_2, x_3 : (G_1 = g^{x_1}) \wedge (H_1 = (h_A)^{x_1}g^{x_2}) \wedge (C_a = \gamma_1^{x_2}\gamma_2^{x_3}))$. The above zero-knowledge proof suggests that the ciphertext $\langle G, H\rangle$ is properly constructed and it encrypts the same value that is committed into C_{a_1}. In similar fashion, Alice will prove a statement about the ciphertext $C_{1,2}$ which recall that is defined as follows: $C_{1,2} = E_{pk_A}(a_1^2) = \langle G_2, H_2\rangle = \langle g^{r_2}, (h_A)^{r_2}g^{a_1^2}\rangle$. Alice will provide a zero-knowledge proof for the following statement: $\mathsf{PK}(x_1, x_2, x_3 : (G_1 = g^{x_1}) \wedge (H_1 = (h_A)^{x_1}g^{x_2}) \wedge (G_2 = g^{x_3}) \wedge (H_2 = (h_A)^{x_3}g^{x_2 \cdot x_2}) \wedge (C_a = \gamma_1^{x_2}\gamma_2^{x_3}))$. The above zero-knowledge proof suggests that the value that is encrypted into $\langle G_2, H_2\rangle$ is the product of the value that is encrypted into the ciphertext $\langle G_1, H_1\rangle$ and the value that is committed into C_{a_1}. This statement together with the previous one suggest that the ciphertext $\langle G_2, H_2 \rangle$ contains the square of the value a_1. In a similar fashion Alice can prove the validity of the remaining ciphertexts $C_{i,j}$ for $i = 1, \ldots, |A|$ and $j = 1, \ldots, |B|$. Note that during the course of the executions of all these steps a number of zero-knowledge proofs are generated by Alice and directed to Bob. We assume of course that Bob will terminate the protocol if one of these proofs is found to be false. Finally observe that all of the above modifications in step $2A\forall A$ do not change the communication complexity in the asymptotic sense since the combined length of all the zero-knowledge proofs is $\mathcal{O}(|A| \cdot |B|)$.

This completes the description on how step $2A\forall A$ is modified. The modifications that are required in the other steps of the compiler construction are of similar nature and we will not include them in this extended abstract. Nevertheless the principal ideas are the same. Note that in all steps, Alice will prove the consistency of her ciphertexts with respect to the UC-commitments $\{C_a\}_{a \in A}$. Similarly Bob will prove the consistency of his ciphertexts with respect to the UC-commitments $\{C_b\}_{b \in B}$. The UC-commitments need only be exchanged during the first round of communication and subsequent steps by either player can refer to the originally exchanged commitments. Observe that Bob is not using his values directly but instead he is using them through the coefficients $t_0, \ldots, t_{|B|}$ of the polynomial f that has the values $b \in B$ as roots. This will require for Bob to prove that the polynomial f has as roots the values that he has UC-committed to. This can be done in the similar fashion as above. Finally, in steps $2A\forall B$ and $2B\forall A$, where one of the players selects the random elements r_i, the two players must generate such random elements collaboratively to ensure the required distributional property.

Given the above set of modifications to the steps of our protocol, it can be proven secure in the malicious setting. Indeed, we can provide now a simulator that can transform any real-world implementation of Alice or Bob to an ideal-world implementation using the extractability properties of the UC-commitment (while at the same time simulating the other player).

5   Applications

Subset Inclusion Predicate. The client wishes to check whether it holds that $C \subseteq S$. There are four possible QMQ's each one yielding two different protocols, depending on which player starts. Note that below a "round" is two communication flows (e.g., from Alice to Bob and back). Moreover, we will classify schemes on the relative sizes of C, S compared to the universe.

- $\forall x \in C : x \in S$. The client plays the role of Alice and the server plays the role of Bob. If Alice (client) starts, the communication complexity is $|C| \times |S| + 1$ in 1 round. On the other hand, if Bob (server) starts, the communication complexity is $|S| + 3$ in 1.5 rounds. This protocol has better communication complexity but is worse in terms of round complexity. This QMQ is suited for **small** C, S.
- $\forall x \in \overline{S} : x \in \overline{C}$. The server plays the role of Alice and the client plays the role of Bob. If Alice (server) starts, the communication complexity is $|\overline{C}| \times |\overline{S}| + 2$ in 1.5 rounds. Nevertheless, if Bob (client) starts, the communication complexity is $|\overline{C}| + 2$ in 1 round, i.e., this the preferred of the two. This QMQ is suited for **large** C, S.

- $\neg\exists x \in C : x \in \overline{S}$. The client plays the role of Alice and the server plays the role of Bob. If Alice (client) starts, the communication complexity is $|C| \times (|\overline{S}|+1)$ in $|C|$ rounds. If Bob (server) starts, the communication complexity is $|C| \times (|\overline{S}| + 2)$ in $|C| + 0.5$ rounds. This QMQ is suitable for **small** C and **large** S and in particular when C is smaller than $\overline{S}$.
- $\neg\exists x \in \overline{S} : x \in C$. The server plays the role of Alice and the client plays the role of Bob. If Alice (server) starts, the communication complexity is $|\overline{S}| \times (|C| + 1)$ in $|\overline{S}| + 0.5$ rounds. If Bob (client) starts, the communication complexity is $|\overline{S}| \times (|C| + 2)$ in $|\overline{S}|$ rounds. This QMQ is suitable for **small** C and **large** S and in particular when $\overline{S}$ is smaller than C.

Disjointness Predicate. The client wishes to check if $C \cap S \overset{?}{=} \emptyset$. There are four possible QMQ's each one yielding two different protocols depending on which player starts:

- $\exists x \in C : x \in S$. The client plays the role of Alice and the server plays the role of Bob. If Alice (client) starts, the communication complexity is $|C| \times (|S| + 1)$ in $|C|$ rounds. If Bob (server) starts, the communication complexity is $|C| \times (|S| + 2)$ in $|C| + 0.5$ rounds. This QMQ is suited for **small** C, S and in particular when C is smaller than S.
- $\exists x \in S : x \in C$. The server plays the role of Alice and the client plays the role of Bob. If Alice (server) starts, the communication complexity is $|S| \times (|C| + 1)$ in $|S| + 0.5$ rounds. If Bob (client) starts, the communication complexity is $|S| \times (|C| + 2)$ in $|S|$ rounds. This QMQ is suited for **small** C, S and in particular when S is smaller than C.
- $\neg\forall x \in C : x \in \overline{S}$. The client plays the role of Alice and the server plays the role of Bob. If Alice (client) starts, the communication complexity is $|C| \times |\overline{S}| + 1$ in 1 round. Players can choose this protocol if client's set and the complement of server's set are small. If Bob (server) starts, the communication complexity is $|\overline{S}| + 3$ in 1.5 rounds. These two protocols are suited for the case of a **large** S, the first one being preferable when C is rather small.
- $\neg\forall x \in S : x \in \overline{C}$. The server plays the role of Alice and the client plays the role of Bob. If Alice (server) starts, the communication complexity is $|\overline{C}| \times |S| + 1$ in 1.5 rounds. If Bob (client) starts, the communication complexity is $|\overline{C}| + 2$ in 1 round and thus this is the preferred of the two. This protocol is suited for the case of a **large** C.

References

1. Mihir Bellare and Oded Goldreich, *On Defining Proofs of Knowledge*, CRYPTO 1992: 390-420.
2. Jan Camenisch, Victor Shoup, *Practical Verifiable Encryption and Decryption of Discrete Logarithms*, CRYPTO 2003: 126-144
3. Ran Canetti and Marc Fischlin, *Universally Composable Commitments*, CRYPTO 2001: 19-40
4. David Chaum, Jan-Hendrik Evertse and Jeroen van de Graaf, *An Improved Protocol for Demonstrating Possession of Discrete Logarithms and Some Generalizations*, EUROCRYPT 1987: 127-141.

5. D. Chaum and T. Pedersen *Wallet databases with observers*, In Advances in Cryptology – Crypto '92, pages 89-105, 1992.
6. Ronald Cramer and Ivan Damgard *Zero-Knowledge Proofs for Finite Field Arithmetic; or: Can Zero-Knowledge be for Free?*, CRYPTO 1998: 424-441.
7. Ronald Cramer, Ivan Damgard, Berry Schoenmakers, *Proofs of Partial Knowledge and Simplified Design of Witness Hiding Protocols*, CRYPTO 1994: 174-187
8. Ronald Cramer, Rosario Gennaro and Berry Schoenmakers, *A Secure and Optimally Efficient Multi-Authority Election Scheme*, EUROCRYPT 1997, pp. 103-118.
9. Ivan Damgard, *Efficient Concurrent Zero-Knowledge in the Auxiliary String Model* EUROCRYPT 2000: 418-430.
10. Ivan Damgard, Jesper Buus Nielsen, *Perfect Hiding and Perfect Binding Universally Composable Commitment Schemes with Constant Expansion Factor*, CRYPTO 2002. pp. 581-596.
11. Alfredo De Santis, Giovanni Di Crescenzo, Giuseppe Persiano and Moti Yung, *On Monotone Formula Closure of SZK*, FOCS 1994: 454-465.
12. T. ElGamal. *A public-key cryptosystem and a signature scheme based on discrete logarithms*, IEEE Transactions on Information Theory, IT-31(4):469–472, July 1985.
13. Bart Goethals and Mohammed Javeed Zaki, *Advances in Frequent Itemset Mining Implementations: Introduction to FIMI03*, FIMI '03, Frequent Itemset Mining Implementations, Proceedings of the ICDM 2003 Workshop on Frequent Itemset Mining Implementations, 19 December 2003, Melbourne, Florida, USA.
14. Lea Kissner AND Dawn Xiaodong Song, *Privacy-Preserving Set Operations*, CRYPTO 2005, pp. 241-257.
15. Sven Laur, Helger Lipmaa and Taneli Mielikainen *Private Itemset Support Counting*, ICICS '05, Vol. 3783 LNCS, pages 97–111, 2005
16. Ronald Fagin, Moni Naor, and Peter Winkler. Comparing information without leaking it. Communications of the ACM, 39(5):77–85, 1996.
17. Michael Freedman, Kobbi Nissim and Benny Pinkas, *Efficient private matching and set intersection*, EUROCRYPT 2004.
18. Shafi Goldwasser, Silvio Micali and Charles Rackoff, *The Knowledge Complexity of Interactive Proof Systems* SIAM J. Comput. 18(1), pp. 186-208, 1989.
19. Oded Goldreich, *Secure Multi-Party Computation*, unpublished manuscript, 2002. http://www.wisdom.weizmann.ac.il/oded/pp.html.
20. Aggelos Kiayias and Antonina Mitrofanova, *Testing Disjointness of Private Datasets*, Financial Cryptography and Data Security 2005, pp. 109-124.
21. D. Malkhi, N. Nisan, B. Pinkas, and Y. Sella. *The Fairplay project*, http://www.cs.huji.ac.il/labs/danss/FairPlay.
22. Moni Naor and Benny Pinkas. Oblivious transfer and polynomial evaluation. In Proc. 31st Annual ACM Symposium on Theory of Computing, pages 245–254, Atlanta, Georgia, May 1999.
23. Berry Schoenmakers and Pim Tuyls, *Practical Two-Party Computation Based on the Conditional Gate*, ASIACRYPT 2004, pp. 119-136.
24. A. C. Yao, *How to generate and exchange secrets*, In Proceedings of the 27th FOCS, pages 162-167, 1986.

Author Index

Lecture Notes in Computer Science

For information about Vols. 1–3918

please contact your bookseller or Springer